THE DOCUMENTARY HISTORY OF THE RATIFICATION OF THE CONSTITUTION

VOLUME II

Ratification of the Constitution by the States

PENNSYLVANIA

THE DOCUMENTARY HISTORY OF THE RATIFICATION OF THE CONSTITUTION

Volume II

Ratification of the Constitution by the States

Pennsylvania

Edited by Merrill Jensen

MADISON
STATE HISTORICAL SOCIETY OF WISCONSIN
1 9 7 6

Manufactured in the United States of America by
Worzalla Publishing Company, Stevens Point, Wisconsin

LIBRARY OF CONGRESS CATALOGING IN PUBLICATION DATA
Main entry under title:

The Documentary history of the ratification
of the Constitution.

Includes indexes.
CONTENTS: v. 1. Constitutional documents
and records, 1776–1787. –v. 2. Ratification
of the Constitution by the States: Pennsylvania.
1. United States–Constitutional history–Sources.
I. Jensen, Merrill.

KF4502.D63 342'.73'029 75–14149
ISBN 0–87020–153–0 (v. 1)

Preface

Pennsylvania was the focus of national attention during the first few weeks after the Constitutional Convention adjourned on 17 September 1787. The Constitution was read to the Pennsylvania Assembly on 18 September, and eleven days later the Assembly voted that delegates to a state convention would be elected on 6 November, and that the Convention would meet in Philadelphia on 20 November. The prompt action of the Pennsylvania legislature, and the force it used to secure a quorum, was reported throughout the United States.

Pennsylvania also took the lead in the national debate over the Constitution. Within days after the Constitutional Convention adjourned, Pennsylvanians began filling their newspapers, and pamphlets and broadsides, with arguments for and against the Constitution. Pennsylvania publications circulated widely, and material from them was reprinted throughout the United States before writers in most states had begun to supply their own printers with more than occasional pieces about the Constitution. As the debate got under way in other states, the dependence on Pennsylvania material decreased, although Federalist essays such as Tench Coxe's "An American Citizen," and Antifederalist essays such as Samuel Bryan's "Centinel" continued to circulate as a vital part of the national debate.

The debate among Pennsylvanians did not cease with the ratification of the Constitution by the state Convention on 12 December 1787. The amount of material published after ratification was as great as before, and it was characterized by ever-more bitter personal attacks on political leaders. After a brief lull late in the spring of 1788, the debate revived with the ratification of the Constitution by the ninth and tenth states: New Hampshire on 21 June and Virginia on 25 June.

The debate thereafter concerned the election of Senators and Representatives to the Congress of the United States, but all the old arguments were reiterated, and they ranged all the way from the issue of amendments to the Constitution to the alleged corruptness of Robert Morris during the War for Independence. After the establishment of the new government under the Constitution, Pennsylvania leaders continued to oppose one another on both the state and national level as they had before. On the national level most of the Federalists of 1787 became Federalists, and most of the Antifederalists of 1787 became Democratic Republicans.

The documents for the history of the ratification of the Constitution by Pennsylvania consist almost entirely of public records in the form of legislative and convention proceedings and debates; and of newspapers, pamphlets and broadsides. Private correspondence relating to ratification is sparse, although the available letters are invaluable, notably those in the papers of Tench Coxe and Benjamin Rush who supported ratification, and those in the papers of John Nicholson who opposed it.

For the most part, the record is a public one and, with one exception, is limited to Philadelphia and the nearby areas. That exception is Cumberland County, which, like most backcountry counties, was the home of vigorous opponents of the Constitution. The leading inhabitants of the town of Carlisle, and its newspaper, the *Carlisle Gazette,* were Federalists, but many townspeople and the rural inhabitants of the county were active and vocal Antifederalists who managed to make themselves heard and to leave a record for posterity.

Thus the history of ratification by Pennsylvania is first of all to be found in the proceedings and debates of the Assembly and the state Convention, and in the newspapers, pamphlets, and broadsides published in Philadelphia. Secondly, it is the history of ratification as set forth in the deeds and words of the inhabitants of Cumberland County, whose Antifederalists must be taken, lacking other sources, as representative of backcountry opposition to the ratification of the Constitution.

Acknowledgment was made in Volume I to those who have contributed to the gathering of materials for *The Documentary History of the Ratification of the Constitution.* However, special acknowledgment is due to those who have contributed directly to the preparation of this volume. The staffs of the Historical Society of Pennsylvania, the Library Company of Philadelphia, and the library of the Independence Hall National Historical Park, all in Philadelphia, and of the Pennsylvania Historical and Museum Commission in Harrisburg have been unstinting in their help. Thanks are also due to H. Bartholomew Cox for permission to print the notes of debates by Anthony Wayne in his private collection, to the Shippen family for permission to print the letters of William Shippen, Jr., and to the Massachusetts Historical Society for permission to print materials in the papers of Timothy Pickering and Winthrop Sargent.

Finally, grateful acknowledgment is due to those who have helped in every way in the preparation of this volume, and without whose dedicated work it could not have been prepared. They are John P. Kaminski and Gaspare J. Saladino who have served as associate editors, and Esther Anken, Douglas E. Clanin, Richard Leffler, Gail Walter, and Joan Westgate who have served as editorial assistants.

MERRILL JENSEN

Contents

* * * *

THE RATIFICATION OF THE CONSTITUTION BY PENNSYLVANIA

I. The Pennsylvania Assembly and the Constitution, 17–29 September 1787

II. The Debate Over the Constitution in Pennsylvania, 17 September–11 December 1787

III. The Pennsylvania Convention, 20 November–15 December 1787

IV. The Aftermath of Ratification in Pennsylvania

Organization

The Documentary History of the Ratification of the Constitution is divided into four groups of documents:
(1) *Constitutional Documents and Records, 1776–1787;*
(2) *Ratification of the Constitution by the States;*
(3) *Commentaries on the Constitution: Public and Private;*
(4) *Amendments to the Constitution: From Ratification by the States to the Proposal of a Bill of Rights by Congress.* Each of these groups is interrelated, and cross-references are made from group to group.

Constitutional Documents and Records, 1776–1787

This introductory volume to *The Documentary History of the Ratification of the Constitution* consists of constitutional documents and records from 1776 to 1787, beginning with the Declaration of Independence and concluding with documents describing the transmittal of the Constitution to the states by the Confederation Congress on 28 September 1787. The documents are arranged in chronological order within the following sections: (1) The Declaration of Independence; (2) The Articles of Confederation; (3) Ratification of the Articles of Confederation by the States in Congress; (4) Amendments to the Articles of Confederation, Grants of Power to Congress, and Ordinances for the Western Territory; (5) The Calling of the Constitutional Convention; (6) Appointment of Delegates to the Constitutional Convention; (7) The Resolutions and Draft Constitutions of the Constitutional Convention; (8) The Report of the Constitutional Convention; and (9) The Confederation Congress and the Constitution.

Ratification of the Constitution by the States

The documents relating to *Ratification of the Constitution by the States* are arranged as follows: (1) Pennsylvania; (2) Delaware; (3) New Jersey; (4) Georgia; (5) Connecticut; (6) Massachusetts; (7) First Session of the New Hampshire Convention; (8) Rhode Island Referendum; (9) Maryland; (10) South Carolina; (11) Second Session of the New Hampshire Convention; (12) Virginia; (13) New York; (14) First North Carolina Convention; (15) Second North Carolina Convention; (16) Rhode Island Convention.

With three exceptions, the states are placed in the order in which they ratified the Constitution. Pennsylvania is placed first, although Delaware ratified on 7 December, five days before Pennsylvania. The Pennsylvania Assembly was the first state legislature to receive the Constitution and to call a convention, and the means used to call it attracted nationwide attention. Furthermore, the Philadelphia press was for some time the principal source of material for the public debate on the Constitution.

The second exception is the placement of the first session of the New Hampshire Convention (13–22 February 1788) after Massachusetts, which ratified the Constitution on 6 February. The third exception is the popular referendum on the Constitution in Rhode Island on 24 March 1788, which is placed after the first session of the New Hampshire Convention. Thereafter, the states are arranged in the order in which their conventions ratified the Constitution.

The arrangement of documents in the order in which important events occurred is a more meaningful chronological order than one arbitrarily determined by the dates of ratification.

The documents for each state are arranged in the following order: (1) from the receipt of the Constitution after 17 September 1787 to the meeting of the state legislature which called the state convention; (2) the proceedings of the state legislature in calling the state convention; (3) from the legislature's call of the convention to the meeting of the convention; (4) the proceedings of the state convention day by day; (5) official letters transmitting the act of ratification to the Confederation Congress and to other states; and (6) post-convention documents.

Since the history of the ratification of the Constitution by each state is unique, the organization outlined above varies somewhat from state to state.

Ratification of the Constitution by the States: Microform Supplements

Much of the material for each state is repetitious or peripheral and is placed in microform supplements to the volumes of *Ratification of the Constitution by the States.* The documents in these supplements consist of consecutively numbered items arranged, for the most part, in chronological order.

The following is a list of the types of documents included in the microform supplements:

(1) Photographic copies of manuscripts such as notes of debates.

(2) Transcripts of certain letters which contain peripheral information about politics and social relationships.

(3) Newspaper items consisting of ongoing debates that repeat arguments, examples of which are printed in the volumes relating to ratification.

(4) Photographic copies of petitions with the names of signers.

(5) Pamphlets that circulated primarily within one state and which are not printed in either *Ratification of the Constitution by the States* or in *Commentaries on the Constitution*.

(6) Miscellaneous documents such as town records, election certificates, pay vouchers and financial records, attendance records, "recollections" of past events, etc.

Commentaries on the Constitution: Public and Private

The public debate and private commentary about a new government began before the Constitutional Convention met in the spring of 1787, continued during the Convention, and intensified after the Constitution was published in September 1787. The various forms of the public debate—newspapers, pamphlets, and broadsides which circulated in more than one state and throughout the nation—were read and referred to by men in and out of legislatures and conventions. Thus the Constitution was debated on a regional and on the national level as well as within each state. The purpose of these volumes is to place the ratification of the Constitution in this broad context.

These volumes also contain certain private letters. Most private letters were concerned with ratification in particular states and have been placed in *Ratification of the Constitution by the States*. However, other private letters were published and widely debated, gave mens' opinions of the Constitution in general, contained reports of ratification in more than one state, or discussed the means of securing or preventing ratification of the Constitution with or without amendments. Such documents, public and private, are an essential matrix of the history of ratification.

The documents are arranged in chronological order and are numbered consecutively throughout the volumes. A few of these documents are also printed in *Ratification of the Constitution by the States* because of their significance in the state of origin.

Amendments to the Constitution: From Ratification by the States to the Proposal of a Bill of Rights by Congress

The purpose of this selected group of documents is to bridge the gap between the ratification of the Constitution in each state and the proposal of a bill of rights in Congress on 8 June 1789. There is a basic continuity because the debate over the Constitution continued as actively in several states after ratification as it did before and during the state conventions. The debate centered upon the issue of amendments to the Constitution, and if amendments were needed, whether they should be proposed by a second constitutional convention or by the first Congress under the Constitution. These documents therefore provide the essential background for an understanding of the twelve amendments proposed by Congress on 26 September 1789.

This group of documents consists of materials in the following categories: (1) amendments adopted or rejected by state conventions; (2) amendments proposed by individuals and groups after the state conventions; (3) calls for a second constitutional convention; (4) the responses of state legislatures to calls for a second constitutional convention; (5) documents illustrating individual and group attitudes toward the Constitution after ratification; (6) examples of the continuing newspaper and pamphlet debate on the Constitution after ratification; (7) the role of the Confederation Congress in establishing the new government by setting the date for the first federal elections and the place for the first meeting of the government under the Constitution; (8) the first federal elections; (9) the debate over amendments in the first Congress under the Constitution; (10) the amendments proposed in and rejected by Congress; (11) the twelve amendments submitted to the states for consideration.

Editorial Procedures

Literal Reproduction of Official Documents

Official documents such as the Constitution, resolutions of the Confederation Congress, state acts calling conventions, forms of ratification, and proclamations are reproduced as literally as possible. A few other documents, because of their character or importance, are also reproduced as literally as possible. The literal reproduction of such documents is indicated by the symbol "LT" (i.e., literal transcript) in the footnote citation to the source.

Reproduction of Newspaper, Pamphlet, and Broadside Material

Eighteenth century printers sometimes used several varieties of type in a single item—large capitals, small capitals, and italics, as well as ordinary type. No attempt is made to reproduce varieties of type except when capital letters and italics were evidently used for emphasis by the author or the printer. In a few cases we have reproduced, so far as possible, the format of newspaper items.

Newspaper items are usually printed as separate documents, but occasionally more than one item from a single issue is printed under the title and date of the newspaper. In such cases the items are separated by asterisks.

Notes by Contemporaries

Contemporary footnotes and marginal notes are printed as footnotes after the document and immediately preceding editorial footnotes. Eighteenth-century symbols, such as asterisks, daggers, double daggers, etc., have been replaced by letters ("a," "b," "c," etc.), while Arabic numbers are used for editorial footnotes. Notes inserted in the text by authors remain in the text and are enclosed in parentheses.

Salutations, Closings, etc., of Letters

Endorsements, addresses, salutations, and complimentary closings of letters are omitted, except in cases where they provide information important for the understanding or identification of a letter. In such cases they are included in the editorial notes.

Excerpts and Elisions

Many documents, particularly letters, contain material such as family news, business affairs, and the like, which is not relevant to ratification. Hence, such material has been omitted. However, when longer excerpts or entire documents have been printed elsewhere, or are included in the microform supplements, this fact is noted.

Headings for Documents

All headings are supplied by the editors. They are as follows:

(1) Letters: Headings include the names of the writer and the recipient, and the place and date of writing.

(2) Newspaper essays, broadsides, and pamphlets: Headings are usually shortened versions of the full titles, which are given in editorial notes.

(3) Pseudonymous essays: Headings contain the pseudonym, title or short title, and the source if printed in a newspaper. Information and conjectures about the authors of such essays and full titles are placed in editorial notes.

(4) Untitled newspaper items: Headings consist of the short title of the newspaper and the date.

(5) Reports of public meetings: Headings consist of the name and date of such meetings with the source given in editorial notes.

Capitalization, Punctuation, and Italics in Manuscript Materials

Capital letters are used to begin each sentence. Random capitals and italics are removed except when they are evidently used by the author for emphasis. Periods are placed at the ends of sentences instead of dashes, colons, or no punctuation at all. Punctuation is altered within sentences if needed to clarify meaning.

Spelling

With one exception, spelling is made to conform to present-day practice. For example, "labour" and "foederal" are spelled "labor" and "federal." The exception to this rule is the spelling of names of individuals. While it is easy enough to correct the spelling of the names of a "Madison" or a "Washington," there are hundreds of legislators and other men whose names are spelled in various ways in document after document, and sometimes in the same document. The editors therefore follow the practice of the editors of such modern publications as the papers of Thomas Jefferson, John Adams, and Benjamin Franklin, who print the names as they are spelled in each document.

Abbreviations, Contractions, Superscripts, Numbers, Crossed-out Words, and Blank Spaces

Abbreviations such as those for place names ("Phila." for Philadelphia, for example) and military titles are spelled out. Contractions such as "can't," "tis," and "altho" are retained. Superscripts are lowered to the line. Archaic forms such as "yt" and "ye" are spelled out, "&c." is printed "etc.," and "&" is printed "and." Numbers are printed as they appear in the documents. Crossed-out words in documents, if they are significant, are placed in editorial notes. Otherwise they are not reproduced. Spaces intentionally left blank in documents are indicated by an underline.

Brackets

Brackets are used for the following purposes:

(1) Editorial insertions are enclosed in brackets: [Amendment].

(2) Conjectural readings are enclosed in brackets and followed by a question mark: [Amendment?].

(3) Illegible and missing words are indicated by dashes enclosed in brackets: [———].

Legislative Proceedings

The actions of state legislatures relating to ratification are printed under the headings "House Proceedings," "Senate Proceedings," or whatever the name of the "upper" or "lower" house may be, and are followed by the day and date. These proceedings consist primarily of excerpts from the journals of state legislatures but are supplemented by other sources.

When both houses acted on the same day, their actions are placed under the heading: "House and Senate Proceedings." In such cases the proceedings are arranged in the order of action by the two houses so that the progress of a report, a resolution, or a bill through the two houses can be followed in the order in which it occurred.

Messages, resolutions, and reports adopted by one house and sent to the other were often copied in the journals of the house to which they were sent. To avoid duplication in such cases, editorial notes enclosed in brackets are placed at appropriate places in the journals.

No attempt has been made to reproduce literally the *form* of printed or manuscript journals. Lists of names of members of committees, for example, which appear in column form, are printed as paragraphs, and each motion and resolution is set off as a paragraph.

When the first names of men making speeches or motions are not given, they are inserted without using brackets. The full names of speakers are set in italics. When a member is referred to in a general manner, the name is inserted in the proper place in brackets (i.e., "the member from Fayette [John Smilie] said").

We have included in the House and Senate proceedings only those actions relating to ratification. But it should be remembered that the legislatures which called state conventions also carried on their regular business during the same sessions, and usually spent far more time on such business than they did on ratification.

Convention Proceedings

The nature of the sources for the proceedings of state conventions varies from state to state, and sometimes from day to day within a state. In this *Documentary History* the proceedings of a convention, with some exceptions, are printed in the following order:

(1) Official convention journals.

(2) Accounts of convention debates by reporters.

(3) Notes of debates and proceedings by convention members (arranged alphabetically).

(4) Public and private commentaries on a day's proceedings.

In printing the convention journals and debates, the editorial procedures used in printing legislative journals and debates are followed, with some exceptions arising from the nature of the sources.

Cross-references

(1) Each volume of *The Documentary History of the Ratification of the Constitution* is divided into sections indicated by Roman numerals and subsections indicated by capital letters. Cross-references to documents within a single volume are indicated by the Roman numeral and the capital letter. For example: "II:B above," "III:C below," etc.

(2) Cross-references to documents in the first volume of *The Documentary History,* subtitled *Constitutional Documents and Records, 1776–1787,* are indicated by "CDR" followed by the relevant Roman numeral and capital letter. For example: "CDR:II, C."

(3) Cross-references to volumes in *The Documentary History,* subtitled *Ratification of the Constitution by the States,* are indicated by "RCS" followed by the abbreviation of the name of the state. For example: "RCS:Pa."

(4) Cross-references to documents in the microform supplements to *Ratification of the Constitution by the States* are indicated by "Mfm" followed by the abbreviation for the name of the state and the number of the document. For example: "Mfm:Pa. 36."

(5) Cross-references to documents in *Commentaries on the Constitution: Public and Private* are indicated by "CC" followed by the number of the document. For example: "CC:25."

References to Reprinting of Newspaper Items

Many items printed in a state's newspaper were reprinted by other newspapers in the same state and by newspapers in other states. When such reprinting appears significant, the distribution will be indicated in editorial notes.

Chronology, 1786–1790

1786

21 January	Virginia legislature calls meeting to consider granting Congress power to regulate trade.
7 August	Grand committee of Confederation Congress reports amendments to the Articles of Confederation.
11–14 September	Meeting of commissioners at Annapolis, Maryland.
14 September	Commissioners at Annapolis propose that states elect delegates to a convention at Philadelphia in May 1787.
ca. 20 September	Confederation Congress receives report of commissioners at Annapolis.
11 October	Confederation Congress appoints committee to consider report of commissioners at Annapolis.
23 November	Virginia legislature authorizes election of delegates to Convention at Philadelphia.
23 November	New Jersey legislature elects delegates.
4 December	Virginia legislature elects delegates.
30 December	Pennsylvania legislature elects delegates.

1787

6 January	North Carolina legislature elects delegates.
17 January	New Hampshire legislature elects delegates.
3 February	Delaware legislature elects delegates.

10 February	Georgia legislature elects delegates.
21 February	Confederation Congress calls Convention to amend Articles of Confederation.
22 February	Massachusetts legislature authorizes election of delegates.
28 February	New York legislature authorizes election of delegates.
3 March	Massachusetts legislature elects delegates.
6 March	New York legislature elects delegates.
8 March	South Carolina legislature elects delegates.
14 March	Rhode Island legislature refuses to elect delegates.
28 March	Pennsylvania legislature elects Benjamin Franklin to Convention.
23 April–26 May	Maryland legislature elects delegates.
5 May	Rhode Island legislature again refuses to elect delegates.
14 May	Convention meets at Philadelphia: quorum not present.
14–17 May	Connecticut legislature elects delegates.
25 May	Convention begins with quorum of seven states.
29 May	Virginia Resolutions presented to Convention.
29 May	Charles Pinckney's Plan presented to Convention.
13 June	Amended Virginia Resolutions submitted to Convention.
15 June	New Jersey Amendments to Articles of Confederation presented to Convention.
16 June	Rhode Island legislature again refuses to elect delegates.
18 June	Alexander Hamilton's Plan presented to Convention.
19 June	Convention rejects New Jersey Amendments to Articles of Confederation and accepts Amended Virginia Resolutions.

27 June	New Hampshire legislature renews election of delegates.
13 July	Confederation Congress adopts Northwest Ordinance.
24, 26 July	Convention submits resolutions to Committee of Detail.
6 August	Committee of Detail submits draft constitution to Convention.
10 September	Convention submits amended draft constitution of 6 August to Committee of Style.
12 September	Committee of Style submits draft constitution to Convention.
17 September	Constitution signed and Convention adjourns *sine die.*
18 September	Constitution read in Pennsylvania legislature.
20 September	Constitution read in Confederation Congress.
26–28 September	Confederation Congress debates Constitution.
28 September	Congress transmits Constitution to the states.
28–29 September	Pennsylvania calls state convention to meet on 20 November.
17 October	Connecticut calls state convention to meet on 3 January 1788.
25 October	Massachusetts calls state convention to meet on 9 January 1788.
26 October	Georgia calls state convention to meet on 25 December 1787.
31 October	Virginia calls state convention to meet on 2 June 1788.
1 November	New Jersey calls state convention to meet on 11 December 1787.
6 November	Pennsylvania elects delegates to state convention.
10 November	Delaware calls state convention to meet on 3 December 1787.
12 November	Connecticut elects delegates to state convention.

19 November 1787–7 January 1788	Massachusetts elects delegates to state convention.
20 November–15 December	Pennsylvania Convention.
26 November	Delaware elects delegates to state convention.
27 November	Maryland calls state convention to meet on 21 April 1788.
27 November–1 December	New Jersey elects delegates to state convention.
3–7 December	Delaware Convention.
4–5 December	Georgia elects delegates to state convention.
6 December	North Carolina calls state convention to meet on 21 July 1788.
7 December	Delaware Convention ratifies Constitution, 30 to 0.
11–20 December	New Jersey Convention.
12 December	Pennsylvania Convention ratifies Constitution, 46 to 23.
14 December	New Hampshire calls state convention to meet on 13 February 1788.
18 December	New Jersey Convention ratifies Constitution, 38 to 0.
25 December 1787–5 January 1788	Georgia Convention.
31 December	Georgia Convention ratifies Constitution, 26 to 0.
31 December 1787–12 February 1788	New Hampshire elects delegates to state convention.

1788

3–9 January	Connecticut Convention.
9 January	Connecticut Convention ratifies Constitution, 128 to 40.
9 January–7 February	Massachusetts Convention.

16–19 January	South Carolina legislature debates Constitution.
19 January	South Carolina calls state convention to meet on 12 May 1788.
1 February	New York calls state convention to meet on 17 June 1788.
6 February	Massachusetts Convention ratifies Constitution, 187 to 168, and proposes amendments.
13–22 February	New Hampshire Convention: first session.
1 March	Rhode Island legislature calls statewide referendum on Constitution on 24 March.
3–31 March	Virginia elects delegates to state convention.
24 March	Rhode Island referendum: voters reject Constitution, 2,711 to 239.
28–29 March	North Carolina elects delegates to state convention.
7 April	Maryland elects delegates to state convention.
11–12 April	South Carolina elects delegates to state convention.
21–29 April	Maryland Convention.
26 April	Maryland Convention ratifies Constitution, 63 to 11.
29 April–3 May	New York elects delegates to state convention.
12–24 May	South Carolina Convention.
23 May	South Carolina Convention ratifies Constitution, 149 to 73, and proposes amendments.
2–27 June	Virginia Convention.
17 June–26 July	New York Convention.
18–21 June	New Hampshire Convention: second session.
21 June	New Hampshire Convention ratifies Constitution, 57 to 47, and proposes amendments.
25 June	Virginia Convention ratifies Constitution, 89 to 79, and proposes amendments.
2 July	New Hampshire ratification read in Congress; Congress appoints committee to report an act for putting the Constitution into operation.
21 July–4 August	First North Carolina Convention.

26 July	New York Convention Circular Letter calls for second constitutional convention.
26 July	New York Convention ratifies Constitution, 30 to 27, and proposes amendments.
2 August	North Carolina Convention proposes amendments and refuses to ratify until amendments are submitted to Congress and to a second constitutional convention.
13 September	Confederation Congress sets dates for election of President and meeting of new government under the Constitution.
20 November	Virginia legislature requests Congress under the Constitution to call a second constitutional convention.
30 November	North Carolina legislature calls second state convention to meet on 16 November 1789.

1789

4 February	Presidential Electors cast ballots for President and Vice President.
4 March	New Congress meets: quorum not present.
1 April	Quorum present in House of Representatives.
6 April	Quorum present in Senate, and votes for President and Vice President are counted.
30 April	George Washington takes oath of office as President.
21–22 August	North Carolina elects delegates to second state convention.
26 September	Congress adopts twelve amendments to Constitution to be submitted to the states.
16–23 November	Second North Carolina Convention.
21 November	Second North Carolina Convention ratifies Constitution, 194 to 77, and proposes amendments.

1790

17 January	Rhode Island legislature calls state convention to meet on 1 March 1790.

8 February	Rhode Island elects delegates to state convention.
1–6 March	Rhode Island Convention: first session.
13 May	United States Senate passes bill to sever Rhode Island from Union.
24–29 May	Rhode Island Convention: second session.
29 May	Rhode Island Convention ratifies Constitution, 34 to 32, and proposes amendments.

Calendar for the Years 1787—1790

1787

JANUARY

S	M	T	W	T	F	S
	1	2	3	4	5	6
7	8	9	10	11	12	13
14	15	16	17	18	19	20
21	22	23	24	25	26	27
28	29	30	31			

FEBRUARY

S	M	T	W	T	F	S
				1	2	3
4	5	6	7	8	9	10
11	12	13	14	15	16	17
18	19	20	21	22	23	24
25	26	27	28			

MARCH

S	M	T	W	T	F	S
				1	2	3
4	5	6	7	8	9	10
11	12	13	14	15	16	17
18	19	20	21	22	23	24
25	26	27	28	29	30	31

APRIL

S	M	T	W	T	F	S
1	2	3	4	5	6	7
8	9	10	11	12	13	14
15	16	17	18	19	20	21
22	23	24	25	26	27	28
29	30					

MAY

S	M	T	W	T	F	S
		1	2	3	4	5
6	7	8	9	10	11	12
13	14	15	16	17	18	19
20	21	22	23	24	25	26
27	28	29	30	31		

JUNE

S	M	T	W	T	F	S
					1	2
3	4	5	6	7	8	9
10	11	12	13	14	15	16
17	18	19	20	21	22	23
24	25	26	27	28	29	30

JULY

S	M	T	W	T	F	S
1	2	3	4	5	6	7
8	9	10	11	12	13	14
15	16	17	18	19	20	21
22	23	24	25	26	27	28
29	30	31				

AUGUST

S	M	T	W	T	F	S
			1	2	3	4
5	6	7	8	9	10	11
12	13	14	15	16	17	18
19	20	21	22	23	24	25
26	27	28	29	30	31	

SEPTEMBER

S	M	T	W	T	F	S
						1
2	3	4	5	6	7	8
9	10	11	12	13	14	15
16	17	18	19	20	21	22
23	24	25	26	27	28	29
30						

OCTOBER

S	M	T	W	T	F	S
	1	2	3	4	5	6
7	8	9	10	11	12	13
14	15	16	17	18	19	20
21	22	23	24	25	26	27
28	29	30	31			

NOVEMBER

S	M	T	W	T	F	S
				1	2	3
4	5	6	7	8	9	10
11	12	13	14	15	16	17
18	19	20	21	22	23	24
25	26	27	28	29	30	

DECEMBER

S	M	T	W	T	F	S
						1
2	3	4	5	6	7	8
9	10	11	12	13	14	15
16	17	18	19	20	21	22
23	24	25	26	27	28	29
30	31					

1788

JANUARY

S	M	T	W	T	F	S
		1	2	3	4	5
6	7	8	9	10	11	12
13	14	15	16	17	18	19
20	21	22	23	24	25	26
27	28	29	30	31		

FEBRUARY

S	M	T	W	T	F	S
					1	2
3	4	5	6	7	8	9
10	11	12	13	14	15	16
17	18	19	20	21	22	23
24	25	26	27	28	29	

MARCH

S	M	T	W	T	F	S
						1
2	3	4	5	6	7	8
9	10	11	12	13	14	15
16	17	18	19	20	21	22
23	24	25	26	27	28	29
30	31					

APRIL

S	M	T	W	T	F	S
		1	2	3	4	5
6	7	8	9	10	11	12
13	14	15	16	17	18	19
20	21	22	23	24	25	26
27	28	29	30			

MAY

S	M	T	W	T	F	S
				1	2	3
4	5	6	7	8	9	10
11	12	13	14	15	16	17
18	19	20	21	22	23	24
25	26	27	28	29	30	31

JUNE

S	M	T	W	T	F	S
1	2	3	4	5	6	7
8	9	10	11	12	13	14
15	16	17	18	19	20	21
22	23	24	25	26	27	28
29	30					

JULY

S	M	T	W	T	F	S
		1	2	3	4	5
6	7	8	9	10	11	12
13	14	15	16	17	18	19
20	21	22	23	24	25	26
27	28	29	30	31		

AUGUST

S	M	T	W	T	F	S
					1	2
3	4	5	6	7	8	9
10	11	12	13	14	15	16
17	18	19	20	21	22	23
24	25	26	27	28	29	30
31						

SEPTEMBER

S	M	T	W	T	F	S
	1	2	3	4	5	6
7	8	9	10	11	12	13
14	15	16	17	18	19	20
21	22	23	24	25	26	27
28	29	30				

OCTOBER

S	M	T	W	T	F	S
			1	2	3	4
5	6	7	8	9	10	11
12	13	14	15	16	17	18
19	20	21	22	23	24	25
26	27	28	29	30	31	

NOVEMBER

S	M	T	W	T	F	S
						1
2	3	4	5	6	7	8
9	10	11	12	13	14	15
16	17	18	19	20	21	22
23	24	25	26	27	28	29
30						

DECEMBER

S	M	T	W	T	F	S
	1	2	3	4	5	6
7	8	9	10	11	12	13
14	15	16	17	18	19	20
21	22	23	24	25	26	27
28	29	30	31			

1789

JANUARY

S	M	T	W	T	F	S
				1	2	3
4	5	6	7	8	9	10
11	12	13	14	15	16	17
18	19	20	21	22	23	24
25	26	27	28	29	30	31

FEBRUARY

S	M	T	W	T	F	S
1	2	3	4	5	6	7
8	9	10	11	12	13	14
15	16	17	18	19	20	21
22	23	24	25	26	27	28

MARCH

S	M	T	W	T	F	S
1	2	3	4	5	6	7
8	9	10	11	12	13	14
15	16	17	18	19	20	21
22	23	24	25	26	27	28
29	30	31				

APRIL

S	M	T	W	T	F	S
			1	2	3	4
5	6	7	8	9	10	11
12	13	14	15	16	17	18
19	20	21	22	23	24	25
26	27	28	29	30		

MAY

S	M	T	W	T	F	S
					1	2
3	4	5	6	7	8	9
10	11	12	13	14	15	16
17	18	19	20	21	22	23
24	25	26	27	28	29	30
31						

JUNE

S	M	T	W	T	F	S
	1	2	3	4	5	6
7	8	9	10	11	12	13
14	15	16	17	18	19	20
21	22	23	24	25	26	27
28	29	30				

JULY

S	M	T	W	T	F	S
			1	2	3	4
5	6	7	8	9	10	11
12	13	14	15	16	17	18
19	20	21	22	23	24	25
26	27	28	29	30	31	

AUGUST

S	M	T	W	T	F	S
						1
2	3	4	5	6	7	8
9	10	11	12	13	14	15
16	17	18	19	20	21	22
23	24	25	26	27	28	29
30	31					

SEPTEMBER

S	M	T	W	T	F	S
		1	2	3	4	5
6	7	8	9	10	11	12
13	14	15	16	17	18	19
20	21	22	23	24	25	26
27	28	29	30			

OCTOBER

S	M	T	W	T	F	S
				1	2	3
4	5	6	7	8	9	10
11	12	13	14	15	16	17
18	19	20	21	22	23	24
25	26	27	28	29	30	31

NOVEMBER

S	M	T	W	T	F	S
1	2	3	4	5	6	7
8	9	10	11	12	13	14
15	16	17	18	19	20	21
22	23	24	25	26	27	28
29	30					

DECEMBER

S	M	T	W	T	F	S
		1	2	3	4	5
6	7	8	9	10	11	12
13	14	15	16	17	18	19
20	21	22	23	24	25	26
27	28	29	30	31		

1790

JANUARY

S	M	T	W	T	F	S
					1	2
3	4	5	6	7	8	9
10	11	12	13	14	15	16
17	18	19	20	21	22	23
24	25	26	27	28	29	30
31						

FEBRUARY

S	M	T	W	T	F	S
	1	2	3	4	5	6
7	8	9	10	11	12	13
14	15	16	17	18	19	20
21	22	23	24	25	26	27
28						

MARCH

S	M	T	W	T	F	S
	1	2	3	4	5	6
7	8	9	10	11	12	13
14	15	16	17	18	19	20
21	22	23	24	25	26	27
28	29	30	31			

APRIL

S	M	T	W	T	F	S
				1	2	3
4	5	6	7	8	9	10
11	12	13	14	15	16	17
18	19	20	21	22	23	24
25	26	27	28	29	30	

MAY

S	M	T	W	T	F	S
						1
2	3	4	5	6	7	8
9	10	11	12	13	14	15
16	17	18	19	20	21	22
23	24	25	26	27	28	29
30	31					

JUNE

S	M	T	W	T	F	S
		1	2	3	4	5
6	7	8	9	10	11	12
13	14	15	16	17	18	19
20	21	22	23	24	25	26
27	28	29	30			

JULY

S	M	T	W	T	F	S
				1	2	3
4	5	6	7	8	9	10
11	12	13	14	15	16	17
18	19	20	21	22	23	24
25	26	27	28	29	30	31

AUGUST

S	M	T	W	T	F	S
1	2	3	4	5	6	7
8	9	10	11	12	13	14
15	16	17	18	19	20	21
22	23	24	25	26	27	28
29	30	31				

SEPTEMBER

S	M	T	W	T	F	S
			1	2	3	4
5	6	7	8	9	10	11
12	13	14	15	16	17	18
19	20	21	22	23	24	25
26	27	28	29	30		

OCTOBER

S	M	T	W	T	F	S
					1	2
3	4	5	6	7	8	9
10	11	12	13	14	15	16
17	18	19	20	21	22	23
24	25	26	27	28	29	30
31						

NOVEMBER

S	M	T	W	T	F	S
	1	2	3	4	5	6
7	8	9	10	11	12	13
14	15	16	17	18	19	20
21	22	23	24	25	26	27
28	29	30				

DECEMBER

S	M	T	W	T	F	S
			1	2	3	4
5	6	7	8	9	10	11
12	13	14	15	16	17	18
19	20	21	22	23	24	25
26	27	28	29	30	31	

The Ratification of the Constitution by Pennsylvania

Introduction

The debate over the ratification of the Constitution in Pennsylvania was in part a continuation of the debate between two political parties which began with the writing of the Pennsylvania constitution of 1776. By the end of the War for Independence the parties were commonly known as Constitutionalists and Republicans. The Constitutionalists supported the constitution of 1776 and the federal system of the Articles of Confederation, while the Republicans sought to supplant both.

Most of Pennsylvania's colonial leaders opposed independence, either openly or covertly, and lost control of the state in the summer of 1776. New men, with far more radical ideas, seized power and wrote a state constitution that promised, in principle and in specific provisions, a political revolution within Pennsylvania.

The Declaration of Rights prefacing the constitution proclaimed that "all power being originally inherent in, and consequently derived from, the people; therefore all officers of government, whether legislative or executive, are their trustees and servants, and at all times accountable to them." This principle was enumerated in one specific provision after another. The constitution abolished property qualifications for voting and gave all taxpayers and non-taxpaying sons of freeholders the right to vote. The old grievance of inadequate representation for the back country counties was more than redressed. In 1775 the three eastern counties and Philadelphia had twenty-six representatives in the Assembly; the eight western counties, with about half the population of the colony, had but fifteen. The constitution provided that representation should be according to the number of taxable inhabitants; but that until a census could be taken, each county and Philadelphia would have six representatives, thus giving the "West" forty-eight and the "East" twenty-four seats in the legislature.

The constitution retained the single-house legislature of colonial times but replaced the governor with a Supreme Executive Council consisting of a delegate from each county and from the city of Philadelphia. The Council, elected for three-year terms, had certain appointive and administrative powers but no veto power or legislative authority.

The votes and proceedings of the Assembly were to be published weekly. All proposed laws were to be printed for the "consideration of the people," and except in case of "sudden necessity," no law could be enacted in the same session of the Assembly in which it was introduced. Furthermore, the public was free to attend all sessions of the Assembly "except only when the welfare of this state may require the doors to be shut."

The distrust of men in power and the fear of power seekers, so characteristic of the political thought of the age, were reflected by requiring rotation in office. The purpose, declared in the constitution, was to train men for public business, "and moreover the danger of establishing an inconvenient aristocracy will be effectually prevented." Assemblymen could not serve more than four years in seven; members of the Council and county sheriffs no more than three years in seven; and Pennsylvania delegates in Congress who served two consecutive years could not be reelected for three years thereafter.

To safeguard the constitution, the framers made its amendment difficult. The legislature could not alter the constitution or propose amendments. Only the Council of Censors, elected by the people every seven years, could do so. The Council, composed of two delegates from each county and from the city of Philadelphia, could propose amendments, and by a two-thirds vote, it could summon a convention to consider them. But even if the Censors did call a convention, proposed changes had to be published for the public's consideration at least six months before the people elected and instructed delegates to a convention.

Early in September the convention published a draft of the constitution for public consideration. The convention adopted many of the changes suggested, made revisions of its own, and adopted the constitution on 28 September. The constitution aroused the intense opposition of political leaders in eastern Pennsylvania, and within a month they met in Philadelphia and adopted thirty-two resolutions condemning it. They also tried to prevent the new government from functioning. Some delegates to the Assembly, elected in November 1776, boycotted that body, thereby preventing a quorum. Opponents of the constitution also refused to accept local offices, refused to take the oath to support the constitution, and delayed the opening of county courts.

The Republicans began a campaign for a new constitution at once, but not until November 1778 were they able to persuade the Assembly to adopt resolutions providing for a popular referendum on the issue of calling a constitutional convention. The Constitutionalists struck back. Early in 1779 they inundated the Assembly with petitions opposing a convention and filled the newspapers with articles attacking its supporters. This campaign was effective, and in late February 1779 the Assembly rescinded the resolutions calling for the referendum.

In March 1779 the Republicans organized the Republican Society which denounced the constitution as a "monster," the Council of Censors as a "jubilee of tyranny," and the oath to support the constitution as an infringement of the rights of freemen to judge and determine for themselves. They demanded a two-house legislature and the appointment of judges during good behavior, rather than election for limited terms.

Such Republican actions only strengthened the resolve of the Constitutionalists, who stepped up their attacks upon Republican leaders. Constitutionalists excoriated Robert Morris for alleged wartime profiteering, and mobs threatened Republican merchants accused of hoarding and price-gouging. In October 1779 a mob attacked some Republican leaders at James Wilson's house in Philadelphia, and several people were killed and wounded before order was restored.

On the national level, the Constitutionalist-controlled Assembly ratified the Articles of Confederation, which guaranteed the sovereignty of each state, in March 1778. The next month the Supreme Executive Council—presided over by its vice president, Constitutionalist leader George Bryan—concurred in the Assembly's action. The Constitutionalists also opposed Congress' efforts to encroach on the state's sovereignty and resisted attempts of the Continental Army to extend its authority in Pennsylvania.

These actions and policies aroused the opposition of Republicans. They preferred a strong central government with a supreme legislature such as the one John Dickinson proposed to Congress in July 1776, and which James Wilson supported in the congressional debates in 1776 and 1777.

By 1780 military defeats, army mutinies, and runaway inflation convinced the Republicans that the salvation of the state and of the Union depended upon the revision of the state constitution and the strengthening of the central government. Consequently, they strove to gain control of the Assembly, and after partial successes in the elections of 1780 and 1781, they won majorities in 1782 and 1783.

Between 1781 and 1783 the Republicans—led by Robert Morris, whom Congress appointed superintendent of finance in 1781—were so actively engaged in trying to increase the power of the central government that Pennsylvania became the center of a movement to create what came to be called a "national government." The Republicans supported and the Assembly adopted the principal acts by which Congress sought to enhance its power. In April 1781 the Assembly adopted the congressional Impost of 1781, and in the summer of 1783 it ratified the congressional Impost of 1783 and the accompanying amendment to share expenses according to population.

Robert Morris also sought to strengthen the central government by attaching to it the dominant commercial and financial interests of the United States, particularly those in Pennsylvania. Morris believed that a national debt paid from national revenue would be the cement of union and that holders of the debt throughout the United States would unite to support the government which paid the debt. In 1782 the Assembly chartered the Republican-controlled Bank of North America which had been chartered by the Confederation Congress the previous year. Morris hoped that the bank would become the agent of Congress by loaning Congress money, collecting congressional revenue, and using that revenue to pay the national debt.

Late in 1783 the Republicans had an opportunity to change the state constitution because the Council of Censors was scheduled to meet. The Republicans elected a majority of the delegates to the Council in the October 1783 elections but not the two-thirds majority necessary to call a constitutional convention. The Council met from November 1783 through January 1784 and then adjourned until June 1784. When twenty-four members met in June, the Constitutionalists, through a series of fortuitous events, had a majority of four. After three months of heated debate, the Council resolved "That there does not appear to this Council an absolute necessity to call a convention, to alter, explain or amend the constitution."

This Constitutionalist victory marked the beginning of their return to power. In the October 1784 elections they won a majority in the Assembly. In December 1784 the Assembly ratified the temporary grant of commercial power which Congress had requested on 30 April 1784. The Constitutionalists agreed, because of the postwar commercial and economic depression, but in March 1785 they struck at the heart of the Republican political and economic system when the Assembly funded the state debt and assumed the United States debt owed to citizens of Pennsylvania. The act provided that the state would pay the interest on both debts with an emission of paper money, the sale of public lands, an excise tax, a state impost, and a tax on real and personal property. Then in September 1785 the Constitutionalists revoked the charter of the Bank of North America.

In March 1786 the Assembly responded to Virginia's call for a commercial convention by authorizing the Supreme Executive Council to appoint commissioners to meet at Annapolis, Maryland. On 11 April the Council appointed Robert Morris, George Clymer, John Armstrong, Jr., Thomas FitzSimons, and Tench Coxe, all of whom, with the exception of Coxe, were prominent Republicans. Only Coxe attended the convention in September.

The Republicans regained control of the Assembly in the October 1786 elections, and in the spring of 1787 they rechartered the Bank of North America. Meanwhile, in December 1786, the Assembly began consideration of the report of the Annapolis meeting. After it learned that the Virginia legislature had appointed delegates to meet in a convention at Philadelphia, the Assembly, on 30 December, elected Robert Morris, Gouverneur Morris, Thomas Mifflin, James Wilson, Thomas FitzSimons, George Clymer, and Jared Ingersoll deputies to the convention. They were directed to join with other deputies "in devising, deliberating on and discussing all such alterations and further provisions as may be necessary to render the federal constitution fully adequate to the exigencies of the Union and in reporting such act or acts for that purpose to the United States in Congress assembled as when agreed to by them and duly confirmed by the several states will effectually provide for the same." All of the deputies were from the city and county of Philadelphia; and, with the possible exception of Ingersoll, they were all Republicans. On 28 March the Assembly added Benjamin Franklin, who was claimed by both parties as a leader, to the list of deputies.

Two Pennsylvania delegates played leading roles in the Constitutional Convention. James Wilson and Gouverneur Morris each gave more speeches than any other member of the Convention. Wilson played a prominent part in writing the first draft of the Constitution as a member of the Committee of Detail. Morris had a similar role in writing the final draft as a member of the Committee of Style. Benjamin Franklin spoke little; but on the last day of the Convention, Wilson delivered a speech for him in which Franklin sought to conciliate those opposed to the Constitution. Robert Morris, the acknowledged leader of the Pennsylvania Republicans, made no reported speeches.

Before and during the Constitutional Convention, Pennsylvania newspapers were virtually unanimous in their support of the Convention. Newspaper articles enumerated the defects of the central government under the Articles of Confederation and painted a picture of economic and political distress. Other newspaper items contained plans for improving the central government, praise for Convention delegates, and hints about the Convention's proceedings.

Such accounts apparently alarmed some of the leaders of the Constitutionalist Party. A newspaper reported in early August 1787 that meetings were being held in the houses of George Bryan and Jonathan Bayard Smith, and that publications were being distributed "to excite prejudices against the new federal government, and thereby prevent its adoption by this state" (*Independent Gazetteer*, 8 August, Mfm: Pa. 16; see also Mfm:Pa. 20).

During the debate over the Constitution in 1787 and 1788, with a few exceptions, Constitutionalists were Antifederalists and Republicans were Federalists. The strength of the Constitutionalist Party in the fall of 1787 was concentrated in the western counties of Berks, Northampton, Cumberland, Franklin, Dauphin, Westmoreland, Fayette, and Washington, although the party also had some support in the eastern part of the state. Constitutionalist leaders included such westerners as William Findley of Westmoreland, Robert Whitehill of Cumberland, James McLene of Franklin, and John Smilie of Fayette, and such Philadelphians as George Bryan, the Reverend Dr. John Ewing, Dr. James Hutchinson, Jonathan Bayard Smith, John Nicholson, and Thomas McKean. With the exception of McKean, all opposed the new Constitution.

Republicans controlled Philadelphia and Pittsburgh, and the more heavily populated eastern counties of Philadelphia, Bucks, Chester, Montgomery, and Lancaster; and York to the west. The Republican leaders were Robert Morris, James Wilson, George Clymer, Thomas FitzSimons, William Bingham, and Thomas Willing of Philadelphia; Thomas Mifflin of Philadelphia County; John Armstrong, Sr. of Cumberland County; and Hugh H. Brackenridge of Westmoreland County.

After a heated public debate, the Pennsylvania Convention ratified the Constitution on 12 December 1787, but Antifederalists continued to campaign for amendments. The debate over amendments lasted through the elections for the federal House of Representatives. In 1789 and 1790 the new federal Congress adopted much of the financial program of the Pennsylvania Federalists, and their triumph was completed in 1790 when Pennsylvania adopted a new state constitution incorporating ideas of government which Pennsylvania Republicans had fought for since 1776.

Note on Sources

Pennsylvania Legislative Records

The official sources for Pennsylvania legislative history consist of the Minutes of the Supreme Executive Council and the Journals of the General Assembly. The rough and smooth manuscript minutes of the Council for 1787 and 1788 are located in the Division of Public Records of the Pennsylvania Historical and Museum Commission and have been published in the *Minutes of the Supreme Executive Council of Pennsylvania, From its Organization to the Termination of the Revolution* (Vols. XI–XVI of [*Colonial Records*], Harrisburg, Pa., 1852–1853), XV.

The manuscript Journals of the Assembly for the same period are not extant. However, the Journals were published at the end of each session. The Journals relating to the calling of the state Convention are in the *Minutes Of The Third Session Of The Eleventh General Assembly Of The Commonwealth Of Pennsylvania* . . . (Philadelphia, [1787]), and *Minutes Of The First Session Of The Twelfth General Assembly Of The Commonwealth Of Pennsylvania* . . . (Philadelphia, 1787). The Journals relating to the petition campaign requesting the Assembly to reject the ratification of the Constitution by the Convention are in *Minutes Of The Second Session Of The Twelfth General Assembly Of The Commonwealth Of Pennsylvania* . . . (Philadelphia, [1788]).

Pennsylvania is unique among the states in that there are reports of Assembly debates during this period. Thomas Lloyd took notes of the debates in the four sessions between 4 September 1787 and 4 October 1788 and published them as *Proceedings and Debates of the General Assembly of Pennsylvania* (4 vols., Philadelphia, 1787–1788). The first and second volumes contain the debates in September and November 1787 over the calling of the state Convention. Another version is in the *Pennsylvania Herald,* whose editor, Alexander J. Dallas, published his notes of the Assembly debates from time to time.

Personal Papers and Records

The number of letters and other documents of Pennsylvania political leaders and observers is small compared to some other states, but there are several important collections. The papers of John Nicholson, in the Division of Public Records of the Pennsylvania Historical and Museum Commission, are invaluable for the study of opposition to the Constitution outside Philadelphia. The William Irvine Papers in the Historical Society of Pennsylvania contain important letters concerning the opposition, especially in Cumberland County. Other valuable collections in the Historical Society of Pennsylvania are those of such supporters of the Constitution as Tench Coxe, Levi Hollingsworth, and James Wilson. The Pemberton Papers contain material on Quaker opposition to the slave-trade clause of the Constitution.

The Library Company of Philadelphia has the papers of Benjamin Rush; and the papers of Robert Aitken, a Philadelphia printer and bookseller, which contain information on the dissemination of Antifederalist literature. The Robert R. Logan Collection of John Dickinson Papers contains letters concerning Dickinson's publication of the "Letters of Fabius." The library of the Independence National Historical Park has Jasper Yeates's notes of debates in the state Convention.

Several libraries and a private collector outside Pennsylvania have useful material. The Manuscript Division of the Library of Congress has the Shippen Family Papers, which include letters of William Shippen, Jr., a Philadelphia Antifederalist who was married to the sister of Richard Henry Lee of Virginia. The Rare Book Room has a large collection of pamphlets and broadsides. The William L. Clements Library at the University of Michigan and H. Bartholomew Cox of Washington, D.C., each own a part of Anthony Wayne's notes of debates in the state Convention. The Timothy Pickering Papers in the Massachusetts Historical Society contain information on Pickering's support of the Constitution and on attitudes toward the Constitution in Luzerne County.

Newspapers and Magazines

The most important sources for the history of the debate over the Constitution in Pennsylvania are the fifteen newspapers and two magazines that were published in the state at one time or another between September 1787 and June 1788. Ten of the newspapers and the two magazines were published in Philadelphia. The Philadelphia newspapers appeared daily, semiweekly, triweekly, and weekly.

The Philadelphia dailies were Eleazer Oswald's *The Independent Gazetteer; or, the Chronicle of Freedom* and John Dunlap and David C. Claypoole's *The Pennsylvania Packet, and Daily Advertiser*. The *Packet,* a Federalist newspaper, contained little original material about the Constitution. Oswald printed both Federalist and Antifederalist pieces in the *Gazetteer* until mid-November. Thereafter the paper was strongly Antifederalist. It contained more original items than any other Philadelphia newspaper, many of which were reprinted throughout the United States.

The Philadelphia triweeklies were Daniel Humphreys' *The Pennsylvania Mercury and Universal Advertiser,* which had been a weekly before 1 January 1788, and Andrew Brown's *The Federal Gazette, and the Philadelphia Evening Post,* which was published only in March and April 1788. Both were Federalist newspapers. William Spotswood's *The Pennsylvania Herald, and General Advertiser* was a triweekly between 11 September and 6 October 1787, but a semiweekly thereafter. The *Herald* was edited by Alexander J. Dallas, whose published reports of the debates in the Convention led to Federalist attacks upon him and his dismissal as editor in January 1788. Spotswood retired after the issue of 5 February, and the *Herald* ceased publication shortly afterwards.

The Philadelphia semiweeklies were Thomas Bradford's *The Pennsylvania Journal and the Weekly Advertiser,* and Robert Smith and James Prange's *The Evening Chronicle.* Both were Federalist newspapers, judging from the material they reprinted from other newspapers. The *Chronicle*'s last-known issue is that of 7 November 1787.

The Philadelphia weeklies were David and William Hall and William Sellers' *The Pennsylvania Gazette,* Francis Bailey's *The Freeman's Journal: or, the North-American Intelligencer,* and Melchior Steiner's *Gemeinnützige Philadelphische Correspondenz.* The *Gazette* was Philadelphia's leading Federalist newspaper, and news and propaganda pieces were reprinted throughout America. The *Philadelphische Correspondenz* was also Federalist. Bailey's *Journal* was an Antifederalist paper which contained almost no Federalist pieces.

Philadelphia's two magazines were Mathew Carey's *The American Museum, Or Repository Of Ancient And Modern Fugitive Pieces, Prose And Poetical* and Thomas Seddon, William Spotswood, Charles Cist, and James Trenchard's *The Columbian Magazine, Or Monthly Miscellany Containing a View of . . . History, Literature, Manners & Characters . . . .* Both magazines were monthlies which usually appeared between the 7th and 10th of the month following the month given as the date of publication. The *American Museum* was Federalist, with a national subscription list that included many prominent Americans, and it reprinted many of the most important Federalist pieces published in Philadelphia, as well as a few original items. *The Columbian Magazine* contained little about politics.

Four weeklies and one biweekly were published outside Philadelphia. The four weeklies were: John Scull and John Boyd's *The*

Pittsburgh Gazette; George Kline and George Reynolds' *The Carlisle Gazette, and the Western Repository of Knowledge*; Matthias Bartgis and Thomas Roberts' *Pennsylvania Chronicle or the York Weekly Advertiser*; and Anton Stiemer, Johann Albrecht, and Jacob Lahn's *Neue Unpartheyische Lancaster Zeitung, und Anzeigs-Nachrichten*. The biweekly (published once every two weeks) was Michael Billmeyer's *Die Germantauner Zeitung*. The Carlisle and Pittsburgh gazettes were Federalist newspapers published in Federalist towns located in predominately Antifederalist counties. Not enough issues of the *Pennsylvania Chronicle*, which began publication on 24 October 1787, exist to determine its political affiliations. The German-language newspapers were Federalist.

The Constitution was printed in eleven of the state's extant newspapers and in both magazines. In addition to newspaper coverage, the Constitution was also printed in broadsides, pamphlets, and almanacs; and, on 24–25 September, the Assembly authorized the printing of the Constitution in English and in German at state expense.

Pennsylvania printers, particularly those in Philadelphia, also printed pamphlets and broadsides on the need to strengthen the central government and on the merits or defects of the Constitution. Between 17 October 1787 and 27 April 1788, six Philadelphia printers and one in Carlisle published seven pamphlets which were original treatises on the Constitution. Two Philadelphia publishers printed pamphlets of material originating outside Pennsylvania, such as George Washington's letter of June 1783 to the state executives and Luther Martin's "Genuine Information." Philadelphia printers also printed as broadsides such items as "Centinel," "An American Citizen," and "An Old Whig," which had previously appeared in Pennsylvania newspapers.

The Sources for the Pennsylvania Convention

The sources consist of the Journals of the Convention, notes of debates taken by private reporters and delegates, and newspaper summaries of proceedings and debates. There are no private letters or diaries written by members of the Convention or by observers which provide any substantive information.

The printed Journals of the Convention contain an incomplete account of the Convention's proceedings, and no manuscript version has been located. The Convention authorized David and William Hall and William Sellers to publish 3,000 copies in English and Melchior Steiner to publish 2,000 copies in German. The English version is entitled *Minutes of the Convention of the Commonwealth of Pennsylvania . . .* (Philadelphia, 1787), and the German version is entitled *Tagebuch der Convention der Republic Pennsylvanien . . .* (Philadelphia, 1788).

The record of the debates in the Convention is incomplete and scattered except for the notes taken by Alexander J. Dallas of the debates on 27 and 28 November, the first part of the debates on 30 November, and the debates on 12 December. In addition, Dallas printed news stories in the *Pennsylvania Herald* which commented on the proceedings and sometimes included speeches or parts of speeches. Dallas, the editor of the *Herald,* began publishing the full debates of 27 November in the *Herald* on 1 December. He interrupted the publication of the earlier debates to publish the debates of 12 December in the *Herald* on 15 December. In the issue of 5 January 1788, Dallas published the first four speeches given on the morning of 30 November. He was then fired as editor of the *Herald,* and the further publication of his notes of the debates ended.

From the beginning, Dallas aroused the wrath of the Federalists by his short accounts in the *Herald* of daily proceedings in which he sometimes implied that the Antifederalists had won the day in the debates. Federalists declared that Dallas' version of James Wilson's long speech on 24 November, which was published as a pamphlet on 28 November, was "inaccurate" and "misstated." Dallas' report of a speech by Benjamin Rush on 12 December, in the *Pennsylvania Herald* on 15 December, was denounced by Thomas Lloyd as "a gross misrepresentation," while Rush declared that Dallas was guilty of "imprudent conduct" and had misrepresented the proceedings and speeches of the Convention (to Noah Webster, 13 February 1788, Mfm:Pa. 426).

After Dallas was dismissed, Antifederalists charged that it was no mere coincidence that it happened soon after a Federalist meeting in Philadelphia. At the meeting James Wilson allegedly declared that the Antifederalists were "daily increasing in consequence of the publications which issued constantly from the press against the *proposed Constitution*" ("Tom Peep," *Independent Gazetteer,* 10 January 1788, Mfm:Pa. 320). Antifederalists also declared that Dallas' impartial accounts had caused the Federalists "to injure and suppress the *Herald*" (*Pennsylvania Herald,* 30 January 1788, Mfm:Pa. 390). "Centinel" lamented that with the stoppage of Dallas' notes of debates, "the arguments of a Findley, a Whitehill, and a Smilie, that bright constellation of patriots are suppressed, and a spurious publication substituted" ("Centinel" XIII, *Independent Gazetteer,* 30 January 1788).

"Centinel" was referring to the projected publication of the debates by Thomas Lloyd, who had begun to report and publish the debates of the Assembly starting with the session of 4 September 1787. During the Convention Lloyd announced he would publish the debates, but even before they were published, "Centinel" charged that Lloyd's account would be "spurious." When "G. R." attacked "Centinel" for making the charge (*Independent Gazetteer,* 31 January 1788, Mfm:Pa. 393) "Peep, Junior" replied that "I know that Centinel has the *best intelligence,* that he has the whole history of the writing, manufacturing, fabricating, dressing, transcribing, printing, molding, coining and casting anew, and reprinting of this spurious work. . . ." Furthermore, "Mr. Lloyd's character . . . is too well established to need any further illustration" (*Independent Gazetteer,* 5 February, Mfm:Pa. 399).

Lloyd published *Debates of the Convention of the State of Pennsylvania, on the Constitution, Proposed for the Government of the United States. The Speeches of Thomas M'Kean & James Wilson, Esquires: In Which They Have Unfolded the Principles . . . of the Constitution . . .* on 7 February 1788. The 150-page volume contained the major speeches of James Wilson and some of the more temperate speeches of Thomas McKean. No other Federalist speeches were reported, and the only recognition of the Antifederalists was the inclusion of a question John Smilie asked James Wilson during the latter's speech on 11 December.

The New York *American Magazine* reviewed the volume in its March 1788 issue. The reviewer complimented Wilson and McKean on their speeches, and then asked: "why has the compiler suppressed the speeches of the most able men on the opposite party? Are they to appear in the second volume? and if so, will they not be misplaced? It is presumed that the principles of the Constitution, like those of the Christian religion, will bear the severest scrutiny; and that its cause will even gain strength by discussion. The omission of the Antifederal arguments as stated by the opposition may give uneasiness to some warm friends to the Constitution. On this subject however it is necessary to suspend our opinion, till the appearance of the second volume" (Mfm:Pa. 592).

Antifederalist charges that Lloyd's publication was designed as propaganda for the Constitution is borne out by the letters of certain Pennsylvania Federalists who evidently thought Lloyd's version of the debates would be useful in other states. On 24 December Timothy Pickering wrote to Charles Tillinghast in New York that James Wilson's speeches were a "clear and satisfactory explanation" of the Constitution and that they would be published by themselves and earlier than he had expected. "Read them with attention—and you may read them with *confidence,* for he is a *great* and a *good* man"

(CC:288–C). Tench Coxe began distributing printed pages of Lloyd's *Debates* before they were published. On 16 January 1788 he wrote to James Madison in Congress in New York, that he was sending sixty pages "which I am anxious to get into the hands of Mr. [Rufus] King for the use of the gentlemen in the Massachusetts Convention" (RC, Madison Papers, DLC). On 27 January Coxe wrote to Madison again: "From your letter with respect to the Convention at B[oston] I have been anxious to procure the rem[ainde]r of Mr. Lloyd's debates to send to Mr. King. There were some pages more struck off, which I have obtained and cover them to you with a letter to be forwarded as before" (RC, Madison Papers, DLC).

Three members of the Convention—all supporters of the Constitution—took notes of debates. The most complete notes, those taken by James Wilson, are in the Wilson Papers in the Historical Society of Pennsylvania. They consist of three documents. The first document contains forty-seven pages of notes of debates between 26 November and 12 December. Wilson does not report his own speeches and seldom indicates when he spoke. His main concern was to list the arguments of opponents of the Constitution so that he could answer them in set speeches from time to time. Between 3 and 8 December, Wilson numbered all of the Antifederal objections consecutively in his daily notes, listing a total of 240 objections (there were actually 241, number 134 being repeated). These notes were published as an appendix to McMaster and Stone, *Pennsylvania and the Federal Constitution.*

The second document is a six-page outline for Wilson's speech on 4 December. The first four pages, headed "Objections," lists thirty-four numbered Antifederal objections which Wilson compiled from his notes of debates on 28 and 30 November and 1 December. These pages outlined Wilson's speech in the morning; while the last two pages, headed "Reasons for adopting the Constitution," outlined his speech in the afternoon.

The third document is a three-page outline for Wilson's speech on 11 December. This outline, headed "2d List of Objections," consists of twenty-nine general, unnumbered objections compiled by Wilson from his daily notes. After each general objection, Wilson listed (in abbreviated form) the specific objections which fell within the sphere of that general objection. The abbreviated citation for the specific objections included: (1) the page numbers of Wilson's manuscript daily notes on which the objections were listed or (2) the number assigned by Wilson to the objections made between 3 and 8 December.

The notes taken by Anthony Wayne cover the debates between

27 November and 11 December and are by far the most difficult to decipher. Wayne did not begin each day's debates on a new sheet of paper; and occasionally, because of the lack of space, he placed isolated notes of a speech on separate pages with notes from speeches on other days. These isolated notes are sometimes indicated by a hand device. Usually each page was divided vertically with the right column reserved for notes of speeches and the left column for Wayne's own marginal notes. Most marginal notes appear to be Wayne's own thoughts which he did not present in speeches, but some of them appear to be notes of speeches answering specific objections to the Constitution. The notes for 27 November and part of the notes for 30 November and 1 December are in the William L. Clements Library at the University of Michigan. The remainder of Wayne's notes are in the collection of H. Bartholomew Cox, who published the notes of the debates on 6, 7, 8, and 11 December as "The Convention Notes of Anthony Wayne," *Manuscripts,* XVI (1964), 18–25.

The notes taken by Jasper Yeates are in two different depositories. The main collection, in the library of the Independence National Historical Park, contains: (1) drafts of two of his speeches, (2) notes of debates from 30 November to 11 December, and (3) a draft of the form of ratification. Yeates's miscellaneous legal papers at the Historical Society of Pennsylvania contain notes of debates on 26, 27, and 28 November.

The notes in the Independence National Historical Park library have been printed by R. Carter Pittman as "Jasper Yeates's Notes on the Pennsylvania Ratifying Convention, 1787," *William and Mary Quarterly,* 3rd series, XXII (1965), 301–18. Yeates's notes, as printed in this volume, with some variations, agree with Pittman's version except for a two-page draft of a speech which Pittman attributes to James Wilson on 4 December. He states that Lloyd's report of the debate "follows the general outline of the speech reported here by Yeates." However, the evidence indicates that the two pages are the draft of a speech given by Yeates on 30 November. Dallas' report of Yeates's speech (in the *Pennsylvania Herald*) duplicates many of the phrases in the draft, and the references to and quotations from the Constitution are the same.

There is no adequate account of the ratification of the Constitution by Pennsylvania. McMaster and Stone's *Pennsylvania and the Federal Constitution* is compiled largely from the *Independent Gazetteer, Pennsylvania Herald,* and *Pennsylvania Packet.* The volume also contains brief biographical sketches of the members of the Convention prepared by W. H. Egle. Much information about the years preceding ratification is contained in Robert L. Brunhouse, *The Counter-Revolution in Pennsylvania 1776–1790* (Harrisburg, Pa., 1942), Russell J. Ferguson, *Early Western Pennsylvania Politics* (Pittsburgh, Pa., 1938), and E. Bruce Thomas, *Political Tendencies in Pennsylvania 1783–1794* (Philadelphia, Pa., 1938). However, none of these books give more than passing attention to the ratification of the Constitution by Pennsylvania.

Symbols

FOR MANUSCRIPTS, MANUSCRIPT DEPOSITORIES, SHORT TITLES, AND CROSS-REFERENCES

Manuscripts

DS	Document Signed
FC	File Copy
LT	Literal Transcript
MS	Manuscript
RC	Recipient's Copy
Tr	Translation from Foreign Language

Manuscript Depositories[1]

CSmH	Henry E. Huntington Library, San Marino, California
DLC	Library of Congress, Washington, D.C.
DNA	National Archives, Washington, D.C.
MHi	Massachusetts Historical Society, Boston
MiU-C	William L. Clements Library, University of Michigan, Ann Arbor
PCarlH	Cumberland County Historical Society and Hamilton Library Association, Carlisle, Pennsylvania
PHarH	Pennsylvania Historical and Museum Commission, Harrisburg
PHi	Historical Society of Pennsylvania, Philadelphia
PPIn	Independence National Historical Park, Philadelphia
PPL	Library Company of Philadelphia, Philadelphia
ViMtvL	Mount Vernon Ladies' Association of the Union, Mount Vernon, Virginia

Short Titles

Adams, *Defence*	John Adams, *A Defence of the Constitutions of Government of the United States of America* (Philadelphia, 1787).
Assembly *Minutes*	*Minutes of the . . . General Assembly of the Commonwealth of Pennsylvania* [1787, 1788]. For a full citation for each session, see Note on Sources.
Blackstone	William Blackstone, *Commentaries on the Laws of England. In Four Books* (5 vols., Philadelphia, 1771–1772).
Convention *Minutes*	*Minutes of the Convention of the Commonwealth of Pennsylvania . . . for the Purpose of Taking into Consideration the Constitution Framed by the Late Foederal Convention for the United States of America* (Philadelphia, 1787).
Farrand	Max Farrand, ed., *The Records of the Federal Convention* (3 vols., New Haven, Conn., 1911).
Hiltzheimer, *Diary*	Jacob Cox Parsons, ed., *Extracts from the Diary of Jacob Hiltzheimer, of Philadelphia. 1765–1798* (Philadelphia, Pa., 1893).
JCC	Worthington C. Ford, et al., eds., *Journals of the Continental Congress, 1774–1789 . . .* (34 vols., Washington, D.C., 1904–1937).
Lloyd, *Debates*	Thomas Lloyd, comp. and ed., *Debates of the Convention, of the State of Pennsylvania on the Constitution, Proposed for the Government of the United States* (Philadelphia, 1788).
LMCC	Edmund C. Burnett, ed., *Letters of Members of the Continental Congress* (8 vols., Washington, D.C., 1921–1936).
Locke	John Locke, *Two Treatises of Government . . .* (London, 1713).
McMaster and Stone	John B. McMaster and Frederick D. Stone, eds., *Pennsylvania and the Federal Constitution, 1787–1788* ([Philadelphia, Pa.], 1888).
Montesquieu	Charles, Baron de Montesquieu, *The Spirit of Laws* (2 vols., London, 1773).

Necker	Jacques Necker, *De L'Administration des Finances de la France* (n.p., 1785).
Pa. *Statutes*	James T. Mitchell and Henry Flanders, comps., *The Statutes at Large of Pennsylvania from 1682 to 1801* (16 vols., Harrisburg, Pa., 1896–1911).
PCC	Papers of the Continental Congress, 1774–1789 (Record Group 360, National Archives).
RG 11	United States Government Documents Having General Legal Effect (National Archives).
Taylor	Julian P. Boyd and Robert J. Taylor, eds., *The Susquehannah Company Papers* (11 vols., Wilkes-Barre, Pa. and Ithaca, N.Y., 1930–1971).
Thorpe	Francis N. Thorpe, ed., *The Federal and State Constitutions . . .* (7 vols., Washington, D.C., 1909).
Vattel	Emerich de Vattel, *The Law of Nations . . .* (Dublin, 1792).

Cross-references

CC	*Commentaries on the Constitution: Public and Private*
CDR	*Constitutional Documents and Records, 1776–1787*
Mfm	Microform Supplements to RCS
RCS	*Ratification of the Constitution by the States*

1. The symbols are those adopted by the Library of Congress: *Symbols of American Libraries* (10th ed., Washington, D.C., 1969).

Pennsylvania Chronology, 1786–1788

1786

7 March	Assembly committee appointed to consider Virginia's call for a commercial convention.
21 March	Assembly authorizes Supreme Executive Council to appoint five delegates to convention at Annapolis.
11 April	Council appoints Robert Morris, George Clymer, John Armstrong, Jr., Thomas FitzSimons, and Tench Coxe delegates to convention at Annapolis.
20 September	Council receives report of Annapolis Convention.
10 October	Assembly election.
28 October	Assembly receives report of Annapolis Convention.
14 December	Assembly submits report of Annapolis Convention to a committee.
21 December	*Independent Gazetteer* publishes Virginia act of 4 December appointing delegates to convention in Philadelphia in May 1787.
30 December	Assembly elects Thomas Mifflin, Robert Morris, George Clymer, Jared Ingersoll, Thomas FitzSimons, James Wilson, and Gouverneur Morris delegates to convention in May 1787.

1787

21 February	Confederation Congress calls Convention at Philadelphia to amend Articles of Confederation.
28 March	Assembly elects Benjamin Franklin to Convention.
4 September	Assembly session begins.

17 September	Constitutional Convention adjourns *sine die.*
18 September	Constitution read in Assembly.
28 September	Absent members prevent Assembly quorum and call for state convention.
29 September	Absent members returned by force; quorum declared present; and state convention called. Assembly adjourns *sine die.*
9 October	Assembly election.
22 October	Assembly session begins.
6 November	Delegates elected to state convention.
9 November	Assembly refuses to require two-thirds quorum for state convention.
20 November	Pennsylvania Convention meets in Philadelphia.
12 December	Convention rejects amendments to Constitution and votes to ratify 46 to 23.
15 December	Convention adjourns *sine die.*
18 December	Dissent of the Minority of Convention published.
26–27 December	Riots and celebration of ratification at Carlisle.
ca. 27 December	Beginning of petition campaign requesting Assembly to reject Convention's ratification of the Constitution.

1788

19 February	Assembly session begins.
1 March	Antifederalist militiamen march into Carlisle, and rioters released from prison.
17–29 March	Assembly receives and tables petitions signed by more than 6,000 inhabitants of Northampton, Dauphin, Bedford, Franklin, Cumberland, and Westmoreland counties requesting Assembly to reject ratification of Constitution.
29 March	Assembly session ends.

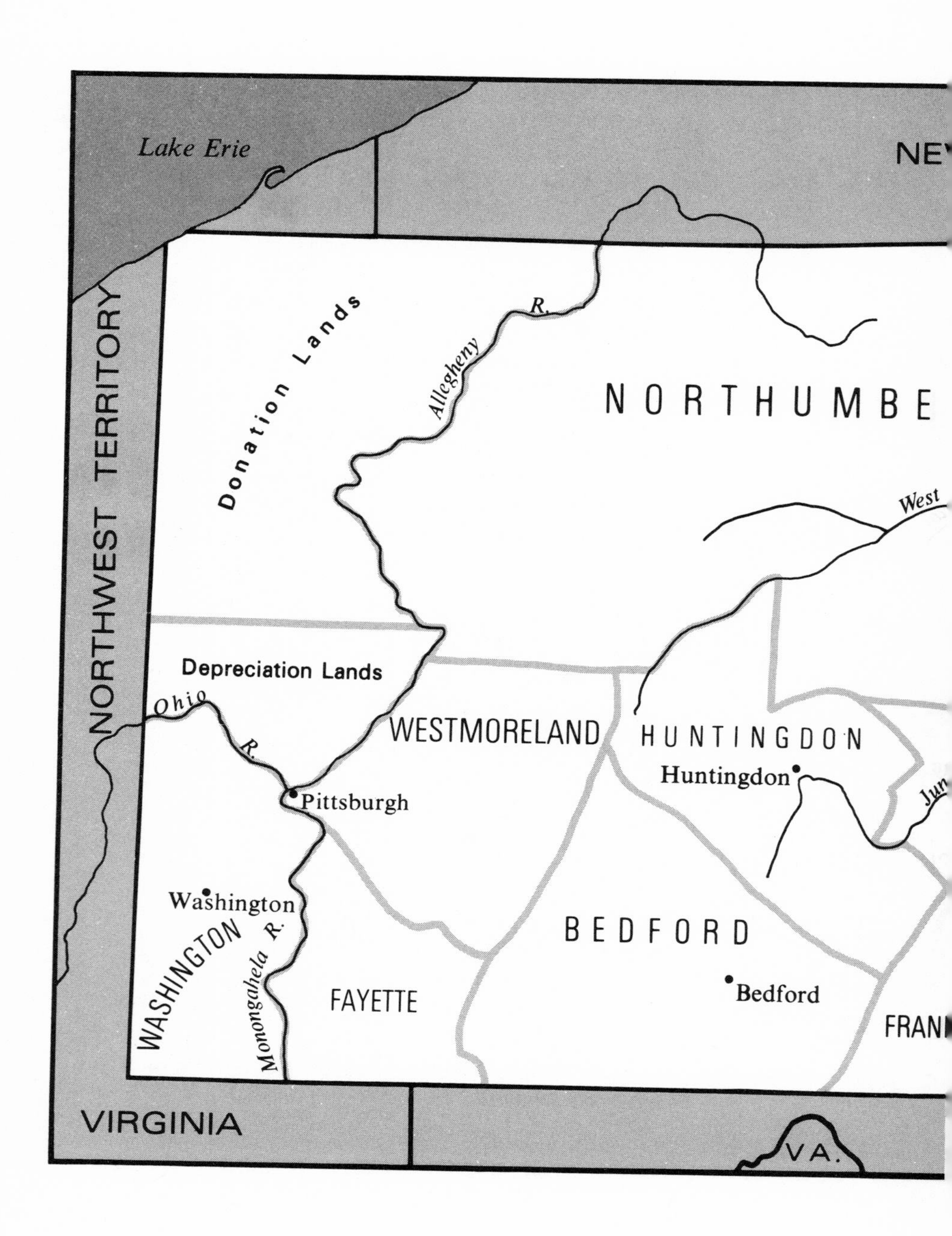

Lake Erie
NEW
NORTHWEST TERRITORY
Donation Lands
Allegheny R.
NORTHUMBE
West
Depreciation Lands
Ohio R.
WESTMORELAND
HUNTINGDON
Huntingdon
Jun
Pittsburgh
Washington
WASHINGTON
Monongahela R.
BEDFORD
Bedford
FAYETTE
FRAN
VIRGINIA
VA.

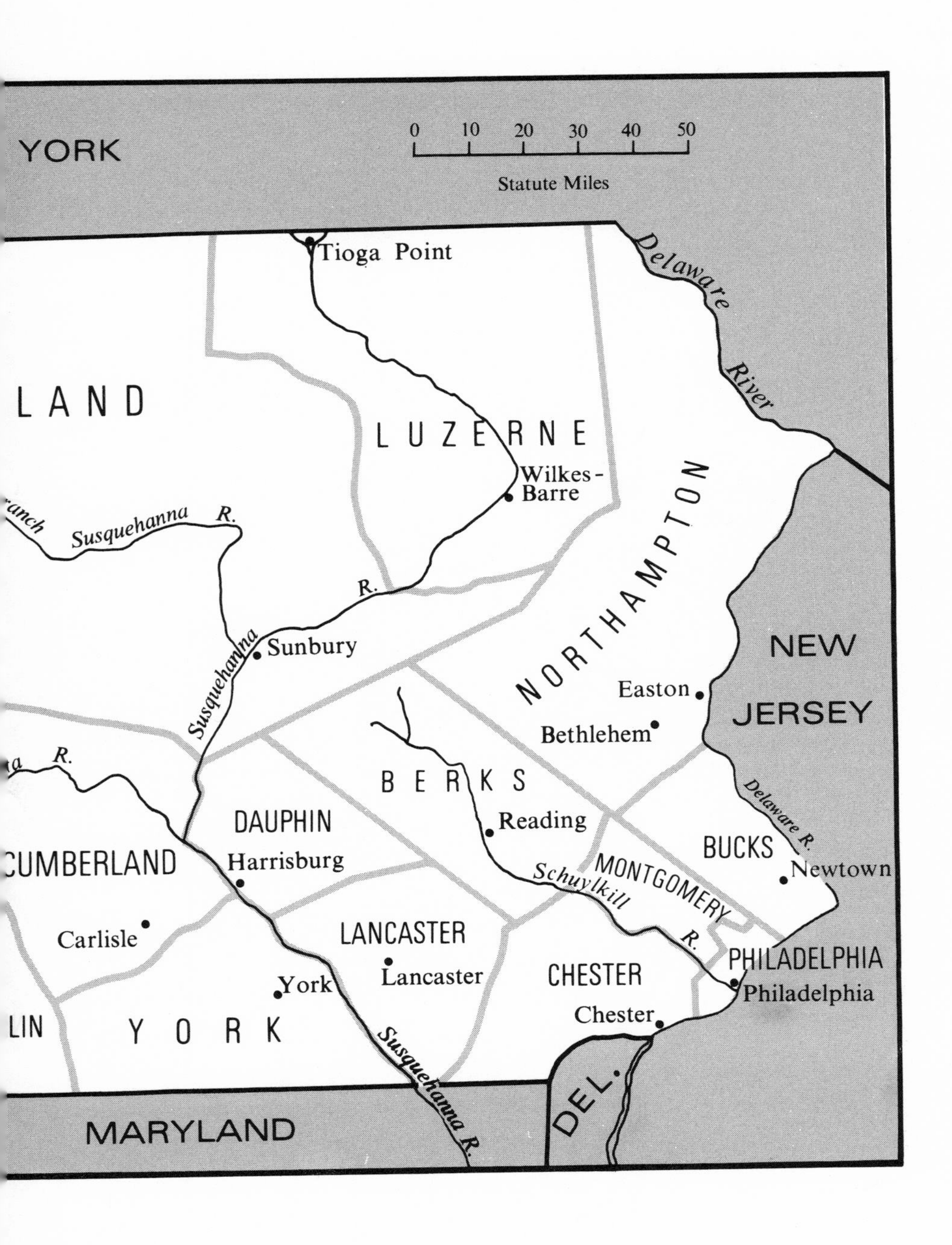
YORK
0 10 20 30 40 50
Statute Miles
Tioga Point
Delaware
River
LAND
LUZERNE
Wilkes-
Barre
Susquehanna
R.
R.
NORTHAMPTON
Sunbury
Susquehanna
NEW
JERSEY
Easton
Bethlehem
R.
BERKS
Delaware R.
DAUPHIN
Reading
BUCKS
CUMBERLAND
Harrisburg
MONTGOMERY
Newtown
Schuylkill
R.
Carlisle
LANCASTER
PHILADELPHIA
Lancaster
CHESTER
York
Philadelphia
Chester
LIN
YORK
Susquehanna R.
DEL.
MARYLAND

I

The Pennsylvania Assembly and the Constitution

17–29 September 1787

Introduction

The third and final session of the 11th General Assembly met from 4 to 29 September 1787. When the Assembly reconvened on 4 September, the Constitutional Convention was still meeting in the legislative chamber. Therefore, the Assembly resolved to meet "above stairs," where it proceeded with its usual business concerning bills for the creation of counties, towns, and ecclesiastical societies, for internal improvements and the erection of public buildings, for altering acts already in force, and to assist private persons.

The Constitutional Convention "broke up" at 4 P.M., 17 September, and the next morning Pennsylvania's Convention delegates delivered a copy of the Constitution and accompanying documents to the Assembly which read them into its Journals. At the end of the reading Benjamin Franklin suggested that the Assembly pass an act ceding land to the United States for the seat of government. The Assembly then adjourned for the day and did not resume consideration of the Constitution until Monday, 24 September, when it began to receive petitions supporting the Constitution.

After the Constitutional Convention adjourned, the central issue in the Assembly was whether or not to remain in session until the Confederation Congress acted on the Constitution. The Federalists wanted to call a state convention before the end of the session on 29 September, while the Antifederalists wanted to delay until after the election of the new Assembly on 9 October.

There were conflicting reports as to what the Assembly would do. On 20 September the *Pennsylvania Herald* reported that "It is said that the General Assembly will break up in the beginning of next week. The important business reported from the Federal Convention will probably be left to the succeeding house." On 22 September the *Independent Gazetteer* declared that "We are informed by good authority, that our legislature have no intention of rising next week as has been reported; so far from it, that they are anxiously waiting the return of the new Federal Constitution from Congress, in order that they may take it under their most serious consideration before they close the present session."

During a debate on 27 September, Robert Whitehill stated that the Assembly "intended to adjourn on Saturday," 29 September.

However, the Federalists were determined to call a state convention whether or not Congress acted, and they controlled the Assembly. They knew that Congress was considering the Constitution and that a majority of the members supported it (see George Clymer's comments in the Assembly Debates (Lloyd), Friday, A.M., 28 September; and William Bingham to Thomas FitzSimons, 21 September, CDR: IX, A).

On Friday morning, 28 September, George Clymer presented resolutions calling a convention to consider the Constitution, establishing the procedures for electing delegates, and setting the time and place for its meeting. After several hours of debate, the Assembly passed only the resolution to call a convention and then adjourned until 4 P.M.

When the members reassembled, they discovered that enough opponents of the Constitution had stayed away to prevent a quorum. The members present then adjourned until Saturday morning. This maneuver was not new in Pennsylvania politics, and it was facilitated by the Pennsylvania constitution. Most state constitutions provided that a majority was enough for a quorum, but the Pennsylvania constitution defined a quorum as two-thirds of the elected members.

Early Saturday morning, 29 September, George Clymer received an unofficial copy of the congressional resolution of the previous day, which transmitted the Constitution to the states. William Bingham, a Pennsylvania delegate in Congress, had sent the resolution by an express rider who arrived in Philadelphia some time between 3 and 7 o'clock Saturday morning (Samuel Hodgdon to Timothy Pickering, 29 September and *Pennsylvania Gazette,* 3 October, both I:C below; and *Pittsburgh Gazette,* 27 October, Mfm:Pa. 167). When the members convened at 9:30, the Assembly still lacked a quorum. The members present then ordered the sergeant at arms and the assistant clerk to bring in the absent members. With the assistance of a mob led by Captain John Barry, the officials forcibly returned James M'Calmont and Jacob Miley to the Assembly, and a quorum was then declared present. Before the Assembly adjourned *sine die* that afternoon, it had voted for the election of delegates to be held on 6 November and for the Convention to meet in Philadelphia on 20 November.

After the adjournment, sixteen of the nineteen seceding assemblymen signed an address, dated 29 September, giving their version of the events of 28–29 September and stating their objections to the Constitution (I:B below). Frederick Antes (who had voted to call a convention), Joseph Powell, and Thomas Kennedy did not sign. On 2 October Eleazer Oswald printed the address as a broadside despite opposition from Philadelphia Federalists (William Bradford to Elias Boudinot, 2 October, Mfm:Pa.88; Charles Tillinghast to Hugh Hughes, 12 October, CC:155). The next day Oswald reprinted the address in the *Independent Gazetteer,* and within a month it was reprinted eleven more times in the state. Melchior Steiner of the *Philadelphische Correspondenz* also printed the address as a broadside in German. (For national circulation of the address, see CC:125–A.)

Six assemblymen answered the address of the seceding assemblymen in the *Pennsylvania Packet* on 8 October (I:B below). This reply was reprinted seven times in Pennsylvania and nine times outside the state. (For other replies to the address, see "The Protest of the Minority," 3 October, II:A below; "An Independent Citizen" and an anonymous writer in the *Pittsburgh Gazette,* Mfm:Pa. 118, 168; Pelatiah Webster's pamphlet, CC:125–B; "Federal Constitution," CC:150–B.)

The published defenses of the seceding members were few; and, for the most part, they relied upon the arguments used in the address itself. The Assembly was attacked for having acted without official word from Congress and for resorting to violence to secure a quorum (*Pennsylvania Herald,* 6 October; William Findley's "An Assemblyman," and "One of the Dissenting Assemblymen," Mfm: Pa. 166, 224).

As the first state to call a convention, Pennsylvania attracted national attention. Federalists throughout the country censured the seceding assemblymen, but they also criticized the majority for its intemperance. Antifederalists defended the actions of the seceding members because the majority had used undue haste in calling a convention. (For Federalist commentaries by Edward Carrington, James Madison, and Nicholas Gilman, see CC: 185, 187, 215. For Antifederalist commentaries by Richard Henry Lee and George Mason, see CC:132, 179.)

Members of the Assembly, 1786–1787

City of Philadelphia
- William Will
- Robert Morris
- Thomas FitzSimons
- George Clymer
- Jacob Hiltzheimer

County of Philadelphia
- Thomas Mifflin
- Isaac Gray
- William Robinson, Jr.
- John Salter
- George Logan

County of Bucks
- Samuel Foulke
- Gerardus Wynkoop
- John Chapman
- Valentine Upp

County of Chester
- James Moore
- Richard Willing
- Robert Ralston
- Samuel Evans
- Richard Thomas
- Townsend Whelen

County of Lancaster
- Samuel J. Atlee
- Alexander Lowrey
- Adam Hubley
- Emanuel Carpenter
- Joseph Work
- George Ross

County of York
- David McConaughy
- Michael Schmyser
- David McClellan
- Joseph Lilley
- Henry Tyson
- Adam Eichelberger

County of Cumberland
- Robert Whitehill
- Thomas Beale
- Thomas Kennedy
- David Mitchell

County of Berks
- Joseph Hiester
- Philip Kreemer
- Gabriel Hiester
- David Davis
- Daniel Clymer

County of Northampton
- Peter Trexler, Jr.
- Thomas Mawhorter
- Robert Brown
- Peter Burkhalter

County of Bedford
- John Piper
- Joseph Powell
- John Cannon

County of Northumberland
- Frederick Antes
- Samuel Dale

County of Westmoreland
- William Findley
- James Barr
- Hugh H. Brackenridge

County of Washington
- Alexander Wright
- John McDowell
- John Flenniken [?]
- James Allison

County of Fayette
- Theophilus Philips
- John Gilchrist

County of Franklin
- Abraham Smith
- James M'Calmont

County of Montgomery
- Charles Moore
- Samuel Wheeler
- James Hockley
- Jacob Reiff

County of Dauphin
- Robert Clark
- Jacob Miley
- John Carson

County of Luzerne
- John Franklin

A. THE ASSEMBLY CALLS THE STATE CONVENTION

The Pennsylvania Assembly
Monday
17 September 1787

Assembly Proceedings[1]

A letter from the honorable the members representing this state in the Federal Convention was read; and on motion, and by special order, the same was read the second time, as follows, viz.:

"Philadelphia, 17th September, 1787

"Sir: The Convention having decided on the form of a Constitution, to be recommended to the consideration of the United States, we take the earliest moment to communicate this important intelligence to the Assembly of the Commonwealth of Pennsylvania, and to request you would inform that Honorable House, that we shall be ready to report to them at such time and place as they may direct.

"With perfect respect, we have the honor to be, sir, your most obedient and humble servants, B. Franklin, Robert Morris, Thomas Mifflin, George Clymer, Jared Ingersoll, Thomas Fitzsimons, Gouverneur Morris, James Wilson."

Whereupon on motion of Thomas Fitzsimons, seconded by Adam Hubley,

Ordered, That eleven o'clock tomorrow morning be assigned for receiving the said report.

Adjourned until half past nine o'clock tomorrow, A.M.

1. The Assembly Proceedings, taken from the *Minutes,* are cited by date only. The account in Thomas Lloyd's *Debates* (Mfm:Pa. 45) is not printed here because it is almost identical with the Proceedings. For a description by an assemblyman, see Jacob Hiltzheimer Diary, 17 September, Mfm:Pa. 46.

Newspaper Report of Assembly Proceedings

The Speaker [Thomas Mifflin] presented a letter to the House from their delegates in Convention, of the following purport, viz., that they were happy in being able to inform the House, that the Convention had agreed upon the Constitution of a federal government for the United States, and that the delegates were ready to report to the legislature, at any time that should be appointed.

Upon motion, and special order, this letter was taken up for a second reading, when Mr. Fitzsimons observed, that as this measure was essentially interesting to the people, and as it had already exercised a great share of public patience, he should propose that tomorrow morning at 11 o'clock be appointed for receiving the report of the delegates which being seconded by Mr. Hubley was accordingly agreed to.

Mr. Fitzsimons then mentioned that it was the wish of the delegates to the Federal Convention, after the accomplishment of so arduous a task, to enjoy a social meeting; which, on account of the departure of some of them this evening, had been appointed for today's dinner. He hoped, therefore, that the House would agree to an adjournment in order that the Speaker and the other members of the House that were delegates might have it in their power to attend this appointment. Accordingly the House adjourned to meet tomorrow morning at half past 9 o'clock. [*Pennsylvania Herald,* 18 September]

The Pennsylvania Assembly
Tuesday
18 September 1787

Assembly Proceedings[1]

On motion of William Findley, seconded by William Will,

Ordered, That Mr. Piper and Mr. C. Moore be a committee, to introduce the honorable the deputies representing this state in the Federal Convention into the Assembly chamber, for the purpose of reporting to this House the Constitution agreed to by the Convention for the government of the United States.

. . . .

Ordered, . . . That the deputies from this state to the late General Convention may be introduced.

The honorable the deputies representing this state in the late Federal Convention being introduced, His Excellency the President [Benjamin Franklin] of this commonwealth addressed the Speaker in the following words:

"Sir: I have now the very great satisfaction of delivering to you, and to this Honorable House, the result of our deliberations in the late Convention. We hope and believe, that the measures recommended by that body will produce happy effects to this commonwealth, as well as to every other of the United States."

His Excellency then presented to the Speaker the Constitution,[2] agreed to in Convention, for the government of the United States, which was read, as follows, viz.,

[The Constitution and the two accompanying documents signed by George Washington are inserted in the Proceedings at this point.]

His Excellency the President of the state then addressed the Speaker in the words following, viz.,

"Sir: Your delegates in Convention conceive it their duty, to submit in a more particular manner to the consideration of this House, that part of the Constitution just now read, which confers on the Congress exclusive legislation over such district as may become the seat of government of the United States. Perhaps it would be advisable to pass a law, granting the jurisdiction over any place in Pennsylvania, not exceeding ten miles square, which, with the consent of the inhabitants, the Congress might choose for their residence. We think, sir, that such a measure might possibly tend to fix their choice within the bounds of this commonwealth, and thereby essentially benefit the citizens of Pennsylvania."[3]

Adjourned until half past nine o'clock tomorrow, A.M.

1. Lloyd's *Debates* (Mfm:Pa. 48) are not printed here because they are almost identical with the Proceedings.

2. The six-page Dunlap and Claypoole broadside (CC:76).

3. For the Assembly's action upon this recommendation, see Assembly Proceedings, Friday, A.M., 28 September and Saturday, 29 September.

Newspaper Reports of Assembly Proceedings

Yesterday the frame of government was reported by the delegates of Pennsylvania, agreeably to their instructions, to the General Assembly of this state and read publicly in the presence of a large crowd of citizens, who stood in the gallery of the Assembly room, and who testified the highest pleasure in seeing that great work at last perfected, which promises, when adopted, to give security, stability, and dignity to the government of the United States. [*Pennsylvania Gazette*, 19 September][1]

* * * *

On motion of Mr. Findley, Colonel Piper and Dr. Moore were appointed to introduce the delegates to the Federal Convention, at the time appointed for receiving their report.

. . . .

Precisely at 11 o'clock, Colonel Piper and Dr. Moore introduced His Excellency Dr. Franklin, Robert Morris, George Clymer, James Wilson, Thomas Fitzsimons, Jared Ingersol, and Governeur Morris, esquires, the delegates to the Federal Convention, when His Excellency addressed himself to the Speaker to the following effect: "Sir, we have now the honor to present to this House the plan of government for the United States, which has been determined upon by the Federal Convention. We sincerely hope and believe that the result of the labors of that honorable body will tend to promote the happiness and prosperity of this commonwealth in particular, and of the United States in general."

Mr. Fitzsimons then stated the propriety of the report being read by a member of the delegation and proposed the Speaker for that purpose, who accordingly read it to the House.

[The Constitution and the accompanying documents appear at this point.]

As soon as the Speaker had concluded, Dr. Franklin rose and delivered a letter from the delegates to the House, which being read, consisted of a recommendation to the legislature, "that a law should be immediately passed vesting in the new Congress a tract of land of ten miles square, by which that body might be induced to fix the seat of federal government in this state—an event that must be highly advantageous to the Commonwealth of Pennsylvania."

The delegates having withdrawn, on motion of Mr. Findley, the House adjourned, till tomorrow morning at half past 9 o'clock. [*Pennsylvania Herald*, 20 September][2]

1. Reprinted: *Pennsylvania Mercury*, 21 September. For other accounts, see Mfm:Pa. 52. By 16 October several accounts of this day's events were reprinted sixteen times from Maine to Maryland.

2. This account was reprinted with slight variations in the *Pennsylvania Packet*, 21 September. Only the portion concerning a cession of land was reprinted in the *Pennsylvania Mercury*, 21 September and *Lancaster Zeitung*, 26 September. By 22 October the House proceedings, particularly those concerning the cession of land, were reprinted twenty times from Maine to South Carolina.

The Pennsylvania Assembly
Monday
24 September 1787

Assembly Proceedings

The House met pursuant to adjournment.[1]

Petitions from 250 inhabitants of Germantown, in the county of Philadelphia, were presented to the chair and read, as follows, viz.,[2] "To the Honorable the Representatives of the Freemen of Pennsylvania, in General Assembly met.

"The Petition and Declaration of the Citizens of Germantown, respectfully show, that your petitioners have seen, with great pleasure, the proposed Constitution of the United States, and as they conceive it to be wisely calculated to form a perfect union of the states, as well as to secure to themselves and posterity the blessings of peace, liberty and safety, they have taken this method of expressing their earnest desires that the said Constitution may be adopted, as speedily as possible, by the State of Pennsylvania, in the manner recommended by the resolution of the late Honorable Convention."

Ordered to lie on the table.

. . . .

On motion of William Findley, seconded by William Will,

Resolved, That three thousand copies of the Constitution for the government of the United States, recommended by the late Honorable Convention, be printed in the English language, and five hundred copies thereof in the German, to be distributed throughout this state for the information of the inhabitants thereof.

Ordered, That Mr. Will, Mr. Hubley and Mr. Kreemer be a committee to procure a translation of the said Constitution into the German language.

1. The House had adjourned on Friday afternoon.
2. For other petitions, see Mfm:Pa. 61. Subsequent entries in the Proceedings for the 26th, 27th, and 28th of September indicate that petitions "of a similar tenor" to the Germantown petition of the 24th were read.

Assembly Debates

The House met pursuant to adjournment.

A petition was presented from two hundred and fifty inhabitants of Germantown, as follows:

[See Assembly Proceedings, 24 September.]

William Findley moved, that the House would direct one thousand copies in English, and five hundred copies in German, of "the Constitution agreed to in Convention, for the government of the United States," to be printed and distributed among the citizens of Pennsylvania.

Hugh H. Brackenridge would add to the motion, that a committee be appointed to engage a proper person to translate the plan into the German language; which was agreed to, and Messrs. Will, Hubley, and Kreemer were appointed.

The Pennsylvania Assembly
Tuesday
25 September 1787

Assembly Debates

Robert Whitehill thinking the number, ordered yesterday to be published of the plan of the federal government, is too small, he moved to add two thousand more to that motion.

Hugh H. Brackenridge observed, that this paper had been published in all the gazettes, as well as in handbills; from which he concluded, that the number of fifteen hundred, ordered yesterday, would be enough to convey the information generally through the state; as it was also probable, that it would be reprinted in the gazettes at Pittsburgh and Carlisle. He observed, that the Constitution and statement of the comptroller, printed for the purpose of being distributed through the state, were not the more generally spread—as such orders of the House did not accomplish their object, he was of opinion it would be as well to keep the money in the treasury.

Robert Whitehill contended, that the circulation of newspapers was but small and not adequate to convey that full information which the present subject required.

The southwest part of Chester County and Lancaster County, he thought, were hitherto unacquainted with the result of the deliberations of the Convention; the newspaper in Carlisle may circulate it in Cumberland County, but Northampton, Northumberland, and the other back counties can know nothing of it. He was for saving the public money, as much as any member; but wished to give the people an opportunity of thinking for themselves on this important subject. Keeping money in the treasury does not give information to the people, which, at this time, is so extremely necessary.

DANIEL CLYMER moved to amend the motion by adding a thousand copies in German; whereupon,

It was ordered "That two thousand copies in English and one thousand in German be printed in addition."[1]

1. Lloyd's *Debates* are the sole source for the Assembly's action on printing additional copies of the Constitution.

The German language printing was done by Michael Billmeyer, publisher of the *Germantauner Zeitung*. The English printing was probably done by Hall and Sellers of the *Pennsylvania Gazette*, printers to the Assembly.

The Pennsylvania Assembly
Wednesday
26 September 1787

Assembly Proceedings

The House met pursuant to adjournment.

Petitions from 249 inhabitants of the townships of Germantown, Oxford and Lower Dublin, in the county of Philadelphia, were read, of a similar tenor with those read September 24th from 250 inhabitants of Germantown.[1]

Ordered to lie on the table.

1. Lloyd's *Debates* record that "George Logan presented a petition from two hundred and forty-nine inhabitants of Lower Dublin and Oxford townships soliciting the House to take measures for adopting the Federal Constitution." Lloyd mentions only one petition, but six petitions were presented. The clerk's endorsement on the Germantown petition indicates that Oxford submitted four petitions and Lower Dublin and Germantown one each. The endorsement gives the total number of petitioners as 249. (See Mfm:Pa. 61 for the petitions.)

The Pennsylvania Assembly
Thursday
27 September 1787

Assembly Proceedings

Petitions from 3681 inhabitants of the city of Philadelphia, the district of Southwark, and townships of the Northern Liberties, Moyamensing, Passyunk, etc. in the county of Philadelphia, were read of a similar tenor with the petition of 250 inhabitants of Germantown read September 24th.[1]

Ordered to lie on the table.

1. Lloyd's *Debates,* which are essentially the same as the Proceedings, indicate that George Clymer presented the petitions. An account by Dallas is in the *Pennsylvania Herald,* 2 October (Mfm:Pa. 72).

The Pennsylvania Assembly
Friday
28 September 1787

Assembly Proceedings, A.M.[1]

Petitions from 130 inhabitants of the district of Southwark, and the township of the Northern Liberties, and of the grand jury and others, inhabitants of the county of Montgomery, were read, of a similar tenor with those presented September 24th from 250 of the inhabitants of Germantown.

Ordered to lie on the table.

. . . .

A motion was made by George Clymer, seconded by Gerardus Wynkoop, in the words following, viz.:

"Whereas the Convention of deputies from the several states composing the Union, lately held in this city, have published a Constitution for the future government of the United States, to be submitted to conventions of deputies chosen in each state by the people thereof, under the recommendation of its legislature, for their assent and ratification; and whereas it is the sense of great numbers of the good people of this state, already signified in petitions and declarations to this House, that the earliest steps should be taken to assemble a convention within the state, for the purpose of deliberating and determining on the said Constitution:

"Resolved, That it be recommended to such of the inhabitants of the state as are entitled to vote for representatives to the General Assembly, that they choose suitable persons to serve as deputies in a state convention, for the purpose herein before mentioned; that is, for the city of Philadelphia and the counties respectively, the same number of deputies that each is entitled to of representatives in the General Assembly.

"That the elections for deputies as aforesaid be held at the several places in the said city and counties, as are fixed by law for holding the elections of representatives to the General Assembly, and that they be conducted under the same officers, and according to the regulations prescribed by law for holding the elections for said representatives, and at the times herein mentioned, viz., For the city of Philadelphia, the counties of Philadelphia, Chester, Bucks, Lancaster, Berks, Montgomery, Northampton, Northumberland, Dauphin, Luzerne, York, Cumberland and Franklin, on the day of the general election of representatives [9 October] to the General Assembly. For the counties of Bedford, Huntingdon,[2] Westmoreland, Fayette and Washington, on the ________ day of October.[3]

"That the persons so elected to serve in convention shall assemble on the last day of November, at the State House, in the city of Philadelphia.

"That the proposition submitted to this House by the deputies of Pennsylvania in the General Convention of the states, of ceding to the United States a district of country within this state, for the seat of the general government, and for the exclusive legislation of Congress, be particularly recommended to the consideration of the convention.

"That it be recommended to the succeeding House of Assembly, to provide for the payment of any extraordinary expenses which may be incurred by holding the said elections of deputies."

And on the question, "Will the House adopt the first resolution?" the yeas and nays were called by Thomas Fitzsimons and Daniel Clymer, and were as follow, viz.:

YEAS [43]
William Will
Thomas Fitzsimons
George Clymer
Jacob Hiltzheimer
Isaac Gray
William Robinson, Jr.
John Salter
George Logan
Samuel Foulke
Gerardus Wynkoop
John Chapman
Valentine Upp
James Moore
Richard Willing
Robert Ralston
Samuel Evans
Richard Thomas
Townsend Whelen
Alexander Lowrey
Adam Hubley
Emanuel Carpenter
Joseph Work
George Ross
James Clemson
David M'Conaughy
Michael Schmyser
David M'Clellan
Joseph Lilley
Joseph Heister
Philip Kreemer
Gabriel Heister
David Davis
Daniel Clymer
Peter Trexler, Jr.
Peter Burkhalter
John Canon
Frederick Antes
Hugh H. Brackenridge
Charles Moore

Samuel Wheeler
James Hockley
Jacob Reiff
John Carson

NAYS [19]
Robert Whitehill
Thomas Kennedy
David Mitchell
Robert Brown
John Piper
Joseph Powell
Samuel Dale
William Findley
James Barr
Alexander Wright
John M'Dowell
John Flenniken
James Allison
Theophilus Philips
John Gilchreest
Abraham Smith
James M'Calmont
Robert Clark
Jacob Miley

So it was carried in the affirmative.[4]

Ordered, That the further consideration of the said motion be postponed.

Adjourned until four o'clock, P.M.

1. For accounts by assemblymen, see Jacob Hiltzheimer Diary, 28 September, I:A below; "Address of the Seceding Assemblymen," I:B below; Hugh H. Brackenridge's "Narrative," 27 October, Mfm:Pa. 167; and "One of the Dissenting Assemblymen" [William Findley?], 14 November, Mfm:Pa. 224. For newspaper reports which vary in extent and nature, see Mfm:Pa. 75.

Alexander J. Dallas' report of proceedings and debates in the *Pennsylvania Herald* (Mfm:Pa. 74), which was the fullest of the newspaper accounts, was reprinted in the *Pennsylvania Packet* and in part in the *Pennsylvania Gazette* within a few days. Outside Pennsylvania it was reprinted in part eighteen times from Maine to Virginia by 31 October. Reports from other Pennsylvania newspapers were reprinted in fourteen newspapers from Vermont to Georgia by 27 October.

2. Huntingdon County was created on 20 September 1787.

3. The resolutions, as printed in Lloyd's *Debates,* call for the election in the western counties "on the fourth Tuesday in October" (i.e., 23 October).

4. Tench Coxe reported that "There were 34 Republicans and 9 Constitutionalists in the 43. The *principal* Germans were among the nine. The western members chiefly composed the 19" (to James Madison, 28–29 September, I:C below). The nine Constitutionalists were William Will, Samuel Foulke, Gabriel Hiester, Philip Kreemer, Joseph Hiester, David Davis, Peter Trexler, Jr., Peter Burkhalter, and Frederick Antes. For newspaper comments on the vote, see *Pennsylvania Gazette,* 3 October, I:C and II:A below; and Mfm:Pa. 94, 127, 135.

Assembly Debates, A.M.

Isaac Gray presented the petition and declaration of the magistrates and grand jury of the county of Montgomery, requesting the House to agree to some measure for calling a convention to adopt the new confederation.

William Robinson presented a similar one from thirty-one inhabitants of Southwark.

Which were all read and ordered to lie on the table.

. . . .

On CALLING a CONVENTION

GEORGE CLYMER: The House cannot, sir, have forgotten a business of the highest magnitude, which was recommended to their attention by the Federal Convention, and I am persuaded they will readily concur in taking the necessary measures for calling a convention of the citizens of Pennsylvania, to deliberate upon that plan of government which has been presented to this House; for which reason I shall submit the following resolutions.

"Whereas the Convention of deputies from the several states composing the Union, lately held in this city, have published a Constitution for the future government of the United States, to be submitted to conventions of deputies chosen in each state by the people thereof, under the recommendation of its legislature, for their assent and ratification, and whereas it is the sense of great numbers of the good people of this state, already signified in petitions and declarations to this House, that the earliest steps should be taken to assemble a convention within the state, for the purpose of deliberating and determining on the said Constitution.

"Resolved, That it be *recommended* to such inhabitants of the state as are entitled to vote for representatives to the General Assembly, that they *choose suitable persons to serve as deputies in a state convention,* for the purpose herein before mentioned; that is, for the city of Philadelphia and the counties respectively, the same number of deputies that each is entitled to, of representatives in the General Assembly.

"Resolved, That the elections for deputies as aforesaid be held at the several places in the said city and counties, as is fixed by law for holding the elections of representatives to the General Assembly, and that the same be conducted by the officers who conduct the said elections of representatives, and agreeably to the rules and regulations thereof.

"Resolved, That the election of deputies aforesaid shall be held for the city of Philadelphia, and for the counties of Philadelphia, Bucks, Chester, Lancaster, York, Cumberland, Berks, Northampton, Northumberland, Montgomery, Franklin, and Dauphin, on the ninth day of October next, and the election for deputies for the counties of Bedford, Huntingdon, Westmoreland, Washington, and Fayette, be held on the fourth Tuesday in October next.[1]

"Resolved, That the persons so elected to serve in convention shall assemble on the ________, at the State House, in the city of Philadelphia.[2]

"Resolved, That the proposition submitted to this House by the deputies of Pennsylvania in the General Convention of the states, of ceding to the United States a district of country within this state, for the seat of the general government, and for the exclusive legislation of Congress be particularly recommended to the consideration of the convention.

"Resolved, That it be recommended to the succeeding House of Assembly, to make the same allowance to the attending members of the convention, as is made to the members of the General Assembly, and also to provide for the extraordinary expenses which may be incurred by holding the said elections."

These resolutions being seconded by Gerardus Wynkoop, they were by agreement stated as distinct propositions, and on the question, Will the House agree to the following:

"Resolved, That it be *recommended* to such of the inhabitants of the state as are entitled to vote for representatives of the General Assembly, that they *choose suitable persons to serve as deputies in a state convention,* for the purpose herein before mentioned; that is, for the city of Philadelphia and the counties respectively, the same number of deputies that each is entitled to of representatives in the General Assembly.

"Resolved, That the elections for deputies as aforesaid be held at the several places in the said city and counties, as are fixed by law for holding the elections of representatives to the General Assembly, and that the same be conducted by the officers who conduct the said elections of representatives, and agreeably to the rules and regulations thereof."

ROBERT WHITEHILL answered, *no.* He then rose and said: The House, sir, ought to have time to *consider* on this subject, before they determine; for which reason I move to postpone *the consideration* until we meet again, and that may be this afternoon, as the session is drawing so near to a close.

THOMAS FITZSIMONS: I will submit it to the House, whether it is proper to delay this business for the reason assigned by the member from Cumberland [Robert Whitehill]. If the gentlemen are not prepared to say what time the election for delegates shall be held, at least the general principle, or that such convention is proper, must be well enough understood to warrant an immediate determination. It will be observed, that the ordinary business of the state is pretty well gone through, and the House likely to dissolve tomorrow. But the subject brought forward by my worthy colleague [George Clymer] is a business of the highest consequence, and the House must see how eligible it will be to give it the sanction of the legislature. The only object of our consideration is, whether the election shall be held with that propriety which may perhaps be best effected by the representatives pointing out the mode for the conduct of the people.

We are not, I conceive, to consider, whether calling a convention is proper or improper; because that I look upon as a measure inevitable, even should not the Assembly consent, but it will be well for us to appoint the mode by which such choice shall be conducted. These are distinct propositions; and on the first every gentleman must have determined, but on the other every member will have an opportunity of offering his reasons, when it comes before us in the next resolution. Perhaps, sir, it may be necessary to alter the times, from what is there mentioned, to more distant periods; of this the gentlemen from the several counties will be better able to judge than I can pretend to, and I am sure I shall give no opposition to every reasonable extension of the time. I hope it will not be thought necessary, that anything should be said in commendation of the new Constitution prepared for the government of the United States. This, sir, is not the object of our discussion or deliberation, and was it, I think, sir, my abilities could not enable me to do justice to the subject; but the feelings of every member will more forcibly convince his judgment than all the argument which could be offered. From the number of petitions on your table, it may be clearly inferred, that it is the wish and expectation of the people, that this House should adopt speedy measures for calling a convention. I do not, therefore, see a necessity for saying much on a subject so well felt and understood within and without, but cheerfully submit it to the members to say, whether they will proceed now or in the afternoon.

Daniel Clymer: The worthy gentleman from the city [Thomas FitzSimons] has submitted the subject to the feelings of the House, and I agree with him, argument will not more clearly show the advantages that must result from the adoption of the Federal Constitution, than what suggests to the mind of every person within these walls. Nor have I a doubt, sir, but every member will do justice to those feelings, and cheerfully assent to calling a convention, for their own as well as for the future happiness and welfare of the citizens of Pennsylvania. The gentleman observes, it is the general wish of the people, that we should go forward in the measure. Here, sir, I firmly believe him; for, I think, it has but few opposers, very few indeed! I have heard, sir, that only four or five leading party men in this city are against it,[3] whose names I should be glad to know, that their characters might be examined; for I am confident, they will be hereafter ashamed to show their faces among the good people, whose future prosperity they wish to blast in the bud. The reason of their opposition, though not positively known, can be well conjectured; and let them be careful, lest they draw upon themselves the odium of that people, who have long indulged their rioting upon public favor. But, sir, the adoption of this measure is a matter of so much consequence to America, that I am satisfied it will meet the hearty concurrence of this House.

WILLIAM FINDLEY: Whatever gentlemen say with respect to the importance of this subject is argument to prove, that we should go into it with deliberation. And if it is of so much importance, and so well understood out of doors, the House then certainly ought not to be surprised into it. The gentleman from Berks [Daniel Clymer] has spoken warmly against opposing the present measure, in a manner as if intended to prevent men from speaking their minds. He has charged some leading characters in this city with giving opposition. If he means me as one of them (Mr. D. Clymer interrupted him, addressing the Speaker with: No, sir, upon my honor, I did not mean him). Well then, I don't consider that part of his speech as not addressed to the House, but merely to the gallery. But, sir, I consider what has been said of the wishes of the people, as applying to the plan of government, and not to the present question. If I understand it right, we are not at present to judge of the merits of the plan, but on the proper and adequate measure of conducting the people into it. Of the plan I believe there can be no doubt of its being wisely calculated for the purposes intended, but nothing is perfect, and this may be as well as could be expected, and I consider it as very deserving the commendation it received; but this can be no reason for hurrying on the measure with such precipitancy. If it is of the importance it is said to be, surely the House will not refuse to postpone for the present, in order that there may be time to make it as agreeable as possible.

DANIEL CLYMER: I said, sir, the matter was well understood, if we might judge from the sentiments of the people, and there was but little opposition, and that from a few men, who will be ashamed hereafter to come forward and avow their secret machination; so, sir, I say still—nor can any gentleman aver to the contrary. With respect to the postponement of the business till the afternoon, I will ask where is the necessity? Every member must be confident that, with or without his consent, the measure will be adopted; for it is too generally agreeable, and too highly recommended, to be assassinated by the hand of intrigue and cabal. And if it must be adopted, why can it not be done as well this morning as in the afternoon? Or do some gentlemen want an opportunity of consulting with their associates, how far it is agreeable. If there are objections to the time of holding elections, it may be altered. I think sufficient time is not allowed to the county, which I am honored by representing; many others may be in the same predicament, but this can be accommodated.

Yet the general principle is so clear, that nothing is left for consideration or discussion.

GERARDUS WYNKOOP: I suppose, sir, there is not a member of this House but what has pretty fully considered the present business. This I am led to believe from its importance and the length of time which has elapsed since it was communicated to the House. Now if every member has made up his mind, what reason can there be for further consideration? And if the members do not declare they have not yet made up their minds on the propriety of calling a convention, I shall vote for going on with the business.

ROBERT WHITEHILL: It is very well known, that this business is a matter of great importance and deserves the serious attention of the House. But however well the people may be said to be acquainted with the design and intention, yet I don't know how far that may be the case. This, sir, is a very large and extensive state, and I may venture to say, that so far from being the general voice of the people, that not one in twenty know anything about it. I believe a great many people in and about the city have signed petitions in favor of it, but that is but a small part of the whole state.

But to waive the question on the propriety of the measure, it will appear clear, sir, when we come to consider, whether it should be held in so many distant counties on the day of the general election, that it cannot be done; and the members ought to have an opportunity of asking or consulting themselves on that, which would be more proper.

The gentlemen that have brought forward this motion must have some design, as they cannot digest the postponement, or why not leave the members at liberty to consult, or acquire further information? If this is a concerted plan, and it must go through as it stands, we cannot help it; but if it is to be made agreeable to what may be right, on due consideration, why not allow time to consider of it? I believe if time is allowed, we shall be able to show, that this is not the proper time for calling a convention, and I don't know any reason there can be for driving it down our throats, without an hour's preparation. It appears to me to be a plan not fit for discussion, or why refuse to allow it to be postponed? I hope, when the House comes to consider how it has been introduced, they will allow us the time we desire.

DANIEL CLYMER: The gentleman has misunderstood me for I did not speak of the state at large, when I said the people understood it and were in favor of it; though I have not the smallest doubt, but it will receive their warmest approbation, when they hear of it.

THOMAS FITZSIMONS: I did wish, and still hope, the House will pretty unanimously agree to the resolutions which are before us. When we took the business up, I flattered myself the decision would not be delayed, because every member had [had] time enough to consider this subject, since it was first introduced to our attention. But if it is the opinion of any considerable number of gentlemen, that it should lay over till the afternoon, I will not press it. I am sure the arguments made use of by the member from Cumberland [Robert Whitehill] offer no sufficient inducement for a delay. The plan of the new confederation has laid upon your table near a fortnight, and it can be nothing more or less than a confession of inattention, not to say neglect of duty, for gentlemen to plead they have not considered it; for surely the subject was so important, that they must have turned it in their minds and know what is proper to decide on this occasion. The House is also so near its dissolution, that if the measure is to be effected, very little time remains for it; though as I observed before, I do not think it lies with the House to determine, whether a convention shall be called or no. This, I think, sir, forms no part of our deliberations. But it is my wish, that the legislature should take the lead and guide the people into a decent exercise of their prerogative; and surely, sir, it cannot be a matter of such high consideration as to require much time in determining the day on which elections should be held for nominating persons to form a state convention. And, I conceive, this is the single point which we have to consider; for I repeat again, that I do not think it is in our power; nay, I am sure it is not in our power to prevent the people from adopting what may be a lasting benefit to themselves and a certain treasure to posterity. But I think that taking the lead in this business will be an honor not only to this legislature, but to the state also. It is not only honorable but convenient and advantageous; and I submit it to the majority of this House to conclude, whether we shall, by proceeding, obtain for ourselves and constituents these advantages, which even our neglect cannot prevent.

GEORGE CLYMER: The resolutions, Mr. Speaker, which I presented to you, contain separate and distinct propositions. Directing the elections to be held at a short day goes upon the supposition that there is time to communicate the necessary information. If this is not well founded, of consequence it must be altered; but I hope no kind of hesitation can be made, as to the propriety of adopting the first, which goes on the principle, that such a convention is necessary for the better union and happiness of the several states of America. To hesitate upon this proposition will give a very unfavorable aspect to a measure on which our future happiness, nay, I may almost say, our future existence, as a nation, depends. If the time, sir, is not agreeable for holding elections, as mentioned in the second resolution, it cannot operate to prevent our entering upon the first. I therefore hope gentlemen will withdraw their opposition and let a degree of unanimity prevail, which may be an inducement to others steadily to cooperate in perfecting a work, that bids fair to relieve our embarrassments and carry us to a height of prosperity we have hitherto been strangers to.

[Alexander J. Dallas' report of Clymer's speech, *Pennsylvania Herald,* 2 October (Mfm:Pa. 74): Sir, The resolutions before you may be divided into two propositions—first, whether the House will call a convention, and secondly, in what manner it shall be done. On the first of these propositions the House is certainly prepared to decide, and the other may be left till the afternoon. I therefore propose a division of the question in order to accommodate the arguments of the gentlemen who think it necessary to consult upon the times and places of holding the election.]

HUGH H. BRACKENRIDGE: Before the division of the propositions, I had made up my mind to be in favor of the postponement; but it now appears clear to me, that we may decide upon the general principle, to wit, shall a convention of the people be called? With respect to this point, every member must have made up his mind fully, because it is a measure, that from the first was apparent and must have occupied the attention of every individual who had but seen the plan. This, as was remarked before, has been on your table many days, and from its magnitude and importance must have been a subject of reflection to the members, who wished to perform the duty they owed to their God, their conscience, and fellow citizens, so that voting now on a subject already well understood cannot be difficult; and, in my opinion, we are as well prepared to determine upon the principle as we shall be after dinner.

ROBERT WHITEHILL: The gentleman from Westmoreland [Hugh H. Brackenridge], as well as the others who have spoken in favor of the resolutions, seemed generally of opinion, that they ought to be adopted without further consideration, concluding that every member is prepared to determine on the propriety thereof. But this, sir, is not the case; for I own, that I have not prepared myself to take up this business, because I did not expect any notice would be taken of it for Congress ought to send forward the plan before we do anything at all in this matter. For of what use was sending it forward to them unless we meant to wait their determination. Now as these measures are not recommended by Congress, why should we take them up? Why should we take up a thing, which does not exist? For this does not exist, that is before us, nor can it until it is ratified by Congress. I have no doubt for my part, but Congress will adopt it; but if they should make alterations, and amendments in it, is there anyone can say then, what sort of a plan it will be? And as this may happen, I hope the House, when they come to consider seriously, will see the impropriety of going on at present. It will appear, that it is necessary to give time for Congress to deliberate before they recommend. It does appear that Congress have not recommended it; and the recommendation of Congress ought to be waited for in a matter that concerns the liberties and rights of the people of the United States. I say this recommendation is not come forward to the House, nor we don't know when (if ever) it will. We do not know that Congress may be able to go thro with it this long time yet, and why are we to determine on it before we know whether they will allow of such change of the Confederation? We do not know that Congress are even sitting or whether they will be in session.[4] And before we proceed to measures of this importance, do let us know what we are going on, and let us not sport away the rights and liberties of the people altogether. I say, is it not better to go safely on the business, and let it lie over till the next house; when we have adjourned, let our constituents think of it and instruct their representatives to consider of the plan proper to be pursued. Will not the next house be as able to determine as we are? And I would wish the members to consider, that it never was supposed at our election, that we had the power to determine on such a measure. When we come to consider, it does appear to me better to leave it over to the next house, and they will be better able, and better instructed, what to do in this case. And what is the consequence the gentlemen propose by this hurry, that the State of Pennsylvania shall have the honor of taking the lead. This may be preserved, sir, as well by letting it lie over; for, can the other states go into it before us? Can the State of Georgia receive it as soon, and send it forward for ratification, as we can? No, to be sure they cannot. Therefore this hurry does appear too great in my opinion; because, if it is delayed, our determination can still be brought forward sooner than that of any other state. If there are any objections of moment against calling the convention at present, let us be prepared to make them; we may do that better, perhaps, by deferring only till the afternoon for tho gentlemen say they have had time, and have made up their minds, yet that has not been my case, and I don't see why the business should be hurried upon us at this rate. I hope when gentlemen consider, they will agree to postpone for the present.

HUGH H. BRACKENRIDGE: I conceive, sir, that the member [Robert Whitehill] has wandered from the point, whenever he went into remarks upon the new Constitution; but I did not interrupt, nor do I mean now to reply to those observations, because I would not follow him in a subject which is not before the House. But if it should be necessary to speak on the general principles, I trust that he would be fully answered. At present, sir, I understand the question to be, whether sufficient time has not elapsed to give every member, who respects his duty, sufficient opportunity to have made up his mind on the propriety of calling a convention of the people. If this is the case, the House will not surely postpone.

Daniel Clymer: The member from Cumberland [Robert Whitehill] seems to think it highly improper, that we should proceed in this business until Congress shall recommend it to our attention and have given it the stamp of their approbation; but this, sir, is extremely fallacious. For if Congress are to determine the point, where was the necessity for the Federal Convention to recommend calling state conventions? Or pray, sir, were the delegates to that important undertaking ordered even to report to Congress? No, sir, they were not. But I take it that their reason for having done so was that as they meant to report to the people of the United States at large, they thought Congress would be a proper channel to convey it to every part from New Hampshire to Georgia and I think the mode of conveyance very proper; but I never entertained an idea, that it was submitted to their cognizance, as the gentleman says, for alteration or amendment. He supposes too, that the convention of the state may adopt some part of the frame of government and refuse the other. But not so, sir, they must adopt *in toto* or refuse altogether for it must be a plan that is formed by the United States, which can be agreeable to all, and not one formed upon the narrow policy and convenience of any one particular state. Such, sir, is the Constitution lately presented to you, framed by the collective wisdom of a continent, centered in a venerable band of patriots, worthies, heroes, legislators and philosophers—the admiration of a world. This, sir, is a subject the member from the city [Thomas FitzSimons] did well to submit to your feelings. Vain is every attempt to do justice to its merits. No longer shall thirty thousand people engage all our attention—all our efforts to procure happiness. No! The extended embrace of fraternal love shall enclose three millions, and ere fifty years are elapsed thirty millions, as a band of brothers! And will the State of Pennsylvania, will a few of her inhabitants I should say, attempt to defeat this long-expected and wished-for moment, by entering into a discussion of the minutiae? How her interest is preserved? Why, sir, to form a happy Union, the weakest eye must perceive the necessity of mutual concessions—mutual sacrifices. Had the late Convention not been composed of gentlemen of liberal sentiments, patriotism, and integrity, it might never have been perfected. Had each been studious of accommodating the Constitution to the circumstances and wishes of the state they represented, nothing could have been effected. Do we not hear, that disposed as they were to make a sacrifice of the local interests to the general welfare, that five weeks elapsed before they could determine the proportion of representation. If these gentlemen met with such difficulties, who possessed the information and knowledge of the continent, can it be supposed the United States would submit to the amendments and alterations to be made by a few inhabitants of Pennsylvania? Could it be expected that Virginia (the Dominion of Virginia, as some people in derision call it, though I say it is a land of liberty, a land of patriots, and the nurse of science) I say will you expect, sir, that Virginia and the Southern States shall coincide with alterations made only for the benefit of Pennsylvania? No! Away with such idea, and let that unanimity prevail at its adoption that it did at its formation. It is improper for gentlemen to say, we ought not to enter on this business until it is ratified by Congress. This, sir, is not the case, and let me, as setting my argument on a foundation of solidity, call your attention to the recommendation made by the united sense and wisdom of our continent to this legislature. Remember how strong the language of the venerable Franklin, when he addressed you to enforce this recommendation. Remember the advantage and prosperity held out to Pennsylvania, for her early and cheerful concurrence in a measure, whose perfections are so clearly seen as to make hesitation criminal. Will all the art of sophistry prove an inferiority to the present Confederation, which, upon trial, is found to be loose and ineffectual? Shall we, by chicane and artful procrastination, defeat the measure so loudly demanded by every circumstance of happiness or preservation. Better would it be, Mr. Speaker, to join in the glorious sentiment of that gallant officer, who having quitted his station, and gained a signal victory over his enemy, and when called to account for his breach of orders, answered, that man holds his life too dear, who would not sacrifice it for his country's safety.

If it is the interest of a few individuals to keep up the weak and shattered government, which brings on us the contempt of every surrounding tribe and the reproach and obloquy of every nation, let them exert their opposition, but it will be all in vain, for should even this House refuse, I think it the duty of people, as they value their present and future welfare, to come forward and do that justice to themselves which others would deny them.

As this subject is now before us, let us not hesitate, but eagerly embrace the glorious opportunity of being foremost in its adoption. Let us not hesitate; because it is damping the ardor with which it should be pursued. Sir, it is throwing cold water on the flame, that warms the breast of every friend of liberty and every patriot who wishes this country to acquire that respect to which she is justly entitled.

As we have taken up this matter, let us go through; for our determination may have weight with our sister states, and they will follow where we take the lead, the honor of agreeing first to a measure, that must entitle to posterity security for their property—no longer subject to the fluctuation of faithless paper money and party laws, security to their liberty, and security to their personal safety. These are blessings which will engage the gratitude of posterity to venerate your ashes. Excuse me, sir, for being warm; it is a matter I have much at heart, and a subject which I almost adore; and let the consequences to me be what they may, I must give it my support; for it has my most hearty concurrence, and to every part and particle I do pronounce a willing and a grateful AMEN.

I am against the postponement of the question, as to the principle; but as to that part of the resolution relating to the time, I shall move for an alteration, as my colleagues and myself think the period too short.

THOMAS FITZSIMONS: I was inclined to delay the business until the afternoon; but from all that has been said, I believe it must be the opinion of the House, that it will be proper to decide upon the first resolution before we adjourn. As to the Constitution itself, I believe the proper place for discussing that will be in the convention, so that nothing need be added on that head. If the time mentioned for the elections is supposed improper, that may be accommodated to the gentleman's [Daniel Clymer] wishes by amendments.

The question, will the House agree to the postponement? was put, and only nine rose in favor of it. So it was determined in the negative.[5]

HUGH H. BRACKENRIDGE: You will please to recollect, sir, that, when I was up last, I observed that one of the arguments of the member from Cumberland [Robert Whitehill] might easily be obviated. As that was an improper time to reply to him, I declined doing it; but I mean now to enter on this subject, as I consider it fully before us.

ROBERT WHITEHILL interrupted him with saying he had said nothing against the principles of the proposed plan, but that we were not ready to take it up.

HUGH H. BRACKENRIDGE: The gentleman must suppose me a fool to think I was going into a defense of the principles of the new form of government. No, sir, that I take to be seated above either the reach of his arguments or information.

It is wholly upon another point I mean to remark. He has said, if I could select what he said, that we ought not to take up the present question, nor adopt the resolution, until we heard from Congress; and his argument was, that this should be left to a future house to complete. Now this I mean to answer, and hope to show perfectly, that neither premises or conclusion is well founded. There is also another question, which seems to lie at the bottom of his argument, namely, that it is necessary at the same time, for the state to wait until an improvement of the congressional government is recommended by Congress. This, sir, I conceive, would be a question lying at the bottom of the subject, which occupies our present consideration. But I have not been able to discover any principle on which an idea of this nature can be founded. What particular right have Congress to recommend an improvement of the federal government? They may recommend, but I should suppose it comes under no part of the authority delegated to them; and therefore that it was going wholly out of the province assigned to them. I should suppose it indelicate for the superior *power* to solicit more. We know they are invested with the power of recommending by the Confederation; but who would recommend from that body, that it should be gratified with more extensive power? I should, I say, presume it must come from them, not with the highest degree of delicacy. In the next place, taking it for granted that it should come entirely from them, what is the foundation, or what must be the foundation of a recommendation of that nature? Is it because they have become sensible, that the present powers are not sufficient to conduct the affairs of the United States, and that a more vigorous and energetic government became necessary? Who ought to be the best judges of this necessity? Men in Congress reflecting abstractedly or the body of the people, on this continent, feeling and knowing this necessity. I therefore think it would be advisable to be guided in an alteration rather by this maxim, than by the other. If a thing, sir, ought to be done, it is little matter whether it be from the reflection of Congress or the feeling and sensibility of the people; and I own, that I always feel a contempt for those languid and trammeled sentiments, which move but like a piece of mechanism. And what are the consequences of taking up the subject, without waiting the result of congressional deliberation? We lead the way, and do great honor to ourselves, in marking the road to obtain the sense of the people, on a subject that is of the greatest moment to them and to their posterity. How did this business first originate? Did Virginia wait the recommendation of Congress? Did Pennsylvania, who followed her in the appointment of delegates, wait the recommendation of Congress? The Assembly of New York, when they found they had not the honor of being foremost in the measure, revived the idea of its being necessary to have it recommended by Congress, as an excuse for their tardiness (being the seat of the federal government), and Congress, to humor them, complied with their suggestions.[6] How it happened to take effect in the other states, I do not positively say; but I am rather inclined to believe it was adopted from the influence of example, rather than from the recommendation of Congress, which happened to take place in the interval between the sittings of the legislatures. But we never heard, that it was supposed necessary to wait their recommendations. No such argument was made use of on this floor when the law was passed. The delegates to the Convention were appointed without the recommendation of Congress; and they reported the result of their deliberations to this House. What reason then is there for waiting any longer to determine, whether it is proper to call a convention, to consider of it or not? I don't see, for my part, what Congress have to do with it, though doubtless I should not object to waiting a few days to hear their opinion. This has been done even until now, which is so near the close of our session, as to make a longer delay improper, therefore, waiting their recommendation is no argument for prolonging the consideration of the subject before us. But there is certainly strong reasons, why we should call up and determine the question, whether a convention should be called or not. The advantages to the state are, that it will be to her honor to take the lead in adopting so wise a plan, and it will be an inducement for other states to follow. We no doubt remember the influence the example of Virginia and Pennsylvania had in getting a general delegation appointed, and that example will no doubt as generally be followed in adopting the result, for it is everywhere fully and sensibly felt, that an alteration in the federal government is requisite, and I think there can be little hesitation in agreeing to the resolution for calling a convention. As for the day of election, that is but a secondary consideration and may be determined when it comes before us. We surely shall unanimously agree to the first resolution at this time, for delay would argue a lukewarmness, that must be injurious to the cause. Every person who should hear we had the subject ten days before us and, notwithstanding, avoided entering upon it, must conclude we are unfriendly to it; and it will be cause of triumph to our enemies, who wait only to see us refuse that government, which alone can save us from their machinations.

As it is fully in our power to appoint the mode and manner of calling the convention, I hope gentlemen will turn their thoughts, and say what is the proper time, for if it is delayed until the next house, it will be some time far advanced into another year before a convention can sit to ratify the plan for our future government, by which means the force of example would be for delay, and a measure so extremely necessary would be left exposed or perhaps neglected, unless the ardor of our citizens should induce them to do what our timidity would decline. The influence which this state may acquire by decision will be lost, and many of the advantages lessened by an unnecessary delay.

WILLIAM FINDLEY: I do not intend to reply to the arguments used in favor of the present measure, but only examine the ground on which we stand. When the question was on postponement, I did not think it right that gentlemen should have introduced the observations which they did, nor that the manner of speaking, which some used, was proper. It was only addressed to the passions, and in my reply I do not mean to justify such language, by using what may be similar. No, sir, I intend to address the judgment, and not the passions of any man. I have no doubt, *but a convention might be called, and will be called. That it ought to be called, and will be called,* is seen so clearly, that I shall add nothing to enforce it; therefore, I take it, that the propriety of calling a convention is not the question before us. After declaring my sentiments so far, I shall proceed, sir, now to examine the ground on which we stand. I believe we stand on federal ground; therefore, we are not in a state of nature. If we were in a state of nature, all the arguments produced for hastening this business would apply; but as we are not, I would observe, that the most deliberate manner of proceeding is the best manner. But the manner in which this subject has been introduced is an indeliberate manner and seems to argue, that we are not on federal ground. The design of carrying this through, I say, sir, is a presumption, that we are in a state of nature; if that is the case, then it can only be proper to use this expedition. What I mean, sir, by a state of nature is with respect to the Confederation, or union of the states, and not any wise alluding to our particular state government. Now my opinion is, sir, that we are on federal ground, that the Federal Convention was a federal convention, that it had the powers of a federal convention, and that they were limited to act federally, that they have acted agreeable to the limitation, and have acted federally. I know by some of the arguments which have been used, that some gentlemen suppose otherwise. Well then, sir, we will have recourse to the Confederation itself, and then to the law which appointed delegates to the Convention, and let them decide whether we are on federal ground or not.

The sixth Article of the Confederation says, "No two or more states shall enter into any treaty, confederation, or alliance whatever between them, without the consent of the United States in Congress assembled, specifying, accurately, the purposes for which the same is to be entered into, and how long it shall continue." It may be said this don't apply. Well let us examine what it says further in the thirteenth Article. "The Articles of Confederation shall be inviolably observed by every state, and the Union shall be perpetual; nor shall any alteration at any time hereafter be made in any of them, unless such alteration be agreed to in a congress of the United States, and be afterwards confirmed by the legislatures of every state." Now did we act in conformity with these articles by passing the law appointing delegates to the Convention, or did we not? I say we did. I know the contrary has been said, but let us have recourse to our own act. I don't mean, as I said before, to reply particularly to any arguments, but to establish the point that we have all along acted upon federal principles, and that we ought to continue federal, and I have no doubt but we shall. But what says the preamble of the law? Hear our own words, sir: "Whereas the general assembly of this commonwealth, taking into their serious consideration the representations heretofore made to the legislatures of the several states in the union, by the United States in Congress assembled," etc. It has been mentioned that we took it up in consequence of Virginia's having engaged in the measure; and as the reasons are only mentioned in the preamble, they may not deserve much attention, but the second section of the law decides this point. The words are, after enumerating the persons, that they are hereby constituted and appointed deputies from this state, with powers to meet such deputies as may be appointed and authorized by the other states to assemble in the said Convention at the city aforesaid, and to join with them in devising, deliberating on, and discussing all such alterations and further provisions as may be necessary to render the Federal Constitution fully adequate to the exigencies of the Union; and in reporting such act or acts for that purpose, to the United States in Congress assembled, as when agreed to by them, and duly confirmed by the several states, will effectually provide for the same.[7]

Now I consider it as a question of importance, whether we are to take up the new Constitution as being in a state of nature or acting on federal ground, whether we stand unconnected or subordinate to the present Confederation. If we are bound by that, it obliges us to continue on federal ground. I should conceive, that we are still bound by the Confederation, and that the conduct of the House has hitherto been federal; that the Convention was federal as appears by their appointment and their report to Congress. Did they, sir, address their report to this House? No, sir, they did not. It is true, sir, we were honored with a report from our own delegates. No, sir, I retract the word—the delegates were honored; they did themselves the honor of communicating the result of their deliberations. But did the Convention address this House? No, sir, they did not. They addressed Congress, as they were ordered to do. Hitherto the business has been in a federal channel, and this, sir, is the first step that places us upon unfederal ground. The report is before Congress, and it is to be presumed Congress will agree to it, but has such a length of time elapsed as to induce us to suspect they will not concur or to justify our going into it without their recommendation? We may act, sir, without due deliberation and hurry on without consideration, but Congress will not. I know the propriety of waiting to hear from them must have weight with every member, and I ask every gentleman in this House, will they take upon themselves to doubt of the acquiescence of Congress, in order to furnish an argument for dispatch? If any will, let him say so and take the consequences upon his character. No doubt can be entertained but Congress will recommend as the acquisition of power is a desirable object with them. Their disposition must be to promote the present plan, but they must wish to preserve the appearance of decency on such a subject. I ask, can any gentleman suppose but what Congress will come readily into it? They who have been many years recommending and requiring, nay I may say, begging for such powers as are now proposed to be given them, cannot change their disposition and decline receiving an increase. Well, what does all this tend to prove; have we not all along been a federal state, remarkably so? And shall we be the first to step out of our way wantonly, and without any reason? Certainly we will not.

However, I suppose some gentlemen will say it is necessary for Pennsylvania to show a ready compliance on the present occasion—that it is absolutely necessary to supersede the existing Confederation. Why, sir, we know that nothing, no argument, no opposition can withstand the plea of necessity; well, but the absolute necessity must arise from the dangers we are in. Now where are any dangers to be avoided while Congress are going only through their usual forms to recommend this measure? They must have time to read and consider the plan; it must go through the usual course of business. Circular letters must be prepared and sent with authenticated copies of the new form of government. I am of opinion all this will be done with proper speed, and the communications will be made as soon as possible. Why send the plan to Congress at all, if we must act upon it without their approbation? If the present Confederation is not adequate to the great national purposes, it is fair to put it in competition with the proposed one. We know it was framed by good and wise men, and so was this. Wise and great men were employed in framing both. Nay, some of the same men prepared them, but as time and experience have shown a revision to be necessary, has it not been entered into a federal ground? And will the State of Pennsylvania quit this to answer the concealed purposes of those who urge on the present measure? No, I hope not, but they will agree to leave it to another house, by which time the usual formalities may be given it by the United States. Surely Pennsylvania can take it up early enough to prevent any damage that is feared. In doing so, we act federally. What are held out as inducements to act with such precipitation, as some members say the *honor* of being foremost; but I would rather say the *dishonor* of acting unfederally; and will any federal purposes be answered by a breach of the Confederation, which can counterbalance the disgrace of being the first to dissolve the Union? And, sir, it is not convenient that one state should enter into this measure any length of time before the others. This is one reason of waiting the recommendation of Congress, for then the new Constitution comes officially and all are prepared to go hand in hand in perfecting the work. But will a name justify us for a breach of faith unnecessarily, and no necessity is alleged to justify the measure. Sir, in acting the part I do in supporting federal measures, I am justified by every citizen, who will think with deliberation on a subject of this importance. I have supposed the gentlemen who support the resolutions before you have some object in view which is not understood. I have a right for such suspicion, or why was it delayed to the last but one day of the sessions? We do not treat this subject which is allowed to be of importance with any respect; we treat it rather as a matter of no importance when we hurry it on in this manner. Why, sir, even the trifling business of appointing a prothonotary or register is made the order of the day. Certainly then we treat this with indignity.

There must be some reasons for this, but though I cannot see it, I may suppose it, and I would ask the gentlemen whether it is that they may have the merit of promoting a business which appears to be very popular; but will this consist with our federal engagements. I would go further and assign another reason against it, but I may be supposed to touch it with indelicacy. It may be asked, was this House elected with a view of entering into matters of this importance? I say this may be indelicate as the House have elected delegates to Convention, but then, sir, I have showed they had that right by the Articles of Confederation, so that the House so far did their duty. It is true they happened in their choice of delegates to choose a number of their own members; but in this they were also justified for one reason; perhaps they thought them better judges of what would be for the benefit of a state they regulated by their legislation.

I believe nothing was improper in this; but, I remember, it was lamented that some persons were not chosen better to represent the country interest. And it is these very men, who now come forward with the resolutions, they, no doubt, are able to decide; but I think they should indulge others with time for a like consideration—therefore, I hope they will agree to let it lie over to the next house. I don't think that it will be then too late, and few or none of the other states can be forwarder than ourselves in calling a convention.

GEORGE CLYMER: We now, Mr. Speaker, have heard all the commonplace arguments against adopting the Federal Constitution; and among this mass of matter, what has the gentleman [William Findley] attempted to establish? I think, sir, it may be reduced to these two points: first, that the legislature of Pennsylvania is not adequate to calling a convention, though generally desired; and the other is, that the measure of calling a convention, if gone into, is antifederal and shows an impropriety in the conduct of the House in not waiting the result of the deliberations of Congress. Sir, I have as great respect for federal measures and for Congress as that gentleman can pretend to, but waiting their report, sir, I believe will be to attend to forms and lose the substance. A little calculation will serve to demonstrate this and show the impropriety of waiting the report of that body. At the same time a due regard to decency has been had by postponing this business to so late an hour. If this House order a convention, it may be deliberated and decided some time in November, and the Constitution may be acted under by December. But if it is left over to the next house, it will inevitably be procrastinated until December, 1788. No man, I presume, would be willing that our Union and existence should remain so long in jeopardy or run the risk of a final ruin.

If this business is neglected by the present House and suffered to pass over to the next, it will undoubtedly have the appearance of our being unfriendly to the new Constitution, or will be owning to the world that we are not willing to decide in its favor. The gentleman [William Findley] supposes wrong, when he says, that the reason for bringing it forward now is that Congress are not favorable to the measure. It originated on no such apprehension; on the contrary we know that Congress are favorable, and I have been informed by a gentleman of information, lately from [New] York, that the members of Congress were unanimous in approving it;[8] but that the formality which accompanies their decisions is of such a nature as to require a longer time for making official communications.

The other argument, that it is unfederal to call a convention without the approbation of Congress, is not supported, for he agrees that should Congress disapprove, there is still a way left of laying it before the people, which amounts to a full proof that Congress is considered only as a vehicle to communicate the information generally to the United States. In this light the gentleman will find the Convention addressed them; if he turns over to the resolutions accompanying the Constitution, it is there declared as their opinion that it should be addressed to a convention of delegates chosen in each state by the people thereof, under the recommendation of its legislature; and when agreed to in such manner by nine states, it shall then be in force. Thus we see there is no power vested in Congress to prevent the states going into it separately and independently. The idea which he has taken up may be traced undoubtedly in the original Confederation, but he will not find it at all attended to by the Convention. Waiting to receive a recommendation of the measure from Congress must even, by that gentleman, be esteemed merely as a compliment, which I think, by the delay already made, has been fully complied with; so that I think little remains but that the House patronize the calling a convention by agreeing to the first resolution, and no man, I apprehend, in favor of federal measures will oppose this; and when the second comes before us, we may determine the time for holding the election.

WILLIAM ROBINSON:[9] The arguments of the gentleman [William Findley] who objects to the present measure is not against the propriety of calling a convention, but only that this is an improper time; and it appears that he supposes further that we are not acting consistent with our federal engagements in deciding on this subject, before it is recommended by Congress, because, as he says, we quit the federal ground on which we have hitherto trodden and act as if we were in a state of nature with respect to the Confederation existing between the thirteen states. Now, sir, I must oppose these arguments by asserting, in the first place, that we have not acted hitherto on federal ground; that the appointment made by this house of delegates to Convention was not federal, nor any one step taken by us has been in conformity with the Articles of Confederation. And all this I think, sir, I shall be able to prove to your satisfaction and to a full refutation of every pretext, which the gentleman from Westmoreland [William Findley] has set up to defeat the proposed measure at the present. The gentleman has introduced to your attention the thirteenth Article of the Confederation, and concludes from it that we are acting unfederally if we do not wait their decision. Now I mean to prove by this Article, that we have not acted hitherto in conformity with it, but that at the very first onset, we entered new ground, and the Articles of this Confederation (it says) shall be *inviolably observed,* and the Union shall be *perpetual,* nor shall any alteration, at any time hereafter be made in any of them, unless such alteration be agreed to in a Congress of the United States and be afterwards *confirmed* by the LEGISLATURE OF EVERY STATE.

From this is plainly inferred, that alterations ought to have *originated* with *Congress* and by them been *recommended* to the several LEGISLATURES. Here is no provision for leaving it to *another body of men* to recommend *alterations* to *state conventions.* Here is no provision for making an engagement binding as soon as entered into by nine states assembled in *conventions.* No, sir, the Constitution proposed is no *alteration* of any *particular article* of the *Confederation,* which is the only thing provided for. The Federal Convention did not think of amending and altering the present Confederation, for they saw the impropriety of vesting one body of men with the necessary powers. Hence resulted the necessity of a different organization. America had been taught by dear-bought experience that she could never hope for security or prosperity under articles of Union that were no longer binding; that suited the convenience of each particular state and was slighted or condemned as petulance or caprice dictated. America has seen the Confederation totally inadequate to the purposes of an equal general government, incapable of affording security either within or without. Attempts in vain have been made to obtain the assent of all the states to measures which have at one time or another been agreed by them severally, yet retracted by some, when a prospect of success appeared. Hence resulted the necessity of taking up this business on original ground. Hence resulted the necessity of having again recourse to the AUTHORITY OF THE PEOPLE. *Under this impression, sir, the* CONVENTION *originated.* Virginia passed a law appointing delegates to join with the delegates of such other states as, influenced by her example and convinced of the necessity of having a more effective federal government, should concur therein. Virginia, sir, was not authorized by Congress to make such appointment, nor did Pennsylvania wait for that authority; but this reason, which is inserted in the preamble of the bill, was thought sufficient to justify our conduct and was the real inducement for passing the law. "And whereas the legislature of the state of Virginia have already passed an act of that commonwealth, empowering certain commissioners to meet at the city of Philadelphia, in May next, a convention of commissioners, or deputies, from the different states; and the legislature of this state are fully sensible of the important advantages which may be derived to the United States, and every of them, from *co-operating with the commonwealth of Virginia,* and the other states of the confederation, in the said design."

Finally, sir, the recommendation of Congress was obtained for calling the Convention; but this was a power not vested in them by any article of the Confederation, under which they ought to act. In this, sir, they departed from that federal conduct, which the member from Westmoreland [William Findley], by mistake, asserts has hitherto been pursued. Having, sir, not hitherto proceeded one step on federal ground, is it to be expected that federal ground should now be resumed? But, sir, if we were to proceed under the most earnest recommendation of Congress, to call a *state convention,* we proceed contrary to the principle laid down in the 13th Article, which declares the alteration must be CONFIRMED BY THE LEGISLATURE; so, whether Congress recommend or do not recommend, if *a convention is called* (which every gentleman agrees is proper), we act inconsistent with the Articles of Confederation. For is it anywhere said, that *conventions of the people* shall be called to determine such alterations as are submitted by Congress? No, sir, THE LEGISLATURES are to decide, and moreover, it must be confirmed by *all of them* before it can have effect. Now is this a circumstance that can be reasonably expected after the disunion and obstinacy, which has heretofore taken place? The new Constitution declares, when nine states concur, it shall be binding on them; so that whatever way we proceed in, it must be clear we proceed without regard to the Confederation.

With respect to the recommendation of Congress, I think it is generally believed they will recommend, but it is only mere formality that could require us to wait it. Even was it federal, which it is not, let us suppose that Congress were to refuse recommending, would it drop to the ground? And suppose we decline calling a convention, will not the people call one themselves? They surely will, and have an undoubted right so to do. And the only question before us is, what advantage will arise from calling that *convention now*? The people who reside near the seat of government have generally applied to you to direct this affair. Now, should we treat their application with a silent neglect, it will argue that the General Assembly are unfriendly to a more federal and effective government. If it should not carry that idea to the people about us, who may have fuller information, it certainly will to the extremes of the state and other distant places. It will tend to damp that ardor, which the proposed plan has universally inspired. The State of Pennsylvania is of great weight, her influence would be extended, nor has she ever relaxed her federal exertions, she would become still of greater importance in the Union, and her example on the present question may fix the liberty, prosperity and happiness of united America; while sun and moon endureth.

A tardiness will lose us these advantages, and by referring to another house, we may not see it effected until many other states that have formed a better judgment of its importance shall have acceded and eclipsed our fame.

THOMAS FITZSIMONS: I think too highly of the good sense of this House to suppose it necessary to say anything to prove to them that their *agreement* to calling a convention is *not unfederal,* as every member must have fully considered the point before this time; nor I do not think a single gentleman supposes that it would be unfederal. Though the member from Westmoreland [William Findley] has taken some pains to persuade us that Pennsylvania has been hitherto a federal state, and that we are about to depart from that conduct, and to run before even prosperity itself. I think it greatly to the honor of Pennsylvania that she deserves the gentleman's commendation by having always stood foremost in support of federal measures, and I think it will redound still more to her honor to enter foremost into this new system of Confederation, seeing the old is so dissolved or rotten as to be incapable of answering any good purpose whatsoever. Has the gentleman ever looked at the new Constitution? If he has, he will see it is not an alteration of an article in the old, but that it departs in every principle from the other. It presupposes, sir, that no Confederation exists; or if [it] does exist, it exists to no purpose; as it can answer no useful purpose, it cannot provide for the common defense, nor promote the general welfare. Therefore, arguments that are intended to reconcile one with the other, or make the latter an appendage to the former, are but a mere waste of words. Does the gentleman suppose, that the Convention thought themselves acting under any provision made in the Confederation for altering its articles? No, sir, they had no such idea. They were obliged, in the first instance, to begin with the destruction of its greatest principle, *equal representation.* They found the Confederation without vigor and so decayed that it was impossible to graft a useful article upon it; nor was the *mode,* sir, as prescribed by that Confederation, which requires alterations to originate with Congress. They found at an early period that no good purpose could be effected by making such alterations as were provided by the first articles of Union. They also saw that what alterations were necessary could not be ratified by the legislatures, as they were incompetent to ordaining a form of government. They knew this belonged to the people only, and that the people only would be adequate to carry it into effect. What have Congress and the legislatures to do with the proposed Constitution? Nothing, sir, they are but the mere vehicles to convey the information to the people.

The Convention, sir, never supposed it was necessary to report to Congress, much less to abide their determination.[10] They thought it decent to make the compliment to them of sending the result of their deliberations, concluding the knowledge of that would be more extensively spread through their means, not that I would infer there is the least doubt of the most hearty concurrence of that body. But, should they decline, and the State of Pennsylvania neglect calling a convention, as I said before, the authority is with the people, and they will do it themselves; but there is a propriety in the legislatures providing the mode by which it may be conducted in a decent and orderly manner.

The member from Westmoreland [William Findley] agrees that a convention ought to take place. He goes further and declares that it must and will take place but assigns no reason why it should not early take place. He must know that any time after the [state] election will be proper, because at that time the people, being collected together, have full opportunity to learn each other's sentiments on this subject. Taking measures for calling a convention is a very different thing from deciding on the plan of government. The sentiments of the people, so far as they have been collected, have been unanimously favorable to its adoption, and its early adoption, if their representatives think it a good one. If we set the example now, there is a great prospect of its being generally come into; but if we delay many ill consequences may arise. And I should suppose, if no better arguments are offered for the delay than what has been advanced by the gentleman on the other side of the House, that we will not agree to it. As to the time of election, that has been all along conceded, and gentlemen will propose such time as they think proper.

William Findley: I wish to make a few observations, sir, on what has been said by the several gentlemen who support the motion, and to offer some further reasons in favor of delay. One gentleman [George Clymer] says, it will be procrastinated, if laid over to the next house, into another year. In that, sir, I will agree with him, if he means the beginning, but not if the middle or latter end. The same gentleman says, that no one in favor of federal measures would oppose it. Now, sir, I profess myself in favor of federal measures, and I believe the members of the House are generally so; and it is for that very reason that I wish to defer it, in order that we may accomplish in a federal manner. The gentleman further says, that if Congress disapprove of it, there is still a way left of having it adopted, but if Congress should disapprove, will it be contended that we have acted properly in agreeing to a measure without consideration. Congress certainly take no more time than is necessary, and they must know how the legislature of Pennsylvania is circumstanced. They know we are near our dissolution, and never can imagine that even if they were to determine on recommending, that we have time to decide on that recommendation.

As to what the gentleman from the county [Philadelphia] (William Robinson) says of the Federal Convention's not being a federal convention, I have but little to reply. I stated some facts to prove they were a federal convention acting under the Confederation, both by its injunctions and by the law. He charges Congress also with not having acted agreeable to the Confederation; but he has not shown us why that body should wantonly step out of the way when, by the 13th section [i.e., Article], they were able to effect every alteration which was required. But, for my part, I think their conduct was federal and their resolution conformable to the Confederation. Neglecting to adopt the measure of calling a convention is said by him to carry the idea of this state's being unfriendly to the proposed Constitution; but why should it have this effect? Is it not known that the usual method of determining any matter of a public nature is, by a due consideration and repeated deliberation, conformable with our constitution? Can a hasty decision be expected? No, it is expressly prohibited. Why then must it be inferred from delay that we are unfriendly?

The member from the city (Thomas Fitzsimmons) says, that every member must have considered this subject. I will say, that every member has not considered it. For my part I have read it over not with a view of considering it in this House, and as for the object before us, I never thought of it at all, taking it for granted that the session was so far expired that time was not left to receive it from Congress or deliberate upon it. I know that it is the province of the convention to consider of the merits of the plan, and I suppose that they will have good reasons assigned for their determination, whether it be to reject or adopt it, so that I shall add nothing on this head. The gentleman goes further and informs us, that the Federal Convention did not act under the Confederation, which he says is dissolved and rotten, and they paid no respect to it in their deliberations. I know this matter does not come properly before the House; but, sir, I cannot forbear remarking upon these words. I should think it unwise to throw out the dirty water, sir, before we get clean. If the Confederation is dissolved, there is no bond to keep us together, even while we deliberate on the new. But, sir, our Confederation is not dissolved, though it may be defective. We remember, it was framed in time of war, and every requisite for the time of peace may not have been adverted to; and we should remember it served, and served us faithfully, through a difficult and protracted war. Let us, therefore, not censure it too highly, as we have been advantaged by it, nor despise it and say it is dissolved and rotten; for, sir, when I go into my new house, I wait till it is finished and furnished before I quit the humble cabin that has served me many a cold and weary day; and when I bid it an adieu, it is becoming to speak respectfully of it, because it was true and faithful to the last.

Now with respect to the propriety of waiting the recommendations of Congress and whether we are acting federally or not are questions, in my opinion, of high importance. The gentlemen say also, that the subject is important; but how do they treat it? They treat it, sir, as a trifle, whilst we, by desiring due deliberation, treat it as important. Ask the gentlemen, sir, what they are about to do? They mean to summon an election of delegates at so short a day that people have not the least time to consult together even on a proper representation. Perhaps the city and county of Philadelphia may have time sufficient, but no other can. If a majority of the people of Pennsylvania are favorable to the new Constitution, how can they find out the sentiments of those, whom they wish to represent them? Perhaps they may elect persons who will give it every opposition, and it may be, sir, that the very persons who are pressing this business forward do it to inspire a confidence that they are its supporters, when they mean, if opportunity shall offer, to destroy it. I ask the members of this House, is it reasonable to suppose proper time is allowed? Let every member ask himself, if the people can choose delegates with any kind of judgment? The people generally are disposed to have a government of more energy. How far the proposed one may answer their idea, I think we ought to let them consider. They have a right to think and choose for themselves. Shall we then deprive them of their right? Surely not. Let them then have time, and they no doubt will act right and refuse or adopt the plan of government held out to them.

HUGH H. BRACKENRIDGE: With respect to the expediency of immediate decision on this question, it has been sufficiently observed, that the example of Pennsylvania would be a great inducement to the other states to come speedily into its adoption; on the contrary, a delay with us will occasion a delay in the other legislatures. The gentleman [William Findley] allows we labor under inconveniences by the present mode of government; let his object then be to remove the difficulties and hasten their termination by a speedy application of the only remedy the case admits of. I cannot see, Mr. Speaker, whence the gentlemen (Robert Whitehill and William Findley) are so averse to a measure that the one owns is necessary and the other cannot state a single objection against.

All efforts to restore energy to the federal government have proved ineffectual, when exerted in the mode directed by the 13th Article of the Confederation, and it is in consequence of this, that recourse is once more had to the *authority of the people.* The first step toward obtaining this was antifederal; the acquiescence of Congress was antifederal; the whole process has been antifederal so far as it was not conducted in the manner prescribed by the articles of Union. But the first and every step was *federal,* inasmuch as it was sanctioned by the PEOPLE OF THE UNITED STATES. The member from Westmoreland [William Findley] pleases his fancy with being on federal ground, pursuing federal measures, and being a very federal sort of person; he concludes we are not in a state of nature, because we are on federal ground. But, sir, we are not on federal ground but on the wild and extended field of nature, unrestrained by any former compact, bound by no peculiar tie, at least so far are we disengaged, as to be capable of forming a constitution, which shall be the wonder of the universe. It is on the principle of self-conservation that we act. The former Articles of Confederation have received sentence of death, and though they may be on earth, yet are inactive and have no efficacy. But the gentleman would still have us to be bound by them, and tells you your acts must correspond with their doctrine; this he proves, sir, from the 13th Article, but in this he is like some overstudious divines, who in commenting on their text turn it to different shapes and force it to prove what it never meant, or in the words of the poet:

As Critics! learned Critics view,
In Homer, more than Homer knew.

He will not suffer the old to be dissolved, until the new is adopted; he will not quit his old cabin till the new house is furnished, not if it crumbles about his ears. But, sir, we are not now forsaking our tenement, it is already been forsaken, and I conceive we have the power to proceed, independent of Congress or Confederation. But as to the second object, whether the time is proper, as stated in the resolution, I do not say that it is, because I conceive it too short for several counties distant from this city; but this subject will come forward with propriety after the present question is agreed to.

WILLIAM FINDLEY: The proposed plan is not now before us; therefore we have nothing to say on that subject. But, sir, I would still suppose the old Confederation is in existence. The new says, that when nine states agree, it shall be binding on them; that is to say, we shall not go out of the old until the new is so far completed. Then, sir, for my part I would retire from under the old, but not till then, when I would bid it an honorable and friendly adieu, for its meritorious services. Then I would cheerfully pay that attention to the new, which a more perfect edifice deserves. I would then support or act under it as occasion might require.

ROBERT WHITEHILL: I shall make but a very few observations on this business, as enough has already been said I apprehend to convince the House of the propriety of delay, if any consideration can effect it. I believe, sir, we are under the Confederation, and when we come to consider the Articles of that Confederation, as well as the law passed appointing delegates to Congress, we shall have reason to conclude, that we are on federal ground and not in a state of nature. In the sixth Article it is expressly declared, that no state shall enter into any confederation without the consent of Congress; this is sufficient to satisfy the House that they ought not to proceed without the approbation of Congress. I say, when we come to consider that the states appointed delegates in consequence of the recommendation of Congress, and that they reported to Congress agreeably to their orders, every member must be convinced that it is a federal measure; and this way of going out of it must be contrary to all right and propriety. We have Articles of Confederation, sir, and we are bound by them; we are acting, sir, a very wrong part to deny this; they are our government. They have the necessary powers by the Confederation, and I say their recommendation is necessary; and unless we have it, nothing can be done toward establishing the new Constitution.

DANIEL CLYMER said the new Constitution had nothing to do with the present question, which was simply, will the House take the proper means to have a convention of the people called to deliberate on the propriety of receiving or refusing the new plan of confederation?

The question was now put, Will the House agree to the resolution? And the yeas and nays being called by Daniel Clymer and Thomas Fitzsimmons are as follows:

Yeas. Will, Fitzsimmons, [G.] Clymer, Hiltzeimer, Gray, Robinson, Salter, Logan, Foulke, Wynkoop, Chapman, Upp, Moore, Willing, Ralston, Evans, Thomas, Wheelen, Lowry, Hubley, Carpenter, Work, Ross, Clemson, M'Conaghy, Schmyser, M'Lellan, Lilley, G. Heister, Kreemer, J. Heister, Davis, D. Clymer, Trexler, Burkhalter, Cannon, Antis, Brackenridge, Moore, Wheeler, Hockley, Riffe [Reiff], Carson. 43.

Nays. Whitehill, Kennedy, Mitchell, Brown, Piper, Powel, Dale, Findley, Barr, Wright, M'Dowel, Flannaken, Allison, Phillips, Gilchrist, Smith, M'Calmont, Clarke, Miley. 19.

After which the House adjourned till 4 o'clock in the afternoon.

1. The Proceedings do not give the date proposed for the election of delegates in the five westernmost counties.

2. The Proceedings give 30 November as the date.

3. See "Daniel Shays to the Antifederal Junto," 25 September, II:A below.

4. On 24 September Assemblyman Thomas FitzSimons heard from William Bingham in Congress that Congress would begin consideration of the Constitution on 26 September, but not all members of the Assembly seem to have known it. See Bingham to FitzSimons, 21 September and the note thereto, CDR:IX, A.

5. The Proceedings record neither the motion nor the vote. There is also some question as to the number of assemblymen who voted for postponement. Tench Coxe reported that twelve assemblymen voted for it (to James Madison, 28–29 September, I:C below).

6. For the resolution of Congress on 21 February calling the Convention, see CDR:V, C.

7. For the Pennsylvania Act of 30 December 1786 electing delegates to the Convention, which Findley quotes and summarizes, see CDR:VI, C.

8. On 26 September the *Independent Gazetteer* printed a widely circulated report that there was "no disposition in Congress to affect any alteration in the new Constitution, but to give it to the states as it was received from the Convention" (CC:99). However, the opposition in Congress was very real. See CDR:IX, A and B.

9. Robinson, a lawyer, represented Philadelphia County in the Assembly from 1785 to 1789 and in 1791 was commissioned a judge of the Court of Common Pleas for the city and county of Philadelphia.

10. The requirement that the Confederation Congress approve the work of the Convention was contained in all the resolutions of the Convention and the draft constitution of 6 August. The requirement was dropped on 31 August by a vote of eight states to three.

The Pennsylvania Assembly
Friday
28 September 1787

Assembly Proceedings, P.M.

Mr. Speaker with forty-four members met, and the roll being called, it appeared that the following members were absent, viz.: Mr. Whitehill, Mr. Kennedy, Mr. Mitchell, Mr. Piper, Mr. Powell, Mr. Dale, Mr. Findley, Mr. Barr, Mr. Wright, Mr. M'Dowell, Mr. Flenniken, Mr. Allison, Mr. Philips, Mr. Gilchreest, Mr. Smith, Mr. M'Calmont, Mr. Clark, Mr. Antes and Mr. Miley; and there not being a quorum,[1]

Ordered, That the sergeant at arms collect the absent members.

The Speaker left the chair for half an hour.

The sergeant at arms having returned, the Speaker resumed the chair, and the sergeant at arms reported, that he had seen all the absent members at the house of Alexander Boyd[2] (except Mr. Philips and Mr. Smith), that he informed them the Speaker and forty-four members being met, and not forming a quorum, he was directed to collect the absent members, and in obedience to his orders required them to attend. Mr. Whitehill replied, there was no house; and that they, the members to whom his message was directed, had not made up their minds, and for that reason would not attend.

It was moved and seconded, to adjourn.

Adjourned until half past nine o'clock tomorrow, A.M.

1. Sixty-eight men had been elected to the Assembly, and forty-six were required for a quorum.

2. Some western members stayed at Major Alexander Boyd's boarding house. For Boyd's boarding house as a meeting place of Antifederalists, see Tench Coxe to James Madison, 28–29 September, I:C below; "The Protest of the Minority," 3 October, II:A below; and Mfm:Pa. 181. For the attitude of Philadelphians towards the western assemblymen, see Mfm:Pa. 699.

Assembly Debates, P.M.

Mr. Speaker took the chair, when it appeared there were but 44 members met, which not being a quorum,

GERARDUS WYNKOOP observed that the House had under their consideration a business of the highest importance, and as he remarked the absent members were mostly those, who had given it opposition in the forenoon, he suspected they had withdrawn themselves by design, he would therefore move, that the sergeant at arms be sent for them. This being unanimously agreed to, the sergeant was dispatched in search of the following members of the General Assembly of Pennsylvania; namely:

From Cumberland: Robert Whitehill, Thomas Kennedy, David Mitchel.

From Bedford: John Piper, [Joseph] Powell.

From Northumberland: Frederick Antis (who voted in favor of calling the Convention), Samuel Dale.

From Westmoreland: William Findley, James Bar.

From Washington: Alexander Wright, John M'Dowel, John Flennaken, James Allison.

From Fayette: Theophilus Philips, John Gilchrist.

From Franklin: Abraham Smith, James M'Calmont.

From Dauphin: Robert Clarke, and Jacob Miley.

The Speaker left the chair until the return of the sergeant at arms, who was immediately examined at the bar of the House.

MR. SPEAKER: Well, sergeant, have you seen the absent members?

SERGEANT: Yes, sir, I saw R. Whitehill, Kennedy, Mitchel, Piper,

Powell, Dale, Findley, Bar, Wright, M'Dowell, Flennaken, Allison, Gilchrist, M'Calmont, R. Clark, Antis, and Miley.

MR. SPEAKER: What did you say to them?

SERGEANT: I told the gentlemen that the Speaker and the House had sent for them; and says they, there is no house.

MR. SPEAKER: Did you let them know they were desired to attend?

SERGEANT: Yes, sir, but they told me they could not attend this afternoon, for they had not made up their minds yet.

DANIEL CLYMER: How is that?

SERGEANT: They had not made up their minds this afternoon to wait on you.

MR. SPEAKER: Who told you this?

SERGEANT: Mr. Whitehill told me the first.

MR. SPEAKER: Where did you see them?

SERGEANT: At a house in Sixth Street, Major Boyd's, I think.

DANIEL CLYMER: You say Mr. Whitehill told you first there was no house, who told you afterward?

SERGEANT: Mr. Clark said they must go *electioneering* now.

DANIEL CLYMER: I would be glad to know what conversation there was among them, and who was there?

SERGEANT: There was a member of Council with them, Mr. [James] M'Laine, and he asked me who sent you?

MR. SPEAKER: Was no other person in the room?

SERGEANT: Yes, I saw Mr. [John] Smiley there.

DANIEL CLYMER: Was there no private citizens?

SERGEANT: No, sir.

DANIEL CLYMER: There was none then but MEN IN PUBLIC OFFICES?

SERGEANT: No.

DANIEL CLYMER: Well, and pray what did the Honorable Mr. Smiley say?

SERGEANT: He said nothing.

DANIEL CLYMER: Could all the persons in the room hear Mr. M'Laine['s] question?

SERGEANT: Yes, sir.

DANIEL CLYMER: And did they seem pretty unanimous in their determination not to come, that is, did it appear so to you?

SERGEANT: Yes, sir, as I understood it nearly.

DANIEL CLYMER: Did you hear of anyone willing to come?

SERGEANT: No, sir.

[SPEAKER]: Sergeant, you may retire.

The Speaker now recapitulated the unfinished business and wished to know what the members would choose to do.

GERARDUS WYNKOOP would be glad to know, if there was no way to compel men, who deserted from the duty they owed their country, to a performance of it, when they were within the reach of the House. If there is not, then *God be merciful to us!!!*

ALEXANDER LOWREY believed there was a law to compel the absent members to serve, which was passed in the year 1777;[1] but upon investigation this law was found wholly inadequate, and upon search it appeared, that the only penalty to which such men were liable was a forfeiture of one-third of one-day's pay, being the sum of five shillings Pennsylvania currency; and this is inflicted under one of the rules for the regulation of the members' conduct.

WILLIAM ROBINSON: I believe, sir, that punishment is not in our power, nor can we compel their presence, so that we have nothing left but to adjourn; but before this I would wish to make a few observations. This House, sir, have this forenoon agreed to call a convention of the people of this state, in order to deliberate upon a new form of confederation. I would remark, that this business is not of such a nature as to require a law to carry it into effect, it being merely to lay down the mode by which the citizens may proceed in their choice in a manner best suited to their convenience. This business, sir, is of that important nature to all the citizens of the United States, that it must not be suffered to fail by the secession of nineteen of your members, though sorry I am that our Journals are again to be stained by recording the conduct of an unmanly minority.[2] But passing this over, I think there will be a propriety of meeting again, and under our respective signatures recommend this measure to our constituents. Fully impressed with the idea of its importance and necessity, I cannot but strongly recommend its adoption and leave these men to suffer the stings of conscience, and that contempt and displeasure of their constituents, which they have drawn upon themselves.

Adjourned until tomorrow half past nine.

1. The act passed in January 1777 was entitled "An Act To Enable A Smaller Number Of The Members Of Assembly Than A Quorum To Collect The Absent Members And Issue Writs For Filling Vacancies Occasioned By Neglect Or Refusal." The act (and its supplement passed in October of the same year) applied only to obtaining a quorum at the opening of a session (Pa. *Statutes,* IX, 28–29, 146–47).

2. See Assembly Debates, Saturday, 29 September, n. 4.

Jacob Hiltzheimer Diary, Philadelphia, 28 September[1]

Forenoon attended at the Assembly. It was proposed by Mr. George Clymer that this House recommend to the people to choose a convention as soon as convenient to deliberate and to confer on the Federal Constitution as recommended by the late Honorable Convention. This occasioned a long debate; the speakers in favor of it were the two Clymers, Fitzsimmons, Robinson, and Brackenridge; against it, R. Whitehill and William Findlay. On the votes being taken forty-three were for it and nineteen against it. The House then adjourned to four o'clock in the afternoon. Half an hour after the Speaker took the chair, and the members' names being called, it was found that eighteen of those who had voted against the Convention stayed away, and one of the forty-three, Mr. Antes; Mr. Bower [Brown] was the only one who appeared in the House that voted against it in the forenoon. Therefore, no quorum being present, the House adjourned to half past nine tomorrow.

1. *Diary*, 133. Hiltzheimer, a former street commissioner of Philadelphia, was elected to the Assembly from Philadelphia in October 1786 and served for eleven consecutive years.

The Pennsylvania Assembly
Saturday
29 September 1787

Assembly Proceedings[1]

Mr. Speaker with forty-three members met, and the roll having been called, it appeared there was no quorum.

On motion, Resolved, That the sergeant at arms require the members absenting themselves to attend, and that the assistant clerk accompany the sergeant.

The Speaker left the chair for a short time.

The assistant clerk and sergeant at arms being returned, the assistant clerk reported, they had been to the house of Major Alexander Boyd; that he there saw Mr. M'Calmont and Mr. Miley, informed them of the resolution of Congress dated September 28th instant,[2] and published this day, which Mr. M'Calmont said he had [not] seen or heard of. The assistant clerk told the two members of his instruction, requiring them to attend; they answered, they would not attend. Before he got to Boyd's house, he saw Mr. Piper and some other members, does not recollect who, and followed them to the corner of Arch and Seventh streets, then saw Mr. Piper, Mr. Findley and Mr. Barr walking towards Market Street. Mr. Findley looked round and, perceiving him, mended his pace, and turned the corner of Seventh down Market

Street, but before he could arrive at the corner of Seventh Street, lost sight of Mr. Findley. He then informed Mr. Piper and Mr. Barr of the resolution of Congress before mentioned, and told them the Speaker and members present had sent for them; they said they would not attend. From thence he proceeded to the lodgings of Mr. Whitehill and there saw a woman, who said Mr. Whitehill was above stairs; she went up and, returning, said he was not at home. At Mr. Whitehill's lodgings he saw Mr. Mitchell and acquainted him with his message; Mr. Mitchell answered, he would not attend. He also saw Mr. M'Dowell and acquainted him with the order requiring the attendance of members absenting themselves, who said he would consider and do what was just. He found Mr. Dale and Mr. Antes at their lodgings, and, after informing them as he had done the others, Mr. Dale said he would not attend as he was going out of town. Mr. Antes said the resolve of Congress was not come officially, therefore he would not attend. He likewise saw Mr. Clark, and having acquainted him in the same way with the rest, he answered he would not attend.

Mr. M'Calmont and Mr. Miley appeared in the Assembly chamber,[3] and there being a quorum, the House resumed the consideration of the remainder of the motion postponed yesterday.

And in debating the following resolution, viz.:

"Resolved, That the persons so elected to serve in Convention shall assemble on the third Tuesday of November, at the State House, in the city of Philadelphia."

It was moved by James M'Calmont, seconded by Alexander Lowrey, to strike out the words "at the State House, in the city of Philadelphia," and in lieu thereof to insert, "at the courthouse, in the borough of Lancaster."[4]

And on the question, "Will the House agree to the amendment," the yeas and nays were called by James M'Calmont and Daniel Clymer, and were as follow, viz.:

YEAS [15]
Alexander Lowrey
Adam Hubley
Emanuel Carpenter
Joseph Work
George Ross
James Clemson
David M'Conaughy
Michael Schmyser
David M'Clellan
Joseph Heister
Gabriel Heister
John Canon
James M'Calmont
Jacob Miley
John Carson

NAYS [30]
William Will
Robert Morris
Thomas Fitzsimons
George Clymer
Jacob Hiltzheimer

Isaac Gray
William Robinson, Jr.
John Salter
George Logan
Samuel Foulke
Gerardus Wynkoop
John Chapman
Valentine Upp
James Moore
Richard Willing
Robert Ralston
Samuel Evans
Richard Thomas
Townsend Whelen
Joseph Lilley
Philip Kreemer
David Davis
Daniel Clymer
Peter Trexler, Jr.
Peter Burkhalter
Hugh H. Brackenridge
Charles Moore
Samuel Wheeler
James Hockley
Jacob Reiff

So it was carried in the negative, and the resolution adopted.

And in debating the preamble to the motion,

It was moved by George Clymer and Hugh H. Brackenridge to insert after the words "and ratification," the words, "And whereas Congress, on Friday, the twenty-eighth instant, did unanimously resolve, that the said Constitution be transmitted to the several legislatures of the states, to the intent aforesaid."

It was carried in the affirmative, and the original motion, as amended, adopted as follows, viz.:[5]

"WHEREAS the Convention of Deputies from the several states composing the union, lately held in this city, have published a constitution for the future government of the United States, to be submitted to conventions of deputies chosen in each state by the people thereof, under the recommendation of its legislature, for their assent and ratification: And whereas Congress, on *Friday*, the twenty-eighth instant, did unanimously resolve, that the said constitution be transmitted to the several legislatures of the states, to the intent aforesaid: And whereas it is the sense of great numbers of the good people of this state, already signified in petitions and declarations to this House, that the earliest steps should be taken to assemble a convention within the state, for the purpose of deliberating and determining on the said constitution:

"*Resolved,* That it be recommended to such of the inhabitants of the state as are entitled to vote for representatives to the General Assembly, that they chuse suitable persons to serve as deputies in a state convention, for the purpose herein before mentioned; that is, for the city of *Philadelphia,* and the counties respectively, the same number of deputies that each is entitled to of representatives in the General Assembly.

"*Resolved,* That the elections for deputies as aforesaid be held at the several places in the said city and counties, as are fixed by law for holding the elections of representatives to the General Assembly, and that the same be conducted by the officers who conduct the said elections of representatives, and agreeably to the rules and regulations thereof; and that the election of deputies as aforesaid shall be held for the city of *Philadelphia,* and the several counties of this state, on the first *Tuesday* of *November* next.

"*Resolved,* That the persons so elected to serve in Convention shall assemble on the third *Tuesday* of *November,* at the State-House, in the city of *Philadelphia.*

"*Resolved,* That the proposition submitted to this House by the deputies of *Pennsylvania* in the General Convention of the states, of ceding to the United States a district of country within this state, for the seat of the General Government, and for the exclusive legislation of Congress, be particularly recommended to the consideration of the Convention.[6]

"*Resolved,* That it be recommended to the succeeding House of Assembly, to make the same allowance to the attending members of the Convention as is made to the members of the General Assembly, and also to provide for the extraordinary expences which may be incurred by holding the said elections.[7]

"Whereupon, *Resolved,* That 3000 copies of the resolutions which the House have this day adopted, for calling a Convention on the Foederal Constitution, recommended to them by Congress, be struck off, and transmitted by the Clerk to the members of the city of *Philadelphia,* and the different counties of this state; 2000 of said copies to be in the *English,* and 1000 in the *German* language."

1. For accounts by assemblymen, see Jacob Hiltzheimer Diary, 29 September, Mfm:Pa. 81; "Address of the Seceding Assemblymen," I:B below; and "One of the Dissenting Assemblymen," [William Findley?], 14 November, Mfm:Pa. 224. For contradictory accounts by assemblymen William Findley and Hugh H. Brackenridge, see Mfm:Pa. 166, 167, 196, 197. On 2 October Alexander J. Dallas of the *Pennsylvania Herald* (Mfm:Pa. 79) published a detailed account of the Assembly's proceedings which was reprinted in four Pennsylvania newspapers by 10 October. Outside Pennsylvania it was reprinted, in part, ten times from Maine to South Carolina by 25 October. For other newspaper accounts, see Mfm:Pa. 80.

2. This resolution was not the official copy sent by Congress to the state executives, but was a copy which William Bingham sent to George Clymer. The official copy was received by the Supreme Executive Council after the Assembly adjourned on 29 September. In the next Assembly, Antifederalists, led by James McLene and William Findley, inserted the official copy in the *Minutes* to demonstrate that the Federalists had acted before official word was received from Congress (Mfm:Pa. 90).

3. M'Calmont and Miley were returned to the Assembly chamber by force. See the Assembly Debates immediately below.

4. Antifederalist efforts to move the Convention from Philadelphia to Lancaster continued (William Shippen, Jr. to Thomas Lee Shippen, 7–18 November, II:D below; and Mfm:Pa. 193).

5. The resolutions have been transcribed literally from the Assembly *Minutes*. They were printed as a broadside by Hall and Sellers of the *Pennsylvania Gazette* (Mfm:Pa. 78), and Melchior Steiner of the *Philadelphische Correspondenz*. They were reprinted eight times in Pennsylvania and nineteen times from Rhode Island to Georgia by 27 October.

6. On 1 October some Germantown inhabitants sent a petition to Congress offering buildings to Congress (Mfm:Pa. 86). For Carlisle's interest in the federal capital, see John Montgomery to William Irvine, 9–13 October, II:B below. For the state Convention's action, see Convention Proceedings, 11, 14, and 15 December.

7. See "An Act to Provide for the Wages of Members of the State Convention, and to Defray the Expences of Holding the Same," 10 November, Mfm:Pa. 210–A.

Assembly Debates

Mr. Speaker took the chair and, on calling over the roll, it appeared there were but forty-four members present, namely, all those who appeared yesterday, but Mr. Robert Brown from Northampton, who has now withdrawn himself. And by order, the sergeant at arms, accompanied by the assistant clerk, was dispatched in pursuit of the seceding members. But first George Clymer presented to the chair the unanimous resolution of Congress, which he said had been agreed to yesterday and was forwarded by Mr. [William] Bingham to him express, having chosen this mode in preference to the ordinary conveyance by post. Whereupon,

The following resolution was read and sent by the assistant clerk to the seceding members (as was observed by the Speaker) in order to remove that objection, which they had taken yesterday against the measure.

[A copy of the congressional resolution of 28 September appears at this point.]

The Speaker left the chair, and in a few minutes James M'Calmont and Jacob Miley entered the House. The Speaker resumed the chair, and the roll was called, when the following gentlemen answered to their names.

From the city of Philadelphia: Messrs. Will, Morris, Fitzsimmons, G. Clymer, and Hiltzeimer.

From the county of Philadelphia: Messrs. Gray, Robinson, Salter, and Logan.

From Bucks: Messrs. Foulke, Wynkoop, Chapman, and Upp.

From Chester: Messrs. J. Moore, Willing, Thomas, Ralston, Evans, and Wheelen.

From Lancaster: Messrs. Lowry, Hubley, Carpenter, Work, Ross, and Clemson.

From York: Messrs. M'Conaughty, Schmyser, M'Lellan, and Lilley.

From Cumberland: None.

From Berks: Messrs. J. Heister, Kreemer, G. Heister, Davis, and D. Clymer.

From Northampton: Messrs. Trexler, and Burkholter.

From Bedford: Mr. Cannon.

From Northumberland: None.

From Westmoreland: Mr. Brackenridge.

From Washington: None.

From Fayette: None.

From Franklin: Mr. M'Calmont.

From Montgomery: Messrs. J. Wheeler, C. Moore, Hockley, and Riffe [Reiff].

From Dauphin: Messrs. J. Miley, and Carson.

Being 45, and with the Speaker 46, the number which constitutes a quorum.

After reading over the Minutes of yesterday,

JAMES HOCKLEY presented a petition and memorial from forty-three inhabitants of the county of Montgomery, desiring the House would take the necessary measures to have a convention of the people assembled as speedily as possible.

Which was read and ordered to lie on the table.

The committee appointed to select such business from the files of the House as would be proper to recommend to the attention of the succeeding General Assembly made report, which was also read and ordered to lie on the table.

JAMES M'CALMONT informed the House, that he had been forcibly brought into the Assembly room, contrary to his wishes, this morning by a number of the citizens, whom he did not know, and that therefore, he begged he might be *dismissed* the House.[1]

ALEXANDER LOWREY: I hope, as the gentleman says he was forcibly brought, he will give some reason why force was necessary to make him do his duty; and what reason can he give now he is here, that should induce us to part with him again? Surely his being brought by force and against his wishes is not a reason that he should be suffered to go off again.

THOMAS FITZSIMONS would be glad to know if any member of the House was guilty of forcing the gentleman from the determination of absenting himself; if there was, he thought it necessary that the House mark such conduct with their disapprobation. But we are to consider, sir, that the member is now here, and that the business of the state cannot be accomplished if anyone is suffered to withdraw; from which consideration I conclude, it will be extremely improper for any member to leave this House until the laws and other unfinished business is completed.

WILLIAM ROBINSON: I believe my sentiments, sir, are well known on the subject of the new Federal Constitution, and I yesterday declared my strong disapprobation of the conduct of those members, who, by leaving the House, have forsaken that obligation they owe their God, their country, and their conscience. But at the same time that I decidedly condemn their conduct, I would not wish to act by any means unfair in completing that business which they have neglected. No, sir, I consider that there are but forty-five members here if the gentleman is retained by compulsion. He cannot, sir, be detained against his will; and if the member is so callous as to refuse the calls of his country to do her service, and forsakes his duty, when much is required, he must stand responsible to his constituents, and to his God, and must suffer the general odium and reproach of every friend to decency or order. But, sir, we have no authority to confine him within these walls; if any gentleman suppose so, they will find upon a due consideration that their opinion is not well founded. If any improper method has been used to bring him here, and he is detained against his will, I do conceive we are not a house.

HUGH H. BRACKENRIDGE: It may be a proper question for the House to discuss, whether their officers by force have brought this member here or whether other members have by violence compelled him. I suppose in either of these cases, the House might have cognizance. But if the member has been conducted by the citizens of Philadelphia to his seat in the legislature, and they have not treated him with the respect and veneration he deserves, it must lie with him to obtain satisfaction, but not with us. The gentleman [James M'Calmont] by answering to his name, when the roll was called, acknowledged himself present, and forms a part of the House. Well, sir, I conceive the question is, what is to be done now he is here, for how he came here can form no part of our inquiry, whether his friends brought him (and I should think they could not be his enemies, who would compel him to do his duty and avoid wrong), I say, sir, whether his friends brought him, or by the influence of good advice persuaded him to come, and he did come; or whether to ease his difficulty in walking to this room, they brought him in a sedan chair, or by whatever ways or means he introduced himself among us. All we are to know is that he is here, and it only remains for us to decide, whether he shall have leave of absence. Now, if the gentleman can show that his life will be endangered by staying with us (for I should think the loss of health on the present occasion an insufficient reason) we may grant him the indulgence he asks for—waiving the whole story of his coming, I presume the House can immediately decide whether he may retire or not.

JAMES M'CALMONT: I desire that the rules may be read, and I will agree to stand by the decision of the House.

The rules were read accordingly, and it appeared that every member who did not answer on calling the roll should pay two shillings and six pence, or, if there was not a quorum without him, five shillings.[2]

JAMES M'CALMONT then rose from his place, and putting his hand in his pocket took out some loose silver and said, well, sir, here is your five shillings, so let me go.

This ludicrous circumstance occasioned a loud laugh in the gallery. And the Speaker told him that the person[3] who had been appointed to receive the fines was not in his place; but if he was, the member ought not to pay it, as he had not broke the rule, which declared those persons only finable, who did not appear and answer to their names; he had done both and therefore might retain his money.

THOMAS FITZSIMONS hoped the member would not be dismissed; for he thought no one man ought to be allowed to break up the Assembly of Pennsylvania, which could be done agreeable to constitution, only by the time expiring for which it was chosen.

ASSISTANT CLERK: The sergeant at arms and assistant clerk had, by this time, returned from hunting up the seceding members, and appearing in the House, the clerk was examined at the bar, and related as follows:

I went, sir, in pursuance of your order, with the sergeant at arms, in search of the absent members. First, sir, I went to Major Boyd's and there saw Mr. Miley and Mr. M'Calmont. I informed them that the Speaker and members present had sent me for them and showed them the resolution of Congress. They told me in answer, that they *would not attend.* Before I got from that door, I saw Colonel Piper and some other member, who I do not recollect, at a great distance. I went after them to the corner of Arch and Sixth streets. I saw Mr. Bar, and Mr. Findley, Colonel Piper, and some other member going toward Market Street. *Mr. Findley looked round and saw me, as I supposed, for he mended his pace.* I followed Mr. Piper and Mr. Bar, who kept on to Market Street, and soon turned the corner; before I got there, *I lost sight of Mr. Findley, who, I supposed had got into some house.* I went forward after Piper and Bar, and came up with them and told them of the unanimous resolution of Congress, but they answered me in the same manner, that they *would not attend.* From them I went to Mr. Whitehill's lodging and saw a woman that I supposed to be the maid of the house. *She informed me, that Mr. Whitehill was upstairs; she went up, and stayed some time; when she returned and told me he was not at home.* I saw also Mr. Clark and

Mr. M'Dowell in the street, and Mr. M'Dowell told me, he would consider of the matter, and he would do what he thought just. I saw Mr. Mitchell at Mr. Whitehill's lodging, and he said he *would not attend.* Mr. Dale, and Mr. Antis I found at their lodgings, and Mr. Dale told me *he would not attend.* Mr. Antis said, this resolution of Congress had not come officially, and therefore *he would not attend.*

DANIEL CLYMER asked, if Mr. M'Calmont had offered any excuse, when he was desired to attend?

CLERK: No, he said, he had heard of the resolution of Congress but *he would not attend.*

Thus ended the report of the clerk.

GEORGE LOGAN entered into a long detail of the benefits and advantages which would result from the adoption of the proposed confederation; when several of the members desired he would confine himself to the question. He went on to remark, that the member was a part of the House, he had answered to his name, and after this it lay entirely with the House, whether they would dismiss him or no.

WILLIAM ROBINSON: I do not conceive the question to be, whether he shall be dismissed or not; but as the doors are open, he may go out, and if he does, he is only responsible to his constituents for his conduct. I conceive he cannot be detained as in prison, and it rests with the gentleman whether he will stay or go.

GERARDUS WYNKOOP expressed some amaze at the argument of the gentleman. The member, Mr. M'Calmont, had sworn to do the duties he was delegated to; there had been nothing of force in that, and he should not, for his part, think himself at liberty to withdraw, until the business was completed, nor could he think any member ought. He would call on the gentleman to assign his reasons for absconding from his duty, at the bar of the House, where he might be heard as to his complaint; but the House could not be formed without him.

JAMES M'CALMONT replied, he was not to be called to the bar of this House, he had to answer for his conduct at another bar.

DANIEL CLYMER was of opinion the member was within the power of the House by being present and instanced the case of General Gansell, who was arrested by the sheriff's officers in a protected place. The determination of the judges was that as he was taken, he should be confined until the debt was paid; though he had his action for damages against the officers, who had broken the law of the realm in arresting him. So, he was for punishing every person who had ill treated the gentleman; however faulty his conduct was, it belonged not to individuals to punish; that was to be left to the judges, who, no doubt, will see the laws properly executed.

THOMAS FITZSIMONS was a friend to good order and decorum, but he believed the gentleman's complaint was not to be redressed by the House. The member himself has trespassed, maybe inadvertently, since he had taken his seat. He had perhaps offered the greatest indignity to the legislature of Pennsylvania which could be offered. He has, sir, tendered you a fine of five shillings in order to be permitted to destroy the business, if not the good government of the state. On this, sir, I will make no reflections; the member is now here, and we may determine that he shall stay, not only on constitutional ground, but from the law of nature that will not suffer any body to destroy its own existence prematurely.

WILLIAM ROBINSON: The question, sir, is whether the member shall have leave of absence. Now suppose the House determine that he shall not, and yet he should attempt to withdraw. Certainly you will not lock your doors. (Thomas FitzSimons interrupted with, yes, sir, if no other method could retain him.)

This can't be proper, sir, for it appears to me inconsistent with the rules of every house to return a person as a member by compulsion. With respect to calling a convention, I apprehend the recommendation of forty-four members will have as good effect, as if the consent of that gentleman was obtained; for the citizens of Pennsylvania will not lose their rights or liberty, because nineteen members absconded this House. But, sir, I can't admit the idea that there is a house, while the member declares he is retained by compulsion, but as long as he answers to his name, and keeps his seat, there surely is a house.

DANIEL CLYMER would ask, if the power to refuse leave of absence did not imply a power to detain the person, and whether in that case, if it was necessary to lock the doors, the House would not be justifiable. An anecdote had occurred to him, which he would wish to communicate, though somewhat foreign. *It was remarkable, that three years back from yesterday, a similar secession had taken place; the same number of members, namely nineteen, had then absconded, and there was the same number of laws, ready to be compared at the table.*[4]

GEORGE CLYMER was decidedly of opinion, even had not the gentleman submitted himself to the decision of the House, that they were competent to use measures to compel his stay.

The Speaker now stated the question.

WILLIAM ROBINSON had all along agreed that the member was in the power of the House, after answering to his name, but he had supposed him to be held by compulsion, and if so, then they were not a house.

JAMES M'CALMONT now rose and made towards the door. Mr. Fitzsimons addressed him, but so as not to be heard, and the gallery called out *stop him,* there being a number of citizens at the door he went toward. The commotion subsided in a few seconds, and Mr. M'Calmont returned to his seat, to wait the decision of the House.

THOMAS FITZSIMONS informed the Speaker, that Mr. M'Calmont had told him, he had occasion to go out and was willing to go in company with the sergeant at arms; he thereupon hoped the gentleman's wish might be complied with.

The Speaker put the question, shall Mr. M'Calmont have leave of absence? which was determined almost, if not quite, unanimously, in the negative.

The House now proceeded to compare and enact a number of bills, which were lying engrossed on the table.

On motion the House resumed the consideration of the unfinished resolutions which were presented yesterday, by Mr. G. Clymer, when the one fixing the day for holding the election of delegates to convention was read.

Hugh H. Brackenridge moved to insert the first Tuesday in November, to be the day throughout the state.

GERARDUS WYNKOOP thought the last Tuesday in October, would allow sufficient time, but Daniel Clymer approved of the most distant day. None of the gentlemen were anxious about the week, and therefore agreed the question should be on the first Tuesday in November.

JAMES M'CALMONT thought this much too early and moved successively for the last Tuesday, the third Tuesday, and second Tuesday in December, without being seconded.

The question was therefore taken on the *first Tuesday in November,* which was agreed to.

On appointing the place where the convention should sit, it was proposed by James M'Calmont to alter it from the city of Philadelphia, to Carlisle, but in this he was not seconded. He then moved for Lancaster, and after some time was seconded by Alexander Lowry. The yeas and nays were called by him on this question, and are:

Yeas. Lowry, Hubley, Carpenter, Work, Ross, Clemson, M'Conaghy, Schmyser, M'Lellan, J. Heister, G. Heister, Cannon, M'Calmont, Miley, Carson. 15.

Nays. Will, Morris, Fitzsimmons, [G.] Clymer, Hiltzeimer, Gray, Robinson, Salter, Logan, Foulke, Wynkoop, Chapman, Upp, Moore, Willing, Ralston, Evans, Thomas, Wheelen, Lilley, Kreemer, Davis, D. Clymer, Trexler, Burkhalter, Brackenridge, Moore, Wheeler, Hockley, and Riffe [Reiff], 30.

So it was determined in the negative, and afterward the resolution was agreed to as it stood.

GEORGE CLYMER now moved to insert these words in the preamble, "And whereas Congress on Friday the twenty-eighth instant, did unanimously resolve, that the said Constitution be transmitted to the several legislatures of the states to the intent aforesaid." Which being done, the committee who had been appointed to see the seals set to the laws reported they had performed this service.

The warrant for their pay was delivered to the members present, and Mr. M'Calmont received those intended for the members who had withdrawn themselves. Thus closed the business of the eleventh General Assembly of Pennsylvania:

When on motion of Daniel Clymer, the House came to the following resolution.

"*Resolved unanimously,* That the thanks of this House be presented to the Speaker for his able, upright, and faithful discharge of the important duties of his station."

To which the Speaker returned for answer:

"Gentlemen: Your Speaker is extremely gratified to find the General Assembly of Pennsylvania approve his endeavors to discharge the duties of his station. He has not been wanting in his efforts to render that satisfaction, which you now declare his conduct has given you. This mark of your approbation is a great reward for the highest exertions of an honest man, and it is the only reward an honest man can either receive or wish for."

The House now adjourned *sine die.*

1. Only three individuals, Captain John Barry, Michael Morgan O'Brien, and Major William Jackson, have been identified as being among those citizens who forcibly returned M'Calmont and Miley to the Assembly (Charles Swift to Robert E. Griffiths, 18 October, II:C below). O'Brien, an Irish immigrant, was a Philadelphia merchant and Jackson had been secretary of the Constitutional Convention.

2. The rule reads: "Every member actually attending the session shall be in his place at the time the House stands adjourned to, or within half an hour thereof, on the penalty, if a quorum without him, of *two shillings and six-pence,* if not, of *five shillings.* A member having withdrawn, while the House is sitting, without leave, shall forfeit *five shillings.* Excuses, however, may be admitted" ([12th] Assembly *Minutes,* 10 November 1787, p. 39).

3. James Barr, one of the seceding members, had been designated to receive such fines (Mfm:Pa. 79).

4. This incident occurred on 28 September 1784. When the Constitutionalists realized that they could not prevent a Republican attempt to revise the test laws, nineteen of them left the Assembly, forcing an adjournment for lack of a quorum. The next day the Assembly failed to secure a quorum and adjourned *sine die.* Two of the seceding members, Abraham Smith and Frederick Antes, also seceded in September 1787.

Appendix

James M'Calmont's Appeal to the Supreme Executive Council, 3 October 1787–16 February 1788

James M'Calmont, who had been brought into the General Assembly by a mob, petitioned the Supreme Executive Council for redress. On 3 October the Council voted 8 to 3 to direct Attorney General William Bradford, Jr. "to commence a prosecution against Captain John Barry and such other persons as shall be found to have been principally active" in the mob. Three councillors declared that the Council should not interfere in a trivial matter which did not endanger the state and which made the Council an instrument of politics.

On 20 October, Bradford drew up warrants against Barry and certain unnamed persons and applied to Chief Justice Thomas McKean for a precept. McKean declined to issue one until he knew who the unnamed persons were. Earlier in the month McKean had refused to issue warrants against Barry and the others reportedly because "the mass of the people were so incensed at their [the seceding assemblymen's] conduct, that tumult and further outrage would be the inevitable consequence." Sometime during the week of 10 December, a judge finally issued a warrant for Barry, who was preparing to leave for the Far East as captain of the ship *Asia,* owned by Robert Morris. Whether or not the warrant was ever served is unknown, but on 14 December Barry's ship sailed from Philadelphia for Canton, China. On 16 February 1788, Attorney General Bradford asked the advice of the Council about the suit pending against Barry. The Council resolved "That the attorney general be informed that Council do not wish to interfere but that they leave the matter entirely with him to act as he shall judge best." The case was closed.

For documents concerning the above events, see Mfm:Pa. 91.

B. THE ADDRESS OF THE SECEDING ASSEMBLYMEN AND THE REPLY OF SIX ASSEMBLYMEN

The Address of the Seceding Assemblymen[1]

Gentlemen: When in consequence of your suffrages at the last election we were chosen to represent you in the General Assembly of this Commonwealth, we accepted of the important trust, with a determination to execute it in the best manner we were able, and we flatter ourselves we acted in such a manner as to convince you, that your interests with that of the good of the state has been the object of our measures.

During the fall and spring sessions of the legislature, on the recommendation of the Congress of the United States, your representatives proceeded to the appointment of delegates to attend a convention to be held in the city of Philadelphia, for the purposes of revising and amending the present Articles of Confederation, and to report their proceedings to Congress, and when adopted by them, and ratified by the several states to become binding on them as part of the Confederation of the United States. We lamented at the time that a majority of our legislature appointed men to represent this state who were all citizens of Philadelphia, none of them calculated to represent the landed interest of Pennsylvania, and almost all of them of one political party, men who have been uniformly opposed to that constitution for which you have on every occasion manifested your attachment. We were apprehensive at the time of the ill consequences of so partial a representation, but all opposition was in vain. When the Convention met, members from twelve states attended and, after deliberating upwards of four months on the subject, agreed on a plan of government which was sent forward by them to Congress, and which was reported to the House by the delegates of Pennsylvania as mere matter of information, and printed in the newspapers of the city of Philadelphia; but the House had not received it officially from Congress, nor had we the least idea that, as the annual election was so near, we should be called upon to deliberate, much less to act on so momentous a business; a business of the utmost importance to you and your posterity. We conceived it required the most minute examination and mature consideration, and that it ought to be taken up by the next house. Judge then of our surprise on finding the last day but one in the sessions, a member of the House [George Clymer] who had been a delegate in the Convention, without any previous notice or any intimation of his intentions to the House, offer a resolution recommending the calling a convention to consider of the proposed Constitution, and to direct the electing members for the same, at so early a period as the day of your annual election, thus attempting to surprise you into a choice of members—to approve or disapprove of a Constitution, which is to entail happiness or misery forever without giving time to the greatest part of the state even to see, much less to examine the plan of government.

Our duty to ourselves and our regard for your dearest interests induced us to oppose the measure by every possible argument that we could suggest at the time; but all our efforts were insufficient even to produce a postponement until the afternoon. We urged and urged in vain the constant practice of the House when any important business was to be brought on, of giving previous notice and making it the order of the day sometime beforehand; that no bill however trifling was passed without three readings, and without this formality which gave the members time and opportunity to think on the subject; that the rules were adhered to so strictly that even the building of a bridge, or the laying out a road, could not be determined on without this form; but this the most important of all matters was to be done by surprise and, as we conceived, with design to preclude you from having it in your power to deliberate on the subject. Our anxiety for your interests was great, but notwithstanding the firmest and most determined opposition, no respite could be obtained, and the first resolution was adopted by a majority of the House, when they adjourned till the afternoon to complete the business. In these circumstances we had no alternative; we were under a necessity of either returning to the House and, by our presence, enabling them to call a convention before our constituents could have the means of information or time to deliberate on the subject, or by absenting ourselves from the House, prevent the measure taking place. Our regard for you induced us to prefer the latter, and we determined not to attend in the afternoon. We conceived that at the time we were chosen you had no view to this business, and we could see no inconvenience nor loss of time from deferring a matter of such importance and which would in its consequences affect or, perhaps, annihilate our own constitution, as well as that of every constitution in the Union to a house chosen after the people had some knowledge of the plan, especially as the next house will meet at so early a period, and a convention could be called by them time enough to meet in a few months, which would be as early as any state in the Union and would be allowing you time to make up your minds on a matter which appeared to us to require so much deliberation. Thus circumstanced and thus influenced, we determined the next morning again to absent ourselves from the House, when James M'Calmont, Esquire, a member from Franklin, and Jacob Miley, Esquire, a member from Dauphin, were seized by a number of citizens of Philadelphia, who had collected together for that purpose; their lodgings were violently broken open, their clothes torn, and after much abuse and insult, they were forcibly dragged through the streets of Philadelphia to the State House, and there detained by force, and in the presence of the majority, who had, the day before, voted for the first of the proposed resolutions, treated with the most insulting language; while the House so formed proceeded to finish their resolutions, which they mean to offer to you as the doings of the legislature of Pennsylvania. On this outrageous proceeding we make no comment. The inhabitants of Franklin and Dauphin have been grossly insulted by the treatment of their members. We know the feelings of the people of these counties are sufficiently keen; it becomes us not to add to them by dwelling longer on the subject; but as our conduct may, and we have no doubt, will be misrepresented, we thought it our duty to lay before our constituents, to whom alone we are accountable, a real state of facts; that they may judge for themselves. We need not tell you, that we could have no interested motive to influence our conduct. A sense of that duty which we owed to you and to ourselves could have alone induced us to submit to the variety of abuse and insults which many of us have experienced, for not consenting to a measure that might probably have surprised you into a surrender of your dearest rights. Our conduct has at least had the good effect to lengthen out the time of election, and induced them to postpone the election for members of the convention until the first Tuesday in November next; whereas the resolution first proposed directed it to be holden for all the counties east of Bedford on the day of the annual election, nine days from the time of proposing the measure.

We cannot conclude without requesting you to turn your serious attention to the government now offered to your consideration. "We are persuaded that a free and candid discussion of any subject tends greatly to the improvement of knowledge, and that a matter in which the public are so deeply interested cannot be too well understood. A good constitution and government is a blessing from heaven and the right of posterity and mankind; suffer then, we entreat you, no interested motive, sinister view or improper influence to direct your determinations or bias your judgments." Provide yourselves with the new Constitution offered to you by the Convention; look it over with attention that you be enabled to think for yourselves. We confess when the legislature appointed delegates to attend the Convention, our ideas extended no further than a revision or amendment of the present Confederation, nor were our delegates, by the acts of Assembly appointing them, authorized to do more as will appear by referring to the said act, the second section of which describes their powers in the following words, viz.:

"2. Be it enacted, and it is hereby enacted by the representatives of the Freemen of the Commonwealth of Pennsylvania in General Assembly met, and by the authority of the same, That Thomas Mifflin, Robert Morris, George Clymer, Jared Ingersoll, Thomas Fitzsimons, James Wilson and Governeur Morris, esquires, are hereby appointed deputies from this state to meet in the Convention of the deputies of the respective states of North America, to be held at the city of Philadelphia, on the second day of the month of May next. And the said Thomas Mifflin, Robert Morris, George Clymer, Jared Ingersoll, Thomas Fitzsimons, James Wilson and Governeur Morris, esquires, or any four of them are hereby constituted and appointed deputies from this state, with powers to meet such deputies as may be appointed and authorized by the other states to assemble in the said convention at the city aforesaid, and to join with them in devising, deliberating on, and discussing all such alterations and further provisions as may be necessary to render the foederal constitution fully adequate to the exigencies of the Union; and in reporting such act or acts for that purpose, to the United States in Congress assembled, as when agreed to by them, and duly confirmed by the several states, will effectually provide for the same."[2]

You will therefore perceive that they had no authority whatever from the legislature to annihilate the present Confederation and form a constitution entirely new, and in doing which they have acted as mere individuals, not as the official deputies of this commonwealth. If, however, after mature deliberation, you are of opinion that the plan of government which they have offered for your consideration is best calculated to promote your political happiness and preserve those invaluable privileges you at present enjoy, you will no doubt choose men to represent you in convention who will adopt it; if you think otherwise you will, with your usual firmness, determine accordingly.

You have a right, and we have no doubt you will consider whether or not you are in a situation to support the expense of such a government as is now offered to you, as well as the expense of your state government or whether a legislature consisting of three branches, neither of them chosen annually, and that the Senate, the most powerful, the members of which are for six years, are likely to lessen your burthens or increase your taxes or whether in case your state government should be annihilated, which will probably be the case, or dwindle into a mere corporation, the continental government will be competent to attend to your local concerns? You can also best determine whether the power of levying and imposing internal taxes at pleasure will be of real use to you or not or whether a continental collector assisted by a few faithful soldiers will be more eligible than your present collectors of taxes? You will also, in your deliberations on this important business, judge whether the liberty of the press may be considered as a blessing or a curse in a free government, and whether a declaration for the preservation of it is necessary or whether in a plan of government any declaration of rights should be prefixed or inserted? You will be able likewise to determine, whether in a free government there ought or ought not to be any provision against a standing army in time of peace or whether the trial by jury in civil causes is become dangerous and ought to be abolished and whether the judiciary of the United States is not so constructed as to absorb and destroy the judiciaries of the several states? You will also be able to judge whether such inconveniences have been experienced by the present mode of trial between citizen and citizen of different states as to render a continental court necessary for that purpose or whether there can be any real use in the appellate jurisdiction with respect to fact as well as law? We shall not dwell longer on the subject; one thing however it is proper you should be informed of; the Convention were not unanimous with respect to men though they were as states. Several of those who have signed did not fully approve of the plan of government, and three of the members, viz., Governor Randolph and Colonel George Mason of Virginia, and Eldredge [*sic*] Gerry, Esquire of Massachusetts, whose characters are very respectable, had such strong objections as to refuse signing. The Confederation no doubt is defective and requires amendment and revision, and had the Convention extended their plan to the enabling the United States to regulate commerce, equalize the impost, collect it throughout the United States, and have the entire jurisdiction over maritime affairs, leaving the exercise of internal taxation to the separate states, we apprehend there would have been no objection to the plan of government.

The matter will be before you, and you will be able to judge for yourselves. "Show that you seek not yourselves, but the good of your country, and may He who alone has dominion over the passions and understandings of men enlighten and direct you aright, that posterity may bless God for the wisdom of their ancestors."

James M'Calmont	John Gilchrist
Robert Clark	Abraham Smith
Jacob Miley	Robert Whitehill
Alexander Wright	David Mitchel
John M'Dowell	John Piper
John Flenniken	Samuel Dale
James Allison	William Findley
Theophilus Philips	James Barr[3]

Saturday, September 29th, 1787

1. Broadside, Rare Book Room, DLC. The full title is: *An Address of the Subscribers Members of the late House of Representatives of the Commonwealth of Pennsylvania to their Constituents* [Philadelphia, 1787]. The broadside in the Library of Congress, annotated "published & sold Oct. 2. 1787," is the only extant broadside copy.

2. For the complete text of the act, passed 30 December 1786, see CDR:VI, C. For another criticism of the delegates to the Constitutional Convention for violating their instructions, see "An Old Constitutionalist," 26 October, Mfm:Pa. 162.

3. Thomas Kennedy is listed among the signers in the German version of this address.

The Reply of the Six Assemblymen, Pennsylvania Packet, 8 October[1]

Mr. [William] Findley, Mr. [Robert] Whitehill, and others, members of the late General Assembly, making a disorderly secession from the House, with intention to put an end to its deliberations upon the subject of calling a state convention, for the purpose of considering the system offered for the general government of the United States, they have, in a public address, rested their justification on these two points:

1st. The irregularity of taking up the Constitution framed by the Convention, without the special permission of Congress—the Assembly having in the appointment of deputies to the Convention proceeded but upon the recommendation of Congress.

2d. The unfitness of the deputies appointed. The addressers lamenting at the time when the choice was made, that they were all citizens of Philadelphia, and none of them *calculated* to represent the landed interest of the state.

Having been also members of the House, and competent to judge with respect to these points of justification, we beg leave to state all the necessary facts concerning them for the information of the public.

As to the first—on a communication of the proposition of Virginia, for holding a general convention, a bill for the appointment of the deputies was reported by a committee, of which Mr. Findley and Mr. Whitehill were members, and passed into a law on the 30th of December last. The law, as set forth in the preamble, stood upon "*Representations of Congress heretofore made,*" and on the proposition of Virginia; but the special recommendation of Congress, to send the deputies to the proposed convention, made no part of the preamble. This recommendation not having passed Congress until the 21st day of February following, when that body, for the first time, recognized the convention. In the next session, on the 28th of March, a supplementary law passed the House; but its only object was to add another deputy to the number already chosen, and its only reference was to the original act.[2]

As the representations of Congress spoken of in the preamble to the law, of the first session, were only such as had been frequently made of the weakness of the general government, and of the necessity that arose of endowing it with greater powers, but gave no special license to the states to send deputies to the convention proposed by the State of Virginia, it follows that in the appointment of the deputies the Assembly acted independently of Congress, or of its recommendation. It is in vain, for the reasons before mentioned, that the addressers attempt, by a general reference to the transactions of both sessions, to cover their assertion upon this head. It is an artifice more unworthy than the most naked falsehood!

As little can be said in support of the second, their disapprobation of the deputies, which a state of nominations and votes will evince. The original intention of the House was to send seven deputies, though afterwards that number was, by the supplementary law, increased to eight. To supply the seven places, twelve persons stood in nomination. They, with the votes for each, were as follow:

*Jared Ingersoll	61	John Bayard	25
Charles Pettit	25	*Thomas Fitzsimons	37
*Robert Morris	63	*James Wilson	35
*George Clymer	63	*Governeur Morris	33
*Thomas Mifflin	63	Benjamin Franklin	10
Thomas M'Kean	26	William Findley	2

Of whom those marked with an * were elected.[3]

As to four of these persons, there appears from the votes to have been a general agreement, 63 being the number composing the House; so that no real controversy took place but as to the remaining three. Between these opposite three then must have lain the question with the House, with respect to the fitness to represent the landed interest; and for this they might all have been fit, except in the circumstance of city residence, the candidates generally holding considerable landed property within the state, the whole body of candidates, Mr. Finley excepted, being inhabitants of Philadelphia; and as to that gentleman, the solitary nominee from the country. He seems then, from the state of the votes, to have been out of the question, which is the more extraordinary, if, as the addressers must be understood, a country residence was indispensable to represent the landed interest of the state.

But the truth is, that at the time of election no such lamentation was made by the sixteen or any others that the candidates were citizens of Philadelphia, or otherwise unqualified to represent the landed interest; for it is well known, that both Mr. Findley and Mr. Whitehill were of opinion that the choice should be confined to the city of Philadelphia and its neighborhood, as it would not be convenient for persons living at a distance to attend a convention; the former declaring a seat there would not suit him, which, perhaps, may account for the fewness of his votes.

This being the state of facts relating to these points, can we suppose a depravation of mind equal to such impositions and deceptions, or ought we not rather to suppose, in these instances, that the addressers were not at the pains to read what was prepared to their hands?

It is urged, in argument against the House, that the deputies having exceeded the terms of their powers that the system they agreed to ought not to be taken up. It is not easy to determine to what the powers of the deputation from Pennsylvania, and from the other states (for they are in the same predicament), did really extend; but any argument brought from an excess in the exercise of the powers against the object of them cannot be that of good sense or integrity. A man of understanding, or a good patriot, will examine only whether or not the system actually offered is calculated to better the condition of our country. Indeed one would think the system being no more than a proposition, which none are bound to yield to, tho all ought to consider, that the Convention have not really transgressed their powers, they certainly might make whatever propositions they pleased.

The addressers resent the harsh treatment of the House to the two of their body who were forced back to their seats, by some of the citizens from without. They suffered no such treatment. On the contrary, the House showed a wonderful good temper on so provoking an occasion when a misdemeanor had been committed of a kind, which, tho it has hitherto escaped even the slightest punishment, is deserving of the highest; when the addressers had by their conduct violated the first condition of all political society, which obliges the few to give way to the many; when they had offended in the double capacity of citizens of the United States and of Pennsylvania, in setting a dangerous example of riot and turbulence to the continent; and, as much as lay in their feeble means, attempting to dissolve the government under which they live.

William Will[4]	Jacob Hiltzheimer
Thomas Fitzsimons	Daniel Clymer
George Clymer	William Robinson, Jr.

Dr. Franklin's not having been chosen at the first election, was owing to a misunderstanding among the members, with respect to his willingness to serve, but on better information, in the next session, it was the unanimous desire of the House that he should be added, which gave occasion to the supplementary law.

1. This item was dated "Philadelphia, October 6, 1787."
2. For the Pennsylvania act of 30 December 1786, see CDR:VI, C.
3. These votes were not recorded in either the Assembly *Minutes* or in the newspaper report of Assembly proceedings.
4. William Will was high sheriff of Philadelphia from 1780 to 1783 and 1791 to 1794 and served in the Assembly from 1785 to 1788.

C. PUBLIC AND PRIVATE COMMENTARIES ON THE PROCEEDINGS OF THE ASSEMBLY ON 28–29 September 1787

**Tench Coxe to James Madison,
Philadelphia, 28–29 September**[1]

I troubled you with a few lines by Mr. Moore, in which I promised myself the pleasure of sending you the third number of the American Citizen,[2] which I have now the pleasure to enclose. Our House is at this moment on the adoption of the plan. A motion to postpone was made by our Western members, but on the question only 12 were for the postponement. The House are now proceeding, and the resolution before them is to this effect: "that the House *recommend* to the people of Pennsylvania the calling a convention agreeably to the plan proposed by the late Federal Convention for the purpose of considering the new Constitution, etc."

A second resolution is to follow fixing the times of election and meeting. There is *very* little doubt that it will be carried. I have none indeed. Mr. [William] Findley stated his ideas on the subject fully, and went so far as to say that he thought a convention ought to be called and expected it would be called. He made no observation unfavorable to the new Constitution.

[P.S.] The *only* ground of opposition was not having the Constitution before the House from Congress.

29th. Our Assembly on a division on the first question were 43 for it and 19 against; Mr. [Robert] Morris was not in the House. There were 34 Republicans and 9 Constitutionalists in the 43. The *principal* Germans were among the nine. The Western members chiefly composed the 19. This took place about two o'clock when the House adjourned till after dinner. On the call of the roll there appeared but 45 members, 46 is a quorum. This appearing designed to prevent the second resolution fixing the time, manner, etc. of electing and convening the state convention, the sergeant at arms was sent for the 17 absentees who were found together at the house [of] a great Constitutional partisan, a Major [Alexander] Boyd, with two Constitutional members of the Council from the Western counties, Messrs. J[ames] McClane and [John] Smilie. They received the Speaker's message from the sergeant but refused to go to the House. The House adjourned till this morning at 1/2 past nine.

It appears probable to me from the information I have been able to collect that Judge [George] Bryan was with the 17 prior to the sergeant's finding them, but not at the time. A Mr. [Robert] Whitehill, one of the Constitutional leaders, certainly was at his [Bryan's] house at dinner.

It appears from these facts, that the Western people have a good deal of jealousy about the new Constitution, and it is very clear that the men who have been used to lead the Constitutional[ists] are against it decidedly. I am sorry for anything that appears irregular, or looks like an interruption of peace, but I have no doubt of a large majority of the Convention adopting the new frame of government *in toto*. One thing will certainly follow: the rending the Constitutional Party to pieces when the animosities among them will be more bitter from their former cordiality.

The enclosed paper has also the resolution of the House at large.

The arrival of the recommendation of Congress before ten o'clock today would be a most happy circumstance.

1. RC, Madison Papers, DLC. The letter was delivered to Madison in New York by Major [Aquila?] Giles.

2. See the third number of "An American Citizen," 26–29 September, II:A below.

Samuel Hodgdon to Timothy Pickering, Philadelphia, 29 September (excerpt)[1]

Yesterday the question for calling a convention to determine on the adoption of the Constitution lately recommended was put. [William] Findley and [Robert] Whithill at the head of 17 others opposed it, but finding the previous question carried, they did not return in the afternoon to the adjournment. The sergeant at arms was sent to command their attendance. Hearing they were at [Alexander] Boyd's, he went there, found them, and delivered his message. Whitehill answered that as there was no house, his orders were impertinent and would not be complied with. This answer being communicated, the Speaker and members forty-five in number, they adjourned until [9:30] o'clock this morning. At 7 o'clock an express arrived from New York, with the agreeable news that Congress (eleven and a half states being present) had unanimously agreed to recommend the new Constitution to the United States. This I suppose will bring the members to the House at the adjournment today, and finish the resolution of yesterday for calling the convention.

Today again the *nineteen* refused giving their attendance. An order was signed for taking them into custody by the sergeant at arms, and the clerk of the House was directed to attend him. A number of volunteer gentlemen also attended him. The whole proceeded to Boyd's where *two* only were found. These were apprehended and brought by force of arms and seated. One of them rose, and plead[ed] duress, and tendered his fine of 5 shillings and demanded liberty to depart, but he was immediately silenced, and the business was introduced and passed as you will perceive by the enclosed paper. This conduct has put an *end* to the Constitutional interest in this city. The principals in the business are universally despised, and their abettors hide their heads.[2] The House having finished this and some other business dissolved themselves, and writs are out for holding an election on the ninth of next month, at which time [John] *Franklin*[3] may try what interest he has yet in your county [Luzerne].

1. RC, Pickering Papers, MHi. Hodgdon was Pickering's business partner.
2. See also Hodgdon to Pickering, 4 October, Mfm:Pa. 91.
3. See "Daniel Shays to the Antifederal Junto," 25 September, n. 1, II:A below.

Pennsylvania Herald, 29 September[1]

A correspondent laments the scandal to which our legislature was yesterday exposed by the wanton desertion of *nineteen* of its members. It is thus that the affairs of government may be transferred from the majority to the minority, and the public business must either be transacted conformably to the will of a few men; or, conformably to their will, it must be left undone. The maxim of necessity, which has hitherto been employed to palliate so gross a violation of civil polity, could have no operation in the present case, for the question was merely as to the mode of proceeding to appoint the delegates of a convention, which the House had already agreed it was proper and necessary to summon. Could the matter of *form,* therefore, be magnified into the *necessity,* which excuses an attack upon the fundamental principles of government? Or, was it the mortification of a previous defeat, which introduced this attempt to counteract the end, by denying the means requisite to accomplish it? Whatever was the motive, every honest citizen will deprecate the consequences; and we have only to hope, continues our correspondent, that this event, manifesting the evils of a weak and inefficient government, will excite a constant and universal attachment to a plan of a contrary description. In the meantime, let it be left to the seceding party to reconcile to their constituents and their consciences, a measure which, to a man of plain sense and common honesty, appears a willful deviation from the legislative duties they were appointed to perform.

1. Reprinted in the *Pennsylvania Gazette,* 3 October and *Pennsylvania Mercury,* 5 October, and outside Pennsylvania in eight newspapers from New Hampshire to South Carolina by 18 October.

Pennsylvania Gazette, 3 October[1]

On Saturday last, at three o'clock, A.M. an express, forwarded by the Honorable Mr. [William] Bingham, one of the delegates from Pennsylvania, arrived in this city from Congress, with the resolution, recommending to each state to call a convention, to take into consideration the federal government. It was read in the Assembly on Saturday forenoon, where it was adopted, with only *two* objecting votes.

From the time the resolution of Congress was passed till its adoption by the State of Pennsylvania was only *twenty* hours. Such is the zeal of Pennsylvania to show her attachment to a vigorous, free, and wise frame of national government.

In consequence of the arrival of the unanimous resolution of Congress, and the adoption of it by our Assembly, the bells of Christ Church rang during the greatest part of Saturday. Many hundred citizens of the first character attended in the lobby, and at the door of the State House, during the deliberations of the House on the calling of a convention, and testified their joy upon the resolves being passed for that purpose by three heartfelt cheers. In short, unusual joy appeared in every countenance (three or four officers of government excepted) and the day exhibited everywhere the most agreeable marks of the speedy resurrection of the prosperity and happiness of Pennsylvania.

1. Reprinted in whole or in part three times in Pennsylvania and thirty-four times from Maine to South Carolina.

Louis-Guillaume Otto to Comte de Montmorin, New York, 10 October[1]

The public was still occupied with the perusal of the new Constitution and seemed disposed to admire it on the whole, when the imprudence of the legislative Assembly of Pennsylvania all at once revived the jealousy and the anxiety of the democratic party. By a peculiarity which is difficult to account for, Pennsylvania had only been represented in the General Convention by citizens from the county of Philadelphia; the other counties whose interests have always been different from those of the capital were hardly satisfied with this, and when the question was taken in the legislature to order the election of a convention to ratify the new Federal Constitution, their representatives took a decision to stay away. The majority immediately sent a bailiff of the chamber to compel the members of the minority to surrender to the Assembly; the populace, taking part in this quarrel, carried some people off to the legislative chamber. This violent proceeding furnished very heated debates and the next day a justificatory account was published signed by 17 dissident members, in which they indulged in the most alarming observations against the aristocratic party and even against the members of the General Convention.[2]

The conduct of the two factions has been equally disapproved of by true patriots. In forcing the minority to consent to the ratification of the new government without investigation, the legislature made use of a harshness and a precipitancy that should render this government very suspect. On the other hand, the minority did not have any right to disregard the summons of the chamber, and in spreading misgivings on the new Constitution from the beginning it could strike it a fatal blow. These members were highly disapproved of by their constituents and they have been replaced by other men;[3] but the alarm is sounded, the public is on its guard and they begin to examine strictly what they would have adopted almost blindly.

These dissidents, sir, avail themselves of a very embarrassing argument to weaken the new Constitution. They are saying that the members of the Convention exceeded their powers in drafting a *new Constitution,* that their goal should only have been to *propose amendments to the Articles of Confederation which the well being of the Union might have required.* Instead of limiting themselves to this task, they have consolidated the states, seized all power from the legislative assemblies, authorized the establishment of an army and perhaps of an arbitrary taxation.

Pennsylvania, sir, is the only state which suffered some jolts by the publication of the new Constitution. The parties which have existed there for such a long time seem to take on a new vigor. The people there have always been against the establishment of a high chamber and a governor capable of balancing the excessive preponderance of the legislative Assembly. The questions which necessarily result from the scrutiny of the new government revive old quarrels on the balance of the three branches of administration.

1. RC (Tr), Correspondance Politique, États-Unis, Vol. 32, ff. 368–69, Archives du Ministère des Affaires Étrangères, Paris, France. Otto had been French chargé d'affaires since 1785 and was France's principal diplomatic agent in the United States until the arrival in January 1788 of the Comte de Moustier as minister plenipotentiary. The Comte de Montmorin was the French Minister of Foreign Affairs.

2. Otto refers to the "Address of the Seceding Assemblymen," I:B above.

3. Otto, writing the day after the state election, was wrong. Only two of the seventeen seceding members eligible for reelection to the Assembly were defeated.

II

The Debate Over the Constitution in Pennsylvania

17 September–11 December 1787

Introduction

Pennsylvanians began lining up in support of and in opposition to the Constitution as soon as the Constitutional Convention adjourned. The first public meeting to support the Constitution was held in Philadelphia on 20 September. On the 26th the first major attack upon the Constitution was published in the *Freeman's Journal.* The same day Tench Coxe published "An American Citizen" Number I, the first major defense of the Constitution, in the *Independent Gazetteer.* On 2 October sixteen of the nineteen assemblymen who refused to attend the Assembly on 28–29 September in an attempt to prevent the calling of a state convention published an address defending their action. They denounced the violence used to secure a quorum and the calling of a convention before the Confederation Congress had transmitted the Constitution to the states officially. They concluded the address by outlining their objections to the Constitution. The address was reprinted twelve times in Pennsylvania and sixteen times from New Hampshire to Virginia.

On 5 October Samuel Bryan published the first of the "Centinel" essays in the *Independent Gazetteer.* The essays of "Centinel" were the most outspoken attacks by a Pennsylvanian on the motives of the members of the Constitutional Convention and on the nature of the Constitution, and were used by opponents of the Constitution from Massachusetts to Georgia, as well as in Pennsylvania. On 6 October, the day after the first "Centinel" appeared, James Wilson delivered a speech in the State House Yard that became the "official" Federalist interpretation of the Constitution throughout the United States.

Meanwhile, Pennsylvanians were campaigning for the annual Assembly election on 9 October, a campaign which was looked upon, in part at least, as a referendum on the Constitution. The Federalists denounced the nineteen assemblymen who had seceded from the Assembly and all other candidates who might oppose the Constitution. Nevertheless, fifteen of the seventeen seceders eligible for reelection were returned by the voters, and the opposition gained a few additional seats, although the Federalists retained control of the new Assembly.

The campaign for seats in the state Convention began as soon as the Assembly elections were over, and there are records of meetings to nominate candidates in several parts of the state. According to two newspaper accounts, assemblymen who supported the Constitution deliberately chose not to run for Convention seats. In any event, not a single "Federalist" assemblyman was elected to the Convention. Furthermore, James Wilson was the only one of the eight delegates to the Constitutional Convention who ran for and was elected to the state Convention.

In contrast, four Antifederalist assemblymen from the 11th and 12th assemblies, and five Antifederalist councillors from the immediately preceding Supreme Executive Council and the then sitting Council were elected to the Convention. All voted against ratification.

The election of Convention delegates on 6 November was a clear victory for those who called themselves Federalists, a victory that was widely recognized as deciding the outcome of the Convention before it began. An indication of the heat of the campaign for Convention seats was the election night riot in Philadelphia in which a mob attacked Major Alexander Boyd's boarding house where many of the western members of the Assembly lodged when the Assembly was in session. The march of a mob on Boyd's house on 29 September and the return of two seceding members to the Assembly by the mob was publicized throughout the United States, but not a single Philadelphia newspaper reported the riot on election night, 6 November.

In November, prior to the Convention, opponents of the Constitution in the new Assembly tried to establish the requirement that the quorum in the Convention be two-thirds of the elected members, the constitutionally required quorum for the Assembly. The attempt failed, as did an effort to block adjournment of the Assembly while the Convention was in session.

From the adjournment of the Constitutional Convention on 17 September to the meeting of the state Convention on 20 November, the Constitution was debated from many points of view. However, by mid-October a central issue was that of amendments to the Constitution and, particularly, the need for or lack of a need for a bill of rights. By the time the Convention met on 20 November, most of the arguments that were to be used in the Convention debates had been set forth repeatedly and at length. The newspaper debate continued after the Convention met, but there is no evidence that it had any effect on either the debates or the decisions of the Convention. On the other hand, the decision of the Convention to ratify the Constitution did not diminish the public debate, which continued for months after the Convention adjourned on 15 December 1787.

A. PUBLIC AND PRIVATE COMMENTARIES ON THE CONSTITUTION

17 September–6 October 1787

By 29 September when the Assembly called the state Convention, Philadelphia newspapers had printed many articles about the Constitution, some of which circulated nationally. Advocates of the Constitution maintained that it would herald an era of stability at home and respectability abroad; be a bulwark against tyranny and protect the rights, liberties, and property of all people; and insure and guarantee the liberties won by the War for Independence.

Opponents declared that Congress' vast powers, especially the power of direct taxation and the power to create a standing army, would be inimical to the rights, liberties, and property of the people. Moreover, the Constitution failed to guarantee the right of trial by jury in civil cases, and above all, that it was a "consolidated" rather than a "federal" government.

Simultaneously with the beginning of the newspaper debate, public meetings to consider the Constitution were held in and around Philadelphia. The result was a petition campaign asking the Assembly to call a state convention. Between 24 and 29 September petitions signed by more than 4,000 inhabitants of the city of Philadelphia and Philadelphia and Montgomery counties were presented to the Assembly (Mfm:Pa. 61).

During the ten days after the Assembly called the state Convention, Philadelphia Federalists and Antifederalists outlined many of the arguments for and against the Constitution that were used throughout the debate over ratification in Pennsylvania, and in many other states as well. The three principal statements were the "Address of the Seceding Assemblymen" (I:B above), "Centinel" I (II:A below), and James Wilson's Speech in the State House Yard on 6 October (II:A below). According to the *Massachusetts Centinel* of 31 October: "The *essence* and *quintessence* of all that can be objected to the American Constitution are comprised in the address of the Pennsylvania *seceders,* and a complete answer to them and the other Antifederalists, may be found in the address of Mr. Willson." "Other Antifederalists" presumably included "Centinel" I.

Samuel Bryan, formerly clerk of the General Assembly, was the author of "Centinel," although contemporaries attributed the essay to his father, George Bryan (*Pennsylvania Gazette,* 31 October, Mfm: Pa. 178). "Centinel" I, first published in the *Independent Gazetteer* on 5 October, was also published as broadsides in English and German, and reprinted in the *Carlisle Gazette,* 24 October, and excerpted in the

Freeman's Journal, 12 December. (For national circulation of "Centinel" and for its authorship, see CC:133. The eighteen "Centinel" essays, between 5 October 1787 and 9 April 1788, are printed in *Commentaries on the Constitution.*)

For an example of a Pennsylvania Federalist reply to "Centinel" I, see "A Federalist," 10 October (II:C below). (See also, CC:158, 218; Mfm:Pa. 152, 156, 161.)

On 6 October James Wilson discussed the Constitution in a speech to a public meeting called to nominate candidates for the Assembly election on 9 October. The speech was published in an extra edition of the *Pennsylvania Herald* on 9 October. The *Herald* stated that the speech "is the first authoritative explanation of the principles of the NEW FEDERAL CONSTITUTION, and as it may serve to obviate some objections, which have been raised to that system, we consider it sufficiently interesting for publication in the present form." Responding to an "extensive demand," the *Herald* reprinted the speech the next day, and within a few weeks the speech was reprinted ten more times in the state and many times throughout the United States. (For national circulation, see CC:134.)

For examples of Pennsylvania Antifederalist replies to Wilson's speech, see "A Democratic Federalist," 17 October (II:A below), and "An Officer of the Late Continental Army," 6 November (II:C below); and "Centinel" II (CC:190).

Samuel Hodgdon to Timothy Pickering, Philadelphia, 17 September (excerpt)[1]

Today the Convention is dissolved. The enclosed is the result of their deliberations. Tho I do not know of any opportunity to address you, yet I write supposing it possible that I may hear of a conveyance when unprepared. This morning the new Constitution was read in our House of Assembly, to a crowded audience, and seems to be generally approved, indeed we have been in high glee ever since; bells ringing and congratulations in every street. I think it is a well-digested paper, and abundantly more equal to our wants than the Confederation Articles. I wish your opinion after an attentive reading.[2]

1. RC, Pickering Papers, MHi. The letter is dated 17 September, but evidently part of it was written on the 18th when the Constitution was read to the Assembly.

2. For Pickering's views on the Constitution, see his letter to Charles Tillinghast, 24 December, CC:288–C.

Thomas Mifflin to Silas Talbot, Philadelphia, 19 September (excerpt)[1]

I take the earliest opportunity of enclosing to you the result of the deliberations of the late Convention. May your state [New York] adopt it as soon as your neighbors of New Jersey and Connecticut who I am told will lose no time in giving it their sanction. We are determined here to admire it and to take it for better [or] for worse. Clear it is that unless we immediately agree to it America will repent our neglect.

1. RC, Talbot Papers, Marine Historical Association, Mystic, Connecticut. Mifflin was Speaker of the Assembly. Talbot, a New York landowner, had been first an army officer and then a naval officer during the Revolution.

Matthew M'Connell to William Irvine, Philadelphia, 20 September[1]

I have been favored with yours of the 13th and purchased the bolting cloth, for which I paid five pounds ten shillings and delivered it and the letter for your brother to Mr. Bryson. I should have answered your letter sooner but waited to try if I could find what effect the rising of the Convention might have upon state and continental credit. People interested in these matters seem very much staggered, however, continental certificates have rose to be very current at 2/6, and I was this morning offered 2/9 for five thousand dollars by a stranger who has lately began to purchase. Our new loan are 4/ but very few sellers and as few purchasers. Paper money cannot be said to be better than 25 percent discount.

It appears to me that if the new federal government is adopted all certificates will be alike, that is, the debt Pennsylvania has adopted must revert back to the United States and rest upon their funds. This would derange all our funding and land office laws it is true, but perhaps it might be as well for the creditors in the end, provided Congress get stable and permanent funds. The new government will abridge the powers of state legislatures, and I suppose in some measure impair their constitutions. These things I am afraid the people will not readily consent to, and yet if they do not I am of opinion America cannot exist as one nation; so that I see great difficulties every way, and independent of the funding systems adopted by Pennsylvania and New York.[2] These are my own private opinions. I have not met with anybody yet who chose to speak very freely on the subject. I suppose Congress will have it under consideration very shortly.

P.S. [I] should be happy to know [how] the continental lands sell at auction.

1. RC, Irvine Papers, PHi. M'Connell, a Philadelphia merchant, was the author of *An Essay on Domestic Debts . . .* (Philadelphia, 1787). Irvine, a native of Carlisle,

was a Pennsylvania delegate to Congress. For other letters concerning the effect of the Constitution on public securities, see Mfm:Pa. 64, 124, 169.

2. See M'Connell to Irvine, 25 September, Mfm:Pa. 65.

James Pemberton to John Pemberton, Philadelphia, 20 September (excerpt)[1]

The expectation of our politicians has been much turned towards the determination of this Convention, the members of which being under an injunction of secrecy, their proceedings have been kept very close. How they will now relish the plan, time will make manifest, but the late Congress had become so very low in general estimation, a change with enlarged powers and a proper balance seemed to be absolutely necessary. But yet, unless there is an increase of virtue among the people, all the efforts of human wisdom and policy will avail little to promote their real happiness and welfare. I have given thee these outlines of the new plan of a federal government with a view to mention that we entertained a hope that its establishment would have been more conspicuous on the principles of equity and moral justice by a provision against the iniquitous slave trade. But the influence of the Southern governments has diverted them from that very important object, so far as to obtain a prohibition against the Congress meddling therewith for 21 years, as appears by the ninth section of the first Article of the plan which says, viz.:

"The migration, or importation of such Persons as any of the States now existing shall think proper to admit, shall not be prohibited by Congress prior to the year 1808, but a [tax] or duty may be imposed on such importation, not exceeding ten dollars for each person" which is further defended by a fifth Article, which after liberty given for the mode of proposing future amendments to this intended Constitution, sets forth a proviso, that "no amendment which may be made prior to the year 1808 shall in any manner affect the first and fourth clauses in the ninth Section of the first Article."[2]

1. RC, Pemberton Papers, PHi. James and John Pemberton, the sons of Israel Pemberton, were leaders of Philadelphia's Quaker community. John Pemberton was in Scotland. This letter is the first of a series the brothers exchanged concerning the Constitution and the slave trade. Preceding the above excerpt is a description of the structure of the new government with a brief mention of its powers (Mfm:Pa. 55).

2. For further examples of the concern of Pennsylvania and Rhode Island Quakers about the Constitution and the slave trade, see CC:Vol. II, Appendix.

Philadelphia, Southwark, and Northern Liberties Meeting, 20 September[1]

At a meeting of a very respectable number of the inhabitants of the different wards of this city, the district of Southwark and township of the Northern Liberties, the following petition and declaration was unanimously agreed to be circulated, and when signed, to be presented to the honorable the representatives of the freemen of the Commonwealth of Pennsylvania in General Assembly met.

To[2] the Honorable the *Representatives* of the *Freemen* of the Commonwealth of *Pennsylvania* in *General Assembly* met,

The Petition and Declaration of the Inhabitants of Philadelphia and of the Districts of Southwark and the Northern Liberties.

Respectfully showeth, That your petitioners have seen, with great pleasure, the proposed Constitution of the United States, and as they conceive it to be wisely calculated to form a perfect union of the states, as well as to secure to themselves and posterity, the blessings of peace, liberty and safety, they have taken this method of expressing their earnest desires, that the said Constitution may be adopted as speedily as possible, by the State of Pennsylvania, in the manner recommended by the resolution of the late Honorable Convention.

1. *Pennsylvania Packet,* 21 September. The *Independent Gazetteer* also printed this item on the same day. By 16 October this report of the first known public meeting to consider the Constitution was reprinted or reported five other times in Philadelphia, once in Lancaster, and thirty-nine times from Maine to South Carolina.

The date of the meeting is not given, but it probably occurred on 20 September, the day before it was reported in the *Packet* and the *Gazetteer,* both daily newspapers.

2. From this point on, the text, with minor variations, is identical with the printed petitions circulated in the area.

Germantown Meeting, 21 September[1]

At a meeting of a respectable number of the citizens of Germantown, Dr. Charles Bensel in the chair, the Constitution of the United States being read,

Resolved unanimously, That we do highly approve of the proposed Constitution of the United States, and that we will concur with our fellow citizens in Philadelphia in praying the legislature immediately to adopt the measures recommended by the late Honorable Convention, for carrying the same into execution.

1. *Pennsylvania Packet,* 22 September. Bensel was a Germantown physician. The *Independent Gazetteer* and the *Evening Chronicle* also printed the item on

22 September, and by 15 October accounts of the meeting had been printed in two other Pennsylvania newspapers and in twenty-one newspapers from Portland, Maine, to Charleston, South Carolina.

David Redick to William Irvine, Philadelphia, 24 September[1]

The new plan of government proposed by the Convention has made a bustle in the city and its vicinity. All people, almost, are for swallowing it down at once without examining its tendencies.

I have thought it unsafe within the wind of hurricane to utter a syllable about it: but to you sir I may venture to say that, in my opinion, the day on which we adopt the present proposed plan of government, from that moment we may justly date the loss of American liberty. Perhaps my fears hath contributed principally to this opinion. I will change the moment that I see better. My dear sir, why is not the liberty of the press provided for? Why will the Congress have power to alter the plan or mode of choosing Representatives? Why will they have power to lay direct taxes? Why will [they] have power to keep standing armies in time of peace? Why will they have power to make laws in direct contradiction to the forms of government established in the several states? Why will they have power to collect by law ten dollars for ever[y] German or Irishman which may come to settle in America? Why is the trial by jury destroyed in civil causes before Congress? And, above all, I cannot imagine why the people in this city are so very anxious to have it adopted instantly before it can be digested or deliberately considered. If you were only here to see and hear those people, to observe the means they are using to effect this purpose, to hear the Tories declare they will draw their sword in its defense, to see the [Quakers?] running about signing declarations and petitions in favor of it before the[y] have time to examine it, to see gentlemen running into the country and neighboring towns haranguing the rabble. I say were you to see and hear these things as I do you would say with me that the very soul of confidence itself ought to change into distrust. If this government be a good one or even a tolerable one, the necessities and the good sense of America will lead us to adopt it; if otherwise give us time and it will be amended and then adopted; but I think the measures pursued here is a strong evidence that these people know it will not bear an examination and therefore wishes to adopt it first and consider it afterward. I hope Congress will be very deliberate and digest it thoroughly before they send it recommended to the states. I sincerely hope that such gentlemen as were members of Convention and who have seats in Congress may not be considered as very proper judges of their own works.

[I pray?] a spirit of wisdom and a spirit of integrity pervade Congress, more especially at this time.

1. RC, Irvine Papers, PHi. Redick represented Washington County in the Supreme Executive Council. Later he supported the Constitution (Thomas Scott to Benjamin Rush, 3 March 1788 and *Pittsburgh Gazette*, 15 March 1788, Mfm:Pa. 476, 531).

Independent Gazetteer, 24 September[1]

If party is unavoidable in free governments, it is now to be hoped, says a correspondent, that in future it will be carried on at least with less virulence. The eagerness that so unanimously has been shown to promote a federal government and insure the prosperity and liberty of America must evince the patriotism of the individuals who compose, both the Constitutional and Republican parties in this city, and ought to endear them to each other.

1. This item was also printed in the *Pennsylvania Packet* the same day and by 11 October it was reprinted three times in Philadelphia and ten times from New Hampshire to New York.

Daniel Shays to the Antifederal Junto in Philadelphia, Independent Gazetteer, 25 September[1]

Tioga point, 15*th September,* 1787.[2]

My dear Friends, It is with great concern that I have heard that you are composed of only *five* members, and that a great body of citizens who once followed you in every thing, have lately joined the federal party. Rest assured, they never were sound at bottom, that is, they never were attached to *themselves* above all things, or they never would have left you at this trying juncture.[3]

My advice to you upon this occasion is, give the new government all the opposition that lies in your power. For this purpose, if you are applied to to sign a petition to your Assembly to recommend the adoption of it,—you must say "*you* have not read it;" or if you have, that "you want time to consider of it."

Besides this, you must *snarle* at the Convention in every company, and write letters to the frontier countries, where the people is most easily deceived, and alarm them with a number of hard words, such as *aristocracy, monarchy, oligarchy,* and the like, none of which they will understand.

You must tell them further, that by the constitution of Pennsylvania, which *you* are sworne to support (and no wonder, for its treasury supports *you*) the federal government cannot be adopted in Pennsylvania.[4] Even the *people* themselves cannot consent to any alterations of the constitution; for the constitution is above them all, and above every thing else, except you, five gentlemen, who live by it, and who may break it, and twist it, and turn it when ever it suits your interest and party.

You must try further to put off the recommendation of a Convention, till the next session of your Assembly. This will give you time to look about you, and perhaps to throw a lock upon one of the wheels of the great continental waggon; for you may depend upon it your wheelbarrow, and the new flying machine, cannot long travel the same road together.

With great regard, and sincere wishes for your success in every thing that tends to anarchy, distress, poverty, and tyranny, I am your friend and humble servant, DANIEL SHAYS.

1. LT. This fictitious letter was reprinted in the *Pennsylvania Gazette* on 26 September, the *Carlisle Gazette* on 17 October, and in eight newspapers from Massachusetts to South Carolina. For the national circulation, see CC:94. For a similar piece, see "Wat Tyler, A Proclamation," 24 October, II:C below. From the language in the letter, especially the next to last paragraph, there is a possibility that Benjamin Rush was the author. He used similar language in a letter to Timothy Pickering on 30 August 1787: "The new federal government like a new continental wagon will overset our state dung cart, with all its dirty contents (reverend and irreverent) and thereby restore order and happiness to Pennsylvania" (Philadelphia, RC, Pickering Papers, MHi).

2. Tioga Point was in the Wyoming Valley of Pennsylvania, an area claimed and settled by Connecticut people before the War for Independence. After years of violence, a commission appointed by Congress awarded jurisdiction to Pennsylvania in 1782. The settlers, led by John Franklin, who was looked upon in eastern Pennsylvania as the equivalent of Daniel Shays, attempted to create an independent state in 1787. (See Taylor, IX, X.)

3. Among the principal opponents of the Constitution in Philadelphia were George Bryan, James Hutchinson, Reverend John Ewing, John Nicholson, Charles Pettit, and Jonathan Bayard Smith. For other examples of the argument that opposition was negligible, see "Southwark," 3 October, II:A below; and Mfm:Pa. 94, 129.

4. The assertion that Antifederalists opposed the Constitution because they held state offices was a common Federalist argument.

Pennsylvania Gazette, 26 September[1]

In the city and neighborhood of Philadelphia, a petition to our Assembly to call a convention in order to adopt this government has been almost unanimously signed. The zeal of our citizens in favor of this excellent Constitution has never been equalled, but by their zeal for liberty in the year 1776. Republicans, Constitutionalists, Friends, etc. have all united in signing this petition. It is expected the new government will abolish party and make us, once more, members of one great political family.

1. This item was reprinted in the *Pennsylvania Mercury,* 28 September and the *Philadelphische Correspondenz,* 2 October. Twenty-one newspapers from Vermont to South Carolina reprinted a version of it by 22 October.

An American Citizen, On the Federal Government I, II, III, Independent Gazetteer, 26–29 September

These essays by Tench Coxe were the first major defenses of the Constitution published in the United States. They were printed in the *Independent Gazetteer* on 26, 28, and 29 September, and reprinted in the *American Museum,* the *Pennsylvania Gazette,* and the *Carlisle Gazette* by 7 November. The *Philadelphische Correspondenz* printed German translations of the first essay on 13 November, the second on 20 November, and the third probably on 27 November, in an issue not extant. The three essays were reprinted, with a fourth essay by Coxe, in an anthology, *Addresses to the Citizens of Pennsylvania,* 21 October. See Coxe to Madison, 21 October, II:C below; and CC:100 A–C, 109, 112, 183 A–C for national distribution.

An American Citizen I

It is impossible for an honest and feeling mind, of any nation or country whatever, to be insensible to the present circumstances of America. Were I an East Indian, or a Turk, I should consider this singular situation of a part of my fellow creatures, as most curious and interesting. Intimately connected with the country, as a citizen of the Union, I confess it entirely engrosses my mind and feelings.

To take a proper view of the ground on which we stand, it may be necessary to recollect the manner in which the United States were originally settled and established. Want of charity in the religious systems of Europe and of justice in their political governments were the principal moving causes which drove the emigrants of various countries to the American continent. The Congregationalists, Quakers, Presbyterians and other British dissenters, the Catholics of England and Ireland, the Huguenots of France, the German Lutherans, Calvinists, and Moravians, with several other societies, established themselves in the different colonies, thereby laying the ground of that catholicism in ecclesiastical affairs, which has been observable since the late Revolution. Religious liberty naturally promotes corresponding dispositions in matters of government. The constitution of England, as it stood on paper, was one of the freest at that time existing in the world, and the American colonies considered themselves as entitled to the fullest enjoyment of it. Thus when the ill-judged discussions of latter times in England brought into question the rights of this country, as it stood connected with the British Crown, we were found more strongly impressed with their importance and accurately acquainted with their extent, than the wisest and most learned of our brethren beyond the Atlantic. When the greatest names in Parliament insisted on the power of that body over the commerce of the colonies, and even the right to bind us in all cases whatsoever, America, seeing that it was only another form of tyranny, insisted upon the immutable truth, that taxation and representation are inseparable, and while a desire of harmony and other considerations induced her into an acquiescence in the commercial regulations of Great Britain, it was done from the declared necessity of the case, and with a cautious, full and absolute saving of our voluntarily suspended rights. The Parliament was persevering, and America continued firm till hostilities and open war commenced, and finally the late Revolution closed the contest forever.

Tis evident from this short detail and the reflections which arise from it, that the quarrel between the United States and the Parliament of Great Britain did not arise so much from objections to the form of government, *though undoubtedly a better one by far is now within our reach,* as from a difference concerning certain important rights resulting from the essential principles of liberty, which the constitution preserved to all the subjects actually residing within the realm. It was not asserted by America that the people of *the island of Great Britain* were slaves, but that *we,* though possessed absolutely of the same rights, were not admitted to enjoy *an equal degree of freedom.*

When the Declaration of Independence completed the separation between the two countries, new governments were necessarily established. Many circumstances led to the adoption of the republican form, among which was the predilection of the people. In devising the frames of government it may have been difficult to avoid extremes opposite to the vices of that we had just rejected; nevertheless many of the state constitutions we have chosen are truly excellent. Our misfortunes have been, *that in the first instance we adopted no national government at all,* but were kept together by common danger only, *and that in the confusions of a civil war we framed a federal constitution now universally admitted to be inadequate to the preservation of liberty, property, and the Union.* The question is not then how far our state constitutions are good or otherwise—the object of our wishes is *to amend and supply the evident and allowed errors and defects of the federal government.* Let us consider awhile, that which is now proposed to us. Let us compare it with the so much boasted British form of government, and see how much more it favors the people and how completely it secures their rights, remembering at the same time that we did not dissolve our connection with that country so much on account of its constitution as the perversion and maladministration of it.

In the first place let us look at the nature and powers of the head of that country, and those of the ostensible head of ours.

The British king is the great bishop or supreme head of an established church, with an immense patronage annexed. In this capacity he commands a number of votes in the House of Lords, by creating bishops, who, besides their great incomes, have votes in that assembly, and are judges in the last resort. They have also many honorable and lucrative places to bestow, and thus from their wealth, learning, dignities, powers and patronage give a great luster and an enormous influence to the Crown.

In America our President will not only be *without* these influencing advantages, *but they will be in the possession of the people at large, to strengthen their hands in the event of a contest with him.* All religious funds, honors and powers are in the gift of numberless, unconnected, disunited, and contending corporations, wherein the principle of perfect equality universally prevails. In short, danger from ecclesiastical tyranny, that longstanding and still remaining curse of the people—that sacrilegious engine of royal power in some countries, can be feared by no man in the United States. In Britain their king is for life. In America our President will always be *one of the people* at the end of four years. In that country the king is hereditary and may be an idiot, a knave, or a tyrant by nature, or ignorant from neglect of his education, yet cannot be removed, for *"he can do no wrong."* In America, as the President is to be one of the people at the end of his short term, so will he and his fellow citizens remember, *that he was originally one of the people; and that he is created by their breath.* Further, he cannot be an idiot, probably not a knave or a tyrant, for those whom nature makes so, discover it before the age of thirty-five, until which period he cannot be elected. It appears we have not admitted that he can do no wrong, but have rather presupposed he may and will sometimes do wrong, by providing for *his impeachment, his trial, and his peaceable and complete removal.*

In England the king has a power to create members of the upper house, who are judges in the highest court, as well as legislators. Our President not only cannot make members of the upper house, but their creation, like his own, is by *the people* through their representatives, and a member of assembly may and will be as certainly dismissed at the end of his year for electing a weak or wicked Senator, as for any other blunder or misconduct.

The king of England has legislative power, while our President can only use it when the other servants of the people are divided. But in all great cases affecting the national interests or safety, his modified and restrained power must give way to the sense of two-thirds of the legislature. In fact it amounts to no more, than a serious duty imposed upon him to request both houses to reconsider any matter on which he entertains doubts or feels apprehensions; and here the people have a strong hold upon him *from his sole and personal responsibility.*

The president of the upper house (or the chancellor) in England is appointed by the king, while our Vice President, who is chosen *by the people* through the Electors and the Senate, *is not at all dependent on the President,* but may exercise equal powers on some occasions. In all royal governments an helpless infant or an inexperienced youth may wear the crown. *Our President must be matured by the experience of years,* and being born among us, his character at thirty-five must be fully understood. Wisdom, virtue, and active qualities of mind and body can alone make him the first servant of a free and enlightened people.

Our President will fall very far short indeed of any prince in his annual income, which will not be hereditary, but *the absolute allowance of the people passing through the hands of their other servants from year to year as it becomes necessary.* There will be no burdens on the nation to provide for his heir or other branches of his family. Tis probable, from the state of property in America and other circumstances, that many citizens will *exceed* him in show and expense, those dazzling trappings of kingly rank and power. He will have no authority to make a treaty without *two-thirds of the Senate,* nor can he appoint ambassadors or other great officers *without their approbation,* which will remove the idea of *patronage and influence,* and of personal obligation and dependence. The appointment of even the inferior officers may be taken out of his hands by an act of Congress at any time; he can create no nobility or titles of honor, nor take away offices during good behavior. *His person is not so much protected as that of a member of the House of Representatives; for he may be proceeded against like any other man in the ordinary course of law.* He appoints *no officer of the separate states.* He will have no influence *from placemen in the legislature,* nor can he prorogue or dissolve it. He will have no power *over the treasures of the state*; and lastly, as he is *created* through the Electors by the people at large, *he must ever look up to the support of his creators.* From such a servant with powers so limited and transitory, there can be no danger, especially when we consider the solid foundations on which our national liberties are immovably fixed by the other provisions of this excellent Constitution. Whatever of dignity or authority he possesses is *a delegated part of their majesty and their political omnipotence, transiently vested in him by the people themselves for their own happiness.*

An American Citizen II

We have seen that the late Honorable Convention, in designating the nature of the chief executive office of the United States, *have deprived it of all the dangerous appendages of royalty,* and provided for *the frequent expiration of its limited powers.* As our President bears *no resemblance to a king,* so we shall see the Senate have *no similitude to nobles.*

First then not being hereditary, their *collective* knowledge, wisdom and virtue are not precarious, *for by these qualities alone are they to obtain their offices*; and they will have none of the *peculiar* follies and vices of those men *who possess power merely because their fathers held it before them,* for they will be educated (under equal advantages and with equal prospects) among and on a footing with the other sons of a free people. If we recollect the characters, who have, at various periods, filled the seats of Congress, we shall find this expectation *perfectly reasonable.* Many *young* men of genius and *many characters of more matured abilities, without fortunes,* have been honored with that trust. *Wealth has had but few representatives there, and those have been generally possessed of respectable personal qualifications.* There have also been many instances of persons, not eminently endowed with mental qualities, who have been sent thither *from a reliance on their virtues, public and private.* As the Senators *are still to be elected by the legislatures of the states,* there can be no doubt of *equal safety and propriety* in their future appointment, especially as no further pecuniary qualification is required by the Constitution.

They can hold *no other office* civil or military under the United States, nor can they join *in making provisions for themselves,* either by creating new places or increasing the emoluments of old ones. As their sons are not to succeed them, they will not be induced to aim at an increase or perpetuity of their powers, at the expense of the liberties of the people of which those sons will be a part. They possess *a much smaller share of the judicial power* than the upper house in Britain, for they are not, as there, the highest court in civil affairs. Impeachments *alone* are the cases cognizable before them, and in what other place could matters of that nature be so properly and safely determined? The judges of the federal courts will owe their appointments to the President and Senate, therefore may not feel so perfectly free *from favor, affection and influence* as the upper house, who receive their power from the people, through their state representatives, and are immediately responsible to those assemblies, and finally to the nation at large. Thus we see when a daring or dangerous offender is brought to the bar of public justice, the people *who alone can impeach him by their immediate representatives* will cause him to be tried, *not by the judges appointed in the heat of the occasion,* but by two-thirds of *a select body, chosen a long time before, for various purposes by the collected wisdom of their state legislatures.* From a pretense or affection of extraordinary purity and excellence of character *their word of honor* is the sanction under which these high courts in other countries have given their sentence. But with us, like the other judges of the Union, like the rest of the people *of which they are never to forget they are a part,* it is required that they be on oath.

No ambitious, undeserving or unexperienced youth can acquire a seat in this house by means of the most enormous wealth or most powerful connections, *till thirty years have ripened his abilities and fully discovered his merits to his country*—a more rational ground of preference surely than mere property.

The Senate, though more independent of the people as to *the free exercise of their judgment and abilities* than the House of Representatives, by the longer term of their office, must be older and more experienced men, and the public treasures, *the sinews of the state,* cannot be called forth by their original motion. They may *restrain the profusion or errors* of the House of Representatives, *but they cannot take the necessary measures to raise a national revenue.*

The people, through the Electors, *prescribe* them such a President as shall be *best qualified to control them.*

They can only, by conviction on impeachment, *remove and incapacitate a dangerous officer,* but the punishment of him as a criminal *remains within the province of the courts of law to be conducted under all the ordinary forms and precautions,* which exceedingly diminishes the importance of their judicial powers. They are *detached,* as much as possible, from *local* prejudices in favor of their respective states by having *a separate and independent vote,* for the sensible and conscientious use of which, every member will find *his person, honor and character* seriously bound. He cannot shelter himself, *under a vote in behalf of his state,* among his immediate colleagues. As there are only *two,* he cannot be voluntarily or involuntarily governed *by the majority of the deputation.* He will be obliged, by wholesome provisions, *to attend his public duty,* and thus in great national questions *must give a vote* of the honesty of which he will find it necessary to convince his constituents.

The Senate *must always receive the exceptions of the President* against any of their legislative acts, which, without *serious deliberation and sufficient reasons,* they will seldom disregard. They will also feel a considerable check *from the constitutional powers of the state legislatures,* whose rights they will not be disposed to infringe, since they are the bodies *to which they owe their existence,* and are moreover to remain *the immediate guardians of the people.*

And lastly the Senate will feel *the mighty check of the House of Representatives*—a body *so pure in its election,* so intimately connected, by its interests and feelings, *with the people at large,* so guarded against *corruption and influence*—so much, from its nature, *above all apprehensions,* that it *must ever be able to maintain the high ground assigned to it by the Federal Constitution.*

An American Citizen III

In pursuing the consideration of the new Federal Constitution, it remains now to examine the nature and powers of the House of Representatives—*the immediate delegates of the people.*

Each member of this truly popular assembly will be chosen by about six thousand electors, *by the poor as well as the rich.* No decayed and venal borough will have an *unjust* share in their determinations. No old *Sarum* will send thither a Representative *by the voice of a single elector.*[a] As we shall have no royal ministries to purchase votes, so we shall have no votes for sale. *For the suffrages of six thousand enlightened and independent freemen are above all price.* When the increasing population of the country shall render the body too large at the rate of one member for every thirty thousand persons, they will be returned at the greater rate of one for every forty or fifty thousand, which will render the electors still more incorruptible. For this regulation is only designed to prevent a *smaller number* than thirty thousand from having a Representative. Thus we see a provision follows, that no state shall have less than one member; for if a new and greater number should hereafter be fixed on, which shall exceed the whole of the inhabitants of any state, such state, without this wholesome provision, would lose its voice in the House of Representatives, a circumstance which the Constitution renders *impossible.*

The people of England, whose House of Commons is filled with military and civil officers and pensioners, say their liberties would be perfectly secured by triennial parliaments. *With us no placemen can sit among the Representatives of the people, and two years are the constitutional term of their existence.* Here again, lest wealth, powerful connections, or even *the unwariness of the people* should place in this important trust an undeserving, unqualified or inexperienced youth, the wisdom of the Convention has proposed *an absolute incapacity till the age of twenty-five.* At twenty-one a young man is made the guardian of his *own* interests, *but he cannot for a few years more be entrusted with the affairs of the nation.* He must be an inhabitant of the state that elects him, that he may be intimately acquainted with their *particular circumstances.* The House of Representatives is not, *as the Senate,* to have a president chosen *for them* from *without* their body, *but are to elect their speaker from their own number.* They will also appoint *all their other officers.* In great state cases, they will be *the grand inquest of the nation,* for they possess *the sole and uncontrollable power of impeachment.* They are neither *to wait the call* nor *abide the prorogations and dissolutions of a perverse or ambitious prince,* for they are to meet at least once in every year, and sit on adjournments to be agreed on between themselves and the other servants of the people. Should they differ in opinion, the President, who is a temporary fellow servant and not their hereditary master, has *a mediatorial power* to adjust it for them, *but cannot prevent their constitutional meeting within the year.* They can compel the attendance of their members, that their public duty may not be *evaded* in times of difficulty or danger. The vote of each Representative can be always known, as well as the proceedings of the House, *that so the people may be acquainted with the conduct of those in whom they repose so important a trust.* As was observed of the Senators, they cannot make *new* offices *for themselves,* nor increase, *for their own benefit,* the emoluments of old ones, *by which the people will be exempted from needless additions to the public expenses on such sordid and mercenary principles.* They are not to be restrained from *the firm and plain language* which becomes the independent representatives of freemen, *for there is to be a perfect liberty of speech.* Without their consent *no monies can be obtained, no armies raised, no navies provided.* They *alone* can originate bills for drawing forth the revenues of the Union, and *they will have a negative upon every legislative act of the other house.* So far, in short, as the sphere of federal jurisdiction extends, they will be controllable *only by the people,* and in contentions with the other branch, so far as they shall be right, *they must ever finally prevail.*

Such, my countrymen, are some of *the cautionary provisions* of the frame of government your faithful Convention have submitted to your consideration—such *the foundations of peace, liberty and safety,* which have been laid by their unwearied labors. They have guarded you against *all servants* but those "whom choice and common good ordain," against *all masters* "save preserving Heaven."

(a) *This is the case with that British borough.*

The First Newspaper Attack upon the Constitution and the Response, 26 September–4 October

On 26 September, the day that "An American Citizen" I appeared in the *Independent Gazetteer,* an anonymous writer in the *Freeman's Journal* published the first major newspaper criticism of the Constitution. Two days later "Tar and Feathers," in the *Independent Gazetteer,* attacked the anonymous writer. The following day, 29 September, the *Gazetteer* printed an item by "Fair Play" attacking "Tar and Feathers" and another item by "Nestor" replying to the anonymous essay in the *Freeman's Journal* on the 26th. "Tar and Feathers" replied to "Fair Play" in the *Gazetteer* on 2 October, and "Fair Play" responded in the same paper on 4 October. As "Tullius," the author of the anonymous essay of 26 September replied in the *Freeman's Journal* on 10 October (Mfm:Pa. 120).

Freeman's Journal, 26 September[1]

The writer of the following remarks has the happiness and respectability of the United States much at heart, and it is with pleasure he has seen a system promulged by the late Convention, which promises to insure those blessings. But as perfection is not the lot of human nature, we are not to expect it in the new Federal Constitution. Candor must confess, however, that it is a well-wrought piece of stuff, and claims, upon the whole, the approbation of all the states. Our situation is critical, and demands our immediate care. It is therefore to be hoped that every state will be speedy in calling a convention—*speedy* because the business is momentous and merits the utmost deliberation.

The following strictures on the proposed Constitution are submitted with diffidence. Excepting a single instance, they regard points of an inferior magnitude only; and as the writer is not possessed of any of the reasons which influenced the Convention, he feels the more diffident in offering these.

Remarks

Article I. section 2 (3d clause). "The number of Representatives shall not exceed one for every 30,000." If we consider the *vast* extent and *increasing* population of the United States, it will appear that a representation upon this principle (though proper to *begin* with) cannot last very long. It must grow far too unwieldy for business and the Constitution must therefore be mended and patched with new work. Let your government be invariably fixed; so far, at least, as human foresight can go, and age will secure it respect and veneration from the multitude. In framing a government, we should consider a century to come as but a day, and leave the least possible for posterity to mend. Errors sanctified by long usage are not easily relinquished. Their age attaches the people and renders a reform difficult. There is even danger in reforming the errors of a government, but there is more in letting them alone. Hence we ought to aim at PERMANENCY in every part of a constitution intended to endure. *In America representation ought to be in a ratio with population,* and this should be provided for in the government of the United States.

Section 4 (1st clause). "The *times, places,* and manner of holding Elections for Senators and Representatives, shall be prescribed in each State by the Legislature thereof; but the Congress may at any time by law make or *alter* such regulations, except as to the places of chusing Senators." A general uniformity of acting in confederation (whenever it can be done with convenience) must tend to federalize (allow me the word) the sentiments of the people. The *time,* then, might as well have been fixed in Convention—not subject to *alteration* afterwards. Because a day may be chosen by Congress which the constitution or laws of a state may have appropriated to *local* purposes, not to be subverted or suspended. Leaving the *places* subject to the alteration of Congress may also lead to improper consequences and (*humanum est errare*) tempt to sinister views. Who in Pennsylvania would think it advisable to elect Representatives on the shore of Lake Erie; or even at Fort Pitt?

Second clause. "The Congress shall assemble *at least once* in every year, and such meeting shall be on the first Monday in *December.*" Here is a kind of solecism; as the late period of assembling hardly admits of a prorogation and reassembling in the same year. But as probably a *federal* year is meant, it should have been so expressed. *December* is an objectionable month, too, for the representatives of so many distant states to meet in; the depth of winter forbids the convenience of water, and the communication by land is expensive, inconvenient, and often obstructed at this season. Much time would necessarily be lost in bringing the members together.

Section 9 (22d clause). "No *Capitation* or other direct tax shall be laid, unless," etc. I confess here a great disappointment. When I began to read this clause, I did not doubt that the poll tax would share the fate of *ex post facto* laws and bills of attainder. I am sorry to find myself mistaken. For a capitation tax is *impolitic* and *unjust*; it is a tax upon population, and falls indiscriminately upon the poor and the rich; the helpless, who cannot work, and the robust, who can. The poll taxes of the Eastern States have forced many thousands of their valuable citizens to emigrate. and made those disaffected who stayed behind.

Article 3. section 2 (3d clause). "The trial of all crimes, except in cases of impeachment, shall be by *Jury*." I sincerely wish the Convention had said, *a "Jury" of* THIRTEEN, *a* MAJORITY *of whom shall determine the verdict*. Is it not extravagantly absurd to expect that twelve men shall have but one opinion among them upon the most difficult case? Common sense revolts at the idea, while conscience shudders at the prostitution of an oath thus sanctified by law! Starve, or be perjured! say our courts. The monstrous attachment of the people to an English jury shows how far the force of prejudice can go and the encomiums which have been so incessantly lavished upon it should caution us against borrowing from others, without the previous conviction of our own minds.

Tar and Feathers, Independent Gazetteer, 28 September

An anonymous scribbler, in the *Freeman's Journal* of last Wednesday, has daringly attacked the new Federal Constitution, in making objections to supposed faults, or defects, therein, which this *mock-patriot* himself acknowledges to be *trivial and of very small importance*. Why then in the name of wonder has he started them at this awful crisis; when, the fate of America depends on the unanimity of all classes of citizens, in immediately establishing this hitherto unequalled, and I am happy to add, this *popular* form of government? Certainly, with a design to sow dissensions among the weak, the credulous, and the ignorant, since no other effect can be produced by his Antifederal remarks, at this stage of the business.

I repeat it sir, the proposed Federal Constitution is a masterpiece in politics, and loudly proclaims the wisdom of its authors. But even if it were imperfect, none of my fellow citizens are stupid enough to think it, like the laws of the Medes and Persians, irrevocable and unalterable. No, it has one article which wisely provides for future amendments and alterations whenever they shall appear necessary. I can easily perceive, that the author of these silly remarks is the same person who formerly attacked the Convention, under the signature of "Z,"[2] before the result of their deliberations was known. Need we wonder then, to find him carping at their works when published?

This *Antifederalist* should reflect, that his name may yet be known, and himself branded with infamy as an enemy to the happiness of the United States; I would therefore advise him to choose some other subject for his remarks in future, if he wishes to escape the just resentment of an incensed people, who perhaps may honor him with a coat of TAR and FEATHERS.

Fair Play, Independent Gazetteer, 29 September

I am a federal man in the truest sense of the word. I wish to see the United States in possession of a general government which may insure to them strength and liberty at home and respectability abroad, but I do not agree with a writer in your paper of this day, that every person who objects to some parts, or even to the whole, of the *aristocratical* plan proposed by the late Convention ought to have "a coat of *Tar and Feathers*." Tar and feathers, I believe, never made a convert to any system whatever, whether *religious* or *political*; and that must be a most *noble* form of government indeed which requires such infamous measures to support and establish it! That would be a *mob* government with a witness!

At the glorious period of our *independence*, the newspapers were filled with publications against as well as for that salutary measure: and I am clearly of opinion, that the LIBERTY OF THE PRESS—the great bulwark of all the liberties of the people—ought never to be restrained (notwithstanding the Honorable Convention did not think fit to make the least declaration in its favor) and that on every occasion truth and justice should have FAIR PLAY.

Nestor, Independent Gazetteer, 29 September

That the opinion of the people becomes of great moment, either to impart applause or obtain condemnation on the proceedings of those who have been signally employed in national service, is a maxim established by experience; but it is generally best understood and attended to by men of base intentions, who, to favor some deep design, take care to varnish out a scheme of deception with the apparent colors of truth, whereby the multitude seeing the object through false lights alone are often ensnared and led to adopt sentiments repugnant to their dearest interest. In the *Freeman's Journal* of Wednesday last, a writer well acquainted with this principle has, with daring effrontery, attempted to make strictures on our *new Constitution,* in order to tarnish, with his corrosive ink extracted from an Antifederal heart, the luster of our august Convention. Instigated either by the private designs of some party or by hatred to the national character of America, he has set out, with the nimble feet of counterfeit probity, to exhibit imaginary defects and to raise in the mind of the unthinking citizen groundless conjectures, which, if not checked in time, may become so deeply seated, that the joint force of truth and pure demonstration can scarce be able to erase them; or until, perhaps, the injury done to our country be of such magnitude, that it will be equally indifferent whether the deception be or be not discovered.

In the exordium, he says: "The writer of the following remarks has the happiness and respectability of the United States much at heart, and it is with pleasure he has seen a system promulged by the late Convention, which promises to insure those blessings. But as perfection is not the lot of human nature, we are not to expect it in the new Federal Constitution. Candor must confess however that it is *a well-wrought piece of stuff,* and claims upon the whole the approbation of all the states. Our situation is critical and demands our immediate care. It is therefore to be hoped that every state will be speedy in calling a convention—speedy because the business is momentous, and merits the utmost deliberation." It is pleasant to observe with what affected tenderness and diffidence this writer attempts to remark upon the imperfections of our new Constitution; but, with all his candor in allowing it to be a *well-wrought piece of stuff,* I fear there are some who will be apt to think that his design is to seduce the people; as the devil is painted in his temptation of Saint Anthony, in the modest habit of a fair face, and the charming form of virgin innocence, but his cloven foot is very visible to those who can take their eyes off the object of seduction. "It is therefore to be hoped (says he) that every state will be speedy in calling a convention"—but for what? Why to follow the example of this writer, to remark upon and to condemn several articles of the new Constitution; and finally to reject the whole of such a *well-wrought piece of stuff.* I appeal to the understanding and ask, is not this the language and true meaning of the writer?

Before he begins his futile remarks, he says: "The following strictures on the proposed Constitution are submitted with diffidence. Excepting a single instance, they regard points of an inferior magnitude only; and as the writer is not possessed of any of the reasons which influenced the Convention, he feels the more diffident in offering these remarks." Here is a matter of curiosity undoubtedly; this gentleman *is not possessed of any of the reasons which influenced the Convention,* and yet, I affirm it, there is not another person in America besides himself unacquainted with them. There is not a man in America or even in Europe, possessed of common sense, that has heard of the meeting of that honorable body, but knows the reasons and motives which influenced every member of it. Yes, the very enemies of America know them well and will, I trust, soon feel their effects to their mortification. The reasons and motives which influenced the Convention were "to form a more perfect union, establish justice, ensure domestic tranquility, provide for the common defence, promote the general welfare, and to secure the blessings of liberty to themselves and their posterity, and to promote the lasting welfare of that country so dear to us all." These, I say, were their motives, and where is the wretch so base as to suppose they were influenced by any other. Perhaps the writer may pretend to say that he meant no more in this paragraph than *he is not possessed of any of the reasons which influenced the Convention to adopt those articles on which he has thought proper to make his strictures.* Now if this even were his meaning, the general answer given above will still apply; for the same motives, which influenced the Convention to frame the whole body of this noble Constitution, must necessarily have influenced them in framing every article of it, namely, the good of their country. Is not such a writer either an insidious enemy to his country or willfully wicked?

But let us examine what he has to say against the Constitution, and we will find that his objections are groundless and absurd. His first remark is upon Article 1, section 2: "The number of representatives shall not exceed one for every 30,000." After exhibiting a long paragraph of unmeaning sentences in the discussion of this subject, he concludes: "In America representation ought to be in a ratio with population." Now the very article against which he objects manifestly provides, that the representation shall be in the direct ratio of the population. It seems to me that this gentleman's idea of the term *ratio* is to be explained by some learned definition of his own, with which I hope he will soon favor the literati; and then perhaps he will demonstrate the representation in America must increase in the *duplicate* ratio or proportion of the number of inhabitants. Such a learned Antifederal gentleman! *O princeps asinorum!*

It would indeed be spending time in a useless manner to remark upon all his strictures which are equally erroneous. I shall therefore pass over his second and third, and conclude with taking some notice of his fourth or last remark, which is on, "Article 3, section 2. *The trial of all crimes except in cases of impeachment, shall be by jury.* I sincerely wish (says he) the Convention had said, a jury of thirteen, a majority of whom shall determine the verdict. Is it not extravagantly absurd to expect that twelve men shall have but one opinion among them upon the most difficult case? Common sense revolts at the idea, while conscience shudders at the prostitution of an oath thus sanctioned by law! starve or be perjured! say our courts. The monstrous attachment of the people to an English jury, show how far the force of prejudice can go, and the encomiums which have been so incessantly lavished upon it, should caution us against borrowing from others, without the previous conviction of our own minds." Here is a complete specimen of this man of diffidence and candor; here we see him throwing off the mask and stepping forth with dauntless courage, and attacking with sophistical declamation the first privilege of freemen; the noblest article that ever entered the constitution of a free country; a jewel whose transcendent luster adds dignity to human nature. No, sir, common sense does not revolt at the idea, common sense and experience confirm the excellency of this law every day. In short your own condemnation of it is manifestly a negative proof of its goodness. *Sit perpetua hac lex.* But plunge this Janus, this double-faced wretch (who, under the pretense of patriotism and candor, writes only with a view to embarrass the mind, and so prevent the adoption of the new Constitution) into the mines a thousand yards deep; and there let the injured ghost of Columbia incessantly torment the monster.

Tar and Feathers, Independent Gazetteer, 2 October

When we had the honor of addressing you a few days since, we hoped our caution to the modern TORIES, alias ANTIFEDERALISTS, might not be amiss. It has, however, attracted the notice of your correspondent, *Fair Play,* who observes that "we never made a convert, either in religion or politics." Well sir, it is granted. We would ask this gentleman whether the sword, either of war or of justice, has ever made proselytes to any opinion? Certainly not in a greater degree than we have. Yet it is often found expedient to use these means (in punishing those on whom remonstrance and reason were thrown away) for the same purpose that Jehovah sent the deluge in Noah's days. Laughable indeed would it be to suppose that no villain, however dignified among villains, ought to be punished, but with a view to reclaim *him.* There is a point of more consequence to be considered, and that is to expel from society a monster who is unfit to associate with men, and thereby *to deter others* from treading in *his* steps. That we have frequently during the Revolution terrified the *Tories,* or *Antifederalists* of those times, into a moderate line of conduct is well-known. True indeed, we did not make many converts to whiggism (although we have often decorated the backs of those gentry), neither did the sword.

If you trace our history, sir, you will find that we have been faithful allies to America throughout the late war; but were never well relished by the *Tories* and a few *sham* or *lukewarm Whigs.* Should our country again demand our aid, we shall cheerfully obey the summons. At the same time permit us to declare that we will never attack any *real friend* to *America,* however different his sentiments may be from the throng; nor will we ever assist in shackling the liberty of the press, but, on the contrary, will exert ourselves to the last in defense of *that most invaluable privilege of freemen.*

When on Friday last eighteen or nineteen human asses, who are a disgrace to Pennsylvania, basely deserted the trust reposed in them by an unwarrantable revolt from the Assembly, we confess candidly that nothing could have given us more pleasure than to have been employed in chastising these disciples of SHAYS: Wretches, who were not influenced in their defection by the laudable motives which actuated the citizens of Rome when they revolted and were appeased by the institution of those popular magistrates styled tribunes; nor by that patriotic spirit which prompted the illustrious English barons to extort Magna Charta from their tyrannical king, John. No sir, these *tools of sedition,* whose *ignorance* is still greater than their *obstinacy,* evidently copied after those despicable incendiaries, Jack Straw and Wat. Tyler,[3] in endeavoring to introduce *anarchy* into these states, that they might be an easy prey to *their lord* and *master,* DANIEL SHAYS. Against such traitors to their delegated trust, we would willingly be engaged.

To conclude, we cannot help lamenting the monstrous ingratitude of the Americans in neglecting many of the best friends of the Revolution, and among the rest, their faithful allies TAR AND FEATHERS.

Fair Play, Independent Gazetteer, 4 October

Your correspondent, who has assumed the signature of *Tar and Feathers,* seems to allow that his mode of administering *justice* never made a convert; yet persists in his diabolical plan of endeavoring to inflame the minds of the people against those who happen to differ from him on political subjects. Perhaps, like the fox who lost his tail and strove to persuade the rest of his species to have theirs cut off also, he himself has undergone the *discipline* he is now so anxious to bestow on others. I wonder whether this gentleman (though I much doubt he has any claim to the epithet) ever had the honor of bearing either "the sword of war or of justice." One would be apt to conclude he never had; otherwise he could not be so destitute of those excellent qualifications which constitute the character of a good soldier and an impartial judge. Generous minds will ever rouse with indignation against such *monsters* as wish to interrupt the peace of society by flying in the face of all law and authority. And I must confess the *new Constitution* comes in a very "questionable shape," when attended with such furious advocates as *"Tar and Feathers."* Brave men and good citizens will never associate with the most abandoned of the human species, for such we must deem those creatures who contend for *mob* governments, to abuse an individual because he entertains a different opinion from themselves, or because he has firmness and honesty enough to avow his *own* sentiments. None but the mere *echoes* and tools of party and faction would engage in such dirty business.

It is a fact, I believe, that will not be denied, that many of those who arrange themselves under the banners of those who call themselves *Federalists* were either *downright Tories, lukewarm Whigs,* or disaffected to the cause of America and the Revolution; and who now eagerly wish to seize the present opportunity to gratify their revenge and to retaliate on the *real Whigs* of 1775 and 1776. And I am the more inclined to espouse this opinion, because the author of *Tar and Feathers* aims to destroy the distinction of *Whig* and *Tory,* and to establish one more odious, viz. *Federalists* and *Antifederalists.*[4]

The *new* friends to the *tarring and feathering* system seem to direct their resentment against the *Tories. "Laughable indeed would it be to suppose,"* that they had not well examined and sought for a few of that class of beings among their own party to begin with. Look at home first Mr. *Tar and Feathers,* and try to work a reformation there before you begin to *deal damnation* abroad. There invoke the *Great Jehovah* to forgive thy past crimes and follies; and presume no more thou blasphemous wretch to compare your infamous doctrine of *expedients* with the purpose of that DEITY, "who sent the deluge in the days of Noah."

I shall conclude for the present, Mr. Oswald, with observing, that I consider this daemon of discord as some cowardly *"villain," "however dignified among villains"*—some ferocious monster, whose nerves do not admit of his heading a *tarring and feathering mob,* but who, at the same time, would rejoice to see anarchy and confusion prevailing and triumphing over peace and good order among the citizens of Philadelphia.

1. The writer was possibly Major George Turner. The copy of the *Independent Gazetteer,* 29 September, in the Rare Book Room of the Library of Congress contains an annotation to "Nestor's" reply to the essay which identifies the writer as "Major T-rn-r." Turner was a South Carolina Revolutionary War officer

who moved to Philadelphia after the war. He was accused of writing the "Centinel" essays, but he denied it (Mfm:Pa. 597, 598). Late in 1789 President Washington appointed him to a judgeship in the Northwest Territory.

2. On 22 August the *Freeman's Journal* published an item by "Z" which was aimed primarily at the leaders of the Republican Party (Mfm:Pa. 23). "Halter" published an answer in the *Independent Gazetteer* on 30 August (Mfm:Pa. 29).

3. Straw and Tyler were leaders of the Peasant's Revolt in England in 1381.

4. For more on the use of the party labels "Federalist" and "Antifederalist," see "A Federalist," 10 October, II:C below.

Thomas Duncan to William Irvine, Carlisle, 3 October (excerpt)[1]

We have this moment received intelligence of the resolution of the Assembly for calling a convention and of the very improper conduct of the representatives on this side the Susquehanna. The people in general seem well disposed to the Federal Constitution, and I believe it will be a difficult task for their former leaders to prevent them from exerting themselves to adopt it. [William] Brown is bellowing against it, but his audience is very small. [Ephraim] Blain appears its friend. [John] Jordon is lukewarm, but a great majority of the people cry out for its immediate adoption. The first impression made on their minds is in its favor, and first impressions are not easily removed. The Constitutionalists are splitting here about a councillor—[Robert] Whitehill against [Frederick] Watts. The people on the hills against those in the valley. The Republicans are not able to do more than hiss them on and foment their divisions at this election—and I think will fight under General Watts's banner merely to disappoint Robert.

1. RC, Irvine Papers, PHi. Duncan was a lawyer in Carlisle and a former law student of Jasper Yeates, a Lancaster County Federalist. Brown, a member of the Supreme Executive Council from Dauphin County, represented that county in the Pennsylvania Convention and voted against ratification of the Constitution. Blaine was commissary general of the Northern Department during the Revolution and a Cumberland County landowner. Jordan was a Cumberland County lawyer and judge of the Court of Common Pleas. General Watts, who had served in the Assembly, was elected to represent Cumberland County in the Supreme Executive Council on 9 October 1787.

The Protest of the Minority, Pennsylvania Gazette, 3 October[1]

Dissentient:

1st. Because, by the diminution of the power of the state of Pennsylvania, we shall have fewer offices, and smaller salaries, to bestow upon our friends.

2d. Because, like the Declaration of Independence, the measure, if a right one, is *premature*.

3d. Because the new Federal Constitution puts an end to all future emissions of paper money, and to tender laws, to both of which many of us owe our fortunes, and all of us our prospects of extrication from debt and exemption from gaol, or the benefit of the bankrupt law.

4th. Because, by the new Constitution of the United States, we shall be compelled to pay our taxes, whereas we now pay nothing towards the support of government, and yet are handsomely supported out of the state treasury.

5th. Because the new Constitution was not submitted to the consideration of the Antifederal junto in Philadelphia before it was sent to Congress, to each individual whereof America is under greater obligations than to General Washington.

6th. Because, by the 6th section of the 1st Article of the Constitution of the United States, it is made impossible for persons in power to create offices for themselves, or to appoint themselves to offices. This we conceive to be an evident departure from the free and excellent constitution of Pennsylvania, by which it is lawful for assemblymen and councillors to appoint themselves or their sons to all, or to any of the offices of the state.

7th. Because a disaffected member of the Federal Convention from Virginia [George Mason], in a closet conversation with R[obert] Whitehill, disapproved of the federal government, and we hold it to be our duty rather to follow his advice, than the inclinations of our constituents.[2]

8th. Because, from the power claimed by the new Constitution, Congress will have a right to suppress all "domestic insurrections" in particular states, by which means we shall be deprived of the only means of opposing the laws of this state, especially laws for collecting taxes.

F[indle]y, W[hitehi]ll, and Co.[3]

Major [Alexander] B[oy]d's Cellar, September 29, 1787.

1. The full title is "The Protest of the Minority, who objected to calling a Convention, for the purpose of adopting the foederal Constitution." This item was reprinted eight times from Vermont to South Carolina by 7 November.

2. For Mason's meetings with Whitehill and other Antifederalist leaders, see George Washington to James Madison, 10 October 1787 and George Mason to Thomas Jefferson, 26 May 1788, RCS:Va.

3. For other attacks upon Findley and Whitehill and for a defense, see Mfm:Pa. 102, 106, 107.

Southwark, Pennsylvania Gazette, 3 October

The following comparison of the characters and conduct of the Tories and the Antifederal junto may serve to show that they are animals of the same breed, and should be equally despised by all true friends to their country.

1st. The principal Tories were *officers of government*—so are the Antifederalists: witness, Messrs. [George] Bryan, J[onathan] B[ayard] Smith, [John] Nicholson, etc.

2d. The Tories said, the *time* for opposing Great Britain was not come—the Antifederalists say, "more time for considering the new government is necessary than is allowed by the resolves of the Assembly."

3d. The Tories said our grievances were all *imaginary* in the year 1776—the Antifederalists say the same of the defects of our present governments and of the universal distress and complaints of the people.

4th. The Tories tried to prevent an appeal to the people by calling a convention to form a new government in Pennsylvania in the year 1776—the Antifederalists are trying every art to prevent an *appeal to the people* to alter the present constitution of Pennsylvania so as to make it fit the new federal government.

5th. The Tories despised the proceedings of conventions and town meetings and called them nothing but *mobs*—the Antifederalists despise the Convention of the United States and call the petitions and resolves of our citizens the acts of mobs and fools.

6th. The Tories thought they alone were inspired with a knowledge in government—the Antifederalists entertain the same exalted opinion of themselves.

7th. The Tories were deserted by all their friends who were honest—the Antifederalists, in like manner, have been deserted by the party which they once led and now stand alone like four or five dead and rotten trees in an old field.

It is to be hoped the Antifederalists will end their career as some of the Tories, whom they resemble in so many particulars, have done, viz.—in poverty—in exile—or in that state of *dependence* which is inflicted upon treason in Pennsylvania.

Pennsylvania Gazette, 3 October[1]

It is with singular pleasure that we inform the public, that our German fellow citizens, in every part of the state, are in favor of the federal government. Honest and industrious men everywhere love order and dislike paper money laws and constitutions. Among the nineteen absconders from the Assembly, there was but *one* German.[2] Berks and Northampton counties have taken leave of the Antifederal junto.[3] These ancient counties, inhabited chiefly with sober and industrious Germans, have shown themselves to be firm friends to the Constitution of the United States.

1. This item was reprinted three times in Pennsylvania and in seventeen newspapers from Maine to South Carolina by 30 October. (For similar items, see Mfm: Pa. 135, 178, 207.)

2. Frederick Antes of Northumberland County, who seceded from the Assembly although he had voted to call the Convention. (See also *Pennsylvania Gazette,* 17 October, II:B below.)

3. See Northampton County Meeting, 22 October, II:D below.

Centinel I, Independent Gazetteer, 5 October[1]

Friends, Countrymen and Fellow Citizens: Permit one of yourselves to put you in mind of certain *liberties* and *privileges* secured to you by the constitution of this commonwealth, and to beg your serious attention to his uninterested opinion upon the plan of federal government submitted to your consideration, before you surrender these great and valuable privileges up forever. Your present frame of government secures to you a right to hold yourselves, houses, papers and possessions free from search and seizure, and therefore warrants granted without oaths or affirmations first made, affording sufficient foundation for them, whereby any officer or messenger may be commanded or required to search your houses or seize your persons or property, not particularly described in such warrant, shall not be granted. Your constitution further provides "that in controversies respecting property, and in suits between man and man, the parties have a right *to trial by jury, which ought to be held sacred."* It also provides and declares, *"that the people have a right of* FREEDOM OF SPEECH, *and of* WRITING *and* PUBLISHING *their sentiments, therefore* THE FREEDOM OF THE PRESS OUGHT NOT TO BE RESTRAINED." The constitution of Pennsylvania is *yet* in existence, *as yet* you have the right to *freedom of speech,* and of *publishing your sentiments.* How long those rights will appertain to you, you yourselves are called upon to say, whether your *houses* shall continue to be your *castles;* whether your *papers,* your *persons* and your *property* are to be held sacred and free from *general warrants,* you are now to determine. Whether the *trial by jury* is to continue as your birthright, the freemen of Pennsylvania, nay, of all America, are now called upon to declare.

Without presuming upon my own judgment, I cannot think it an unwarrantable presumption to offer my private opinion, and call upon others for theirs; and if I use my pen with the boldness of a freeman, it is because I know that *the liberty of the press yet remains unviolated,* and *juries yet are judges.*

The late Convention have submitted to your consideration a plan of a new federal government. The subject is highly interesting to your future welfare. Whether it be calculated to promote the great ends of civil society, viz., the happiness and prosperity of the community; it behooves you well to consider, uninfluenced by the authority of names. Instead of that frenzy of enthusiasm, that has actuated the citizens of Philadelphia, in their approbation of the proposed plan, before it was possible that it could be the result of a rational investigation into its principles; it ought to be dispassionately and deliberately examined, and its own intrinsic merit the only criterion of your patronage. If ever free and unbiased discussion was proper or necessary, it is on such an occasion. All the blessings of liberty and the dearest privileges of freemen are now at stake and dependent on your present conduct. Those who are competent to the task of developing the principles of government ought to be encouraged to come forward, and thereby the better enable the people to make a proper judgment; for the science of government is so abstruse, that few are able to judge for themselves; without such assistance the people are too apt to yield an implicit assent to the opinions of those characters, whose abilities are held in the highest esteem, and to those in whose integrity and patriotism they can confide; not considering that the love of domination is generally in proportion to talents, abilities, and superior acquirements; and that the men of the greatest purity of intention may be made instruments of despotism in the hands of the *artful and designing.* If it were not for the stability and attachment which time and habit gives to forms of government, it would be in the power of the enlightened and aspiring few, if they should combine, at any time to destroy the best establishments, and even make the people the instruments of their own subjugation.

The late Revolution having effaced in a great measure all former habits, and the present institutions are so recent, that there exists not that great reluctance to innovation, so remarkable in old communities, and which accords with reason, for the most comprehensive mind cannot foresee the full operation of material changes on civil polity; it is the genius of the common law to resist innovation.

The wealthy and ambitious, who in every community think they have a right to lord it over their fellow creatures, have availed themselves, very successfully, of this favorable disposition; for the people thus unsettled in their sentiments, have been prepared to accede to any extreme of government; all the distresses and difficulties they experience, proceeding from various causes, have been ascribed to the impotency of the present Confederation, and thence they have been led to expect full relief from the adoption of the proposed system of government; and in the other event, immediate ruin and annihilation as a nation. These characters flatter themselves that they have lulled all distrust and jealousy of their new plan, by gaining the concurrence of the two men in whom America has the highest confidence, and now triumphantly exult in the completion of their long meditated schemes of power and aggrandizement. I would be very far from insinuating that the two illustrious personages alluded to, have not the welfare of their country at heart; but that the unsuspecting goodness and zeal of the one, has been imposed on, in a subject of which he must be necessarily inexperienced, from his other arduous engagements; and that the weakness and indecision attendant on old age, has been practiced on in the other.[2]

I am fearful that the principles of government inculcated in Mr. [John] Adam's treatise, and enforced in the numerous essays and paragraphs in the newspapers, have misled some well-designing members of the late Convention.[3] But it will appear in the sequel, that the construction of the proposed plan of government is infinitely more extravagant.

I have been anxiously expecting that some enlightened patriot would, ere this, have taken up the pen to expose the futility, and counteract the baneful tendency of such principles. Mr. Adams's *sine qua non* of a good government is three balancing powers, whose repelling qualities are to produce an equilibrium of interests, and thereby promote the happiness of the whole community. He asserts that the administrators of every government will ever be actuated by views of private interest and ambition, to the prejudice of the public good; that therefore the only effectual method to secure the rights of the people and promote their welfare is to create an opposition of interests between the members of two distinct bodies, in the exercise of the powers of government, and balanced by those of a third. This hypothesis supposes human wisdom competent to the task of instituting three coequal orders in government, and a corresponding weight in the community to enable them respectively to exercise their several parts, and whose views and interests should be so distinct as to prevent a coalition of any two of them for the destruction of the third. Mr. Adams, although he has traced the constitution of every form of government that ever existed, as far as history affords materials, has not been able to adduce a single instance of such a government; he indeed says that the British constitution is such in theory, but this is rather a confirmation that his principles are chimerical and not to be reduced to practice. If such an organization of power were practicable, how long would it continue? Not a day, for there is so great a disparity in the talents, wisdom and industry of mankind, that the scale would presently preponderate to one or the other body, and with every accession of power the means of further increase would be greatly extended. The state of society in England is much more favorable to such a scheme of government than that of America. There they have a powerful hereditary nobility and real distinctions of rank and interests; but even there, for want of that perfect equality of power and distinction of interests, in the three orders of government, they exist but in name; the only operative and efficient check, upon the conduct of administration is the sense of the people at large.

Suppose a government could be formed and supported on such principles. Would it answer the great purposes of civil society? If the administrators of every government are actuated by views of private interest and ambition, how is the welfare and happiness of the community to be the result of such jarring adverse interests?

Therefore, as different orders in government will not produce the good of the whole, we must recur to other principles. I believe it will be found that the form of government which holds those entrusted with power, in the greatest responsibility to their constituents, the best calculated for freemen. A republican, or free government, can only exist where the body of the people are virtuous, and where property is pretty equally divided. In such a government the people are the sovereign and their sense or opinion is the criterion of every public measure; for when this ceases to be the case, the nature of the government is changed, and an aristocracy, monarchy, or despotism will rise on its ruin. The highest responsibility is to be attained, in a simple struction [*sic*] of government, for the great body of the people never steadily attend to the operations of government, and for want of due information are liable to be imposed on. If you complicate the plan by various orders, the people will be perplexed and divided in their sentiments about the source of abuses or misconduct. Some will impute it to the Senate, others to the House of Representatives, and so on, that the interposition of the people may be rendered imperfect or perhaps wholly abortive. But if, imitating the constitution of Pennsylvania, you vest all the legislative power in one body of men (separating the executive and judicial) elected for a short period, and necessarily excluded by rotation from permanency, and guarded from precipitancy and surprise by delays imposed on its proceedings, you will create the most perfect responsibility; for then, whenever the people feel a grievance they cannot mistake the authors, and will apply the remedy with certainty and effect, discarding them at the next election. This tie of responsibility will obviate all the dangers apprehended from a single legislature, and will the best secure the rights of the people.

Having premised thus much, I shall now proceed to the examination of the proposed plan of government, and I trust, shall make it appear to the meanest capacity, that it has none of the essential requisites of a free government; that it is neither founded on those balancing restraining powers, recommended by Mr. Adams and attempted in the British constitution, or possessed of that responsibility to its constituents, which, in my opinion, is the only effectual security for the liberties and happiness of the people; but on the contrary, that it is a most daring attempt to establish a despotic aristocracy among freemen, that the world has ever witnessed.

I shall previously consider the extent of the powers intended to be vested in Congress, before I examine the construction of the general government.

It will not be controverted that the legislative is the highest delegated power in government, and that all others are subordinate to it. The celebrated Montesquieu establishes it as a maxim, that legislation necessarily follows the power of taxation. By section 8, of the first Article of the proposed plan of government, "the Congress are to have power to lay and collect taxes, duties, imposts and excises, to pay the debts and provide for the common defence and *general welfare* of the United States; but all duties, imposts and excises, shall be uniform throughout the United States." Now what can be more comprehensive than these words? Not content by other sections of this plan, to grant all the great executive powers of a confederation, and a STANDING ARMY IN TIME OF PEACE, that grand engine of oppression, and moreover the absolute control over the commerce of the United States and all external objects of revenue, such as unlimited imposts upon imports, etc.; they are to be vested with every species of *internal* taxation. Whatever taxes, duties and excises that they may deem requisite for the *general welfare* may be imposed on the citizens of these states, levied by the officers of Congress, distributed through every district in America; and the collection would be enforced by the standing army, however grievous or improper they may be. The Congress may construe every purpose for which the state legislatures now lay taxes, to be for the *general welfare,* and thereby seize upon every object of revenue.

The judicial power by 1st section of Article 3 "shall extend to all cases, in law and equity, arising under this Constitution, the laws of the United States, and treaties made or which shall be made under their authority; to all cases affecting ambassadors, other public ministers and consuls; to all cases of admiralty and maritime jurisdiction, to controversies to which the United States shall be a party, to controversies between two or more states, between a state and citizens of another state, between citizens of different states, between citizens of the same state claiming lands under grants of different states, and between a state, or the citizens thereof, and foreign states, citizens or subjects."

The judicial power to be vested in one Supreme Court, and in such Inferior Courts as the Congress may from time to time ordain and establish.

The objects of jurisdiction recited above are so numerous, and the shades of distinction between civil causes are oftentimes so slight, that it is more than probable that the state judicatories would be wholly superseded; for in contests about jurisdiction, the federal court, as the most powerful, would ever prevail. Every person acquainted with the history of the courts in England knows by what ingenious sophisms they have, at different periods, extended the sphere of their jurisdiction over objects out of the line of their institution, and contrary to their very nature; courts of a criminal jurisdiction obtaining cognizance in civil causes.

To put the omnipotency of Congress over the state government and judicatories out of all doubt, the 6th Article ordains that "this constitution and the laws of the United States which shall be made in pursuance thereof, and all treaties made, or which shall be made under the authority of the United States, shall be the *supreme law of the land,* and the judges in every state shall be bound thereby, any thing in the constitution or laws of any state to the contrary notwithstanding."

By these sections the all-prevailing power of taxation, and such extensive legislative and judicial powers are vested in the general government, as must in their operation, necessarily absorb the state legislatures and judicatories; and that such was in the contemplation of the framers of it, will appear from the provision made for such event, in another part of it; (but that, fearful of alarming the people by so great an innovation, they have suffered the forms of the separate governments to remain, as a blind). By section 4th of the 1st Article, "the times, places and manner of holding elections for senators and representatives, shall be prescribed in each state by the legislature thereof; *but the Congress may at any time, by law, make or alter such regulations, except as to the place of chusing senators.*" The plain construction of which is, that when the state legislatures drop out of sight, from the necessary operation of this government, then Congress are to provide for the election and appointment of Representatives and Senators.

If the foregoing be a just comment, if the United States are to be melted down into one empire, it becomes you to consider whether such a government, however constructed, would be eligible in so extended a territory; and whether it would be practicable, consistent with freedom? It is the opinion of the greatest writers, that a very extensive country cannot be governed on democratical principles, on any other plan, than a confederation of a number of small republics, possessing all the powers of internal government, but united in the management of their foreign and general concerns.

It would not be difficult to prove, that anything short of despotism could not bind so great a country under one government; and that whatever plan you might, at the first setting out, establish, it would issue in a despotism.

If one general government could be instituted and maintained on principles of freedom, it would not be so competent to attend to the various local concerns and wants, of every particular district; as well as the peculiar governments, who are nearer the scene and possessed of superior means of information. Besides, if the business of the *whole* Union is to be managed by one government, there would not be time. Do we not already see, that the inhabitants in a number of larger states, who are remote from the seat of government, are loudly complaining of the inconveniencies and disadvantages they are subjected to on this account, and that, to enjoy the comforts of local government, they are separating into smaller divisions.

Having taken a review of the powers, I shall now examine the construction of the proposed general government.

Article I, section I. "All legislative powers herein granted shall be vested in a Congress of the United States, which shall consist of a senate and house of representatives." By another section, the President (the principal executive officer) has a conditional control over their proceedings.

Section 2. "The house of representatives shall be composed of members chosen every second year, by the people of the several states. The number of representatives shall not exceed one for every 30,000 inhabitants."

The Senate, the other constituent branch of the legislature, is formed by the legislature of each state appointing two Senators, for the term of six years.

The executive power by Article 2, section I is to be vested in a President of the United States of America, elected for four years. Section 2 gives him "power, by and with the consent of the senate to make treaties, provided two thirds of the senators present concur; and he shall nominate, and by and with the advice and consent of the senate, shall appoint ambassadors, other public ministers and consuls, judges of the Supreme Court, and all other officers of the United States, whose appointments are not herein otherwise provided for, and which shall be established by law, &c." And by another section he has the absolute power of granting reprieves and pardons for treason and all other high crimes and misdemeanors, except in case of impeachment.

The foregoing are the outlines of the plan.

Thus we see, the House of Representatives are on the part of the people to balance the Senate, who I suppose will be composed of the *better sort,* the *wellborn,* etc. The number of the Representatives (being only one for every 30,000 inhabitants) appears to be too few, either to communicate the requisite information of the wants, local circumstances and sentiments of so extensive an empire, or to prevent corruption and undue influence, in the exercise of such great powers; the term for which they are to be chosen, too long to preserve a due dependence and accountability to their constituents; and the mode and places of their election not sufficiently ascertained, for as Congress have the control over both, they may govern the choice, by ordering the *Representatives* of a *whole* state, to be *elected* in *one* place, and that too may be the most *inconvenient.*

The Senate, the great efficient body in this plan of government, is constituted on the most unequal principles. The smallest state in the Union has equal weight with the great states of Virginia, Massachusetts, or Pennsylvania. The Senate, besides its legislative functions, has a very considerable share in the executive; none of the principal appointments to office can be made without its advice and consent. The term and mode of its appointment will lead to permanency; the members are chosen for six years, the mode is under the control of Congress, and as there is no exclusion by rotation, they may be continued for life, which, from their extensive means of influence, would follow of course. The President, who would be a mere pageant of state, unless he coincides with the views of the Senate, would either become the head of the aristocratic junto in that body, or its minion; besides, their influence being the most predominant, could the best secure his reelection to office. And from his power of granting pardons, he might screen from punishment the most treasonable attempts on the liberties of the people, when instigated by the Senate.

From this investigation into the organization of this government, it appears that it is devoid of all responsibility or accountability to the great body of the people, and that so far from being a regular balanced government, it would be in practice a *permanent* ARISTOCRACY.

The framers of it, actuated by the true spirit of such a government, which ever abominates and suppresses all free enquiry and discussion, have made no provision for the *liberty of the press,* that grand *palladium of freedom* and *scourge of tyrants,* but observed a total silence on that head. It is the opinion of some great writers, that if the liberty of the press, by an institution of religion, or otherwise, could be rendered *sacred,* even in *Turkey,* that despotism would fly before it. And it is worthy of remark, that there is no declaration of personal rights, premised in most free constitutions; and that trial by *jury* in *civil* cases is taken away; for what other construction can be put on the following, viz., Article III, section 2d. "In all cases affecting ambassadors, other public ministers and consuls, and those in which a State shall be party, the Supreme Court shall have *original* jurisdiction. In all the other cases above mentioned, the Supreme Court shall have *appellate* jurisdiction, both as to *law and fact.*" It would be a novelty in jurisprudence, as well as evidently improper to allow an appeal from the verdict of a jury, on the matter of fact; therefore, it implies and allows of a dismission of the jury in civil cases, and especially when it is considered, that jury trial in criminal cases is expressly stipulated for, but not in civil cases.

But our situation is represented to be so *critically* dreadful, that however reprehensible and exceptionable the proposed plan of government may be, there is no alternative between the adoption of it and absolute ruin. My fellow citizens, things are not at that crisis; it is the argument of tyrants. The present distracted state of Europe secures us from injury on that quarter, and as to domestic dissensions, we have not so much to fear from them, as to precipitate us into this form of government, without it is a safe and a proper one. For remember, of all *possible* evils, that of *despotism* is the *worst* and the most to be *dreaded.*

Besides, it cannot be supposed, that the first essay on so difficult a subject, is so well digested, as it ought to be. If the proposed plan, after a mature deliberation, should meet the approbation of the respective states, the matter will end; but if it should be found to be fraught with dangers and inconveniencies, a future general convention, being in possession of the objections, will be the better enabled to plan a suitable government.

Who's here so base, that would a bondman be?
If any, speak; for him have I offended.
Who's here so vile, that will not love his country?
If any, speak; for him have I offended.

1. The quotations from the Constitution are printed as they are given by "Centinel." For the national circulation of the essay, see CC:133.

2. The reference is to George Washington and Benjamin Franklin. For Federalist replies, see "A Federalist," 10 October, II:C below and CC:150–A. For "Centinel's" rejoinder, see "Centinel" II, 24 October, CC:190. The second half of this paragraph, beginning "These characters . . . ," was omitted from the German translation. See *Pennsylvania Gazette,* 24 October, II:C below.

3. The reference is to Adams's *A Defence of the Constitutions of Government of the United States of America* (CC:16).

James Wilson's Speech in the State House Yard, Philadelphia, 6 October[1]

Mr. Wilson then rose, and delivered a long and eloquent speech upon the principles of the Federal Constitution proposed by the late Convention. The outlines of this speech we shall endeavor to lay before the public, as tending to reflect great light upon the interesting subject now in general discussion.

Mr. Chairman and Fellow Citizens: Having received the honor of an appointment to represent you in the late Convention, it is perhaps, my duty to comply with the request of many gentlemen whose characters and judgments I sincerely respect, and who have urged, that this would be a proper occasion to lay before you any information which will serve to explain and elucidate the principles and arrangements of the Constitution, that has been submitted to the consideration of the United States. I confess that I am unprepared for so extensive and so important a disquisition; but the insidious attempts which are clandestinely and industriously made to pervert and destroy the new plan, induce me the more readily to engage in its defense; and the impressions of four months constant attention to the subject have not been so easily effaced as to leave me without an answer to the objections which have been raised.

It will be proper, however, before I enter into the refutation of the charges that are alleged, to mark the leading discrimination between the state constitutions and the Constitution of the United States. When the people established the powers of legislation under their separate governments, they invested their representatives with every right and authority which they did not in explicit terms reserve; and therefore upon every question, respecting the jurisdiction of the house of assembly, if the frame of government is silent, the jurisdiction is efficient and complete. But in delegating federal powers, another criterion was necessarily introduced, and the congressional authority is to be collected, not from tacit implication, but from the positive grant expressed in the instrument of union. Hence it is evident, that in the former case everything which is not reserved is given, but in the latter the reverse of the proposition prevails, and everything which is not given, is reserved. This distinction being recognized, will furnish an answer to those who think the omission of a bill of rights, a defect in the proposed Constitution: for it would have been superfluous and absurd to have stipulated with a federal body of our own creation, that we should enjoy those privileges, of which we are not divested either by the intention or the act, that has brought that body into existence. For instance, the liberty of the press, which has been a copious source of declamation and opposition, what control can proceed from the federal government to shackle or destroy that sacred palladium of national freedom? If indeed, a power similar to that which has been granted for the regulation of commerce, had been granted to regulate literary publications, it would have been as necessary to stipulate that the liberty of the press should be preserved inviolate, as that the impost should be general in its operation. With respect likewise to the particular district of ten miles, which is to be made the seat of federal government, it will undoubtedly be proper to observe this salutary precaution, as there the legislative power will be exclusively lodged in the President, Senate, and House of Representatives of the United States. But this could not be an object with the Convention, for it must naturally depend upon a future compact, to which the citizens immediately interested will and ought to be parties; and there is no reason to suspect that so popular a privilege will in that case be neglected. In truth then, the proposed system possesses no influence whatever upon the press, and it would have been merely nugatory to have introduced a formal declaration upon the subject—nay, that very declaration might have been construed to imply that some degree of power was given, since we undertook to define its extent.

Another objection that has been fabricated against the new Constitution, is expressed in this disingenuous form—"the trial by jury is abolished in civil cases." I must be excused, my fellow citizens, if upon this point, I take advantage of my professional experience to detect the futility of the assertion. Let it be remembered then, that the business of the Federal Convention was not local, but general; not limited to the views and establishments of a single state, but coextensive with the continent, and comprehending the views and establishments of thirteen independent sovereignties. When, therefore, this subject was in discussion, we were involved in difficulties which pressed on all sides, and no precedent could be discovered to direct our course. The cases open to a trial by jury differed in the different states, it was therefore impracticable on that ground to have made a general rule. The want of uniformity would have rendered any reference to the practice of the states idle and useless;

and it could not, with any propriety, be said that "the trial by jury shall be as heretofore," since there has never existed any federal system of jurisprudence to which the declaration could relate. Besides, it is not in all cases that the trial by jury is adopted in civil questions, for causes depending in courts of admiralty, such as relate to maritime captures, and such as are agitated in courts of equity, do not require the intervention of that tribunal. How then, was the line of discrimination to be drawn? The Convention found the task too difficult for them, and they left the business as it stands, in the fullest confidence that no danger could possibly ensue, since the proceedings of the Supreme Court are to be regulated by the Congress, which is a faithful representation of the people; and the oppression of government is effectually barred, by declaring that in all criminal cases the trial by jury shall be preserved.

This Constitution, it has been further urged, is of a pernicious tendency, because it tolerates a standing army in the time of peace. This has always been a topic of popular declamation; and yet, I do not know a nation in the world, which has not found it necessary and useful to maintain the appearance of strength in a season of the most profound tranquillity. Nor is it a novelty with us; for under the present Articles of Confederation, Congress certainly possesses this reprobated power, and the exercise of that power is proved at this moment by her cantonments along the banks of the Ohio. But what would be our national situation were it otherwise? Every principle of policy must be subverted, and the government must declare war, before they are prepared to carry it on. Whatever may be the provocation, however important the object in view, and however necessary dispatch and secrecy may be, still the declaration must precede the preparation, and the enemy will be informed of your intention, not only before you are equipped for an attack, but even before you are fortified for a defense. The consequence is too obvious to require any further delineation, and no man, who regards the dignity and safety of his country, can deny the necessity of a military force, under the control and with the restrictions which the new Constitution provides.

Perhaps there never was a charge made with less reasons than that which predicts the institution of a baneful aristocracy in the federal Senate. This body branches into two characters, the one legislative, and the other executive. In its legislative character it can effect no purpose, without the cooperation of the House of Representatives; and in its executive character, it can accomplish no object, without the concurrence of the President. Thus fettered, I do not know any act which the Senate can of itself perform, and such dependence necessarily precludes every idea of influence and superiority. But I will confess that in the organization of this body, a compromise between contending interests is discernible; and when we reflect how various are the laws, commerce, habits, population, and extent of the confederated states, this evidence of mutual concession and accommodation ought rather to command a generous applause, than to excite jealousy and reproach. For my part, my admiration can only be equalled by my astonishment, in beholding so perfect a system, formed from such heterogeneous materials.

The next accusation I shall consider is that which represents the Federal Constitution as not only calculated, but designedly framed, to reduce the state governments to mere corporations, and eventually to annihilate them. Those who have employed the term corporation upon this occasion are not perhaps aware of its extent. In common parlance, indeed, it is generally applied to petty associations for the ease and conveniency of a few individuals; but in its enlarged sense, it will comprehend the government of Pennsylvania, the existing union of the states, and even this projected system is nothing more than a formal act of incorporation. But upon what pretense can it be alleged that it was designed to annihilate the state governments? For, I will undertake to prove that upon their existence, depends the existence of the federal plan. For this purpose, permit me to call your attention to the manner in which the President, Senate, and House of Representatives are proposed to be appointed. The President is to be chosen by Electors nominated in such manner as the legislature of each state may direct; so that if there is no legislature, there can be no Electors, and consequently the office of President cannot be supplied. The Senate is to be composed of two Senators from each state chosen by the legislature; and therefore if there is no legislature, there can be no Senate. The House of Representatives is to be composed of members chosen every second year by the people of the several states, and the electors in each state shall have the qualifications requisite for electors of the most numerous branch of the state legislature. Unless, therefore, there is a state legislature, that qualification cannot be ascertained, and the popular branch of the Federal Constitution must likewise be extinct. From this view, then it is evidently absurd to suppose, that the annihilation of the separate governments will result from their union; or, that having that intention, the authors of the new system would have bound their connection with such indissoluble ties. Let me here advert to an arrangement highly advantageous, for you will perceive, without prejudice to the powers of the legislature in the election of Senators, the people at large will acquire an additional privilege in returning members to the House of Representatives—whereas, by the present Confederation, it is the legislature alone that appoints the delegates to Congress.

The power of direct taxation has likewise been treated as an improper delegation to the federal government; but when we consider it as the duty of that body to provide for the national safety, to support the dignity of the Union, and to discharge the debts contracted upon the collective faith of the states for their common benefit, it must be acknowledged, that those upon whom such important obligations are imposed, ought in justice and in policy to possess every means requisite for a faithful performance of their trust. But why should we be alarmed with visionary evils? I will venture to predict, that the great revenue of the United States must, and always will be raised by impost, for, being at once less obnoxious, and more productive, the interest of the government will be best promoted by the accommodation of the people. Still however, the objects of direct taxation should be within reach in all cases of emergency; and there is no more reason to apprehend oppression in the mode of collecting a revenue from this resource, than in the form of an impost, which, by universal assent, is left to the authority of the federal government. In either case, the force of civil institutions will be adequate to the purpose; and the dread of military violence, which has been assiduously disseminated, must eventually prove the mere effusion of a wild imagination or a factious spirit. But the salutary consequences that must flow from thus enabling the government to receive and support the credit of the Union will afford another answer to the objections upon this ground. The State of Pennsylvania particularly, which has encumbered itself with the assumption of a great proportion of the public debt, will derive considerable relief and advantage; for, as it was the imbecility of the present Confederation, which gave rise to the funding law, that law must naturally expire when a competent and energetic federal system shall be substituted. The state will then be discharged from an extraordinary burthen, and the national creditor will find it to be his interest to return to his original security.

After all, my fellow citizens, it is neither extraordinary or unexpected, that the Constitution offered to your consideration should meet with opposition. It is the nature of man to pursue his own interest, in preference to the public good; and I do not mean to make any personal reflection, when I add, that it is the interest of a very numerous, powerful, and respectable body to counteract and destroy the excellent work produced by the late Convention. All the offices of government, and all the appointments for the administration of justice and the collection of the public revenue, which are transferred from the individual to the aggregate sovereignty of the states, will necessarily turn the stream of influence and emolument into a new channel. Every person, therefore, who either enjoys or expects to enjoy a place of profit under the present establishment, will object to the proposed innovation; not, in truth, because it is injurious to the liberties of his country, but because it affects his schemes of wealth and consequence. I will confess, indeed, that I am not a blind admirer of this plan of government, and that there are some parts of it which, if my wish had prevailed, would certainly have been altered. But, when I reflect how widely men differ in their opinions, and that every man (and the observation applies likewise to every state) has an equal pretension to assert his own, I am satisfied that anything nearer to perfection could not have been accomplished. If there are errors, it should be remembered, that the seeds of reformation are sown in the work itself, and the concurrence of two-thirds of the Congress may at any time introduce alterations and amendments. Regarding it then, in every point of view, with a candid and disinterested mind, I am bold to assert, that it is the best form of government which has ever been offered to the world.

Mr. Wilson's speech was frequently interrupted with loud and unanimous testimonies of approbation, and the applause which was reiterated at the conclusion evinced the general sense of its excellence, and the conviction which it had impressed upon every mind.

1. *Pennsylvania Herald,* 9 October, Extra. (CC:134 for national circulation.)

Independent Gazetteer, 6 October[1]

Another correspondent observes, that although the tide seems to run so high at present in favor of the new Constitution, there is no doubt but the people will soon change their minds when they have had time to examine it with coolness and impartiality.

Among the *blessings* of the new-proposed government our correspondent enumerates the following: 1. The *liberty of the press* abolished.[2] 2. A standing army. 3. A Prussian militia. 4. No annual elections. 5. Fivefold taxes. 6. No trial by jury in civil cases. 7. General search warrants. 8. Excise laws, customhouse officers, tide and land waiters, cellar rats, etc. 9. A free importation of Negroes for one and twenty years. 10. Appeals to the supreme continental court, where the rich may drag the poor from the furthermost parts of the continent. 11. Elections for Pennsylvania held at Pittsburgh or perhaps Wyoming. 12. Poll taxes for our heads, if we choose to wear them. 13. And *death* if we dare to complain.[3]

1. CC 136 for national circulation.
2. For a reply to this charge, see "Avenging Justice," 17 October, II:C below.
3. For a Federalist counterpart of this Antifederalist item, see "A Slave," 25 October, CC:197–A.

B. THE ASSEMBLY ELECTION
9 October 1787

Federalists and Antifederalists made the Constitution a major issue in the election. The Federalists, with their leadership virtually intact, retained control of the Assembly and the Council, although their majority was somewhat smaller than it had been in the previous Assembly. In addition to gaining some seats in the Assembly, the Antifederalists reelected most of their leaders, some of whom had been among the seceding members. They returned William Findley and James M'Calmont to the Assembly. Abraham Smith, who was not eligible for reelection to the Assembly, was elected to the Council. Of the eligible seceding members, only Joseph Powell and Samuel Dale were not reelected; while Robert Whitehill, also a seceding member, but not eligible for reelection, lost his bid for a Council seat. However, former councillor James McLene's election to the Assembly was an Antifederalist triumph. The turnover was the smallest it had been since the Revolution: seventy percent of the members of the previous Assembly were reelected.

Carlisle Meeting, 3 October[1]

At a meeting of the inhabitants of the borough of Carlisle, in the county of Cumberland, convened at the courthouse, Major General John Armstrong was unanimously chosen chairman.[2]

The business of the meeting was opened by Colonel [Robert] Magaw,[3] and the Constitution of the United States, formed by the late Convention, was read, and the following resolutions unanimously entered into:

Resolved, That the said Constitution is most warmly approved of by this meeting, and that this meeting entertain the highest sense of the public virtue and patriotism of the majority of the House of Assembly in calling immediately a convention of this state, in pursuance of the recommendation of the Federal Convention.

Resolved, That it is the opinion of this meeting, that the withdrawing or absenting of a member of Assembly, in order to defeat any resolution or act of the legislature, is an offense most destructive to good government and the happiness and true interest of the state. And that any member who is guilty of such desertion and breach of trust is unworthy of the confidence of the people and unfit to represent them.[4]

A committee was unanimously chosen to form a ticket for a councillor and representatives of this county for the ensuing year.

By the unanimous order of the meeting, John Armstrong, chairman.

We can assure the public that the meeting was the most large and respectable that has been in this place since the Declaration of Independence, and that the greatest unanimity and concord prevailed amongst the people. This has inspired the true lovers of their country with the hope that here party spirit is extinct.

1. *Pennsylvania Packet,* 15 October. The *Packet's* report was reprinted or summarized eight times in Pennsylvania by the second week in November and reprinted ten times from New Hampshire to New York by 1 November. For the national distribution of a short account of this meeting in the *Pennsylvania Gazette* on 10 October, see CC:150–E.

2. Armstrong, a resident of Carlisle, had been a brigadier general in the Continental Army and had represented Pennsylvania in the Continental Congress.

3. Magaw, a lawyer, had commanded a battalion during the Revolution and was prominent in military affairs in Cumberland County. His brother, Samuel, was vice-provost of the University of Pennsylvania.

4. The reference is to the county's representatives, Robert Whitehill, Thomas Kennedy, and David Mitchell, who had seceded from the Assembly on 28 September.

Philadelphia Meeting, 6 October

According to advertisement, a very great concourse of people attended at the State House on Saturday evening, to fix upon a ticket of representatives for the ensuing General Assembly.

Mr. [John] Nixon was chosen chairman and Mr. Tench Coxe secretary of the meeting.

Mr. [William?] Jackson having spoken, Mr. [Francis] Gurney reported from a commitee that had been previously appointed, the following names, which were separately offered to the consideration of the citizens present, and approved of, viz.: William Will, Thomas Fitzsimons, George Clymer, Jacob Hiltzheimer, William Lewis.

On motion of Mr. [John] Donaldson, the citizens of the respective wards were requested to meet on Monday evening, to appoint proper persons for making out and circulating a sufficient number of tickets in favor of the above persons.

[At this point the *Herald* printed James Wilson's Speech in the State House Yard, Philadelphia, 6 October, II:A above.]

Doctor [Benjamin] Rush then addressed the meeting in an elegant and pathetic style describing our present calamitous situation and enumerating the advantages which would flow from the adoption of the new system of federal government. The advancement of commerce, agriculture, manufactures, arts and sciences, the encouragement of emigration, the abolition of paper money, the annihilation of party, and the prevention of war were ingeniously considered as the necessary consequences of that event. The doctor concluded with an emphatic declaration that "were this the last moment of his existence, his dying request and injunction to his fellow citizens would be, to accept and support the offered Constitution."

Mr. Gurney moved, that a committee be appointed to write and publish answers, under the authority of their names, to the anonymous pieces which have appeared against the Federal Constitution. But, Mr. Donaldson observing that it would be improper to expose any particular gentleman to a personal attack, Colonel Gurney's motion was withdrawn.

The thanks of the meeting being presented to the chairman, the business of the evening was closed. [*Pennsylvania Herald,* 9 October, Extra]

* * * *

A correspondent finds occasion to remark the difference between words and actions, in reviewing the proceedings of the meeting lately held at the State House. It was the favorite theme of declamation, and the great source of claps and huzzas, that the adoption of the new plan of federal government would annihilate party. But mark the result, not a man was chosen without the pale of the Republican association, and the name of a respectable citizen was lost in the echoes of *no, no,* because he has hitherto been esteemed an advocate for the constitution of Pennsylvania. It is undoubtedly true, continues our correspondent, that the Republican Party predominates so effectually in this city, that it can accomplish any object which it undertakes; but to render this power permanent, it must be exercised with candor, consistency, and prudence. It is to be hoped, therefore, that the election of delegates to the Convention will be conducted upon those principles; and that, on the one hand, men will not be appointed to sit in judgment upon their own work, while, on the other, only the friends to the Revolution will be employed for transacting a business which is the immediate consequence of that glorious event. [*Pennsylvania Herald,* 13 October]

John Montgomery to William Irvine, Carlisle, 9, 13 October[1]

This is one of the important days throught this State it is truly So to us in this County [Cumberland] the members of which has Disgreaceed them Selves and us by thire late Conduct in Philad by Seeseeding or absenting themselves from thire Duty when the important affair of the new Plan of government was the object you will See by the inclosed Resolve our Disaprobation of such Conduct and the ticket we intend to run in this place but I have my fears that it will not genrl Carried and that [Thomas] Kennedy & [David] Mitchl will be Chosen again which if they are will be Disgreasfull to the County the plan is univarssally aproved off and I have not the Least Doubt but that it will be aproved off in this State indeed I think that thire Cant bee Devise a Better ones

Mr. Donal has done nothing nor appears to make any indistory he wont Sell his wheat under 5/ Pr Bushals and none Can afford to give that price I am sorry to trouble you about this matter but as you Know my Setuation youll Excuse me

13th

my fears are realised the County has Sent the Same Creatures too the assembly that Disgreasd themselves and the County in the late assembly our ticket failed the same Kind of animals will be Sent to the Convention [Robert] whithill [Jonathan] hoge & [John] Harris are named And I have not the least Doubt of thire Being Choosen what a pack of sorry Scoundrals perhaps Alexander McKieghen [McKeehan] or John moore will be the 4th Convention man the former is Commisr for the County blessed times[2]

I am much Dilighted with the Prospect of the Eastren people Setling on the west of the ohio I hope that Mr Sims [John Cleves Symmes] will also Succeed they People will be an Excelent Barrieerr to those on the East Side[3]

James McClean & [James] McCalmont is in the assembly for Franklin County and I Dont Exspect one republican on this Side Susquana only from york County

Shou'd be glad to Know the Sucssess the new plan of goverment has had in the Estran States and in that in which Congrass now have thire Seat if aproved by those States I am of opinion that it will be adopted what woud you think of the Publick works for a feadrel town it woud not be a Crime I Sepose to make Such a proposition but it Distroy our hops of haveing it for a College as you are now a Congrass will move in that affair I wish that it was Determined in favr of the College [Dickinson College].

1. RC (LT), Irvine Papers, PHi. Montgomery, a burgess of Carlisle, was elected to the Assembly in 1782 and 1783.

2. Whitehill, Hoge, and Harris were probably nominated at the Stoney Ridge Convention (Ephraim Blaine to Benjamin Rush, 15 October, II:D below). Hoge and Harris were also nominated at a Cumberland County meeting on 25 October (II:D below). They were elected and voted against ratification. Whether or not

McKeehan and Moore ran for the fourth Convention seat is unknown. The man elected, John Reynolds, also voted against ratification.

3. Montgomery refers to the 2,000,000 acres which John Cleves Symmes of New Jersey had bought from Congress.

Richard Butler to William Irvine, Carlisle, 11–12 October (excerpt)[1]

The new Constitution for the United States seems now to engross the attention of all ranks. The better or wiser kind of people wish its adoption, but the *Whitehill-ites* are doing all they can against it, paper against paper, and almost man against man. I suppose never was an election begun under worse auspices or with the appearance of more confusion and difference of opinion. The generality of the people would go right *if let alone,* and although I cannot say that every part of it pleases me and many others, we think it had better be tried than cobbled or tinkered, but these filthy puppies have (to carry their point) brought it and our d[amne]d [state] constitution together which makes it a kind of sacrilege to say a word in its favor to the very people it would most immediately help, *the mechanics.* The great commotion of this county [Cumberland] is not yet fully seen or can it till the returns for assemblymen comes in which is hourly expected. If it comes in time you shall have it. I have forwarded the new form to Pittsburgh with several papers and the resolves of this town meeting, but it is feared that [William] Findley and his copartners in iniquity are gone up fraught with opposition papers. God only knows what will be the event, but I am not out of hope yet. I find by *sad experience* there is no likelihood of interest being paid on the certificates. Whether it is a state trick to sell the lands, the fault of the treasurer, or poverty in reality I don't know, but some are swearing and some laughing about it; *but I want the money.* I presume you have had hot work in Congress about this new *apparition.* Some I suppose are frighted and others see it as a guardian angel. I suspect some from the *Dominion* [Virginia] will be averse to it. The party in this state have gone great lengths; indeed Mr. [Robert] Whitehill almost said to a friend of ours, G[enera]l A________g [John Armstrong], that G[enera]l W[ashingto]n was a fool and Mr. F[rankli]n a dotard. He was not quite so plain but bordered close. Thus these gentry go on.

the 12th. The returns are not all in, but from every account [Thomas] Kennedy, [Thomas] Beals, [David] Mitchel and [John] Oliver goes. *A hopeful set* and highly to the honor of Cumberland.

Your little family are well. Poor Ric'd much disappointed again. The ticket proposed for Carlisle, or rather by it, was Ric'd Postle [thwaite], James Dunlap and another whose name I [forget?] but they had no chance.[2] I'll pester you no longer with this *stuff.*

1. RC, Irvine Papers, PHi. A Continental Army officer during the Revolution, Butler became a brevet brigadier general in 1783 and soon thereafter was appointed superintendent of Indian affairs for the Northern District.

2. Beale, Kennedy, and Mitchell had served in the previous Assembly, the latter two being among the seceding members. Beale was not in the Assembly when it voted to call the Convention. James Dunlop was a Revolutionary War officer who served for a time in Irvine's battalion. In 1787 he was judge of the Court of Common Pleas of Cumberland County.

Pennsylvania Gazette, 17 October[1]

It is with great pleasure we inform our customers that from the returns already come to hand of the late elections in this state, there is a large majority of persons strongly attached to the new Federal Constitution.

Mr. R[obert] Whitehill, who was rejected from a seat in the [Supreme Executive] Council by the county of Cumberland, for refusing to concur in calling a convention and for deserting the Assembly, was so confident of being returned by his late constituents, that he had taken lodgings for himself in a private house in this city for three years, the term of service in the Council agreeable to the constitution of Pennsylvania.

The rejection of Messrs. [Frederick] Antes and [Samuel] Dale, in the county of Northumberland, was occasioned by their desertion of their duty in the Assembly.[2] Previous to the election, the following advertisement was pasted up in all the places of public resort in the county:

"Northumberland, October 1787.

"A handsome reward and reasonable expenses will be paid to any person who will apprehend and bring to justice seventeen of the members of Assembly lately fled from their duty. There were nineteen in the whole, but, fortunately for themselves, two of these deluded creatures were taken up in the city and conveyed to the place from whence they came. The remainder are scattered to and fro on the earth, being, as the swine of old, possessed and had they ran into the Delaware, it would have been well for their country. They are now at large, and with the poison of their tongues (if not speedily prevented) will taint the minds of their late constituents, as they are suffered to go forth as lying prophets to delude and misguide the unwary sons of men. Satan-like, when he found his kingdom would be curtailed by a Saviour, he even had the effrontery upon the mount to endeavor to seduce our Lord Himself, by offering Him all the kingdoms of the world, if He would fall down and worship him. And as these weak tools of party are of opinion that, through the effects of the late glorious Constitution, when it shall begin to operate, their adherents will no longer pay that homage to ignorance they have hitherto done, but will join hand in hand with the ever memorable forty-four true-born sons of America, who are not affected with that green eyed hell-born jealousy; that a WASHINGTON and his colleagues, whose interest and political salvation are inseparable from ours, would tender a constitution to their brethren fraught with such evils as is by that diabolical junto set forth. Alas for it! our government has no mode of punishing such miscreants."

1. The first paragraph was reprinted in the *Philadelphische Correspondenz,* 23 October and *Lancaster Zeitung,* 24 October. Outside Pennsylvania the *Gazette's* account was reprinted, in whole or in part, fourteen times from Maine to Georgia by 8 November.

2. It is unlikely that Antes ran for the Assembly. Under the state constitution he was not eligible to sit in that body because he had been elected in each of the four previous years (see also Mfm:Pa. 158).

C. PUBLIC AND PRIVATE COMMENTARIES ON THE CONSTITUTION

10 October–10 November 1787

Between 10 October and the election of Convention delegates on 6 November, the terms "Federalist" and "Antifederalist" were as commonly used as "Republican" and "Constitutionalist." During this period Pennsylvanians reiterated the Federalist and Antifederalist arguments which had been presented during the first week of October in the "Address of the Seceding Assemblymen" (I:B above); "Centinel" I (II:A above); and James Wilson's speech in the State House Yard (II:A above).

The Federalists controlled most of Pennsylvania's newspapers and the bulk of the material published supported the Constitution. However, the Antifederalists published more major items during this period, principally in the *Independent Gazetteer*. Five major Antifederalist pieces were published on a single day—17 October. They were: "A Democratic Federalist" and "The Chronicles of Early Times" (both in II:C below); "An Old Whig" II (CC:170); "Montezuma" (Mfm:Pa. 140); and a pamphlet by John Nicholson (Mfm:Pa. 141). Other important items were "M.C." 27 October and "An Officer of the Late Continental Army," 6 November (both in II:C below); "Centinel" II (CC:190); and "An Old Whig" I, III–V (CC:157, 181, 202, 224). "Centinel" II, "An Old Whig" IV–V, and "An Officer of the Late Continental Army" were also printed as broadsides (for still other Antifederalist items, see Mfm:Pa. 154, 162, 164). Pennsylvania printers also reprinted major Antifederalist pieces from the *New York Journal*, such as "Cato" II; "Brutus" I; and "A Republican to James Wilson" I (CC:153, 178, 196).

While the Antifederalists published more major items than the Federalists, the latter had the advantage in the great number of squibs and short items containing optimistic reports of the prospect for ratification in various states (for examples, see *Pennsylvania Gazette*, 10 October, CC:150 A–L, and CC:Vol. I, Appendix). Moreover, Federalist newspapers were filled with reports of actions and sentiments favoring the Constitution reprinted from out-of-state newspapers (for examples, see CC:123, 156).

The principal writings by Pennsylvania Federalists during this period were "One of the People," 17 October and "Wat Tyler, A Proclamation," 24 October (both in II:C below); "Federal Constitution," 10 October (CC:150–B); and pamphlets by Noah Webster, signed "A Citizen of America" (17 October, Mfm:Pa. 142) and by Pelatiah Webster, signed "A Citizen of Philadelphia" (18 October, CC:125–B).

On 21 October Tench Coxe's "An American Citizen" IV was first printed in a broadside anthology which contained reprints of some of the major Federalist items that had been published between 26 September and 10 October (CC:183-A). For other important Federalist items, see Mfm:Pa. 127, 152, 161, 165, 175, 183. Some major out-of-state Federalist items, such as "Curtius" (CC:111) and Governor John Hancock's speech to the Massachusetts General Court (CC:177), were also widely reprinted in Pennsylvania.

A Federalist, Independent Gazetteer, 10 October

The CENTINEL, in your paper of last Friday,[1] compliments the citizens of Philadelphia, when he says, "A frenzy of enthusiasm has actuated them, in their approbation of the proposed Federal Constitution, before it was possible that it could be the result of a rational investigation." This, however, is trivial compared with the sequel, wherein he charges the worthy and very patriotic characters, of whom the late Convention was composed, with a conspiracy against the liberty of their country; not even the *immortal* WASHINGTON, nor the *venerable* FRANKLIN escapes his satire; but both of them, says this insidious enemy to his country, were *non compos mentis,* when they concurred in framing the new Federal Constitution. When he ventured to make these assertions against characters so very respectable, he should have been able to support the charge. One of his objections to this Constitution is that each state is to have two Senators and not a number proportioned to its inhabitants; here, he has fallen into a terrible inconsistency, not recollecting that such is the mode of electing members of the Supreme Executive Council, in this state, where every county appoints one, and only one, without any regard had to the number of taxable inhabitants in the respective counties. Yet, he has gone so far in panegyrics upon the constitution of this state, as to maintain that a similar one would be the best that could be devised for the United States.

Had the different members of the Convention entertained sentiments thus *narrow, local, contracted* and *selfish,* each would have proposed the constitution of his own state, and they would never have united in forming that *incomparable* one which is now exhibited to our view, and which, *without partiality to any particular state, is adapted to the general circumstances of all.*

I am happy to find the distinction of *Republican* and *Constitutionalist* in this city has given way to the more important one of *Federalist* and *Antifederalist;*[2] such a worthy example will, I trust, be imitated through every part of this state.

To conclude, sir, if some person of better abilities should not step forth in defense of the form of government proposed by the Convention, I shall hold myself bound, in duty to the welfare of my country, to expose, upon a future occasion, the *weakness* and *futility* of CENTINEL'S arguments, together with the motives which urged him to undertake the infamous job.[3] I shall not, however, resort [to] his torrents of personal invective, but shall take notice of the *sophistry* he has made use of, so far as it is calculated to *mislead* the citizens of Pennsylvania, or of the adjacent states.

1. "Centinel" I, 5 October, II:A above.
2. See also William Lewis to Thomas Lee Shippen, 11 October, Mfm:Pa. 125; and Charles Swift to Robert E. Griffiths, 18 October, II:C below.
3. See "A Federalist," 25 October, Mfm:Pa. 161.

The Chronicles of Early Times, Freeman's Journal, 17 October[1]

CHAPTER XIV: And he reported to them faithfully all that had been done, and how the enemies of the mill [Bank of North America] had been put to flight.

10. So the mill was rebuilt, and the friends thereof shouted for joy.

11. Then said Robert the Cofferer [Robert Morris], ye do well to rejoice, for a great work hath been wrought this day amongst us. Perceive ye not how the mill is constructed, so that henceforth we shall be able to grind our adversaries even to powder.

12. And when the multitude were dispersed, there remained yet a few chosen men, amongst whom were James the Caledonian [James Wilson], Thomas the Roman [Thomas FitzSimons], George the Climberian [George Clymer], and Gouvero the cunning man [Gouverneur Morris], and others to whom they might impart all things.

13. And when they had shut to the door of the place in which they were assembled, Robert opened his mouth and spake, saying:

14. Know ye not, that although the mill hath been rebuilt, yet many of the rulers of the people and agents who have adhered to and joined us in building the mill have done so because they expected to receive of the corn when it is ground; others absented themselves through fear or did not oppose us because of dismay. All these rulers may the people change and appoint others to represent them, so that of our mill there may not be left one stone upon another that shall not be again thrown down.

15. But against all these things have I been careful to provide for heretofore in my bed, when deep sleep falleth upon men. I foresaw that after the mill was rebuilded these things would be, and my heart was sore troubled within me, insomuch that my sleep fled from mine eyes.

16. And I gat me up and called upon Gouvero, saying, arouse from thy slumbers, O thou who art cunning to devise, for danger lieth in wait for us.

17. So he arose and gat himself up, and I opened to him all my fears and showed him that after the workmanship of the mill, which had then been begun to be rebuilt was finished, there was danger lest the people should a second time destroy the mill, and take away all the customers thereof to the country mill, for I saw that they could not both stand together.

18. And Gouvero said, fear not these things, neither be dismayed, I also have thought upon these evils and have found a remedy therefor.

19. Then said I, blessed art thou amongst men, O Gouvero! for thy stratagems are wise, thy councils are deep, and thy cunning exceedeth all things!

CHAPTER XV: 1. And Gouvero furthermore added and said,

2. Thou knowest the state of our nation and of our country, that ofttimes when the people from the country round about had brought their corn to our mill, so that it was collected in large granaries, and when the people of other nations who wanted of this corn and came hither from the four winds under heaven, riding upon the waters of the great deep, in ships laden with gaw-gaws, and chains, and bracelets, and rings, and jewels, and mantles, and mantlets, and wimples, and crisping pins, and cauls, and round buttons like the moon, and mufflers, and ornaments for show and not for use, and headbands and tablets, and bonnets, and all manner of gauzes, silks, embroidery, and gay apparel, thou knowest, I say, that the corn thus gathered together was taken from our mill and exchanged with the foreign merchantmen for these things, so that there hath been a great dearth of corn in our land.

3. Thou also knowest that many whose hearts went out after these things, and were set upon gay attire and apparel, and neglected to perform those things which afore time they had been exercised in, and whereby they had earned unto themselves and to their families corn in moderate competency, straightway betook themselves to our mill, where they gat them corn upon the promise of themselves and their friends, that it should be restored to us with usury, by the space of thirty days, at the end of which period they could again draw corn, and with a part thereof repay what they had before received, and so on with facility continuing after the same manner, until corn became so plenty in their houses, that they forgat they had but little at the first. And they also forgat the rock from whence it had been hewn— so they said everyman to his fellow: "lo, I am rich and increased in goods, give me thy note, and I will also give thee mine, whereby we

may go to the managers of the great mill, who assemble themselves weekly together on the fifth day of every week, and there continue to receive from them corn, that we may live as beseemeth us, for lo! it is there in great abundance, and whosoever can borrow his neighbor's note may have thereof as much as he willeth. Blessed be the mill where corn may be thus had in plenty!"

4. So they forgat themselves and did eat, and consume, and waste corn in abundance, but thou also knowest that while their hearts were merry, destruction came upon many of them as a whirlwind, and as a thief in the night, and that in their fall many who had given and endorsed notes fell also. Nay, that so great was the rage for wasting of corn, that every man was upbraided and esteemed as nothing who wasted not corn in like manner with themselves, until it became general throughout all the country and regions round about—insomuch that notwithstanding the managers of the mill whom thou hast appointed, required for surety such as they esteemed to have much corn of their own in store to pay withal, and never let any of the sons of men fall in an unfavorable moment, while our notes or endorsements were thought to be insecure, yet even we are in danger of losing corn also in some cases.

5. These things, and others of like kind, have brought on a day of general calamity. There is no corn in our land to repay the corn which was lent to us by other nations in the day that we went out to battle against our enemies, and every man's inquiry hath been pursuing the cause thereof. Now thou knowest that as it is unnatural for all men to blame their own folly as the cause of their adversity, so the people sought to lay the blame on something else.

6. And it came to pass that it was not long ere the covenant [Articles of Confederation] which had been made between and amongst the twelve tribes and the tribe of Manasseh [Rhode Island], in the day that the Lord delivered them and saved them from the hands of their enemies, was held out [by] many as the cause of all the evils which had come upon the land, and they cried out every man saying, let us alter this covenant, for it hath caused much evil, as ye all behold even at this day.

7. Thou rememberest that under this covenant a wall was built around our mill, and some supposed it would have secured it from the people, but it was weak and the people trampled it down, moreover they said that the wall stood upon improper ground and withal was of none effect.

8. Now therefore let us take away the covenant from before the eyes of the people, and let us make a firm league, so shall we have a

wall around our mill that the people may not approach or injure it; and it shall be built on good ground, the right whereof shall not be questioned or disputed at all forever.

9. We will therein also take away from the country mill both the upper and the nether millstones, and will make cornerstones thereof for the wall which shall be built around our mill. And the walls of the country mill shall be pulled down and destroyed, and the dam thereof shall be broken up and removed, so that the water may run freely to our mill, and the place where it now stands shall know it again no more.

10. And the things which Gouvero had said pleased me well, so we communed together on the way whereby all these things might be accomplished.

11. And I got the rulers of the land to appoint me to be a deputy to meet deputies from other tribes who might choose to assemble for the purpose of revising the great covenant, and proposing alterations therein, and with me Thomas the Roman, James the Caledonian, George the Climberian, and Gouvero the cunning man, all of whom are chosen friends and managers of the mill, and *Jared* [Ingersoll] also who is not of our sheepfold was appointed, but it behooved us so to do that we might succeed the better.

12. And now behold you see how the thing hath prospered, for most of the tribes have appointed deputies and they are shortly to be convened together.

13. But inasmuch as we are all of us brethren of the mill, except *Jared*, and lest peradventure the rumor should go abroad that we have been chosen to represent the interest of the mill and not of the tribe by whom we have been chosen, let us also have Benjamin of the house of Frankland added to the number of the deputies, we shall nevertheless have a majority in the deputies from our tribe, and his name will give respect to our councils—for Benjamin was highly reverenced by all the people.

14. Now they considered that Benjamin was an old man and full of days, and that his body was feeble and bowed down with years, and supposed that his outgoings to the meetings of the deputies of the tribes would not be frequent, and the thing which Robert had proposed pleased them well, and it was done as he had desired.

1. For other examples of attacks on Robert Morris and James Wilson, which mounted after ratification, see Mfm:Pa. 387, 457, 467, 481, 487, 511, 512, 522, 538, and 661. For the relationship of the Bank of North America to Pennsylvania politics, see Brunhouse, *Counter-Revolution, passim.*

Squibs from the Pennsylvania Gazette, 17 October

[The following are examples of the hundreds of often reprinted items known as "squibs."]

By a late calculation, it appears that the reduction of the expenses of the government of Pennsylvania, by the adoption of the new Federal Constitution, will amount to 35,000 £ a year. A sum that will nearly pay the interest of our whole proportion of the debt of the United States.[1]

* * * *

A minister of the Gospel, through the medium of our paper, begs leave to ask, whether men can be serious in regard to the Christian religion, who object to a government that is calculated to promote the glory of GOD, by establishing peace, order and justice in our country?—and whether it would not be better for such men to renounce the Christian name, and to enter into society with the Shawanese or Mohawk Indians, than to attempt to retain the blessings of religion and civilization, with their licentious ideas of government.[2]

* * * *

It is to be hoped (says a correspondent) that the city and counties will avoid choosing such persons as are in Council or in the Assembly to represent the state in the ensuing CONVENTION. Their *oaths* will interfere with their duty in considering the new government, and the session of the Convention will by those means be greatly prolonged. Besides, how disgraceful will it be to a country to appear so barren of sensible and federal citizens as to heap two appointments upon the same persons.[3]

* * * *

We hear that the uniform of the Federalists in this city is to consist of—cloth covered buttons, leather pockets, and plain shirts.[4]

1. By 13 November this item was reprinted four times in Pennsylvania and twenty-two times from New Hampshire to Georgia.
2. Outside Pennsylvania this item was reprinted ten times from New Hampshire to Maryland by 13 November. For another item about the clergy's support of the Constitution, see Mfm:Pa. 177.
3. This item was reprinted once in Pennsylvania and five times from Massachusetts to Maryland by 31 October. For a similar item, see Mfm:Pa. 183.
4. By 8 November this item was reprinted once in Pennsylvania and fifteen times from New Hampshire to Georgia.

One of the People, Pennsylvania Gazette, 17 October[1]

At this important period, on which the existence of America as a people depends, one of the people begs leave to lay before them, in a dispassionate and cool manner, some facts, which may tend to illustrate to them their true interest, and repel the poison which the late dissenters from the House of Assembly, in their insidious and inflammatory address, have endeavored to infect them with.[2]

It is not now a question between those who have distracted the state by the names of Republican and Constitutionalist which calls for your attention; it is a subject of far greater magnitude involving in it not the fate of this state alone, but of all America. A Constitution is offered to the people of the United States by their delegates in Convention. On the awful *fiat* of the people of America does this Constitution now depend. This Convention, composed of the most celebrated characters, the collected wisdom of America, have appealed to you to judge of their proceedings. Suffer not yourselves then to be carried by the artful and designing declaration of sixteen men, whose names are recorded for a disgraceful abandonment of you, their constituents. The Confederation was formed in a hasty manner at a time of danger and distress. It was calculated for the moment when a war raged in our country. It was not calculated for civil purposes, nor for times of peace, and these states were only kept together by a sense of common danger. But the moment peace was established, and that sense of common danger was extinct, it was found inadequate to the government of this extensive country. It wanted that energy which in all governments has been found necessary for the well regulating the people. It exposed us to ruin and distress at home and disgrace abroad. At the peace, the United States were esteemed, revered, and dreaded by foreign nations. America held a most elevated rank among the powers of the earth; but how are the mighty fallen! disgraced have we rendered ourselves abroad and ruined at home. Bankrupt merchants, poor mechanics, and distressed farmers are the effects of the weakness of the Confederation. America saw it and assembled those amongst her sons celebrated for wisdom and a knowledge of government; and she has not been disappointed in her representatives. That assembly has produced a work which immortalizes its fame, which will, if ambition and envy suffer it to be adopted by us, raise us to that station which America should hold among the nations of Europe.

The people of Pennsylvania, in general, are composed of men of three occupations, the farmer, the merchant, the mechanic; the interests of these three are intimately blended together. A government then, which will be conducive to their happiness and best promote their interest, is the government which these people should adopt. The Constitution now presented to them is such a one. Every person must long since have discovered the necessity of placing the exclusive power of regulating the commerce of America in the same body;

without this, it is impossible to regulate their trade. The same imposts, duties and customs must equally prevail over the whole; for no one state can carry into effect their impost laws—a neighboring state could always prevent it—no state could effectually encourage their manufactories—there can be no navigation act. Whence comes it that the trade of this state, which abounds with materials for shipbuilding, is carried on in foreign bottoms? Whence comes it that shoes, boots, made-up clothes, hats, nails, sheet iron, hinges, and all other utensils of iron are of British manufactory? Whence comes it that Spain can regulate our flour market? These evils proceed from a want of one supreme controlling power in these states. They will be all done away, by adopting the present form of government. It will have energy and power to regulate your trade and commerce, to enforce the execution of your imposts, duties and customs. Instead of the trade of this country being carried on in foreign bottoms, our ports will be crowded with our own ships, and we shall become the carriers of Europe. Heavy duties will be laid on all foreign manufactures which can be manufactured in this country, and bounties will be granted on their exportation of our commodities. The manufactories of our country will flourish—our mechanics will lift up their heads, and rise to opulence and wealth. So convinced of this are the mechanics of Philadelphia, that they have petitioned for calling a convention. The farmer is particularly interested in carrying into immediate execution this Constitution. Flour, the staple commodity of the state, is become a drug. No brisk market offers for it, and the tiller of the earth is obliged frequently to sell the produce raised by the sweat of his brow for less than the price of his labor. This is not owing to the want of demand abroad, for it is sufficient, but for the want of power at home to regulate our foreign trade. This power once granted, America would be able to regulate her own market and not receive from any foreign power the small pittance they please to bestow for the staff of life, and America could starve them into a generous price. Lands under the present Confederation have fallen since the peace at least one-third or one-half. It surely is a melancholy consideration to the farmer, to think that the independence which he shed his blood for should reduce the value of his estate near one-half. However melancholy it may be, experience evinces its truth. No foreigner who has money will venture it in a country which has no fixed government. A stable energetic Federal Constitution will cause property again to rise to its real and true value and will invite monied men from all the countries of Europe. Yet to such a Constitution, so fraught with blessings to our distressed country, have our worthy representatives set themselves in battle array and have come forth in a public address armed with the weapons of hypocrisy and palpable falsehood; and fearing to trust the people with a candid inquiry and discussion, have endeavored to strangle the infant in its birth, by opposing the calling of a convention on pretexts the most idle and false that can be imagined. The assertion as to the House not having received official accounts from Congress is false, for an official account most assuredly had arrived and was communicated to them, not at the time of the first debate, but after the adjournment of the House on that evening. That account, too, under the hand of the Secretary of Congress to the Speaker of the Assembly. The House had not dissolved, and business of importance required their attendance—several bills were lying on the table, which had been agreed to and waited for the House to pass them into laws. Their duty, their oaths, called on them to attend. They should, if they thought the calling of a convention improper, have stood in their places and opposed it. They should have attended and entered a protest against it. This was the mode pointed out by the constitution. Their absenting themselves was a desertion of their trust, a betraying of their constituents, and of mischievous consequences to the state, as it directly tends to a dissolution of all government.

How absurd it is to say, that they had not received official information from Congress. Where was such information to be attained? Not in the house of Major [Alexander] Boyd, nor from the major's hands—not in the public streets—but in the State House and from the Speaker. They knew such information was in the House, they knew the Speaker was in possession of it, for he had shown it to them. One here is at a loss what most to be surprised at, the impudence of the falsehood or insult offered the understanding of the people. The complaint of the shortness of the time, and the necessity of consulting the people, is idle. The House were not to determine whether Pennsylvania approved of the Constitution or not. All the power the Assembly were possessed of was to call a convention of the people to consider of the Constitution. In opposing this, they have attempted to take away from the people the power of judging and determining for themselves. Their language amounts to this: "We are better judges what suits the people than they are. We are acquainted with government. We think this a bad form, and will not even submit it to the people;" and yet these are the men who talk of their great regard to your interest, their love of liberty and the constitution. There is one good advice given you in the address, "read the Federal Constitution;" and when it is read, I am convinced every dispassionate man will pronounce that it is not liable to any of the objections its enemies have raised. It is affirmed that the deputies from this state had not power to recommend to the people, under their appointment, a new constitution. The deputies from this state were empowered, they had power to make such *alterations* and *further provisions as may be necessary to render the federal government fully adequate to the exigencies of the Union.* Had objections such as these prevailed, America never would have had a Congress, nor had America been independent. Alterations in government are always made by the people. It is said that this Constitution will annihilate the state government. On what section of the Constitution do these men ground this assertion? It breathes nothing like it—it interferes not with the internal government of any state—it supports and adds a dignity to every government in the United States. They complain of the power granted to Congress of levying taxes. This is a power without which no government can exist. Finance is the very nerve of government, and unless Congress have power to effect the collection of the taxes, the power of assessing and recommending their collection is a shadow.

When Congress, at the conclusion of the war, recommended a duty of five percent, the trifling state of Rhode Island, whose extent is not greater than one of our counties, refused their acquiescence, and this prevented a measure most beneficial to these states, and by which a great part of the federal debt would have been discharged.[3] It is most shameful to say that this tax will be collected by soldiers. The power is not given to a foreign prince, but to a Congress, chosen by the people. Pennsylvania, which has been always highly federal, has suffered by the want of this power. She has ever been most forward in complying with the requisitions of Congress, whilst other states have hung back, preferring the interest of their particular state to that of the Union. The taxes fall heavy on the landed men of this state. A general impost throughout the states will lighten their burthen, and the greater part of our taxes will be paid by duties on foreign manufactures and the luxuries of life. This government will not be attended with greater expense than the present Congress, for under this Constitution they do not sit perpetually, as the Congress now do. The freedom of the press and trials by jury are not infringed on. The Constitution is silent, and with propriety too, on these and every other subject relative to the internal government of the states. These are secured by the different state constitutions. I repeat again, that the Federal Constitution does not interefere with these matters. Their power is defined and limited by the 8th section of the first Article of the Constitution, and they have not power to take away the freedom of the press, nor can they interfere in the smallest degree with the judiciary of any one of the states. It is essentially necessary that the judiciary of the United States should have an appellate jurisdiction both in law and fact, in cases of disputes between a state and citizens of another state, and between citizens of different states. This could not have been done under the old Confederation, but by an application to Congress for a federal court, the expense of which was borne by the party who was cast, and amounted to 5000 £. No man, under these circumstances, would risk an appeal, though his property had been unjustly taken from him by a prejudice so natural to inhabitants of the same state. It is said that this Constitution was disapproved by three persons, and that they refused signing it.[4] However respectable their names may be, they cannot certainly be placed in competition with those of a [George] Washington, a [William] Livingston, a [Benjamin] Franklin, a [James] Maddison, a [John] Rutledge, and a Rufus King; and one of those who refused to sign has been notoriously ill-disposed to any federal government.[5] It was unanimously approved and signed by all the states present—and the only matter of surprise is, that in so large a body only three individuals dissented from it. Such an instance of unanimity upon a great national object can scarcely be paralleled in any country, and can only be ascribed to the influence of that BEING in whose hands are the hearts and understandings of all men. The government which is offered to you is truly republican, and unites complete vigor and the most perfect freedom; for the people have the election of the Representatives in Congress, the legislature the appointment of the Senate, and the people the choice of Electors for electing a President—and in the House of Representatives must all money bills originate.

It is the privilege of every citizen to deliver with freedom his sentiments, and the duty of every lover of truth to detect falsehood. These are the motives which have induced me to endeavor to undeceive you, to state the truth, and guard you against designing ambition. And should my feeble voice be heard amidst the noise of party, and incline my countrymen to judge with coolness and impartiality—should it prevail against the loud brawls of dissimulation and untruth—it will afford the most pleasing sensations the human mind is capable of, as it will preserve this country from the dreadful consequences of rejecting a Constitution, which alone can free them from confusion, anarchy, distress and ruin. Let us accept with gratitude the Constitution offered to us and make a fair trial of it. It is not unchangeable. If upon experiment it is found not to answer the end of all government (the happiness of the people) it can be altered, for two-thirds of the legislatures of the states can effect this change.

1. This item, addressed "To the Freemen of Pennsylvania," was reprinted in the *Philadelphische Correspondenz,* 30 October; *Lancaster Zeitung,* 31 October; and the October *American Museum.* Outside Pennsylvania, it was reprinted in the

Newport Herald, 1 November; Boston *Independent Chronicle,* 1 November; and Boston *American Herald,* 5 November.

2. "Address of the Seceding Assemblymen," I:B above.

3. For the Impost of 1781, see CDR:IV, A.

4. Elbridge Gerry, George Mason, and Edmund Randolph refused to sign the Constitution.

5. Probably George Mason who was attacked earlier. See "Protest of the Minority," 3 October, II:A above.

Avenging Justice, Pennsylvania Gazette, 17 October[1]

As a conclusive answer to the fallacious reasoning of those placemen-scribblers, who have presumed not only to arraign that invaluable frame of government, the Federal Constitution, but to attack and defame the venerable names of Washington and Franklin, be pleased, Messrs. Printers, to insert this single observation.

As in the state governments, all powers which have not been expressly reserved by the constitutions or declarations of rights, are vested in the several legislatures, whose authority is thereby rendered supreme—so the direct reverse of this proposition applies to the government of the United States, as fixed and limited by the Federal Constitution, and no one power or authority, whatever, can be exercised by the Congress, which is not expressly granted by the Constitution.

Where, then, is the ground on which that abominable falsehood is built (published, among others, in the *Independent Gazetteer* of the 6th instant) which charges the Federal Constitution with abolishing the liberty of the press?[2]

How despicable must the cause of that opposition be, which has recourse to such means to effect its purpose! How unworthy to be styled the advocates of freedom are those men whose arguments are founded in such base falsehood, and whose only motive to such unworthy conduct must be the influence of foreign gold, or, if possible, the still baser intention of betraying their country into anarchy, that they may either retain their present unmerited stations or rise upon her ruins. Let them beware—the vengeance of an injured people will not sleep forever—and, whether native or foreigner, when roused, they will feel its force. Abused forbearance will be followed by AVENGING JUSTICE.

1. For an attack upon "Avenging Justice," see "Plain Truth," 24 November, II:F below.

2. II:A above.

A Democratic Federalist, Pennsylvania Herald, 17 October[1]

The arguments of the Honorable Mr. [James] Wilson, expressed in the speech he made at the State House on the Saturday preceding the general election (as stated in the *Pennsylvania Herald*), although extremely *ingenious* and the best that could be adduced in support of so bad a cause, are yet extremely *futile* and will not stand the test of investigation.

In the first place, Mr. Wilson pretends to point out a leading discrimination between the state constitutions and the Constitution of the United States. In the former, he says, every power which is not *reserved* is *given,* and in the latter, every power which is not *given* is *reserved.* And this may furnish an answer, he adds, to those who object that a bill of rights has not been introduced in the proposed Federal Constitution. If this doctrine is true, and since it is the only security that we are to have for our natural rights, it ought at least to have been clearly expressed in the plan of government. The 2d section of the present Articles of Confederation says: *"Each State retains its sovereignty, freedom and independence, and* EVERY POWER, JURISDICTION AND RIGHT WHICH IS NOT BY THIS CONFEDERATION EXPRESSLY, DELEGATED TO THE UNITED STATES IN CONGRESS ASSEMBLED." This declaration (for what purpose I know not) is entirely omitted in the proposed Constitution. And yet there is a material difference between this Constitution and the present Confederation, for Congress in the latter are merely an executive body; it has no power to raise money, it has no *judicial jurisdiction.* In the other, on the contrary, the federal rulers are vested with each of the three essential powers of government—their laws are to be *paramount* to the laws of the different states. What then will there be to oppose to their encroachments? Should they ever pretend to tyrannize over the people, their *standing army* will silence every popular effort; it will be theirs to explain the powers which have been granted to them. Mr. Wilson's distinction will be forgot, denied or explained away, and the liberty of the people will be no more.

It is said in the 2d section of the 3d Article of the federal plan: "The judicial power shall extend to ALL CASES, in *law* and *equity,* arising under this constitution." It is very clear that under this clause, the tribunal of the United States may claim a right to the cognizance of all offenses against the *general government,* and *libels* will not probably be excluded. Nay, those offenses may be by them construed, or by law declared *misprision of treason,* an offense which comes literally under their express jurisdiction. Where is then the safety of our boasted liberty of the press? And in case of a *conflict of jurisdiction* between the courts of the United States and those of the several commonwealths is it not easy to foresee which of the two will obtain the advantage?

Under the enormous power of the new confederation, which extends to the *individuals* as well as to the *states* of America, a thousand means may be devised to destroy effectually the liberty of the press. There is no knowing what corrupt and wicked judges may do in process of time when they are not restrained by express laws. The case of *John Peter Zenger* of New York ought still to be present to our minds to convince us how displeasing the liberty of the press is to men in high power.[2] At any rate, I lay it down as a general rule that wherever the powers of a government extend to the lives, the persons, and properties of the subject, all their rights ought to be clearly and expressly defined, otherwise they have but a poor security for their liberties.

The second and most important objection to the federal plan, which Mr. Wilson pretends to be made *in a disingenuous form,* is the entire *abolition of the trial by jury in civil cases.* It seems to me that Mr. Wilson's pretended answer is much more *disingenuous* than the objection itself, which I maintain to be strictly founded in fact. He says "that the cases open to trial by jury differing in the different states, it was therefore impracticable to have made a general rule." This answer is extremely futile, because a reference might easily have been made to the *common law of England,* which obtains through every state, and cases in the maritime and civil law courts would of course have been excepted. I must also directly contradict Mr. Wilson when he asserts that there is no trial by jury in the courts of chancery. It cannot be unknown to a man of his high professional learning that whenever a difference arises about a matter of fact in the courts of equity in America or England, the fact is sent down to the courts of common law to be tried by a jury, and it is what the lawyers call a *feigned issue.* This method will be impracticable under the proposed form of judicial jurisdiction for the United States.

But setting aside the equivocal answers of Mr. Wilson, I have it in my power to prove that under the proposed Federal Constitution *the trial of facts in civil cases by a jury of the vicinage* is entirely and effectually abolished and will be absolutely impracticable. I wish the learned gentleman had explained to us what is meant by the *appellate* jurisdiction as to law and *fact* which is vested in the superior court of the United States? As he has not thought proper to do it, I shall endeavor to explain it to my fellow citizens, regretting at the same time that it has not been done by a man whose abilities are so much superior to mine. The word *appeal,* if I understand it right in its proper legal signification includes the *fact* as well as the *law,* and precludes every idea of a trial by jury. It is a word of *foreign growth* and is only known in England and America in those courts which are governed by the civil or ecclesiastical law of the *Romans.* Those courts have always been considered in England as a grievance and have all been established by the usurpations of the *ecclesiastical* over the *civil* power. It is well-known that the courts of chancery in England were formerly entirely in the hands of *ecclesiastics,* who took advantage of the strict forms of the common law to introduce a foreign mode of jurisprudence under the specious name of *Equity.* Pennsylvania, the freest of the American states has wisely rejected this establishment and knows not even the name of a court of chancery. And in fact, there cannot be anything more absurd than a distinction between LAW and EQUITY. It might perhaps have suited those barbarous times when the law of England, like almost every other science, was perplexed with quibbles and *Aristotelian* distinctions, but it would be shameful to keep it up in these more enlightened days. At any rate, it seems to me that there is much more *equity* in a trial by jury, than in an appellate jurisdiction from the fact.

An *appeal,* therefore, is a thing unknown to the common law. Instead of an appeal from facts, it admits of a second, or even third trial by different juries, and mistakes in points of *law* are rectified by superior courts in the form of a *writ of error*—and to a mere common lawyer, unskilled in the forms of the *civil law* courts, the words *appeal from law and fact* are mere nonsense and unintelligible absurdity.

But even supposing that the superior court of the United States had the authority to try facts by *juries of the vicinage,* it would be impossible for them to carry it into execution. It is well-known that the supreme courts of the different states, at stated times in every year, go round the different counties of their respective states to try issues of fact, which is called *riding the circuits.* Now, how is it possible that the supreme continental court, which we will suppose to consist at most of five or six judges, can travel at least twice in every year, through the different counties of America, from New Hampshire to Kentucky, and from Kentucky to Georgia, to try facts by juries of the vicinage. Common sense will not admit of such a supposition. I am therefore right in my assertion, that *trial by jury in civil cases is, by the proposed Constitution, entirely done away and effectually abolished.*

Let us now attend to the consequences of this enormous innovation and daring encroachment on the liberties of the citizens. Setting aside the oppression, injustice, and partiality that may take place in the trial of questions of property between man and man, we will attend to one single case, which is well worth our consideration. Let us remember that all cases arising under the new Constitution, and all matters between *citizens of different states,* are to be submitted to the new jurisdiction. Suppose, therefore, that the military officers of Congress, by a wanton abuse of power, imprison the free citizens of America, suppose the excise or revenue officers (as we find in Clayton's *Reports,* page 44 Ward's case that a constable, having a warrant to search for stolen goods, pulled down the clothes of a bed in which there was a woman and searched under her shift),[3] suppose, I say, that they commit similar or greater indignities; in such cases a trial by jury would be our safest resource. Heavy damages would at once punish the offender and deter others from committing the same. But what satisfaction can we expect from a lordly court of justice, always ready to protect the officers of government against the weak and helpless citizen, and who will perhaps sit at the distance of many hundred miles from the place where the outrage was committed? What refuge shall we then have to shelter us from the iron hand of arbitrary power? O! my fellow citizens, think of this while it is yet time and never consent to part with the glorious privilege of trial by jury, but with your lives.

But Mr. Wilson has not stopped here. He has told us that a STANDING ARMY, that *great support of tyrants,* not only was not dangerous, but that it was *absolutely necessary.* O! my much respected fellow citizens! and are you then reduced to such a degree of insensibility, that assertions like these will not rouse your warmest resentment and indignation? Are we then, after the experience of past ages, and the result of the inquiries of the best and most celebrated patriots have taught us to dread a standing army above all earthly evils, are we then to go over all the threadbare commonplace arguments that have been used without success by the advocates of tyranny, and which have been for a long time past so gloriously refuted! Read the excellent Burgh in his political disquisitions[4] on this hackneyed subject, and then say, whether you think that a standing army is necessary in a free country? Even Mr. Hume, an *aristocratical* writer, has candidly confessed that *an army is a mortal distemper in a government, of which it must at last inevitably perish* (2d Burgh, 349); and the Earl of Oxford (Oxford, the friend of France and the *pretender,* the attainted Oxford) said in the British Parliament, in a speech on the mutiny bill, that "while he had breath, he would speak for the liberties of his country, and against courts martial and a standing army in peace as dangerous to the constitution" (ibid., page

455 [356]). Such were the speeches even of the enemies to liberty, when Britain had yet a right to be called free. But, says Mr. Wilson, "It is necessary to maintain the appearance of strength even in times of the most profound tranquility." And what is this more than a threadbare hackneyed argument, which has been answered over and over in different ages and does not deserve even the smallest consideration? Had we a standing army when the British invaded our peaceful shores? Was it a standing army that gained the battle of Lexington and Bunker's Hill, and took the ill-fated [John] Burgoyne? Is not a well-regulated militia sufficient for every purpose of internal defense? And which of you, my fellow citizens, is afraid of any invasion from foreign powers, that our brave militia would not be able immediately to repel?

Mr. Wilson says that *he does not know of any nation in the world which has not found it necessary to maintain the appearance of strength in a season of the most profound tranquility.* If by this *equivocal* assertion, he has meant to say that there is no nation in the world without *a standing army in time of peace,* he has been mistaken. I need only adduce the example of Switzerland, which, like us, is a *republic* whose *thirteen* cantons, like our thirteen states, are under a *federal government,* and which besides is surrounded by the most powerful nations in Europe, all jealous of its liberty and prosperity. And yet that nation has preserved its freedom for many ages, with the sole help of a militia, and has never been known to have a standing army except when in actual war. Why should we not follow so glorious an example, and are we less able to defend our liberty without an army than that brave but small nation, which with its militia alone has hitherto defied all Europe?

It is said likewise, that *a standing army is not a new thing in America. Congress even at this moment have a standing army on foot.* I answer, that *precedent* is not *principle.* Congress have no right to keep up a standing army in time of peace. If they do, it is an infringement of the liberties of the people—*wrong* can never be justified by *wrong*—but it is well-known that the assertion is groundless. The few troops that are on the banks of the Ohio were sent for the express purpose of repelling the invasion of the savages and protecting the inhabitants of the frontiers. It is our misfortune that we are never at peace with those inhuman butchers of their species, and while they remain in our neighborhood, we are always, with respect to them, in a state of war. As soon as the danger is over, there is no doubt but Congress will disband their handful of soldiers. It is therefore not true that Congress keep up a standing army in a time of peace and profound security.

The objection to the enormous powers of the President and Senate is not the least important of all, but it requires a full discussion and ample investigation. I shall take another opportunity of laying before the public my observations upon this subject, as well as upon every other part of the new Constitution. At present I shall only observe that it is an established principle in America, which pervades every one of our state constitutions, that *the legislative and executive powers ought to be kept forever separate and distinct from each other,* and yet in this new Constitution we find there are TWO EXECUTIVE BRANCHES, each of which has *more or less control over the proceedings of the legislature.* This is an innovation of the most dangerous kind upon every known principle of government, and it will be easy for me to convince my fellow citizens that it will, in the first place, create a *Venetian* aristocracy and, in the end, produce an *absolute monarchy.*

Thus I have endeavored to answer to the best of my abilities, the principal arguments of Mr. Wilson. I have written this in haste, in a short interval of leisure from my usual avocations. I have only traced the outlines of the subject, and I hope some abler hand will second my honest endeavors.

1. This item, the first major Antifederalist response to James Wilson's speech of 6 October, was reprinted in the *Pennsylvania Packet* on 23 October, the *New York Morning Post,* 22 October, and the Baltimore *Maryland Gazette,* 26 October.

2. In 1734 Zenger, the printer of *The New-York Weekly Journal,* was charged with seditious libel against the administration of Governor William Cosby, but he was acquitted by a jury. Throughout the Revolutionary Era the Zenger case was cited as an example of the danger of arbitrary power and of the need for guaranteeing the freedom of the press.

3. [J. Clayton], *Reports and Pleas of Assises At Yorke . . .* (London, 1651).

4. James Burgh, an English political and religious reformer, published his *Political Disquisitions* in 1774 and 1775. The three volumes were reprinted in Philadelphia in 1775.

Charles Swift to Robert E. Griffiths, Philadelphia, 18 October (excerpt)[1]

In my letter by the *Pigou* I made a few observations respecting our Convention, and I should have enclosed you all their proceedings, together with the political opinions published since pro and con, but from an apprehension that you would receive them by the packet before mine could arrive and be put to an unnecessary postage. In this country the proposed Constitution has, I believe, a majority of friends amongst the rich and wealthy and amongst the extreme poor. Its enemies are chiefly among the middling class headed by a few interested placemen whose offices and profits will diminish whenever the federal government takes place. In Pennsylvania it is strongly opposed by many (not all) of what was called the Constitutional Party. I say what was called because the distinction now is *"Federal or Antifederal."* When the resolution of Congress recommending the calling a convention for the purposes expressed in the resolutions of the Federal Convention came to our Assembly, a secession took place. The minority, finding the House determined to vote the immediate calling a convention, 16 of them headed by old [William] Finley seceded. The sergeant at arms was dispatched to bring them in, and he, aided by Captain [John] Barry, Michael M. Obrien and Major [William] Jackson seized two of the delinquents [and] brought them by force into the House by which means a quorum was made and the resolutions respecting the calling a convention in November next taken. Those resolutions will be carried into effect; Pennsylvania will call a state convention for the purposes recommend[ed] by the General Convention, and the consequence everybody thinks will be the adoption of the new Constitution. When nine states accede, the President is to be chosen and the government organized. And I've little doubt that will be done this autumn as most of the state legislatures are sitting at this season. You can have no idea of the enthusiastic zeal that prevails in this city. A man hazards ill-usage and insult who dares avow his disapprobation. The [desire?] of the extreme poor and the wealthy for this government may be traced to the same source—the positive disallowance of paper money—a circumstance that always falls heaviest on those classes. The middling sort, being generally in debt or wishing to contract debts, love a currency which by depreciating sanctifies their rapacity and legally authorizes fraud. If anything new occurs before the *Grange* returns I will write.

1. FC, Swift Family Papers, PHi. Endorsed: "Copy of letter Dated Octr: 18th: 1787 to Robert E. Griffiths. Manchester [England]." Swift was a Philadelphia lawyer.

Tench Coxe to James Madison, Philadelphia, 21 October[1]

I received your letter acknowledging the receipt of the three papers in the [*Independent*] *Gazetteer*.[2] At the request of Mr. [James] Wilson, Dr. [Benjamin] Rush and another friend or two, I added a 4th paper calculated to show the general advantages and obviate some of the objections to the system. It was desired by these gentlemen for the purpose of inserting in one of several handbills, which it was proposed to circulate thro our Western counties.[3] I beg leave to enclose you three of them with the same news as in the former case; and wish that you and Colonel [Alexander] H[amilton] may make any use of them, which you think will serve the cause. I also send each of you a pamphlet of Pelatiah Webster's. Tho calculated principally for this state, it has other [merit?].[4]

The opposition here has become more open. It is by those *leaders* of the Constitutional interest who have acted in concert with the Western interest. *The people* of the party in the city are chiefly Federal, tho not so I fear in the counties. However there is no doubt but that a majority, and a very respectable one in our Convention will adopt the Constitution *in toto*. The matter seems likely to be attended with a good deal of warmth in the conversations and publications, perhaps some abuse; but these things will arise on such great occasions. The city members of Convention as proposed are Mr. J. Wilson and Dr. Rush; a Mr. Hilary Baker, a German; a Mr. [George] Latimer formerly of the Constitutional Party, and of great influence among their people here and in some of the counties; and Chief J[ustice Thomas] McKean.[5] The latter, tho of the Constitutional Party, has always approved of two branches, and on this occasion has been called on by some of the Republicans among the Federalists, and has in the most explicit terms approved and engaged to support the plan. A good many people however are averse to him, but as he has a Western influence, as he will show them that one of their men proposed for the Federal Convention has been run by the city, and as he will be a proof that the Federalists do not go upon party distinctions, I think he ought to be and hope he will be elected. I feel great hopes from appearances in Virginia. Colonel [George] Mason's conduct appears to be resented, and Mr. [Edmund] Randolph's is [viewed?] with pain and regret.[6] He is a very amiable, valuable man but I fear will suffer from the circumstance. It seems as if his declining to sign has occasioned a powerful interest to seize the opportunity of overthrowing him by giving countenance to the measures he has declined. The country in this case will be served, but at his expense. If his views were pure, it is to be regretted that he should suffer; if otherwise we must rejoice that it produces or tends to produce public benefits. I remember observing to him that I thought his not signing might lessen the violence of opposition, tho I did not think then nor do I now, that he was right in refusing.

You will oblige me exceedingly by having the enclosed packet for Mr. [Thomas] Jefferson put onto the French mail, which will be closed the 25th inst.

1. RC, Madison Papers, DLC.

2. Madison's letter was dated 1 October. The "three papers" were Coxe's "An American Citizen," I–III, 26–29 September, II:A above.

3. "An American Citizen" IV was first printed by Hall and Sellers on 21 October in a four-page broadside entitled: *Addresses to the Citizens of Pennsylvania. Calculated to shew the Safety—Advantages—and—Necessity of adopting the proposed Constitution of the United States. In which are included Answers to the Objections that have been made to it* (Philadelphia, [1787]). The broadside also contained the first three numbers of "An American Citizen," as well as a number of other major Federalist items which had already been published. "An American Citizen" IV was reprinted in the *Pennsylvania Gazette* and *Independent Gazetteer,* 24 October, the October *American Museum,* and the *Philadelphische Correspondenz,* 4 December. (For its national circulation and the contents of the broadside, see CC:183–A.)

4. "A Citizen of Philadelphia," 18 October, CC:125–B.

5. See "Philadelphia City and County Nomination Tickets," 13 October–3 November, II:D below.

6. On 17 October, four days before Coxe wrote this letter, the *Pennsylvania Gazette, Pennsylvania Herald,* and *Pennsylvania Journal* published brief items attacking Mason and Randolph (CC:171 A–C).

Pennsylvania Gazette, 24 October[1]

We hear with great pleasure, that our German fellow citizens, in the counties inhabited by them on this side the Susquehanna, are to a man in favor of the new federal government, and that they have rejected with indignation the addresses of the sixteen absconders and of the Centinel, notwithstanding the latter had the art to keep back from his translation of it the abuse of Dr. Franklin and General Washington.[2]

If the Germans in Franklin and Cumberland counties have not concurred with their brethren on this side the Susquehanna, in rejecting [James] M'Clane and company from the councils of the state, it is owing to their having been deceived by falsehoods and calumnies propagated among them respecting the new government. It is to be hoped the Germans in Lancaster and York counties will take some pains to undeceive their countrymen and to recover them from the dominion of the enemies of peace, order, industry and property.

1. Outside Pennsylvania this term was reprinted or reported seven times from New Hampshire to Virginia by 15 November.

2. See "Centinel" I, 5 October, n. 2, II:A above.

Wat Tyler, A Proclamation, Pennsylvania Herald, 24 October[1]

WHEREAS it hath been represented unto us that many *evil disposed* men, enemies to our person and authority, have, after great deliberation, devised, and do with strong reason and persuasion recommend unto the people of these states a certain plan or frame of government, evidently calculated to subvert the antient principles of our administration, and to introduce the odious doctrines of national power, honor, and respectability: AND WHEREAS it is the interest and duty of all our true and faithful subjects and friends to oppose, counteract, and defeat this *dangerous and diabolical innovation* upon the *anarchy* of our dominion, THEREFORE we have thought fit, by and with the advice of our dearly beloved Cousins *Jack Straw, Daniel Shays,* and *John Franklin*; to issue this our *vagrant* proclamation, requiring and commanding all and every of our subjects and friends aforesaid, and more especially such of them as are *judges, counsellors, accomptants, constables,* and *public officers* of every denomination, to be zealous and vigilant in their efforts to undermine and destroy the *baneful* system which has been projected as aforesaid. And in our great anxiety for the preservation of those rights and privileges which have ever been held sacred by the freest of all commonwealths, *a mob,* we earnestly recommend to as many of our *learned* subjects as have acquired the art or mystery of writing, the *necessary* task of depreciating, traducing, and defaming: for, as the *silly* prejudice with which men regard a *virtuous* character is apt to make them value the action for the sake of the agent, it will be in vain to attempt the destruction of this *iniquitous* work, till it is *proved,* at least, that the authors were *fools and dotards,* who did not understand, or *knaves and traitors* who would not promote, the welfare of their country. Having then, neither spared *age* for its *wisdom,* or *patriotism* for its *worth,* it is our will and pleasure that our most *clamorous* subjects do proceed, in the next place, to the natural resources of our domination, and oppose to *the inglorious* dictates of truth and reason, the *inexhaustible* artillery of impudent assertion and daring falsehood. Let it be remembered that few men comprehend the science of government, and that, destitute of *judgment,* the people are only to be influenced by their *passions.* Hence arises the *expediency* of resorting to *sound* instead of *sense*; and of bewildering the imagination with visionary terrors, instead of instructing the understanding with rational disquisition, or candid interpretation. It is well known to most of our faithful subjects, that in former times a text of scripture, dexterously quoted, has inflamed the minds of mankind to the most frantic enthusiasm; and our affectionate and illustrious servant, *Lord George Gordon,*[2] has lately demonstrated, that the *stalking horse* of religion may yet be exercised with *excellent* advantage in the cause of tumult and sedition. We do therefore, above all, recommend to our *well disposed* and *industrious* adherents, the selection of such *phrases* and *sentences* as have hitherto excited popular admiration; and that, without regard to the natural correspondence of causes and effects the destruction of the rights and liberties of the nation be inferred, from the means which are employed to secure and preserve them. Thus it may be argued, that because no power is given by the projected plan to controul the freedom of the press, *therefore* the projected plan is calculated to destroy the freedom of the press: because the federal representation of the people will possess the power to declare in what civil cases the trial shall be by jury, *therefore* the trial by jury is abolished in all civil cases: because the power of raising troops for the national protection and defence is delegated to the Congress of the United States, *therefore* the people, and Congress who are a part of the people, will be butchered and enslaved by a standing army: because the several state governments are, from time to time, and at all times to elect and appoint persons to fill the offices of the federal government, *therefore* the several state governments must be eventually annihilated—with many other similar propositions as *fairly* and as *conclusively* deduced from their respective premises.

With these instructions, and confiding in the zeal, faith, and perseverance of our liege subjects, and of all men who know how to estimate the *blessings* of anarchy and licentiousness, and who *wisely* prefer their own temporary interests, to the permanent welfare of the public, we earnestly commend you to the countenance and support of the great father of all sedition, whose triumph over harmony and peace has established an everlasting kingdom.

DONE at our CABBIN at TIOGA on the 5th day of November (being the anniversary of the *fatal* discovery of the *glorious gun powder plot*) annoque domini, 1787.

MAT. TYLER.

Test:
JACK CADE.[3]

1. LT. For a similar piece, see "Daniel Shays to the Antifederal Junto in Philadelphia," 25 September, II:A above. The *Massachusetts Centinel* which reprinted the "proclamation" on 10 November and the Newburyport *Essex Journal* which reprinted it on 14 November followed the *Herald* in using "Mat" rather than "Wat" Tyler.

2. Gordon was an instigator of the riots in 1780 against Parliament's efforts to ameliorate the conditions of English Catholics. The riots, in which hundreds lost their lives, were widely publicized in America.

3. Cade was a leader of a rebellion in England in 1450 which sought judicial and parliamentary reform.

M.C., Pennsylvania Herald, 27 October[1]

The present is universally acknowledged to be a most momentous era, as likely to decide the fate of a world for future ages. This consideration renders it the duty of every individual to submit to the consideration of his fellow citizens whatever he may deem calculated to elucidate the grand subject in general discussion.

The opposition to the new Constitution is said to be made by interested men. This assertion is true only in part. It is possible, indeed, that the most violent, the most active, and the most voluminous writers against the proposed system are generally influenced by sinister and personal considerations. But there are many persons whose apprehensions have been excited by the Centinels, the Old Whigs, the Democratic Federalists, and the Catos,[2] and whose opposition is patriotic and disinterested, as they are fearful for the liberty of posterity and anxious to prevent future encroachments of Congress. To satisfy the minds of those people, I venture, but with great diffidence, to propose a plan, which may possibly remove [a] great part of the present opposition.

Let a meeting of the citizens be called, and a proper committee appointed to frame a bill of rights, for securing the liberty of the press and all other rights which the states hold sacred. Let this bill of rights be transmitted to the several state conventions to be taken into consideration with the new Constitution. Little doubt need be entertained but that it would be universally agreed to.

This measure, if adopted, would draw a line of distinction between the detestable few who would sacrifice the interest and happiness of not only the present, but distant generations to their own emolument, and those who oppose the new system from a patriotic, but perhaps mistaken, dread of danger. The former would be left destitute of the vain covering under which they shelter their want of virtue and public spirit, and the latter would become zealous Federalists.

To the friends of the proposed Constitution, I beg leave to observe, that this measure cannot possibly retard or affect the success of a plan which has justly met with their admiration. Even admitting that no such precaution is really necessary, would it not be advisable to indulge the honest prejudices of many of their fellow citizens? This much, at least, may be said in favor of my plan, that even if it does no good, it can do no possible injury.

I submit it to the candor of the opposers of the new Constitution whether it would not be better to unite in this or some similar plan, than to attempt to defeat the wishes and desires of the continent for an efficient form of government, which is confessedly all that is necessary to restore America to her lost splendor, consequence, credit, and happiness?

Should this hint be attended to and produce the good effect I hope for, I shall esteem it the most fortunate idea that ever occurred to your humble servant, M.C.

1. "M.C." also was printed on the same day in the *Independent Gazetteer, Pennsylvania Journal,* and the *Pennsylvania Packet,* and circulated widely outside the state (CC:203).

2. "Centinel" I, 5 October (II:A above), and II (CC:190); "An Old Whig" I–III (CC:157, 170, 181); "A Democratic Federalist," 17 October (II:C above); and "Cato" I–II (CC:103, 153).

John Humble, Address of the Lowborn, Independent Gazetteer, 29 October[1]

The humble address of the *lowborn* of the United States of America, to their fellow slaves scattered throughout the world—greeting.

Whereas it hath been represented unto us that a most dreadful disease hath for these five years last past infected, preyed upon, and almost ruined the government and people of this our country; and of this malady we ourselves have had perfect demonstration, not mentally, but bodily, through every one of the five senses; for although our sensations in regard to the mind be not just so nice as those of the *wellborn*; yet our feeling, through the medium of the plow, the hoe, and the grubbing axe, is as acute as any nobleman's in the world.

And whereas a number of skilled physicians having met together at Philadelphia last summer for the purpose of exploring and, if possible, removing the cause of this direful disease have, through the assistance of John Adams, Esquire, in the profundity of their great political knowledge, found out and discovered that nothing but a new government consisting of three different branches, namely *king, lords,* and *commons,* or in the American language, *President, Senate,* and *Representatives,* can save this our country from inevitable destruction,

And whereas it hath been reported that several of our *lowborn* brethren have had the horrid audacity to think for themselves in regard to this new system of government, and, *dreadful thought*! have wickedly began to doubt concerning the perfection of this evangelical Constitution, which our political doctors have declared to be a panacea, which (by inspiration) they know will infallibly heal every distemper in the Confederation and finally terminate in the salvation of America.

Now we the *lowborn,* that is, all the people of the United States except 600 or thereabouts *wellborn,* do by this our humble address, declare and most solemnly engage that we will allow and admit the said 600 *wellborn* immediately to establish and confirm this most noble, most excellent and truly divine Constitution. And we further declare that without any equivocation or mental reservation whatever we will support and maintain the same according to the best of our power, and after the manner and custom of all other slaves in foreign countries, namely by the sweat and toil of our body. Nor will we at any future period of time ever attempt to complain of this our *royal* government, let the consequences be what they may. And although it appears to us that a *standing army*, composed of the purgings of the jails of Great Britain, Ireland and Germany, shall be employed in collecting the *revenue* of this our king and government; yet, we again in the most solemn manner declare, that we will abide by our present determination of nonassistance and passive obedience; so that we shall not dare to molest or disturb those military gentlemen in the service of our royal government. And (which is not improbable), should any one of those soldiers when employed on duty in collecting the *taxes*, strike off the arm (with his sword) of one of our *fellow slaves*, we will conceive our case remarkably fortunate if he leaves the other arm on. And moreover because we are aware that many of our fellow slaves shall be unable to pay their *taxes*, and this incapacity of theirs is a just cause of impeachment of treason; wherefore in such cases we will use our utmost endeavors, in conjunction with the *standing army*, to bring such atrocious offenders before our *federal judges*, who shall have power without *jury* or *trial*, to order the said miscreants for immediate execution. Nor will we think their sentence severe unless after being hanged they are also to be both *beheaded* and *quartered*. And finally we shall henceforth and forever leave all *power*, *authority*, and *dominion* over our *persons* and *properties* in the hands of the *wellborn*, who were designed by Province to *govern*. And in regard to the *liberty of the press*, we renounce all claim to it forever more. Amen. And we shall in future be perfectly contented if our *tongues* be left us to lick the feet of our wellborn masters.

Done on behalf of three millions of *lowborn* American slaves. John Humble, secretary.

1. This item was reprinted in the *New York Morning Post* on 14 November and in the *Massachusetts Centinel* on 24 November. For a similar Antifederalist item, see Mfm:Pa. 140.

Gouverneur Morris to George Washington, Philadelphia, 30 October (excerpt)[1]

With respect to this state, I am far from being decided in my opinion, that they will consent. True it is that the city and its neighborhood are enthusiastic in the cause, but I dread the cold and sour temper of the back counties, and still more the wicked industry of those who have long habituated themselves to live on the public, and cannot bear the idea of being removed from the power and profit of state government, which has been and still is the means of supporting themselves, their families, and dependents, and (which perhaps is equally grateful) of depressing and humbling their political adversaries.

1. RC, Washington Papers, DLC (printed CC:213). Shortly after he wrote this letter, Morris and Robert Morris went to Virginia where they remained for several months, reportedly assisting Virginia Federalists (Robert Morris to George Washington, 25 October, Mfm:Pa. 160; William Shippen, Jr. to Thomas Lee Shippen, 18–22 November, II:F below; and Samuel Powel to George Washington, 13 November, CC:255).

Freeman's Journal, 31 October

Extract of a letter from a gentleman in the western country to his friend in this city.

It hath been reported that a number of copies of the proposed Constitution was directed to be printed in the English and German language, to be distributed throughout the state. I wish it were done, that the people might have an opportunity of reading it and judging for themselves. Much time elapses before information can reach the industrious yeomanry of the state that are distant from the seat of government. If a convention is to be chosen, the great body of the people will be ignorant of the plan to be decided upon, and be therefore unable to determine whether they ought to vote for persons who would oppose it or advocate it. If it will bear the examination of the people, who are to be bound thereby, why is such precipitancy used?[1]

1. There is no evidence as to the circulation in the backcountry of copies of the Constitution ordered printed by the Assembly.

Francis Murray to John Nicholson, Newtown, 1 November (excerpt)[1]

I must acknowledge to you that I am greatly changed in regard of my sentiments of the proposed Federal Constitution since I saw you last. And it is in a great measure owing to the Centinel No. 2, the Old Whig No. 2 and 3, and to your pamphlet which I have read; and am well assured that if the election was deferred for four or five weeks longer, a different return for Convention would take place, not only in this county but throughout the states.[2] There is a few of us [who] had a first meeting but have not come to a determination either to run a new ticket (little hopes of carrying of it as the Quakers are entirely in favor of the new Constitution) or entirely to stay at home and not vote.

N.B. I [have] just been reading the fourth letter of the Old Whig

[and] the Democratic Federalist's and am pleased with both and should like something done like the plan proposed by M.C.[3]

1. RC, Nicholson Papers, PHarH. Colonel Francis Murray of Newtown in Bucks County served as county lieutenant in the early 1780s.

2. See "Centinel" II, CC:190; and "An Old Whig" II and III, CC:170, 181. For Nicholson's pamphlet, published on 17 October, see Mfm:Pa. 141. For its circulation and comments about it, see Ebenezer Bowman to Timothy Pickering, 12 November, II:D below; and Mfm:Pa. 141, 413.

3. See "A Democratic Federalist," 17 October, and "M.C.," 27 October, both II:C above; and "An Old Whig" IV, CC:202.

John King to Benjamin Rush, West Conococheague, 5–6 November (excerpt)[1]

A letter from you together with a small pamphlet in answer to the address of the sixteen deserters came to my hand about three days ago, and I have endeavored to make as good use of it as I could.[2] I hope not without some effect. Nothing on that side of the subject had appeared, for so long a time, that we thought there were no Centinels in Philadelphia but the one, and therefore were doing as well as we could for ourselves, both publicly and privately. What may be the consequence, tomorrow will decide.

. . . .

The flames of party blown up by the address and the Centinel have arisen to a great height in this county, tho, I apprehend, not so high as in Cumberland. It is amazing to see how blindly they follow those guides below, and terrify themselves with imaginary evils. The main weight will rest on the lower counties. I fear we will lose the honor of adding a fiat to the excellent Constitution of the United States. November 6. Everything among our people must be seasoned with party, but it is astonishing to think that this great national question should have gotten so entirely involved in it, as it is in this state. I have just returned from the election in [our] district where notwithstanding all the efforts of the Anticons, we have carried, by a considerable majority, John Alison against Abraham Smith.[3] How the matter may turn in the other districts I yet know not.

I hope to hear from you as occasion offers. Our anxiety is great, and will be increased when the Convention meets. I would desire to know their complexion. It will please the Centinel to find some of his party in it which, alas, he had not in the former Convention, when matters underwent only an "*ex parte* discussion." Mr. [John] Montgomery can easily send up a letter by the post any week, who comes to my house, immediately from Carlisle.

1. RC, Rush Papers, PPL. King was pastor of the Presbyterian church at Upper West Conococheague in Franklin County.
2. The reference is to Pelatiah Webster's pamphlet, "A Citizen of Philadelphia," 18 October, CC:125–B.
3. Allison represented Cumberland County in the Assembly from 1780 to 1782 and Franklin County in the Convention, where he voted for ratification. Smith served in the Assembly from 1783 to 1787 and was one of the assemblymen who seceded on 28 September. He was ineligible for reelection to the Assembly in October 1787 and was elected to the Supreme Executive Council.

George Turner to Winthrop Sargent, Philadelphia, 6 November (excerpt)[1]

There are two parties here upon the momentous business now agitating independent America. One party sees nothing but danger and mischief in the proposed Constitution; while the other extols it as a *chef d'oeuvre* in politics. In this case, as in almost every other, there is a middle walk to be trodden, as the directest road to truth. For my part, I like the outlines of the plan, and, being a friend to energy of government, I approve of most of the powers proposed to be given. But, as a friend to the natural rights of man, I must hold up my hand against others. There are certain great and unalienable rights (which I need not enumerate to you) that should have been secured by a declaration or bill of rights. For that sweeping clause [Article VI] (as it has been termed) in the proposed Constitution, which places the authority of Congress over the laws and constitutions of the several states renders, in my opinion, such a declaration an indispensable condition. Mr. [James] Wilson has said that "what is not given is reserved," but I consider this an unfortunate declaration on his part; for the clause alluded to embraces *everything*.[2]

I myself should not fear the operation of the new system; but, to be candid, I should not like to trust it with posterity. As a public creditor, and weighing, like many good citizens, my own private advantage against the public good, I ought to wish for the most speedy adoption of the proposed plan. For tho my opinion of either the faith or gratitude of republics is not the best (an opinion derived from history, and confirmed by *recent facts*), yet payment of my hopeless debt might possibly be obtained sooner under a *real government of any sort,* than one *merely nominal.* But here let you and me pause. It is not fair to tire you with the dull repetition of things which are in everybody's mouth.

P.S. There is the d[evi]l of a scramble in this city of *brotherly love* for the loaves and fishes. Wilson the Lawyer has slipped into the prothonotary's place and Tom Fitzsimons has ousted the celebrated Rittenhouse, the treasurer. *There is a swarm* of office hunters hovering over the secretaryship.[3]

1. RC, Sargent Papers, MHi.
2. Speech in the State House Yard, 6 October, II:A above.
3. Turner crossed out this postscript, probably because the information was incorrect. The incumbent, Jonathan Bayard Smith, defeated James Wilson for the office of prothonotary of the Court of Pleas of the City and County of Philadelphia (Extract of a Letter from Philadelphia, 18 November, *Maryland Journal*, 14 December, II:D below). Thomas FitzSimons did not replace David Rittenhouse as state treasurer. Charles Biddle was elected secretary of the Supreme Executive Council on 7 November (William Shippen, Jr. to Thomas Lee Shippen, 7–24 November, CC:232).

An Officer of the Late Continental Army, Independent Gazetteer, 6 November[1]

Friends, Countrymen, Brethren, and Fellow Citizens: The important day is drawing near when you are to elect delegates to represent you in a convention, on the result of whose deliberations will depend, in a great measure, your future happiness.

This convention is to determine whether or not the Commonwealth of Pennsylvania shall adopt the plan of government proposed by the late Convention of delegates from the different states, which sat in this city.

With a heart full of anxiety for the preservation of your dearest rights, I presume to address you on this important occasion. In the name of sacred liberty, dearer to us than our property and our lives, I request your most earnest attention.

The proposed plan of continental government is now fully known to you. You have read it, I trust, with the attention it deserves. You have heard the objections that have been made to it. You have heard the answers to these objections.

If you have attended to the whole with candor and unbiased minds, as becomes men that are possessed and deserving of freedom, you must have been alarmed at the result of your observations. Notwithstanding the splendor of names which has attended the publication of the new Constitution, notwithstanding the sophistry and vain reasoning that have been urged to support its principles; alas! you must at least have concluded that great men are not always infallible, and that patriotism itself may be led into essential errors.

The objections that have been made to the new Constitution are these:

1. It is not merely (as it ought to be) a CONFEDERATION of STATES, but a GOVERNMENT of INDIVIDUALS.

2. The powers of Congress extend to the *lives,* the *liberties* and the *property* of every citizen.

3. The *sovereignty* of the different states is *ipso facto* destroyed in its most essential parts.

4. What remains of it will only tend to create violent dissensions between the state governments and the Congress, and terminate in the ruin of the one or the other.

5. The consequence must therefore be, either that the *Union* of the states will be destroyed by a violent struggle or that their sovereignty will be swallowed up by silent encroachments into a universal aristocracy; because it is clear, that if two different *sovereign powers* have a coequal command over the *purses* of the citizens, they will struggle for the spoils, and the weakest will be in the end obliged to yield to the efforts of the strongest.

6. Congress being possessed of these immense powers, the liberties of the states and of the people are not secured by a bill or DECLARATION of RIGHTS.

7. The *sovereignty* of the states is not expressly reserved, the *form* only, and not the SUBSTANCE of their government, is guaranteed to them by express words.

8. TRIAL BY JURY, that sacred bulwark of liberty, is ABOLISHED IN CIVIL CASES, and Mr. [James] W[ilson], one of the Convention, has told you, that not being able to agree as to the FORM of establishing this point, they have left you deprived of the SUBSTANCE. Here are his own words: "*The subject was involved in difficulties. The Convention found the task* TOO DIFFICULT *for them, and left the business as it stands.*"[2]

9. THE LIBERTY OF THE PRESS is not secured, and the powers of Congress are fully adequate to its destruction, as they are to have the trial of *libels,* or *pretended libels* against the United States, and may by a cursed abominable STAMP ACT (as the *Bowdoin administration* has done in Massachusetts) preclude you effectually from all means of information.[3] *Mr. W*[ilson] *has given you no answer to these arguments.*

10. Congress have the power of keeping up a STANDING ARMY in time of peace, and Mr. W[ilson] has told you THAT IT WAS NECESSARY.

11. The LEGISLATIVE and EXECUTIVE powers are not kept separate as every one of the American constitutions declares they ought to be; but they are mixed in a manner entirely novel and unknown, even to the constitution of Great Britain; because,

12. In England the king only has a *nominal negative* over the proceedings of the legislature, which he has NEVER DARED TO

EXERCISE since the days of *King William,* whereas by the new Constitution, both the *President General* and the *Senate,* TWO EXECUTIVE BRANCHES OF GOVERNMENT, have that negative and are intended to *support each other in the exercise of it.*

13. The representation of the lower house is too small, consisting only of 65 members.

14. That of the *Senate* is so small that it renders its extensive powers extremely dangerous. It is to consist only of 26 members, two-thirds of whom must concur to conclude any *treaty or alliance* with foreign powers. Now we will suppose that five of them are absent, sick, dead, or unable to attend; *twenty-one* will remain, and eight of these (*one-third,* and *one* over) may prevent the conclusion of any treaty, even the most favorable to America. Here will be a fine field for the intrigues and even the *bribery* and *corruption* of European powers.

15. The most important branches of the EXECUTIVE DEPARTMENT are to be put into the hands of a *single magistrate,* who will be in fact an ELECTIVE KING. The MILITARY, the land and naval forces are to be entirely at his disposal, and therefore:

16. Should the *Senate,* by the intrigues of foreign powers, become devoted to foreign influence, as was the case of late in *Sweden,* the people will be obliged, as the *Swedes* have been, to seek their refuge in the arms of the *monarch* or PRESIDENT GENERAL.

17. ROTATION, that noble prerogative of liberty, is entirely excluded from the new system of government, and great men may and probably will be continued in office during their lives.

18. ANNUAL ELECTIONS are abolished, and the people are not to reassume their rights until the expiration of *two, four* and *six* years.

19. Congress are to have the power of fixing the *time, place* and *manner* of holding elections, so as to keep them forever subjected to their influence.

20. The importation of slaves is not to be prohibited until the year 1808, and SLAVERY will probably resume its empire in Pennsylvania.

21. The MILITIA is to be under the immediate command of Congress, and men *conscientiously scrupulous of bearing arms* may be compelled to perform military duty.

22. The new government will be EXPENSIVE beyond any we have ever experienced, the *judicial* department alone, with its concomitant train of *judges, justices, chancellors, clerks, sheriffs, coroners, escheators, state attornies and solicitors, constables, etc.* in every state and in every county in each state, will be a burden beyond the utmost abilities of the people to bear, and upon the whole.

23. A government partaking of MONARCHY and aristocracy will be fully and firmly established, and liberty will be but a name to adorn the *short* historic page of the halcyon days of America.

These, my countrymen, are the objections that have been made to the new proposed system of government; and if you read the system itself with attention, you will find them all to be founded in truth. But what have you been told in answer?

I pass over the sophistry of Mr. W[ilson], in his equivocal speech at the State House. His pretended arguments have been echoed and reechoed by every retailer of politics, and *victoriously* refuted by several patriotic pens. Indeed if you read this famous speech in a cool dispassionate moment, you will find it to contain no more than a train of pitiful sophistry and evasions, unworthy of the man who spoke them. I have taken notice of some of them in stating the objections, and they must, I am sure, have excited your *pity* and *indignation*. Mr. W[ilson] is a man of sense, learning and extensive information; unfortunately for him he has never sought the more solid fame of *patriotism*. During the late war he narrowly escaped the effects of popular rage, and the people seldom arm themselves against a citizen in vain. The whole tenor of his political conduct has always been strongly tainted with the spirit of *high aristocracy*; he has never been known to join in a truly popular measure, and his talents have ever been devoted to the patrician interest. His lofty carriage indicates the lofty mind that animates him, a mind able to conceive and perform great things, but which unfortunately can see nothing great out of the pale of power and worldly grandeur; despising what he calls the inferior order of the people. Popular liberty and popular assemblies offer to his exalted imagination an idea of meanness and contemptibility which he hardly seeks to conceal. He sees at a distance the pomp and pageantry of courts, he sighs after those stately palaces and that apparatus of human greatness which his vivid fancy has taught him to consider as the supreme good. Men of sublime minds, he conceives, were born a different race from the rest of the sons of men. To them, and them only, he imagines, high heaven intended to commit the reins of earthly government; the remaining part of mankind he sees below at an immense distance; they, he thinks, were born to serve, to administer food to the ambition of their superiors, and become the footstool of their power. Such is Mr. W[ilson], and fraught with these high ideas, it is no wonder that he should exert all his talents to support a form of government so admirably contrived to carry them into execution. But when the people, who possess collectively a mass of knowledge superior to his own, inquire into the principles of that government on the establishment or rejection of which depend their dearest concerns, when he is called upon by the voice of thousands to come and explain that favorite system which he holds forth as an object of their admiration, he comes—he attempts to support by reasoning what reason never dictated, and finding the attempt vain, his great mind, made for nobler purposes, is obliged to stoop to mean evasions and pitiful sophistry. Himself not deceived, he strives to deceive the people, and the treasonable attempt delineates his true character, beyond the reach of the pencil of a *West* or *Peale,* or the pen of a *Valerius.*

And yet that speech, weak and insidious as it is, is the only attempt that has been made to support by argument that political monster THE PROPOSED CONSTITUTION. I have sought in vain amidst the immense heap of trash that has been published on the subject, an argument worthy of refutation, and I have not been able to find it. If you can bear the disgust which the reading of those pieces must naturally occasion, and which I have felt in the highest degree, read them, my fellow citizens, and say whether they contain the least shadow of logical reasoning. Say (laying your hands upon your hearts) whether there is anything in them that can impress unfeigned conviction upon your unprejudiced minds.

One of them only I shall take notice of, in which I find that argument is weakly attempted. This piece is signed "An American Citizen" and has appeared with great pomp in four succeeding numbers in several of our newspapers.[4] But if you read it attentively, you will find that it does not tell us what the new Constitution IS, but what it IS NOT, and extols it on the sole ground that it does not contain ALL the principles of tyranny with which the European governments are disgraced.

But where argument entirely failed, nothing remained for the supporters of the new Constitution but to endeavor to inflame your passions. The attempt has been made and I am sorry to find not entirely without effect. The great names of WASHINGTON and FRANKLIN have been taken in vain and shockingly prostituted to effect the most infamous purposes. What! because our august chieftain has subscribed his name in his capacity of President of the Convention to the plan offered by them to the states, and because the venerable sage of Pennsylvania has *testified* by his signature that *the majority of the delegates of this state* assented to the same plan, will anyone infer from this that it has met with their entire approbation, and that they consider it as the masterpiece of human wisdom? I am apt to think the contrary, and I have good reasons to ground my opinion on.

In the first place we have found by the publication of *Charles Cotesworth Pinckney,* Esquire, one of the *signing* members of the Convention, who has expressed the most pointed disapprobation of many important parts of the new plan of government, that all the members whose names appear at the bottom of this instrument of tyranny have not concurred in its adoption.[5] Many of them might conceive themselves bound by the opinion of the majority of their state, and leaving the people to their own judgment upon the form of government offered to them, might have conceived it impolitic by refusing to sign their names, to offer to the world the lamentable spectacle of the disunion of a body on the decisions of whom the people had rested all their hopes. We KNOW, and the long sitting of the Convention tells us, that (as it is endeavored to persuade us) concord and unanimity did not reign exclusively among them. The thick veil of secrecy with which their proceedings have been covered has left us entirely in the dark, as to the *debates* that took place, and the unaccountable SUPPRESSION OF THEIR JOURNALS, the highest insult that could be offered to the majesty of the people, shows clearly that the whole of the new plan was entirely the work of an *aristocratic majority.*

But let us suppose for a moment that the proposed government was the unanimous result of the deliberations of the Convention—must it on that account preclude an investigation of its merits? Are the people to be dictated to without appeal by any set of men, however great, however dignified? Freedom spurns at the idea and rejects it with disdain. We appeal to the collective wisdom of a great nation, we appeal to their general sense which is easily to be obtained through the channel of a multitude of free presses, from the opinions of *thirty-nine* men, who secluded from the rest of the world, without the possibility of conferring with the rest of their fellow citizens, have had no opportunity of rectifying the errors into which they may have been led by the *most designing* among them. We have seen names not less illustrious than those of the members of the late Convention subscribed to the present *reprobated* Articles of Confederation, and if those patriots have erred, there is no reason to suppose that a succeeding set should be more free from error. Nay the very men, who advocate so strongly the new plan of government, and support it with the infallibility of Doctor Franklin, affect to despise the present constitution of Pennsylvania, which was dictated and avowed by that venerable patriot. They are conscious that he does not entirely approve of the new plan, whose principles are so different from those he has established in our ever-glorious constitution, and there is no doubt that it is the reason that has induced them to leave his respected name out of the *ticket* for the approaching election.

Now then my fellow citizens, my brethren, my friends; if the sacred flame of liberty be not extinguished in your breasts, if you have any regard for the happiness of yourselves, and your posterity, let me entreat you, earnestly entreat you by all that is dear and sacred to freemen, to consider well before you take an awful step which may involve in its consequences the ruin of millions yet unborn. You are on the brink of a dreadful precipice; in the name therefore of holy liberty, for which I have fought and for which we have all suffered, I call upon you to make a solemn pause before you proceed. One step more, and perhaps the scene of freedom is closed forever in America. Let not a set of aspiring despots, *who make us* SLAVES and *tell us tis our* CHARTER, wrest from you those invaluable blessings, for which the most illustrious sons of America have bled and died; but exert yourselves, like men, like freemen and like Americans, to transmit unimpaired to your latest posterity those rights, those liberties, which have ever been so dear to you, and which it is yet in your power to preserve.

1. This essay, dated "Philadelphia, November 3, 1787" and addressed "To the Citizens of Philadelphia," was allegedly written by William Findley, a member of the Assembly. It was reprinted in the *Freeman's Journal,* 7 November and the November *American Museum,* and published as a broadside (CC:231 A–B for circulation outside Pennsylvania and its authorship). For replies to "An Officer," see "Plain Truth," printed immediately below, and Mfm:Pa. 208, 212, 226.

2. Speech in the State House Yard, 6 October, II:A above.

3. In March 1785 the Massachusetts legislature passed a "stamp act" levying duties on legal documents, commercial papers, newspapers, and almanacs.

4. See "An American Citizen" I–III, 26–29 September, II:A above; and "An American Citizen" IV, CC: 183–A.

5. Charles Pinckney, not Charles Cotesworth Pinckney, wrote *Observations on the Plan of Government Submitted to the Federal Convention, in Philadelphia* (CC:166). Excerpts from it were reprinted in the *Pennsylvania Gazette,* 24 October.

Plain Truth: Reply to An Officer of the Late Continental Army, Independent Gazetteer, 10 November[1]

Friend Oswald, Seeing in thy paper of yesterday, twenty-three objections to the new plan of federal government, I am induced to trouble the public once more; and shall endeavor to answer them distinctly and concisely. That this may be done with candor, as well as perspicuity, I request thee to reprint them as they are stated by *"An Officer of the Late Continental Army,"* and to place my answers in the same order.

I shall pass over everything that is not in point, and leave the strictures on friend [James] W[ilson] to those who are acquainted with him. I will only observe that "his lofty carriage," is very likely to be the effect of habit; for I know by experience that a man who wears spectacles must keep his head erect to see through them with ease and to prevent them from falling off his nose.

Now for the objections.

"1. It is not merely (as it ought to be) a CONFEDERATION of STATES, but a GOVERNMENT of INDIVIDUALS."

Answer 1. It is more a government *of the people,* than the present Congress ever was, because, the members of Congress have been hitherto chosen by the legislatures of the several states. The proposed Representatives are to be chosen "BY THE PEOPLE." If therefore it be not a confederation of *the states,* it is a popular compact, something more in favor of liberty. (Article I, section 2.)

"2. The powers of Congress extend to the *lives,* the *liberties* and the *property* of every citizen."

2. Is there a government on earth where the life, liberty and property of a citizen may not be forfeited by a violation of the laws of God and man? It is only when justified by such crimes, that the new government has such power; and all crimes (except in cases of impeachment) are expressly to be TRIED BY JURY, *in the state where they may be committed.* (Article 3, section 2.)

"3. The *sovereignty* of the different states is *ipso facto* destroyed in its most essential parts."

3. Can the sovereignty of each state in all its parts exist, if there be a sovereignty over the whole? Is it not nonsense in terms to suppose an united government *of any kind* over 13 coexistent sovereignties? "It is obviously impracticable in the federal government of these states, to secure all the rights of independent sovereignty to each, and yet provide for the interest and safety of all." (President's letter.)[2]

"4. What remains of it will only tend to create violent dissensions between the state governments and the Congress, and terminate in the ruin of the one or the other."

4. No such dissension can happen unless some state oppose the interests of the whole collectively; and it is to overcome such opposition by a majority of 12 to 1, "to ensure domestic tranquility, to provide for the common defence, promote the general welfare, and secure the blessings of liberty," that the Union is now, and has ever been thought indispensable. (Introduction to the new plan.)

"5. The consequence must therefore be, either that the *Union* of the states will be destroyed by a violent struggle or that their sovereignty will be swallowed up by silent encroachments into a universal aristocracy; because it is clear that if two different *sovereign powers* have a coequal command over the *purses* of the citizens, they will struggle for the spoils, and the weakest will be in the end obliged to yield to the efforts of the strongest."

5. The preceding petition being eradicated, this *consequence* falls to the ground. It may be observed, however, that the revenue to be raised by Congress is not likely to interfere with the taxes of any state. Commerce is the source to which they will naturally apply, because that is one great and uniform object, and they cannot attend to detail. The burden too will, in this way, be scarcely felt by the people. All foreigners who may sell merchandise at a loss (and that often has been, and often will be the case in an extensive degree) will pay the impost in addition to that loss, and the duties on all that may be sold at a profit will be eventually paid by the consumers. Thus the taxes will be insensibly included in the price, and every man will have the power of refusal by not consuming the taxed luxuries.

"6. Congress being possessed of these immense powers, the liberties of the states and of the people are not secured by a bill or DECLARATION of RIGHTS."

6. Notwithstanding all that has been written against it, I must recur to friend W[ilson]'s definition on this subject. A state government is designed for ALL CASES WHATSOEVER, consequently what is not reserved is tacitly given. A federal government is expressly only for FEDERAL PURPOSES, and its power is consequently bounded by the terms of the compact. In the first case a bill of rights is indispensable, in the second it would be at best useless, and if one right were to be omitted, it might injuriously grant, by implication, what was intended to be reserved.

"7. The *sovereignty* of the states is not expressly reserved, the *form* only, and not the SUBSTANCE of their government, is guaranteed to them by express words."

7. When man emerged from a state of nature, he surely did not reserve the natural right of being the judge of his wrongs and the executioner of the punishments he might think they deserved. A renunciation of such rights is the price he paid for the blessings of good government; and for the same reason, state sovereignty (as I have before observed) is as incompatible with the federal Union, as the natural rights of human vengeance is with the peace of society.

"The United States shall guarantee to every state, a republican form of government." That is, they shall guarantee it against monarchical or aristocratical encroachments. Congress can go no further, for the states would justly think themselves insulted, if they should presume to interfere in other alterations which may be individually thought more consistent with the good of the people. (Article 4, section 4.)

"8. TRIAL BY JURY, that sacred bulwark of liberty, is ABOLISHED IN CIVIL CASES, and Mr. [James] W[ilson], one of the Convention, has told you, that not being able to agree as to the FORM of establishing this point, they have left you deprived of the SUBSTANCE.[3] Here is his own words: *'The subject was involved in difficulties. The Convention found the task* TOO DIFFICULT *for them, and left the business as it stands.'* "

8. Trial by jury has been seen to be expressly preserved in criminal cases. In civil cases, the federal court is like a court of chancery, except that it has original jurisdiction only in state affairs; in all other matters it has "appellate jurisdiction both as to law and fact, *with such exceptions and under such regulations as congress shall make.*" (Article 3, section 2.) Nobody ever complained that trials in chancery were not by jury. A court of chancery "may issue injunctions in various stages of a cause," saith Blackstone, "and stay oppressive judgment." Yet courts of chancery are everywhere extolled as the most equitable; the federal court has not such an extent of power, and what it has is to be always under the *exceptions and regulations of the United States in Congress.*

Friend W[ilson] has well observed that it was impossible to make one imitation of thirteen different models, and the matter seems now to stand, as well as human wisdom can permit.

"9. THE LIBERTY OF THE PRESS is not secured, and the powers of Congress are fully adequate to its destruction, as they are to have the trial of *libels,* or *pretended libels* against the United States, and may by a cursed abominable STAMP ACT (as the *Bowdoin administration* has done in Massachusetts) preclude you effectually from all means of information. *Mr. W*[ilson] *has given you no answer to these arguments.*"

9. The liberty of the press in each state can only be in danger from the laws of that state, and it is everywhere well secured. Besides, as the new Congress can only have the defined powers given, it was needless to say anything about liberty of the press, liberty of conscience, or any other liberty that a freeman ought never to be deprived of. It is remarkable in this instance, that among all the cases to which the federal jurisdiction is to extend (Article 3) not a word is said of *"libels or pretended libels."* Indeed in this extensive continent, and among this enlightened people, no government whatever *could* control the press. For after all that is said about "balance of power," there is one power which no tyranny on earth

could subdue if once roused by this great and general grievances, that is THE PEOPLE. This respectable power has preserved the press in Great Britain in spite of government; and none but a madman could ever think of controlling it in America.

"10. Congress have the power of keeping up a STANDING ARMY in time of peace, and Mr. W[ilson] has told you THAT IT IS NECESSARY."

10. The power here referred to is this, "to raise and support armies, *but no appropriation of money to that use shall be for a longer term than two years."* (Article I, section 8.) Thus the representatives of the people have it in their power to disband this army every two years, by refusing supplies. Does not every American feel that no standing army in the power of Congress to raise, could support despotism over this immense continent, where almost every citizen is a soldier? If such an apprehension came, in my opinion, within the bounds of possibility, it would not indeed become my principles to oppose this objection.

"11. The LEGISLATIVE and EXECUTIVE powers are not kept separate [as] every one of the American constitutions declares they ought to be; but they are mixed in a manner entirely novel and unknown, even to the constitution of Great Britain."

11. The first Article of the Constitution defines the legislative, the second, the executive, and the third the judicial powers; this does not seem like *mixing* them. It would be strange indeed if a professed democratist should object, that the President's power is made subject to "the advice and consent of two-thirds of the senate." (Article 2, section 2.)

"12. In England, the king only has a *nominal negative* over the proceedings of the legislature, which he has NEVER DARED TO EXERCISE since the days of *King William,* whereas by the new Constitution, both the *President General* and the *Senate,* TWO EXECUTIVE BRANCHES OF GOVERNMENT, have that negative and are intended to *support each other in the exercise of it."*

12. Whoever will read the 7th section of the 4th Article, will see that the President has only a *conditional* negative, which is effectual or not as two-thirds of the Senate and two-thirds of the Representatives may on reconsideration determine. If the *"two executive branches"* (as they are here called) should agree in the negative, it would not be novel, as to the power of the Senate; for I believe every senate on the continent, and every upper house in the world, may refuse concurrence and quash a bill before it arrives at the executive department. The king of England has an *unconditional* negative, and has often exercised it in his former colonies.

"13. The representation of the lower house is too small, consisting only of 65 members."

13. The Congress on the old plan had but 13 voices, and of these, some were frequently lost by equal divisions. If 65 voices be yet too few, it must follow that the new plan has made some progress towards perfection.

"14. That of the *Senate* is so small that it renders its extensive powers extremely dangerous. It is to consist only of 26 members, two-thirds of whom must concur to conclude any *treaty or alliance* with foreign powers. Now we will suppose that five of them are absent, sick, dead, or unable to attend; *twenty-one* will remain, and eight of these (*one-third* and *one* over) may prevent the conclusion of any treaty, even the most favorable to America. Here will be a fine field for the intrigues and even the *bribery* and *corruption* of European powers."

14. This like the former objection is mere matter of opinion. The instance as to supposed vacancies does not apply, for "if vacancies happen by resignation *or otherwise* during the recess of the legislature of any state, the executive thereof may make temporary appointments until the meeting of the legislature which shall then fill such vacancies." (Article I, section 3.) This provision expressly implies that accidental vacancies shall be *immediately* filled.

"15. The most important branches of the EXECUTIVE DEPARTMENT are to be put into the hands of a *single magistrate,* who will be in fact an ELECTIVE KING. The MILITARY, the land and naval forces are to be entirely at his disposal."

15. It was mentioned as a grievance in the 12th objection that this supposed "elective king," had his powers clogged by the conjunction of another branch; here he is called a *"single magistrate."* Yet the new Constitution provides that he shall act "by and with the advice and consent of the senate" (Article 2, section 2), and can in no instance act alone, except in the cause of humanity by granting reprieves or pardons.

"16. Should the *Senate,* by the intrigues of foreign powers, become devoted to foreign influence, as was the case of late in *Sweden,* the people will be obliged, as the *Swedes* have been, to seek their refuge in the arms of the *monarch* or PRESIDENT GENERAL."

16. The comparison of a little kingdom to a great republic cannot be just. The revolution in Sweden was the affair of a day, and the success of it was owing to its confined bounds. To suppose a similar event in this extensive country, 3000 miles distant from European intrigues, is, in the nature of things, a gross absurdity.

"17. ROTATION, that noble prerogative of liberty, is entirely excluded from the new system of government, and great men may and probably will be continued in office during their lives."

17. How can this be the case, when at stated periods the government reverts to the people, and to the representatives of the people, for a new choice in every part of it.

"18. ANNUAL ELECTIONS are abolished, and the people are not to reassume their rights until the expiration of *two, four* and *six* years."

18. Annual changes in a federal government would beget confusion; it requires years to learn a trade, and men in this age are not legislators by inspiration. One-third of the Senate as well as all the Representatives are to be elected every *two* years. (Article I, section 3.)

"19. Congress are to have the power to fixing the *time, place* and *manner* of holding elections, so as to keep them forever subjected to their influence."

19. Congress are not to have power to fix the place of choosing Senators; and the time, place, and manner of electing Representatives are to be fixed by each state itself. Congress indeed are to have control to prevent undue influence in elections, which we all know but too often happens through party zeal. (Article I, section 4.)

"20. The importation of slaves is not to be prohibited until the year 1808, and SLAVERY will probably resume its empire in Pennsylvania."

20. This is fully answered in my letter to Timothy,[4] but it may not be amiss to repeat that Congress will have no power to meddle in the business til 1808. All that can be said against this offending clause is, that we may have no alteration in this respect for 21 years to come, but 21 years is fixed as a period when we may be better, and in the meantime we cannot be worse than we are now. (Article I, section 9.)

"21. The MILITIA is to be under the immediate command of Congress, and men *conscientiously scrupulous of bearing arms* may be compelled to perform military duty."

21. Congress may "provide for *calling forth* the militia, and may provide for organizing, arming and disciplining it." But the states respectively can only *raise it,* and they expressly reserve the right of "appointment of officers and of training it." Now we know that men conscientiously scrupulous by sect or profession are not *forced* to bear arms in any of the states, a pecuniary compensation being accepted in lieu of it. Whatever may be my sentiments on the present state of this matter is foreign to the point. But it is certain that whatever redress may be wished for, or expected, can only come from *the state legislature,* where, and where only, the dispensing power, or enforcing power, is *in the first instance* placed. (Article [I], section 8.)

"22. The new government will be EXPENSIVE beyond any we have ever experienced, the *judicial* department alone, with its concomitant train of *judges, justices, chancellors, clerks, sheriffs, coroners, escheators, state attornies and solicitors, constables, etc.* in every state and in every county in each state, will be a burden beyond the utmost abilities of the people to bear."

22. This mighty expense would be paid by about one shilling a man throughout the states. The other part of this objection is not intelligible, nothing is said in the new Constitution of a judicial department in *"states* and *counties,"* other than what is already established.

"23. A government partaking of MONARCHY and aristocracy will be fully and firmly established, and liberty will be but a name to adorn the *short* historic page of the halcyon days of America."

23. The 5th Article expressly provides against every danger, by pointing out a mode of amendment when necessary. And liberty will thus be a name to adorn the *long* historic page of American virtue and happiness.

Thus I have answered all the objections, and supported my answers by fair quotations from the new Constitution; and I particularly desire my readers to examine all the references with accurate attention. If I have mistaken any part, it will, I trust, be found to be an error of judgment, not of will, and I shall thankfully receive any candid instruction on the subject. One quotation more and I have done. "In all our deliberations on this subject (saith GEORGE WASHINGTON) we kept steadily in our view, that which appears to us the greatest interest of every true American, the consolidation of our Union, in which is involved our prosperity, felicity, safety, perhaps our national existence. This important consideration, seriously and deeply impressed on our minds, led each state in the Convention to be less rigid on points of inferior magnitude, than might have been otherwise expected; and thus the Constitution which we now present, is the result of a spirit of amity, and of that mutual deference and concession which the peculiarity of our political situation rendered indispensable."[5]

1. This reply, dated "Philadelphia, November 7, 1787," was reprinted in the *Carlisle Gazette,* 21 and 28 November, and in the November *American Museum* (CC:231–B for national circulation).

2. The President of the Convention to the President of Congress, 17 September 1787 (CDR:VIII, A).

3. Speech in the State House Yard, 6 October, II A above.

4. For the debate over the slave trade clause which took place between "Plain Truth" and "Timothy Meanwell" in the *Independent Gazetteer* from 29 October to 7 November, see CC:Vol. II, Appendix.

5. See note 2 above.

D. THE ELECTION OF CONVENTION DELEGATES 6 November 1787

Federalists and Antifederalists campaigned strenuously. They wrote innumerable newspaper articles as well as some broadsides and pamphlets. Most of the items did not refer specifically to the election. Instead, writers continued to attack opposing leaders and their positions on the Constitution, and so too did the meetings held to nominate slates of candidates. On 22 October, a Northampton County Federalist meeting voiced strong support of the Constitution and attacked the assemblymen who had seceded from the previous Assembly (II:D below). In Philadelphia, some leading Federalists required candidates to commit themselves to vote for the Constitution before placing their names on the Federalist ticket (*Pennsylvania Herald,* 7 November and William Shippen, Jr. to Thomas Lee Shippen, 7–18 November, both II:D below).

As most political observers predicted, a large majority of the Convention delegates elected on 6 November supported the Constitution. James Madison reported from New York that he had been informed that the delegates elected "reduced the adoption of the plan in that state to absolute certainty and by a greater majority than the most sanguine advocates had calculated" (to Edmund Randolph, 18 November, CC:270). On 21 November, the second day of the Convention, the *Pennsylvania Gazette* estimated that two-thirds of the members were Federalists (Mfm:Pa. 235).

Despite the Federalist victory, Antifederalists were heartened by the election of some of their principal leaders, and later two Antifederalist newspapers declared that more votes were cast for Antifederalist than for Federalist candidates (*Independent Gazetteer* and *Freeman's Journal,* 5 December, both II:D below).

Only four assemblymen were elected to the Convention, but all were Antifederalist leaders and all voted against ratification. They were Joseph Powell of Bedford and Robert Whitehill of Cumberland counties who had been members of the 11th Assembly, and Joseph Hiester of Berks and William Findley of Westmoreland counties who had been members of the 11th Assembly and were reelected to the 12th Assembly on 9 October.

Three members of the Supreme Executive Council whose terms expired on 8 October were elected to the Convention. They were William Brown of Dauphin, Jonathan Hoge of Cumberland, and John Whitehill of Lancaster counties. John Baird of Westmoreland and John Smilie of Fayette counties were reelected to the Council on 9 October and elected to the Convention. All five men were Antifederalists and all voted against ratification.

No Federalist assemblymen or councillors were elected to the Convention, apparently as a result of deliberate Federalist policy. They claimed that their oaths as assemblymen and councillors to support the state constitution made it improper for them to vote on a Constitution which would abridge the powers of the state government (see "Squibs from the *Pennsylvania Gazette,*" 17 October, II:C above, and "A Marylander," 4 December, II:D below). James Wilson was the only Pennsylvania delegate to the Constitutional Convention elected to the state Convention.

The partisan nature of the election was illustrated by a riot in Philadelphia. At midnight on election night a mob attacked the houses of several Philadelphia Antifederalist leaders and Major Alexander Boyd's boarding house, where western assemblymen and councillors were lodged. On 9 November the Supreme Executive Council directed that a proclamation be issued requiring judges, justices of the peace, and other law enforcement officers to do all in their power to apprehend and punish the rioters. The next day the General Assembly voted to ask the Council to offer a reward for their capture. However, the Federalist assemblymen defeated a resolution asking the Council to direct the attorney general to prosecute the rioters. On 12 November the Council issued a proclamation offering a $300 reward, but no rioters were apprehended.

A short time later, James Wilson was accused of fomenting the riot ("Plain Truth," 24 November, II:F below), a charge echoed by an Antifederalist partisan, "The Scourge," in January 1788 (IV:B below). The same month another writer charged that the Federalists had employed British sailors "to raise a riot" (Mfm:Pa. 378).

No Pennsylvania newspaper ever published an account of the riot, although some newspapers reported the Assembly's proceedings on 10 November concerning it and printed the Council's proclamation of 12 November.

Philadelphia City and County Nomination Tickets, 13 October–3 November

Philadelphia County and City Election Notice, 13 October[1]

Public notice is hereby given, to the freemen of the city and county of Philadelphia,

That in obedience to a resolve of the General Assembly of the State of Pennsylvania of the 29th day of September last to choose suitable persons to serve as deputies in a convention on the Federal Constitution,

A general election is to be held for the city and county aforesaid, on Tuesday the sixth day of November next, for the purpose aforesaid and at the several places in the said city and county as are fixed by law for holding the elections of representatives to the General Assembly, and that said election is to be conducted by the officers who conducted the last general election and agreeable to the rules and regulations thereof, and at which places the electors of the city and county are to choose five persons for the city, and five persons for the county, to serve in a state convention.

Pennsylvania Herald, 31 October[2]

We have been informed that the following tickets will be proposed at the ensuing election for delegates to the state Convention [for the city of Philadelphia]. By the Republicans—Thomas McKean, James Wilson, Benjamin Rush, George Latimer, and Hilary Baker. By the Constitutionalists—Benjamin Franklin, Thomas McKean, David Rittenhouse, Charles Pettit, and George Schlosser.

Philadelphia County Meeting, 2 November[3]

At a meeting of a respectable number of the inhabitants of the county of Philadelphia, at the house of William Lesher in Germantown, on Friday the second of November, agreeably to notice in the public papers, for the purpose of nominating five suitable persons to serve in the ensuing Convention, the following gentlemen were chosen, viz., John Hunn, George Gray, Senior, William M'Pherson, Enoch Edwards, Samuel Ashmead.

Pennsylvania Herald, 3 November[4]

A correspondent is happy to observe that Dr. Franklin is in the list of persons proposed for the state Convention, since it is thought necessary to introduce a member of the Federal Convention to explain the new plan of government. His worth as a patriot and his wisdom as a politician entitle him to that distinction and as he enjoys the *unbounded confidence* of his fellow citizens, it is hoped that no personal consideration will induce him to waive this important service, at so critical a juncture.

City of Philadelphia Meeting, 3 November

At a very numerous meeting of the freemen of the city of Philadelphia at the State House, on Saturday evening the 3d instant, the following ticket was agreed on for the election, to be held this day, for the members of the ensuing state Convention: THOMAS M'KEAN, JAMES WILSON, BENJAMIN RUSH, HILARY BAKER, GEORGE LATIMER.

The most remarkable unanimity appeared on the occasion, not one name being offered to the meeting in opposition. The gentlemen in nomination had previously, and have since, declared their conviction that it is necessary for the safety, happiness, and preservation of liberty and good government of the United States, that the plan of *federal government,* as proposed by the late Honorable Convention, should be adopted without alteration or delay.[5]

* * * *

At a meeting of the friends to the new Constitution held at the State House on Saturday last, Mr. [William?] Jackson, Mr. [Thomas] Fitzsimons, and several other gentlemen were appointed to wait upon the five persons fixed on as delegates to the state Convention and to demand, categorically, "whether they would support and adopt the proposed plan of government in all its parts, without alteration or amendment," and unless they respectively declared in the affirmative, it was resolved to call another meeting to supply the place of such as hesitated or dissented. Colonel [Francis] Gurney informed the meeting that Mr. [Thomas] M'Kean had already unequivocally asserted to several gentlemen, who inquired his sentiments with a view to the present election, that he approved of the new plan of government and would support it in all its parts without alteration or amendment.[6]

1. *Pennsylvania Journal,* 17 October. The notice, also printed the same day in the *Independent Gazetteer,* the *Pennsylvania Gazette,* and the *Pennsylvania Packet,* was dated "Philadelphia, October 13th, 1787" and signed "Joseph Cowperthwait, Sheriff." It was reprinted many times before election day.

2. The *Independent Gazetteer* of 1 November and the *Pennsylvania Journal* of 3 November reprinted this item, while the *Evening Chronicle* of 3 November reprinted only the names of the Constitutionalist ticket. All the Republicans were elected and voted for ratification. For an earlier discussion of the Republican ticket, see Tench Coxe to James Madison, 21 October, II:C above.

3. *Independent Gazetteer,* 5 November. Beginning on 23 October the *Gazetteer, Pennsylvania Gazette,* and *Pennsylvania Packet* published notices calling this meeting. All five "gentlemen" were elected and voted for ratification.

4. This item was also printed in the *Evening Chronicle* on the same day, and in the *Independent Gazetteer* and *Pennsylvania Packet* on 5 November. Outside Pennsylvania it was reprinted fourteen times from New Hampshire to South Carolina by 4 December.

5. This account is from the *Independent Gazetteer,* 6 November.

6. This account is from the *Pennsylvania Herald,* 7 November. The *Evening Chronicle* also printed this item on the same day. Outside Pennsylvania it was reprinted eight times from New Hampshire to South Carolina by 29 November. For Antifederalist comments about McKean's promise, see William Shippen, Jr. to Thomas Lee Shippen, 7–18 November, II:D below; Tench Coxe to James Madison, 21 October, II:C above; and Mfm:Pa. 190.

Cumberland County Nominations, 13–25 October

Ephraim Blaine to Benjamin Rush, Carlisle, 15 October (excerpt)[1]

I have no news worth communicating, only our Stoney Ridge Convention have formed a ticket for our members of Convention, a majority of which I fear will be against federal measures.

Carlisle Meeting, 22 October[2]

On Monday evening last a number of the inhabitants of Carlisle met at Mr. [Joseph R.] Postlethwait's tavern, when it being agreed that, as many freeholders from several parts of the county [Cumberland] will necessarily attend in the town during the court, it would be the most proper time for calling a general meeting and taking the sense of the people at the present important crisis respecting the new federal government. Therefore, the freeholders and other electors of this county are requested to meet at the courthouse, tomorrow [25 October] at half an hour after eight o'clock in the morning, in order that a proper ticket may be formed for members of the state Convention.

Cumberland County Meeting, 25 October[3]

In pursuance of notice published in our last paper, a respectable number of the inhabitants of this county met at the courthouse, on Thursday last, in order to form a ticket of members for the ensuing state Convention. Major General [John] Armstrong, being unanimously chosen chairman, opened the business of the meeting and, in a short but animated address, exhorted us to unite and act as one man for the public good at the present most important crisis; and assured us that a cool dispassionate temper of mind and a determination to consider the good of our country, as infinitely to be preferred to the narrow interests of party, were absolutely necessary to enable us to act such a part as we can reflect upon with satisfaction, and for which we may be held in respect by our fellow citizens.

A committee was then chosen, consisting of three members from each township present, to name proper persons to represent this county in the ensuing state Convention. This committee agreed to meet at Mr. Semple's tavern the same evening.

At the hour appointed, a number of gentlemen from different townships met accordingly and proceeded to the choice of four gentlemen to represent this county in the ensuing state Convention—

when a majority agreed to recommend the following gentlemen to their respective townships, viz., John Harris, Esquire; Jonathan Hoge, Esquire; William Brown, Esquire, Juniata [Dauphin County]; John Reynolds, Esquire.[4]

1. RC, Rush Papers, PPL. The Antifederalist Stoney Ridge Convention, held on or before 13 October, nominated Robert Whitehill, Jonathan Hoge, and John Harris (John Montgomery to William Irvine, 9–13 October and n. 2, II:B above). Stoney Ridge was in East Pennsboro township, about six miles east of Carlisle, and was probably on or near Robert Whitehill's estate. Whitehill was known as "the country member from Stoney Ridge."

2. *Carlisle Gazette,* 24 October.

3. Ibid., 31 October.

4. Harris, Hoge, and Reynolds were elected, along with Robert Whitehill, and all voted against ratification. William Brown of Juniata was elected from Dauphin County and voted against ratification.

Northampton County Nominations, 22 October[1]

At a meeting of sundry respectable inhabitants of the county of Northampton, held at Bethlehem, October 22d 1787, for to agree upon the nomination of persons, to be returned, to serve in the state Convention, as appointed by the Honorable House of Assembly; and to support such nomination at the election for that purpose.

Peter Rhoads, Esquire was unanimously chosen chairman.

The business of the meeting was opened by the chairman, and the Constitution of the United States, as formed by the late Convention, being read, the following resolutions were unanimously entered into:

Resolved, That this meeting do most warmly and cordially approve of the said Constitution, and that they esteem it the only salvation of this country, on which the existence of the United States of America, as a people, depends.

Resolved, That this meeting entertain the highest sense of the public virtue and patriotism of the majority of the House of Assembly, in calling immediately a convention of this state in pursuance of the recommendation of the Federal Convention.

Resolved, That it is the opinion of this meeting that the withdrawing or absenting of any member of Assembly, who was sworn to serve his country to the best of his abilities, tends to subvert all order and the fundamental principles of good government and establishes precedents of aristocratic powers, for a minority, to defeat the proceedings of a majority.

Resolved, That this meeting nominate four persons, proposed by a committee, appointed for that purpose, as candidates, for to serve in the said state Convention, and that each person present engages to support this ticket at the ensuing election and, as much as in him lieth, to prevent all fraud and deceit at the said election.

Resolved, That each of the candidates, nominated as aforesaid, do make public declaration before this meeting that if it should be his lot to be elected as member of the said Convention, he will use his utmost endeavors that the said Constitution be ratified.

And the said four candidates accordingly severally made the said declaration before this meeting.

Resolved, That the chairman sign these resolves, and that the same be printed and published.

1. *Independent Gazetteer,* 26 October. The resolves were signed: "Peter Rhoads, Chairman." Rhoads had been a member of the Pennsylvania constitutional convention of 1776 and of the Assembly from 1777 to 1781. This item was reprinted six times in Pennsylvania and once in New Jersey by 7 November. The nomination ticket has not been located, but it probably consisted of John Arndt, Stephen Balliot, David Deshler, and Joseph Horsfield. All were elected and all voted to ratify. For the nomination of Balliot, see Alexander Patterson to Charles Stewart, 10 November, Mfm:Pa. 214.

Chester County Nominations, 24 October–1 November

Agricola, To the Freemen of Chester County, 24 October[1]

Permit a person whose interests are inseparable with your own to advise you on the subject of the approaching election for deputies to the Convention. You are perhaps generally acquainted that at the late county meeting convened at the courthouse [6 October], for the purpose of forming a ticket for persons to represent you in Assembly, the object of the meeting having been accomplished, General [Anthony] Wayne, who presided as chairman, suggested the expediency of forming a ticket for deputies to the Convention to obviate the necessity of calling the people together at a future day. This proposition obtained the unanimous concurrence of the meeting, and the committees previously nominated from each of the districts composing the county were ordered to prepare a ticket for the conventional election, which they did and presented the following ticket to the chair, viz., *Anthony Wayne, William Gibbons, Thomas Bull, John Hannum, Richard Downing,* Jr. and *Thomas Cheney,* whose names were separately offered to the meeting at large for their approbation, which was I believe unanimously assented to.[2] I would not wish to flatter the gentlemen who compose this ticket, nor detract from the merits of any other gentleman in the county, when I assert that a better ticket could not have been formed, nor persons at this crisis found more worthy of your confidence. That this sentiment is prevalent in the county I believe no person will deny, which presages that unanimity which has hitherto characterized the friends of equal liberty and crowned their efforts with success. But, my friends, the Antifederal junto of East Whiteland, leagued with some others of the same political creed in the county, have issued an advertisement requesting you to attend at the close of the Supreme Court to form a ticket, or rather to undo what has been already done, hoping at least to produce some division, and knowing full well that their numbers are too insignificant to effect anything without previously disseminating divisions among you. There is this consolation to be drawn, that when the county at large comes to be possessed of the knowledge from whence the advertisement alluded to originated, they will treat it with that contempt it deserves. That Judas-like complacence and electioneering indifference which pervaded the Antifederal junto, at the late election, was only a prelude to the vigorous exertions they intend making on the day of election to defeat the ticket already formed. That you may evince to the world on the day of election that you are not to be made dupes by any daemon of discord is the fervent desire of AGRICOLA. Chester County, October 21, 1787.

A Friend to Efficient Government, To the People of Chester County, 31 October[3]

A writer in Hall and Sellers' paper of the 24th inst., under the signature of Agricola, addresses you on the subject of the ensuing election for deputies to the state Convention, and blames the people of East Whiteland for publishing an advertisement desiring you to meet during the sitting of the Supreme Court to form a ticket against the said election. No inhabitant of East Whiteland or Antifederalist was concerned in framing the advertisement complained of. The writers were actuated by the purest motives and a wish to lend a helping hand to establish an efficient government in the United States. But it would seem that Agricola and his coadjutors have kindly saved you the trouble of meeting by making a ticket previous to the late general election without apprising you of such business being intended, and speaks of committees being previously nominated for each of the districts composing the county, when, in fact, no persons were authorized by all the districts to attend. One, I know, made no nomination, and if it had, would not have sent such men as presumed to represent it.

I am as far removed from flattery or detraction as Agricola, and highly esteem some of the persons proposed, but I know the county is not so barren as to be obliged to make use of either of their names in forming a ticket at least equal, and I think superior, and one in which you may repose full confidence. That Judas-like complacence and electioneering indifference, of which that writer speaks, can be understood by himself only. I am as much interested as any of you and earnestly desire that, throwing aside all party, you will endeavor to choose the most suitable men in the county—men of abilities equal to the great task, if such can be found, whose conduct in private life will not disgrace the virtuous and the good electors of Chester County. Chester County, October 25, 1787.

John Hannum to Anthony Wayne, Turk's Head, 1 November[4]

The most insidious attempt has this day been made by the Antifederal junto, stimulated thereto by their grand master Judge [George] Bryan, to disseminate divisions amongst us (knowing their numbers to be too insignificant to effect anything without previously disarming us) by sowing divisions amongst us; and that they have effected their fell purposes in part is much to be feared.[5] That they have acted with more cunning and address this day than heretofore will appear to you in a very striking manner when I inform you of the mode of their proceeding. Yesterday being the day for forming a ticket agreeable to a notification given by some anonymous writer who did not think proper to come and open the business of the day, notwithstanding which a very great number of persons met and determined [that] should any person who was opposed to the ticket formed at the late county meeting intimate a wish to make a change, they would enter on the business and sanctify what was done the 6 of October, which would have certainly been effected from the determination which generally pervades. Antifederal sagacity led them to believe it would certainly have been the case for which reason they prudently deferred it, often declaring [that] they were easy and knew of no dissension. But next morning, finding the people generally gone and the remainder off their guard, they made sham committees from the different districts of the county and ushered in their new ticket; which, could I believe they intended to [run], or that the people would generally run, I should be perfectly easy. But I concluding, as I am sure they have done, that a division will [ensue?] at the day of election amongst us whereby they may get in at least their Bryanites, for rest assured that party will not run one single person either formed this day nor that formed the 6th October. No my friend, they have their [———] robins and which they intend vigorously to push on that day. One of the junto disclosed the secret. Only turn your eyes to persons that formed the ticket and you will find their matchless effrontery equal to their accustomed treachery [and you?] will have abundant reasons to be satisfied with the [ticket enclosed herein?]. For the Red Lion District: Samuel Cunigham, John Culbertson, William Hunter, and William Clingan, Esquire; for the Turk's Head, Aaron Musgrove, Daniel Cornog; for Chester, Thomas Levis, Esquire; for Chatham all Anticonstitutionals, their names I do not remember except F[———].[6] Just remember, so far being promised, and I think your faith must be sufficient to remove mountains to suppose they will run any persons that are not perfectly Antifederalist. I am assured that you have the weal of our country too much at heart to suffer those "Daymons of Discord" from spreading their poison in your neighborhood, and that you will effectually heal the wounds they have made.

1. *Pennsylvania Gazette,* 24 October.
2. The six men were elected to the state Convention and voted to ratify.
3. *Pennsylvania Gazette,* 31 October.
4. RC, Wayne Papers, MiU-C. Colonel John Hannum, who was elected to the state Convention, represented Chester County in the Assembly in 1781, 1782, 1783, and 1785. General Anthony Wayne, also elected to the state Convention, represented Chester County in the Assembly in 1784 and 1785.
5. George Bryan was in Chester County at this time as a justice of the Pennsylvania Supreme Court, then on circuit.
6. Hannum refers to nominating tickets drawn up in Chester County's four election districts and identifies them by the sites where the elections were held. The Red Lion was the second district; Turk's Head the first district; Chester the fourth district; and Chatham the third district.

Samuel Cunningham was a member of the Pennsylvania constitutional convention of 1776 and of the Assembly in 1776 and 1777. Major John Culbertson served in the Assembly for several years during the Revolution. William Clingan, a Constitutionalist, was a member of the Continental Congress from 1777 to 1779 and a justice of the peace from 1757 to 1786. Thomas Levis was a justice of the peace, and before and during the Revolution he held such county offices as sublieutenant, treasurer, assessor, and commissioner.

Newspaper Reports of the Election of Convention Delegates on 6 November

Pennsylvania newspapers did not print the names of all the sixty-nine delegates elected to the state Convention. By 20 November, four Philadelphia newspapers—the *Independent Gazetteer, Pennsylvania Herald, Pennsylvania Journal,* and *Pennsylvania Packet*—had reported the names of fifty-five delegates elected in Philadelphia and in twelve of the state's eighteen counties. The reports in four other Philadelphia newspapers—the *Freeman's Journal, Pennsylvania Gazette, Pennsylvania*

Mercury, and *Philadelphische Correspondenz*—were somewhat less full. By 21 November, two western newspapers, the *Carlisle Gazette* and *Lancaster Zeitung,* had printed the names of fifty and fifty-eight delegates, respectively. (See Mfm:Pa. 200 for other examples of reports such as those printed below.)

Independent Gazetteer, 8 November[1]

Tuesday last came on the election for five persons to represent this city in the ensuing state Convention. On the close of the poll, at the State House, the votes stood as follows, viz.:

George Latimer	1215
Benjamin Rush	1211
Hilary Baker	1204
James Wilson	1203
Thomas M'Kean	1157
Benjamin Franklin	235
Charles Pettit	150
David Rittenhouse	148
John Steinmetz	137
James Irvine	132

Pennsylvania Gazette, 14 November (excerpt)[2]

Nothing shows the weakness of the Antifederal junto more than the above state of the votes of our city. With their utmost exertions and industry, their whole number of votes amounted only to 150. Dr. Franklin, who was run in their ticket as a decoy, was left out of the Federal ticket, only because his infirmities and present station would have made it improper to put him in the chair of the Convention, and he could not have been there without being president. Mr. [John] Steinmetz, who is a Federalist, was low in votes only from being in Antifederal company.[3]

Lancaster Zeitung, 14 November (excerpt)[4]

In an election held last Tuesday for delegates to a state Convention the following gentlemen were elected:

For Lancaster County	votes
Stephan Chambers	691
Robert Coleman	691
John Hubley	689
Sebastian Graff	681
Jasper Yates	653
John Whitehill	379

York County	
Henrich Schlegel [Henry Slagle]	916
Thomas Campbell	899
Thomas Hartley	864
Benjamin Pedan	666
David Grier	649
John Black	649
Berks County	
Nicolaus Lutz	604
John Ludwig	594
Abraham Lincoln	560
John Bischoff [Bishop]	488
Joseph Hiester	440

1. The results of the election in Philadelphia, but without the votes, were printed on 7 November in the *Evening Chronicle, Freeman's Journal,* and *Pennsylvania Gazette* (Mfm:Pa. 200). Outside Pennsylvania, these first reports were reprinted or reported fourteen times from Massachusetts to Georgia by 6 December.

2. The omitted portions give the votes in Philadelphia and the names of the delegates elected in ten counties (see Mfm:Pa. 200 for the complete report).

3. Steinmetz, a wealthy German merchant, had served earlier in the Assembly as a Constitutionalist.

4. Tr. Omitted here are the votes for the city of Philadelphia and the names of the delegates elected from Dauphin County.

William Shippen, Jr. to Thomas Lee Shippen, Philadelphia, 7, 13, 15, and 18 November (excerpts)[1]

Last evening T[homas] McKean, J[ames] Wilson, G[eorge] Latimer, B[enjamin] Rush, and H[ilary] Baker were chosen city members of the Convention, but not before they had given their honor to vote for the adoption of the new Constitution *in toto.* 5 were chosen for the county on the same terms; could you have supposed the Chief [Justice McKean] would be made such a slave of? When the election was over, honest [William] Findley and other country members who lodged at [Alexander] Boyd's were insulted at 12 o'clock, the windows broken with large stones, etc. The houses of G[eorge] Bryan, [John] Ewing, [James] Hutchinson were attacked by a violent noise and they abused, their wives frightened, etc. Does not this give us a foretaste of this blessed Constitution? However, tis supposed when all the elections thro the state are known, there will not be more than a majority of 5 or 6 in favor of receiving it as it stands. Findley, [Robert] Whitehill, etc. will come down well prepared to oppose it. There will be a very respectable minority and a severe and pointed protest—and if they succeed in their first motion, which will be to adjourn the Convention to Lancaster or Reading,[2] perhaps they will find a majority against it, which your Uncle R[ichard] H[enry] L[ee] ardently prays may be the case. He went from hence yesterday on his way to Virginia determined to prevent its adoption in Virginia. While here he had a long interesting conference w[ith] Findley, [James] McClean, [Charles] Pettit, Hutchinson, Bryan, [John] Smiley, and Ab[raham] Smith at my house.[3] I apprehend if the Constitution is adopted in this state it will produce a mighty convulsion.

[13 November] The Convention is chosen and there appears to be a much greater majority in favor of the new Constitution than was expected.

[15 November] The Assembly have offered a reward of 300 dollars for apprehending the rioters who insulted the members at Boyd's house. The Republicans could not defend the traitors tho they loved the treason. Tomorrow a motion is to be made in the House to move the seat of government to Lancaster and tis thought there will be a majority for it, a happy consequence of the mob.[4]

[18 November] Findley, Smilie and Whitehill are chosen for the Convention and will be strenuous in their opposition. [Hugh H.] Brackenridge had but 3 votes and D[aniel] Clymer 10. I am thus particular because I suppose you wish to know all on political movements.

1. RC, Shippen Family Papers, DLC (printed CC:232). Shippen was a Philadelphia physician. His son, Thomas Lee Shippen, was in Europe.

2. See also Mfm:Pa. 193.

3. What transpired at this meeting is unknown. Lee, Shippen's brother-in-law, wrote Shippen on 2 October that he would be in Philadelphia on 6 November (CC:122), and enclosed a copy of the amendments to the Constitution he had presented to Congress on 27 September (CDR:IX, A).

4. Neither the Assembly *Minutes* nor Lloyd's *Debates* for 16 November, or for the remainder of the session, record a motion to move to Lancaster.

Samuel Baird to John Nicholson, Norristown, 9 November[1]

It is with the deepest concern, my dear sir, that I have heard of the insult offered to you a few nights since. And in a particular manner so on account of Mrs. Nicholson, whose situation must have been truly distressing. I hope the perpetrators will be detected and severely punished.

Every man who has a regard for the peace and good order of society must in the highest degree reprobate such conduct. The moment a person is liable to insult for his sentiments on public affairs, that moment liberty is at an end. And sooner than see a faction powerful enough to do so, and evade punishment, I would with pleasure see another Caesar proclaim himself perpetual dictator.

A difference in opinion will ever obtain among mankind; and in all free countries parties will arise and will be distinguished by names which sometimes have but little reference to their general principles. But so far from thinking these dangerous, I think they are beneficial to the state and become otherwise only when, as above alluded to, government does not support its dignity and protect the individual. Surely it would have been in the power of the magistrates and constables to have put a stop to such villainous proceedings. Write me by the first opportunity. Let me know all on any that are supposed to have been concerned, and my good sir do bring [Mrs. N?] up to see us, if it is any how possible.

Mrs. B[aird] presents her compliments to Mrs. Nicholson. Do not forget to bring up some members of Assembly and Council with you.

1. RC, Nicholson Papers, PHarH. Baird was a justice of the peace of Montgomery County.

Benjamin Rush to John Montgomery, Philadelphia, 9 November (excerpt)[1]

I am sorry to inform you that I was misinformed last evening with respect to the election in Berks County. Every man in their ticket is Antifederal.[2] Men capable of believing that George Bryan is infallible, and that the President of the United States will *black* their faces, seize their plantations, press their wagons, and afterwards sell them for slaves at public vendue.

How long, how long!, wilt thou. But I will not intrude a prayer into my letter. Instead of it, I shall conclude with a text of Scripture which applies directly to the *beast,* and his companion the *red* dragon "Having great wrath, because their time was short." *All will end well,* no less with our federal government than with our college [Dickinson College].

1. RC, Rush Papers, PPL.
2. All five men elected from Berks County voted against ratification. Berks County continued to oppose the Constitution after ratification (Mfm:Pa. 325).

Supreme Executive Council Minutes, 9 November

A proclamation was also directed to issue requiring all judges, justices, etc. to use their utmost endeavors to apprehend and bring to exemplary punishment the persons who were concerned in the riot in the night of the sixth instant.

The Pennsylvania Assembly Saturday 10 November 1787

Assembly Proceedings[1]

A motion was made by Thomas Kennedy, seconded by James M'Lene, in the words following, viz.:

Whereas it appears to this House, by the complaint of divers of the members, supported by the affidavits of the Honorable John Beard [Baird], Esquire,[2] and Major Alexander Boyd, that on the night of Tuesday, the sixth day of November instant, about midnight, a number of persons unknown committed a violent riot and most outrageous assault upon the dwelling-house of the said Alexander Boyd, in which three of the members of the Honorable Supreme Executive Council and four of the members of this House lodged, and were then abed and asleep (until awaked by the said rioters); at the same time throwing out the most indecent and violent threats and abuse towards the said members, to the great contempt of this government, and especially of the said Supreme Executive Council and of this House. Therefore,

Resolved, That the said affidavits be transmitted to His Excellency the President in Council, and that it be recommended to His Excellency and the honorable members of the Supreme Executive Council to offer a reward, by proclamation, of ________ pounds for the discovery of the perpetrators of the said outrage and contempt, so that they may be brought to punishment, or of ________ pounds for the discovery of any one of them, and that this House will provide for the payment of the said rewards; and that it be also recommended to the Supreme Executive Council to direct the attorney general to prosecute the said rioters, and every of them, when discovered.

It was then moved by George Clymer, seconded by Thomas Fitzsimons, that the same be referred to a committee, to report thereon.

And on the question, Shall the same be referred to a committee? The yeas and nays were called by Mr. M'Lene and Mr. M'Calmont, and were as follow, viz.:

YEAS [33]

1 George Clymer
2 Thomas Fitzsimons
3 Jacob Hiltzheimer
4 William Lewis
5 William Will
6 William Robinson, Jr.
7 John Salter
8 George Logan
9 Richard Peters
10 Gerardus Wynkoop
11 Samuel Foulke
12 Valentine Upp
13 Robert Ralston

14 James Moore
15 Richard Thomas
16 Samuel Evans
17 Richard Willing
18 Townsend Whelen
19 Alexander Lowrey
20 Adam Hubley
21 Joseph Work
22 Jacob Erb
23 John Hopkins
24 William Mitchell
25 David M'Clellan
26 Joseph Lilley
27 Joseph Reed
28 Thomas Clingan
29 Peter Trexler, Jr.
30 Samuel Maclay
31 Jacob Reiff
32 John Carson
33 John Paul Schott

NAYS [30]
1 John Chapman
2 James Clemson
3 David Mitchell
4 Thomas Beale
5 Thomas Kennedy
6 John Oliver
7 Gabriel Heister
8 David Davis
9 Joseph Sands
10 Philip Kreemer
11 Peter Burkhalter
12 John Piper
13 John White
14 William Findley
15 James Barr
16 John Irvine
17 John M'Dowell
18 James Allison
19 Alexander Wright
20 John Flenniken
21 Theophilus Philips
22 John Gilchreest
23 James M'Lene
24 James M'Calmont
25 Robert Lollar
26 Benjamin Rittenhouse
27 Peter Richards
28 Jacob Miley
29 Robert Clark
30 Hugh Davison

So it was carried in the affirmative.

Whereupon, Ordered, That Mr. Clymer, Mr. Peters, Mr. G. Heister, Mr. Lollar and Mr. Rittenhouse be a committee, to report thereon.

. . . .

The committee to whom was referred, this forenoon, the motion respecting the insult offered to some members of this House, made report, which was read; and on motion, and by special order, the same was read the second time, as follows, viz.:

The committee, to whom was referred the motion made by Mr. Kennedy, respecting the insult offered to some members of this House, propose the following resolution:

Whereas complaint has been made to this House by James M'Calmont, James M'Lene, John Piper and William Findley, esquires, members thereof, that on the night of Tuesday, the sixth instant, the house of Major Boyd, of this city, in which they resided, was riotously attacked by a number of persons, to the said members unknown, and themselves abused and insulted by reproachful language:

Resolved, That such outrageous proceeding is highly disapproved of by this House, and is a breach of the privilege of its members.

Resolved, That this resolution, together with the affidavits which the said members have thought proper to produce on the subject, be transmitted to the Supreme Executive Council, and that Council be requested to issue a proclamation, offering such rewards as they may deem necessary for apprehending the perpetrators of the said outrage, in order that they may be brought to punishment, and that this House will provide for the payment of such rewards.

It was then moved by James M'Lene, seconded by Philip Kreemer to add the following resolution, viz.:

Resolved, That the Supreme Executive Council be requested to direct the attorney general to prosecute the prepetrators of the outrage aforesaid, and every of them, when discovered and apprehended.

And on the question, Will the House agree to the same? The yeas and nays were called by Mr. M'Lene and Mr. M'Calmont, and were as follow, viz.:

YEAS [26]
1 William Mitchell
2 Joseph Reed
3 David Mitchell
4 Thomas Beale
5 Thomas Kennedy
6 John Oliver
7 Gabriel Heister
8 David Davis
9 Joseph Sands
10 Philip Kreemer
11 Peter Trexler, Jr.
12 Peter Burkhalter
13 John Piper
14 William Findley
15 James Barr
16 John M'Dowell
17 James Allison
18 John Flenniken
19 Theophilus Philips
20 John Gilchreest
21 James M'Lene
22 James M'Calmont
23 Robert Lollar
24 Peter Richards[3]
25 Jacob Miley
26 Robert Clark

NAYS [34]
1 George Clymer
2 Thomas Fitzsimons
3 Jacob Hiltzheimer
4 William Lewis
5 William Will
6 William Robinson, Jr.
7 John Salter
8 George Logan
9 Richard Peters
10 Gerardus Wynkoop
11 John Chapman
12 Samuel Foulke
13 Valentine Upp
14 Robert Ralston
15 James Moore
16 Richard Thomas
17 Samuel Evans
18 Richard Willing
19 Townsend Whelen
20 Alexander Lowrey
21 Adam Hubley
22 Joseph Work
23 James Clemson
24 Jacob Erb
25 John Hopkins
26 David M'Clellan
27 Samuel Maclay
28 John White
29 John Irvine
30 Alexander Wright
31 Jacob Reiff
32 John Carson
33 John Paul Schott
34 Hugh Davison

So it was carried in the negative, and the report adopted.

1. For another account, see Alexander Dallas' report in the *Pennsylvania Herald,* 14 November, Mfm:Pa. 210–B, which was reprinted in the *Pennsylvania Packet,*

16–17 November, *Carlisle Gazette,* 26 December, and the *New York Morning Post,* 21 November.

2. Baird, the councillor from Westmoreland County who had been elected to the Convention, was one of the western members living at Major Boyd's.

3. The *Debates* record Rittenhouse as voting rather than Richards.

Assembly Debates

JAMES MCLENE considered himself bound to state some facts to the House, on which they might take such order as they pleased. He was asked by the Speaker if it related to the order of the day, which was the election of a treasurer for the ensuing year? Mr. McLene answered in the negative; when Mr. Wynkoop, from a desire to hear what labored in the member's mind, moved to postpone the order of the day, with an intention to permit the member to relate what he was desirous of.

Whereupon, the order of the day was postponed; when Mr. McLene proceeded to relate how the house in which he lodged was attacked by a mob last Tuesday night. This being a disagreeable circumstance, the members, his fellow lodgers, and some members of the Executive Council who were with them, had consulted and concluded upon the propriety of bringing it to the notice of the House, that they might show their disapprobation of such conduct if they disapproved. The design of the rioters he could not ascertain, unless it was to put them in fear of their lives; however be it as it might, after the deliberation which they had among themselves, he conceived it his duty to state it to the House, and he did not hesitate to believe it would meet with their disapprobation.

WILLIAM FINDLEY was one of the lodgers at Major Boyd's, and could assure the House of the truth of what the gentleman had stated, but they had gone further, and should support it by the testimony of two gentlemen who had sworn to the facts on this occasion.

Whereupon he handed the depositions to the chair of the Honorable John Beard [Baird], Esquire and Major Alexander Boyd, which being severally read, as follows:[1]

Philadelphia, ss.

"On this ninth day of November, A.D. 1787, before me Plunket Fleeson, Esquire being one of the justices of the peace in and for the city and county of Philadelphia, and residing in the said city, cometh *the hon. John Beard,* who is one of the members of the Supreme Executive Council of this Commonwealth, and the said *John,* being duly sworn on the holy gospel, doth depose, testify and say, that he this deponent doth lodge with *Alexander Boyd,* and that being in bed at the dwelling of the said *Alexander,* in Sixth-Street from Delaware river, in the city of Philadelphia, on Tuesday night last, the 6th instant, and being fallen asleep he was disturbed and awaked by a confused noise, at first seeming to him to be the report of guns fired, made by riotous persons in the street, at and near the same dwelling, and heard the glass of the lower story of the house breaking, by throwing of stones against the same; that this deponent still lying in his bed and not rising, heard some persons in the street say *'here the damned rascals live who do all the mischief,'* or words to like effect. That the disturbance aforesaid, did not continue after this deponent awaked as aforesaid, above a minute, after which the deponent heard the rioters aforesaid departing hastily, as the sound of their feet indicated, towards Mulberry-Street [Arch Street]; and that the *honorable John Smilie, and Abraham Smith, together with James M'Calmont, James M'Lene, John Piper, and William Findley, Esquires,* representatives in the general assembly of this state, do also lodge with the said *Alexander Boyd,* and were all in bed, as this deponent hath good reason to believe, in the dwelling of the said *Alexander* aforesaid, at the time of the outrage and riot so as aforesaid committed, and further saith not."

Philadelphia, ss.

"On this ninth day of November, in the year of our Lord one thousand seven hundred and eighty seven, before me Plunket Fleeson, Esq. being one of the justices of peace, in the city and county of Philadelphia, residing in the said city—cometh *Alexander Boyd,* of Sixth-street from Delaware river in the said city, Esq. who being solemnly sworn with uplifted hand, doth depose, testify and say, that on the night of Tuesday last, being the sixth of this present month of November, this deponent together with the *honorable John Smilie, John Beard* and *Abraham Smith,* members of the Supreme Executive Council; and *James M'Calmont, James M'Lean, John Piper,* and *William Findley, Esquires,* representatives in the General Assembly of the state of Pennsylvania, who lodge with this deponent, were gone to bed in his dwelling in Sixth-street aforesaid; that this deponent was fallen asleep, when about twelve o'clock midnight, a great noise in the adjoining street awaked this deponent, who thereupon immediately *jumped* out of his bed, and raising the sash of a window towards the street of the third floor of the House, he saw a considerable number of men in the street, of whom twelve or fifteen were nigh to the door of this deponent's dwelling, and that divers of the persons, so as aforesaid assembled, did then and there speak reproachfully of the gentlemen who were lodged with this deponent, and did say that here is the House where the damned rascals lodge who do all the devilment, or words to the like effect; adding *that they ought to be all hanged.* That hearing the window rise and seeing this deponent at the window, as this deponent believes, this deponent heard one of the same persons say, *there is one of the damned rascals putting his head out of the window.* That a man who lives nigh to this deponent, at this moment coming out of his dwelling, and approaching the mob aforesaid, the persons who composed the same, ran northerly towards Mulberry-street [Arch Street], and this deponent saw them no more. That this deponent was awaked as aforesaid, by the noise aforesaid, and by the throwing of large stones against the front door of his dwelling, some of which stones drove in the sash over the same door and fell in his entry, and one of them was at least *ten pounds* in weight. And that this deponent was not able to distinguish any of the aforesaid rioters, so as to know their names, or who they or any of them were. And further this deponent saith not."

THOMAS KENNEDY, if he was seconded, would present a resolution on this subject, which he had in his possession; he was seconded by James M'Calmont, and the motion was read as follows:

Whereas it appear to this House, by the complaint of divers of the members supported by the affidavits of the Honorable John Beard, Esquire and Major Alexander Boyd, that on the night of Tuesday the 6th day of November instant about midnight, a number of persons unknown, committed *a violent riot and most outrageous assault upon the dwelling house* of the said Alexander Boyd, in which three of the members of the Honorable Supreme Executive Council and four of the members of this House lodged, and were there abed and asleep (until awaked by the said rioters) at the same time throwing out the *most indecent and violent threats and abuse* towards the said members, to the great contempt of this government, and *especially* of the said Supreme Executive Council and this House, therefore,

Resolved, That the said affidavit be transmitted to His Excellency the President in Council, and that it be recommended to His Excellency and the honorable members of the said Supreme Executive Council, to offer a reward by proclamation of ________ pounds, for discovering of the perpetrators of the said outrage and contempt, so that they may be brought to punishment, or of ________ pounds for the discovery of any one of them; and that this House will provide for the payment of the said rewards; and that it be also recommended to the Supreme Executive Council to direct the attorney general to prosecute the said rioters, and every of them, when discovered.

GEORGE CLYMER was of opinion, that this House ought not to be backward in expressing their disapprobation of such conduct as was alleged by the members who lodged at the house of Mr. Boyd; but he apprehended it was not proper to take any notice of the members of

Council, because that branch of the government would attend to what respected their own body, for which reason he concluded, that part of the resolution that related to them ought to be omitted.

RICHARD PETERS: I am extremely willing that the House should express every degree of disapprobation that is proper, as I think such outrage very scandalous. I have no doubt but the gentlemen on this floor are disposed to do whatever is right; but as it is a new subject, I should wish the members to consent to allow us a little time to consider what is proper to be done; some amendment or alteration may be necessary, and I leave it to the gentlemen to say how far it may answer their own views, to have it gone into with some degree of deliberation; for my own part, I am not prepared to vote, as I have not made up my mind further than that it was a very scandalous thing; therefore I hope for a little time, either by postponing or deferring the motion for another time.

THOMAS FITZSIMONS had no doubt but the House would show a disapprobation of the conduct of any person, who should act in the unwarrantable manner which the people are alleged to have done on Tuesday night; but he thought the business was introduced in a way not common, beside it was improper for the House to go so far as the resolution extended; if the House had cognizance of the crime, it could extend no further than to their own members, and the rioters could only be punished by them for a breach of privilege, the other matter must be left to the laws; he observed also, that the preamble did not agree with the subsequent matter, and therefore it ought to be committed; for as a solemn act of this House, it ought to be done with correctness, especially as it is to be a reflection upon the *police* of the city of Philadelphia, which is so trammeled as not to possess the power of keeping good order within its limits; for these reasons sir I shall move you that the motion and affidavits be committed.

GEORGE CLYMER seconded the motion to commit, as he observed the House were to assent to a number of facts without their knowledge, and which respected members of the Executive Council as much as the members of the House.

JAMES MCLENE hoped the House would not agree to commit, whenever a postponement of any business was proposed to the House; if it was supported by any substantial reason, he should have no objection; but the reasons now assigned were of no weight, as on this occasion the matter is simply this, that I wish the House to show an early disapprobation if they disapprove; and I lament that it was so long neglected, I did think of bringing it before the House yesterday, but it seemed that we had other business which occupied all our time and prevented me; now the gentlemen say, they will not wish to delay the business; if anything is improper in the language of the motion, amendments can be proposed at the table, and all proper alterations can be adopted. I think the House cannot adopt proper measures too soon on this occasion, nor can I be so uncharitable as to think it is the wish or intention of any gentleman in this House to give it the go-by.

WILLIAM LEWIS: It is sometimes impossible to make up one's mind on an important subject the moment it is offered to consideration. The one now introduced has occupied very little of any former attention of mine, and I must own I do not feel a wish to be compelled to a decision, until I have had a little more time to examine how the question stands. I observe the gentleman has in some degree blamed himself for the delay of the business to this time; he who has had so much time to consider, will no doubt acquiesce in indulging others with the same; at present, I labor under some difficulty about the propriety of our interfering, if it is to be considered merely as an outrage; the laws of the land are fully adequate to its punishment; but if it is to be considered as a breach of privilege, the punishment must be by the House; if this is the point of view in which it is set, I think the offenders ought to be inquired after and punished severely; be the crime which it may, I am clear it deserves correction, and no doubt but what there will be a proper disposition to inflict it.

THE SPEAKER [Thomas Mifflin] would just suggest to the House, if the complaint was understood to be a breach of privilege, the propriety of ordering the attorney general to prosecute, when the cognizance was only in the General Assembly.

THOMAS FITZSIMONS: If this House, sir, enters into a resolution, which is to affect the police of the city of Philadelphia, and to affect it in a very disagreeable manner, on what grounds are we to stand? Is a partial affidavit—an affidavit perhaps insufficient of itself to convict any person before any of your courts of justice—to be the cause of such decision? The gentleman does not think it a matter of little consequence to affix a stigma upon the citizens, without hearing one word in their defense, or without receiving that kind of evidence necessary to support the charge of the veriest petit larceny. The recommendation of a prosecution to Council, should be extremely well-grounded, before it is entered into, and the House ought to have ascertained the facts, and be well satisfied of the truth; if this is not done already, the House must see the necessity for committing in order to effect it. The gentleman [James McLene] says he hopes we have no wish to give the business the go-by—that is not the question, sir, but we are determined to meet everything fairly, and do what on due deliberation shall be judged proper; these are the reasons which occur to me to prove it necessary to commit; but I can assure the gentleman I have no intention to give it the go-by. I only wish to do what is right, and until last evening, I never heard that such a thing had happened.

WILLIAM FINDLEY was of opinion, from the precedents in Parliament which he had consulted, that nothing more was necessary than the complaint of a member rising in his place; and that offering the affidavits of the two gentlemen who had sworn to the insulting language offered us, was wholly out of the question, or more than was necessary, in case of a breach of privilege. I say from the custom of Parliament nothing more is necessary, than for the members to complain of the insult; the affidavits were taken in order to make the charge more permanent. I only mention this, because it has been thought that an inquiry into the truth of the facts stated, should take place by a committee before the House decided.

THOMAS FITZSIMONS had been absent when the business was introduced and knew nothing of the affidavits, or of any complaint made by the members; he just came in when the motion made by Mr. [Thomas] Kennedy was reading.

RICHARD PETERS wanted to know what to do; he had so little time to consider, that he could not make up his mind, on what would be the proper mode to pursue this business in; he was very far from the wish insinuated by the member from Franklin (James M'Lene) of giving it the go-by—but surely the gentleman might agree to allow him time to consider how to act, and suffer the motion to be committed for that purpose, as well as to examine how far there was a necessity for amendment.

THOMAS FITZSIMONS wished it to be committed in order to have the facts ascertained from the evidence of the members. He apprehended the gentlemen need not fear but the House would act with propriety in their case, after they had considered what that propriety was.

GEORGE CLYMER was struck with the inaccuracy of the style in which the motion was framed, and he suspected that the necessary accuracy could not be obtained by loose amendments proposed at the table. The gentleman who introduced the matter [Thomas Kennedy], and he who pressed the immediate adoption [James McLene] will both recollect that it is not the act of an individual, but the act of the House if adopted; and that neither of them would be specially answerable for the ill manner in which he conceived it to be drawn.

THOMAS KENNEDY did not wish to hurry the matter, but he thought the object of the motion was pretty well understood; but if it was so inaccurately drawn as to make it necessary to refer it to a committee for correction, he hoped the gentleman who discovered its faults might be appointed as one of the committee.

GEORGE CLYMER hoped he should not.

JAMES MCLENE was not particularly concerned in the matter, and therefore would say no more, but the House might commit or neglect it altogether as they saw fit. He should only just mention, that he introduced it to know if the gentlemen were equally solicitous with himself in supporting the honor of the House—as an individual he was regardless of the insult, but the objection that the members of Council ought not to be noticed, who were equally insulted, he did not understand; however he believed that body would take measures to support their own dignity, and had indeed began; therefore he apprehended a delay of the business in the House would be telling the world, that this House was not inclined to secure the safety of its members from the violence of a mob.

THOMAS FITZSIMONS begged leave to ask the gentlemen whether Council had not actually determined on the subject before the House; he understood they had—but no doubt that gentleman has more certain information.

JAMES MCLENE declared he did not know that they had.

The question on commitment was taken, and the yeas and nays were as follows:

Yeas. Messrs. Clymer, Fitzsimons, Hiltzheimer, Lewis, Will, Robinson, Salter, Logan, Peters, Wynkoop, Foulke, Upp, Ralston, Moore, Thomas, Evans, Willing, Whelen, Lowrey, Hubley, Work, Erb, Hopkins, W. Mitchell, M'Lellan, Lelly, Reed, Clingan, Trexler, Riffe [Reiff], Maclay, Carson and Schott.—33.

Nays. Messrs. Chapman, Clemson, D. Mitchell, Beale, Kennedy, Oliver, G. Heister, Kreemer, Davis, Sands, Burkhalter, Piper, White, Findley, Barr, Irvine, M'Dowel, Allison, Wright, Flennagan, Philips, Gilchrist, M'Lene, M'Calmont, Lollar, Richards, Rittenhouse, Miley, Clark and Davison.—30.

Whereupon it was referred to the following gentlemen to make report:

Messrs. Peters, Clymer, Lollar, Rittenhouse and G. Heister.

THOMAS FITZSIMONS thought it would be proper, and absolutely necessary, that the members who complained of the insult should express precisely what abuse they had received, in order that the committee might be able to state their report upon some positive foundation, and that the House might the better determine how far they were right.

WILLIAM FINDLEY, one of Major Boyd's lodgers, informed the House, that he had already mentioned the statement to be just as declared by the member from Franklin (James M'Lene). There were two other members that lodged with them, who might declare also.

JAMES M'CALMONT, another of the Major's lodgers, said he agreed also to the general statement which had been made to the House.

And COLONEL JOHN PIPER, the other of Major Boyd's lodgers, joined and corroborated the statement as made by his colleagues; he added, that he was asleep, but awaked by the noise of the stones thrown, as he apprehended against the doors and windows, and in the morning when he got up he found the door much hurt, and the glass broke to pieces that was over the door, and lying all strewed in the entry, with a number of stones that had broke through.

He also observed, a few minutes after, that the clock struck twelve.

. . . .

The committee to whom was referred this forenoon the motion respecting the insult offered to some members of this House, made report by their chairman, Mr. Clymer; who observed, that the committee had shown a disposition to pay every attention to the subject, yet had not delayed for a moment making their report. The report was read as follows:

The committee to whom was referred the motion made by Mr. Kennedy, respecting the insult offered to some members of this House, propose the following resolution:

Whereas complaint has been made to this House by James M'Calmont, James M'Lene, John Piper and William Findley, esquires, members thereof, that on the night of Tuesday the 6th instant, the house of Major Boyd, of this city, in which they resided, was riotously attacked by a number of persons to them unknown, and themselves abused and insulted by reproachful language:

Resolved, That such outrageous proceedings is highly disapproved of by this House, and is a breach of the privilege of its members.

Resolved, That this resolution be transmitted to the honorable the Supreme Executive Council, together with the affidavits which the said members have thought proper to produce on the subject, and be requested to issue a proclamation, offering such rewards as they may deem necessary, for apprehending the perpetrators of the said outrage, in order that they may be brought to punishment.

RICHARD PETERS thought it would be more honorable to the gentlemen to have the House decide upon that complaint, as coming from themselves; but he confessed he was at a loss to say whether the insult was a breach of privilege or not, because he did not know whether they were abused for their conduct as members, either in the present House or in the *former* one, or whether the abusive language alluded to them, or the members of Council who were their fellow lodgers.

JAMES MCLENE desired the latter part of Mr. Kennedy's motion, and the latter part of the report to be both read, and then inquired what reason had induced the committee to leave out that resolution, which directed Council to order the attorney general to prosecute.

GEORGE CLYMER: It was the idea of the committee that Council would order it without direction; and indeed it appears to be a matter of course, in consequence of offering a reward for the apprehension of the rioters.

JAMES MCLENE was not satisfied with the reason assigned by the gentleman, and therefore moved that a resolution to this effect might be added to the report of the committee.

Resolved, That it be also recommended to the Supreme Executive Council, to direct the attorney general to prosecute the said rioters, and every of them, when discovered.

THOMAS FITZSIMONS submitted, with deference to the House, whether it would not be best for the legislature to attend to what related to themselves, and not interfere with the executive in directing them to perform what it will be their duty to do without any directions.

RICHARD PETERS declared the reason for not mentioning in the report a prosecution for the outrage, was because it was conceived more proper to leave the punishment of that to the laws, which were fully adequate to execute justice on the offenders.

JAMES MCLENE did not mean to press the amendment, but he conceived it would be very proper for the House to express fully their disapprobation; and if they think the rioters ought to be punished, it must certainly be proper to order a prosecution.

WILLIAM LEWIS: Mr. Speaker, I am decidedly against the amendment proposed by the member from Franklin [James McLene], and I would beg leave to offer my reasons for this opposition. The offense being of such a nature as to require us to take unusual means to obtain a knowledge of the offenders, and to make it perfectly advisable to offer a reward for their apprehension; and the disposal of all public monies whatsoever being entirely with us, is the ground upon which I conceive the report of the committee stands. It therein is stated, that a number of persons, by abuse and otherwise, had been guilty of a breach of privilege, and in order to do justice to ourselves and punish the perpetrators, Council are called on to offer a reward; but when they are apprehended, before whom are they to be brought for trial and under what authority are they to be punished for their outrage? Does the gentleman think the attorney general can be opposed to them for the crime mentioned in the report? I am sure, sir, he cannot. The attorney general cannot prosecute before any of your courts of justice, an offense which doth not belong to the cognizance of the courts, therefore *he* cannot prosecute the offenders for the crime mentioned by the House in their directions to Council.

The report brings forward a charge against the rioters, and this House are desired to go further, assent to the charge, and order the prosecution. I shall not mention now the inconsistency there appears, in ordering Council to perform what it must be their duty to do. If, as perhaps is the case, the offense may not amount to a breach of privilege, for the treatment the gentlemen received perhaps was not offered to them in consequence of their conduct as members of *this House,* but on some other account. In this case it amounts to no more than a high misdemeanor, though of a very serious nature, being an attack upon a person's dwelling at midnight. Now let me ask how is this to be prosecuted? I should imagine the report states everything that is possible for us to do; at least it requires everything that we ought to do. The mean is adequate to the end; a reward is offered, and there is no doubt but that it will be equal to the object in view. There is no doubt either but what the officers respectively will do their duty when called upon to do it, without a special order of the legislature.

The gentleman [James McLene] recommends to the Supreme Executive Council, that they order the attorney general to prosecute; this, sir, is what I hope this nor any future House of Assembly will ever do. For it is sufficient that a man at the hour of trial has to defend himself against the injured laws of his country, without the extraordinary weight lying upon him of an order of the legislature to his condemnation. It has been considered (and justly considered) that an individual appears before the tribunal of justice in unequal circumstances to what the system of our laws and constitution require, when the weight of a prejudication of the representatives of the state, and the mandate of Council lay against him. It must be in the recollection of every gentleman, the precedent of Timothy Matlack, late secretary to Council.[2] I recollect well being of counsel for him, that we complained much, and with reason of a similar order of a former House. I thought it justified me from the weighty manner in which it was brought forward, to object to the trial from the prepossession which the judges and jury must have received by that improper interference. The judges were of opinion with me, that an individual has not a due equality, when he has not only to defend himself against what appears before the court in the common course of law, but against all the weight of the most solemn and deliberate act which the legislature can offer against him.

If the offense amounts to a breach of privilege, sir, the attorney general cannot prosecute, because the House itself will punish the perpetrators. If it is not a breach of privilege, but an infraction of your laws, those laws will punish with all severity. Is the gentleman [James McLene] apprehensive that Council will not do their duty or does he suspect the attorney general? Has that officer ever given him reason to believe he shrinks from the weighty trust reposed in him; no, sir, I dare answer for him he will execute that trust with his wonted abilities on the present occasion, without being stimulated by orders either from this House or from the Executive Council. They will be prosecuted to conviction, if the evidence will support the charge, without adding the solemnity of a decision of the legislature against them; a decision I contend which no persons ought to have to combat with on their trial, be they great or be they small. But be they great or be they small, no man ought to lay under a stigma imposed by the legislature, until convicted in due course of law; it is unjust, and I sincerely hope it never may be again attempted in this country, or any country whatsoever.

JAMES MCLENE hoped the House would agree to the amendment he had proposed, and not refuse on account of the argument made use of by the gentleman last up [William Lewis], which if allowed must prove too much, as he says, he contended against the improper weight placed over the late secretary of Council on his trial; but I apprehend there is a great difference between the settlement of an account, as was his case, and a violent and outrageous assault upon the members of government, as the present case. I say if his argument is allowed of any weight, it goes against the resolutions and report altogether; for if a person is not to have the resolution of the House against him, ordering the attorney general to prosecute, of what signification is it that you offer a reward to apprehend him? It amounts to nothing to say the rioters may be brought before the House; for as the House mean to rise in a few days, it is probable it may not be sitting when they are apprehended. He did not know what was meant to be done by the report, or why the resolution he had proposed to add was left out by the committee; he hoped the gentlemen had not an intention to screen the offenders from any sort of punishment whatsoever.

WILLIAM LEWIS declared he had no intention to screen any man from due punishment, who had been guilty of crimes either against an individual or against the honor and dignity of government; nor did his arguments leave room for such an illiberal and unfounded insinuation. To say that they prove (if they prove anything) that the whole proceeding is wrong, I deny; and I trust every person who hears me will join in that sentiment. I will also say, sir, that if *that* gentleman's [James McLene's] arguments prove anything, they prove that he either did not understand me or entirely and willfully perverts what he did understand.

I said that the disposal of the public money belonged to the legislature in all cases whatsoever; that it was properly our duty to provide for, and direct a reward for the apprehension of the perpetrators of the outrage; and as the violence was leveled at members of the legislature, it became right to call on the Executive Council to offer such rewards; but after having done this, in which I conceive at the present we are justifiable, shall we proceed further and add to the weight which is already against these men, that solemn and tremendous act by which we ordered the prosecution?

I considered the offenders guilty of crimes of such magnitude, that they merit punishment severely; but I did not think there was any ground to suppose the attorney general would be less alert in performing his duty, and rendering the state those services for which his abilities so eminently qualify him, on this occasion, than on the many others entrusted to his care; nor did I think the Executive Council, from anything which we have seen in their former conduct, needed to be urged in the defense of their own dignity, or in attending to the due execution of the law.

I submit it again, and I submit it with confidence, whether my arguments can be tortured into the meaning which *that* gentleman was pleased to give them and with equal confidence I submit to this House whether the awful weight of violated laws are not sufficient for the worst of men to combat with and whether it would not be subversive of good government to exert such an unusual and objectional measure against any man, as a vote by the legislature of the nature that is now proposed? Because it is putting a man upon his trial with the prejudice of a predetermination made by the supreme authority of the land, and the minds of both judges and jury are warped accordingly. Because every man must be led to conclude the person so circumstanced is guilty of what is alleged against him, and guilty too in the most unequivocal and decided manner. Need I ask what probability in such case there can be, of an acquittal even if the suspected person is innocent?

Now if the facts are as thus stated, and which I believe is undeniable, and consequences so unjust may result from them, can an advocate for such dangerous measures be found within these walls? If the persons are guilty of the crimes brought against them and are convicted, they will be punished according to those laws which they have violated. If they are apprehended and brought before this House for the insult offered against its dignity, by the attack upon one or more of its members, the House will punish them in an exemplary manner, be they who they may; for it was not only a riot, but an outrage of an aggravated nature, to attack a dwelling at that dead hour of the night; and instead of wishing to screen the perpetrators, I wish they may be punished in an exemplary manner, to prevent such dangerous practices in future; but I do not wish to direct the attorney general or Council how to act, as in the one case, namely, breach of privilege, they cannot interfere, and in the other it would be unwarrantably cruel, and contrary to the magna charta of our liberties laid down in the constitution.

THOMAS FITZSIMONS: There is in this case, Mr. Speaker, a clear distinction that the member from Franklin [James McLene] does not seem to take into consideration. The person who shall be taken in consequence of the proclamation which the House is about to direct, will be brought before the House, who are competent to inflict a proper punishment for the breach of privilege; consequently we should have no occasion for the attorney general in this case. If they are to be punished for a violation of the laws, it will be a matter of course that the attorney general prosecutes on behalf of the commonwealth; and is there any ground for apprehending a neglect in that officer? There can be no occasion for us to direct Council to stimulate him to do his duty. It must be a reflection on that gentleman, if the amendment is added to the report of the committee; therefore I believe the House will not agree to it. My worthy colleague [William Lewis] has stated further and weighty objections, which no doubt will influence the House to reject the amendment, if the member [James McLene] who made it refuses to withdraw it.

RICHARD PETERS conceived it would be more honorable for the gentleman [James McLene] to have an unanimous vote of the House on this occasion, than suffer a division; for which reason he hoped the motion for the amendment would be withdrawn, as he believed in that case the report of the committee would be generally agreed to.

WILLIAM ROBINSON marked the same distinction which had been drawn by the members from the city, and concluded that the House must be persuaded that the motion was nugatory in one case, and improper in the other, and moreover it must be grounded on a suspicion of neglect both of Council and the attorney general, which was unwarrantable, as neither had hitherto given cause to believe they were regardless of their oaths. He hoped the gentleman [James McLene] was so far convinced of this, as to induce him to withdraw his motion.

JAMES MCLENE looked upon himself entitled to say a few words. He observed gentlemen had insisted much upon its being more honorable for him to have an unanimous vote of the House, than a divided one; he would only observe it was not his honor as an individual which he sought, but the honor of the House; and as for the hint thrown out, that the resolution was laying blame on the Executive Council and attorney general, he did not see it in that light, nor had he any doubt but they would do their duty. He only wanted to know the disposition of the House, and whether they want these people to be punished or not; as for the breach of privilege, if the House allow the outrage to be of that nature, he hoped they would take care to inflict a proper punishment; what respected the violation of the law, he was willing to leave the law to redress.

The question on the amendment was now taken, and the yeas and nays being called, are as follows:

Yeas. Messrs. W. Mitchell, Reed, D. Mitchell, Beale, Kennedy, Oliver, G. Heister, Kreemer, Davis, Sands, Trexler, Burkhalter, Piper, Findley, Barr, M'Dowell, Allison, Flenaken, Philips, Gilchrist, M'Lene, M'Calmont, Lollar, Rittenhouse,[3] Miley, Clark. 26.

Nays. Messrs. G. Clymer, Fitzsimons, Hiltzheimer, Lewis, Will, Robinson, Salter, Logan, Peters, Wynkoop, Chapman, Foulke, Upp, Ralston, Moore, Thomas, Evans, Willing, Whelen, Lowrey, Hubley, Work, Clemson, Erb, Hopkins, M'Lellen, Maclay, White, Irvine, Wright, Riffe [Reiff], Carson, Schott, Davison. 34.

So the amendment was lost.

The question was now taken on the report, which was unanimously agreed to.

1. The depositions are transcribed literally.

2. The reference is to an incident in 1782. The Republican-controlled Assembly accused Constitutionalist Matlack, secretary to the Supreme Executive Council, of not turning over to the state treasurer all the money collected from marriage and tavern licenses, and censured him as unworthy of public trust or confidence. In 1783 a new Assembly declared the censure unconstitutional and annulled the proceedings brought against Matlack.

3. The *Minutes* record Richards as voting rather than Rittenhouse.

Supreme Executive Council Minutes, 12 November

The following drafts of two proclamations were read and approved, viz.:[1]

Pennsylvania ss By the President and the Supreme Executive Council of the Commonwealth of Pennsylvania.

A Proclamation

Whereas it appears to us that about midnight between Tuesday the sixth and Wednesday the seventh instant a most daring riot was committed by a Large company of disorderly and evil minded persons unknown at and on the dwelling of Major Alexander Boyd in sixth

Street in the City of Philadelphia which company violently assaulted the same House by throwing stones thereat and damaging the same to the great disturbance and annoyance of the Honorable John Baird, Abraham Smith and John Smilie members of Council and of James McLene James McCalmont William Findley and John Piper Esquires members of the General Assembly of this Commonwealth who were there asleep within the same dwelling. And whereas it is manifest that the said rioters did perpetrate the riot and outrage aforesaid with design to affront and injure the Gentleman aforesaid in as much as they at the same time declared that they knew that they were lodgers with the said Alexander Boyd and did speak concerning them in the most contumelious and threatening terms.

And whereas, the General Assembly of this State have transmitted to Council the following resolutions entered into by them on this occasion . . . Vizt . . .

Saturday November the tenth 1787 The commitee to whom was referred this forenoon the motion respecting the insult offered to some members of this House made report which was read and on Motion and by special order the same was read the second time and unanimously adopted, as follows . . . Vizt . . .

Whereas complaint hath been made to this House by James McCalmont James McLene, John Piper, and William Findley Esquires Members thereof that on the night of Tuesday the sixth instant the House of Major Boyd of this City in which they resided was riotously attackted by a number of persons to the said members unknown and themselves abused and insulted by reproachfull Language.

Resolved That such outrageous proceedings is highly disapproved of by this House and is a breach of the priviledge of its members.

Resolved That this resolution together with the affidavits which the said members have thought proper to produce on the subject be transmitted to the Supreme Executive Council and that Council be requested to issue a proclamation offering such rewards as they may deem necessary for apprehending the perpetrators of the said outrage in order that they may be brought to punishment and that this House will provide for the payment of such rewards.

And Whereas it is Highly proper that the Authors of such high contempts so inconsistent with the dignity and good order of Government and of the most pernicious example should be immediately discovered and brought to condign Punishment We do therefore by this our proclamation offer and promise the reward of three hundred dollars for the discovery of the rioters aforesaid so that they be duly convicted of the same offence to be paid out of the public Treasury of this Commonwealth to the person or persons who shall furnish the Necessary information concerning the premises, and we do hereby charge and require all Judges Justices Sheriffs and Constables to make diligent search and enquiry after and to use their utmost endeavors to apprehend and secure the said rioters their aiders abettors and comforters so that they may be dealt with according to Law.

Given in Council under the hand of the President and the Seal of the state at Philadelphia this twelfth day of November in the Year of our Lord one thousand seven hundred and eighty seven.

Attest Charles Biddle Secry Benjamin Franklin

1. The proclamation is transcribed literally. It was published as a broadside and by 5 December was printed three times in both the *Independent Gazetteer* and the *Freeman's Journal,* and once in the *Pennsylvania Packet* and the *Lancaster Zeitung*. It was reprinted in the *New York Journal,* the *Massachusetts Gazette,* and the Boston *American Herald* by 10 December. Four of the seven newspapers were Antifederalist.

The other proclamation mentioned called for the arrest of Thomas Francis for murdering Andrew Crusius, a Spanish sailor, at the house of Margaret Bayley in Southwark.

Ebenezer Bowman to Timothy Pickering, Wilkes-Barre, 12 November (excerpt)[1]

I am happy to inform you the people here have made choice of you (by a great majority) to represent them in Convention. I was particularly busy at the election of military officers, but was determined not to be active again in that way and should have kept my resolution had I not been informed the evening before the election that a plan was on foot to send a Constitutionalist. I then thought it my duty, not merely as an inhabitant of this county of Luzerne, but as a citizen of the United States and a well wisher to the federal Union, to exert myself to prevent, if possible, a person being chosen who would object to the proposed Constitution. Christopher Hurlbut[2] was the person proposed, and, being in favor as well with the opposers as the supporters of government, it appeared highly probable he would be chosen. As you had informed [Matthias] Hollenback and Doctor [William Hooker] Smith[3] that it would not be convenient for you to attend (if chosen), no proposal of the kind had been made, but at that late period it was necessary that some person should be run in whom the people would be most likely to unite, or the other party would succeed. You was proposed and it took generally with the people. The only objection was that your attendance would interfere with the business of the county, and this was removed by assuring them you was not expected under three weeks.

It is my sincere wish that you would attend, and I am sure you will, provided it appears by the returns that any considerable number of Constitutionalists are chosen. The other commissioners may come in with safety and the business of the county go on.

I received by Doctor Smith (from you) a number of *Addresses to the Citizens of Pennsylvania*[4] and distributed them among the people, but had it not been your particular desire I should not have done it, for I had carefully avoided letting them know that any objections were made to the Constitution as I knew they were so prone to opposition that they would readily join in any to prevent that excellent plan from taking place; and altho the *Addresses* contain sufficient to convince any rational mind of the excellence of the proposed Constitution, yet as they discover that some persons oppose it, I thought they would do more hurt than good in this place. The comptroller general [John Nicholson] sent four pamphlets into this settlement, each containing the new Constitution with a number of full futile remarks upon it. Had he known the character of those to whom he sent them, I am sure he would not have taken so much trouble (Colonel [Zebulon] Butler, Doctor Smith, Esquire [Obadiah] Gore, and Esquire Hollenback).[5] Gore, as he is a person of some inquiry, undoubtedly read his, but the other three I am convinced never have. I had the curiosity to inquire of Butler just before the poll was opened, concerning the pamphlets he had received from Nicolson. It turned out as I expected, he was not able to determine whether it was on the Constitution or an almanac. Upon the whole, Mr. Nicolson has really lost his pamphlets, and as he has shown his good will in this last struggle, I think it but reasonable that his brethren (of the Constitutional Party) should make him some amends.

1. RC, Pickering Papers, MHi (printed: Taylor, IX, 269–72). Bowman, a Luzerne County lawyer, managed Pickering's legal business while Pickering was in Philadelphia. After the election, Pickering's wife wrote to him: "From what I have heard I find no reason to alter my former opinion. Your being chosen a member of the Convention was owing to Mr. Bo[w]man['s] exertions. No person appearing to interest himself for him, and the persons that were proposed [were] such whose characters he was not pleased with. From anything I have as yet discovered in Mr B I take him to be an honest man and a friend to his country and a friend to you. This is saying a great deal for a lawyer" (Wilkes-Barre, 8 November, RC, Pickering Papers, MHi).

2. Hurlbut of Nanticoke was a surveyor and justice of the peace.

3. Smith was a Wilkes-Barre surgeon and physician and a justice of the peace. Hollenback was a Wilkes-Barre merchant and landowner and justice of the peace. He supported Pickering for Convention delegate from Luzerne (to John Nicholson, 13 November, Mfm:Pa. 141).

4. CC:183–A.

5. Butler was appointed lieutenant of Luzerne County in August 1787. Gore, a blacksmith, was a justice of the peace in the early 1780s and an assemblyman from 1788 to 1791.

Samuel Baird to John Nicholson, Norristown, 13 November[1]

I received your favor by Mr. [William] Irvin but was sorry to find it dated so early as the 12th. I can readily excuse you as the hurry you must be in is certainly great.

I observe a John Black from York returned as a member of Convention. Pray is this our old master?[2] And is the clergy going to turn politicians? The blending them has had effects sufficiently terrible to make us avoid it. But this good little man (if it should be him) I am sure will be an exception. Confined to their closets and mixing but little with the vicious part of mankind for whom government is formed (or at best, mankind assuming, generally speaking, a more virtuous turn in their company) few of them have notions extensive enough to make good politicians. I could have wished an answer to mine of the 13th but make no doubt your situation was such as to make it inconvenient. If you print the state of the finances I will thank you for one.

1. RC, Nicholson Papers, PHarH.
2. The Reverend John Black, pastor of the Upper Marsh Creek Presbyterian Church, voted for ratification.

Carlisle Gazette, 14 November[1]

A correspondent observes that he is happy in having it in his power to inform the public that the county of Franklin has discovered by their conduct at the last election that they are in reality friends to order and just government. The choice they have made of representatives for the state Convention fully evinces the truth of this observation, viz., John Allison and Richard Baird, esquires, who are gentlemen of unblemished characters, well acquainted with the science of government, steadily attached to the interest of their county, and consequently advocates for the new Federal Constitution.[2] They have also treated the conduct of their representatives in the late House of Assembly with a degree of resentment becoming the citizens of a free state; particularly that of their absconding from the House, contrary to the well-known principles of government, and at a period when business of the greatest importance lay before them.[3] For this reason they are prevented from having a seat in the Convention, although some of them had, previous to their late departure from the county, offered themselves as candidates for that important office. This shows that the citizens of Franklin County have too much sense to be imposed on [by] Antifederal influence or the produ[ctions] of designing men, notwithstanding the pains which have been taken to circulate and support them.

The State of Pennsylvania, I am confident will adopt the new system by a large majority; and, from every information which I can collect, it will be adopted by a sufficient majority of the other states. If so, we shall soon taste the sweets of independence so dearly purchased; we shall soon see anarchy and confusion flying before a government whose powers will be coequal with its extent. The Antifederalists will then be convinced that such a government is more safe, and more respectable, than that which admits of popular licentiousness. They will then acknowledge that safety cannot exist in a government where there is no check but the voice of the people at large.

1. Reprinted in four Philadelphia newspapers by 11 December.
2. Allison voted for, and Bard against, ratification.
3. The reference is to Abraham Smith and James M'Calmont. Neither was elected to the Convention, but M'Calmont was reelected to the Assembly and Smith (ineligible for reelection to the Assembly) was elected to the Supreme Executive Council in October.

Extract of a Letter from Philadelphia, 18 November, Maryland Journal, 14 December[1]

I am very anxious to know how your state stands affected with regard to the new proposed Constitution. The political phrensy with which Pennsylvania was seized on its first appearance begins now sensibly to abate. The people get every day more and more information upon the subject; and I make no doubt, that if we had only a short respite of three months, the new Constitution would be entirely rejected; but matters have been carried on with such high-handed precipitation, that I am much afraid we shall pass the Rubicon, and that our eyes will not be fully opened until it is too late. The returns of members for the Convention that have come to hand are generally of an aristocratic complexion, and there will certainly be a majority of the *wellborn* party. Mr. [James] W[ilso]n and Dr. [Benjamin] R[us]h are returned for the city; their daring attempts to deceive the people, by the most insidious speeches, have been rewarded with trust and honors. Our friends have endeavored to carry the venerable Dr. Franklin, but he did not get more than 235 votes. Notwithstanding the great use that is made of his name to support the new system, it is very certain that he is far from approving of it. This the *wellborn* know, and it is the reason why they have left him out of the ticket. This great patriot is as much attached as ever to democratic principles, and every day brings forth some new instance of it. I shall relate one in particular which appears to me very striking. The aristocratics being, for the first time, very strong in our Executive Council, had formed the noble design of turning out every officer of the *democratic* party. They began with Mr. [Peter] Wikoff, the city auctioneer, who had only been about three or four months in office, and who could not be charged with any fault except paying the state duties and his customers with the utmost punctuality.[2] But they were most anxious to displace Jonathan Bayard Smith, Esquire, the prothonotary of this county, an excellent patriot, a Whig in the worst of times, and one who is avowedly opposed to the new Constitution; and no less a man than Mr. Wilson, was the candidate for his office. Yesterday the election came on, and the votes being taken, Council were equally divided, when Dr. Franklin, to the great mortification of the *Wilsonites,* gave his casting vote in favor of Mr. Smith.[3]

Next Tuesday our Convention meets, and as I told you before, I am afraid they will adopt the new Constitution, as I am sure there is a majority of them who are predetermined in its favor. There will be, however, a very respectable minority, and among them, I am proud to name Messrs. [William] Findley, [Robert] Whitehill, and [John] Smiley, whose names, if I am not mistaken, will do an everlasting honor to Pennsylvania. Yet, I fear, those great patriots, notwithstanding all their exertions, will not be able on this occasion to stem the torrent of prejudice created by influence. You need not look up to Pennsylvania for your political salvation from the danger that threatens us all. As the other states have not acted with so much precipitation, it is by them that we expect to be saved from impending ruin. Here I am ready to exclaim with the great Shakespeare:

Methinks our Country sinks beneath the Yoke.
It weeps, it bleeds, and each new Day a Gash
Is added to its Wounds.—Bleed!—bleed!—poor Country!
Grim Tyranny erect thy Basis sure,
For Goodness dares not check thee———. MACBETH.

1. This item was headed: "Extract of a Letter from a Gentleman in Philadelphia, to his Friend in Cecil County [Maryland], dated November 18, 1787." It was reprinted in the *New York Morning Post,* 24 December and the *Virginia Independent Chronicle,* 26 December, both Antifederalist newspapers.

2. The Supreme Executive Council appointed Wikoff auctioneer of the city of Philadelphia on 13 April 1787 and replaced him on 14 November with John Patton. (For a defense of Wikoff, see Mfm:Pa. 243.)

3. See also William Shippen, Jr. to Thomas Lee Shippen, 7–24 November, CC:232. The office of prothonotary was lucrative. (See Mfm:Pa. 16, 85, 294.)

Extract of a Letter from Washington County, Carlisle Gazette, 21 November

The gentleman who delivers this to you will inform you that James Marshal, James Edgar, Thomas Scott, esquires and General [John] Nevill are chosen to represent this county in the ensuing Convention.[1] Such a choice does us honor in my opinion. But these gentlemen are all Constitutionalists, you will say? Very true, and so am I, and yet I am as decidedly in favor of an efficient federal government as any man in Pennsylvania. It must be the rump of the Constitutionalists, who, as a party, are adverse to the federal government, formed by the late Federal Convention. I must confess that I think it is not altogether free from faults, although I warmly approve of it in general as an excellent system, well calculated "to form a more perfect union, establish justice insure domestic tranquility, provide for the common defence, and secure the blessings of liberty to ourselves and posterity." The people are as they ought to be, the fountain of power in the Constitution—the power to amend faults as they are, or shall be discovered, forms part of it. Publications more calculated to inflame than to inform our minds have been sent up from Philadelphia and circulated with uncommon industry in this part of the country; but our own good sense prevented them from making much impression upon us. We can discover a wolf, altho the beast should be in sheep's clothing. We are told that the fugleman is the fabricator of some of these pieces. If so, I dare say, he will attempt to drill our members as soon as they reach the city; but I dare assure you, that at least three of them will act according to the dictates of their own dispassionate uninfluenced judgments. They are all men of sound understanding. I had some conversation with one of them yesterday on the subject when my vanity led me to point out what I thought imperfections in the proposed Federal Constitution. "True," said he, "but if we reject this Constitution, have we any chance of getting a better?" I believe we cannot collect in America a band of better or wiser patriots than those who sat in the Federal Convention. That man must have a nefarious heart who could accuse or suspect such men of "the most daring attempt to establish a despotic aristocracy among freemen that the world ever witnessed." That patriot band will be held in grateful remembrance by united America, when such a daring accuser will either sink into insignificancy and oblivion; or if he should be remembered, it will only be as Judas amongst the Apostles.

I have so high an opinion of the integrity of our other member that

I trust he will, upon this occasion, be superior to the influence of party, and that his political deportment will be as dignified and independent as his moral deportment is just and respectable.

1. Marshel and Edgar voted against, while Scott and Nevill voted for ratification.

Jacob Eyerly, Jr. to John Arndt, Nazareth, 24 November[1]

As Mr. Ulrich Hauser goes to Philadelphia I embrace this opportunity to send a few lines to you, according to our agreement.

You will undoubtedly have had a pleasant journey, if I judge right, from the respectable company, that went together, and if I may give credit to what I have heard, from your meeting together at Bethlehem on Sunday last.[2] I have since received the papers and seen the list of most of the members of this state. As much as I know of them, I believe there are men of both parties, both Federalists and Antifederalists, who will have an opportunity to appear as orators, and display their abilities, etc.

You will certainly have begun to do business, and I am anxious to know how you go on and whether you will have a decided majority in favor of the Constitution, or not. Please therefore to send me an answer by the bearer without fail and inform me of your proceedings. I shan't omit by every good opportunity to send a few lines and should be glad to hear of you, that you may have good success in your proceedings, as every friend to his country must certainly wish to see a good government established.

Excuse me, for not writing more, as it is bedtime, and my eyes are full of sleep.

Give my compliments to all good friends especially Mr. William Henry and Mr. Joseph Horsefield. . . .

1. RC, Northampton County, Misc. Box, PHi. Eyerly represented Northampton County in the Pennsylvania House of Representatives in the 1790s. Arndt, treasurer and recorder of Northampton County, was elected to the Convention where he voted for ratification. He was a member of the Council of Censors in 1783–1784.

2. Probably a meeting of Northampton County delegates to the Convention, all of whom voted for ratification.

Samuel Vaughan, Jr. to James Bowdoin, Philadelphia, 30 November (excerpt)[1]

The Convention has been met some days here. The majority, and that a large one, are for the proposed Constitution, but a troublesome minority will lengthen out their deliberations or rather retard the adoption of it. The time being short that was allotted before the meeting of the Convention for the choice of its members, the back counties were under the necessity of returning their Assembly members who were then at this place;[2] and these are the persons who were most active for the continuation of the test law, the emission of paper money and the cancelling the Bank [of North America] charter, etc., etc. of the same complexion. However it is far from being considered as an unfortunate circumstance, as it will disseminate much light among the people on this important subject. I have the pleasure to enclose Mr. [James] Wilson's first speech, and will forward the debates complete as soon as the Convention is broke up and they are printed.[3] The enclosed part, I must observe, is, however, very inaccurate, and not only parts are omitted and the leading points often lost for want of seizing the exact expression, but some parts are absolutely misstated.

1. RC, Bowdoin-Temple Papers, MHi. Vaughan was the son of a wealthy West Indian merchant. Bowdoin was governor of Massachusetts from April 1785 to May 1787.

2. Joseph Hiester of Berks County and William Findley of Westmoreland County were the only assemblymen elected on 9 October elected to the Convention.

3. Vaughan refers to Wilson's speech of 24 November which was published as a pamphlet on 28 November (see Convention Debates, 24 November, III below).

A Marylander, Maryland Gazette (Baltimore), 4 December (excerpt)[1]

The Convention is now sitting in Pennsylvania, and though that state unhappily is convulsed by the continual struggles of two great contending parties, yet *generally speaking,* they have shown a disposition to choose *disinterested men,* by excluding *salary officers* and *assemblymen,* from an apprehension that a desire to retain their personal consequence and prevent a diminution of their incomes might tempt them to oppose any alteration of our present governments, however expedient or necessary. Persons known to be deeply interested in public securities are there thought improper, because they might wish for any general government, however contradictory to the principles of freedom, merely to appreciate the papers in their hands. Several registers of wills are chosen Convention men in that state, from an idea that all testamentary cases will certainly remain entirely in the state governments, therefore they are considered as impartial persons. The chief judge of the Supreme Court [Thomas McKean] is chosen for the city of Philadelphia because, being a decided friend to the new Constitution, he is supposed to be actuated by patriotic motives, as he acts diametrically contrary to his own *immediate* interest.

No assemblyman in Pennsylvania, who is a friend to the Federal Constitution, would consent to serve in the Convention because it was agreed upon before the late general election, therefore they considered it *extremely indelicate and improper* (though not *criminally* so) to assist personally in a responsible situation to abridge the powers of the state government, after having recently sworn to support, maintain and defend it to the utmost of their power. Three or four assemblymen only, of that state, are deputed to the Convention, but every one of them is vehemently opposed to the federal government, or to any alteration of their own constitution, though the worst in the Union, except that of Georgia. Pennsylvania now acts with more propriety than in 1776, when a majority of the counties laid down a rule and strictly adhered to it, to choose no man of fortune or book learning in the convention, from a fear of their framing a government unfavorable to the liberties of the poor people, as if some knowledge of ancient and modern governments, and the causes of their prosperity and decline, ought to keep any man out of a public station.

1. For the complete article, see RCS:Md.

Independent Gazetteer, 5 December

A correspondent observes, that the virtuous 24, who compose the minority of the Convention, obtained their seats in that body, by a much greater number of the votes of the people of Pennsylvania, than the 44 who compose the majority; yes the 24 had above 1000 more votes than the 44—and in Lancaster and other counties, which are there represented by part of those 44, the votes were nearly equally divided, between those who were in favor and those who were opposed to this government. Whilst in some other counties, few would vote for any members, as they declared that they had not time to make up their minds on this important business, so as to determine upon a proper choice of representatives. In the very large and populous county of Chester, there were but 500 votes given, and in Philadelphia County but 500; in Bucks, Northampton and Montgomery, not one-sixth part of the people voted, and by every account from the different parts of the state, the few that have been in favor of the proposed government have very much decreased and are changing their sentiments daily—that Whigs and Tories are now alarmed, and that in a month's time there will not remain 500 people in all Pennsylvania in favor of the new government, except those who expect offices under it. And it is now reduced to a certainty that North and South Carolina, Virginia, Maryland, New York and Rhode Island will reject *this new scheme* of office making. The legislature of Maryland have called their deputies of the late Convention to give an account of their dark proceedings in that Convention; it is expected we shall hear from thence in a few days some important secrets. So that it is not very material, adds our correspondent, how this affair is decided by our Convention, who may only expose their arbitrary principles without any danger to their constituents.

Freeman's Journal, 5 December

A correspondent informs us, that the 24 virtuous characters who compose the minority in the Convention are all men whose souls have been *tried* in the late glorious war (and that they are men of understanding, I believe the office hunters know to their sorrow). These 24 patriots obtained their seats in that body by above 1000 more votes than the whole 44 did. And we find that in Lancaster, York, Northumberland, and other counties, from which some of the 44 came, that the votes were nearly equally divided between those warmly opposed to the proposed Constitution and those who were in favor of it; and in some other counties, from which others of the 44 came, such as Montgomery, Chester, Bucks, Northampton, and Philadelphia counties, that not above one-fifth of the people would vote, or give any countenance to this Convention, as they considered it was called in a riotous, illegal manner, as well as with dangerous and unconstitutional precipitancy. And at this moment, from every account received from all parts of the state, it appears, that the few who had been in favor of the proposed plan (Whigs and Tories) are daily changing their sentiments concerning it, and declare they have been deceived; so that in a month there will not be 500 people in the state who will wish to have it adopted, except those who expect offices under it. But it is expected (and beyond a doubt it will be the case) that the greater part of the 44 will vote against this scheme of office making, although very great pains has been taken to deceive them in this town.

E. THE ASSEMBLY AND THE ISSUE OF A QUORUM IN THE CONVENTION

8–10 November 1787

The 11th General Assembly did not provide for paying the Convention delegates before it adjourned *sine die* on 29 September. Therefore a bill to pay the delegates was introduced in the 12th General Assembly, which secured a quorum on 24 October. During debate on the bill on 9 November, the Antifederalists, led by James McLene and William Findley, proposed that the quorum in the Convention be two-thirds of the delegates elected, the same quorum required by the state constitution for the Assembly. The Federalists defeated the proposal, and on 10 November the Assembly ordered the engrossing of an act to pay the Convention delegates. (For documents on this subject other than those printed below, see Mfm:Pa. 210–A.)

Antifederalists made other attempts at obstruction. For example, on 3 November James McLene tried but failed to stop the adjournment of the Assembly on 6 November to permit the State House to be used as a polling place for the election of Convention delegates (Mfm:Pa. 186). Three weeks later, McLene again failed when he tried to prevent adjournment of the Assembly during the Convention (Mfm:Pa. 236).

The Pennsylvania Assembly
Thursday
8 November 1787

Assembly Debates

It was moved by Robert Lollar, to take up for a third reading, the bill entitled, "an act to provide for the wages of the state Convention and to defray the expences of holding the same."

James McLene moved to postpone.

GEORGE CLYMER hoped the gentleman would assign some reason to induce the House to comply with his motion, for certainly it was not because *he* moved the postponement, that the members should acquiesce.

JAMES MCLENE had not seen the bill till this minute, when it was put into his hand; if bills are printed for public consideration it was but right to allow time for deliberation.

GEORGE CLYMER had no objection to allowing time, if the member was unprepared, tho it was a bill of the most simple nature, and contained but one clause, whose object was well-known from the title.

The bill was accordingly postponed.

THOMAS FITZSIMONS: I shall move you, sir, that this bill be made the order of the day for tomorrow, as I wish to avoid all unnecessary delay; there is but little business before the House, and that little may be soon done, nor can we sit here long for nothing, only to increase the public expenses, already sufficiently burthensome.

Whereupon, Ordered, That the forementioned bill be the order of the day for tomorrow.[1]

1. The Assembly *Minutes* (Mfm:Pa. 210–A), which state that the act was read the third time on this day, are in error.

The Pennsylvania Assembly
Friday
9 November 1787

Assembly Debates[1]

Agreeably to the order of the day, the House took up for a third reading, the bill entitled, "an act to provide for the wages of the state convention, and to defray the expences of holding the same."

On considering the enacting clause, providing for the payment of their wages, etc. it was moved by James M'Lene [and seconded by William Findley] to amend, by inserting, that a quorum of the said Convention shall be the same as the quorum of the General Assembly, conformable to the 10th and 12th sections of the constitution of this commonwealth.

THOMAS FITZSIMONS: I very much doubt, Mr. Speaker, whether the legislature possesses the power mentioned in the gentleman's amendment. What right have we to say what number shall constitute a quorum in the Convention? The object of the law before us is only to provide for the expense that must necessarily attend their sitting; this, sir, cannot be effected but by law, as it is a disposal of the public money; but what right has the House to form rules and regulations for that body? Certainly they have none—nor could any directions be given them by law. When the measure of collecting a convention was adopted, the House went no further than to recommend it; a law for this purpose would have been improper, and a resolution was used; as the legislature have not hitherto attempted to make a law for regulating the proceedings of the Convention, the House will not certainly come into it now. I conceive the gentleman to be entirely wrong in his object, at least it strikes me in that light, and I cannot think of agreeing to any interference of the nature he proposes.

THOMAS KENNEDY conceived that the business of the House at present was to make provision for the pay of the members of Convention; and as the regulations had been nothing hitherto but by resolution, it would be improper to add anything in the law. He did not think that the resolution for calling a convention was in the power of the House, but now it was done, he would leave them to act as they pleased, as he wished everything to the advantage of the people.

GEORGE CLYMER: The amendment, sir, is extremely foreign to the design of the present bill, and being so, it is very improper to be grafted upon it; but setting this objection aside, though it is of some weight, let me ask what would be the consequence of acknowledging the principle held up in the amendment? If the House, sir, has the right to lay down rules for the conduct of the members of the Convention, and to order the attendance of two-thirds of the members to constitute a quorum, at the same time, and by the same rule, they may enjoin, as essential to form the Convention, the attendance of every member; and thus it must be left to the discretion of this House, whether that body shall have the power or ability to adopt a plan of federal government, for which they are expressly chosen. There is nothing in the constitution of the state, which gives to the General Assembly the power of regulating a convention; it had not an idea of it at the time it was framed. The rules and regulations of that body must be left to themselves, and any law we may make must in itself be void and nugatory from the very nature of the case.

JAMES MCLENE: I confess, sir, when I offered this amendment, I had no expectation of its meeting with opposition from any quarter of the House; the authority of the House was used to call the Convention, and I believe that authority was as good as any that could be employed for the purpose; as to the propriety of having a convention, there can be no doubt about it, nor do I mean to make any. The gentlemen from the city say we have no right to make rules and regulations for the government of that body. Why, sir, the amendment says nothing about it: the Convention will certainly make those themselves; they will appoint their own officers, and agree upon what mode they will conduct their business in; but then certainly this House ought to ascertain what number shall be a quorum. Or is it the wish of the gentlemen that a few of the near counties shall get together and decide upon the business before the others can attend? For my part, I cannot see the reason why they should wish to have the business done in this manner, nor how they can reconcile it to that propriety which a business of this importance demands. I have no doubt but all the counties will send deputies, and that the gentlemen they send will attend here as directed by the resolution of the late House; every gentleman will therefore see the propriety of the proposed amendment, and I mean nothing by it but to have the state fairly represented in Convention. As I said before, I hope gentlemen do not wish a few of the near counties to get together and decide before the others come down; this is surely very unfair and improper. For my own part, I believe the amendment ought to be adopted, and I hope the House will agree to it.

RICHARD PETERS: I am struck with surprise at the conduct of the member from Franklin [James McLene], that he should think the House have the power to direct the Convention. That the House, and no other body, sir, has power to provide the means of paying the expenses of the Convention is clear, because the money of our constituents cannot be disposed of by any other means. But we have no right to say how many of that Convention shall be a quorum to proceed on the business for which they are elected, nor to make rules for them to act by. Suppose we should direct their attendance under severe penalties, would it be proper, or would not such an interference be absurd and nugatory? Would the members elected by an authority paramount to the legislature, the sovereign authority of the people, unshackled by the restraint of a previous constitution: I say, sir, would not the Convention contemn your order? I hope, sir, when the Convention meet, they will stand on solid ground, and not, by the hurry the gentleman apprehends, defeat in a great measure the object of their appointment. I have confidence in them, that if but a few meet they will not, by a hasty decision, determine, because it will lose that respectability and consequence which a full representation must give to their ratification of the Federal Constitution.

Calling a convention, sir, was recommended by the legislature, and the sovereignty of the people has decided upon that recommendation; it is not an act of the legislature that the Convention exists, it is the act of the people, who, meeting in the several counties, have given it stability by sending deputies. No law was equal to obtain this end; the legislature could not by their power, as defined in the constitution of this state, have accomplished this object; nothing but the consent of the people was equal to it, and this has been obtained. The gentleman must know that a vote of the Convention could not have so much weight if adopted in the manner he has insinuated; nor can he suspect that the members will decide on the meeting of a small number, as they must dearly see the consequences of such determination; for which reason, sir, I object to the amendment, not only as unnecessary, but perfectly nugatory, if it is agreed to.

WILLIAM FINDLEY: I believe the members of the Convention will be free to adopt whatever rules and regulations they may think proper, and that this House has not the power to subject them to any penalties for their conduct; but this is not the question proposed by the amendment; if it was, I readily agree with the gentlemen who oppose it, that the interference would be improper. But the House on a former occasion did direct the Convention as to the time when they should meet and the place where; yet I can't think any penalty could arise, if they were to make alterations in these particulars. I observed this argument against rules and regulations has gone thro all that has been said in opposition to the motion, but I think it don't apply; for the object of the amendment was never thought by me when I seconded it, to make rules and regulations. The Assembly direct the Convention to meet at such a time: now this time happens to be so short, that the members from the backcountry cannot come in time; and tho the time is about the same as ordered by the constitution for the meeting of the General Assembly after their election, yet that is an inconvenience which may be justly complained of. I think the time for their meeting is fixed at two weeks, but in this case the inconvenience is increased, as the moment they meet they enter into the business which is already prepared for them, but in the House of Assembly the quorum of two-thirds must be waited for, and before business of any consequence can be gone into, a committee is appointed to wait on Council, and when the business is forwarded to the House, it must be read several times, deliberated on, and three times considered in a bill, before it can be passed into a law, which delay is safe in the one case but not in the other, because the business is of another nature. It is already recommended that they may meet at such a time, and those who meet are not confined to any particular number to proceed to business; yet it is true when met here they are at liberty to go where they please—but still I think as to the number they ought to be restricted; there has been much done already by the legislature in this business, and it will be right to gratify the people further; and let the number be respectable, something more than a bare majority to decide on business of this importance, so interesting to the state and to every individual. All I wish for in supporting the amendment, is fair play to be done generally to all; and we know the time is so short for them to meet in, that many of the counties cannot be represented before the others decide, and there may be no occasion for them at all. The manner in which this business may be conducted is ground of jealousy to the people, and it may be inferred from the shortness of the time, that there was private designs to carry this measure, without the assent or participation of the back counties. I say there is ground to suppose, that the near counties may go through the business without any respect to the others, and that is ground for apprehension. Now by the amendment I wish to put it out of the power of a few to transact this business without the concurrence of the rest, and thereby remove that ground of suspicion and jealousy, which the people entertain of the designs of those who wish to press this measure improperly.

THOMAS FITZSIMONS thought the ground of jealousy mention[ed] by the gentleman just seated [William Findley], did not exist, or was removed—the former House only recommend[ed] to the people calling a convention, and recommended too that the Convention should meet two weeks afterward. The people, by complying with that recommendation, show their approbation, and are not jealous of the appointment. Had the House passed a law for obtaining a convention, the gentleman would at that time have told you that you had no right to pass a law for this purpose, and that it was a violation of the constitution, which vested the legislature with no power that could effect it—yet that gentleman now tells you that it is proper for the House to graft upon the bill before you directions to the Convention, with which the legislature has nothing to do. If acting by law in relation to the Convention was improper in the first instance, it must be equally so in the present; if it was urged then, that the House had not the power of calling a convention by law, certainly the gentleman will not expect his argument to be regarded now. He will recollect a convention was only recommended to the choice of the people, and if any of the counties had declined appointing deputies and disregarded the recommendation of the legislature, they might have done so without censure; and here he will take a distinction between recommending a conduct to the people and attempting to tie their deputies down in a manner which the House can have no pretensions to. The amendment proposed might be recommended, but even of that there is no necessity, as the deputies will no doubt possess wisdom and integrity sufficient to direct them how to act in the great charge committed to them by the citizens of Pennsylvania.

ROBERT LOLLAR[2] acknowledged it was a matter of such nicety, that he scarcely knew what to say. He was convinced that requiring so large a number might leave it in the power of a few to put the state to a great expense by keeping the rest waiting for them, but yet it was known that business of this importance should be conducted by a respectable majority of the delegates. In case the members were generally met, I would entertain no objection that the business should be sanctioned with the presence of two-thirds of the members; but at the same time I expect when they are met, that the nature of the business is such, and so well understood by them, that they will not undertake to transact it, without both sufficient number and sufficient time; and I cannot think they would go into the consideration without having the state fully represented; and I must confess that I have sufficient confidence in the gentlemen that are appointed by the freemen of the state, to believe they will do only what is right, without being directed by us; they will have too much respect for their own deliberations, to make them appear in a light manner to their constituents; they cannot wish to do what the motion is intended to prevent.

GEORGE LOGAN: The objection of the gentleman last up [Robert Lollar] is I think nearly this, that it enables the minority to keep the majority waiting, or in other words, to dictate to them and prevent them from proceeding to business; this I think is his objection, and a very sufficient reason it is against the amendment, but I see no necessity for its being proposed; for suppose it was enacted in the bill before us, it cannot be of any use because it is not binding on them; it is contrary to the constitution for the House to interfere, and it is contrary to the very nature of government, because it puts it in the power of a minority to rule the majority. What reason can any person have to advocate a proposition like this? I know a number of persons take every means in their power to defeat the adoption of the Federal Constitution, and I believe they will be equally indefatigable to prevent the members from attending this Convention. But, Mr. Speaker, the business of forming rules belongs to that body alone; and when a majority of delegates have met I hope they will proceed in the business, as I think it their duty, and not come into a method of transacting it which will put it into the power of a minority to dictate to the majority. I should be led to believe that these gentlemen are the advocates of an aristocracy indeed, who can recommend measures calculated only for its support.

JAMES MCLENE: The arguments which have been used that it is contrary to the constitution I can see no weight in, and therefore shall not reply to any of them, but with regard to the observation which is made of the distinction between the House recommending to call a convention, and giving directions as to the number of that convention which is to constitute a quorum when met, I shall only remark, that because the House had the right to command the people in the first, it does not follow that they have no right to direct the other; and allowing the power in one instance, is but a bad argument to contend with in the latter—however I shall merely content myself on the question with saying yes, and calling the yeas and nays; all I mean by the amendment is fair play, and that every part of the delegates of the people may assemble before the business shall be decided by a few. I have as good reason too, sir, for supposing the gentlemen wish for this advantage to get their measure adopted, as they have to suspect me of a design to enable the minority to rule over the majority—but I don't wish that; I only wish fair play, and that every part of the state may be fairly represented before the business is decided on.

RICHARD PETERS: I am at a loss to perceive the gentleman's object. I would ask the member from Westmoreland [William Findley], does he apprehend that the delegates have not time to come down between their election and the first meeting? This seems to be his principal reason for advocating the amendment, and yet the time is as much as allowed to the members of Assembly. Does the gentleman suspect that they will not come with equal celerity on this occasion, and has he any particular ground for such suspicion? His argument of want of time cannot be allowed any weight, when gentlemen consider that they have as much time for their first meeting as the Assembly, and a day more.

WILLIAM ROBINSON: The gentleman from Franklin [James McLene] mentions a distinction that has been taken, but he has not replied to the substance nor stated it fairly, tho even as he stated it, the distinction may be allowed as far as it goes. But no answer has been to this point, tho it has been several times repeated by the gentlemen who have already spoken on the subject, "that the law would be nugatory in itself, which should pretend to bind the deputies in Convention"; and most clearly it would be so, because the power by which they are constituted is superior to those defined by the constitution to be in the House. The calling a convention was not specially in the legislature; they were sensible their power did not extend to oblige by law the people to do an act never intended by the authority of our frame of government; they therefore did not attempt it by law—therefore they only *recommended* a measure which they were satisfied the general good of the United States demanded, and *this* more for the sake of preserving good order and decorum, and to point out some general rule which if the people approved they might comply with, than for anything else, for the people alone were equal to ordering a convention; to make any law to this effect would have been as nugatory then, as this amendment would be now if it was agreed to. The people have shown their highest approbation of the measure recommended, by going into the election; that is so far as I know, but I believe all the counties in the state have generally acquiesced in it, and I have little doubt of the due attendance of those gentlemen whom their fellow citizens have selected to a work of this importance. The question therefore now is, whether the House shall *pass a law* to define the number which shall constitute a quorum, and enable them to do business. But as the Convention don't assemble under the authority of the House, but under an authority superior to the authority of the legislature, under the authority of the people, as if they were in a state of nature, and about to form a government for themselves hereafter; if this is the case, no authority that is inferior can pretend to bind them in any of their rules or actions; it will be therefore contemptible for us to interfere in a business where this interference is beyond our reach, in a case which nothing but the necessity discovered by the people would justify them in undertaking.

WILLIAM FINDLEY did not expect they were to go into a discussion of the theory of appointing a convention; the less that was said about it the better, and therefore he would take no further notice of it. I own myself obliged to the gentleman from the country (Richard Peters) for discovering how ignorant we are on a business of this kind; but what I mean at present, is to explain the words I used which he has referred to. He has assigned as a reason, that the Convention have time enough to meet in, because the length of it is the same as what the Assembly have, and a day more; it is true that is the case—but when I made the observation, I complained it was an inconvenience, that the constitution had affixed so short a period for the meeting of the Assembly, but then the inconvenience is not so great as in the present case; because when the Assembly do meet they have to appoint committees, and some time expires before any business of importance can be even prepared; they have to originate laws, and can do nothing conclusively for a length of time, sufficient to enable the whole to meet. Men that are the best prepared to set off on the execution of the trust consigned to them—men who have their horses ready for the journey, cannot get down in the time allowed; but there is another reason, which requires more time for these gentlemen. The prothonotaries of the counties are directed immediately to notify the members of Assembly of their appointment, but this direction is omitted in the resolution for calling a convention, and the delegates are left to the accidental reports they may hear from their neighbors; for no one is obliged to give them notice of their election. I say, the members of Assembly from the distant counties, cannot attend in time, that is therefore no reason that the delegates in Convention can do so. I had thought the House would come cheerfully into the amendment, in order to prevent the jealousy and suspicion occasioned by the precipitancy of the measure; give the Convention time to assemble, and I have no doubt but they will perform their duty with the prudence and discretion which they ought.

WILLIAM LEWIS: If the question before the House, Mr. Speaker, was as is apprehended by the gentlemen who advocate the amendment, to put it in the power of the delegates of the neighboring counties to assemble, and finish the business before the distant ones could attend; and if it was in the power of the legislature to control their proceedings, I should not be found in opposition. But I take it for granted, those surmises are totally unfounded, and that on the ground that the people of Pennsylvania have full security in the integrity and wisdom of those gentlemen in whom they have placed an unbounded confidence, by delegating them to transact this important and interesting business. They have no doubt considered well how far each of them are worthy of that confidence, by a review of their characters and an acquaintance with their sentiments, and elected none in whom they had not a firm belief of their ability and veracity. For my own part, I have the most perfect reliance on the members to that Convention, and assure myself, they wish their meeting to be as full as possible, in order to give dignity and force to their decisions, which a partial representation must of consequence diminish. Now, as I can't see any ground for supposing the measure will be improperly hurried by the gentlemen in whom our constituents repose such especial trust, and because I see they must destroy, in a great measure, the desirable object in view, if any unwarrantable expedition is used, I shall not consent to instruct them in what they are to do.

Whether it is reasonable or not, that a quorum of representatives of an independent state should consist of the number mentioned in the amendment, or whether a less majority or a bare majority would be more advisable, I shall not undertake to say, because it is a matter with which this House has nothing to do, inasmuch as it particularly relates to a frame of government or constitution of society. No law declaring for a majority of two-thirds could be obligatory upon the people, though the House of Assembly are undoubtedly compelled to submit to this regulation, because when our government was framed, it was then declared and stipulated, that two-thirds of the members from all the counties who elected, should be requisite to form the existence of a general assembly. The gentlemen who support the amendment, have not distinguished in the point they noticed; they argue indeed, that as the House did direct calling a convention, that they have the power also to direct the regulation of that body. But this, Mr. Speaker, I apprehend does not follow; the situation of our affairs had become such, as to make it necessary for the people to seek security under some mode of government other than what obtained amongst us. A form has been laid down by the collected wisdom of a Federal Convention appointed to correct the evil; nay, to save the Union from impending ruin; and a mode was devised by them to make it necessary for each legislature in the several states to declare whether they would or would not recommend to their constituents, the calling a convention to ratify the frame of government presented them. The House had therefore a right under this exercise of sovereign authority by the people, to say whether or not they approved what was proposed to them to act upon. The House satisfied of the propriety of the measure, proceed under the same authority to recommend to the citizens of Pennsylvania, that they delegate proper persons to a state convention; but the House had no power to pass a law obliging the inhabitants to hold such election; they had even no right to say the people should or should not choose deputies. If the legislature had declared they should make choice, the people might refuse; and did we say they should not, the forbiddance must be futile; it being not the fact that the Convention originated or is supported by the authority of the Assembly, so no act of ours can in anywise be binding upon them; the business came into existence under the people—the mode of interference for the legislatures was laid down, in conformity with which the late House recommended an election for deputies, and the people have generally met as recommended, as far as my information extends; perhaps all have held an election, and when the members are met, they will be under an authority different from that of the legislature; they will be under an authority paramount to the authority of this House—by which I would be understood to mean the supreme original authority of the people at large, who have a right to delegate to them all powers which they judge it proper to invest deputies with, appointed to adopt and concur in a plan of government, which promises them and their posterity perfect security, liberty and happiness. The Assembly then, sir, did proper to determine on recommending, whether a convention should be called or not, because they were required to make this decision; but they have no right to proceed further, and lay down rules and regulations for that convention, because that body stands on superior ground to what we occupy, inasmuch as they are bound to no forms by a previous constitution.

But let me turn a moment to ask the advocates for this restriction, what may be the consequences if this doctrine is allowed? If they possess the right to say that two-thirds shall be a quorum, they possess the right of saying also that nine-tenths must be the number; nay, they may go further, and require the presence and consent of every individual. And what consequences will result from a power of this nature? It will enable the legislature to defeat the intentions of the people; and although every county having chosen delegates, and they are disposed to ratify the Constitution, yet it is rendered impracticable by such interference; wherefore the less authority supersedes its paramount, and suppresses a measure resting upon authority superior to what itself possesses; it is not only irrational but absurd, to suppose a right of this kind vested in the legislature; beside, if this power is acknowledged, it goes even to prevent that body from sitting at all, or to be adjourned for seven years to come, and by such law defeat the wishes of the people. I don't think, sir, that either the member [James McLene] who introduced the amendment, or the gentleman [William Findley] who seconded it, have any intentions of this nature by their motion, but I bring these consequences into view, that the House may see from them the impossibility of possessing powers which the amendment infers we have. I submit it to every gentleman on this floor, and I submit it with confidence, that the House from its relation to the people, and to the Convention, can have no right to make laws for the conduct of a superior body, and because such power involves in it a confession that we may prevent the Convention from deliberating on what they have been chosen for. It is impossible from these circumstances, that the Convention can be within the power of the House, but rests upon the people in general; it is a matter not mentioned in our constitution, which nowhere assigns us such powers, nor had any of the kind in contemplation at its formation. It is impossible that the Convention can be within the power of the House, because it originates upon higher authority than a legislative; and because it would be dangerous it should, as it involves an acknowledgment of a right to defeat the supreme power of the people. It is also certain, that if the House had this power, there exists no occasion for exercising it, as the deputies to Convention are worthy of our confidence; and the inconvenience it is supposed to correct, could not take place, as it must defeat the object of those who might attempt it—from all which reasons I conclude, that the amendment is improper and nugatory, wherefore the House will reject it.

The question was now taken on the amendment, which was determined in the negative.

The Speaker asked Mr. M'Lean if he persisted in his call for the yeas and nays, but he declined it. However the following members rose in its support:

Messrs. M'Lene, Findley, Piper, M'Calmont, Miley, Beale, Clark, M'Dowell, Flamaker [Flenniken] and Allison.—10.[3]

1. The Assembly *Minutes* for 9 November (Mfm:Pa. 210–A) are not printed because they add little to the *Debates*. For Dallas' account in the *Pennsylvania Herald*, see Mfm:Pa. 210–A.

2. Lollar's speech is inserted here where Thomas Lloyd intended it to be. The speech appears in the "Errata" of the *Debates* with the notation that it was "accidentally omitted."

3. At this point the *Minutes* (Mfm:Pa. 210–A) state that the House ordered that the act be engrossed. On the 10th the engrossed act was brought into the Assembly and the Speaker was directed to sign it. (For the act see Mfm:Pa. 210–A.)

F. PUBLIC AND PRIVATE COMMENTARIES ON THE CONSTITUTION AND THE CONVENTION
7 November–11 December 1787

Between the election of delegates on 6 November and the meeting of the Convention on 20 November, the number of Pennsylvania Federalist and Antifederalist publications decreased, while the major essays reprinted from newspapers in other states increased. The number of major original and reprinted items was about evenly divided between the Federalists and Antifederalists, although in terms of squibs and news reports from other states, the Federalists had the advantage (for examples of squibs, see CC:233–B, 258, 259).

The principal Pennsylvania Federalist publication during this period was a pamphlet by Pelatiah Webster (8 November, CC:244), answering "Brutus" I (CC:178), a New York Antifederalist. Webster's pamphlet, like his first pamphlet (CC:125–B) which answered the "Address of the Seceding Assemblymen" (I:B above), was signed "A Citizen of Philadelphia." Other important Federalist items were the answer to "An Officer of the Late Continental Army" by "Plain Truth," 10 November (II:C above); "The Prayer of an American Citizen," 7–10 November (CC:235); and "G," 10 November (Mfm:Pa. 217). Federalist material reprinted from out-of-state newspapers included "The Federalist" I–III (CC:201, 217, 228), and Roger Sherman and Oliver Ellsworth's letter to the Governor of Connecticut (CC:192). Between 12 and 21 November six Pennsylvania newspapers reprinted an item from the *New Jersey Journal,* 7 November (CC:233–A) reporting George Washington's only speech in the Constitutional Convention.

The principal Pennsylvania Antifederalist publications were "Philadelphiensis" I, 7 November (printed immediately below); "Centinel" III, 8 November (CC:243); "One of the Dissenting Assemblymen [William Findley?], 14 November (Mfm:Pa. 224); and "One of the Late Army," 14 November (Mfm:Pa. 225). Antifederalist items reprinted from out-of-state newspapers included "Brutus, Jr." (CC:239); "Cincinnatus to James Wilson, Esquire," I–II (CC:222, 241); and Elbridge Gerry's letter to the Massachusetts General Court (CC:227). Gerry's letter, outlining his objections to the Constitution, was reprinted ten times in Pennsylvania between 16 November and 26 December.

During the meeting of the Convention (20 November–15 December), the number of major Federalist newspaper essays continued to decline, while there was a resurgence in the number of Antifederalist items published. The need to amend the Constitution became the principal issue. Between 2 October and the opening of the Convention, many Antifederalists had demanded amendments, and some had called for a second constitutional convention. For examples, see "Address of the Seceding Assemblymen" (I:B above); "Centinel" I, 5 October (II:A above); "A Democratic Federalist," 17 October, "M.C.," 27 October, "An Officer of the Late Continental Army," 6 November (all in II:C above); "Philadelphiensis" I, 7 November (printed immediately below); "An Old Whig" I–V (CC:157, 170, 181, 202, 224); and Mfm:Pa. 140, 141, 164, 225.

To counteract the Antifederalist campaign, "A Plain Citizen," 22 November (II:F below) asked the Convention not to propose amendments and discouraged the idea of calling a second constitutional convention. Other Federalists discussed issues designed to divert attention from the question of amendments, while still others ridiculed Antifederalist leaders.

Antifederalists reacted with essays emphasizing the need for amendments. They realized that the Convention would ratify the Constitution, but they argued that it should recommend amendments. A few days after the Convention convened, several Philadelphia Antifederalists purchased more than one hundred copies of the pamphlet *Letters from a Federal Farmer to the Republican,* published in New York on 8 November. The author stressed the need for "a complete federal bill of rights." Copies of the pamphlet were given to some members of the Convention. (See Mfm:Pa. 240. For the pamphlet's author and national circulation, see CC:242.)

On 28 November, the same day the Convention debated the issue of a bill of rights, "An Old Whig" VII (II:F below) outlined the procedure for calling a second constitutional convention to consider and propose amendments to the Constitution. A pamphlet signed "A Federal Republican," published the same day (excerpt, II:F below), also supported a second convention. On 3 and 5 December two Philadelphia newspapers reprinted George Mason's objections to the Constitution (CC:276 A–C). Mason's principal objection was the lack of a "declaration of rights." For other Antifederalist writings which stressed the need for amendments as well as other issues, see "An Old Whig" VI (CC:292); "Philadelphiensis" II–IV (CC:302, 320, 342); "Centinel" IV–V (CC:311, 318); "Alfred" (CC:345); and "Algernon Sydney" I (Mfm:Pa. 234).

In early December Antifederalist petitions from Cumberland County and the Philadelphia area were sent to the Convention requesting that it adjourn without ratifying the Constitution. These petitions (II:F below) requested a bill of rights and additional time for the people to consider the Constitution. The Cumberland County petition was read to the Convention, but there is no record that the Convention ever received the Philadelphia petition. The Convention debated the issue of amendments but refused to allow any amendments to be placed on its Journals. Amendments remained an issue long after the Convention ratified the Constitution.

Philadelphiensis I, Freeman's Journal, 7 November[1]

When the advocates of a cause use their endeavors to stop a free and thorough investigation of the subject, we as naturally and as justly infer that the cause is a bad one, as that two and two make four. A good cause, like pure gold, may be tried in the fire and yet retain its full weight and value, or like the utensils of husbandry grow brighter and fitter for use the more it is handled. The application of this observation in respect to the friends of the new Constitution is easy. They see that the more this new scheme of government is discussed, the more tyrannical and ill-adapted to the present circumstances of America does it appear. We find, say they, that to reason in favor of the Constitution is only to give its enemies more latitude to condemn; for although we could call in to our aid a sufficient stock of sophistical arguments and circumstances, by which we might dispose the incautious part of the people to join us in establishing this government, yet we have already experienced that by such means we defeat ourselves; as we thereby give a greater scope for those of more penetration to write against the Constitution. The advocates of this government have also tried an expedient which has been known to succeed upon some occasions, namely, to answer *reason* and *argument* with scurrility and personal invective; but even here they have failed, for the magnitude of the object is so great, as to reduce every little circumstance of that kind to a mere point. In little matters this sort of procedure might do well enough, but in an affair of such vast importance to the whole continent of America its operation is nugatory.

In this desperate situation of affairs, it need not to be wondered at, that the friends of this despotic scheme of government were driven to the last and the only alternative from which there was any probability of success; namely, the abolition of the *freedom of the press.* And accordingly we find, in the *Independent Gazetteer* of the 29th of October, a writer who signs himself A Pennsylvania Mechanic says,[2] "It appears, by a late eastern paper, that the publisher of the *Massachusetts Gazette* is determined to publish no sentiments on this important subject (viz. the new Constitution), unless the writers leave their names with the printer, that anyone that may be desirous of knowing the author, may be informed. No honest man, no true friend to America or to the liberty or happiness of mankind can object to this. For your imitation, gentlemen, I humbly propose the conduct of this your worthy brother, the publisher of the *Massachusetts Gazette.*"[3] This Pennsylvania Mechanic one would take to be a blacksmith, whose true employment is to construct chains to confine to perpetual slavery the freemen of America; but, be that as it may, we find that he can soon call in more of his fellow craftsmen to his assistance, who even seem to be more expert at their occupation than our mechanic abovementioned. One of these tradesmen has given us a small portion of his skill in the business of chainmaking in the

Independent Gazetteer of the 31st of October, under the signature of Galba,[4] which small scrap of his workmanship I beg leave to transcribe that we may be the better able to judge of its excellency. He says, "Mr. Oswald, The hint in your paper of last Monday, that everyone ought to leave his name with the printer who writes for or against the new form of government proposed by the honorable Convention, is only in my opinion right in part; for what reason is there that the patriotic gentlemen who write in favor of a scheme of government that holds forth peace, happiness and prosperity to our distressed country, should, by leaving their names with the printers, be exposed to the malevolence of those wretches who pretend to find fault with it. Indeed, I think it perfectly right that those who wantonly write against it should leave their names, that they may be justly exposed to the contempt and indignation of their fellow citizens, as enemies and traitors to their country; and I hope every patriotic printer in the Union will for the future pay proper attention to the justness and absolute propriety of this hint."

Stop and pause a little, *Galba*. I really believe you were not in your right senses when you wrote this, your hint; for if you had been studying for seven years how you might effectually injure the new Constitution, you could not have hit on a thought more to your purpose. Your zeal has transported you so far beyond the bounds of propriety and discretion, that the haughtiest lordling and friend to arbitrary government in America must hang down his head and blush upon reading your ill-timed hint. I assure you, sir, I think you have explained yourself right cleverly; you have given us a specimen of the genius and spirit of our new government. Here we see pretty plainly through your excellent regulation of the press, how things are to be carried on after the adoption of the new Constitution. All the writings must be on ONE SIDE. The new Constitution appears so glorious and immaculate to *Galba,* that all those who have sufficient spirit to avow their sentiments on the occasion are to be called traitors and enemies to their country, if they do not just think as he does. And to render them still more odious and execrable, he would have the printers throughout the Union to publish their names with their pieces should any of them have the imprudence to write on the subject. I wonder that *Galba* did not propose a suit of tar and feathers; but as the tailors have of late become a little bashful about trying on this sort of apparel, and the conceit is therefore a little stale, he would have those obnoxious writers to leave their names with the printers, that they may be clothed by their fellow citizens with *indignation and contempt,* as with a garment; whilst he would have the patriotic writers in favor of the Constitution entirely exempted from such an abstracted kind of a *coat* and *jacket*. We thank you, *Galba,* for your kind and very liberal hint; for it certainly merits our attention. I make no doubt but it is the wish of a thousand of our wellborn as well as of yourself, that the printers would comply with your request. Such a thought is natural enough; it must naturally be the wish of every *little petty tyrant* in the United States. But most of the printers in Philadelphia are men of sentiment, they are lovers of liberty and the rights of mankind and will necessarily despise such hints, and treat them with the contempt they deserve. There is such a degree of meanness in the requisition, especially in that of *Galba-Longhead,* as must insult the understanding and integrity of every independent printer who sees it.

Galba, your hint was rather calculated for the meridian of Boston than that of Philadelphia, and I doubt not but you and the Boston printers have one and the same object—*self is an old fellow.* This trite saying, I think, will apply. In Boston the liberty of the press is now completely abolished; and hence all other privileges and rights of the people will in a short time be destroyed. No wonder then, that the printers in Boston would exert themselves in favor of this new government. Their present condition is a drawing in miniature of that in which the adoption of the new Constitution will certainly place the whole Union; so that after the nature of the prince of darkness, they wish to have all their fellow citizens in the same dreadful situation with themselves. [Benjamin] Russell, the printer of the *Massachusetts Centinel,* has the effrontery to insult the freemen of America so far as to say in his paper of October the 10th "That, aiming thereby to be just, he is determined not to give place to any piece against the new Constitution, except the writer leave his name to be made public if desired."[5] Russell, I would not hire a mob to bear you aloft as an object of hatred and contempt, nor would I bribe them to hang you in effigy, although you really deserve it. I am sensible of the danger of inflaming the multitude in a free government, for when a public tumult has once been raised, justice has often been sacrificed to appease it; so that I do not intend to raise a fatal prejudice against you. My intention is to consider the nature and consequences of your conduct as an advocate for the new Constitution, which, as far as it respects the liberty of the press, has done more prejudice to your cause than its enemies can do by the violence of their accusations, however well they may be founded.

On so momentous a subject as the new Constitution, it is as plain as any axiom in geometry, that it is of no importance whether or not a writer gives his name; it is with the illustrations and arguments he affords us, and not with his name, we have any concern. Besides, this practice would tend to draw off the mind of the writer from the calm investigation of the subject, to recriminations and personal invectives. And, moreover, men of ability, and of a modest, timid or diffident cast of mind would be deterred altogether from publishing their sentiments. Of what use could it be to the public to know the name of the writer of the piece signed Lucius, that Russell refused to publish? Certainly of no use at all. *Non quis sed quid.* It was not with the author of Lucius that the freemen of Massachusetts had anything to do, but with his reasoning; which, if it were just, ought not to be suppressed, and if it were fallacious should be refuted. Let candor and impartiality be the characteristics of our printers, in respect to this new government, which involves in its consequences the happiness or misery of millions yet unborn. This is the line of conduct which men of honor and integrity will naturally pursue, and I find an unspeakable satisfaction when I every day behold the printers of Philadelphia following this plan almost to a man. And hence I am led to conclude, that the *Pennsylvania Mechanic* and his successor *Galba* must find their hints to be a little premature; such doctrine might have suited finely about the time of the mock ringing of the bells in this city, for joy and gladness, that Congress had recommended the adoption of this new plan of government to the different states (which, by the by, they unluckily forgot to recommend to this present hour). The gentlemen who are friends to the new Constitution had better not blab so freely, especially in regard to the freedom of the press; they ought to wait until this government of governments is once established, and then instead of a coat and jacket of *contempt* and *indignation* they may speak boldly about a gallows, a gibbet, or at least a dungeon, for such writers as the *Old Whig* or *Centinel,* who have dared to speak like freemen. I wonder that our *wellborn* should allow such mean fellows to write against this their government— such base wretches ought not to live in the same country with *gentlemen*; and as soon as our new government is confirmed, these vile enemies to its *splendor* and *dignity* shall quit their capering, I'll warrant them; a federal soldier with a fixed bayonet will soon give such daring dogs their quietus. Ah! what glorious days are coming; how I anticipate the brilliancy of the American court! Behold that gilded chariot set with diamonds and drawn by eight Arabian horses. Off with your hats you poltroons, here is the President going in state to the senate-house to confirm the law for the *abolition of the liberty of the press.* Men and brethren will not these things be so? Yes, most assuredly, if we adopt the new Constitution in its present form. These things will be so. Rouse then, rouse my fellow citizens, and show yourselves to be freemen. This is the most important object that ever presented itself to your understanding. The independence of America, which God himself vouchsafed through his infinite mercy to confer upon us, must end in a curse, if this tyrannical government be suffered to be established. But forbid it heaven!

I was told, last Saturday evening [3 November], by a gentleman of veracity whom I met at the meeting at the State House, that several persons had waited that day on Mrs. [Eleazer] Oswald,[(a)] for the purpose of requesting her not to publish any pieces against the new Constitution, at the same time intimating that if she persisted, she would forfeit their interests; and that in consequence of her spirited reply, several had that very day withdrawn their subscriptions for the paper.[6] This is truly an alarming circumstance. Where is the freeman in America that this is not sufficient to rouse from a state of supineness? My brethren, be circumspect on this momentous occasion, "And, take unto you the whole armor of God, that ye may be able to withstand in the evil day, and having done all to stand. Stand therefore, having your loins girt about with truth, and having on the breastplate of righteousness. And your feet shod with the preparation of the gospel of peace. Above all, taking the shield of faith, wherewith ye shall be able to quench all the fiery darts of the wicked." *Amen.*

(a) Colonel Oswald being abroad.

1. The *Independent Gazetteer* printed "Philadelphiensis" on the same day but without the last paragraph. The *Carlisle Gazette* reprinted "Philadelphiensis" on 5 December. The author was presumably Benjamin Workman, an Irish immigrant, almanac-maker, and tutor at the University of Pennsylvania. He published eleven more essays by 9 April 1788. All of them are printed in *Commentaries on the Constitution* (CC:237 for more on the author).

2. See Mfm:Pa. 170.

3. On 16 October the publisher of the *Massachusetts Gazette* declared that he would not print unsigned articles about the Constitution if authors did not leave their names (CC:165).

4. For "Galba," see Mfm:Pa. 174; and for a reply to "Galba," see Mfm:Pa. 185.

5. For this item, not reprinted in Pennsylvania, see RCS:Mass. For Russell's reply to "Philadelphiensis" and for "Philadelphiensis' " rejoinder, see CC:237 B–C.

6. Mrs. Elizabeth Oswald was the daughter of John Holt, publisher of *The New-York Journal* before the Revolution.

A Freeman, Pennsylvania Gazette, 7 November

I have been informed that a certain *clergyman,*[1] who presides over a literary institution in this city and well known for his Antifederal disposition, has commanded two of his pupils to destroy their speeches which they had prepared for the ensuing commencement, because they contained some sentiments in favor of the proposed glorious Federal Constitution. I wish, therefore, to be acquainted whether the *political* as well as the literary and moral conduct of his scholars is under the control of this man, or, if these commands are submitted to, may we not expect that he will attempt next to invade the rights of conscience and bias their *religious* opinions?

1. "A certain clergyman" was the Reverend John Ewing, a Presbyterian minister and provost of the Constitutionalist-controlled University of Pennsylvania. For other attacks, see Mfm:Pa. 118, 183, 276.

Pittsburgh Meeting, 9 November[1]

At a meeting of the inhabitants of Pittsburgh, at the house of Messrs. Tannehills, for the special purpose of taking the sense of this town with respect to the system of confederate government proposed by the late Convention at Philadelphia.

General John Gibson[2] in the chair.

It was considered that having had an opportunity of hearing on both sides the strictures which have been made upon this system of government in conversation, in the gazettes, and in other writings, on mature deliberation, we are of opinion that it is the result of much political wisdom, good sense and candor in those who framed it; that we have no reason to expect anything better from any other body of men assembled in convention; that from the necessity of *mutual concession* with the different states, it is not probable that anything more equal could be formed; that our prosperity depends on our speedy adoption of some mode of government more efficient than that which we now possess; that of all people it becomes us of the western country more especially to desire an object of this kind; as from the weakness of Congress to take proper measures with the courts of Spain and Britain, we are on the one hand deprived of the advantages of the Mississippi trade, which is our natural right, and on the other, are liable to the incursions of the savages, the posts on the lakes not being yet delivered up according to treaty.[3]

Resolved therefore unanimously, That it is our ardent wish and hope that this system of government may be speedily adopted.

Signed by order of the meeting, John Gibson, chairman.

1. *Pittsburgh Gazette,* 17 November. This item was reprinted four times in Pennsylvania and fourteen times outside Pennsylvania by 7 February 1788. For a description of the meeting, written in February 1788 by Alexander Fowler, see Mfm:Pa. 414.

2. Gibson was a tavern keeper and a major general of militia. He served in the

Pennsylvania constitutional convention of 1789–1790 and in 1800 was appointed secretary of the Indiana Territory.

3. For a newspaper discussion of the Mississippi trade, see "G," *Pittsburgh Gazette,* 10 November, Mfm:Pa. 217.

Alexander Fowler to John Nicholson, Pittsburgh, 10 November[1]

I have been under the necessity of drawing on you in favor of Mr. Samuel Colhoun[2] for £5.14.9 which you will please pay should you have received the interest on my certificates. Our Western Luminary, the malevolent [Hugh H.] B[rackenrid]ge, seems determined to show his teeth on all occasions, but fortunate for us humble men, he has not power to bite. I know not what our new proposed frame of government may do in favor of such characters. God forbid that we should be so much allured by *names* as to forget measures, or so blindfolded as to worship a sign post at the expense of our liberties. I am alarmed at the spirit of faction in this extreme corner of the state introduced by our new made monitor, but notwithstanding his insidious attempts, we have been enabled to return such men to the Convention as will not betray their trust, nor give countenance to any form of government that may tend either to annihilate or even abridge our privileges. I enclose you a paper this moment handed to me from the printers stuffed with malevolent ribaldry, the production of our Western Bard.[3] He is determined to give our weavers and farmers no quarters. I wish to see more of them here and fewer of his fraternity. I was told by the late worthy Mr. [Joseph] Reed that Brackenridge had wrote himself out of credit in Philadelphia.[4] If the people have common penetration or resentment, he must soon be in the like situation here. History, in my opinion, can scarcely produce a man so eminent for vanity, so prone to corruption and servility, as well as every other baneful quality proper to dignify a contemptible tool. On his appearance in this country I considered him as a man of virtue and was his fast friend. I am not now his enemy, but I despise him, as I ever have and ever will engines of oppression.

I should be happy to hear from you on all occasions when you can spare time, and pray, enclose me such political pieces as you may think useful or worth reading. Mr. Colhoun waits for my letter therefore must conclude.

1. RC, Nicholson Papers, PHarH. Fowler, a Pittsburgh merchant, had left the British army and joined the American army during the Revolution. In the late 1790s he was one of Pittsburgh's leading Democratic-Republicans.

2. Calhoun was a Pittsburgh merchant.

3. Fowler refers to Brackenridge's attack upon the seceding members in the *Pittsburgh Gazette*, 3–10 November (Mfm:Pa. 197). For another letter by Fowler critical of Brackenridge, see Mfm:Pa. 249.

4. Reed, president of the Supreme Executive Council from 1778 to 1781, probably referred to the enemies that Brackenridge had made in 1779 while editor of *The United States Magazine* in Philadelphia.

William Shippen, Jr. to Thomas Lee Shippen, Philadelphia, 18, 22 November (excerpts)[1]

Your friend [William] Jackson will not offer himself for trial till he is so accomplished as to meet the best lawyers on the most difficult argument. I imagine the truth is he is looking out for some lucrative place under the new Constitution, despairing of success at the bar.[2] You would be surprised to see what violent hatred is conceived by all the Federalists against everyone who dares to speak a word against the new Constitution; tis as great as the Tories ever had against the Whigs. They would hang them all and yet all the arguments they have in its favor are comprehended in these 3: that great and good men were 4 months framing it, that anarchy and distress will follow its rejection, and that we never can hope to see so good a one if this is not received—and they add if it is found not to be a good one it can be altered. In one of the pieces I send these are well answered, yet the people in general are satisfied and frightened and will adopt it. There certainly should be a bill of rights prefixed securing the liberty of the press, the liberty of conscience and trial by jury, the legislative and executive power should be more independent of each other, and expensive vexatious suits be prevented. It would then be an excellent Constitution don't you think so my son?[3]

[22 November] Prager at last fixes his departure on Saturday [24 November] and I am making a packet for my young barrister. In it you will find the debates of our last session of A[ssembly] taken by T[homas] Lloyd, an *American Museum* for October, and all the papers against and for the new Constitution: Brutus said to be by R[ichard] H[enry] Lee or [John] Jay, Cincinnatus by A[rthur] Lee, Old Whig and Centinel by a club—[George] Bryan, [John] Smilie, [James] Hutchn [Hutchinson], etc. 61 members of the Convention met the 2d day. [Frederick Augustus] Mulenberg the President. Your grandfather[4] is this minute standing at the window reading the morning paper, a perfect Antifederalist since he saw R. H. L[ee] and desires his love to his grandson. He left your dear mother as well as usual and the rest all well. He is now reading aloud a law case which he says I may send to Tom.

11 o'clock, just returned from the concert where Mrs. Morris told

me her sons would be in London this winter. You must find them out and attend to them. Bobby and Gouvero gone to Virginia to aid the Federalists.[5]

1. RC, Shippen Family Papers, DLC (printed CC:232).
2. The reference is probably to Major William Jackson, who had served as secretary to the Constitutional Convention.
3. For Thomas Lee Shippen's views, see his letters to his father, 6 and 20 November, CC:354–D and H.
4. William Shippen, Sr. was a Germantown physician who had served in the Continental Congress with Richard Henry Lee.
5. See Gouverneur Morris to George Washington, 30 October, n. 1, II:C above.

A Plain Citizen, To the Honorable the Convention of the State of Pennsylvania, Independent Gazetteer, 22 November[1]

The fate of America is now suspended, as it were, in a balance, and awaits its final doom from you and the conventions of the different states; with whom it rests, either to entail misery on millions yet unborn or to transmit your dear-bought liberties, inviolate, to your latest posterity.

Consider, then, gentlemen, the importance of the business before you. Behold! your bleeding country supplicates your aid to snatch her from the verge of destruction, and cries for your helping hands to guide her tottering footsteps from the brink of ruin! Behold! the various orders of mechanics, the manufacturers, the merchants, and the husbandmen of America, at the recital of whose calamities humanity shudders!

Behold! the American name insulted and despised by all the world! Nay more—Behold! our federal government, the laughingstock and footstool of desperate and abandoned villains at home! And, surely, you will not hesitate to adopt every measure which may be calculated to relieve the sufferings of your distressed fellow citizens, to vindicate the honor and dignity of your injured country, and, to render her once more respectable among the nations of the earth.

The Constitution, which is now submitted to your consideration, is proposed to answer the above purposes; in discussing this, I trust you will bear in mind, that you are to determine upon a form of government calculated, not to suit the sinister views of any particular state, but to promote the general interest and happiness of the United States.

This proposed Constitution has, for some time past, been a general topic of argumentation and has engaged the attention of many able writers, both for and against it; but I am sorry to find that a majority of these have not been guided by that calm and moderate reason, which the magnitude of the subject deserved.

Many of the advocates for the new Constitution are transported, by an immoderate zeal, beyond the bounds of reason and scruple not to assert that it has neither faults nor imperfections, as if it were like the Jewish theocracy, the immediate work of heaven.

The Convention were not possessed of arrogance enough to think this, more than any other human work, entirely free from faults, and, therefore, have provided for its future amendment, in such particulars as the sense of the people may, at any time, require.

Its opponents have had recourse to the most wretched stratagems to prejudice the people against it. They have made use of the most unmerited calumny and detraction in charging the worthy patriots of the Federal Convention with "insidious" and "long-meditated designs of enslaving their fellow citizens." When I found the enemies of the new Constitution, instead of confining themselves to argument, thus endeavoring to blacken some of the most respectable characters America can boast of, I confess their cause appeared, to me, to be a very bad one, for reason needs not the assistance of slander to enforce her arguments.

This Constitution comes before you sanctioned by names which do honor to human nature; but, since all are liable to err, let the merits of the system itself, and the situation of your country, be your only criterion.

An idea has been held out by some, who, perhaps may be well-meaning people, that the different state conventions may alter and amend the Constitution at pleasure. As this mistaken notion will, probably, be carried, by some members, into your honorable house, permit me to bestow a few remarks upon it.

That the Convention have given no power to the citizens of any state to make the smallest alteration in the proposed plan of government is an incontrovertible fact; well knowing that the different states, unless when convened together, can never be unanimous in anything. This is evident from the contempt with which many of them have, from time to time, treated the requisitions of Congress. When the impost was required, it was only granted by some of the states, and that upon such terms as each of them pleased. Is there, then, the smallest probability that the alterations, which might please any particular state, would be accepted by the others? Certainly, there is not.

If one state has a right to propose amendments, so have the other twelve; supposing them all to enjoy and exercise this privilege, in its utmost extent, what would be the consequence? The petty interests of a single state, not the welfare and happiness of the Union, would predominate in each state convention; so that, instead of the present regular and federal plan, we should have a parcel of narrow, partial and illiberal proposals, jumbled together in one confused chaos, which would require no less than the omnipotent *fiat* of Jehovah to reduce them to order or to consistency with each other.

I conceive, with due submission to your wisdom, that the chief object you are to consider is whether it will be more conducive to the happiness of your country to adopt the proposed Constitution, as it is, or to reject it and continue to encounter all the evils with which we are beset, under the present Confederation. And, here, you have many powerful incentives to urge the adoption of the new plan.

Our situation is truly alarming and not to be trifled with; liberty, in these states, has been changed into licentiousness, and this, if some remedy be not speedily adopted, cannot fail to shackle the freeborn sons of America with the chains of slavery. I repeat it; unless a firm federal government shall be immediately established, slavery is inevitable. The people are distressed beyond measure; their patience is nearly exhausted; and they are now as anxious to get rid of the present form of federal government, as they formerly were to shake off the yoke of Britain.

Is there not reason, then, to fear that if the proposed Constitution shall be rejected, they will enroll themselves under the banners of some enterprising ruffian, and, at one bold stroke, annihilate all government and introduce anarchy into these states? Should this ever be the unhappy fate of our country, liberty must take her flight from amongst us never, never to return again, and we must become the abject slaves of some hardy villain, who will give us a government and laws, at the point of the bayonet. May Heaven guide *your* councils and avert the impending danger.

Nor are these groundless chimeras of a disturbed brain. Let any man reflect coolly upon the situation of Massachusetts last winter and of Pennsylvania at the present moment; let him inquire into the sentiments of the people in general, who have long murmured against the present plan of government, and look up to the proposed Constitution, as the only relief for all their calamities. I say, let him weigh well these circumstances and declare, if he can, that my apprehensions are vain.

It has been suggested, that another Federal Convention should be called, to revise the proposed plan of government.[2] To this, it is sufficient to answer that a considerable time would be required to carry it into effect, and that, in the meantime, the popular frenzy might rise to extremes and be productive of the most serious consequences. Besides, it is by no means probable, that men, of sufficient prudence and abilities, would be found, hardy enough, to undertake the task, after the virulence, and scurrility the worthy members of the late Convention have experienced; not even the illustrious SAVIOR OF HIS COUNTRY has been exempted from the most illiberal torrents of abuse, that envy or malice, could suggest.

In short, gentlemen, I hope you will find many urgent reasons for ratifying the new Constitution. If it should even be found imperfect in some particulars, I trust you will nevertheless adopt it, when you consider, that the members of Congress, under this Constitution, will represent the people more effectually than even the members of the late Federal Convention; and may be instructed, by their constituents, to make such alterations and amendments in it, as may be found expedient, still further to secure the blessings of liberty to America; which, when ratified by the people, as in the present instance, shall become a part of the Federal Constitution. The members, who shall be first chosen, under the new plan, may be instructed, for this purpose, by the people, if found necessary. That real patriotism, and wisdom, may guide your councils is the sincere wish of A Plain Citizen.

1. "Plain Truth," printed immediately below, implies that James Wilson was "A Plain Citizen."

2. See "Centinel" I, 5 October, II:A above; and "An Old Whig" IV–V, 27 October and 1 November, CC:202, 224.

Plain Truth, Independent Gazetteer, 24 November

Mr. Oswald: A writer in your paper of Thursday last, presents a long inflammatory address to our Convention;[1] I have with some little pains dissected, this high sounding studied performance, which although it contains the essence and quintessence of all the decenter essays yet wrote in favor of the new Constitution, I find all the arguments therein urged in favor of adopting it, may be reduced to the two worn-out and often refuted ones, viz. the great names of all the *great men* of the great Convention and the pressing necessity of adopting any efficient government however despotic and dangerous to the liberties of the people it might be. An essay which you republished from the *New York Journal* in your paper of the 14th instant—under the signature of Brutus, Junior—is well worth everybody's attention; it contains a full and clear answer to these two fallacious arguments.[2]

The writer before mentioned has the modesty in this address to declare that the people of Pennsylvania, represented and assembled in this honorable Convention, "have not the power of proposing any alterations, or right to say what sort of government they would like"; for, says he, "that power has not been given them by our late Grand Convention, and it properly belongs to" (the great men in) "the federal conventions." He here discovers himself and his principles, although he endeavors to conceal them, and affects to have a large share of candor.

This writer further says, that calumny and detraction have constantly been used instead of argument and reason by the writers against his favorite plan of government. Here he does not show more candor than he did in his speech to the town meeting, when he said "that the regulation of trial by jury was too difficult for the Great Convention," who only sat 4 months.[3] I say when he talks of calumny he forgets his own productions, viz. the pieces signed Awaiting Vengeance, Tar and Feathers, and numerous others denouncing the most dreadful threats against any who should dare even to lisp their sentiments about the Constitution.[4] He forgets the numerous paragraphs he has wrote for a certain weekly paper which contained the most glaring falsehoods, about Messrs. [George] Mason, [Elbridge] Gerry, [Edmund] Randolph, [George] Clinton, [Richard Henry] Lee, etc. and all others who opposed the violent measures used by the advocates of this his favorite plan.[5] He forgets the decent conversation of himself and his associates in this city, etc. this two months past. And I am sure he must forget on the other hand that the Old Whigs, Centinels, Brutuses, Cincinnatuses, and twenty other pieces are plain, sound and argumentative, adapted to the smallest understandings.

This gentleman does not now recollect anything about the late riot, in which, it is certain, those most urging for the adoption of the new Constitution and the leaders of them were concerned, and very likely himself if report says true. Was this in character to make a midnight attack upon the lodgings of the western assemblymen and councillors, because they would not agree with them in the new Constitution.[6]

1. "A Plain Citizen," 22 November, printed immediately above.
2. "Brutus, Jr.," 8 November (CC:239).
3. See James Wilson's Speech in the State House Yard, 6 October, II:A above.
4. "Awaiting Vengeance" has not been located, but an article signed "Avenging Justice," 17 October (II:C above) denies the need for a bill of rights. See also "Tar and Feathers," 28 September and 2 October, II:A above.
5. The reference is probably to the *Pennsylvania Gazette,* which printed attacks upon George Mason and Richard Henry Lee (for examples, see CC:171–B, 280).
6. See "The Scourge," 23 January, IV:B below.

A Democratic Federalist, Independent Gazetteer, 26 November[1]

The examination of the principle of liberty and civil polity is one of the most delightful exercises of the rational faculties of man. Hence the pleasure we feel in a candid, unimpassioned investigation of the grounds and probable consequences of the new frame of government submitted to the people by the Federal Convention. The various doubts, which the subject has created, will lead us to consider it the more by awakening our minds to that attention with which every freeman should examine the intended constitutions of his country.

Several zealous defenders of liberty in America, and some of them of the *first* reputation, have differed from the bulk of the nation in their speculative opinions on the best constitution for a legislative body. In Pennsylvania this question has formed *the line of division* between two parties, in each of which are to be found men of sound judgment and very general knowledge. As this diversity of opinion has not arisen from any peculiarity in our situation or circumstances, it must have been produced by the imperfections of our political researches and by the fallibility of the human mind, ever liable to unfavorable influence even from laudable and necessary passions. The sincere and zealous friend of liberty is naturally in love with a refined democracy, beautiful and perfect as a theory, and adapted to the government of the purest beings; and he views with jealousy, apprehension and dislike not only *real* deviations from democratic principles, but *the appearance* of aristocracy. Hence the idea of an *upper* house (a term erroneously adopted from the British constitution) has been disagreeable and even alarming to many, who were equally friends to perfect and real liberty and to an effective government. Among the various regulations and arrangements of the new Federal Constitution the *peculiar* ground on which the Senate is placed is on this account the most striking and perhaps estimable. A careful comparison of our *second* branch, as proposed by the Convention, with the upper house in the British constitution, will show, I hope, that there is something like *a middle ground* on which the wise and good of both opinions may meet and unite.

The ancestors of the upper house in England originally derived all their power from the feudal system. Possessed by lawless force of extensive domains, which, after a certain period, became hereditary in their families, they established a permanent power through *the military service* of their tenants, for upon those terms were all the lands of the kingdom once held under them. When the address and spirit of the people, exerted upon every proper occasion, obtained for them the interesting privileges of holding in their families also the tenanted estates of the lords, and of alienating their tenancies to such as would perform the conditions on which they were held—when, by the extinction of the families of some of the barons, their tenants remained in possession of their lands—when by the increase of the property, the knowledge and the power of the tenants (or Commons of England) and from other favorable circumstances, the people of that country obtained a portion of that independence which Providence intended for them, such of their nobles as stood the shock, which fell from these circumstances on their order, were formed into a separate independent body. They claimed an absolute right to act in their proper persons, and not by representatives, in the formation of the laws. Being from their wealth, their hereditary power to legislate and judge, and their extraordinary learning in those times, perfectly independent of the rest of the nation, they have often been useful in checking the encroachments of the crown, and the precipitation and inadvertance of the people. In that country they have really held *the balance* between the king and the Commons. But though such a balance may be proper in a royal government, it does not appear necessary *merely in that view* in a genuine republic—which ought to be a government of laws. Yet there are striking and capital advantages resulting from a second, not an *upper* house, if they can be obtained without departing, in our practice, from the real principles of liberty. The arts and influence of popular and unworthy men; too hasty, careless, incautious and passionate proceedings; breaches of wholesome order and necessary form are evils we must wish to avoid, if to be effected without the hazard of greater. Let us examine how far the *peculiar* constitution of our federal Senate will give us the advantages of a second legislative branch without subjecting us to the dangers usually apprehended from such bodies, that the sincere friends of freedom and mankind in America, if there is no longer reason for their differing upon a point of speculation may harmonize and unite.

The federal Senate, from the nature of our governments, will not be hereditary, nor will they possess, like the British barons, a power originally usurped by lawless violence and supported by military tenants. They will not necessarily have even an influential property, for they will have a greater number of fellow citizens, as rich as themselves; and no qualification of wealth exists in the Constitution at present, nor can it be introduced without the consent of *three-fourths of the people of the Union.* It cannot be apprehended, that the people at large of these free commonwealths will consent to disqualify themselves for the senatorial office, which God and the Constitution have intended they should fill. The members of the

Senate should certainly be men of very general information, but through the goodness of Providence, numbers will be found in every state, equally well qualified in that respect to execute a trust for which two persons only will be necessary. Instead of their possessing all the knowledge of the state, an equal proportion will be found in some of the members of the House of Representatives, and even a greater share of it will often adorn persons in private walks of life. They will have no distinctions of rank, for the persons over whom a Senator might be weak enough to affect a superiority will be really equal to him and may in a short time change situations with him. The Senator will again become a private citizen and the citizen may become a Senator—nay more—a president of the Senate or President of the Union. The upper house in England have an interest different and separate from the people and, whether in the execution of their office or not, are a distinct body of men, a superior order. Many little circumstances tend to favor and promote this unjust and preposterous distinction. If an ambassador is sent to their court by France or Spain, he is a nobleman of his own country, and a nobleman must be sent from England in return, which operates as a deprivation of the rights of every well-qualified commoner in the kingdom. This is a hardship, which *cannot* arise from our second branch, but exists in Britain not only in the case particularized, but in regard to many other employments of honor and profit. But a greater and more essential distinction between the upper house in England and our federal Senate yet remains. The members of the former claim and possess all their powers and honors in their *own* right, their own *hereditary* right, while the new Constitution renders our Senate merely a *representative* body without one distinction in favor of the birth, rank, wealth or power of the Senators or their fathers. There has arisen out of the particular nature of our affairs, a *peculiar* happiness in the formation of this body. The federal Senate are *the representatives of the sovereignties of their respective states.* A second branch, *thus constituted,* is a novelty in the history of the world. Instead of an hereditary upper house, the American Confederacy has created a body, the temporary representatives of their component sovereignties, dignified only by their being the immediate delegates and guardians of sovereign states selected from the body of the people for that purpose, and for no reasons, but their possessing the qualifications necessary for their station. We find then in this body, none of the evils of aristocracy apprehended by those who have drawn their reasonings from an erroneous comparison with the upper house of Britain, and all the benefits of a second branch, without hazarding the rights of the people in the smallest particular. As our federal Representatives and state legislatures will be composed of men, who, the moment before their election, were a part of the people and who on the expiration of their time, will return to the same private situations, so the members of cur federal Senate will be elected from out of the body of the people, without one qualification being made necessary, but mere citizenship, and at the expiration of their term will again be placed in private life. The Senate, therefore, will be as much a democratic body as the House of Representatives, with this advantage, that they will be elected by the state legislatures to whom, on account of their superior wisdom and virtue, the people at large will have previously committed the care of their affairs.

The plan of federal government proposed by the Convention has another merit of essential consequence to our national liberties. Under the old Confederation, the people at large had no voice in the election of their rulers. The collected wisdom of the state legislatures will hereafter be exercised in the choice of the Senate, but our federal Representatives will be chosen *by the votes of the people themselves.* The Electors of the President and Vice President of the Union may also, by laws of the separate states, be put on the same footing.

The separation of the judicial power from the legislative and executive has been justly deemed one of the most inestimable improvements in modern polity; yet no country has ever completely accomplished it in their actual practice. The British peers are criminal judges in cases of impeachment, and are a court of appeal in civil cases. The power of impeachment, vested in our federal Representatives, and the right to hear those cases, which is vested in the Senate, can produce no punishment in person or property, *even on conviction.* Their whole judicial power lies within a narrow compass. They can take no cognizance of a private citizen and can only declare any dangerous public officer no longer worthy to serve his country. To punish him for his crimes, in body or estate, is not within their constitutional powers. They must consign him to a jury and a court, with whom the deprivation of his office is to be no proof of guilt.

The size of the Senate has been considered by some, as an objection to that body. Should this appear of any importance it is fortunate that there are reasons to expect an addition to their number. The legislature of Virginia have taken measures preparatory to the erection of their western counties into a separate state, from which another good consequence will follow, that the free persons, which will remain within the Dominion of Virginia, will perhaps be nearly or quite as well represented in the Senate as Pennsylvania or Massachusetts. Should Vermont, at some future time, be also introduced into the Union, a further addition to the number of our Senators will take place. If therefore there is any importance in the objection to the size of our federal Senate, or if any such objection prevails in the minds of the people, it is in a way of being removed.

The executive powers of the Union are separated in a higher degree from the legislative than in any government now existing in the world. As a check upon the President, the Senate may disapprove of the officers he appoints, but no person holding *any office* under the United States can be a member of the federal legislature. How differently are things circumstanced in the two houses in Britain where an officer of any kind, naval, military, civil or ecclesiastical, may hold a seat in either house.

This is a most enlightened time, but more especially so in regard to matters of government. The divine right of kings, the force of ecclesiastical obligations in civil affairs, and many other gross errors, under which our forefathers have lain in darker ages of the world, are now done away. The natural, indefeasible and unalienable rights of mankind form the more eligible ground on which we now stand.

The United States are in this respect *"the favored of Heaven."* The Magna Charta, Bill of Rights, and common law of England furnished in 1776 a great part of the materials out of which were formed our several state constitutions. *All these* were more or less recognized in the old Articles of Confederation.

On this solid basis is reared the fabric of our new federal government. These taken together form THE GREAT WHOLE OF THE AMERICAN CONSTITUTIONS, the fairest fabric of liberty that ever blessed mankind, immovably founded on a solid rock, whose mighty base is laid at the center of the earth.

1. This item, headed: "Thoughts on the Federal Senate, &c." was reprinted in the *Freeman's Journal,* 5 December; Middletown, Conn., *Middlesex Gazette,* 31 December, and the *Maryland Journal,* 8 February 1788. For other Pennsylvania items defending the Senate, see "An American Citizen" II, 28 September, II:A above, and "A Supplement to the Essay on Federal Sentiments," 23 October, Mfm:Pa. 151.

It is possible that Tench Coxe wrote "A Democratic Federalist." On the address page of a letter he wrote on 26 November, Coxe stated: "The enclosed paper is also mine. I wish you would have it republished in New York, but do not mention the writer, as my attempt to *conciliate* our Constitutionals (the design of the paper) may be deemed uniting with them. You know I am of no party" (to David L. Franks, CC:290-B).

Cumberland County Petition to the Pennsylvania Convention, 28 November[1]

The following petition has been signed in this town [Carlisle] by everyone to whom it was presented, except three or four persons, and has been forwarded to the Convention. The respectable names affixed to it comprehend all the clergy, principal burgesses, members of the learned professions and principal inhabitants of this place; men, who possess the means of information, and are entirely exempt from any private or party interest. It must therefore give to the public a pleasing assurance of the excellence of the proposed government, where so remarkable an unanimity of sentiments has prevailed.

To the Honorable the Deputies of the Freemen of Pennsylvania, met in Convention, at Philadelphia, on the third Tuesday of November, for the purpose of deliberating on the Constitution proposed for the future government of the United States, by the Grand Convention.

The Representation and Petition of the Subscribers Freemen of the County of Cumberland, in the Commonwealth of Pennsylvania.

Respectfully show, that your petitioners being deeply impressed at this interesting period with the magnitude of the question, which is to be decided in your honorable house; think it a duty which they owe to their country, and to the sense they entertain of their own honor and integrity, to express to your honorable body, their humble sentiments on this great national measure.

Your petitioners therefore beg leave to represent that they have the strongest conviction that the new federal government offers the most flattering prospect to your petitioners of restoring system, firmness and energy, to the present embarrassed and relaxed Union; of reviving our declining commerce, of supporting our tottering credit, of relieving us from the pressure of an unequal and inefficacious taxation, of giving us concord at home, and rendering us great and respectable in the eye of the world.

That your petitioners, with the most pure and patriotic motives, wish for its unanimous adoption, not that (however highly they admire) they contend that it is free from all imperfection; but as they consider it as the most perfect that could be expected, and as they are convinced that there is not the most remote probability, that the wisdom of the states, or even of a majority of them, can be again collected, nor if it were possible to collect the same number of men, equally virtuous and equally wise from the different states, is it probable that they would be able to agree upon a constitution better adapted to the purpose of the Union and more free from imperfections than that which is now submitted to your determination. Your petitioners, relying on the wisdom of your honorable house, rest in the most perfect security, that the Constitution will be approved of and ratified by the Convention of Pennsylvania.

1. *Carlisle Gazette,* 28 November.

An Old Whig VII, Independent Gazetteer, 28 November[1]

Many people seem to be convinced that the proposed Constitution is liable to a number of important objections; that there are defects in it which ought to be supplied, and errors which ought to be amended; but they apprehend that we must either receive this Constitution in its present form, or be left without any continental govvernment whatsoever. To be sure, if this were the case, it would be most prudent for us, like a man who is wedded to a bad wife, to submit to our misfortune with patience, and make the best of a bad bargain. But if we will summon up resolution sufficient to examine into our true circumstances, we shall find that we are not in so deplorable a situation as people have been taught to believe, from the suggestions of interested men, who wish to force down the proposed plan of government without delay, for the purpose of providing offices for themselves and their friends. We shall find, that, with a little wisdom and patience, we have it yet in our power, not only to establish a federal constitution, but to establish a good one.

It is true that the Continental Convention has directed their proposed Constitution to be laid before a convention of delegates to be chosen in each state, "for their assent and ratification," which seems to preclude the idea of any power in the several conventions, of proposing any alterations, or indeed of even rejecting the plan proposed, if they should disapprove of it. Still, however, the question recurs, what authority the late Convention had to bind the people of the United States, to any particular form of government, or to forbid them to adopt such form of government as they should think fit. I know it is a language frequent in the mouths of some heaven-born Phaetons amongst us, who like the son of Apollo, think themselves entitled to guide the chariot of the sun; that common people have no right to judge of the affairs of government; that they are not fit for it; that they should leave these matters to their superiors. This, however, is not the language of men of real understanding, even among the advocates for the proposed Constitution; but these still recognize the authority of the people, and will admit, at least in words, that the people have a right to be consulted. Then I ask, if the people in the different states have a right to be consulted, in the new form of continental government, what authority could the late Convention have to preclude them from proposing amendments to the plan they should offer? Had the Convention any right to bind the people to the form of government they should propose? Let us consider this matter.

The late Convention were chosen by the general assembly of each state; they had the sanction of Congress. For what? To consider what alterations were necessary to be made in the Articles of Confederation. What have they done? They have made a new constitution for the United States. I will not say, that in doing so, they have exceeded their authority; but on the other hand, I trust that no man of understanding amongst them will pretend to say, that anything they did or could do, was of the least avail to lessen the rights of the people to judge for themselves in the last resort. This right is, perhaps, unalienable, but at all events, there is no pretense for saying that this right was ever meant to be surrendered up into the hands of the late Continental Convention.

The people have an undoubted right to judge of every part of the government which is offered to them. No power on earth has a right to preclude them; and they may exercise this choice either by themselves or their delegates legally chosen to represent them in the state convention. I venture to say that no man, reasoning upon *revolution* principles, can possibly controvert this right.

Indeed very few go so far as to controvert the right of the people to propose amendments; but we are told that the thing is impracticable; that if we begin to propose amendments there will be no end to them; that the several states will never agree in their amendments; that we shall never unite in any plan; that if we reject this we shall either have a worse or none at all; that we ought therefore to adopt this *at once,* without alteration or amendment. Now these are very kind gentlemen, who insist upon doing so much good for us, whether we will or not. Idiots and maniacs ought certainly to be restrained from doing themselves mischief, and should be compelled to that which is for their own good. Whether the people of America are to be considered in this light, and treated accordingly, is a question which deserves, perhaps, more consideration than it has yet received. A contest between the patients and their doctors, which are mad or which are fools, might possibly be a very unhappy one. I hope at least that we shall be able to settle this important business without so preposterous a dispute. What then would you have us do, it may be asked? Would you have us adopt the proposed Constitution or reject it? I answer that I would neither wish the one nor the other. Though I would be far from pretending to dictate to the representatives of the people what steps ought to be pursued, yet a method seems to present itself so simple, so perfectly calculated to obviate all difficulties, to reconcile us with one another, and establish unanimity and harmony among the people of this country, that I cannot forbear to suggest it. I hope that most of my readers have already anticipated me in what I am about to propose. Whether they have or not, I shall venture to state it, in the humble expectations that it may have some tendency to reconcile honest men of all parties with one another.

The method I would propose is this:

1st. Let the conventions of each state, as they meet, after considering the proposed Constitution, state their objections and propose their amendments.

So far from these objections and amendments clashing with each other in irreconcilable discord, as it has been too often suggested they would do, it appears that from what has been hitherto published in the different states in opposition to the proposed Constitution, we have a right to expect that they will harmonize in a very great degree. The reason I say so is, that about the same time, in very different parts of the continent, the very same objections have been made, and the very same alterations proposed by different writers, who I verily believe, know nothing at all of each other, and were very far from acting a premeditated concert, and that others who have not appeared as writers in the newspapers, in the different states, have appeared to act and speak in perfect unison with those objections and amendments, particularly in the article of a bill of rights. That in short, the very same sentiments seem to have been echoed from the different parts of the continent by the opposers of the proposed Constitution, and these sentiments have been very little contradicted by its friends, otherwise than by suggesting their fears, that by opposing the Constitution at present proposed, we might be disappointed of any federal government or receive a worse one than the present. It would be a most delightful surprise to find ourselves all of one opinion at last; and I cannot forbear hoping that when we come fairly to compare our sentiments, we shall find ourselves much more nearly agreed than in the hurry and surprise in which we have been involved on this subject, than we ever suffered ourselves to imagine.

2d. When the conventions have stated these objections and amendments, let them transmit them to Congress and adjourn, praying that Congress will direct another convention to be called from the different states, to consider of these objections and amendments, and pledging themselves to abide by whatever decision shall be made by such future convention on the subject; whether it be to amend the proposed Constitution or to reject any alteration and ratify it as it stands.[2]

3d. If a new convention of the United States should meet, and revise the proposed Constitution, let us agree to abide by their decision. It is past a doubt that every good citizen of America pants for an efficient federal government—I have no doubt we shall concur at last in some plan of continental government, even if many people could imagine exceptions to it; but if the exceptions which are made at present shall be maturely considered and even be pronounced by our future representatives as of no importance (which I trust they will not); even in that case, I have no doubt that almost every man will give up his own private opinion and concur in that decision.

4th. If by any means another continental convention should fail to meet, then let the conventions of the several states again assemble and at last decide the great solemn question whether we shall adopt the Constitution now proposed, or reject it? And, whenever it becomes necessary to decide upon this point, one at least who from the beginning has been invariably anxious for the liberty and independence of his country will concur in adopting and supporting this Constitution, rather than none; though I confess I could easily imagine, some other form of confederation, which I should think better entitled to my hearty approbation; and indeed I am not afraid of a worse.

1. "An Old Whig" was also printed in the *Freeman's Journal* on the same day. (CC:301 for the author and national circulation.) Between 12 October and 6 February 1788 eight numbers of "An Old Whig" were published, all of which are printed in *Commentaries on the Constitution*.

On 28 November the *Gazetteer* and the *Journal* also printed "Philadelphiensis" II (CC:302) which declared that the Constitution did not protect religious freedom and liberty. The two succeeding numbers of "Philadelphiensis" (CC:320, 342), published on 5 and 12 December, argued for amendments.

2. "An Old Whig" first recommended a second constitutional convention in his fourth and fifth numbers, 27 October and 1 November (CC:202, 224), which were also published as broadsides.

A Federal Republican, A Review of the Constitution, 28 November (excerpt)[1]

Hitherto we have been considering the blemishes of the Constitution as they statedly exist—other objects are derived from omission. Among these the grand one, upon which is indeed suspended every other, is the omission of a bill of rights.

The remarker upon the address of the sixteen members has answered their objection with much force. "I answer (says he) *this is not true,* it contains a declaration of many rights, and very important ones, i.e., that people shall be obliged to fulfill their contracts, and not avoid them by *tenders* of anything less than the value stipulated—that no *ex post facto* laws shall be made, etc."[2]

The gentleman has here very wittily mistaken the sense of the two terms right and obligation.

They are correlative terms and between two parties. Whenever the former applies to the one, the latter of necessity applies to the other. Whatever anyone has a *right* to expect from me, I am *obliged* to render him. He might as well have said that the Constitution gave the people a *right* to submit to Congress in everything, and that we have a *right* to pay the last farthing of compliance to their despotic whims.

What he mentions is the enforcing of *obligation* and not the declaring of *right*.

One of the learned members of the late Convention, the Honorable Mr. [James] Wilson, observes in his speech that all powers which are not by the Constitution given up to Congress are reserved for the disposition of the several states.[3] This observation is wise and true, because properly speaking it should be so. In entering into the social compact, all rights which are not expressly given up to the governors are reserved to the people. That it is so from a just construction it is easy to discover.

But notwithstanding, if the people are jealous of their rights, where will be the harm in declaring them? If they be meant, as they certainly are, to be reserved to the people, what injury can arise from a positive declaration of it? Although in reasoning it would appear to be unnecessary, yet if the people prefer having their rights stately defined, it is certainly reasonable that it should be done. I am well acquainted with the logical reason that is general[ly] given for it.

It is said that the insertion of a bill of rights would be an argument against the present liberty of the people.

To have the rights of the people declared to them would imply that they had previously given them up or were not in possession of them.

This indeed is a distinction of which the votaries of scholastic philosophy might be proud—but in the political world, where reason is not cultivated independently of action and experience, such futile distinctions ought not to be agitated.

In fact, it does not exist, for I should think it is as rational to declare the right of the people to what they already possess, as to decree to them any new rights. If the people do really possess them, there can be no harm in expressing what is meant to be understood.

A bill of rights should either be inserted, or a declaration made that whatever is not decreed to Congress is reserved to the several states for their own disposal.

In this particular, the Articles of the present Confederation have an evident advantage. The second Article says, that "each state retains its *sovereignty, freedom and independence,* and every *power, jurisdiction, and right, which is not* by this confederation *expressly declared* to United States in Congress assembled."[4]

This will appear the more proper, if we consider that these *are rights* in which all the states are concerned. It is thought proper to delegate to Congress supreme power on all occasions where the *natural* interests of the states are concerned, and why not for the same reason grant and declare to the states a bill of *those rights* which are also *mutual*?

At any rate it is certain that no injury can arise from it, and to do it would be satisfactory and wise.

On the whole, my fellow citizens, this Constitution was *conceived* in wisdom; the thanks of the United States are justly due to the members of the late Convention.

But let their productions pass again through the furnace.

Do not give them even the opportunity of depriving you of your rights and privileges, and that, without breaking over any restraint imposed by the Constitution.

Because this once granted they will be fully enabled in the present age to lay the gentle foundation of despotic power, and after a temporary interval of seeming humanity between you and succeeding generations, to rivet upon *them* the chains of slavery beyond the possibility of a rupture.

To guard against this, I could wish to see the proposed Constitution revised and corrected.

If the states are not to be *confederated,* let them be reduced to one compact body.

And if a perfect consolidation of the states is to take place, if the people are to become the source of power, and if Congress is to represent them as the head of this grand body politic, in the name of all that is dear to freemen, permit not the veins through which the life of government itself is to flow from the *heart* to the *head* be any way obstructed—let the passages be free and open that *vital* heat may *animate* every *limb*.

That if all the states were to offer their objections, the Constitution would be reduced to nothing, is an ill-founded idea.

The good-natured simularity which the citizen of America discovered between this Constitution and a piece of painting is perfectly erroneous.[5]

All painting is addressed to the *sense* and relished by *taste* which is various and fluctuating—but this Constitution is addressed to the *understanding* and judged of by *reason* which is fixed and true.

The Constitution is for the most part good, and perhaps many of the objections which have been made to it arise from our not being able to discern *clearly* the collective interest of the states.

Some of them, however, in all probability, exist beyond contradiction.

Let the convention of each state make its exceptions, then let a future and general one receive them all and reconcile them with as much wisdom as possible.

This would certainly be some refinement.

It *could* do no *harm,* but *might* do much *good.*

To conclude, my friends and fellow citizens, have [the] proposed Constitution revised, corrected and amended—have every dubious expression be made plain and clear—have every power accurately defined and well understood, and your own rights and privileges clearly stated or a declaration made that all powers that are not by this Constitution delegated to Congress are reserved for your own disposal.

Then, and not till then, will impartial justice rule over our land, and America become the theater of equity and wisdom, as she has already been the field of patriotism and bravery.

This once obtained, we shall be happy and free, and having enjoyed the blessings of peace and plenty under the ample shade of the tree of *liberty,* we shall deliver them down unimpaired by the corrosive influence of time to the latest posterity.

1. Printed CC:303. The full title of the pamphlet is *A Review of the Constitution Proposed by the Late Convention Held at Philadelphia 1787, By a Federal Republican* (Philadelphia, 1787). Advertisements in the *Freeman's Journal* and *Pennsylvania Herald* on 28 November indicate that the pamphlet was published on that day. The foreword, signed by "the AUTHOR," is dated "Philadelphia, Oct. 28, 1787."

2. The quotation is from Pelatiah Webster's pamphlet of 18 October (CC:125–B). Except for "*ex post facto,*" Webster did not use italics. Earlier in the pamphlet "A Federal Republican" declared that Webster's "whole performance is colored with the ridiculous. He is no doubt a friend to Shaftsbury's position, and feels that it is easier to *laugh* than to *reason.*"

3. Speech in the State House Yard, 6 October, II:A above.

4. CDR:II, B.

5. This is a reference to *Examination into the Leading Principles of the Federal Constitution* . . . By A Citizen of America [Noah Webster], p. 52 (Mfm:Pa. 142).

Many Customers, Independent Gazetteer, 1 December[1]

It has been often said, concerning the proposed Constitution, that those who complained of its faults should suggest amendments. A number of citizens, warmly desirous of promoting the establishment of a well-organized federal government and perceiving in each other sentiments inclining to harmony, formed a committee of their own members to examine and consider the proposed Constitution, with instructions to report such amendments, and such only, as they should deem absolutely necessary to safety in the adoption of it, paying equal regard to its practicability and efficiency as a system of government, on the one hand, and to those rights which are essential to free citizens in a state of society on the other.

The report having been read, a motion was made to adopt it; but after some debate, in which some of the members declared that their minds had already undergone some changes, and that their opinions were not yet satisfactorily established, it was thought proper that further time should be taken to deliberate and advise with their fellow citizens on a subject of such high importance and general concernment.

It was therefore agreed that the question should be postponed for further consideration, and that in the meantime the report be published. By giving it a place in your paper you will oblige MANY CUSTOMERS.

The committee to whom was referred the plan proposed by the late General Convention, for the government of the United States, report,

That in the examination of the said plan, they have conceived it to be their duty to exercise the freedom which the magnitude of the trust reposed in them required; at the same time, that they have kept constantly in mind the respect and deference due to the great characters who formed the plan, and that candor and liberality of construction which are necessary in forming a just opinion of a national compact in which the citizens of every state in the Union, having an equal interest, are equally parties.

Under these impressions, your committee have taken the said plan into their most serious consideration; and though they find much in it which merits approbation, yet the duty they owe to their constituents and to their country obliges them to propose some alterations, which they should deem necessary considering it merely with regard to practicability as a system of government. And when to this consideration are added the propriety of preserving to the respective states so much of their sovereignty as may be necessary to enable them to manage their internal concerns, and to perform their respective functions as members of a federal republic, and of preserving to individuals such rights as are essential to freemen in a state of society, the necessity of making such alterations appear to your committee irresistibly strong.

There are four points in which your committee apprehend alterations are absolutely necessary before the plan can with safety be put in operation, namely: respecting elections, internal taxation, the judicial department, the legislative power, so far as it is independent of the House of Representatives.

Divers other amendments might with propriety be proposed, some of which might be comprehended in a bill of rights or table of fundamental principles so declared and established as to govern the construction of the powers given by the Constitution; but your committee avoid to mention them in detail, because if suitable amendments are made respecting the points enumerated, the necessity for going further on the present occasion, though not entirely done away, will be so far diminished as that it may be thought advisable to leave them to future consideration on such suggestions as time and experience shall offer.

Your committee therefore proposes the following amendments:

Article I, section 4. Strike out these words—*but the Congress may at any time by law make or alter such regulations, except as to the place of chusing senators.*

Article I, section 8. Strike out *tax* and *excises* (and so throughout the plan make such amendments as may be necessary in conformity with this idea. At the end of the clause, add—"To make requisitions, in the proportion aforesaid, on the several states in the Union, for such supplies of money as shall be necessary, in aid of the other revenues, for these purposes; leaving to the states respectively, the mode of levying and collecting the same: Provided that if any state shall neglect or refuse to pass an act for complying with any such requisition, or shall otherwise neglect or refuse to pay its quota of any such requisition within the time therein limited, it shall be in the power of the Congress on any such delinquency, by law, to direct the levying and collecting of such quota, together with such farther sum as may be necessary to defray the expense thereof, and interest from the time it ought to have been paid, from the persons and estates of the inhabitants of such delinquent state, according to the mode of assessment by law established in such state; or in default of such establishment, by such modes and means as the Congress shall by law establish for that purpose."

Article 3, section 2, clause 1st. Strike out the words, *between citizens of different states.* After the words "between a state," strike out, *or the citizens thereof.*

Clause 2d. Strike out, *both as to law and fact.*

These two clauses will then stand as follows:

"The judicial power shall extend to cases in law and equity, arising under this constitution, the laws of the United States, and treaties made or which shall be made, under their authority; to all cases affecting ambassadors, other public ministers and consuls; to all cases of admiralty and maritime jurisdiction; to controversies to which the United States shall be a party; to controversies between two or more states; between a state and citizens of another state; between citizens of the same state claiming lands under grants of different states; and between a state and foreign states, citizens or subjects.

"In all cases affecting ambassadors, other public ministers and consuls, and those in which a state shall be party, the supreme court shall have original jurisdiction. In all the other cases before-mentioned, the supreme court shall have appellate jurisdiction, with such exceptions and under such regulations as the Congress shall make."

Article 6, clause 2. After the word "notwithstanding," insert, "provided that every such treaty which shall hereafter be made shall have been laid before the House of Representatives and have obtained the approbation of so many of the members of that House as shall be a majority of the whole number elected."

And your committee submit the following resolutions to consideration.

That the foregoing amendments to the plan of government formed by the late General Convention be transmitted to the United States in Congress assembled.

That Congress be requested to recommend to the several states in the Union that delegates be elected by the people of the said states respectively, to meet in general convention at ________ on the ________ day of ________ next, take into consideration the said amendments together with such amendments as shall be proposed by the several state conventions, and to revise and amend the said plan of government in such manner as they shall agree upon, not altering the form as it now stands farther than shall be necessary to accommodate it to such of the amendments which shall be so proposed to them, as they, or the representation of any nine or more states, shall agree to adopt; and that in case the plan so agreed upon shall be assented to by the vote of every state which shall be represented in such convention, they shall have power, without further reference to the people, to declare the same the constitution or frame of government of the United States, and it shall thereupon be accepted and acted upon accordingly.

1. This item was also printed in the *Pennsylvania Herald* on the same day and reprinted in the *Pennsylvania Packet,* 4 December; *New York Morning Post,* 10 December; *Massachusetts Centinel,* 15 December; *New York Journal,* 20 December; and the *Salem Mercury,* 25 December. See comments upon it by "Columbus," 8 December, II:F below.

Cumberland County Petition to the Pennsylvania Convention, 5 December[1]

Messieurs Printers: In perusing your useful paper of the 28th instant [November], I observed a petition signed, as is said, by the clergy, principal burgesses, members of the learned professions, and principal inhabitants of this place; and that except three or four persons to whom it was presented, all unanimously signed said petition. In order that it may be seen whether this is actually the case or not, I request you would insert the following petition, signed by upwards of one hundred and seventy in Carlisle, who, in their humble opinion, possess equally good means of information, and are as free from any private or party interest as these respectable signers. In complying with the above, you will oblige one of your readers.

To the Honorable Convention of the State of Pennsylvania.

The Petition of the Subscribers Inhabitants of the County of Cumberland.

Most humbly showeth: That they consider the present political circumstances of the United States, as very interesting to every citizen who sincerely desires to support our Union, and at the same time to secure to the people the future enjoyment of their unalienable rights and liberties; and as the good of the people is the great end of all good government, and that must be best which affords the best security to their rights and freedom; a solicitude for their own permanent political happiness, and that of their fellow citizens, has induced your petitioners to lay before your honorable house some objections to the adoption of the Constitution, as proposed by the late Continental Convention.

And first: There is no declaration of rights, to secure to the people the liberty of worshiping God according to their consciences; and the sixth Article of said Constitution declares "that this Constitution and the Laws of the United States which shall be made in pursuance thereof, etc." Therefore the bill of rights contained in the constitutions of the several states are no security, nor are the people secured in the privileges of the common law.

Secondly: The eighth section of the first Article of this Constitution declares, that the Congress shall have power to make all laws necessary and proper for carrying into execution the foregoing powers, and all other powers vested by this Constitution in the government of the United States, or in any department or officer thereof. This, as we conceive, unlimited powers given to Congress, in which they are to be the judges of what laws shall be necessary and proper, uncontrolled by a bill of rights, submits every right of the people of these states, both civil and sacred to the disposal of Congress, who may exercise their power to the expulsion of the jury–trial in civil causes—to the total suppression of the liberty of the press; and to the setting up and establishing of a cruel tyranny, if they should be so disposed, over all the dearest and most sacred rights of the citizens.

Thirdly: The fourth section of the first Article provides, that the times, places, and manner for holding elections, for Senators and Representatives, shall be prescribed, etc. Here appears to be scarcely the shadow of representation provided, because the Congress may at their pleasure, order the election for the Representatives of the State of Pennsylvania, to be held in Philadelphia, where it will be impossible for the people of the state to assemble for the purpose; and thus the citizens of Philadelphia would be represented, and scarcely any part else of the commonwealth. The MANNER and TIME may prevent three-fourths of the present electors of the state, from giving a vote as long as they live.

These objections, with many others which might be made, induce your petitioners to pray this honorable Convention not to adopt the said proposed plan, until a bill of rights shall be framed and annexed, so as to secure to the citizens of each state, such rights as have been mentioned (we mean to say) those relating to conscience, trial by jury, in civil causes, as well as in criminal cases; the liberty of the press, and such other liberties as to you may seem necessary to be secured and preserved. And your petitioners as in duty bound shall ever pray, etc., etc.

1. *Carlisle Gazette,* 5 December. This petition was a response to the petition published in the *Gazette* on 28 November (II:F above). It appears to have been presented to the Convention on 12 December (Convention Proceedings, 12 December, III below). For an Antifederalist attack upon the Convention's refusal to consider the amendments recommended in this petition, see "Philadelphiensis" V, 19 December, CC:356.

A Farmer, Pennsylvania Gazette, 5 December[1]

It is no matter to the public whether I am Federal or not, but I must beg leave to say our state Convention proceed in a very expensive way in their duty. If, as a member said the other day,[2] they had not got through six words, after spending two thousand dollars of the public money, it will cost a pretty penny before it is got through. I expect there will not be a shilling left to pay the public debts, wages of other officers, etc., etc., for it must take them many months at this rate. The gentlemen have surely been able to reflect sufficiently on the subject, to form a judgment upon all the lesser and more simple matters, and there can be but few points on which to doubt or deliberate; for the objections, however strongly made, are confined to a small number. The people in general seem to consider the *first* question at least to be, whether the Federal Constitution shall be adopted as it stands. If not, then amendments to be recommended would be proper, but not till then. I think it must cost the state twenty-five thousand dollars at least, if they proceed in the present way. Four months would not suffice, at the rate the house goes on. We are very unfortunate in this state, in doing everything more expensively than our neighbors. These things might do in the war, but really the times are now too hard, and the country cannot bear it. Wheat is falling to nothing, for want of trade, and taxes very heavy.

1. This item, dated "Montgomery county, Dec. 3," was reprinted in the *Pennsylvania Packet,* 7 December; *New York Journal,* 8 December; and Baltimore *Maryland Gazette,* 21 December. For other complaints of the high cost of the Convention, see Mfm:Pa. 256, 257.
2. See John Smilie's speech, Convention Debates, 30 November, III below.

One of the Gallery, Pennsylvania Packet, 5 December[1]

I have constantly attended the debates in Convention on the grand question—*Will Pennsylvania assent to and ratify the Federal Constitution proposed by the late General Convention, or not?*—and I have received much entertainment and instruction from the able and learned speakers for and against this important proposition.

It appears to me that this debate may, if the parties are so inclined, be continued for any indefinite length of time. For, whilst the ingenuity of the three gentlemen,[2] who have alone spoke in opposition to the new Constitution, can furnish new objections, or reiterate those which have been made, they will insist that the final question shall not be proposed.

But I would ask, to what purpose are these debates instituted and continued? Is it at all probable that a convert will be made from either side; or, if there should, can the converted member vote according to his conviction? I apprehend he cannot. Pennsylvania has already determined the question. The several counties of the state have sent forward their delegates—not to debate on the proposed Constitution, but to announce the votes of those counties respectively. The voice of the people alone must decide on the proposed federal government, and there is no other way by which the voice of the people of Pennsylvania can be obtained but by means of delegates, elected in the several counties and sent forward to announce—not their own opinions, but the will of the counties to which they respectively belong. The present Convention, therefore, is not a deliberative body. The members are to be considered only as tickets containing the votes of the counties for the adoption or rejection of the proposed Constitution. Suppose one of the opponents should, from information or by argument, be really convinced that it would be for the good of the people that they should assent to and ratify the new system of federal government. Could he in honor, or upon any justifiable principle, vote for it on the final question, when he knows that his constituents have elected him in perfect confidence that he will give the voice of his county against it? That the people have considered their delegates to Convention in this light is evident: for I believe in no one instance has a delegate been appointed who had not previously declared himself a Federalist or an Antifederalist, and, in some instances, even a personal promise has been taken that the delegate should absolutely vote according to the declared will of the electors. So that, I think, Pennsylvania has already decided the question; and nothing remains but to receive and count over the votes of the counties transmitted by their delegates.

I have a great respect for the Convention as a body; but, if considered individually, some members may be found in it, whom no county in this or any other state would trust with a discretionary vote on a point of such great importance.

To what purpose, then, all this reasoning on the subject; these smart altercations, objections, replications, and adjournments, from day to day? It appears to me, as I said before, that the state hath already determined respecting the proposed Constitution; and woe be to that member of this Convention who shall presume to vote contrary to what he knew to be the will of his constituents at the time of his election.

1. This item, dated "December 3d," was answered by "Ego," 8 December, II:F below.
2. William Findley, John Smilie, and Robert Whitehill.

Columbus, Pennsylvania Herald, 8 December[1]

"Be the workmen that they may be, let us speak of the work."
BACON'S ESSAYS.

A late publication in your paper, in the form of a report of a committee,[2] has afforded both information and satisfaction to divers of your readers. It were to be wished that societies, of the kind of that to which the committee reported, were formed in every neighborhood, and that more time had been taken by the people, by such or other means, to possess themselves of a more accurate knowledge of a subject so highly interesting to every individual, before the men were fixed upon who should possess the power of deciding for them on a subject of the highest sublunary importance to them and their posterity.

The members of the General Convention had the matter several months under daily discussion and debate. Every thought which occurred to anyone was communicated to and examined by everyone, so that everyone had time and opportunity to trace the purport and tendency of every clause and sentence, separately considered, as well as the probable effect and influence of the whole; but these deliberations were kept within their walls with the secrecy of a conclave. The people expected the result would be an amendment of the federal compact, on such points only as had been generally spoken of as defective. Their minds had been prepared for such amendments as they could easily judge of and come to a speedy decision upon. But, instead of the old instrument being repaired and amended, we are called upon to consider it as totally dissolved, and its component parts reduced to a state of nature.

The Constitution proposed in its stead is confessedly, even by the framers of it, a NOVELTY in the practice of legislation, essentially different, both in principles and organization, from any system of government heretofore formed, either by force, fraud, accident, or the deliberate consent of a people. It *may* be, as some of its sanguine advocates have asserted, the *best* form that was ever offered to a people; but we should remember, that what *may* be, may *not* be; and however ready we may be to adopt measures on the credit of others in matters of lighter moment, the subject before us is certainly a matter of too much consequence to be decided upon without thorough examination, and more deliberation than the citizens of Pennsylvania have had an opportunity of exercising. For although a few individuals who were in the General Convention may have given it a sufficient degree of investigation to satisfy their own minds; yet it may be fairly said of the people at large, that they could not possibly have given it a due degree of examination at the time that they were in a manner surprised into a kind of surrender of the right of further deliberation, by the election of delegates to express their final decision. It has been said that a small proportion only of the voters in the state (hardly a sixth part) gave their suffrages on this occasion;[3] and it may fairly be presumed, circumstances considered, that a large proportion of those who did not vote declined it because they found themselves unqualified from the mere want of such information as every citizen ought to possess before he gives his weight on either side, on a question of so much importance.

Will the members of the state Convention, thus possessed of the power, run hastily into the adoption, *in toto,* of a plan of government which, in the opinion of a large proportion of their constituents, cannot with safety be put in operation without very essential amendments? Or will they not rather assent either to make the necessary amendments the condition of their agreeing to the plan; or to adjourn for a reasonable time, in order to obtain the deliberate sense of their constituents on a matter of so much importance? Those who mean to act fairly can hardly withhold their assent to such an adjournment, except it be on the score of expense and the trouble of reassembling; but surely these are considerations too light to be placed in opposition to the object. The delay can occasion no real loss of time as to the final event, because the accession of other states will be necessary to give operation to the plan; and we know that divers of the state conventions will not meet to deliberate upon it before May or June. Why then should we be denied a reasonable time for deliberation? If the system be a good one and calculated to promote the happiness of the people, the more it is examined and understood, the more generally will it be approved of; but if it should be otherwise, it can hardly be expected that the people would acquiesce in a determination which they might suppose had been unfairly obtained.

1. This item was also printed in the *Pennsylvania Packet* the same day, and reprinted in the *Independent Gazetteer,* 10 December and the *New York Journal,* 24 December.
2. See "Many Customers," 1 December, II:F above.
3. See the *Independent Gazetteer,* 5 December, II:D above.

Ego, Pennsylvania Packet, 8 December

I have attended some of the debates of the Convention, as well as your correspondent in this day's paper, who signs himself "One of the People."[1]

I have listened with attention to the monotonous and pertinacious [Robert] Whitehill, to the zealous [John] Smilie, and to the candid, thoughtful [William] Findley. On the other side of the room I have heard with conviction the clear and rational arguments of the Chief Justice [Thomas McKean], the good sense of [Jasper] Yates, the fervency of [Stephen] Chambers, the pathos and imagination of [Benjamin] Rush, the nervous thinking and correct eloquence of [James] Wilson. I have heard in the gallery the whispers of approbation circulate, as true Federal sentiments have been well expressed or happily introduced by the members; I have seen those who wished for the establishment of the proposed government return more zealous for it than before. I have seen those who went there undetermined depart in full decision to support it. I have inquired abroad for the opponents of the plan and have found them almost uniformly the possessors or expectants of office, with their nearest friends and connections. I have seen the presses loaded with Antifederal compositions and the federal government almost left to defend itself. I have sought for the effect so many publications must have had on the public mind, and have almost everywhere met with confessions, that objectionable as it might be, in the present situation of things we could not expect a better. I have seen the farmer storing his grain, the merchant suspending his enterprises, and the men of ready money hoarding up their cash till the operation of the government should give activity and confidence to the people of this country in their dealings abroad and with each other. I have seen the landholders assemble and make an offer of territory, and I have witnessed the hopes of the manufacturers and mechanics that their offer may be accepted.[2] I have noticed an anxiety lest Pennsylvania, often the leader, and always amongst the foremost in useful and distinguished measures, should suffer two of her weakest sisters to anticipate her laurels. I have at length heard something like murmurs that the people of Pennsylvania should spend their time in debates, which being conducted without order, promise no certain end, in which the issue of the argument can only be guessed at from the countenance of the members, and the final vote upon the acceptance or rejection of the whole cannot possibly (for the reasons given) be influenced by this discussion of its parts. And I have heard it said that however suitable these disquisitions might be in an academy of petty critics or a divan of trembling slaves (where the evidence and ingenuity in one, or the exercise of freedom by the other, might consist in the dissection of a sentence or the explanation of a *synonyma),* yet it would be more manly, more characteristic of a convention of freemen, at once to put the question—"Shall we be happy or miserable, powerful or contemptible? Shall Pennsylvania adopt or reject the federal government?"

1. See "One of the Gallery," 5 December, II:F above. "Ego" was dated 5 December.
2. This meeting was probably held at William Lesher's in Germantown on 4 December (Jacob Hiltzheimer Diary, 4 December, Mfm:Pa. 254). The meeting, originally called for 30 November, was supposed "to take into consideration the propriety of signifying their approbation of the county [Philadelphia] being offered to Congress as a seat of government, in which to exercise their jurisdiction, agreeable to the terms of the proposed Federal Constitution" (Mfm:Pa. 248). For an earlier offer by some Germantown residents on 1 October, see Mfm:Pa. 86.

Philadelphia County Petition to the Pennsylvania Convention, 11 December[1]

Such of the citizens of Pennsylvania as are not clearly ascertained of the propriety of adopting the proposed Constitution, without amendment or further consideration, may think it proper to join in the following petition:

To the Honorable the Delegates of the State Convention.

The petition of the citizens of Pennsylvania humbly showeth:

That your petitioners, highly sensible of the benefits arising from good government, and perceiving that there were defects in the federal compact established in the infancy of our independency, assented with alacrity to a revision of the Articles of Confederation, in full confidence that such amendments would be made therein as would give sufficient strength and energy to the federal head, without infringing those rights of sovereignty in the several states which are necessary for the purposes of internal government, and the performance of their respective functions as members of a federal union; or such rights of individuals as are necessary to distinguish free citizens from the subjects of despotism.

That the plan proposed by the General Convention, instead of offering to our consideration such amendments as were generally expected and might be easily understood, contains a total abolition of the existing Confederation, and is in itself, as a late writer expresses it, "a novelty in the practice of legislation, essentially different, both in principles and organization, from any system of government heretofore formed." And although it may be an improvement on all those which have preceded it, and better calculated for political happiness than our present system of Confederation is capable of being made, yet your petitioners conceive it is no less the *duty* than the *right* of every citizen to examine it with care and attention, and deliberately consider its probable operations and effects, before he assents to the adoption of a system of such infinite importance. Accident, fraud, or force may impose on a people a system of government to which they will yield obedience no longer than they are restrained from opposition by a power that deprives them of the freedom of citizens. But when a free people deliberately frame a government for themselves, or adopt as their deliberate choice, a system which they have carefully investigated and understand, they are bound to the observance of it by other ties than those of fear. Confident of acting in general concert, and of deriving reciprocal benefits, every individual will then more cheerfully yield obedience to the laws and perform the duties of a citizen. Hence it is of the highest importance that the proposed system of government should be well understood by the people in every state before it be adopted.

But your petitioners conceive that the people of Pennsylvania have not yet had sufficient time and opportunity afforded them for this purpose. Many of those who have had the best opportunity that the shortness of the time would admit, find their minds yet unsatisfied on some important points, though they may highly approve of the general structure. Others, who felt a general approbation at first view, now think some amendments essentially necessary; but the great bulk of the people, from the want of leisure from other avocations; their remoteness from information, their scattered situation, and the consequent difficulty of conferring with each other, cannot yet have duly investigated and considered a system of so much magnitude, which involves so many important considerations as to require not only more time than they have yet had since it was promulged, but the combined force of many enlightened minds, to obtain a right understanding of it.

Your petitioners hope they shall be excused if they mention on this occasion some other matters which have retarded the calm investigation which a subject of this importance ought to receive. The disorderly proceedings in the city, and the unaccountable zeal and precipitation used to hurry the people into a premature decision, spread an amazement through the country, which excited jealousies and suspicions from which they could neither easily nor speedily recover. Those who became partisans in the business had their minds too much agitated to act with deliberation, and the election of delegates was rushed into before the greater part of the people had sufficiently recovered from their surprise to know what part to take in it, or how to give their suffrages. They therefore remained inactive. Your petitioners wish to be understood, however, as being far from intending to invalidate the election, or to intimate any irregularity in the members chosen, whom they respect both individually and as a body, and in whose desire to promote the welfare and happiness of the people they have much confidence; but they conceive it will operate as a strong argument in favor of the measure they request.

Your petitioners beg leave to suggest that the suspension of your final determination for a few months will not occasion any delay to the Union, as divers of the states, whose determinations are of equal importance with that of Pennsylvania, will not meet in convention on this business in less than five or six months. The people of these states have wisely determined to deliberate before they delegate the power of decision. But the people of Pennsylvania, deprived of this privilege, are reduced to the necessity of asking as a favor, what they ought to have enjoyed as a right; and they confide in your wisdom and prudence to afford them an opportunity of forming, collecting and expressing their sentiments by petitions or instructions before you come to a determination which may preclude further deliberation.

Your petitioners therefore pray that the honorable Convention will be pleased to adjourn till some day in April or May next, in order to obtain the deliberate sense of the citizens of Pennsylvania on the plan of government proposed by the late General Convention.

1. *Pennsylvania Packet,* 11 December. This item was printed by the *Independent Gazetteer* on the same day. It was reprinted in the *Freeman's Journal,* 12 December; *Pennsylvania Herald,* 12 December; and the *New York Journal,* 18 December. The *Salem Mercury* printed a summary of it on 25 December. The *Pennsylvania Herald* prefaced its printing: "We are informed that many petitions are circulating in the counties, and some in this city, praying the Convention to adjourn the ultimate decision of the important question before them till April or May next; but from the complexion of that body, the prayer will hardly be granted even if it arrives before their dissolution, which will probably take place tomorrow or Friday." The *Herald's* preface was reprinted in the *Albany Gazette,* 20 December; *Massachusetts Gazette,* 25 December; and the Charleston *Columbian Herald,* 27 December.

The petition, which was never submitted to the Convention, probably circulated only in Philadelphia and its environs. Christopher Marshall of Philadelphia stated that he "Visited at Jos. Warner's with a petition to be signed, praying the members of the Convention for to adjourn some time forward so as they and the people [will] have time to consider it" (MS, Marshall Diary, 10 December, PHi).

III

The Pennsylvania Convention

20 November–15 December 1787

Introduction

The Pennsylvania Convention was called to meet in Philadelphia on Tuesday, 20 November, but only thirty-eight of the sixty-nine delegates elected were present that day. The proceedings began on Wednesday when sixty delegates assembled. The Convention was in session for a total of twenty-two days.

During the first week the delegates elected officers, adopted rules, and appointed printers to publish the Convention Journals. On 21 November the Convention elected its President. Frederick A. Muhlenberg received thirty votes, Thomas McKean twenty-nine, and George Gray one. The validity of the election was questioned since no one had received a majority of votes, but after "a short conversation," it was voted that Muhlenberg "should be conducted to the chair."

Crucial procedural matters were raised and decided during the first week. On Saturday, 24 November, Thomas McKean moved "that this Convention do assent to and ratify the Constitution . . . ," not for the purpose of securing an immediate vote, "but merely to bring the object of our meeting fully and fairly into discussion." Then on Monday, the 26th, McKean moved that the Constitution be considered article by article, and both the Federalists and Antifederalists agreed.

The Antifederalists then moved that the Convention follow Assembly procedure and first consider the Constitution in the committee of the whole to allow "a more free and candid discussion," and to enable the delegates to vote on specific provisions of the Constitution. Federalists argued in reply that the practice of the Assembly was not a precedent for the Convention, and that a committee of the whole would result in considerable expense and delay by going over "the same ground" twice. Furthermore, James Wilson and Benjamin Rush maintained that the Constitution was a single proposition, therefore it was unnecessary to go into a committee of the whole because the separate sections of the Constitution could not be voted on separately and amendments could not be proposed. The Federalists also insisted that the Convention was not authorized to do anything except to ratify or reject the Constitution as a whole. The Antifederalist motion was defeated by a vote of forty-four to twenty-four. The next day, 27 November, the Antifederalists moved that the Convention delegates, like the Assembly delegates; be permitted to enter on the Journals their reasons for voting to ratify or to reject the Constitution. This motion was defeated forty-four to twenty-two.

After the defeat of these Antifederalist proposals, the Convention adopted McKean's motion of 26 November to consider the Constitution article by article. However, this decision was largely ignored, for most of the speakers discussed the Constitution as a whole during the course of the debates.

Only twelve of the sixty-nine delegates are recorded as taking part in the debates: beginning on 24 November, James Wilson, Thomas McKean, Benjamin Rush, and six other Federalists defended the Constitution; while William Findley, John Smilie, and Robert Whitehill attacked it.

The opponents of the Constitution argued that the delegates to the Constitutional Convention had disobeyed their instructions and created a "consolidated" rather than a "federal" government; that their purpose was to create an "aristocracy" in the United States in contravention of the principles of the Declaration of Independence; that the state governments would be virtually annihilated if the Constitution were adopted; and that the lack of a bill of rights in the Constitution would mean that the central government could deprive the people of such cherished liberties as freedom of speech, freedom of religion, and freedom of the press.

The supporters of the Constitution, led by James Wilson, argued that the power of the Convention was derived from the people of the United States; that the government was a federal government with limited powers; that a bill of rights was unnecessary because it was a federal government; and that unless the Constitution were adopted, the United States could never achieve stability and prosperity at home or win the respect of foreign powers.

On 4 December, after the Convention had been in session for two weeks, President Muhlenberg suggested that the proceedings would "meet with a more full and expeditious investigation, by a general statement of the objections to it [the Constitution], and a subsequent reply to those objections." Muhlenberg's suggestion was acted upon. Between 4 and 8 December, William Findley, John Smilie, and Robert Whitehill gave lengthy speeches detailing their objections to the Constitution. These objections were summarized and answered by Thomas McKean on 10 December and by James Wilson on 11 December.

On 12 December, after closing speeches by the Antifederalists, Thomas Hartley and Stephen Chambers moved that the original question, as moved by McKean on 24 November, be considered. Robert

Whitehill then presented petitions signed by 750 inhabitants of Cumberland County praying that the Constitution not be adopted without amendments. Whitehill then moved that the Convention adjourn so that the people could consider a list of fifteen amendments which he presented to the Convention. His motion was rejected by a vote of forty-six to twenty-three, and the proposed amendments were not entered on the Journals. Hartley and Chambers' motion was then taken up, and the Constitution was adopted by a vote of forty-six to twenty-three. On 13 December, the ratification was announced to the public, and the ratification certificates were signed.

During the last two days of the Convention, 14–15 December, the delegates considered and adopted a resolution to cede a ten mile square tract of land to Congress for the seat of the new government under the Constitution. The Convention also offered Congress the temporary use of any public buildings in the state until Congress established its permanent residence.

On 15 December these resolutions, with the state's ratification, were ordered sent to the Confederation Congress. The printing of 5,000 copies of the Constitution and the Convention's ratification was authorized, and a committee was appointed to supervise the publication of the Convention's Journals. After adopting a resolution of thanks to President Muhlenberg, the Convention adjourned *sine die.*

The Arrangement of the Debates

The overall record of the debates is scattered and incomplete aside from Alexander J. Dallas' reports of debates on 27, 28, part of 30 November, and on 12 December, and the reports of James Wilson's and Thomas McKean's speeches in Thomas Lloyd's *Debates.* Newspaper reports of day-to-day proceedings and the notes taken by James Wilson, Anthony Wayne, and Jasper Yeates often agree as to the order in which certain men spoke, but they do not always list all the speakers, and they vary considerably as to what was said. Nevertheless, it is possible to reconstruct, although not always with certainty, the course of most of the debates.

The debates are not arranged reporter by reporter as in Farrand's *Records of the Federal Convention.* Instead, they are arranged in the order in which men spoke, and all of the reports of each speech are placed together, beginning, usually, with the most complete report. For example: the *Pennsylvania Herald,* Anthony Wayne, James Wilson, and Jasper Yeates all record that Robert Whitehill was the first speaker on 30 November. The debates for that day therefore begin with Whitehill's speech as reported by the *Herald,* followed by the reports of Wilson, Wayne, and Yeates.

Occasionally the notes available make it difficult, if not impossible, to determine with precision the order in which men spoke. In such cases the notes of debates are placed in what seems, from the contents of the notes, to be the logical order.

Photographic copies of Anthony Wayne's, James Wilson's, and Jasper Yeates's manuscript notes of debates are placed in the microform supplement to this volume to enable those who wish to do so, to ponder the problems involved in rendering such notes intelligible (Mfm:Pa. 263, 264, 265).

The debaters often referred to parts of the Constitution and to sources such as Blackstone's *Commentaries* and Montesquieu's *Spirit of Laws.* These references are usually abbreviated and sometimes erroneous. Thus a reference to the Constitution might be noted as "A.I,2." Such a reference would be printed as "Article I, section 2." Quotations from the Constitution and other sources are printed as they appear in the notes of debates. When there are substantive errors in such quotations, editorial notes will so indicate. References to such works as those of Blackstone and Montesquieu have been checked, whenever available, in editions available to the delegates, and citations to volume and page numbers of such contemporary editions have been placed in brackets immediately after the references given by the notetakers.

Aside from the full debates printed by Dallas, there are several newspaper stories in which versions of some speeches are given, as well as comments on the day's proceedings. Where appropriate, reports of speeches have been removed from the stories and placed in the debates. Complete copies of such newspaper stories that are not printed below, are placed in the microform supplement (Mfm:Pa. 266).

A. PROCEEDINGS AND DEBATES OF THE CONVENTION

The Pennsylvania Convention Tuesday 20 November 1787

Convention Proceedings

This being the day appointed by the legislature of this state for the meeting of the Convention, a number of gentlemen delegated for that purpose met accordingly at the State House.

And adjourned to three o'clock P.M. tomorrow.[1]

1. The *Pennsylvania Herald,* 21 November, reported that thirty-eight members of the Convention had met on the 20th; and that "A motion was made to meet at 10 o'clock [on 21 November], but a member observing that those persons now on their road could not be arrived so soon, the motion was lost." For other accounts, see Mfm:Pa. 230, 266.

The Pennsylvania Convention Wednesday 21 November 1787

Convention Proceedings

Sixty of the gentlemen elected to serve in the Convention met.

The returns of the elections held for the city of Philadelphia and the several counties of this state were read, by which it appears that the following gentlemen were returned as delegates for the Convention for the said city and counties, respectively, viz.:[1]

For the City of Philadelphia
George Latimer
Benjamin Rush
Hilary Baker
James Wilson
Thomas McKean

For Philadelphia County
William Macpherson
John Hunn
George Gray
Samuel Ashmead
Enoch Edwards

For Bucks County
Henry Wynkoop
John Barclay
Thomas Yardley
Abraham Stout

For Chester County
Thomas Bull
Anthony Wayne
William Gibbons
Richard Downing
Thomas Cheyney
John Hannum

For Lancaster County
Stephen Chambers
Robert Coleman
Sebastian Graff
John Hubley
Jasper Yeates
John Whitehill

For York County
Henry Slagle
Thomas Campbell
Thomas Hartley
David Grier
John Black
Benjamin Pedan

For Cumberland County
John Harris
John Reynolds
Robert Whitehill
Jonathan Hoge

For Berks County
Nicholas Lutz
John Ludwig
Abraham Lincoln
John Bishop
Joseph Hiester

For Northampton County
John Arndt
Stephen Balliot
Joseph Horsfield
David Deshler

For Bedford County
James Martin
Joseph Powell

For Northumberland County
William Wilson
John Boyd

For Westmoreland County
William Findley
John Baird
William Todd

For Washington County
James Marshel
James Edgar
Thomas Scott
John Nevill

For Fayette County
Nathaniel Breading
John Smilie

For Franklin County
Richard Bard
John Allison

For Montgomery County
Jonathan Roberts
John Richards
Frederick A. Muhlenberg
James Morris

For Dauphin County
William Brown
Adam Orth
John A. Hanna

For Luzerne County
Timothy Pickering

For Huntingdon County
Benjamin Elliott

The Convention proceeded to elect a president.

The ballots being counted, it appeared that Frederick Augustus Muhlenberg, Esquire was duly elected.

An invitation to the President and members of the Convention from the faculty of the University of Pennsylvania, requesting their company at a commencement to be held tomorrow, was read.

Agreed to attend in a body, at ten o'clock tomorrow.

Adjourned until nine o'clock, A.M.

1. The spelling of the names of delegates has been changed to conform to the way they wrote their names, in cases where their signatures have been located, and corrected from other sources when signatures are not available.

Newspaper Report of Proceedings and Debates

Sixty members of the Convention being assembled, Mr. M'Kean proposed that the returns should be read over, whereupon it was found that the following persons were duly elected, viz.

[At this point appears the list of delegates as printed in the Convention Proceedings, 21 November.]

The members then proceeded by ballot to the election of a president, when there appeared 30 votes for Mr. Muhlenberg, 29 for M'Kean, and one for Mr. Gray.[1] General Wayne doubted, whether 30 votes could be deemed the sense of the meeting, as it was not a majority of 60, the number of delegates present, which occasioned a short conversation upon the subject; but at length, the question being taken, "Whether Mr. Mullenbergh should be conducted to the chair?" it was determined in the affirmative. It was then proposed to proceed to the choice of a clerk, but that business was deferred on motion of Mr. Smilie. Dr. Rush moved "that a committee be appointed to request the attendance of some minister of the Gospel tomorrow morning, in order to open the business of the Convention with prayer." This was considered by several gentlemen as a new and unnecessary measure, which might be inconsistent with the religious sentiments of some of the members, as it was impossible to fix upon a clergyman to suit every man's tenets, and it was neither warranted by the example of the General Assembly or of the convention that framed the government of Pennsylvania. To these observations Dr. Rush replied that he hoped there was liberality sufficient in the meeting to unite in prayers for the blessing of Heaven upon their proceedings, without considering the sect or persuasion of the minister who officiated; and with respect to precedent, he remarked that it might be taken from the conduct of the first and every succeeding Congress, who certainly deserved our imitation. "That the convention who framed the government of Pennsylvania did not preface their business with prayer is probably the reason," added the Doctor, "that the state has ever since been distracted by their proceedings." Mr. Smilie objected to the absurd superstition of that opinion, and moved a postponement which was accordingly agreed to.[2] An invitation was read from the trustees of the University requesting the attendance of the members at the ensuing commencement, which was unanimously accepted, and the Convention adjourned to meet tomorrow morning at 9 o'clock, in order to proceed in a body to the college hall. [*Pennsylvania Herald,* 24 November][3]

1. George Gray, a tavernkeeper and descendant of a wealthy Quaker family, served in the Assembly from 1774 to 1776 and from 1780 to 1785, and was Speaker in 1783–1784.

2. For an attack on Rush's position, see "Tim Quandary," Mfm:Pa. 287.
3. The *Herald's* report was reprinted in the *Independent Gazetteer* on 27 November, and excerpts were reprinted five times in Pennsylvania, three times in Massachusetts, and once in New Jersey. A shorter account in the *Pennsylvania Packet* on 22 November and the *Lancaster Zeitung* on 28 November was reprinted sixteen times from New Hampshire to Georgia by 7 December.

The Pennsylvania Convention
Thursday
22 November 1787

Convention Proceedings

Convention met and proceeded to the University Hall, attended commencement, and returned to their chamber.

On motion of Anthony Wayne, seconded by Robert Whitehill,

A committee was appointed to report rules and regulations for conducting the business of the Convention.

The committee consisted of Benjamin Rush, James Wilson, George Gray, Anthony Wayne, and Robert Whitehill.

Adjourned until half past nine o'clock tomorrow, A.M.

The Pennsylvania Convention
Friday
23 November 1787

Convention Proceedings[1]

Convention met pursuant to adjournment and proceeded to elect a secretary.

The ballots being taken, it appeared that James Campbell, Esquire was duly elected.

A petition from Thomas Lloyd was read praying to be appointed assistant secretary.

On motion of John Smilie, seconded by Robert Whitehill,

The further consideration thereof was postponed.

Petitions from Andrew Burkhard, James Martin, Nicholas Weaver, Joseph Fry, and Frederick Snyder, respectively praying to be appointed messenger or doorkeeper were read.[2]

The Convention proceeded to the choice of a messenger and doorkeeper, and the ballots being taken, it appeared that Andrew Burkhard was duly elected messenger and Joseph Fry doorkeeper.

The committee appointed yesterday, to bring in rules and regulations, made report; and the same being read was by special order taken up, read by paragraphs, and agreed to, as follows.

I. When the President assumes the chair, the members shall take their seats.

II. At the opening of the Convention each day, the Minutes of the preceding day shall be read, and are then in the power of the Convention to be corrected; after which any business addressed to the chair may be proceeded to.

III. Every petition, memorial, letter, or other matter of the like kind, read in the Convention, shall be deemed as lying on the table for further consideration, unless any special order be moved therein.

IV. A motion made, and seconded, shall be repeated by the President. A motion shall be reduced to writing, if the President, or any two members, require it. A motion may be withdrawn by the member making it, before any decision is had on it.

V. No member speaking shall be interrupted, but by a call to order by the President, or by a member, through the President.

VI. No member to be referred to in debate by name.

VII. The President himself, or by request, may call to order any member who shall transgress the rules. If a second time, the President may refer to him by name. The Convention may then examine and censure the member's conduct, he being allowed to extenuate or justify.

VIII. Every member actually attending the Convention shall be in his place at the time to which the Convention stands adjourned, or within half an hour thereof.

IX. The name of him who makes, and the name of him who seconds a motion, shall be entered on the Minutes.

X. No member shall speak more than twice to a question, without leave.[3]

XI. Every member of a committee shall attend at the call of his chairman.

XII. The yeas and nays may be called and entered on the Minutes, when any two members require it.

On motion of Thomas M'Kean, seconded by John Smilie,

Ordered, That the doors of the Convention be left open during the session.[4]

On motion of Thomas M'Kean, seconded by John Smilie,

Ordered, That the Constitution, as proposed by the late Federal Convention, be read.

It was read accordingly.

On motion of James Wilson, seconded by Jasper Yeates,
It was made a rule of the Convention to meet at ten o'clock, A.M.
Adjourned until ten o'clock tomorrow.

1. A brief account of the proceedings was printed in the *Pennsylvania Packet,* 27 November.

2. Weaver had been sergeant at arms, and Fry had been doorkeeper of the General Assembly since November 1784. On 25 October 1787 Weaver lost his post to James Martin. Although Martin was not elected messenger or doorkeeper of the Convention, he was paid £6.15.0 for "services to the Convention" (Mfm:Pa. 268). Snyder was doorkeeper of the Supreme Executive Council.

3. Rule X was repealed on 26 November.

4. On 21 November the *Pennsylvania Herald* reported: "It has been doubted, says a correspondent, whether the doors of the ensuing Convention will be kept open; but from the very constitution of that body, it cannot be otherwise; for the plan of the federal government is to be submitted to *the people,* yet as it would be highly inconvenient, if not impracticable, to lay it before the citizens at large, it is agreed to submit it to a part for the whole. Whatever therefore is transacted by the Convention is, in fact, transacted by the people, and to exclude them from hearing what passes is in effect excluding them from a share in their own act. Besides this reason, it will doubtless be remembered that the secret proceedings of the Federal Convention, by preventing its members from a knowledge of the sentiments of the people, which might have guided their decisions, has probably been the source of all the opposition that is now made to the plan of government devised by that body." Between 24 November and 4 December this item was reprinted outside Pennsylvania seven times from Massachusetts to New York. It was reprinted in the *Independent Gazetteer* on 18 December. On the "bad appearance" of the secrecy of the Constitutional Convention, see Mfm:Pa. 234.

Newspaper Reports of Proceedings

The Convention being met, pursuant to adjournment, on motion of Mr. M'Kean, they proceeded to the choice of a secretary, when Mr. James Campbell was duly elected. Mr. Burt [Burkhard] was afterwards appointed messenger and Mr. Fry doorkeeper. An application from Thomas Lloyd to be made assistant clerk was read, and a motion complying with the same was postponed.

The committee appointed yesterday to frame rules for regulating the Convention made their report, which was adopted.

On motion of Mr. M'Kean, seconded by Mr. Smilie, Resolved That the doors of the Convention be kept open.

On motion of Mr. M'Kean, the Constitution proposed for the federal government was taken up and read by the clerk.

Mr. Wilson then moved that the time of meeting and adjourning should be fixed, observing that with respect to the time of adjournment, it had been found necessary in the Federal Convention to make a rule that at 4 o'clock they should break up, even if a member was in the middle of his speech, and he proposed that two o'clock should be the hour now limited for adjournment; but after a short conversation, it was agreed that the Convention should meet at 10 o'clock each morning, leaving the hour of adjournment unspecified.

The Convention adjourned to meet tomorrow morning at 10 o'clock. [*Pennsylvania Herald,* 24 November][1]

* * * *

The Convention having proceeded to ballot for a secretary—on casting up the votes there appeared 46 for James Campbell,[2] late captain in the Pennsylvania line, 15 for [William] Temple Franklin, 7 for ________ Webb.

Whereon, James Campbell, Esquire was declared duly elected secretary.

This appointment is certainly a good federal feature and highly honorable to the members, as marking their gratitude and approbation of gallantry and military service. [*Independent Gazetteer,* 24 November]

* * * *

A correspondent cannot help taking notice that however well intentioned the gentlemen of the state Convention might be, who proposed Mr. Franklin as their secretary; there was certainly a great impropriety in letting his name be run without previously mentioning it to him and obtaining his consent. As it is more than probable that had that gentleman expressed a wish on the subject, his character and abilities would have commanded a more respectable number of votes.

Another correspondent supposes that Mr. Franklin was put in nomination by the same Antifederal junto who put his respectable grandfather at the head of their ticket for members of the state Convention; and with the same view—that of insinuating that he was opposed to the new plan of government. Is it not scandalous that such characters should be so trifled with! [*Independent Gazetteer,* 26 November]

1. Reprinted five times in Pennsylvania and, in part or in whole, seven times from Maine to New Jersey.

2. On 24 November William Shippen, Jr. wrote his son, Thomas Lee Shippen, that "Campbell, alias *young Jackson,* is chosen secretary to the Convention. [William] T[emple] Franklin had but 17 votes" (CC:232). Campbell is possibly the man who was appointed to the office of secretary to the Commission for Indian Treaties in 1784. At that time Campbell was said to be "a student of the law," whose abilities were "greater than common at his age which is but seventeen or eighteen" (LMCC, VIII, 854). He was admitted to the Philadelphia bar in June 1788.

The Pennsylvania Convention
Saturday
24 November 1787

Convention Proceedings

The Convention met pursuant to adjournment.

On motion of Thomas M'Kean, seconded by John Hannum,

The Constitution, as proposed by the late Convention, was read a second time, together with a letter from the secretary of Congress to the president of this state.[1]

It was moved by Thomas M'Kean, and seconded by John Allison,

That this Convention do assent to and ratify the Constitution agreed to on the 17th of September last by the Convention of the United States of America held at Philadelphia.

On motion of adjournment by John Smilie, seconded by Robert Whitehill,

Adjourned until three o'clock on Monday next, P.M.

1. Charles Thomson's Circular Letter to the Executives of the States, New York, 28 September (CDR:IX,A) transmitting the Constitution.

Convention Debates

THOMAS MCKEAN: Mr. President, there will perhaps be some difficulty in ascertaining the proper mode of proceeding to obtain a decision upon the important and interesting subject before us. We are certainly without precedent to guide us; but the utility of the forms observed by other public bodies will be an inducement to adhere to them, where a variation of circumstances does not render a variation of the mode essentially necessary. As far, therefore, as the rules of the legislature of Pennsylvania will apply to the constitution and business of this body, I shall recommend their adoption, but I perceive that in a very great degree we shall be obliged, for conveniency and propriety, to resort to new regulations, arising from the singularity of the subject offered to our consideration. For the present, however, I shall move you sir, that we come to the following resolution: "Resolved, That this Convention do adopt and ratify the Constitution of federal government as agreed upon by the Federal Convention at Philadelphia on the 17th day of September, 1787." This measure,

Mr. President, is not intended to introduce an instantaneous decision of so important a question, but merely to bring the object of our meeting fully and fairly into discussion. It is not my wish that it should be determined this day, nor do I apprehend it will be necessary that it should be determined this day week; but it is merely preparatory to another motion[1] with which I shall hereafter trouble you, and which, in my opinion, will bring on that regular and satisfactory investigation of the separate parts of the proposed Constitution, which will finally enable us to determine upon the whole. [Dallas' Debates, *Pennsylvania Herald,* 28 November][2]

McKean: The subject, now, Mr. President, comes fully and fairly before us. Our first object must be to ascertain the proper mode of proceeding to obtain a final decision. We are without precedent to guide us, yet those forms observed by other public bodies, so far as they are eligible, may generally be proper for us to adhere to. So far, therefore, as the rules of the legislature of Pennsylvania apply with convenience to our circumstance, I acquiesce in their adoption.

I now think it necessary, sir, to make you a motion, not that I apprehend it can be determined until a full investigation of the subject before us is had. This motion will be, sir, that this Convention do *assent to* and *ratify* the Constitution agreed to on the 17th of September last by the Convention of the United States of America held at Philadelphia.

Upon this motion being seconded, sir, the consideration of the Constitution will be necessarily drawn on. Every objection that can be suggested against the work will be listened to with attention, answered, and perhaps obviated. And finally, after a full discussion, the ground will be ascertained on which we are to receive or reject the system now before you. I do not wish this question to be decided today; tho perhaps it may be determined this day week. I offer you this for the sake of form, and shall hereafter trouble you with another motion that may bring the particular parts of this Constitution before you for a regular and satisfactory investigation. [Lloyd, *Debates,* 24–25][3]

* * * *

James Wilson: The business of the Convention being brought before that honorable body on Saturday last by motion of the Honorable Mr. M'Kean (recited in our last), Mr. Wilson attracted the attention of the house by a speech which the celebrated Roman orator would not have blushed to own. He began by pointing out the difficulties that the late Convention had to encounter; the diversity of opinion, interest, and prejudice they had to combat. He sketched the different forms of ancient and modern republics, and showed how imperfect models they were for our imitation; he proved to demonstration, that there was not among them one confederated republic; he mentioned these difficulties (he said) not to make a parade of the merits of the Convention in surmounting them but to show how visionary—how idle it is to expect that under them a government could be framed unexceptionable in all its parts to each individual of so extensive an empire. He forcibly contrasted the imbecility of our present Confederation with the energy which must result from the proffered Constitution. After defining (with an accuracy which marked his acquaintance with governmental history) the different kinds of government, and pointing out their respective advantages and wants, he concluded a speech which had justly won the admiration of his audience, by saying, that the late Convention had in view, and, he hoped, had in some measure executed a Constitution whose energy would pervade the Union and restore credit and happiness to a distracted empire. [*Pennsylvania Packet,* 27 November][4]

Wilson: As soon as Mr. M'Kean's motion had been read from the table, Mr. Wilson rose, and, in a long and elaborate speech, delineated the general principles upon which the Federal Constitution has been founded. The difficulties which the late Convention had to encounter were pointed out, in the extent of the country, its population, and independent establishments, the various and contending habits, prejudices, and interests of the people, and the want of an applicable example in any of the ancient or modern institutions of governments. The republics of former times, as well as the existing confederations of the Swiss cantons, the United Netherlands, and the Germanic body, were shown to be incapable of furnishing a precedent, and the three simple species of governments, the monarchical, aristocratical, and democratical, were accurately reviewed to demonstrate that they did not singly afford a rule adequate to the exigencies and dominion of the continent. Mr. Wilson then entered into a disquisition of the nature and properties of civil society, civil liberty, and civil government, and, closing this part of his speech with a definition of what, for the first time, he designated by the term of "federal liberty," he observed that the same principles which applied in resigning a portion of the natural rights of individuals to form society would apply in resigning a portion of the civil liberty of each state to form a federal republic; because in both cases the good of the whole must be preferred to a part, and, in truth, more liberty is gained by associating, than is lost by the natural rights which it absorbs. Having ably discriminated between the advantages and disadvantages of every known species of government, Mr. Wilson observed that it was the object of the Convention to form such a system as would admit the one but exclude the other, and therefore a federal republic naturally presented itself to their approbation. The result of their opinions lying for the discussion of the Convention, it would certainly be asked, after investigating other governments, of what description is the proposed plan? To which Mr. Wilson answered, in its principles, it is surely democratical; for, however wide and various the firearms of power may appear, they may all be traced to one source, the people. [Dallas' Debates, *Pennsylvania Herald,* 28 November]

There are two long versions of the above speech by James Wilson. A pamphlet version was published on 28 November. The other version was published in Lloyd's *Debates* in February 1788. Both versions are printed below after Jasper Yeates: Draft of Speech, 24–26 November.

* * * *

JOHN SMILIE: When Mr. Wilson had concluded, Mr. Smilie rose and entered into a severe animadversion upon the nature of the motion offered by Mr. M'Kean, which however, he observed, was consistent with the system of precipitancy that had uniformly prevailed in respect to the important subject before the Convention. He observed that we were repeatedly told of the peculiar advantages which we enjoy in being able deliberately and peaceably to decide upon a government for ourselves and our posterity, but we find every measure that is proposed leads to defeat those advantages and to preclude all argument and deliberation in a case confessedly of the highest consequence to the happiness of a great portion of the globe. What, continued he, can be the object of the motion? Is it to bring on a hasty and total adoption of the Constitution? Let it be remembered that the Federal Convention consumed four months in framing it, and shall we not employ a few days in deciding upon it? If it is that noble, that perfect system, we have been told it is, why interfere with the fullest investigation of its principles, since, in that case, the better they are understood, the more they will be approved. The most common business of a legislative body is treated with greater delicacy, being submitted to repeated discussion upon different days, and are we on a point of such magnitude to determine without information, to agree *in toto* to so complicated a system before we have weighed and examined its constituent parts? No, sir, it is our duty to go coolly and circumstantially into the consideration of this business, and by comparing it, at least, with the circumstances and exigencies of our country, ask with firmness, "Is such a sacrifice of civil liberty necessary to the national honor and happiness of America?" For my part, I think otherwise, though, at the same time I am sensible of the expediency of giving additional strength and energy to the federal head. But we are not so situated as to be obliged to accept any terms, and if this plan is such as we ought not to accept, I hope this Convention will have candor and fortitude enough to reject it. [Dallas' Debates, *Pennsylvania Herald,* 28 November]

* * * *

THOMAS MCKEAN followed Mr. Smilie and remarked that the object of his motion was declared when it was proposed. It was not to preclude, but to promote a free and ample discussion of the federal plan. But as to the precedents which are pointed out from the legislature of Pennsylvania to guide our proceedings, if they were always right, which I do not think they are, still no parallel can be drawn between the nature of their business and ours, consequently their rules cannot apply. We do not come here to legislate; we have no right to inquire into the power of the late Convention or to alter and amend their work; the sole question before us is, whether we will ratify and confirm, or, upon due consideration reject, in the whole, the system of federal government that is submitted to us. But because this is the only question which we can decide, does it follow that we are not minutely to investigate its principles in every section and sentence? No sir, that will be our duty before we conclusively say whether we will ratify or reject; but precedents in point of proceeding cannot be drawn from any part of the world, for we are the first people who have ever peaceably assembled upon so great and interesting an occasion. [Dallas' Debates, *Pennsylvania Herald,* 28 November]

* * * *

ROBERT WHITEHILL stated that, in his opinion, the object of the motion had been misunderstood by the member from Fayette [John Smilie], which was undoubtedly intended to bring the subject fairly before the Convention. Indeed I cannot perceive how we can decide upon the whole without having first considered every part, and in order to do that with conveniency and effect, I presume a motion to go into a committee of the whole Convention, which I mean to propose, will be adopted. Notwithstanding the arrangements, there may be reasonable objections urged against the proposed plan, and if it is found that it conveys to the federal government rights and liberties which the people ought never to surrender, I hope no speculative argument will seduce us into a confirmation, which bind ourselves and our posterity forever. [Dallas' Debates, *Pennsylvania Herald,* 28 November]

1. McKean's motion was printed in the *Pennsylvania Packet* on 26 November with the comment that "it was not expected to be immediately agreed to." On 26 November McKean moved "That this Convention do now proceed to consider the Constitution referred to their consideration, by articles."

2. Dallas' version of the debates on 24 November was reprinted in full in the *Independent Gazetteer,* 29 November; *Pennsylvania Journal,* 1 December; *Carlisle Gazette,* 5 December; and *Pittsburgh Gazette,* 22 December. Dallas misdated the debates as taking place on 27 November.

3. Lloyd misdated McKean's speech as taking place on 26 November.

4. The *Packet's* account of Wilson's speech was reprinted in the *Pennsylvania Gazette,* 28 November, *Lancaster Zeitung,* 5 December, and sixteen times from New Hampshire to South Carolina by 22 December.

Jasper Yeates: Draft of Speech, 24–26 November

Yeates apparently drafted the following speech to be delivered on Monday, 26 November to support Thomas McKean's motion on 24 November to ratify the Constitution. However, McKean moved on Monday morning to consider the Constitution article by article. There is no evidence that Yeates delivered the speech.

Mr. President: I rise in support of the motion made by the honorable member [Thomas McKean] that this Convention do assent to and ratify the Constitution of the United States as lately agreed to on the 17 September last by the Convention of the United States.

The intentions of the member have been fully and clearly stated. No precipitation or hurry is affected. A fair dispassionate, deliberate discussion of the principles of the system proposed to us is desired by all; and that the most ample time should be given for the bringing forward and investigating every objection that can be made to the new Constitution. Precipitation and hurry on the one hand and affected delay and unnecessary procrastination on the other should equally be avoided.

The primary question then will be in what form or shape our deliberations shall be conducted—whether we shall proceed to the discussion in full Convention as a body delegated for this express purpose, or whether pursuing the general system of the House of Assembly on bills before them, we shall resolve ourselves into a committee of the whole, choose a chairman, take it up paragraph by paragraph, collect the votes on each paragraph, and make report to the Convention of our proceedings and resolutions.

I am strongly inclined to pursue the first mode on principles of propriety, ease, and public utility.

We are not met here to amend or alter the Constitution. We have no such power delegated to us. We do not resemble the legislature in this particular, nor are their precedents binding on us. The powers which carried into exercise necessarily produce this effect with them of resolving themselves into a committee of the whole to alter, amend, and improve any particular bill, do not exist with us. The cause ceasing with us, the effect must cease also. We are brought here for the discussion of a simple point and in the event to determine whether we will ratify or reject the Constitution offered to us. This is the grand question which we are to solve.

If we go into a committee of the whole we shall, after spending considerable time on the system, have to travel the same ground over again in Convention, and thereby incur unnecessary expense as well as a considerable loss of time.

But why debate it paragraph by paragraph? Surely there [are,] at least, some things [in] it [that are] unexceptionable, etc. [Yeates's Papers, PPIn]

James Wilson's Speech on 24 November

Wilson's speech was summarized by Alexander J. Dallas in the *Pennsylvania Herald* on 28 November. On the same day Thomas Bradford published a much longer version in a pamphlet derived from Dallas' notes. The pamphlet circulated throughout the country. Although no Pennsylvania newspaper reprinted the pamphlet, eleven newspapers in Massachusetts, New Hampshire, Rhode Island, Connecticut, and New York had reprinted it by 7 January 1788. (For national circulation and the responses to the speech, see CC:289.)

The pamphlet version created controversy immediately. Two days after it appeared, Samuel Vaughan, Jr. in Philadelphia wrote to James Bowdoin in Massachusetts that the pamphlet was "very inaccurate, and not only parts are omitted and the leading points often lost for want of seizing the exact expression, but some parts are absolutely misstated" (30 November, II:F above). On 3 December the *Independent Gazetteer* published an advertisement signed by Thomas Lloyd in which he disclaimed responsibility for the pamphlet and pledged to give Wilson's speech "without mutilation or misrepresentation" in his version of the Convention *Debates*, which, he said, was then at the press (Mfm:Pa. 252). Lloyd's version, however, was not published until 7 February 1788.

The speech evoked a partisan response varying from condemnation by "Centinel" to praise by Francis Hopkinson. "Centinel" charged that Wilson and his cohorts were "aspiring despots" who were hoping "to gull" the people out of their liberties and accused Wilson of "sophistry" and drawing distinctions which existed only in "his own fertile imagination" ("Centinel" V, 4 December, CC:318). Hopkinson declared that "Wilson exerted himself to the astonishment of all hearers. The powers of Demosthenes and Cicero seemed to be united in this able orator" (to Thomas Jefferson, 14 December, Mfm:Pa. 262). See also Mfm:Pa. 242 for other comments on the speech.

Version of Wilson's Speech by Alexander J. Dallas[1]

As the only member of this respectable body, who had the honor of a seat in the late Federal Convention, it is peculiarly my duty, Mr. President, to submit to your consideration, the general principles that have produced the national Constitution, which has been framed and proposed by the assembled delegates of the United States, and which must finally stand or fall by the concurrent decision of this Convention, and of others acting upon the same subject, under similar powers and authority. To frame a government for a single city or state is a business both in its importance and facility, widely different from the task entrusted to the Federal Convention, whose prospects were extended not only to thirteen independent and sovereign states, some of which in territorial jurisdiction, population, and resource equal the most respectable nations of Europe, but likewise to innumerable states yet unformed, and to myriads of citizens who in future ages shall inhabit the vast uncultivated regions of the continent. The duties of that body, therefore, were not limited to local or partial considerations but to the formation of a plan commensurate with a great and valuable portion of the globe.

I confess, sir, that the magnitude of the object before us filled our minds with awe and apprehension. In Europe the opening and extending the navigation of a single river has been deemed an act of imperial merit and importance; but how insignificant does it seem when we contemplate the scene that nature here exhibits, pouring forth the Potomac, the Rappahannock, the Susquehanna, and other innumerable rivers to dignify, adorn, and enrich our soil. But the magnitude of the object was equalled by the difficulty of accomplishing it, when we considered the uncommon dexterity and address that were necessary to combat and reconcile the jarring interests that seemed naturally to prevail, in a country which, presenting a coast of 1500 miles to the Atlantic, is composed of 13 distinct and independent states, varying essentially in their situation and dimensions, and in the number and habits of their citizens. Their interests too, in some respects really different, and in many apparently so; but whether really or apparently, such is the constitution of the human mind, they make the same impression, and are prosecuted with equal vigor and perseverance. Can it then be a subject for surprise that with the sensations indispensably excited by so comprehensive and so arduous an undertaking, we should for a moment yield to despondency, and at length, influenced by the spirit of conciliation, resort to mutual concession, as the only means to obtain the great end for which we were convened? Is it a matter of surprise that where the springs of dissension were so numerous, and so powerful, some force was requisite to impel them to take, in a collected state, a direction different from that which separately they would have pursued?

There was another reason, that in this respect, increased the different tempers and dispositions of the people for whom they acted. But, however widely they may differ upon other topics, they cordially agree in that keen and elevated sense of freedom and independence, which has been manifested in their united and successful opposition to one of the most powerful kingdoms of the world. Still it was apprehended by some, that their abhorrence of constraint would be the source of objection and opposition; but, I confess, that my opinion, formed upon a knowledge of the good sense, as well as the high spirit of my constituents, made me confident that they would esteem that government to be the best, which was best calculated eventually to establish and secure the dignity and happiness of their country. Upon this ground, I have occasionally supposed that my constituents have asked the reason of my assent to the several propositions contained in the plan before us. My answer, tho concise, is a candid, and, I think a satisfactory one—because I thought them right; and thinking them right, it would be a poor compliment, indeed, to presume they could be disagreeable to my constituents—a presumption that might occasion a retort to which I wish not to expose myself, as it would again be asked, "is this the opinion you entertain of those who have confided in your judgment? From what ground do you infer that a vote right in itself would be disagreeable to us?" And it might with justice be added, "this sentiment evinces that you deserved not the trust which we reposed in you." No sir! I have no right to imagine that the reflected rays of delegated power can displease by a brightness that proves the superior splendor of the luminary from which they proceed.

The extent of country for which the new Constitution was required produced another difficulty in the business of the Federal Convention. It is the opinion of some celebrated writers that to a small territory, the democratical; to a middling territory (as Montesquieu has termed it), the monarchical; and, to an extensive territory, the despotic form of government is best adapted. Regarding then, the wide and almost unbounded jurisdiction of the United States, at first view, the hand of despotism seemed necessary to control, connect, and protect it; and hence the chief embarrassment arose. For, we knew that, although our constituents would cheerfully submit to the legislative restraints of a free government, they would spurn at every attempt to shackle them with despotic power.

In this dilemma, a federal republic naturally presented itself to our observation as a species of government which secured all the internal advantages of a republic, at the same time that it maintained the external dignity and force of a monarchy. The definition of this form of government may be found in Montesquieu, who says, I believe, that it consists in assembling distinct societies, which are consolidated into a new body capable of being increased by the addition of other members; an expanding quality peculiarly fitted to the circumstances of America.

But, while a federal republic removed one difficulty, it introduced another, since there existed not any precedent to assist our deliberations; for, though there are many single governments, both ancient and modern, the history and principles of which are faithfully preserved and well understood, a perfect confederation of independent states is a system hitherto unknown. The Swiss cantons, which have often been mentioned in that light, cannot properly be deemed a federal republic, but merely a system of united states. The United Netherlands are also an assemblage of states; yet, as their proceedings are not the result of their combined decisions, but of the decisions of each state individually, their association is evidently wanting in that quality which is essential to constitute a federal republic. With respect to the Germanic body, its members are of so disproportionate a size, their separate governments and jurisdictions so different in nature and extent, the general purpose and operation of their union so indefinite and uncertain, and the exterior power of the House of Austria so prevalent, that little information could be obtained or expected from that quarter. Turning then to ancient history, we find the Achaean and Lycian leagues, and the Amphyctionic Council bearing a superficial resemblance to a federal republic; but of all these, the accounts which have been transmitted to us are too vague and imperfect to supply a tolerable theory, and they are so destitute of that minute detail from which practical knowledge may be derived, that they must now be considered rather as subjects of curiosity, than of use or information.

Government, indeed, taken as a science may yet be considered in its infancy; and with all its various modifications, it has hitherto been the result of force, fraud, or accident. For, after the lapse of six thousand years since the Creation of the world, America now presents the first instance of a people assembled to weigh deliberately and calmly, and to decide leisurely and peaceably, upon the form of government by which they will bind themselves and their posterity. Among the ancients, three forms of government seem to have been correctly known, the monarchical, aristocratical, and democratical; but their knowledge did not extend beyond those simple kinds, though much pleasing ingenuity has occasionally been exercised, in tracing a resemblance of mixed government in some ancient institutions, particularly between them and the British constitution. But, in my opinion, the result of these ingenious refinements does more honor to the moderns in discovering, than to the ancients in forming the similitude. In the work of Homer, it is supposed by his enthusiastic commentators, the seeds of every science are to be found, but, in truth, they are first observed in subsequent discoveries, and then the fond imagination transplants them to the book. Tacitus, who lived towards the close of that period, which is called ancient, who had read the history of all antecedent and contemporary governments, who was perfectly competent to judge of their nature, tendency, and quality, Tacitus considers a mixed government as a thing rather to be wished than expected; and, if ever it did occur, it was his opinion, that it could not last long. One fact, however, is certain, that the ancients had no idea of representation, that essential to every system of wise, good, and efficient government. It is surprising, indeed, how very imperfectly, at this day, the doctrine of representation is understood in Europe. Even Great Britain, which boasts a superior knowledge of the subject, and is generally supposed to have carried it into practice, falls far short of its true and genuine principles. For, let us inquire, does representation pervade the constitution of that country? No. Is it either immediately or remotely the source of the executive power? No. For it is not any part of the British constitution, as practiced at this time, that the king derives his authority from the people. Formerly that authority was claimed by hereditary or divine right; and even at the Revolution [of 1688], when the government was essentially improved, no other principle was recognized, but that of an original contract between the sovereign and the people—a contract which rather excludes than implies the doctrine of representation. Again, is the judicial system of England grounded on representation? No. For the judges are appointed by the king, and he, as we have already observed, derives not his majesty or power from the people. Lastly, then, let us review the legislative body of that nation, and even there, though we find representation operating as a check, it cannot be considered as a pervading principle. The Lords, acting with hereditary right, or under an authority immediately communicated by regal prerogative, are not the representatives of the people, and yet they, as well as the sovereign, possess a negative power in the paramount business of legislation. Thus the vital principle of the British constitution is confined to a narrow corner, and the world has left to America the glory and happiness of forming a government where representation shall at once supply the basis and the cement of the superstructure. For, representation, sir, is the true chain between the people and those to whom they entrust the administration of the government; and, though it may consist of many links, its strength and brightness never should be impaired. Another, and perhaps the most important obstacle to the proceedings of the Federal Convention arose in drawing the line between the national and the individual governments of the states.

On this point a general principle readily occurred, that whatever object was confined in its nature and operation to a particular state ought to be subject to the separate government of the states, but whatever in its nature and operation extended beyond a particular state ought to be comprehended within the federal jurisdiction. The great difficulty, therefore, was the application of this general principle, for it was found impracticable to enumerate and distinguish the various objects to which it extended; and as the mathematics, only, are capable of demonstration, it ought not to be thought extraordinary that the Convention could not develop a subject involved in such endless perplexity. If however, the proposed Constitution should be adopted, I trust that in the theory there will be found such harmony, and in the practice such mutual confidence between the national and individual governments, that every sentiment of jealousy and apprehension will be effectually destroyed. But sir, permit me to ask, whether on the ground of a Union, the individual or the national government ought most to be trusted? For my part, I think it more natural to presume that the interest of each would be pursued by the whole, than the reverse of the proposition, that the several states would prefer the interest of the confederated body, for in the general government each is represented, but in the separate governments, only the separate states.

These difficulties, Mr. President, which embarrassed the Federal Convention are not represented to enhance the merit of surmounting them, but with a more important view, to show how unreasonable it is to expect that the plan of government should correspond with the wishes of all the states, of all the citizens of any one state, or of all the citizens of the united continent. I remember well, sir, the effect of those surrounding difficulties in the late Convention. At one time the great and interesting work seemed to be at a stand, at another it proceeded with energy and rapidity, and when at last, it was accomplished, many respectable members beheld it with wonder and admiration. But having pointed out the obstacles which they had to encounter, I shall now beg leave to direct your attention to the end which the Convention proposed.

Our wants, imperfections, and weakness, Mr. President, naturally incline us to society, but it is certain; society cannot exist without some restraints. In a state of nature each individual has a right, uncontrolled, to act as his pleasure or his interest may prevail, but it must be observed that this license extends to every individual, and hence the state of nature is rendered insupportable by the interfering claims and the consequent animosities of men, who are independent of every power and influence, but their passions and their will. On the other hand, in entering into the social compact, though the individual parts with a portion of his natural rights, yet, it is evident that he gains more by the limitation of the liberty of others, than he loses by the limitation of his own; so that in truth, the aggregate of liberty is more in society, than it is in a state of nature.

It is then, sir, a fundamental principle of society, that the welfare of the whole shall be pursued and not of a part, and the measures necessary to the good of the community must consequently be binding upon the individuals that compose it. This principle is universally allowed to be just with respect to single governments, and there are instances in which it applies with equal force to independent communities; for the situation and circumstances of states may make it as necessary for them, as for individuals, to associate. Hence, Mr. President, the important question arises—are such the situation and circumstances of the American states?

At this period, America has it in her power to adopt either of the following modes of government: she may dissolve the individual sovereignty of the states and become one consolidated empire; she may be divided into thirteen separate, independent, and unconnected commonwealths; she may be erected into two or more confederacies; or, lastly, she may become one comprehensive federal republic.

Allow me, sir, to take a short view of each of these suppositions. Is it probable that the dissolution of the state governments and the establishment of one consolidated empire, would be eligible in its nature and satisfactory to the people in its administration? I think not, as I have given reasons to show that so extensive a territory could not be governed, connected, and preserved, but by the supremacy of despotic power. All the exertions of the most potent emperors of Rome were not capable of keeping that empire together, which in extent was far inferior to the dominion of America. Would an independent, an unconnected situation, without any associating head, be advantageous or satisfactory? The consequences of this system would at one time expose the states to foreign insult and depredations, and, at another, to internal jealousy, contention, and war. Then let us consider the plan of two or more confederacies which has often been suggested, and which certainly presents some aspects more inviting than either of the preceding modes, since the subjects of strife would not be so numerous, the strength of the confederates would be greater, and their interests more united. But even here when we fairly weigh the advantages and the disadvantages, we shall find the last greatly preponderating; the expenses of government would be considerably multiplied, the seeds of rivalship and animosity would spring up and spread the calamities of war and tumult through the country; for tho the sources of rancor might be diminished, their strength and virulence would probably be increased.

Of these three species of government, however, I must observe, that they obtained no advocates in the Federal Convention, nor can I presume that they will find advocates here, or in any of our sister states. The general sentiment in that body, and, I believe, the general sentiment of the citizens of America, is expressed in the motto which some of them have chosen, UNITE OR DIE; and while we consider the extent of the country, so intersected and almost surrounded with navigable rivers, so separated and detached from the rest of the world, it is natural to presume that Providence has designed us for an united people, under one great political compact. If this is a just and reasonable conclusion, supported by the wishes of the people, the Convention did right in proposing a single confederated republic. But in proposing it, they were necessarily led not only to consider the situation, circumstances, and interests of one, two, or three states, but of the collective body; and as it is essential to society, that the welfare of the whole should be preferred to the accommodation of a part, they followed the same rule in promoting the national advantages of the Union in preference to the separate advantages of the states. A principle of candor, as well as duty, lead to this conduct; for, as I have said before, no government, either single or confederated can exist, unless private and individual rights are subservient to the public and general happiness of the nation. It was not alone the State of Pennsylvania, however important she may be as a constituent part of the Union, that could influence the deliberations of a Convention, formed by a delegation from all the United States, to devise a government adequate to their common exigencies and impartial in its influence and operation. In the spirit of union, inculcated by the nature of their commission, they framed the Constitution before us, and in the same spirit, they submit it to the candid consideration of their constituents.

Having made some remarks upon the nature and principles of civil society, I shall now take a cursory notice of civil liberty, which is essential to the well-being of civil government. The definition of civil liberty is, briefly, that portion of natural liberty which men resign to the government, and which then produces more happiness than it would have produced if retained by the individuals who resign it; still however leaving to the human mind the full enjoyment of every privilege that is not incompatible with the peace and order of society. Here I am easily led to the consideration of another species of liberty, which has not yet received a discriminating name, but which I will venture to term "federal liberty." This, sir, consists in the aggregate of the civil liberty which is surrendered by each state to the national government; and the same principles that operate in the establishment of a single society, with respect to the rights reserved or resigned by the individuals that compose it, will justly apply in the case of a confederation of distinct and independent states.

These observations have been made, Mr. President, in order to preface a representation of the state of the Union, as it appeared to the late Convention. We all know, and we have all felt, that the present system of confederation is inadequate to the government and the exigencies of the United States. Need I describe the contrasted scene which the Revolution has presented to our view? On the one hand, the arduous struggle in the cause of liberty terminated by a glorious and triumphant peace; on the other, contention and poverty at home, discredit and disgrace abroad. Do we not remember what high expectations were formed by others and by ourselves, on the return of peace? And have those honorable expectations from our national character been realized? No! What then has been the cause of disappointment? Has America lost her magnanimity or perseverance? No. Has she been subdued by any high-handed invasion of her liberties? Still I answer no; for, dangers of that kind were no sooner seen, than they were repelled. But the evil has stolen in from a quarter little suspected, and the rock of freedom, which stood firm against the attacks of a foreign foe, has been sapped and undermined by the licentiousness of our own citizens. Private calamity and public anarchy have prevailed; and even the blessing of independency has been scarcely felt or understood by a people who have dearly achieved it.

Shall I, sir, be more particular in this lamentable history? The commencement of peace was likewise the commencement of our distresses and disgrace. Devoid of power, we could neither prevent the excessive importations which lately deluged the country, nor even raise from that excess a contribution to the public revenue; devoid of importance, we were unable to command a sale for our commodities in a foreign market; devoid of credit, our public securities were melting in the hands of their deluded owners, like snow before the sun; devoid of dignity, we were inadequate to perform treaties on our own part or to compel a performance on the part of a contracting nation.

In short, sir, the tedious tale disgusts me, and I fondly hope it is unnecessary to proceed. The years of languor are over. We have seen dishonor and destruction, it is true, but we have at length penetrated the cause, and are now anxious to obtain the cure. The cause need not be specified by a recapitulation of facts; every act of Congress and the proceedings of every state are replete with proofs in that respect, and all point to the weakness and imbecility of the existing Confederation; while the loud and concurrent voice of the people proclaims an efficient national government to be the only cure. Under these impressions, and with these views, the late Convention were appointed and met; the end which they proposed to accomplish, being to frame one national and efficient government, in which the exercise of beneficence, correcting the jarring interests of every part, should pervade the whole, and by which the peace, freedom, and happiness of the United States should be permanently insured. The principles and means that were adopted by the Convention to obtain that end are now before us and will become the great object of our discussion. But on this point, as upon others, permit me to make a few general observations.

In all governments, whatever is their form, however they may be constituted, there must be a power established from which there is no appeal and which is therefore called absolute, supreme, and uncontrollable. The only question is, where that power is lodged? A question that will receive different answers from the different writers on the subject. Sir William Blackstone says it resides in the omnipotence of the British Parliament or, in other words, corresponding with the practice of that country, it is whatever the British Parliament pleases to do. So that when that body was so base and treacherous to the rights of the people as to transfer the legislative authority to Henry VIII, his exercising that authority by proclamations and edicts could not strictly speaking be termed unconstitutional, for under the act of Parliament his will was made the law, and therefore, his will became in that respect the constitution itself. But were we to ask some politicians who have taken a faint and inaccurate view of our establishments, "Where does this supreme power reside in the United States?" they would probably answer, "in their constitutions." This however, tho a step nearer to the fact, is not a just opinion; for, in truth, it remains and flourishes with the people; and under the influence of that truth we, at this moment, sit, deliberate, and speak. In other countries, indeed, the revolutions of government are connected with war and all its concomitant calamities. But with us, they are considered as the means of obtaining a superior knowledge of the nature of government and of accomplishing its end. That the supreme power therefore should be vested in the people is, in my judgment, the great panacea of human politics. It is a power paramount to every constitution, inalienable in its nature, and indefinite in its extent. For, I insist, if there are errors in government the people have the right not only to correct and amend them, but likewise totally to change and reject its form; and under the operation of that right, the citizens of the United States can never be wretched beyond retrieve, unless they are wanting to themselves.

Then let us examine, Mr. President, the three species of simple governments, which, as I have already mentioned, are the monarchical, aristocratical, and democratical. In a monarchy, the supreme power is vested in a single person; in an aristocracy, it is possessed by a body, not formed upon the principle of representation, but enjoying their station by descent, by election among themselves, or in right of some personal or territorial qualification; and, lastly, in a democracy, it is inherent in the people, and is either exercised by themselves or by their representatives. Each of these systems has its advantages and its disadvantages. The advantages of a monarchy are strength, dispatch, and unity; its disadvantages are expense, tyranny, and war. The advantages of an aristocracy are experience and the wisdom resulting from education; its disadvantages are the dissension of the governors and the oppression of the people. The advantages of a democracy are liberty, caution, industry, fidelity, and an opportunity of bringing forward the talents and abilities of the citizens without regard to birth or fortune; its disadvantages are dissension and imbecility, for the assent of many being required, their exertions will be feeble, and their councils too soon discovered.

To obtain all the advantages, and to avoid all the inconveniences of these governments, was the leading object of the late Convention. Having therefore considered the formation and principles of other systems, it is natural to inquire, of what description is the Constitution before us? In its principles, sir, it is purely democratical; varying indeed, in its form, in order to admit all the advantages and to exclude all the disadvantages which are incidental to the known and established constitutions of government. But when we take an extensive and accurate view of the streams of power that appear through this great and comprehensive plan, when we contemplate the variety of their directions, the force and dignity of their currents, when we behold them intersecting, embracing, and surrounding the vast possessions and interests of the continent, and when we see them distributing on all hands, beauty, energy, and riches, still, however numerous and wide their courses, however diversified and remote the blessings they diffuse, we shall be able to trace them all to one great and noble source, THE PEOPLE.

Such, Mr. President, are the general observations with which I have thought it necessary to trouble you. In discussing the distinct propositions of the federal plan, I shall have occasion to apply them more particularly to that subject, but at present, I shall conclude with requesting the pardon of the Convention for having so long intruded upon their patience.

1. *The Substance of a Speech Delivered by James Wilson, Esq. Explanatory of the General Principles of the Proposed Federal Constitution; Upon a Motion Made by the Honorable Thomas M'Kean, In the Convention of the State of Pennsylvania. On Saturday the 24th of November, 1787* (Philadelphia, 1787).

Version of Wilson's Speech by Thomas Lloyd[1]

The system proposed, by the late Convention, for the government of the United States is now before you. Of that Convention I had the honor to be a member. As I am the only member of that body, who have the honor to be also a member of this, it may be expected that I should prepare the way for the deliberations of this assembly by unfolding the difficulties which the late Convention were obliged to encounter, by pointing out the end which they proposed to accomplish, and by tracing the general principles which they have adopted for the accomplishment of that end.

To form a good system of government for a single city or state, however limited as to territory or inconsiderable as to numbers, has been thought to require the strongest efforts of human genius. With what conscious diffidence, then, must the members of the Convention have revolved in their minds the immense undertaking, which was before them. Their views could not be confined to a small or a single community, but were expanded to a great number of states; several of which contain an extent of territory, and resources of population, equal to those of some of the most respectable kingdoms on the other side of the Atlantic. Nor were even these the only objects to be comprehended within their deliberations. Numerous states yet unformed, myriads of the human race, who will inhabit regions hitherto uncultivated, were to be affected by the result of their proceedings. It was necessary, therefore, to form their calculations on a scale commensurate to a large portion of the globe.

For my own part, I have been often lost in astonishment at the vastness of the prospect before us. To open the navigation of a single river was lately thought in Europe, an enterprise adequate to imperial glory. But could the commercial scenes of the Scheldt be compared with those, that, under a good government, will be exhibited on the Hudson, the Delaware, the Potomac, and the numerous other rivers, that water and are intended to enrich the dominions of the United States?

The difficulty of the business was equal to its magnitude. No small share of wisdom and address is requisite to combine and reconcile the jarring interests, that prevail, or seem to prevail, in a single community. The United States contain already thirteen governments mutually independent. Those governments present to the Atlantic a front of fifteen hundred miles in extent. Their soil, their climates, their productions, their dimensions, their numbers are different. In many instances a difference and even an opposition subsists among their interests. And a difference and even an opposition is imagined to subsist in many more. An apparent interest produces the same attachment as a real one; and is often pursued with no less perseverance and vigor. When all these circumstances are seen and attentively considered, will any member of this honorable body be surprised, that such a diversity of things produced a proportioned diversity of sentiment? Will he be surprised that such a diversity of sentiment rendered a spirit of mutual forbearance and conciliation indispensably necessary to the success of the great work, and will he be surprised that mutual concessions and sacrifices were the consequences of mutual forbearance and conciliation? When the springs of opposition were so numerous and strong, and poured forth their waters in courses so varying, need we be surprised that the stream formed by their conjunction was impelled in a direction somewhat different from that, which each of them would have taken separately?

I have reason to think that a difficulty arose in the minds of some members of Convention from another consideration—their ideas of the temper and disposition of the people for whom the Constitution is proposed. The citizens of the United States, however different in some other respects, are well-known to agree in one strongly marked feature of their character—a warm and keen sense of freedom and independence. This sense has been heightened by the glorious result of their late struggle against all the efforts of one of the most powerful nations of Europe. It was apprehended, I believe, by some, that a people so highly spirited, would ill brook the restraints of an efficient government. I confess that this consideration did not influence my conduct. I knew my constituents to be high-spirited, but I knew them also to possess sound sense. I knew that, in the event, they would be best pleased with that system of government, which would best promote their freedom and happiness. I have often revolved this subject in my mind. I have supposed one of my constituents to ask me, why I gave such a vote on a particular question? I have always thought it would be a satisfactory answer to say, "because I judged, upon the best consideration I could give, that such a vote was right." I have thought that it would be but a very poor compliment to my constituents to say—"that, in my opinion, such a vote would have been proper, but that I supposed a contrary one would be more agreeable to those who sent me to the Convention." I could not, even in idea, expose myself to such a retort, as, upon the last answer, might have been justly made to me. "Pray, sir, what reasons have you for supposing that a right vote would displease your constituents? Is this the proper return for the high confidence they have placed in you?" If they have given cause for such a surmise, it was by choosing a representative, who could entertain such an opinion of them. I was under no apprehension that the good people of this state would behold with displeasure the brightness of the rays of delegated power, when it only proved the superior splendor of the luminary, of which those rays were only the reflection.

A very important difficulty arose from comparing the extent of the country to be governed with the kind of government which it would be proper to establish in it. It has been an opinion, countenanced by high authority, "that the natural property of small states is to be governed as a republic; of middling ones, to be subject to a monarch; and of large empires, to be swayed by a despotic prince; and that the consequence is, that, in order to preserve the principles of the established government, the state must be supported in the extent it has acquired; and that the spirit of the state will alter in proportion as it extends or contracts its limits.[(a)] This opinion seems to be supported, rather than contradicted, by the history of the governments in the Old World. Here then the difficulty appeared in full view. On one hand, the United States contain an immense extent of territory, and, according to the foregoing opinion, a despotic government is best adapted to that extent. On the other hand, it was well-known, that, however the citizens of the United States might, with pleasure, submit to the legitimate restraints of a republican constitution, they would reject, with indignation, the fetters of despotism. What then was to be done? The idea of a confederate republic presented itself. This kind of constitution has been thought to have "all the internal advantages of a republican, together with the external force of a monarchical government."[(b)] Its description is, "a convention, by which several states agree to become members of a larger one, which they intend to establish. It is a kind of assemblage of societies, that constitute a *new one,* capable of increasing by means of further association."[(c)] The *expanding* quality of such a government is peculiarly fitted for the United States, the greatest part of whose territory is yet uncultivated.

But while this form of government enabled us to surmount the difficulty last mentioned, it conducted us to another, of which I am now to take notice. It left us almost without precedent or guide; and consequently, without the benefit of that instruction, which, in many cases, may be derived from the constitution, and history and experience of other nations. Several associations have frequently been called by the name of confederate states, which have not, in propriety of language, deserved it. The Swiss cantons are connected only by alliances. The United Netherlands are indeed an assemblage of societies; but this assemblage constitutes *no new one;* and, therefore, it does not correspond with the full definition of a confederate republic. The Germanic body is composed of such disproportioned and discordant materials, and its structure is so intricate and complex, that little useful knowledge can be drawn from it. Ancient history discloses, and barely discloses to our view, some confederate republics—the Achaean League, the Lycian Confederacy, and the Amphyctyonic Council. But the facts recorded concerning their constituions are so few and general, and their histories are so unmarked and defective, that no satisfactory information can be collected from them concerning many particular circumstances, from an accurate discernment and comparison, of which alone legitimate and practical inferences can be made from one constitution to another. Besides, the situation and dimensions of those confederacies, and the state of society, manners, and habits in them, were so different from those of the United States, that the most correct descriptions could have supplied but a very small fund of applicable remark. Thus, in forming this system, we were deprived of many advantages, which the history and experience of other ages and other countries would, in other cases, have afforded us.

Permit me to add, in this place, that the science even of government itself seems yet to be almost in its state of infancy. Governments, in general, have been the result of force, of fraud, and of accident. After a period of six thousand years has elapsed since the Creation, the United States exhibit to the world, the first instance, as far as we can learn, of a nation, unattacked by external force, unconvulsed by domestic insurrections, assembling voluntarily, deliberating fully, and deciding calmly, concerning that system of government, under which they would wish that they and their posterity should live. The ancients, so enlightened on other subjects, were very uninformed with regard to this. They seem scarcely to have had any idea of any other kinds of governments than the three simple forms designed by the epithets, monarchical, aristocratical, and democratical. I know that much and pleasing ingenuity has been exerted, in modern times, in drawing entertaining parallels between some of the ancient constitutions and some of the mixed governments that have since existed in Europe. But I much suspect that, on strict examination, the instances of resemblance will be found to be few and weak; to be suggested by the improvements, which, in subsequent ages, have been made in government, and not to be drawn immediately from the ancient constitutions themselves, as they were intended and understood by those who framed them. To illustrate this, a similar observation may be made on another subject. Admiring critics have fancied that they have discovered in their favorite, Homer, the seeds of all the improvements in philosophy and in the sciences made since his time. What induces me to be of this opinion is that Tacitus—the profound politician Tacitus—who lived towards the latter end of those ages, which are now denominated ancient, who undoubtedly had studied the constitutions of all the states and kingdoms known before and in his time; and who certainly was qualified in an uncommon degree for understanding the full force and operation of each of them, considers, after all he had known and read, a mixed government, composed of the three simple forms, as a thing rather to be wished than expected. And he thinks, that if such a government could even be instituted, its duration could not be long. One thing is very certain, that the doctrine of representation in government was altogether unknown to the ancients. Now the knowledge and practice of this doctrine is, in my opinion, essential to every system that can possess the qualities of freedom, wisdom and energy.

It is worthy of remark, and the remark may, perhaps, excite some surprise, that representation of the people is not, even at this day, the sole principle of any government in Europe. Great Britain boasts, and she may well boast, of the improvement she has made in politics by the admission of representation. For the improvement is important as far as it goes, but it by no means goes far enough. Is the executive power of Great Britain founded on representation? This is not pretended. Before the Revolution [of 1688] many of the kings claimed to reign by divine right, and others by hereditary right; and even at the Revolution nothing further was effected or attempted than the recognition of certain parts of an original contract[(d)] supposed, at some former remote period, to have been made between the king and the people. A contract seems to exclude, rather than to imply, delegated power. The judges of Great Britain are appointed by the Crown. The judicial authority, therefore, does not depend upon representation, even in its most remote degree. Does representation prevail in the legislative department of the British government? Even here it does not predominate; though it may serve as a check. The legislature consists of three branches, the King, the Lords, and the Commons. Of these only the latter are supported by the constitution to represent the authority of the people. This short analysis clearly shows to what a narrow corner of the British constitution the principle of representation is confined. I believe it does not extend further, if so far, in any other government in Europe. For the American states were reserved the glory and the happiness of diffusing this vital principle throughout the constituent parts of government. Representation is the chain of communication between the people and those to whom they have committed the exercise of the powers of government. This chain may consist of one or more links; but in all cases it should be sufficiently strong and discernible.

To be left without guide or precedent was not the only difficulty, in which the Convention were involved, by proposing to their constituents a plan of a confederate republic. They found themselves embarrassed with another of peculiar delicacy and importance; I mean that of drawing a proper line between the national government and the government of the several states. It was easy to discover a proper and satisfactory principle on the subject. Whatever object of government is confined in its operation and effects within the bounds of a particular state should be considered as belonging to the government of that state; whatever object of government extends in its operation or effects beyond the bounds of a particular state should be considered as belonging to the government of the United States. But though this principle be sound and satisfactory, its application to particular cases would be accompanied with much difficulty; because in its application, room must be allowed for great discretionary latitude of construction of the principle. In order to lessen or remove the difficulty arising from discretionary construction on this subject, an enumeration of particular instances, in which the application of the principle ought to take place, has been attempted with much industry and care. It is only in mathematical science that a line can be described with mathematical precision. But I flatter myself that upon the strictest investigation, the enumeration will be found to be safe and unexceptionable; and accurate too in as great a degree as accuracy can be expected in a subject of this nature. Particulars under this head will be more properly explained, when we descend to the minute view of the enumeration, which is made in the proposed Constitution.

After all, it will be necessary, that, on a subject so peculiarly delicate as this, much prudence, much candor, much moderation, and much liberality should be exercised and displayed both by the federal government and by the governments of the several states. It is to be hoped, that those virtues in government will be exercised and displayed, when we consider, that the powers of the federal government and those of the state governments are drawn from sources equally pure. If a difference can be discovered between them, it is in favor of the federal government, because that government is founded on a representation of the *whole* Union; whereas the government of any particular state is founded only on the representation of a part, inconsiderable when compared with the whole. Is it not more reasonable to suppose, that the counsels of the whole will embrace the interest of every part, than that the counsels of any part will embrace the interests of the whole?

I intend not, sir, by this description of the difficulties with which the Convention were surrounded to magnify their skill or their merit in surmounting them, or to insinuate that any predicament in which the Convention stood should prevent the closest and most cautious scrutiny into the performance, which they have exhibited to their constituents and to the world. My intention is of far other and higher aim—to evince by the conflicts and difficulties which must arise from the many and powerful causes which I have enumerated, that it is hopeless and impracticable to form a constitution, which, in every part, will be acceptable to every citizen, or even to every government in the United States; and that all which can be expected is to form such a constitution, as upon the whole, is the best that can possibly be obtained. Man and perfection!—a state and perfection!—an assemblage of states and perfection!—can we reasonably expect, however ardently we may wish, to behold the glorious union?

I can well recollect, though I believe I cannot convey to others the impression, which, on many occasions, was made by the difficulties which surrounded and pressed the Convention. The great undertaking, at some times, seemed to be at a stand; at other times, its motion seemed to be retrograde. At the conclusion, however, of our work, many of the members expressed their astonishment at the success with which it terminated.

Having enumerated some of the difficulties, which the Convention were obliged to encounter in the course of their proceedings, I shall next point out the end, which they proposed to accomplish. Our wants, our talents, our affections, our passions, all tell us that we were made for a state of society. But a state of society could not be supported long or happily without some civil restraint. It is true, that in a state of nature, any one individual may act uncontrolled by others; but it is equally true, that in such a state, every other individual may act uncontrolled by him. Amidst this universal independence, the dissensions and animosities between interfering members of the society would be numerous and ungovernable. The consequence would be, that each member, in such a natural state, would enjoy less liberty, and suffer more interruption, than he would in a regulated society. Hence the universal introduction of governments of some kind or other into the social state. The liberty of every member is increased by this introduction; for each gains more by the limitation of the freedom of every other member, than he loses by the limitation of his own. The result is, that civil government is necessary to the perfection and happiness of man. In forming this government, and carrying it into execution, it is *essential* that the *interest* and *authority* of the whole community should be binding in every part of it.

The foregoing principles and conclusions are generally admitted to be just and sound with regard to the nature and formation of single governments, and the duty of submission to them. In some cases they will apply, with much propriety and force, to states already formed. The advantages and necessity of civil government among individuals in society are not greater or stronger than, in some situations and circumstances, are the advantages and necessity of a federal government among states. A natural and a very important question now presents itself—is such the situation—are such the circumstances of the United States? A proper answer to this question will unfold some very interesting truths.

The United States may adopt any one of four different systems. They may become consolidated into one government, in which the separate existence of the states shall be entirely absorbed. They may reject any plan of union or association and act as separate and unconnected states. They may form two or more confederacies. They may unite in one federal republic. Which of these systems ought to have been formed by the Convention? To support, with vigor, a single government over the whole extent of the United States would demand a system of the most unqualified and the most unremitted despotism. Such a number of separate states, contiguous in situation, unconnected and disunited in government, would be, at one time, the prey of foreign force, foreign influence, and foreign intrigue; at another, the victim of mutual rage, rancor, and revenge. Neither of these systems found advocates in the late Convention. I presume they will not find advocates in this. Would it be proper to divide the United States into two or more confederacies? It will not be unadvisable to take a more minute survey of this subject. Some aspects, under which it may be viewed, are far from being, at first sight, uninviting. Two or more confederacies would be each more compact and more manageable than a single one extending over the same territory. By dividing the United States into two or more confederacies, the great collision of interests, apparently or really different and contrary, in the *whole extent* of their dominion, would be broken, and, in a great measure, disappear in the several parts. But these disadvantages[e] which are discovered from certain points of view, are greatly overbalanced by inconveniences that will appear on a more accurate examination. Animosities, and perhaps wars, would arise from assigning the extent, the limits, and the rights of the different confederacies. The expenses of governing would be multiplied by the number of federal governments. The danger resulting from foreign influence and mutual dissensions would not, perhaps, be less great and alarming in the instance of different confederacies, than in the instance of different though more numerous unassociated states. These observations, and many others that might be made on the subject, will be sufficient to evince, that a division of the United States into a number of separate confederacies would probably be an unsatisfactory and an unsuccessful experiment. The remaining system which the American states may adopt is a union of them under one confederate republic. It will not be necessary to employ much time or many arguments to show, that this is the most eligible system that can be proposed. By adopting this system, the vigor and decision of a wide-spreading monarchy may be joined to the freedom and beneficence of a contracted republic. The extent of territory, the diversity of climate and soil, the number, and greatness, and connection of lakes and rivers, with which the United States are intersected and almost surrounded, all indicate an enlarged government to be fit and advantageous for them. The principles and dispositions of their citizens indicate that in this government, liberty shall reign triumphant. Such indeed have been the general opinions and wishes entertained since the era of independence. If those opinions and wishes are as well-founded as they have been general, the late Convention were justified in proposing to their constituents, *one* confederate republic as the best system of a national government for the United States.

In forming this system, it was proper to give minute attention to the interest of all the parts; but there was a duty of still higher import—to feel and to show a predominating regard to the superior interests of the whole. If this great principle had not prevailed, the plan before us would never have made its appearance. The same principle that was so necessary in forming it is equally necessary in our deliberations, whether we should reject or ratify it.

I make these observations with a design to prove and illustrate this great and important truth—that in our decisions on the work of the late Convention, we should not limit our views and regards to the State of Pennsylvania. The aim of the Convention was to form a system of good and efficient government on the more extensive scale of the United States. In this, and in every other instance, the work should be judged with the same spirit with which it was performed. A principle of duty as well as candor demands this.

We have remarked, that civil government is necessary to the perfection of society. We now remark that civil liberty is necessary to the perfection of civil government. Civil liberty is natural liberty itself, divested only of that part, which, placed in the government, produces more good and happiness to the community than if it had remained in the individual. Hence it follows, that civil liberty, while it resigns a part of natural liberty, retains the free and generous evercise of all the human faculties, so far as it is compatible with the public welfare.

In considering and developing the nature and end of the system before us, it is necessary to mention another kind of liberty, which has not yet, as far as I know, received a name. I shall distinguish it by the appellation of *"federal liberty."* When a single government is instituted, the individuals, of which it is composed, surrender to it a part of their natural independence, which they before enjoyed as men. When a confederate republic is instituted, the communities, of which it is composed, surrender to it a part of their political independence, which they before enjoyed as states. The principles, which directed, in the former case, what part of the natural liberty of the man ought to be given up and what part ought to be retained, will give similar directions in the latter case. The states should resign, to the national government, that part, and that part only, of their political liberty, which placed in that government will produce more good to the whole than if it had remained in the several states. While they resign this part of their political liberty, they retain the free and generous exercise of all their other faculties as states, so far as it is compatible with the welfare of the general and superintending confederacy.

Since *states* as well as *citizens* are represented in the Constitution before us, and form the objects on which that Constitution is proposed to operate, it was necessary to notice and define *federal* as well as *civil* liberty.

These general reflections have been made in order to introduce, with more propriety and advantage, a practical illustration of the end proposed to be accomplished by the late Convention.

It has been too well-known—it has been too severely felt—that the present Confederation is inadequate to the government and to the exigencies of the United States. The great struggle for liberty in this country, should it be unsuccessful, will probably be the last one which she will have for her existence and prosperity, in any part of the globe. And it must be confessed, that this struggle has, in some of the stages of its progress, been attended with symptoms, that foreboded no fortunate issue. To the iron hand of tyranny, which was lifted up against her, she manifested, indeed, an intrepid superiority. She broke in pieces the fetters, which were forged for her, and showed that she was unassailable by force. But she was environed with dangers of another kind, and springing from a very different source. While she kept her eye steadily fixed on the efforts of oppression, licentiousness was secretly undermining the rock on which she stood.

Need I call to your remembrance the *contrasted* scenes of which we have been witnesses? On the glorious conclusion of our conflict with Britain, what high expectations were formed concerning us by others! What high expectations did we form concerning ourselves! Have those expectations been realized? No. What has been the cause? Did our citizens lose their perseverance and magnanimity? Did they become insensible of resentment and indignation at any high-handed attempt that might have been made to injure or enslave them? No. What then has been the cause? The truth is, we dreaded danger only on one side. This we manfully repelled. But on another side, danger not less formidable, but more insidious, stole in upon us; and our unsuspicious tempers were not sufficiently attentive either to its approach or to its operations. Those, whom foreign strength could not overpower, have well-nigh become the victims of internal anarchy.

If we become a little more particular, we shall find that the foregoing representation is by no means exaggerated. When we had baffled all the menaces of foreign power, we neglected to establish among ourselves a government, that would insure domestic vigor and stability. What was the consequence? The commencement of peace was the commencement of every disgrace and distress, that could befall a people in a peaceful state. Devoid of national power, we could not prohibit the extravagance of our importations, nor could we derive a revenue from their excess. Devoid of national importance, we could not procure, for our exports, a tolerable sale at foreign markets. Devoid of national credit, we saw our public securities melt in the hands of the holders, like snow before the sun. Devoid of national dignity, we could not, in some instances, perform our treaties, on our parts; and, in other instances, we could neither obtain nor compel the performance of them on the part of others. Devoid of national energy, we could not carry into execution our own resolutions, decisions, or laws.

Shall I become more particular still? The tedious detail would disgust me. Nor is it now necessary. The years of languor are passed. We have felt the dishonor with which we have been covered. We have seen the destruction with which we have been threatened. We have penetrated to the causes of both, and when we have once discovered them, we have begun to search for the means of removing them. For the confirmation of these remarks, I need not appeal to an enumeration of facts. The proceedings of Congress, and of the several states, are replete with them. They all point out the weakness and insufficiency as the cause, and an *efficient* general government as the only cure of our political distempers.

Under these impressions, and with these views, was the late Convention appointed; and under these impressions, and with these views, the late Convention met.

We now see the great end which they propose to accomplish. It was to frame, for the consideration of their constituents, one federal and national constitution—a constitution, that would produce the advantages of good, and prevent the inconveniences of bad government—a constitution whose beneficence and energy would pervade the whole Union; and bind and embrace the interests of every part—a constitution that would insure peace, freedom, and happiness, to the states and people of America.

We are now naturally led to examine the means by which they proposed to accomplish this end. This opens more particularly to our view the important discussion before us. But previously to our entering upon it, it will not be improper to state some general and leading principles of government, which will receive particular applications in the course of our investigations.

There necessarily exists in every government a power from which there is no appeal; and which, for that reason, may be termed supreme, absolute, and uncontrollable. Where does this power reside? To this question, writers on different governments will give different answers. Sir William Blackstone will tell you, that in Britain the power is lodged in the British Parliament, that the Parliament may alter the form of the government; and that its power is absolute without control. The idea of a constitution, limiting and superintending the operations of legislative authority, seems not to have been accurately understood in Britain. There are, at least, no traces of practice conformable to such a principle. The British constitution is just what the British Parliament pleases. When the Parliament transferred legislative authority to Henry VIII, the act transferring could not in the strict acceptation of the term be called unconstitutional.

To control the power and conduct of the legislature by an overruling constitution was an improvement in the science and practice of government reserved to the American states.

Perhaps some politican, who has not considered, with sufficient accuracy, our political systems, would answer, that in our governments, the supreme power was vested in the constitutions. This opinion approaches a step nearer to the truth; but does not reach it. The truth is, that, in our governments, the supreme, absolute, and uncontrollable power *remains* in the people. As our constitutions are superior to our legislatures; so the people are superior to our constitutions. Indeed the superiority, in this last instance, is much greater; for the people possess, over our constitutions, control in *act,* as well as in right.

The consequence is, that the people may change the constitutions whenever and however they please. This is a right, of which no positive institution can ever deprive them.

These important truths, sir, are far from being merely speculative. We, at this moment, speak and deliberate under their immediate and benign influence. To the operation of these truths, we are to ascribe the scene, hitherto unparalleled, which America now exhibits to the world—a gentle, a peaceful, a voluntary, and a deliberate transition from one constitution of government to another. In other parts of the world, the idea of revolutions in government is, by a mournful and an indissoluble association, connected with the idea of wars and all the calamities attendant on wars. But happy experience teaches us to view such revolutions in a very different light—to consider them only as progressive steps in improving the knowledge of government, and increasing the happiness of society and mankind.

Oft have I viewed, with silent pleasure and admiration, the force and prevalence[(f)] through the United States, that the supreme power resides in the people; and that they never part with it. It may be called the *panacea* in politics. There can be no disorder in the community but may here receive a radical cure. If the error be in the legislature, it may be corrected by the constitution. If in the constitution, it may be corrected by the people. There is a remedy, therefore, for every distemper in government; if the people are not wanting to themselves. For a people wanting to themselves, there is no remedy. From their power, as we have seen, there is no appeal. To their error, there is no superior principle of correction.

There are three simple species of government—monarchy, where the supreme power is in a single person; aristocracy, where the supreme power is in a select assembly, the members of which either fill up, by election, the vacancies in their own body, or succeed to their places in it by inheritance, property, or in respect of some *personal* right or qualification; a republic or democracy, where the people at large *retain* the supreme power, and act either collectively or by representation.

Each of these species of government has its advantages and disadvantages.

The advantages of a monarchy are strength, dispatch, secrecy, unity of counsel. Its disadvantages are tyranny, expense, ignorance of the situation and wants of the people, insecurity, unnecessary wars, evils attending elections or successions.

The advantages of aristocracy are wisdom, arising from experience and education. Its disadvantages are dissensions among themselves, oppression to the lower orders.

The advantages of democracy are liberty, equal, cautious, and salutary laws, public spirit, frugality, peace, opportunities of exciting and producing abilities of the best citizens. Its disadvantages are dissensions, the delay and disclosure of public counsels, the imbecility of public measures retarded by the necessity of a numerous consent.

A government may be composed of two or more of the simple forms above mentioned. Such is the British government. It would be an improper government for the United States; because it is inadequate to such an extent of territory; and because it is suited to an establishment of different orders of men. A more minute comparison between some parts of the British constitution and some parts of the plan before us may perhaps find a proper place in a subsequent period of our business.

What is the nature and kind of that government which has been proposed for the United States by the late Convention? In its principle, it is purely democratical. But that principle is applied in different forms, in order to obtain the advantages and exclude the inconveniences of the simple modes of government.

If we take an extended and accurate view of it, we shall find the streams of power running in different directions, in different dimensions, and at different heights watering, adorning, and fertilizing the fields and meadows thro which their courses are led; but if we trace them, we shall discover, that they all originally flow from one abundant fountain.

In THIS CONSTITUTION, *all authority is derived from the* PEOPLE.

Fit occasions will hereafter offer for particular remarks on the different parts of the plan. I have now to ask pardon of the house for detaining them so long.

[Lloyd's notes and errata]
(a) Montesquieu, b. 8. c. 20. [I, 180–81].
(b) Mont, b. 9. c. 1. 2. [Montesquieu, I, 185–88]. Paley 199. 202 [William Paley, *The Principles Of Moral And Political Philosophy* (4th ed., Dublin, 1788), 380–82].
(c) Montesquieu, b. 9. c. 1. [I, 185–87].
(d) Blackstone, [III], 233.
(e) Errata: "For 'disadvantages' read 'advantages'."
(f) Errata: "after 'prevalance' insert 'of this principle'."

1. Lloyd, *Debates,* 25–40. Lloyd misdated the speech as being given on Monday, 26 November.

The Pennsylvania Convention
Monday
26 November 1787

Convention Proceedings

The Convention met pursuant to adjournment.

It was moved by Thomas M'Kean, and seconded by Stephen Chambers,

That this Convention do now proceed to consider the Constitution referred to their consideration, by articles.

It was moved by George Latimer, seconded by James Wilson,

To repeal the tenth rule of this Convention, viz.,

No member shall speak more than twice to a question, without leave.

On the question being put, it was repealed.

It was moved by Robert Whitehill, seconded by Abraham Lincoln,

That the further consideration of the question now before the Convention be postponed, in order to introduce the following, viz.,

That this Convention resolve itself into a committee of the whole, for the purpose of investigating and considering the aforesaid Constitution by articles and sections, and to make report thereon.

And the question being put, the yeas and nays were called by Robert Whitehill and Abraham Lincoln, and were as follow.

YEAS [24]
1 John Whitehill
2 John Harris
3 John Reynolds
4 Robert Whitehill
5 Jonathan Hoge
6 Nicholas Lutz
7 John Ludwig
8 Abraham Lincoln
9 John Bishop
10 Joseph Heister
11 James Martin
12 Joseph Powell
13 William Findley
14 John Baird
15 William Todd
16 James Marshall
17 James Edgar
18 Thomas Scott
19 Nathaniel Breading
20 John Smilie
21 Richard Bard
22 William Brown
23 Adam Orth
24 John Andre Hanna

NAYS [44]
1 George Latimer
2 Benjamin Rush
3 Hilary Baker
4 James Wilson
5 Thomas M'Kean
6 William M'Pherson
7 John Hunn
8 George Gray
9 Samuel Ashmead
10 Enoch Edwards
11 Henry Wynkoop
12 John Barclay
13 Thomas Yardley
14 Abraham Stout
15 Thomas Bull
16 Anthony Wayne

17 William Gibbons
18 Richard Downing
19 Thomas Cheyney
20 John Hannum
21 Stephen Chambers
22 Robert Coleman
23 Sebastian Graff
24 John Hubley
25 Jasper Yeates
26 Henry Slagle
27 Thomas Campbell
28 Thomas Hartley
29 David Grier
30 John Black
31 Benjamin Pedan
32 John Arndt
33 Stephen Balliot
34 Joseph Horsefield
35 David Deshler
36 William Wilson
37 John Boyd
38 John Nevill
39 John Allison
40 Jonathan Roberts
41 John Richards
42 Frederick A. Muhlenberg
43 James Morris
44 Timothy Pickering

So it was determined in the negative.
Adjourned until ten o'clock tomorrow, A.M.

Convention Debates

THOMAS MCKEAN: There can be only one question before us. The questions on separate paragraphs would preclude a vote of approbation on the whole system. Each paragraph may be discussed; but without taking a question on the whole. A house, convenient on the whole, may be defective in some of its apartments. We come not to compose a new book. [Wilson's Notes, PHi]

* * * *

Moved [by George Latimer] and seconded [by James Wilson] that the tenth rule be repealed. [Wilson's Notes, PHi]

* * * *

[JAMES WILSON]: The matters of form reduced to sound sense. The repeal of the rule or step to obtain the same free debate as in committee. We have another advantage—everything will appear on the Minutes. [Wilson's Notes, PHi]

* * * *

JOHN SMILIE: It would be more proper to go into a committee on the whole, than to repeal the rule. By going into a committee there will be a double investigation. [Wilson's Notes, PHi]

* * * *

ROBERT WHITEHILL: We are not precluded from proposing amendments. We are going to examine the foundations of the building. By proposing amendments we can hear what they say in the other states, and then can accommodate. [Wilson's Notes, PHi]

* * * *

[JAMES WILSON]: We must take the system in the whole, and, as the result of the whole, ratify or not ratify. The General Convention took allowances of power; and were not appointed by the people. To whom shall we propose amendments? Do we know they will be agreeable to our const[ituen]ts? As much time in this as in the other states. [Wilson's Notes, PHi]

* * * *

JOHN SMILIE: In a legal discussion I am inferior to (Mr. MKean). The mode proposed by him is contrary to every idea of order. The mode that will give the *longest* time to consider should be preferred. In convention we can consider only each part *once*. The people of Pennsylvania will be taxed by the Representatives of United States. The freemen of Pennsylvania will *think* and *act*. [Wilson's Notes, PHi]

* * * *

THOMAS SCOTT:[1] We are come to stamp the system with the authority of the people, or to refuse it that stamp. [Wilson's Notes, PHi]

* * * *

JASPER YEATES: Miscellaneous notes

Mr. Smiley. (The word *"Paragraphs"* to be omitted.)

Management.

Object to postponement—to let in a committee of the whole.

Committee of the whole: Objections to—delay and procrastination on one hand, on the other, precipitation and hurry to be avoid[ed].

It takes time and expense.

Paragraphs will not answer the purpose. In a detached point of view, justice cannot be done.

Allegory of the P[eli?] of Building. One chamber.

If distinct parts to be considered, and objections to parts of each section, time will be given to each member to reflect on all the arguments that have been used—and have *reflection* before they give their votes.

44 against 24. [Yeates's Notes, PHi]

1. Scott served as a Westmoreland County justice of the peace in 1774, assemblyman in 1776, and councillor in 1777–1780. He was prothonotary of Washington County from 1781 to 1789 and represented that county in the state House of Representatives in 1791. He served in the United States House of Representatives in 1789–1791 and 1793–1795.

Newspaper Reports of Proceedings and Debates

Yesterday afternoon, in the Convention of this state, it was moved by Mr. M'Kean, seconded by Mr. Chambers, That this Convention do now proceed to consider the proposed Constitution by articles.

After some debate it was moved by Mr. Whitehill, seconded by Mr.

Lincoln, that the aforesaid motion be postponed in order to introduce the following, viz.,

That this Convention resolve itself into a committee of the whole, for the purpose of investigating and considering the aforesaid Constitution by articles and sections, and to make report thereon.

A debate of considerable length now took place, which turned principally on the expediency of resolving the Convention into a committee of the whole. In favor of this measure it was urged, that it would subject the Constitution to a more free and candid discussion, that it would allow more time for the members to make up their minds, and that it would be more consonant to the practice of the legislature of Pennsylvania. Against the motion was urged that, by going into a committee of the whole, no minutes could be taken of the proceedings, and that the people at large would thereby be kept in ignorance of them; that as full liberty was given to each to speak as often as he pleased, there would be the same time given for deliberation in Convention as in the committee; that the practice of the Assembly of Pennsylvania was no precedent for the Convention; that this was a body without a precedent in the history of mankind; and that as the whole Constitution was a single proposition, and that proposition alone before the Convention, it was unnecessary to go into a committee, especially as no question could be taken upon any part of the Constitution, nor any additions made to it, agreeably to the recommendation of the Assembly, under which the Convention sat; although objections to every part of it might be made before the question of ratification was proposed.

The question being at length put, Mr. Whitehill's motion for postponement was lost, the yeas and nays being as follow.

[For the yeas and nays, see the Convention Proceedings.]

The question on Mr. M'Kean's motion was then put, and the motion adopted.

The speakers in favor of the motion for a committee [of the whole] were Mr. Findley, Mr. Smilie and Mr. Whitehill. The speakers against it were Mr. M'Kean, Mr. Wilson, Doctor Rush, and Mr. Chambers. [*Pennsylvania Packet,* 27 November] [1]

* * * *

While the Convention were debating on the propriety of referring the Constitution to a committee of the whole, Mr. Wilson made the following observation: "Shall we, sir, while we contemplate a great and magnificent edifice, condescend like a fly, with its microscopic eye, to scrutinize the imperfections of a single brick?" Mr. Findley, retorting the metaphor, said "Shall we not, sir, when we are about to erect a large and expensive fabric (for as far as it respects us, we are about to erect this mighty fabric of government in Pennsylvania) examine and compare the materials of which we mean to compose it, fitting and combining the parts with each other, and rejecting everything that is useless and rotten?" "That," concluded Dr. Rush, "is not our situation. We are not, at this time, called upon to raise the structure. The house is already built for us; and we are only asked, whether we choose to occupy it? If we find its apartments commodious, and, upon the whole, that it is well calculated to shelter us from the inclemencies of the storm that threatens, we shall act prudently in entering it; if otherwise, all that is required of us is to return the key to those who have built and offered it for our use."

. . . .

It was observed in the Convention, that the Federal Convention had exceeded the powers given to them by the several legislatures; but Mr. Wilson observed, that however foreign the question was to the present business, he would place it in its proper light. The Federal Convention did not act at all upon the powers given to them by the states, but they proceeded upon original principles, and having framed a Constitution which they thought would promote the happiness of their country, they have submitted it to their consideration, who may either adopt or reject it, as they please. [*Pennsylvania Herald,* 28 November][2]

1. Reprinted in the *Pennsylvania Gazette,* 28 November, and outside Pennsylvania, in whole or in part, ten times from Maine to South Carolina.

2. Reprinted in full three times in Pennsylvania and ten times from New Hampshire to South Carolina. Excerpts were reprinted eleven times from Philadelphia to Portland, Maine. One short, unrelated paragraph dealing with rumors of war between England and France is deleted above.

The Pennsylvania Convention
Tuesday
27 November 1787

Convention Proceedings

The Convention met pursuant to adjournment.

On motion of Benjamin Rush, seconded by John Allison,

Ordered, That the seats on the right and left of the President be reserved for members of Congress and of the Supreme Executive Council.

Letters from Messieurs Hall and Sellers, and Messieurs Pritchard and Hall, respectively requesting to be appointed printers to the Convention, were read.

On motion of Stephen Chambers, seconded by William M'Pherson,

The Convention proceeded to elect a printer; the ballots being taken, it appeared that Messieurs Hall and Sellers[1] were duly elected.

On motion of Stephen Balliott, seconded by John Hubley,

Ordered, That a number of copies of the Minutes of this Convention be printed in German.

On motion of Benjamin Rush, seconded by John Arndt,

Ordered, That Mr. Steiner[2] be directed to print the German copies.

On motion of Thomas M'Kean, seconded by John Hubley,

Ordered, That the number of English copies be 3000, the number of German 2000.

On motion, Ordered, That the President be directed to draw on the treasurer, in favor of the secretary, for the sum of one hundred dollars, to enable him to defray the contingent expenses of the Convention, he to be accountable.[3]

On motion of Robert Whitehill, seconded by Abraham Lincoln, to add to the 12th rule of this Convention the following words, viz.: "Any member shall have a right to enter the reasons of his vote on the Minutes on the general question, viz., Whether this Convention will assent to and ratify the Constitution submitted to their consideration?" The question being put, the yeas and nays were called by John Smilie and Robert Whitehill, and were as follow.

YEAS [22]

1 John Whitehill
2 John Harris
3 John Reynolds
4 Robert Whitehill
5 Jonathan Hoge
6 Nicholas Lutz
7 John Ludwig
8 Abraham Lincoln
9 John Bishop
10 James Martin
11 Joseph Powell
12 John Baird
13 William Todd
14 James Marshall
15 James Edgar
16 Nathaniel Breading
17 John Smilie
18 Richard Bard
19 John Richards
20 William Brown
21 Adam Orth
22 John Andre Hanna

NAYS [44]

1 George Latimer
2 Benjamin Rush
3 Hilary Baker
4 James Wilson
5 Thomas M'Kean
6 William M'Pherson
7 John Hunn
8 George Gray
9 Samuel Ashmead
10 Enoch Edwards
11 Henry Wynkoop
12 John Barclay
13 Thomas Yardley
14 Abraham Stout
15 Thomas Bull
16 Anthony Wayne
17 William Gibbons
18 Richard Downing
19 Thomas Cheyney
20 John Hannum
21 Stephen Chambers
22 Robert Coleman

23 Sebastian Graff
24 John Hubley
25 Jasper Yeates
26 Henry Slagle
27 Thomas Campbell
28 Thomas Hartley
29 David Grier
30 John Black
31 Benjamin Pedan
32 John Arndt
33 Stephen Balliott
34 Joseph Horsefield
35 David Deshler
36 William Wilson
37 John Boyd
38 Thomas Scott
39 John Nevill
40 John Allison
41 Jonathan Roberts
42 Frederick A. Muhlenberg
43 James Morris
44 Benjamin Elliott

So it was determined in the negative.

The original question being then put, viz., *"Will this Convention now proceed to consider the Constitution (submitted to their consideration) by articles?"*

It was carried in the affirmative.

The Convention then proceeded to consider the first Article, and after some debate,

Adjourned until ten o'clock tomorrow, A.M.

1. Printers of the *Pennsylvania Gazette.*
2. Printer of the *Philadelphische Correspondenz.*
3. On 29 November Campbell received £37.10.0 "to enable him to defray the contingent expenses of Convention" (RG 28, Records of the Treasury Department, "Account Book, 1787–1788," p. 29, Division of Public Records, PHarH).

Convention Debates

ROBERT WHITEHILL offered a resolution declaring that "upon all questions where the yeas and nays were called, any member might insert the reason of his vote upon the Journals of the Convention." [Dallas' Debates, *Pennsylvania Herald,* 1 December]

Whitehill: Moves that reasons for yeas and nays may be entered on the Journals. [Wilson's Notes, PHi]

* * * *

THOMAS HARTLEY:[1] Sir, before the question on this motion is decided, I should wish to understand how far it extends, and whether, contrary to what I have thought was the sense of the Convention, more than one question will be taken upon the proposed Constitution? If the questions are to be multiplied and protests are to be admitted on each, I shall certainly object to the source of embarrassment, delay, and expense, which this motion will open. But if we are limited to the comprehensive question, "Will you ratify or reject the plan?" then, I think it may be reasonable to allow every man that pleases, to justify his assent or dissent by the motives upon which it may be founded. [Dallas' Debates, *Pennsylvania Herald,* 1 December]

* * * *

THOMAS MCKEAN: When we were choosing our printers a few minutes ago, Mr. President, I did not think it a matter of so much importance, as the adoption of the motion before us would render it; for, if every member whenever he pleases shall be at liberty to load our Journals with long and labored arguments, it will be a profitable business, indeed, for those gentlemen that are appointed to publish them. There can, sir, but one question arise in the discussion of the plan that is submitted to us, which is simply, whether we will ratify or reject it; and if the motion were narrowed to that point, I should have no objection to give it my approbation. But on its present ground we would expose ourselves to a scene of altercation highly unbecoming the character and dignity of this body. [Dallas' Debates, *Pennsylvania Herald,* 1 December]

* * * *

ROBERT WHITEHILL: I hope, sir, the measure I have proposed will, upon consideration, meet with the favor of the Convention, since the arguments by which it is opposed arise chiefly from a presumption that the liberty it affords will be abused. This, Mr. President, ought not to be presumed, but rather that every member entertains so just a sense of his duty to himself and to this Honorable Convention, as to forbear everything, in language or in argument, which will be unbecoming a place in your Journals. In truth, sir, unless we are allowed to insert our reasons, the yeas and nays will be a barren document, from which the public can derive no information, and the minority no justification for their conduct. On the other hand, if we are allowed to state the foundation of our votes, the merits of the Constitution may be proved by the arguments of its advocates, and those who do not consider it to be an immaculate, or even salutary system, will have an opportunity to point out the defects from which their opposition originates. I think, sir, the public have a right in so important a transaction to know the principles upon which their delegates proceed; and it is the just right of every man who is bound by his vote to be permitted to explain it. I cannot, therefore, withdraw or reduce the object of my motion. [Dallas' Debates, *Pennsylvania Herald,* 1 December]

* * * *

THOMAS HARTLEY: Then, sir, if I comprehend the sense of the Convention, we are limited to the one great question which shall decide the fate of the Constitution; and upon that I agree in the propriety of permitting a protest. Let the opponents of the new system state their reasons fully and fairly, it will be the duty of its advocates to refute them upon the same terms, and the record of the whole will be preserved for the information of our constituents. This seems, indeed, to open a door for the renewal of all the arguments which have been previously advanced, but it will answer the same purpose as if protests were entered on each distinct proposition. [Dallas' Debates, *Pennsylvania Herald,* 1 December]

* * * *

ROBERT WHITEHILL: We are now, Mr. President, in the full enjoyment of the powers of the mind, and I hope we shall adopt no measure that will tend to curtail the exercise of our faculties. Upon every question that arises, it is in the power of any member to call the yeas and nays, and whenever a vote is registered in that permanent form, it is of no consequence whether it is in the intermediate or conclusive stages of the business, we ought to be permitted to promulge the reasons which have influenced our decisions. Every argument (and gentlemen seem to have conceded the propriety in one case) that will apply to entitle us to protest on the last question will entitle us to that privilege on any preceding one; for, I consider it rather as a right than an indulgence. But, Mr. President, it is said, that we can only have one question in the business before us. If this is true, I see no cause to proceed further. It will be a great public saving to recur to that question at once, and we shall by such means escape the absurdity of arguing upon distinct propositions without determining anything with respect to them. Sir, there is no reason to suppose an improper use will be made of this necessary privilege. It is intended as the means of justifying to the people, the conduct of those with whom they have entrusted their dearest interests, and if in the manner or the substance it is deficient or improper, the people will pronounce its condemnation. Let them therefore judge; but since we are answerable to them, let us not suppress the means of justification. [Dallas' Debates, *Pennsylvania Herald,* 1 December]

* * * *

BENJAMIN RUSH: I shall certainly, sir, object to any protest, but upon the great question, and even there it is hardly in my opinion proper or necessary. Those, Mr. President, who are in favor of the Constitution will be as anxious to vindicate their opinions as those who are against it; hence, whatever is advanced on one side will draw on a reply upon the other, till the whole debates of the Convention are intruded upon the Journals. The expense and procrastination of this transaction would be intolerable. But, sir, the proceedings of the Convention are stamped with authenticity, and it would be dangerous to suffer protests to be inserted in them which might contain insinuations not founded and consequently produce here what has disgraced the legislature of Pennsylvania, a majority defending themselves from the assertions and misrepresentations of a minority. We know, sir, of what nature the protests will be, and if they bear the complexion of the publications that have lately teemed from the press, I am sure they would not be honorable to this body. The proceedings of the Convention cannot be compared in this respect to the proceedings of the legislature, where protests may lay the foundation of a future revision or repeal of the law to which they object, by laying the necessary information before the people; but we can have no view either to a revision or a repeal, and therefore protests can only serve to distract and perplex the state. If, sir, the proposed plan should be adopted, by this Convention, it will be the duty of every man, particularly those who have opposed it, on the fundamental principles of society, to promote its interests among the people. But, if contrary to my opinion of what is their duty, the minority should persevere in their opposition, I hope they will be left to publish in their own way, without our authority, the motives of their conduct, and let them enjoy all the advantages they may derive from the effects of that publication. [Dallas' Debates, *Pennsylvania Herald,* 1 December]

* * * *

THOMAS MCKEAN: I shall be satisfied, Mr. President, if the object of the motion is confined to the final question, and indeed, I do not perceive to what other motions it can extend. But it is said no harm will proceed from its adoption agreeably to its present general terms. Sir, all laws are made to prevent evil, upon a supposition that it may occur, and in the instance before us I do not only think it probable, but I have no doubt it will occur. We are again told of the conduct of the General Assembly of Pennsylvania, which some gentlemen seem to imagine is an unanswerable argument upon every topic. But even there the practice of protesting has only been introduced since the Revolution, nor was it before known, in any province of America, or in any government in the world. Some compliment has on a former occasion been paid to my legal knowledge, with an intention however to depreciate my knowledge of parliamentary proceedings.[2] But the truth is, sir, that those proceedings have both before and since the Revolution formed a great object of my studies, and it has been my lot to have been engaged likewise considerably in the practice. I therefore repeat, confidently, that no precedent of protesting is to be found anywhere but in Pennsylvania.[3] The Lords in England, indeed, enjoy and frequently exercise the privilege; but the reason is, that they are not a representative body, nor accountable to any power for their legislative conduct but God and their consciences, and therefore from a desire to preserve their fame and honor free from suspicion and reproach, they render this voluntary account of their actions to the world. The same motive, however, does not prevail with a representative body, the members of which are from time to time responsible to their constituents, and may be elected or removed from their trust according to the proof of their fidelity and industry in discharging it. I have seen, sir, language by such means intruded upon the Journals of the legislature of Pennsylvania, which would have disgraced a private club at a tavern. But in the British House of Lords, the language of the protest is under the control of the House, and it is not uncommon to erase sentences and paragraphs, and even whole protests from their records. But Mr. President, there cannot be any necessity for introducing the practice here, unless indeed to indulge the vanity of some gentlemen who wish to turn authors at the public expense, to write discourses upon government and to give them a value and consequence by incorporating them with your proceedings, to which they are not intrinsically entitled. I therefore move, sir, that the motion before you be amended, so as to restrict the right of protesting to the last great question, to adopt or reject the proposed plan.

This motion was seconded by Stephen Chambers. [Dallas' Debates, *Pennsylvania Herald,* 1 December][4]

* * * *

JAMES WILSON: I am equally opposed, Mr. President, to the amendment and to the original motion. I do not wish, however, in any degree to suppress what may be spoken or done in this Convention. On the contrary, I wish our proceedings may be fully known and perfectly understood by our constituents; and, to extend the scale, by all our fellow citizens of the United States. But we ought to pause and consider well before we communicate all this information at the public expense, for as the motion has been opened and explained, under the influence of that rule, our Minutes may be increased to an immense volume, and yet we have just determined that 3000 copies of them shall be printed.[5] I certainly, sir (as well as every other member), will have a right to enter my sentiments and arguments in the manner most satisfactory to myself, and therefore, not only what I may hereafter say, but what I have already said, in order to preserve connection and system in the reasoning, must be admitted. The press is undoubtedly free, but is it necessary to that freedom, that every man's tenets on government should be printed at the public cost? Sir, we are here, as upon many other occasions, referred to the constitution of Pennsylvania; but the privilege indulged in this respect is, in my opinion, one of its exceptionable parts, and the instances of its abuse alluded to by my honorable colleague [Thomas McKean] must excite the indignation of every friend to propriety and decency. Look at the Journals of the legislature of Pennsylvania and you will find altercations there which are adapted to the meridian of Billingsgate. In short, sir, the idea of a protest is not to be found in any other representative body, not even in that of the British House of Commons; and if we must seek a lesson from other constitutions, we might, with great propriety, advert to the one before us by which one-fifth of the members are enabled to call for the yeas and nays, but in no case is it permitted to record the reasons of a vote. Shall we then employ the whole winter in carrying on a paper war at the expense of the state, in spreading clamor and dissension, not only among our own citizens, but throughout the United States? My voice, sir, never shall concur in rendering this room the center from which so many streams of bitterness shall flow. Let the opponents of the proposed plan write as much as they please, let them print when they will, but I trust we shall not agree to indulge them at the expense of those who have sent us hither for a very different purpose. [Dallas' Debates, *Pennsylvania Herald,* 5 December]

Wilson: On the question of entering the reasons on the Journals, 5000 copies already voted, they may be swelled into very large *volumes* at the expense of the state. [Wayne's Notes, MiU-C]

* * * *

JOHN SMILIE: It appears, Mr. President, that on this question the gentlemen are divided among themselves. [Dallas' Debates, *Pennsylvania Herald,* 5 December]

* * * *

THOMAS MCKEAN: No, sir, there shall be no division. I thought the measure totally improper and only proposed the amendment in compliment to the members who urged the general motion. I now withdraw my amendment and leave the question upon its original ground. [Dallas' Debates, *Pennsylvania Herald,* 5 December]

* * * *

JOHN SMILIE: I am sorry, sir, that the honorable member should so suddenly have retracted his amendment, for it was more satisfactory to me than the original motion which I wish still to be narrowed down to the final question, as, indeed, I do not perceive how it can operate on any other subject, and it will then answer every purpose to which it can be applied without leaving room for the objection on account of the extraordinary expense. It will, indeed, appear exceedingly strange upon this important subject, that we should be denied an opportunity of declaring the reasons that influence our votes—while we are responsible, it is our duty, and while we are bound, it is our right. Nor is it liberal or reasonable to presume that any harm can ensue from this privilege; for the apprehensions which are expressed, lest faction and clamor should be excited among the people, are highly unbecoming the citizens of a free government. An excellent author has observed that slavery succeeds sleep, and the moment parties and political contentions subside among the people, from that moment liberty is at an end. I admit, sir, that if the ferment rises to an extreme it is an evil; but as it originates from a blessing, those who wish to preserve their freedom must bear with its inconveniences. But what is the evil so much dreaded? We are told that protests in past times have been a dishonor and a discredit. But to whom have they been such? Certainly to those who wrote them, and so, if anything unworthy should appear in the protests upon your Journals, the authors alone will be liable to the infamy and odium of their productions. But let us suppose, on the other hand, what I believe to be the real ground of opposition, that the protests should produce a change in the minds of the people and incline them to new measures. Is this an event proper either to be evaded or suppressed? I take it, sir, that even after this Convention shall have agreed to ratify the proposed plan, if the people on better information and maturer deliberation should think it a bad and improper form of government, they will still have a right to assemble another body to consult upon other measures and either in the whole, or in part, to abrogate this federal work so ratified. If this is true, and that it is true a worthy member of the late Convention [James Wilson] admits when he says, the people have at all times a power to alter and abolish government,[6] what cause is there to fear the operation of a protest? The reasons may easily be given in public newspapers, which circulate more widely and more expeditiously than our Journals, and from whatever source the information is derived, as the people have the power, they may, and I believe they will, exercise it, notwithstanding the determinations of this body. The allusion to the conduct of the British Commons will not apply, for they are in no instance called upon to enter their yeas and nays; and after all, it appears to me to be congenial with the spirit of a free government, and if the one before us is free, it will be congenial with the principles of the proposed Constitution that where men are bound by a solemn and recorded vote, their reasons should accompany their assent or dissent, and be together transmitted to posterity. [Dallas' Debates, *Pennsylvania Herald,* 5 December]

Smilie: It is impossible to take a vote but on the general question—to be deprived of giving reasons for our *votes.* When party subside our liberties are in danger. The reasons produce a change in the opinion of the people.[a] [Wayne's Notes, MiU-C]

[Wayne's marginal note]
(a) May vote.

* * * *

JAMES WILSON: It is one reason of my opposition to this measure that its objects can be effected in another manner than by inserting them in our Journals, and therefore there is no pretense to load the public with an expense for diffusing what is called necessary information, but which in my opinion will terminate in the acrimony of party. But, sir, if there were no other cause of objection, if the thing were proper in itself, the enormous expense that it would occasion would be a conclusive ground for rejecting it. It is asked, however, what is there to fear? Sir, I repeat, that I have not the least dread at the most public and most general promulgation of what is done and spoken here. We know that the same things may as effectually, and, perhaps, more expeditiously, be disseminated through other channels, but let them not in their course, either involve the public in expense nor derive from our countenance a stamp of authenticity. [Dallas' Debates, *Pennsylvania Herald,* 5 December]

* * * *

ROBERT WHITEHILL: I do not think, Mr. President, that if there is any use in the proposed measure, the expense can be a sufficient reason to defeat it. The people ought to be informed of the principles upon which we have acted, and they ought to know in the clearest manner what is the nature and tendency of the government with which we have bound them. The friends to the Constitution will be pleased to receive arguments in favor of their opinions; those against it will be pleased to show to the world that their opposition does not arise merely from caprice, and the people at large will acknowledge, with thanks, the resulting information upon a subject so important to themselves and their latest posterity. But it is said that there are other means for accomplishing the same end, and that the press is open to those who choose to use it. This surely does not meet the object of the motion. A public paper is of a transient and perishable nature, but the Journals of this house will be a permanent record for posterity, and if ever it becomes a question, upon what grounds we have acted, each man will have his vote justified by the same instrument that records it. But this comparative view cannot take place through the medium of a common newspaper. As, however, it seems the general disposition, I am willing to reduce the motion to the last question, and this at least, I hope will be acceded to. The expense cannot be so great as it is apprehended, and I really consider it essential to the discharge of the commission with which we are entrusted. [Dallas' Debates, *Pennsylvania Herald,* 5 December]

* * * *

THOMAS HARTLEY: On consideration, I do not think it necessary, sir, to determine upon the motion at this time. It has been said on one hand, that there is no precedent but in the British House of Lords and in the legislature of Pennsylvania for the practice of protesting; and on the other hand, it is insisted upon from the example of Pennsylvania and the important nature of the subject in discussion. But, sir, it is certain that much misinformation and misrepresentation have at all times proceeded from public bodies. At present, therefore, I wish the question to be waived, otherwise I shall vote against it, although at a future period, when the reasons are produced, I may be disposed to concur. [Dallas' Debates, *Pennsylvania Herald,* 5 December]

* * * *

ROBERT WHITEHILL: The gentleman's idea of a postponement amounts to this: if we like your reasons when we see them, we will permit you to enter them; if we do not, why we will withhold our consent. It is strange to observe how often members change their opinions on this subject. When I asked a general power to protest, it was said, we will not agree to that, but we think you ought to enjoy it on the last great question; then when we narrow our request to that point, even that is refused. Precedent, sir, cannot be adduced on this occasion, for similar situation never has occurred before in the history of the world, nor do we know of any body of men assembled with similar powers to investigate so interesting a subject. The importance and singularity of the business must place it beyond any former rule. [Dallas' Debates, *Pennsylvania Herald,* 5 December]

* * * *

ANTHONY WAYNE: As it is probable this subject may hereafter be considered in a different and more proper point of view, I am in favor of the postponement. In the interim the usual channels of expressing their disapprobation of this system are open to the opposition. It has already been tried; and I cannot consent that discord and discontent should be propagated through the state at the public expense; particularly as every information may be given in another manner. [Dallas' Debates, *Pennsylvania Herald,* 5 December]

Wayne: The gentlemen are not [at] a loss for the means of giving their reasons. *Vide* the 16 [seceding] members [of the Assembly]. [Wayne's Notes, MiU-C]

* * * *

JAMES WILSON: Sir, I am against the postponement for two reasons—first, because I would not indulge a hope which it is not intended to gratify, and secondly, because I should wish as soon as possible to know the fate of the present motion, that every member may be prepared with his reasons, if it should be adopted, and not have them to look for, at the close of the business. But we are again asked, why suppress the species of information to be propagated by the proposed protests? I thought this question had already been answered satisfactorily when it was said that the public ought not to be loaded with so extraordinary an expense. In truth, sir, the newspapers will answer every proper purpose; and though it is said they are of a transient nature, yet if the reasons are good they will even in that mode be preserved, and if they are bad, I hope we shall not agree to perpetuate at the public cost what ought to be consigned immediately to oblivion. It is added that the expense will be small. Let us inquire then, what will be the consequence of this vote? The minority, dissatisfied with the event of this important business, will first wish to file their reasons, and it would be improper and unjust to deny them the necessary time to digest and arrange them in the best manner. These reasons cannot be answered till they appear, and though they may not possess real merit, they may be plausible and specious, therefore some time will be necessarily given to the majority for framing a replication; and so on through an endless succession of assertion and reply. For my part, I shall certainly expect to be allowed a sufficient time to state my reasons, not only those I have already delivered, but likewise those I may hereafter in the most accurate manner I can; but, as I am perhaps more accustomed to composition than other gentlemen, I shall not ask for that purpose more than two or three months. Shall we then, sir, indulge this procrastinating plan at the expense of 2 or 300 dollars a day, which is the daily expense of this meeting. I hope we shall have a greater regard for the interests of our constituents. [Dallas' Debates, *Pennsylvania Herald,* 5 December]

* * * *

ROBERT WHITEHILL and JOHN SMILIE repeated some of the former arguments and concluded with observing that if the motion was negatived, their constituents would, at least, observe that they were anxious to show the grounds of their conduct which they were refused the opportunity of doing.

On taking the question, there appeared a very great majority against the motion. [Dallas' Debates, *Pennsylvania Herald,* 5 December]

* * * *

THOMAS MCKEAN: On motion to read the first Article of the proposed Constitution for debate, the question was put and carried. The Article being read, Thomas M'Kean said, I rise to request that a spirit of conciliation and coolness may prevail in this discussion. The wisest and best men in all countries and ages have differed on the subject of government. The history of ancient government is somewhat obscure; yet enough has been given us to authorize the conclusion, than no two of them were alike. Though China and Sweden are despotic governments, they are widely different. The monarchies of France and Spain meet in very few points; nor are there any two republics but differ in their forms and powers of government. They all descend from the same parent (*the People*) but they are of various features and complexions. Even in religion we disagree to confine ourselves to one sect—how various are the doctrines, church discipline, and worship of Christians—though we have but one rule, the New Testament—the new Constitution (if you please). And if men think so differently on the most important subject which can interest society, how silly, how extremely narrow is it, that we should quarrel, because we cannot altogether agree on the subject before us. I hope our inquiries will have information for their object, and that our debates will be conducted with decency and the utmost moderation.

This speech must be admired by every friend to order and dispassionate reasoning and will no doubt greatly influence the deliberations of the Convention. [*Pennsylvania Packet,* 29 November] [7]

Mr. McKean then rose and recommended candor and forbearance in the investigation of this important subject. He stated that a difference of opinion was natural to the human mind and was not only to be found in politics, but in religion. He then traced this difference through the various sects of the Christian faith and concluded by expressing his approbation of a legislature constituted by two branches. [Dallas' Debates, *Pennsylvania Herald,* 5 December]

McKean: No two governments exactly alike altho these monarchies, aristocracies and democracies and *despotisms*—China, Sweden and Denmark.

The 13 United States all from the same *source* but differ in their constitutions; so [too in] religion; the Christians are subdivided into a variety of sects and differ in their modes. If mankind differ in religious matters, can it be expected that they will agree in opinion with respect to constitutions? [Wayne's Notes, MiU-C]

McKean: A speech to promote candor and mutual forbearance. No two governments exactly alike.

Division of the legislative power, into two branches, with a qualified negative highly proper. There should be permanency in the magistracies and stability in the laws. [Wilson's Notes, PHi]

McKean: I highly approve of the legislative power being vested in two branches. [Yeates's Notes, PHi]

1. Hartley, a York County lawyer, served in the Assembly, 1779–1780; the Council of Censors, 1783–1784; and in Congress, 1789–1800.

2. See Convention Debates, 26 November, in which John Smilie stated that "In a *legal* discussion I am inferior to (Mr. MKean)."

3. Other state legislatures permitted minorities to enter their protests in their journals. For an example of such a protest, see CDR:VI, M.

4. Dallas' report of the debates up to this point was printed in the *Pennsylvania Herald,* 1 December. His report of the remainder of the debates for the day was printed in the *Herald* on 5 December. The *Herald's* report of the debates was reprinted in the *Independent Gazetteer,* 3, 7 December; and in the *Pennsylvania Packet,* 4, 6 December. On 8 December the *Pennsylvania Journal* reprinted the last portion of the day's debates from the *Herald's* report of 5 December.

5. A total of 5,000 copies had been authorized—3,000 in English and 2,000 in German (Convention Proceedings, 27 November).

6. See Wilson's speech in Convention, 24 November.

7. Various versions of the *Packet's* account of McKean's speech were reprinted twice in Pennsylvania and seven times from New Hampshire to Virginia.

Newspaper Reports of Proceedings and Debates

Yesterday, in Convention, it was moved by Mr. Whitehill, and seconded by Mr. Lincoln, "That a protest should be entered against the motion for ratifying the Constitution, if required."

It was urged in favor of this motion, that it was the practice of the legislature of Pennsylvania, and that the minority might thereby justify their votes to their constituents and to posterity.

Against it, it was said, the practice of the legislature of Pennsylvania was *singular* in this particular, and that it had done more mischief than good in the state; that it would produce long replies from the majority in defense of their votes, and that this would greatly swell the files, and increase the expense of printing our Journals; that entering a protest would only serve to inflame and distract the state unnecessarily upon a question, that, for the present, could not easily be reconsidered or repealed; that the newspapers were open to the minority for protests and addresses, and that they had a much more extensive circulation and influence than the Journal of the Convention could possibly have. The votes being called, there appeared for the question 22; against it 44.

The speakers in favor of the motion were Mr. Whitehill and Mr. Smilie. Against it were, Dr. Rush, Mr. M'Kean, Mr. Wilson, and Colonel Hartley. [*Pennsylvania Gazette,* 28 November][1]

* * * *

Yesterday a motion was made in the Convention that upon the conclusive question for ratifying or rejecting the proposed Federal Constitution, the members should be allowed to enter, with the yeas and nays, the reasons of their vote; but after some debate, in which it was treated on one side as a measure only calculated to increase the expense of the Convention and to disseminate contention among the people, it was lost by a very great majority. The Convention then resolved that they would proceed to the consideration of the Constitution by articles, and the first Article being read, Mr. M'Kean delivered a few prefatory observations, in which he strongly inculcated mutual indulgence and forbearance. The Convention, without entering further into the discussion of the Article before them, adjourned till this day at 10 o'clock, when it will be resumed. [*Pennsylvania Herald,* 28 November][2]

1. Reprinted, in whole or in part, three times in Pennsylvania and twelve times from Maine to Maryland.

2. Reprinted, in whole or in part, in the *Pennsylvania Mercury,* 30 November, and twelve times from New Hampshire to South Carolina.

The Pennsylvania Convention
Wednesday
28 November 1787

Convention Proceedings

The Convention met pursuant to adjournment.

The President laid before the Convention a letter from the ministers and vestry of the German Lutheran Congregation, requesting the attendance of this Convention at Sion Church tomorrow, at nine o'clock, to an examination of the pupils in the German language, etc.

Agreed, That the Convention do attend.

The Convention resumed the consideration of the first Article of the proposed Constitution, and after some debate on the subject of a bill of rights, and the extent of the legislative powers contained in the first Article,

Adjourned until ten o'clock on Friday next, A.M.

Convention Debates

JAMES WILSON: This will be a proper time for making an observation or two, on what may be called the Preamble to this Constitution.

I had occasion, on a former day [24 November], to mention that the leading principle in politics, and that which pervades the American constitutions, is, that the supreme power resides in the people; this Constitution, Mr. President, opens with a solemn and practical recognition of that principle: "WE, THE PEOPLE OF THE UNITED STATES, in order to form a more perfect union, establish justice, &c. DO ORDAIN AND ESTABLISH this constitution, for the United States of America." It is announced in their name, it receives its political existence from their authority—they ordain and establish. What is the necessary consequence? Those who ordain and establish have the power, if they think proper, to repeal and annul. A proper attention to this principle may, perhaps, give ease to the minds of some, who have heard much concerning the necessity of a bill of rights.

Its establishment, I apprehend, has more force, than a volume written on the subject—it renders this truth evident, that the people have a right to do what they please, with regard to the government. I confess, I feel a kind of pride, in considering the striking difference between the foundation, on which the liberties of this country are declared to stand in this Constitution, and the footing on which the liberties of England are said to be placed. The Magna Charta of England is an instrument of high value to the people of that country. But, Mr. President, from what source does that instrument derive the liberties of the inhabitants of that kingdom? Let it speak for itself. The king says, "*we* have *given* and *granted* to all archbishops, bishops, abbots, priors, earls, barons, and to all the freemen of this our realm, these liberties following, to be kept in our kingdom of England forever." When this was assumed as the leading principle of that government, it was no wonder that the people were anxious to obtain bills of rights, and to take every opportunity of enlarging and securing their liberties. But, here, sir, the fee simple remains in the people at large, and, by this Constitution, they do not part with it. [Lloyd, *Debates,* 40–41] [1]

Wilson: Mr. President, I shall now beg leave to trouble you with a few observations upon the Preamble to the proposed Constitution. In delivering my sentiments on a former day [24 November], I had occasion to show that the supreme power of government was the inalienable and inherent right of the people, and the system before us opens with a practical declaration of that principle. Here, sir, it is expressly announced, "We the people of the United States do ordain, constitute, and establish," and those who can ordain and establish may certainly repeal or annul the work of government, which, in the hands of the people, is like clay in the hands of the potter and may be molded into any shape they please. This single sentence in the Preamble is tantamount to a volume and contains the essence of all the bills of rights that have been or can be devised; for, it establishes, at once, that in the great article of government, the people have a right to do what they please. It is with pride, Mr. President, I remark the difference between the terms of this Constitution and the British Declaration of Rights or even their boasted Magna Charta. For, sir, from what source does Magna Charta derive the liberties of the people? The very words of that celebrated instrument declare them to be the gift or grant of the king; and under the influence of that doctrine, no wonder the people should then, and at subsequent periods, wish to obtain some evidence of their formal liberties by the concessions of petitions and bills of right. But here, sir, the fee simple of freedom and government is declared to be in the people, and it is an inheritance with which they will not part. [Dallas' Debates, *Pennsylvania Herald,* 8 December][2]

Wilson: We the People—it is announced in their name, it is clothed with their authority, from whom all power originated and ultimately belong. Magna Charta is the grant of the king. This Constitution is the act of the people and what they have not expressly *granted,* they have *retained.* [Wayne's Notes, Cox Collection]

* * * *

John Smilie: I expected, Mr. President, that the honorable gentleman [James Wilson] would have proceeded to a full and explicit investigation of the proposed system, and that he would have made some attempts to prove that it was calculated to promote the happiness, power, and general interests of the United States. I am sorry that I have been mistaken in this expectation, for surely the gentleman's talents and opportunities would have enabled him to furnish considerable information upon this important subject; but I shall proceed to make a few remarks upon those words in the Preamble of this plan, which he has considered of so super-excellent a quality. Compare them, sir, with the language used in forming the state constitution, and however superior they may be to the terms of the Great Charter of England, still, in common candor, they must yield to the more sterling expressions employed in this act. Let these speak for themselves.

"That all men are born equally free and independent, and have certain natural, inherent and unalienable rights, amongst which are, the enjoying and defending life and liberty, acquiring, possessing and protecting property, and pursuing and obtaining happiness and safety.

"That the people of this state have the sole, exclusive and inherent right of governing and regulating the internal police of the same.

"That all power being originally inherent in, and consequently derived from the people; therefore all officers of government, whether legislative or executive, are their trustees and servants, and at all times accountable to them.

"That government is, or ought to be, instituted for the common benefit, protection and security of the people, nation or community; and not for the particular emolument or advantage of any single man, family, or set of men, who are a part only of that community. And that the community hath an indubitable, unalienable and indefeasible right to reform, alter or abolish government in such manner as shall be by that community judged most conducive to the public weal."[3]

But the gentleman takes pride in the superiority of this short Preamble when compared with Magna Charta. Why, sir, I hope the rights of men are better understood at this day than at the framing of that deed, and we must be convinced that civil liberty is capable of still greater improvement and extension than is known even in its present cultivated state. True, sir, the supreme authority naturally rests in the people, but does it follow that therefore a declaration of rights would be superfluous? Because the people have a right to alter and abolish government, can it therefore be inferred that every step taken to secure that right would be superfluous and nugatory? The truth is that unless some criterion is established by which it could be easily and constitutionally ascertained how far our governors may proceed, and by which it might appear when they transgress their jurisdiction, this idea of altering and abolishing government is a mere sound without substance. Let us recur to the memorable Declaration of the 4th of July 1776. Here it is said:

"When, in the course of human events, it becomes necessary for one people to dissolve the political bands which have connected them with another, and to assume among the powers of the earth, the separate and equal station to which the laws of nature's God entitle them, a decent respect to the opinions of mankind requires that they should declare the causes which impel them to the separation.

"We hold these truths to be self evident; that all men are created equal; that they are endowed by their Creator with certain unalienable rights; that among these are life, liberty, and the pursuit of happiness. That to secure these rights, governments are instituted among men, deriving their just powers from the consent of the governed; that whenever any form of government becomes destructive of these ends, it is the right of the people to alter or to abolish it, and to institute a new government, laying its foundation on such principles, and organizing its powers in such form, as to them shall seem most likely to effect their safety and happiness."

Now, sir, if in the proposed plan, the gentleman can show any similar security for the civil rights of the people I shall certainly be relieved from a weight of objection to its adoption, and I sincerely hope, that as he has gone so far, he will proceed to communicate some of the reasons (and undoubtedly they must have been powerful ones) which induced the late Federal Convention to omit a bill of rights, so essential in the opinion of many citizens to a perfect form of government. [Dallas' Debates, *Pennsylvania Herald,* 8 December]

Smilie: There is no *security* for our rights in this Constitution. Preamble to Declaration of Independence. Why did they [the Constitutional Convention] omit a bill of rights?

With respect to trial by jury and *habeas corpus* there is a bill of rights. Without one, we cannot know when Congress exceed their powers. There is no check but the people. No security for the rights of conscience.

6th Article of the Constitution: This sweeping clause levels all the bills of rights of the several states, and their governments are not confirmed. [Wilson's Notes, PHi]

Smilie: Does this Constitution provide against an alteration? This was essential to be done (*vide* Article 5th, p. 223).[4] Compare this Constitution with the Declaration of Independence.[(a)] No provision for the rights of conscience (*vide* Article 6th, p. 223). [Wayne's Notes, Cox Collection]

> [Wayne's marginal note]
> (a) The Congress were then claiming rights usurped or attempted to be usurped by the king and Parliament of Great Britain, but we now stand on stronger ground.

Smilie: Is there an expression in the Constitution that justifies the people altering the Constitution, if they think proper? Reads the Declaration of Independence. [Yeates's Notes, PHi]

* * * *

THOMAS MCKEAN: I conceived, Mr. President, that we were at this time to confine our reasoning to the first Article, which relates to the legislative power composed of two branches and the partial negative of the President. Gentlemen, however, have taken a more extensive field and have employed themselves in animadverting upon what has been omitted and not upon what is contained in the proposed system. It is asked, sir, why a bill of rights was not annexed to the Constitution? The origin of bills of rights has been referred to, and we find that in England they proceed upon the principle that the supreme power is lodged in the king and not in the people, so that their liberties are not claimed as an inherent right, but as a grant from the sovereign.

The Great Charter rests on that footing and has been renewed and broken above 30 times. Then we find the Petition of Rights in the reign of Charles I and, lastly, the Declaration of Rights on the accession of the Prince of Orange to the British throne. The truth is, sir, that bills of rights are instruments of modern invention, unknown among the ancients, and unpracticed but by the British nation and the governments descended from them. For though it is said that Poland has a bill of rights, it must be remembered that the people have no participation in that government. Of the constitutions of the United States, there are but five out of the thirteen which have bills of rights. In short, though it can do no harm, I believe, yet it is an unnecessary instrument, for, in fact, the whole plan of government is nothing more than a bill of rights—a declaration of the people in what manner they choose to be governed. If, sir, the people should at any time desire to alter and abolish their government, I agree with my honorable colleague [James Wilson] that it is in their power to do so, and I am happy to observe that the Constitution before us provides a regular mode for that event. At present my chief object is to call upon those who deem a bill of rights so essential to inform us if there are any other precedents than those I have alluded to, and if there is not, the sense of mankind and of nations will operate against the alleged necessity. [Dallas' Debates, *Pennsylvania Herald,* 8 December]

McKean: There is no necessity for a bill of rights. [Yeates's Notes, PHi]

* * * *

JAMES WILSON: I am called upon to give a reason, why the Convention omitted to add a bill of rights to the work before you. I confess, sir, I did think that in point of propriety, the honorable gentleman [John Smilie] ought first to have furnished some reasons, to show such an addition to be necessary; it is natural to prove the affirmative of a proposition; and if he had established the propriety of this addition, he might then have asked, why it was not made.

I cannot say, Mr. President, what were the reasons, of every member of that Convention, for not adding a bill of rights; I believe the truth is, that such an idea never entered the mind of many of them. I don't recollect to have heard the subject mentioned, till within about three days of the time of our rising, and even then there was no direct motion offered for anything of this kind. I may be mistaken in this; but as far as my memory serves me, I believe it was the case.[5] A proposition to adopt a measure, that would have supposed that we were throwing into the general government every power not expressly reserved by the people would have been spurned at, in that house, with the greatest indignation; even in a single government, if the powers of the people rest on the same establishment, as is expressed in this Constitution, a bill of rights is by no means a necessary measure. In a government possessed of enumerated powers, such a measure would be not only unnecessary, but preposterous and dangerous. Whence comes this notion, that in the United States there is no security without a bill of rights? Have the citizens of South Carolina no security for their liberties? They have no bill of rights. Are the citizens on the eastern side of the Delaware less free, or less secured in their liberties, than those on the western side? The State of New Jersey has no bill of rights. The State of New York has no bill of rights. The states of Connecticut and Rhode Island have no bills of rights. I know not whether I have exactly enumerated the states who have thought it unnecessary to add a bill of rights to their constitutions; but this enumeration, sir, will serve to show by experience, as well as principle, that even in single governments, a bill of rights is not an essential or necessary measure. But in a government consisting of enumerated powers, such as is proposed for the United States, a bill of rights would not only be unnecessary, but, in my humble judgment, highly imprudent. In all societies, there are many powers and rights, which cannot be particularly enumerated. A bill of rights annexed to a constitution is an enumeration of the powers reserved. If we attempt an enumeration, everything that is not enumerated is presumed to be given. The consequence is, that an imperfect enumeration would throw all implied power into the scale of the government; and the rights of the people would be rendered incomplete. On the other hand, an imperfect enumeration of the powers of government reserves all implied power to the people; and, by that means the constitution becomes incomplete; but of the two it is much safer to run the risk on the side of the constitution; for an omission in the enumeration of the powers of government is neither so dangerous, nor important, as an omission in the enumeration of the rights of the people.

Mr. President, as we are drawn into this subject, I beg leave to pursue its history a little further. The doctrine and practice of declarations of rights have been borrowed from the conduct of the people of England, on some remarkable occasion; but the principles and maxims, on which their government is constituted, are widely different from those of ours. I have already stated the language of Magna Charta. After repeated confirmations of that instrument, and after violations of it, repeated equally often, the next step taken in this business was when the Petition of Rights was presented to Charles I.

It concludes in this manner, "all of which they most humbly *pray* to be allowed, as their rights and liberties, according to the laws and statutes of this realm."[a] One of the most material statutes of the realm was Magna Charta; so that we find they continue upon the old ground, as to the foundation on which they rest their liberties. It was not till the era of the Revolution [of 1688], that the two houses assume an higher tone, and "*demand* and insist upon all the premises as their undoubted rights and liberties."[b] But when the whole transaction is considered, we shall find that those rights, and liberties, are claimed only on the foundation of an original contract, supposed to have been made at some former period, between the king and the people.[c]

But, in this Constitution, the citizens of the United States appear dispensing a part of their original power in what manner and what proportion they think fit. They never part with the whole; and they retain the right of recalling what they part with. When, therefore, they possess, as I have already mentioned, the fee simple of authority, why should they have recourse to the minute and subordinate remedies, which can be necessary only to those, who pass the fee, and reserve only a rent charge?

To every suggestion concerning a bill of rights, the citizens of the United States may always say, WE reserve the right to do what we please. [Lloyd, *Debates,* 41–44]

[Lloyd's notes]
(a) 8th *Parl. Hist.* 150. [*The Parliamentary, or Constitutional History of England. . . ,* VIII (London, 1751), 150.]
(b) 2 *Par. Deb.* 261. [John Torbuck, *A Collection of the Parliamentary Debates in England. . .* (21 vols., London, 1741–1742), II, 261.]
(c) 1 Blackstone, 233. [Blackstone, III, 233.]

Wilson: Mr. President, we are repeatedly called upon to give some reason why a bill of rights has not been annexed to the proposed plan. I not only think that inquiry is at this time unnecessary and out of order, but I expect, at least, that those who desire us to show why it was omitted will furnish some arguments to show that it ought to have been inserted; for the proof of the affirmative naturally falls upon them. But the truth is, sir, that this circumstance, which has since occasioned so much clamor and debate, never struck the mind of any member in the late Convention till, I believe, within three days of the dissolution of that body, and even then, of so little account was the idea, that it passed off in a short conversation, without introducing a formal debate, or assuming the shape of a motion. For, sir, the attempt to have thrown into the national scale an instrument in order to evince that any power not mentioned in the Constitution was reserved would have been spurned at as an insult to the common understanding of mankind. In civil government it is certain that bills of rights are unnecessary and useless, nor can I conceive whence the contrary notion has arisen. Virginia has no bill of rights, and will it be said that her constitution was the less free? [Dallas' Debates, *Pennsylvania Herald,* 12 December]

Wilson: 8 Vol. *Parly. Histy.* 150—Peto of Rights with the King's answer—2 Vol. *Parl. Deb.* 258 [-64].

At the Revolution [of 1688] the rights of the people were considered as founded on a compact (1 Blackst. 233 to this point) [Blackstone, III, 233]. Our government differ[s] from England, and the[refore] a bill of rights may be necessary there; it is not so here. Virginia, Jersey, New York, South Carolina, Connecticut, Rhode Island have no bill of rights. So of New Hampshire and Georgia. An enumeration of the rights of the people would be dangerous—for what are omitted are to be supposed to be excluded. [Yeates's Notes, PHi]

Wilson: A bill of rights not even thought of in the Federal Convention; it was *absurd.* If we undertake to enumerate and omit any part of the rights of a people, their liberties are abridged or incomplete; and what is not expressly mentioned is taken for granted or ceded (*P:D.* 8.V. Page 150 B. [*sic*] of Rights Bl V 2nd 258–261 Do. 1.–333). [Wayne's Notes, Cox Collection]

* * * *

JOHN SMILIE: I beg leave to observe, Mr. President that although it has not been inserted in the printed volume of state constitutions,[6] yet I have been assured by Mr. [George] Mason that Virginia has a bill of rights. [Dallas' Debates, *Pennsylvania Herald,* 12 December]

* * * *

JAMES WILSON: I do not rely upon the information of Mr. Mason or of any other gentleman on a question of this kind, but I refer to the authenticity of the volume which contains the state constitutions, and in that Virginia has no bill of rights. But, sir, has South Carolina no security for her liberties? That state has no bill of rights. Are the citizens of the eastern shore of the Delaware more secured in their freedom or more enlightened on the subject of government than the citizens of the western shore? New Jersey has no bill of rights; New York has none; Connecticut has none, and Rhode Island has none. Thus, sir, it appears from the example of other states, as well as from principle, that a bill of rights is neither an essential nor a necessary instrument in framing a system of government, since liberty may exist and be as well secured without it. But it was not only unnecessary, but on this occasion, it was found impracticable; for who will be bold enough to undertake to enumerate all the rights of the people? And when the attempt to enumerate them is made, it must be remembered that if the enumeration is not complete, everything not expressly mentioned will be presumed to be purposely omitted. So it must be with a bill of rights, and an omission in stating the powers granted to the government is not so dangerous as an omission in recapitulating the rights reserved by the people. We have already seen the origin of Magna Charta, and tracing the subject still further, we find the Petition of Rights claiming the liberties of the people, according to the laws and statutes of the realm, of which the Great Charter was the most material; so that here again recourse is had to the old source from which their liberties are derived, the grant of the king. It was not till the Revolution [of 1688] that the subject was placed upon a different footing, and even then the people did not claim their liberties as an inherent right, but as the result of an original contract between them and the sovereign. Thus, Mr. President, an attention to the situation of England will show that the conduct of that country in respect to bills of rights cannot furnish an example to the inhabitants of the United States, who by the Revolution have regained all their natural rights and possess their liberty neither by grant nor contract. In short, sir, I have said that a bill of rights would have been improperly annexed to the federal plan, and for this plain reason, that it would imply that whatever is not expressed was given, which is not the principle of the proposed Constitution. [Dallas' Debates, *Pennsylvania Herald,* 12 December]

* * * *

JOHN SMILIE: The arguments which have been urged, Mr. President, have not, in my opinion, satisfactorily shown that a bill of rights would have been an improper, nay, that it is not a necessary appendage to the proposed system. As it has been denied that Virginia possesses a bill of rights, I shall on that subject only observe, that Mr. Mason, a gentleman certainly of great information and integrity, has assured me that such a thing does exist, and I am persuaded, I shall be able at a future period to lay it before the Convention. But, sir, the State of Delaware has a bill of rights, and I believe one of the honorable members (Thomas M'Kean) who now contests the necessity and propriety of that instrument, took a very conspicuous part in the formation of the Delaware government. It seems however that the members of the Federal Convention were themselves convinced, in some degree, of the expediency and propriety of a bill of rights, for we find them expressly declaring that the writ of *habeas corpus* and the trial by jury in criminal cases shall not be suspended or infringed. How does this indeed agree with the maxim that whatever is not given is reserved? Does it not rather appear from the reservation of these two articles that everything else, which is not specified, is included in the powers delegated to the government? This, sir, must prove the necessity of a full and explicit declaration of rights; and when we further consider the extensive, the undefined powers vested in the administrators of this system, when we consider the system itself as a great political compact between the governors and the governed, a plain, strong, and accurate criterion by which the people might at once determine when, and in what instance, their rights were violated is a preliminary without which this plan ought not to be adopted. So loosely, so inaccurately are the powers which are enumerated in this Constitution defined, that it will be impossible, without a test of that kind, to ascertain the limits of authority and to declare when government has degenerated into oppression. In that event the contest will arise between the people and the rulers. "You have exceeded the powers of your office, you have oppressed us" will be the language of the suffering citizens. The answer of the government will be short: "We have not exceeded our power; you have no test by which you can prove it." Hence, sir, it will be impracticable to stop the progress of tyranny, for there will be no check but the people, and their exertions must be futile and uncertain; since it will be difficult indeed, to communicate to them the violation that has been committed, and their proceedings will be neither systematical nor unanimous. It is said, however, that the difficulty of framing a bill of rights was insurmountable; but, Mr. President, I cannot agree in this opinion. Our experience, and the numerous precedents before us, would have furnished a very sufficient guide. At present there is no security, even for the rights of conscience, and under the sweeping force of the sixth Article every principle of a bill of rights, every stipulation for the most sacred and invaluable privileges of man, are left at the mercy of government. [Dallas' Debates, *Pennsylvania Herald,* 12 December]

Smilie: Delaware, Massachusetts, Pennsylvania, Maryland, and North Carolina have a bill of right[s].

Trials by jury in criminal cases are reserved and the privilege of the *habeas corpus* act. These are mere parts of our bill of rights and all that are given to us. In this Constitution there is no security for the rights of conscience.

The section of 6th Article sweeps away all the rights we have under the states' governments. [Yeates's Notes, PHi]

* * * *

Robert Whitehill: I differ, sir, from the honorable member from the city [James Wilson] as to the impropriety or necessity of a bill of rights. If indeed the Constitution itself so well defined the powers of the government that no mistake could arise, and we were well assured that our governors would always act right, then we might be satisfied without an explicit reservation of those rights with which the people ought not, and mean not to part. But, sir, we know that it is the nature of power to seek its own augmentation, and thus the loss of liberty is the necessary consequence of a loose or extravagant delegation of authority. National freedom has been, and will be the sacrifice of ambition and power, and it is our duty to employ the present opportunity in stipulating such restrictions as are best calculated to protect us from oppression and slavery. Let us then, Mr. President, if other countries cannot supply an adequate example, let us proceed upon our own principles, and with the great end of government in view, the happiness of the people, it will be strange if we err. Government we have been told, sir, is yet in its infancy; we ought not therefore to submit to the shackles of foreign schools and opinions. In entering into the social compact, men ought not to leave their rulers at large, but erect a permanent landmark by which they may learn the extent of their authority, and the people be able to discover the first encroachments on their liberties. But let us attend to the language of the system before us. "We the people of the United States" is a sentence that evidently shows the old foundation of the Union is destroyed, the principle of confederation excluded, and a new unwieldy system of consolidated empire is set up upon the ruins of the present compact between the states. Can this be denied? No, sir; it is artfully indeed, but it is incontrovertibly, designed to abolish the independence and sovereignty of the states individually, an event which cannot be the wish of any good citizen of America, and therefore it ought to be prevented, by rejecting the plan which is calculated to produce it. What right indeed have we in the manner here proposed to violate the existing Confederation? It is declared that the agreement of nine states shall be sufficient to carry the new system into operation, and, consequently, to abrogate the old one. Then, Mr. President, four of the present confederated states may not be comprehended in the compact; shall we sir, force these dissenting states into the measure? The consequences of that attempt are evidently such as no man can either justify or approve. But reverse the idea—would not those states have a fair pretext to charge the rest with an unconstitutional and unwarrantable abandonment of the nature and obligation of the Union of 1776? And having shown sufficient reason why they could not accede to the proposed government, would they not still be entitled to demand a performance of the original compact between the states? Sir, these questions must introduce a painful anticipation of the confusion, contest, and a civil war, which, under such circumstances, the adoption of the offered system must produce. It will be proper perhaps to review the origin of this business. It was certainly, Mr. President, acknowledged on all hands, that an additional share of power for federal purposes ought to be delegated to Congress, and with a view, to inquire how far it was necessary to strengthen and enlarge the jurisdiction of that body, the late Convention was appointed under the authority, and by legislative acts, of the several states. But, how, sir, did the Convention act upon this occasion? Did they pursue the authority which was given to them? By the State of Pennsylvania that authority was strictly defined in the following words:

"And the said Thomas Mifflin, Robert Morris, George Clymer, Jared Ingorsoll, Thomas Fitzsimons, James Wilson and Governeur Morris, esqrs. or any four of them are hereby constituted and appointed deputies from this state, with powers to meet such deputies as may be appointed and authorised by the other states to assemble in the said convention at the city aforesaid, and to join with them in devising, deliberating on, and discussing all such alterations and further provisions as may be necessary to render the federal constitution fully adequate to the exigencies of the union; and in reporting such act or acts for that purpose, to the United States in Congress assembled, as when agreed to by them, and duly confirmed by the several states, will effectually provide for the same."[7]

Thus, sir, it appears that no other power was given to the delegates from this state (and I believe the power given by the other states was of the same nature and extent) than to increase in a certain degree the strength and energy of Congress, but it never was in the contemplation of any man that they were authorized to dissolve the present Union, to abrogate the state sovereignties, and to establish one comprehensive government, novel in its structure, and, in its probable operation, oppressive and despotic. Can it then be said that the late Convention did not assume powers to which they had no legal title? On the contrary, sir, it is clear that they set aside the laws under which they were appointed, and under which alone they could derive any legitimate authority, they arrogantly exercised any powers that they found convenient to their object, and, in the end, they have overthrown that government which they were called upon to amend in order to introduce one of their own fabrication. [Dallas' Debates, *Pennsylvania Herald,* 12 December]

True it is, Mr. President, that if the people intended to engage in one comprehensive system of continental government, the power to frame that system must have been conferred by them, for the legislatures of the states are sworn to preserve the independence of their respective constitutions, and, therefore, they could not consistently with their most sacred obligations, authorize an act which sacrificed the individual to the aggregate sovereignty of the states. But it appears from the origin and nature of the commission under which the late Convention assembled, that a more perfect confederation was the only object submitted to their wisdom, and not, as it is attempted by this plan, the total destruction of the government of Pennsylvania, and of every other state. So far, sir, the interference of the legislatures was proper and efficient; but the moment the Convention went beyond that object, they ceased to act under any legitimate authority; for, the assemblies could give them none, and it cannot be pretended that they were called together by the people; for till the Preamble was produced, it never was understood that the people at large had been consulted upon the occasion, or that otherwise than through their representatives in the several states, they had given a sanction to the proceedings of that body. If, indeed, the Federal Convention, finding that the old system was incapable of repair, had represented the incurable defects to Congress, and advised that the original and inherent power of the people might be called into exercise for the institution of a new government, then, sir, the subject would have come fairly into view, and we should have known upon what principles we proceeded. At present we find a Convention appointed by one authority, but acting under the arbitrary assumption of another, and instead of transacting the business which was assigned to them, behold they have produced a work of supererogation, after a mysterious labor of three months. Let us, however, sir, attend for a moment to the Constitution, and here we shall find in a single line, sufficient matter for weeks of debate, and which it will puzzle any one member to investigate and define. But, besides the powers enumerated, we find in this Constitution [Article I, section 8] an authority is given to make all laws that are necessary to carry it effectually into operation, and what laws are necessary is a consideration left for Congress to decide. In constituting the representative body, the interposition of the Congress is, likewise, made conclusive; for, with the power of regulating the place and manner of elections [Article I, section 4], it is easy to perceive that the returns will always be so managed as to answer their purpose. It is strange to mark, however, what a sudden and striking revolution has taken place in the political sentiments of America, for, sir, in the opening of our struggle with Great Britain, it was often insisted that annual parliaments were necessary to secure the liberties of the people, and yet it is here proposed to establish a House of Representatives which shall continue for two, a Senate for six, and a President for four years! What is there in this plan indeed, which can even assure us that the several departments shall continue no longer in office? Do we not know that an English Parliament elected for three years, by a vote of their own body, extended their existence to seven,[8] and with this example, Congress possessing a competent share of power may easily be tempted to exercise it. The advantages of annual elections are not at this day to be taught, and when every other security was withheld, I should still have thought there was some safety in the government had this been left. The seats of Congress being held for so short a period, and by a tenure so precarious as popular elections, there could be no inducement to invade the liberties of the people, nor time enough to accomplish the schemes of ambition and tyranny. But when the period is protracted, an object is presented worthy of contention, and the duration of the office affords an opportunity for perpetuating the influence by which it was originally obtained. Another power, designed to be vested in the new government, is the superlative power of taxation, which may be carried to an inconceivable excess, swallowing up every object of taxation, and consequently plundering the several states of every means to support their governments and to administer their laws. Then, sir, can it longer be doubted that this is a system of consolidation? That government which possesses all the powers of raising and maintaining armies, of regulating and commanding the militia, and of laying imposts and taxes of every kind must be supreme and will (whether in twenty or in one year, it signifies little to the event) naturally absorb every subordinate jurisdiction. It is in vain, sir, to flatter ourselves that the forms of popular elections will be the means of self-preservation, and that the officers of the proposed government will uniformly act for the happiness of the people, for why should we run a risk which we may easily avoid? The giving such extensive and undefined power is a radical wrong, that cannot be justified by any subsequent merit in the exercise; for in framing a new system, it is our duty rather to indulge a jealousy of the human character, than an expectation of unprecedented perfection. Let us, however, suppose, what will be allowed to be at least possible, that the powers of this government should be abused, and the liberties of the people infringed. Do any means of redress remain with the states or with the people at large to oppose and counteract the influence and oppression of the general government? Secret combinations, partial insurrections, sudden tumults may arise, but these, being easily defeated and subdued, will furnish a pretense for strengthening that power which they were intended to overthrow. A bill of rights, Mr. President, it has been said, would not only be unnecessary, but it would be dangerous, and for this special reason, that because it is not practicable to enumerate all the rights of the people, therefore it would be hazardous to secure such of the rights as we can enumerate! Truly, sir, I will agree that a bill of rights may be a dangerous instrument, but it is to the views and projects of the aspiring ruler, and not to the liberties of the citizen. Grant but this explicit criterion, and our governors will not venture to encroach—refuse it, and the people cannot venture to complain. From the formal language of Magna Charta we are next taught to consider a declaration of rights as superfluous; but, sir, will the situation and conduct of Great Britain furnish a case parallel to that of America? It surely will not be contended that we are about to receive our liberties as a grant or concession from any power on earth; so that if we learn anything from the English Charter, it is this, that the people having negligently lost or submissively resigned their rights into the hands of the Crown, they were glad to recover them upon any terms. Their anxiety to secure the grant by the strongest evidence will be an argument to prove, at least, the expediency of the measure, and the result of the whole is a lesson instructing us to do by an easy precaution, what will hereafter be an arduous and perhaps an insurmountable task. But even in Great Britain, whatever may be the courtesy of their expressions, the matter stands substantially on a different footing, for we know that the divine right of kings is there, as well as here, deemed an idle and chimerical tale. It is true the preamble to the Great Charter declares the liberties enumerated in that instrument to be the grant of the sovereign, but the hyperbolical language of the English law has likewise declared that "the king can do no wrong," and yet, from time to time, the people have discovered in themselves the natural source of power, and the monarchs have been made painfully responsible for their actions. Will it still be said that the state governments would be adequate to the task of correcting the usurpations of Congress? Let us not, however, give the weight of proof to the boldness of assertion; for, if the opposition is to succeed by force, we find both the purse and the sword are almost exclusively transferred to the general government, and if it is to succeed by legislative remonstrance, we shall find that expedient rendered nugatory by the law of Congress, which is to be the supreme law of the land. Thus, Mr. President, must the powers and sovereignty of the several states be eventually destroyed, and when, at last, it may be found expedient to abolish that connection, which, we are told, essentially exists between the federal and individual legislatures, the proposed Constitution is amply provided with the means in that clause which assumes the authority to alter or prescribe the place and manner of elections [Article I, section 4]. I feel, Mr. President, the magnitude of the subject in which I am engaged, and although I am exhausted with what I have already advanced, I am conscious that the investigation is infinitely far from being complete. Upon the whole, therefore, I wish it to be seriously considered, whether we have a right to leave the liberties of the people to such future constructions and expositions as may possibly be made upon this system; particularly when its advocates, even at this day, confess that it would be dangerous to omit anything in the enumeration of a bill of rights, and according to their principle, the reservation of the *habeas corpus* and trial by jury in criminal cases may hereafter be construed to be the only privileges reserved by the people. I am not anxious, Mr. President, about forms; it is the substance which I wish to obtain; and therefore I acknowledge, if our liberties are secured by the frame of government itself, the supplementary instrument of a declaration of rights may well be dispensed with. But, sir, we find no security there, except in the two instances referred to, and it will not, I hope, any longer be alleged that no security is requisite, since those exceptions prove a contrary sentiment to have been entertained by the very framers of the proposed Constitution. The question at present, sir, is, however, of a preliminary kind; does the plan now in discussion propose a consolidation of the states? And will a consolidated government be most likely to promote the interests and happiness of America? If it is satisfactorily demonstrated, that in its principles or in its operation, the dissolution of the state sovereignties is not a necessary consequence, I shall then be willing to accompany the gentlemen on the other side in weighing more particularly its merits and demerits. But my judgment, according to the information I now possess, leads me to anticipate the annihilation of the several state governments, an event never expected by the people, and which would, I fervently believe, destroy the civil liberties of America. [Dallas' Debates, *Pennsylvania Herald,* 15 December]

Whitehill: If we were sure that the general government would not infringe on the state governments we would be satisfied. Power is of an increasing nature. We are not bound by forms or examples of other countries. We should improve on them.

"We the People etc." changes the principles of [the] *Confederation,* and introduces a *consolidating* and *absorbing* government. Does not this system violate the Confederation? 9 states are sufficient here—

13 were necessary before. May not the other 4 still insist on the Confederation?

The business was intended to give *more* powers to Congress—the powers of the delegates of this state in the Convention. A *general* government was not thought of. Nor to unhinge the state governments. The Convention have made a plan of their own. They have *assumed* the power of *proposing*. Alterations in government should proceed from the people. The Assembly of Pennsylvania are limited in their powers. And this business should have been left to the people.

There is a mode of amendment in the present Confederation.

Article 1, section 1 [and 8]: Power unbounded. Who are to be judges of what is *necessary* and *proper*?

Section 2: Annual parliaments and assemblies necessary. British Parliament *took* 7 years. Present delegates in Congress may be *recalled.* 6 years too long [for the senatorial term].

Section 4: Times and places of election.

The members of the Senate may enrich themselves, for they have a power to tax. Their powers pervade everything. It forms one general consolidating government.

Power of borrowing money—raising armies.

If we give the power; we are wrong; tho the legislature are of our own election.

Could any state oppose the general government? All are to be sworn to observe it.

A bill of rights may be dangerous to the *governors.*

Article VI: This Article *eradicates* every vestige of state government and was *intended* so, for it was deliberated.

Article 1, section 4: This is intended to carry on the business when the state governments are destroyed.

Can we give away the rights of conscience? There is no *reserve* of *it,* tho these reservations [are provided] as to *ex post facto* laws (Article 1, section 9).

Let us *secure* our liberties, and not quarrel about a bill of rights. They are not secured except as to *habeas corpus.* [Wilson's Notes, PHi]

Whitehill: The present Constitution is a violation of our engagements under the Confederation. No state nor Convention had such powers. The act of Assembly gave no such power. This Constitution gives a general consolidated government. The general legislative power is too large and undefined. Annual elections necessary to liberty. Congress may increase the periods of their sitting. Congress ought not to control the times, modes, and places of choosing House of Representatives. Senators may amass wealth by sitting for 6 years. It is the nature of power to exceed its boundaries. What have we to do with Magna Charta or Great Britain? The late Convention deliberately intended to destroy the state governments. Have we a right to give away the rights of conscience? [Yeates's Notes, PHi]

Whitehill: *We the People*—this is setting out very *artfully*.

Objection [to the] 4th section of 1st Article [and?] to the 6th Article.[(a)] [Wayne's Notes, Cox Collection]

[Wayne's marginal note]
(a) 4th section occasioned by an eventual *invasion, insurrection,* etc.

* * * *

JAMES WILSON: I concur most sincerely, with the honorable gentleman [Robert Whitehill] who was last up, in one sentiment, that if our liberties will be insecure under this system of government, it will become our duty not to adopt, but to reject it. On the contrary, if it will secure the liberties of the citizens of America, if it will not only secure their liberties, but procure them happiness, it becomes our duty, on the other hand, to assent to and ratify it. With a view to conduct us safely, and gradually, to the determination of that important question, I shall beg leave to notice some of the objections that have fallen from the honorable gentleman from Cumberland (Robert Whitehill). But, before I proceed, permit me to make one general remark. Liberty has a formidable enemy on each hand; on one there is tyranny, on the other licentiousness. In order to guard against the latter, proper powers ought to be given to government; in order to guard against the former, those powers ought to be properly distributed. It has been mentioned, and attempts have been made to establish the position, that the adoption of this Constitution will necessarily be followed by the annihilation of all the state governments. If this was a necessary consequence, the objection would operate in my mind with exceeding great force. But, sir, I think the inference is rather unnatural, that a government will produce the annihilation of others, upon the very existence of which its own existence depends. Let us, sir, examine this Constitution and mark its proportions and arrangements. It is composed of three great constituent parts, the legislative department, the executive department, and the judicial department. The legislative department is subdivided into two branches, the House of Representatives and the Senate. Can there be a House of Representatives, in the general government, after the state governments are annihilated? Care is taken to express the character of the electors in such a manner, that even the popular branch of the general government cannot exist unless the governments of the states continue in existence.

How do I prove this? By the regulation that is made concerning the important subject of giving suffrage. Article the first, section second, "and the electors in each state, shall have the qualifications for electors of the most numerous branch of the state legislature." Now, sir, in order to know who are qualified to be electors of the House of Representatives, we are to inquire, who are qualified to be electors of the legislature of each state; if there be no legislatures in the states, there can be no electors of them. If there be no such electors, there is [no] criterion to know who are qualified to elect members of the House of Representatives. By this short, plain deduction, the existence of state legislatures is proved to be essential to the existence of the general government.

Let us proceed now to the second branch of the legislative department. In the system before you, the Senators, sir, those tyrants that are to devour the legislatures of the states, are to be chosen by the state legislatures themselves. Need anything more be said on this subject? So far is the principle of each state's retaining the power of self-preservation, from being weakened or endangered by the general government, that the Convention went further, perhaps, than was strictly proper, in order to secure it; for in this second branch of the legislature, each state, without regard to its importance, is entitled to an equal vote. And in the articles, respecting amendments of this Constitution, it is provided "that no state, without its consent, shall be deprived of its equal suffrage in the senate" [Article V].

Does it appear then, that provision for the continuance of the state governments was neglected, in framing this Constitution? On the contrary, it was a favorite object in the Convention to secure them.

The President of the United States is to be chosen by Electors appointed in the different states, in such manner as the legislature shall direct. Unless there be legislatures to appoint Electors, the President cannot be chosen; the idea, therefore, of the existing government of the states is presupposed in the very mode of constituting the legislative and the executive departments of the general government. The same principle will apply to the judicial department. The judges are to be nominated by the President, and appointed by him, with the advice and consent of the Senate. This shows, that the judges cannot exist without the President and Senate. I have already shown that the President and Senate cannot exist without the existence of the state legislatures. Have I misstated anything? Is not the evidence indisputable, that the state governments will be preserved, or that the general government must tumble amidst their ruins? It is true, indeed, sir, although it presupposes the existence of state governments, yet this Constitution does not suppose them to be the sole power to be respected.

In the Articles of Confederation the people are unknown, but in this plan they are represented; and in one of the branches of the legislature they are represented, immediately, by persons of their own choice.

I hope these observations, on the nature and formation of this system, are seen in their full force; many of them were so seen by some gentlemen of the late Convention. After all this, could it have been expected that assertions, such as have been hazarded on this floor, would have been made, "that it was the business of their deliberations, to destroy the state governments, that they employed four months to accomplish this object, and that such was their intentions?" That honorable gentleman [Robert Whitehill] may be better qualified to judge of their intentions than themselves. I know my own, and, as to those of the other members, I believe that they have been very improperly and unwarrantably represented; intended to destroy! Where did *he* obtain his information? Let the tree be judged of by its fruit.

Mr. President, the only proof that is attempted to be drawn from the work itself is that which has been urged from the fourth section of the first Article. I will read it. "The times, places and manner of holding elections, for senators and representatives, shall be prescribed in each state by the legislature thereof; but the congress may at any time, by law make or alter such regulations, except as to the places of chusing senators."

And is this a proof, that it was intended to carry on this government, after the state government should be dissolved and abrogated? This clause is not only a proper, but a necessary one. I have already shown what pains have been taken in the Convention to secure the preservation of the state governments. I hope, sir, that it was no crime, to sow the seed of self-preservation in the federal government; without this clause it would not possess self-preserving power. By this clause the times, places, and manner of holding elections shall be prescribed in each state, by the legislature thereof. I think it highly proper that the federal government should throw the exercise of this power into the hands of the state legislatures; but not that it should be placed there entirely without control.

If the Congress had it not in their power to make regulations, what might be the consequences? Some states might make no regulations at all on the subject. And shall the existence of the House of Representatives, the immediate representation of the people in Congress, depend upon the will and pleasure of the state governments? Another thing may possibly happen, I don't say it will; but we were obliged to guard even against possibilities, as well as probabilities. A legislature may be willing to make the necessary regulations, yet the minority of that legislature may, by absenting themselves, break up the house and prevent the execution of the intention of the majority. I have supposed the case, that some state governments may make no regulations at all; it is possible also that they may make improper regulations. I have heard it surmised by the opponents of this Constitution, that the Congress may order the election for Pennsylvania to be held at Pittsburgh, and thence conclude, that it would be improper for them to have the exercise of the power; but suppose on the other hand, that the Assembly should order an election to be held at Pittsburgh, ought not the general government to have the power to alter such improper election of one of its own constituent parts? But there is an additional reason still, that shows the necessity of this provisionary clause. The members of the Senate are elected by the state legislatures. If those legislatures possessed, uncontrolled, the power of prescribing the times, places, and manner of electing members of the House of Representatives, the members of one branch of the general legislature would be the tenants at will of the electors of the other branch; and the general government would lie prostrate at the mercy of the legislatures of the several states.

I will ask now, is the inference fairly drawn, that the general government was intended to swallow up the state governments, or was it calculated to answer such end, or do its framers deserve such censure from honorable gentlemen? We find on examining this paragraph that it contains nothing more than the maxims of self-preservation, so abundantly secured by this Constitution to the individual states. Several other objections have been mentioned; I will not, at this time, enter into a discussion of them, though I may hereafter take notice of such as have any show of weight. But I thought it necessary to offer at this time, the observations I have made; because I consider this as an important subject; and think the objection would be a strong one, if it was well-founded. [Lloyd, *Debates,* 44–48]

Wilson: I am willing, Mr. President, to agree with the honorable member who has just spoken [Robert Whitehill], that if this system is not calculated to secure the liberties and happiness of the United States, it should not be adopted; but, on the contrary, if it provides an adequate security for the general liberties and happiness of the people, I presume, it ought not to be rejected. Before I comment upon the principles which have brought us to this issue, I beg leave to make one general remark. Liberty and happiness have, sir, a powerful enemy on each hand—on the one hand there is tyranny, on the other, there is licentiousness. To guard against the latter, it is necessary that adequate powers should be given to the government, and to protect us from the former, it is requisite that those powers should be properly distributed. Under this consideration, let us now regard the proposed system; and I freely confess that if its adoption will necessarily be followed by the annihilation of the state governments, the objection is of very great force and ought to be seriously weighed. The inference, however, appears rather unnatural that a government should be expressly calculated to produce the destruction of other governments, upon which its own existence must entirely depend; for, Mr. President, it is capable of demonstration that if the state governments fall, the general government must likewise be involved in one common ruin. Is it not evident, sir, when we particularly examine the structure of the proposed system that the operation of the federal legislature necessarily presupposes the existence of the legislatures of the several states? Can the Congress, the President, or even the judiciary department survive the dissolution of those powers in the separate governments, from which they essentially derive their origin, and on which they must forever depend for their renovation? No, sir! For, we find that the House of Representatives is to be composed of persons returned by the suffrage of freemen who are qualified to vote for the members of the most numerous branch of the state legislature, which legislature must necessarily exist, or the only criterion for supplying the popular department of the federal government will be extinct. The Senate, which is to be chosen by the several legislatures, cannot consequently be appointed unless those legislatures exist; which is likewise the case in respect to the President, as this office is to be filled by Electors nominated by the respective state legislatures. And lastly, the judges are to be commissioned by the President and Senate, who cannot appoint, unless they are themselves first appointed, and that, it appears, must depend upon the existence of the state legislatures. Thus, Mr. President, by a clear deduction, it is evident, that the existence and efficiency of the general government presupposes the existence and full operation of the separate governments; for, you can never prove a person to have been chosen, till you have proved that he was the choice of persons qualified to vote; you cannot prove any man to be entitled to elect a member of the House of Representatives, till you have proved that he is qualified to elect a member of the most numerous branch of the state legislature. But, sir, it has been intimated, that the design of the Federal Convention was to absorb the state governments. This would introduce a strange doctrine indeed, that one body should seek the destruction of another upon which its own preservation depends, or, that the creature should eat up and consume the creator. The truth is, sir, that the framers of this system were particularly anxious, and their work demonstrates their anxiety, to preserve the state governments unimpaired—it was their favorite object; and perhaps, however proper it might be in itself, it is more difficult to defend the plan on account of the excessive caution used in that respect, than from any other objection that has been offered here or elsewhere. Hence we have seen each state, without regard to their comparative importance, entitled to an equal representation in the Senate, and a clause has been introduced, which enables two-thirds of the state legislatures at any time to propose and effectuate alterations in the general system. But, Mr. President, though in the very structure of the plan, the concomitant duration of the state governments is always presupposed, yet their power is not the only one intended to be recognized and established. The power of the people, sir, is the great foundation of the proposed system, a power totally unknown in the present Confederation, but here, it mediately pervades every department, and is immediately exercised in the House of Representatives. I trust it is unnecessary to dwell longer upon this subject; for, when gentlemen assert that it was the intention of the Federal Convention to destroy the sovereignty of the states, they must conceive themselves better qualified to judge of the intention of that body than its own members, of whom not one I believe entertained so improper an idea. Intended it, sir! how was this information obtained? I trust we shall not admit these visionary interpretations, but wisely judge of the tree by its fruit. The only pretense of proof, indeed, has been taken from the work itself, from that section which empowers the Congress to alter the place and manner of election under which, it is said, the national government may be carried on after the state governments are totally eradicated. This, Mr. President, is not only a proper, but a necessary power, for every government should possess the means of self-preservation. We have seen that the states may alter or amend the proposed system if they should find it incompatible with their interest and independency; and the same reason justifies and requires that Congress should have an ultimate control over those elections upon which its purity and existence must depend. What would otherwise be the consequence? One or more states might refuse to make any regulations upon the subject, or, might make such regulations as would be highly inconvenient and absurd—if the election were appointed to be held at Pittsburgh, or, if a minority, tumultuously breaking up the legislatures, should defeat the disposition of the majority to appoint any place for that purpose. Shall Congress have no authority to counteract such notorious evils, but continue in absolute dependence upon the will of a refractory state? I say not, sir, that these are probable events, but as they are certainly possible, it was the duty of the late Convention to provide against the mischief and to secure to the general government a power, in the *dernier resort,* for the more perfect organization of its constituent parts. In short, sir, this system would be nugatory without the provision so much deprecated, as the national government must be laid prostrate before any state in the Union, whose measures might at any time be influenced by faction and caprice. These, therefore, are the reasons upon which it is founded, and in spite of every perversion, it will be found only to contain the natural maxims of self-preservation. I shall take a future opportunity to remark upon the other points of the speech delivered by the member from Cumberland [Robert Whitehill] and upon the general principles of the proposed Constitution. Thus I have thought it proper to remark, in this early stage of the debate, because I am sensible that the imputation of subverting the state governments, either as a principle or a consequence of the plan, must, if well founded, prove a very important objection. [Dallas' Debates, *Pennsylvania Herald,* 19 December]

Wilson: That is a preposterous idea to suppose that this Constitution, when in operation, will annihilate the state governments; when the principle upon which it is founded, and by which it is to be supported, is the actual and active existence of the state governments.

The *Senate* can only be chosen by the respective state legislatures. Should the state *legislatures* be annihilated, *this Constitution* must fall with them.

4th section, 1st Article: If the Constitution did not make this provision, perhaps the state legislatures might not make any regulations, or if a majority of *virtuous* members were for this regulation, a [venal?] minority might *secede.* Therefore the *clause* was necessary for *self-preservation.* [Wayne's Notes, Cox Collection]

Wilson: If the state governments fall, the government of United States falls also, for there can be no election of Representatives unless there are elections in state legislatures, and the Senators can only be chosen by state legislatures. And each state has an equal vote. No state to be deprived of its equal suffrage in the Senate without its consent (Article 6) [i.e., Article V]. The President is to be appointed by Electors chosen by the legislature of each state. If the legislative and executive powers (which clearly depend on the *state governments*) cease to exist; the judicial power must cease also. [Yeates's Notes, PHi]

* * * *

JOHN SMILIE: I am happy, Mr. President, to find the argument placed upon the proper ground, and that the honorable member from the city [James Wilson] has so fully spoken on the question, whether this system proposes a consolidation or a confederation of the states as that is, in my humble opinion, the source of the greatest objection which can be made to its adoption. I agree likewise with him, sir, that it is, or ought to be, the object of all governments to fix upon the intermediate point between tyranny and licentiousness; and therefore, it will be one of the great objects of our inquiry to ascertain how far the proposed system deviates from that point of political happiness. For my part, I will readily confess that it appears to be well guarded against licentiousness, but I am apprehensive it has deviated a little on the left hand and rather invites, than guards against, the approaches of tyranny. I think however, Mr. President, it has been clearly argued that the proposed system does not directly abolish the governments of the several states because its organization, and, for some time perhaps, its operations, naturally presuppose their existence. But, sir, it is not said, nor is [it] thought, that the words of this instrument expressly announce that the sovereignty of the several states, their independency, jurisdiction, and power are at once absorbed and annihilated by the general government. To this position, and to this alone, the arguments of the honorable gentlemen can effectually apply, and there they must undoubtedly hold as long as the forms of state government remain, or, at least, till a change takes place in the Federal Constitution. It is, however, upon other principles that the final destruction of the individual governments is asserted to be a necessary consequence of their association under this general form. For, sir, it is the silent but certain operation of the powers, and not the cautious, but artful tenor of the expressions contained in this system that can excite terror or generate oppression. The flattery of language was indeed necessary to disguise the baneful purpose, but it is like the dazzling polish bestowed upon an instrument of death; and the visionary prospect of a magnificent, yet popular government was the most specious mode of rendering the people accessory to the ruin of those systems which they have so recently and so ardently labored to establish. Hence, sir, we may trace that passage which has been pronounced by the honorable delegate [James Wilson] to the late Convention with exultation and applause; but when it is declared that "We the people of the United States do ordain and establish this Constitution" is not the very foundation a proof of a consolidated government by the manifest subversion of the principle that constitutes a union of states, which are sovereign and independent except in the specific objects of confederation? These words have a plain and positive meaning which could not be misunderstood by those who employed them and therefore, sir, it is fair and reasonable to infer that it was in the contemplation of the framers of this system to absorb and abolish the efficient sovereignty and independent powers of the several states in order to invigorate and aggrandize the general government. The plan before us, then, explicitly proposes the formation of a new Constitution upon the original authority of the people and not an association of states upon the authority of their respective governments. On that ground, we perceive that it contains all the necessary parts of a complete system of government, the executive, legislative, and judicial establishments; and when two separate governments are at the same time in operation, over the same people, it will be difficult indeed to provide for each the means of safety and defense against the other, but if those means are not provided, it will be easily foreseen that the stronger must eventually subdue and annihilate the weaker institution. Let us then examine the force and influence of the new system and inquire whether the small remnant of power left to the states can be adequate even to the trifling charge of its own preservation. Here, sir, we find the right of making laws for every purpose is invested in the future governors of America, and in this is included the uncontrolled jurisdiction over the purses of the people. The power of raising money is indeed the soul, the vital prop of legislation, without which legislation itself cannot for a moment exist. It will, however, be remarked that the power of taxation, though extended to the general government, is not taken from the states individually. Yes, sir! But it will be remembered that the national government may take from the people just what they please, and if anything should afterwards remain, then indeed the exigencies of the state governments may be supplied from the scanty gleanings of the harvest. Permit me now, sir, to call your attention to the powers enumerated in the 8th section of the first Article, and particularly to that clause which authorizes the proposed Congress "to lay and collect taxes, duties, imposts, and excises, to pay the debts and provide for the common defence and general welfare of the United States." With such powers, Mr. President, what cannot the future governors accomplish? It will be said, perhaps, that the treasure, thus accumulated, is raised and appropriated for the general welfare and the common defense of the states; but may not this pretext be easily perverted to other purposes since those very men who raise and appropriate the taxes are the only judges of what shall be deemed the general welfare and common defense of the national government? If then, Mr. President, they have unlimited power to drain the wealth of the people in every channel of taxation, whether by imposts on our commercial intercourse with foreign nations or by direct levies on the people, I repeat it, that this system must be too formidable for any single state, or even for a combination of the states, should an attempt be made to break and destroy the yoke of domination and tyranny which it will hereafter set up. If, indeed, the spirit of men, once inflamed with the knowledge of freedom, should occasionally blaze out in remonstrance, opposition, and force, these symptoms would naturally excite the jealousy of their rulers and tempt them to proceed in the career of usurpation till the total destruction of every principle of liberty should furnish a fit security for the exercise of arbitrary power. The money which has been raised from the people may then be effectually employed to keep them in a state of slavish subjection. The militia, regulated and commanded by the officers of the general government, will be warped from the patriotic nature of their institution, and a standing army, that most prevailing instrument of despotism, will be ever ready to enforce obedience to a government by which it is raised, supported, and enriched. If, under such circumstances, the several states should presume to assert their undelegated rights, I ask again, what balance remains with them to counteract the encroachment of so potent a superior? To assemble a military force would be impracticable for the general government, foreseeing the attempt would anticipate the means, by the exercise of its indefinite control over the purses of the people; and, in order to act upon the consciences as well as the persons of men, we find it is expressly stipulated that every officer of the state government shall be sworn to support the Constitution of the United States. Hence likewise, sir, I conclude that in every point of rivalship, in every contention for power on the one hand, and for freedom on the other, the event must be favorable to the views and pretensions of a government gifted with so decisive a preeminence. Let us, however, regard this subject in another light. What, Mr. President, will be the feelings and ideas of the people when by the operation of the proposed system they are exposed to such accumulated expense for the maintenance of the general government? Is it not easy to foresee that however the states may be disposed individually to preserve the parade of independence and sovereignty, the people themselves will become indifferent, and at last, averse to the continuance of an expensive form, from which they derive no advantage? For, sir, the attachment of citizens to their government and its laws is founded upon the benefits which they derive from them, and it will last no longer than the duration of the power to confer those benefits. When, therefore, the people of the respective states shall find their governments grown torpid and divested of the means to promote their welfare and interests, they will not, sir, vainly idolize a shadow nor disburse their hardened wealth without the prospect of a compensation. The constitutions of the states having become weak and useless to every beneficial purpose will be suffered to dwindle and decay, and, thus if the governors of the Union are not too impatient for the accomplishment of unrivalled and absolute dominion, the destruction of state jurisdiction will be produced by its own insignificance. Having now, Mr. President, shown that eventually this system will establish a consolidated government, though the intention is not expressly avowed, I will take some notice of the honorable member's [James Wilson] principle culled from the mode of election which is here prescribed. Sir, we do not upon this occasion contend for forms which it is certain may exist long after the substance has forever perished. It is well remembered that the Roman senate continued to meet in all its ceremonies long after they had lost their power and the liberty of Rome had been sacrificed to the most horrid tyranny. Such, sir, must be the case with the state legislatures, which will necessarily degenerate into a mere name, or, at most, settle in a formal board of electors periodically assembled to exhibit the servile farce of filling up the federal representation. [Dallas' Debates, *Pennsylvania Herald,* 19 December]

Smilie: This Constitution goes too far in favor of tyranny. We admit that the *form* of the state governments must subsist, but their *efficiency* and *power* must be destroyed by the superabundant power of the general government.

It is not a federal government—not a confederation. It is a [complete?] government—legislative, judicial, executive. Its powers extend to almost all legislative acts, to *taxes*; and leave only to the states what they please. Article I, section 8: "collect Taxes"—"to make all Laws necessary &c." Who are to be the judges of what is necessary for the welfare of United States?

The state governments cannot make head against the general government. Power will not *lessen.* A power of appropriating money, raising armies, and commanding the militia. Could the state governments oppose this?

There will be a rivalship between the general and state governments. On each side they will endeavor to increase their power. Oaths to be taken to the general government. The state governments will lose the attachment of their citizens by losing their power. The people will not support them; but will suffer them to dwindle to nothing. The *forms* of *government* may subsist after the *substance* is gone as in the senate of Rome. The state elections will be ill-attended. The state governments will be *mere* electors. Will *one* consolidated government be a proper one for the United States? [Wilson's Notes, PHi]

Smilie: The federal government does not immediately abolish the state governments but eventually it will produce it. Instead of the word "People" in the Preamble, it should be "State." This shows the Convention intended to destroy the state governments. The general government have such extensive powers in point of taxation, that the states can do but little—they can only tax the little that is left, if anything. The power of raising armies, the power of Congress over the militia of each state, is formidable to liberty. If state governments cannot raise money enough to pay their officers, they will not serve those governments without salaries. The forms of government may subsist when the substance is gone as in the case of ancient Rome. [Yeates's Notes, PHi]

Smilie: This Constitution has fully guarded against *licentiousness,* but it had gone to the left hand, i.e., in favor of *tyranny.* It is a complete system of government in itself and not a *confederation.*

The powers of levying taxes, etc. takes away all power on that head from the state legislatures (8th section, 1 Article, *vide* the *first* and *last* paragraphs). If they have the power of laying and collecting taxes, they leave nothing to the state governments. The forms of government may exist after, long after, the liberties of the people are done away. Instance the *Roman* Republic when the *senate* were but a *name*—the senate—were hereditary or by the appointment of the prince.[(a)] [Wayne's Notes, Cox Collection]

> [Wayne's marginal note]
> (a) Answer: Who are the members that constitute this body—the *people* or their representatives? Can they do any act that they themselves are not bound by; and if they lay excessive *taxes,* the people will have it in their power to return other *men* (*vide* section 7th of 1st [Article] for the originating of *revenue bill*).

* * * *

THOMAS MCKEAN: The first objection offered, Mr. President, to the adoption of the proposed system arises from the omission of a bill of rights; and the gentlemen in the opposition have gone (contrary, I think to their former wishes, which were to discuss the plan minutely section after section) from the immediate objects of the first Article into an investigation of the whole system. However, as they have taken this wide and extensive path, I shall, though reluctantly, pursue them. It appears then, sir, that there are but seven nations in the world which have incorporated a bill or declaration of rights into their system of government. The ancients were unacquainted with any instrument of that kind, and, till the recent establishment of the thirteen United States, the moderns, except Great Britain and Poland (if the *Pacta Conventa* of that kingdom may be so considered) have not recognized its utility. Hence, sir, if any argument is to be drawn from the example of other countries, we find that far the greatest number, and those most eminent for their power and wisdom, have not deemed a declaration of rights in any degree essential to the institution of government or the preservation of civil liberty. But, sir, it has already been incontrovertibly shown that on the present occasion a bill of rights was totally unnecessary, and that it might be accompanied with some inconveniency and danger if there was any defect in the attempt to enumerate the privileges of the people. This system proposes a union of thirteen sovereign and independent states in order to give dignity and energy to the transaction of their common concerns. It would be idle, therefore, to countenance the idea that any other powers were delegated to the general government than those specified in the Constitution itself, which, as I have before observed, amounts in fact to a bill of rights—a declaration of the people in what manner they choose to be governed. I am happy, Mr. President, to find that no objection has been taken to the forms and structure of the proposed system, to the two branches of legislation, the unity of the executive power, and the qualified negative upon laws which is vested in the President. Objections on this subject, indeed, might easily have been answered since it is evident without the distribution of powers here made, the legislature would naturally have absorbed the authority of every other department, but particularly of the executive. It has, I am persuaded, been satisfactorily proved by my honorable colleague [James Wilson], that the suggestions which represent this system as being expressly calculated to annihilate the sovereignty and independence of the states are groundless and delusive; for he made it evident that the existence of the states is a thing without which the federal functions cannot be organized and supplied, and therefore, the dissolution of the individual and general governments must be concurrent—if the state legislatures fail, the Congress of the United States must likewise be at an end, inasmuch as the annihilation of that power which is alone competent to elect must be followed by the annihilation of the body which is the object of its election. But it is argued that the power of changing the time and place of elections transfers to Congress an authority which ought exclusively to reside in the respective states, and which will eventually enable that body to act independent of the several governments. In this respect, sir, it must be remembered that in the first instance the states are authorized to regulate the time, place, and proceedings of elections, and while they act with propriety there can be little reason to suppose Congress will officiously interfere. But, if, as it has been suggested by the honorable member from the city [James Wilson] an inconvenient situation should be appointed for holding the election, or if the time and manner should be made inconsistent with the principles of a pure and constitutional election, can it be doubted that the federal government ought to be enabled to make the necessary reform in a business so essential to its own preservation and prosperity? If, for instance, the states should direct the suffrage of their citizens to be delivered *viva voce,* is it not necessary that the Congress should be authorized to change that mode, so injurious to the freedom of election, into the mode by ballot, so happily calculated to preserve the suffrages of the citizens from bias and influence? This was one object, I am persuaded, which weighed with the late Convention in framing this clause; and we farther collect their solicitude to prevent, as much as possible, an undue influence of wealth and talents in the important choice of Representatives from that regulation which expressly declares that the day of election shall be the same throughout the United States. By this means it is evident that the influence which is naturally acquired by extraordinary talents, activity, and wealth will be restricted in its operation, and the great men of one district deprived of all opportunity to interfere in the elections of another. Reviewing then, sir, the objections to the power given to the proposed government for superintending the time, place, and manner of choosing its members, they seem to be the offspring of fancy, unsupported by real or probable argument, while the power itself is proved to be a wise and rational subject of delegation. It is next said, Mr. President, and it is reasoned upon as a fact, that the Congress will enjoy over the thirteen states, an uncontrolled power of legislation in all cases whatsoever; and it is repeated, again and again, in one common phrase, that the future governors may do what they please with the purses of the people, for there is neither restriction nor reservation in the Constitution which they will be appointed to administer. Sir, there is not a power given in the Article before us that is not in its expression, clear, plain, and accurate, and in its nature proper and absolutely necessary to the great objects of the Union. To support this assertion, permit me to recapitulate the contents of the Article immediately before us. First, then, it is declared that "the Congress shall have power to lay, and collect taxes, duties, imposts and excises, to pay the debts and provide for the common defence and general welfare of the United States." Thus, sir, as it is not the object of this government merely to make laws for correcting wicked and unruly men, but to protect the citizens of an extensive empire from exterior force and injury, it was necessary that powers should be given adequate to the discharge of so important a duty. But the gentlemen exclaim that here lies the source of excessive taxation, and that the people will be plundered and oppressed. What is there, however, that should render it a more dangerous trust in the hands of the general than of a particular government? For, is it not as much in the power of the state legislatures at this day to do all this mischief, as it will be hereafter in the power of Congress? The truth is, sir, that the great restraint upon excessive taxation arises from this consideration, that the same act by which a representative imposes a tax upon his constituents extends to himself and all his connections, friends, and acquaintances, so that he never will attempt to lay a greater burthen upon the people than he is convinced is necessary for the public service and easy to be borne. Besides this natural security, which applies equally to the individual and the general government of the states, the people will, from time to time, have it in their power to remove those persons who have promoted any measure that tends to injure and oppress them. In short, sir, it seems that the honorable members are so afraid the Congress will do some mischief that they are determined to deny them the power to do any good. But we must divest ourselves of this extravagant jealousy, and remember that it is necessary to repose some degree of confidence in the administration of a government from which we expect the revival of commerce, the encouragement of arts, and the general happiness of the people. To whose judgment, indeed, could be so properly referred the determination of what is necessary to accomplish those important objects, as the judgment of a Congress elected, either directly or indirectly, by all the citizens of the United States? For if the people discharge their duty to themselves, the persons that compose that body will be the wisest and best men amongst us; the wisest to discover the means of common defense and general welfare, and the best to carry those means into execution without guile, injustice, or oppression. But is it not remarkable, Mr. President, that the power of raising money which is thought dangerous in the proposed system is, in fact, possessed by the present Congress, though a single house without checks and without responsibility. Let us now proceed, sir, to the succeeding detail of the powers of the proposed government. That Congress shall have the power to borrow money on the credit of the United States is not objected to, nor are the powers to regulate trade, to establish a general rule of naturalization, and to enact uniform laws on the subject of bankruptcies. The power to coin money and regulate its value must be esteemed highly advantageous to the states, for hitherto its fluctuation has been productive of great confusion and fraudulent finesse. But when this power has established a certain medium throughout the United States, we shall know the extent and operation of our contracts, in what manner we are to pay, or to be paid; no illicit practice will expose property to a sudden and capricious depreciation, and the traveler will not be embarrassed with the different estimates of the same coin in the different districts through which he passes. The punishment of forgery and the establishment of post offices and post roads are subjects confessedly proper to be comprehended within the federal jurisdiction, and the power of securing to authors and inventors the exclusive right to their writings and discoveries could only with effect be exercised by the Congress. For, sir, the laws of the respective states could only operate within their respective boundaries, and therefore, a work which had cost the author his whole life to complete, when published in one state, however it might there be secured, could easily be carried into another state in which a republication would be accompanied with neither penalty nor punishment—a circumstance manifestly injurious to the author in particular, and to the cause of science in general. The next powers enumerated are those for constituting tribunals inferior to the Supreme Court, for defining and punishing piracies and offenses against the law of nations, and for declaring war, to which no objection has been made, and, I am persuaded, none can be made with reason and propriety. But, sir, the power to raise and support armies has occasioned infinite opposition and has been clothed in all the terrors which a jealous and heated imagination could conceive. Is it not necessary however, Mr. President, that some power should exist capable of collecting and directing the national strength against foreign force, Indian depredations, or domestic insurrection? If that power is necessary, where could it otherwise reside, what other body is competent to carry it effectually into operation? For my part, sir, I can perceive that the power is absolutely necessary to support the sovereignty and preserve the peace of the Union, and, therefore, I will not idly argue against its use from the possible abuse, an argument, which, as it applies to every other power as well as that under our immediate consideration, would supersede all the attributes of government and defeat every purpose of society. [Dallas' Debates, *Pennsylvania Herald,* 22 December]

Having thus, Mr. President, recapitulated the powers delegated by the proposed Constitution, it appears to me that they are necessary to the objects of the Union, and therefore entitled to our confirmation. Nor am I, sir, impressed with the opinion, which has given so much pain to the worthy gentlemen in the opposition, that the powers are so vaguely expressed, so indefinite and extensive in their nature that they may hereafter be stretched to every act of legislation, and construed to imply something beyond what is here specified. To evince that the powers enumerated in this Article are all the powers given to the proposed Congress, we need only refer to the clause in the section which I have just discussed [Article I, section 8] that grants to that body a right of exclusive jurisdiction in any district of ten miles, which shall hereafter, with the consent of the inhabitants, become the seat of federal government. Does not this clearly prove, sir, that their right of exclusive jurisdiction is restricted to that district, and that with respect to the United States at large, their jurisdiction must be measured by the powers actually contained in the instrument before us? For, no proposition can, surely, be more clear than this, that in every grant, whatever is not mentioned must, from the nature of the thing, be considered as excluded. But, sir, we are repeatedly told that, however specious the enumeration may be, yet by the sixth Article, a general authority is given to the acts of the proposed government which renders its powers supreme and unlimited. Let us attend to this assertion and compare it with the Article referred to. There it is said, Mr. President, that "this constitution, and the laws of the United States, which shall be made in pursuance thereof, and all treaties made, or which shall be made under the authority of the United States, shall be the supreme law of the land; and the judges in every state shall be bound thereby, any thing in the constitution or laws of any state, to the contrary notwithstanding." Now, sir, what does this prove? The meaning which appears to be plain and well expressed is simply this, that Congress have the power of making laws upon any subject over which the proposed plan gives them a jurisdiction, and that those laws, thus made in pursuance of the Constitution, shall be binding upon the states. With respect to treaties, I believe there is no nation in the world in which they are not considered as the supreme law of the land, and, consequently, obligatory upon all judges and magistrates. They are a common concern, and obedience to them ought to be a common duty. As indeed, the interest of all the states must be uniformly in the contemplation of Congress, why should not that body be authorized to legislate for all? I earnestly hope, sir, that the statutes of the federal government will last till they become the common law of the land, as excellent and as much valued as that which we have hitherto fondly denominated the birthright of an American. Such, Mr. President, are the objects to which the powers of the proposed government extend. Nor is it entirely left to this evident principle, that nothing more is given than is expressed, to circumscribe the federal authority. For, in the ninth section of the first Article, we find the powers so qualified that not a doubt can remain. In the first clause of that section, there is a provision made for an event which must gratify the feelings of every friend to humanity. The abolition of slavery is put within the reach of the federal government; and when we consider the situation and circumstances of the Southern States, every man of candor will find more reason to rejoice that the power should be given at all, than to regret that its exercise should be postponed for twenty years. Though Congress will have power to declare war, it is here stipulated that "the privilege of the writ of *Habeas Corpus* shall not be suspended, unless when in cases of rebellion or invasion, the public safety may require it"; and men will not be exposed to have their actions construed into crimes by subsequent and retrospective laws, for it is expressly declared that "no bill of attainder or *ex post facto* law shall be passed." Though Congress will have the power to lay duties and taxes, yet, "no capitation or other direct tax shall be laid, unless in proportion to the census or actual enumeration of the states, nor can any tax or duty be laid on articles of exportation." This wise regulation, sir, has been successfully practiced by England and Ireland; while the commerce of Spain by a different conduct has been weakened and destroyed. The next restriction on the powers of Congress respects the appropriation of the public funds. "For no money shall be drawn from the treasury, but in consequence of appropriations made by law; and a regular statement and account of the receipts and expenditures of all public money shall be published from time to time." What greater security could be required or given upon this important subject? First, the money must be appropriated by law, then drawn for according to that appropriation, and lastly, from time to time, an account of the receipts and expenditures must be submitted to the people, who will thus be enabled to judge of the conduct of their rulers and, if they see cause to object to the use or the excess of the sums raised, they may express their wishes or disapprobation to the legislature in petitions or remonstrances, which, if just and reasonable, cannot fail to be effectual. Thus, sir, if any power is given, you cannot in my opinion give less—for less would be inadequate to the great objects of the government, and would neither enable Congress to pay the debts or provide for the common defense of the Union. The last restriction mentioned prohibits Congress "from granting titles of nobility, and the officers of the proposed government from accepting without the consent of Congress, any present, emolument, office or title of any kind whatever, from any king, prince, or foreign state." The section which follows these qualifications of the powers of Congress prescribes some necessary limits to the powers of the several states; among which, I find with particular satisfaction, it is declared that "no state shall emit bills of credit, or make any thing but gold and silver coin a tender in payment of debts." By this means, sir, some security will be offered for the discharge of honest contracts and an end put to the pernicious speculation upon paper emissions—a medium which has undermined the morals and relaxed the industry of the people, and from which one-half of the controversies in our courts of justice has arisen. Upon the whole, Mr. President, I must repeat, that I perceive nothing in this system which can alarm or intimidate the sincerest friend to the liberties of his country. The powers given to the government are necessary to its existence and to the political happiness of the people—while the objections which are offered, arise from an evident perversion of its principles and the presumption of a meaning which neither the framers of the system nor the system itself ever meant. True it is, sir, that a form more pleasing and more beneficial to the State of Pennsylvania might be devised; but let it be remembered, that this truth likewise applies to each of our sister states, whose separate interests have been proportionally sacrificed to the general welfare. And after all, Mr. President, though a good system is certainly a blessing, yet the wealth, the prosperity, and the freedom of the people must ultimately depend upon the administration of the best government. The wisdom, probity, and patriotism of the rulers will ever be the criterion of public prosperity; and hence it is, that despotism, if well administered, is the best form of government invented by human ingenuity. We have seen nations prosperous and happy under monarchies, aristocracies, and governments compounded of these, and to what can we ascribe their felicity but the wise and prudent conduct of those who exercise the powers of government? For experience will demonstrate that the most perfect system may be so perverted as to produce poverty and misery, and the most despotic so executed as to disseminate affluence and happiness among the people. But, sir, perfection is not to be expected in the business of this life; and it is so ordered by the wisdom of Providence that as our stay in this world seldom exceeds three score and ten years, we may not become too reluctant to part with its enjoyments, but by reflecting upon the imperfections of the present, learn in time to prepare for the perfections of a future state. Let us then, Mr. President, be content to accept this system as the best which can be obtained. Every man may think and many a man has said, that he could make it better; but, sir, as I observed on a former occasion with respect to religion, this is nothing more than opinion, and every person being attached to his own, it will be difficult indeed to make any number of men correspond in the same objects of amendment. The excellent letter which accompanies the proposed system will furnish a useful lesson upon this occasion. It deserves to be read with attention and considered with candor. Allow me therefore, sir, to close the trouble which I have given you in discussing the merits of the plan with a perusal of this letter—in the second paragraph of which the reason is assigned for deviating from a single body for the federal government.

"In CONVENTION.

"SIR,

"We have now the honor to submit to the consideration of the United States in Congress assembled, that constitution which has appeared to us the most adviseable.

"The friends of our country have long seen and desired, that the power of making war, peace and treaties, that of levying money and regulating commerce, and the correspondent executive and judicial authorities should be fully and effectually vested in the general government of the union: but the impropriety of delegating such extensive trust to one body of men is evident—Hence results the necessity of a different organization.

"It is obviously impracticable in the federal government of these states, to secure all rights of independent sovereignty to each, and yet provide for the interest and safety of all—Individuals entering into society, must give up a share of liberty to preserve the rest. The magnitude of the sacrifice must depend as well on situation and circumstance, as on the object to be obtained. It is at all times difficult to draw with precision the line between those rights which must be surrendered and those which may be reserved; and on the present occasion this difficulty was encreased by a difference among the several states as to their situation, extent, habits and particular interests. In all our deliberations on this subject we kept steadily in our view, that which appears to us the greatest interest of every true American, the consolidation of our union, in which is involved our prosperity, felicity, safety, perhaps our national existence. This important consideration, seriously and deeply impressed on our minds, led each state in the convention to be less rigid on points of inferior magnitude, than might have been otherwise expected, and thus the constitution, which we now present, is the result of a spirit of amity, and of that mutual deference and concession which the peculiarity of our political situation rendered indispensible.

"That it will meet the full and entire approbation of every state, is not perhaps to be expected; but each will doubtless consider, that had her interests been alone consulted, the consequences might have been particularly disagreeable or injurious to others: that it is liable to as few exceptions as could reasonably have been expected, we hope and believe: that it may promote the lasting welfare of that country so dear to us all, and secure her freedom and happiness, is our most ardent wish.—With great respect, we have the honour to be, sir,

Your Excellency's most
obedient humble servants,
GEORGE WASHINGTON, President.

By unanimous Order of the CONVENTION."

I confess, sir, that reading this letter and examining the work to which it refers, though there are some points that I might wish had been otherwise, yet, upon the whole, I am struck with wonder and admiration, that this Constitution should have been rendered so unexceptionable as it is, and that so many men, the representatives of states differing essentially in their views and interests, should have concurred in presenting it to their country.[9] [Dallas' Debates, *Pennsylvania Herald,* 26 December]

McKean: There has been no objection to *two* branches in the legislature, nor to the mode of choosing them or the President.

The powers are *well-defined* and *necessary.*

The great guard against excessive taxation is that he that *lays, pays*—and frequent election.

To prevent mischief, we will not give the power of doing good.

Who are to [be] the judges? Those who are chosen because they are capable of being so.

Administration of government is of as much *practical* importance as its *nature.* [Wilson's Notes, PHi]

McKean: There are but 7 governments in the world who have a *bill of rights* and 5 of these are among the 13 United States.

The gentlemen contend that the Constitution will annihilate the state governments, yet they make no objection to the mode of *electing* the members, but to the *time* and the alteration, which may be made by Congress. It's proper that *Congress* should have that power to prevent the undue influence [of wealth and talents]. [Wayne's Notes, Cox Collection]

McKean: There are but 7 governments in the world which have a bill of rights.

The powers of Congress cannot be so safely vested in any other body—they are the objects of our own choice and have our confidence.

The enumeration of their powers exclude the rest *admissio unius est exclusio alterisis*. Their powers are absolutely to our existence as a confederate government. [Yeates's Notes, PHi]

1. Lloyd misdated the debate as taking place on 28 October.
2. Dallas' report of the debates on 28 November was printed in the *Pennsylvania Herald* on 8, 12, 15, 19, 22, and 26 December. Dallas' report was reprinted in full by the *Independent Gazetteer*, 10, 13, 18, 20, 24, and 27 December; the *Pennsylvania Packet*, 10, 13, 17, 20, 24, and 27 December. Excerpts were reprinted in the *Pennsylvania Journal*, 12, 15, and 19 December; *Carlisle Gazette*, 19 and 26 December; and eight newspapers in New York, Massachusetts, and Vermont.
3. Smilie's quotations are from articles I, III, IV, and V of the Pennsylvania Declaration of Rights in the Pennsylvania constitution of 1776 (Thorpe, V, 3082–83).
4. The reference is to the printed Assembly *Minutes* in which the Constitution was printed under the entry for 18 September 1787. Articles V and VI appear on page 223 of the *Minutes*.
5. On 12 September Elbridge Gerry and George Mason moved that a committee be appointed to prepare a bill of rights. The motion was defeated ten states to one (Farrand, II, 588). See also CC:75.
6. *The Constitutions of the Several Independent States of America. . .* (Philadelphia, 1781). This volume, printed by Francis Bailey "by order of Congress," was reprinted in Boston (1785) and New York (1786). The Virginia Bill of Rights was omitted in all three editions.
7. For the act of 30 December 1786, see CDR:VI, C.
8. A reference to the Septennial Act of 1716 which changed the term of members of Parliament from three to seven years.
9. For attacks on McKean's speech, see Mfm:Pa. 250, 301, and 371; and "Poplicola," Boston *American Herald*, 24 December; and "The Republican Federalist" V, *Massachusetts Centinel*, 19 January 1788.

Newspaper Reports of Proceedings and Debates

In the Convention on Wednesday last, the debates were chiefly confined to the question of a bill of rights for the Federal Constitution. In favor of it was said, it was common and necessary, that it existed in Great Britain, and that it would be an additional security for our liberties. Against it was urged, that bills of rights in England were a gift of the Crown, that the liberties of the people in that country originated with the king; but that the case was widely different in the United States. Here liberty originated with the people. Why then should the people by a bill of rights convey or grant to *themselves* what was their own inherent and natural right? It was further said, that only five of the thirteen states had bills of rights in their constitutions, and that even those were adopted at a time when we were ignorant of the nature and forms of government. Several objections were made by Mr. Whitehill to the Congress having the power of altering the times and places of electing the House of Representatives. To which Mr. Wilson replied, that it was necessary for Congress to possess this power, as the means of its own preservation, otherwise an invasion, a civil war, a faction, or *a secession of a minority of the Assembly* might at any time prevent the representation of a state in Congress.

It was further urged by Mr. Whitehill, that the Federal Constitution annihilated the state governments. To this Mr. Wilson replied, by observing, that the Congress and the state governments must stand or fall together, for that the election of the President, Senators, and House of Representatives all made the state governments essential to the very existence of Congress.

The speakers against the Constitution showed great ingenuity and zeal, while the advocates of it, Mr. Wilson and Mr. M'Kean, showed equal candor and a profound knowledge of the principles and forms of government. [*Pennsylvania Packet,* 30 November]

* * * *

On Wednesday Mr. M'Kean closed a long speech on the legislative Article of the new Constitution, with this striking observation. "Though a good system of government is certainly a blessing, yet it is on the *administration* of the best system that the freedom, wealth, and happiness of the people depend. DESPOTISM, if wisely administered, is *the best form of government invented by the ingenuity of man,* and we find that the people under absolute and limited monarchies, under aristocracies, and mixed governments are as contented and as prosperous as we are, owing, undoubtedly, to the wisdom and virtue of their rulers. In short, the best government may be so conducted as to produce misery and disgrace, and the worst so administered as to insure dignity and happiness to a nation."

On the same day, [Robert Whitehill][1] in an elegant, ingenious, and argumentative speech traced some of the leading defects in the Constitution and endeavored to show that, if not in express terms, yet by inevitable consequence, it would terminate in a consolidation and not a confederation of the states. To this objection (which Mr. Wilson agreed, if taken upon true grounds, was a very serious and important one), the argument respecting the necessary relation between the state legislatures and the federal branches of government was repeated, the latter of which could not exist, it was said, if the former were annihilated. "But," added Mr. Smilie, "let us review the history of Rome, and we shall find, after the most absolute and horrid tyranny was established on the imperial throne, the ancient forms of the commonwealth were preserved; its senate still met and were flattered with a show of authority, but we know the power and dignity of that once illustrious body were dwindled to a name. So, here Mr. President, the shadow of state government may long be retained when the substance is totally lost and forgotten."

"Liberty and happiness," says Mr. Wilson, "have a powerful enemy on each hand; on the one hand tyranny, on the other licentiousness. To guard against the latter, it is necessary to give the proper powers to government; and to guard against the former, it is necessary that those powers should be properly distributed." "I agree," replies Mr. Smilie, "that it is, or ought to be, the object of all governments to fix upon the intermediate point between tyranny and licentiousness; and, I confess, that the plan before us is perfectly armed to repel the latter, but I believe it has deviated too much on the left hand, and rather invites than guards against the approaches of tyranny." [*Pennsylvania Herald,* 1 December][2]

1. The *Herald* mistakenly attributed this speech to John Smilie instead of to Robert Whitehill.
2. Reprinted in the *Pennsylvania Packet,* 3 December, and, in full or in part, twelve times from New Hampshire to Georgia.

The Pennsylvania Convention
Thursday
29 November 1787

Newspaper Report of Convention Proceedings

The state Convention, having accepted an invitation from the German Lutheran Academy, attended the public commencement at the church in Race [Sassafras] Street on Thursday last. [*Pennsylvania Herald,* 1 December]

Timothy Pickering to John Pickering, Philadelphia, 29 November (excerpt)[1]

The Convention of this state is sitting; I am the member for Luzerne County. The Federal Constitution will be adopted by a great majority. The Antifederalists have got only about 22 votes out of 69 on some subordinate questions; and some of those, I have no doubt, will join the Federalists on the great question of ratification.

1. RC, Pickering Papers, MHi. On the same day that Pickering wrote this letter to his brother, he wrote his wife that "I cannot tell when the Convention will

rise, but not under ten days or a fortnight, as I should guess" (RC, Pickering Papers, MHi). A week later, on 6 December, Pickering again wrote his wife that "The Convention is still sitting; but I think will rise next week" (RC, Pickering Papers, MHi).

William Shippen, Jr. to Thomas Lee Shippen, Philadelphia, 29 November (excerpt)[1]

The Convention are now warmly engaged in defending and abusing the new Constitution. The speakers for it are Wilson, McKean, Chambers, Hartley and against it Smilie, Findley, and Whitehill. Upon a division yesterday on a motion of Whitehill to discuss it in a committee of the whole Convention—43 rose against it; 24 only for it. That I imagine will be the state of the vote when the question is put to adopt or reject it *in toto*—44 to 25, for it.[2] Altho it will be adopted here by so great a majority, it is by no means certain that 9 states will agree to it as it now stands. [Thomas] Lloyd is taking down the debates in shorthand and you shall have them as soon as published. The fear of anarchy and not having so good an one if this is rejected are the 2 great reasons that operate on men's minds, and altho I think this fear is imaginary, nothing can remove it. Never was there a finer field for the display of eloquence and abilities, than the opposition of this system affords.

1. RC, Shippen Family Papers, DLC. The remainder of the letter deals with personal family matters and the prospects of ratification in other states (CC:232n).
2. For similar predictions, see CC:314, 334.

The Pennsylvania Convention
Friday
30 November 1787

Convention Proceedings

The Convention met pursuant to adjournment,

And resumed the consideration of the first Article of the proposed Constitution. After some debate on the rate of representation prescribed in it, on the eventual operation of the powers therein granted to Congress, upon the state governments, and on the time for which revenues may be appropriated,

Adjourned until ten o'clock tomorrow, A.M.[1]

1. Although the Journals do not mention it, Henry Wynkoop moved to stop debate on the first Article of the Constitution and to begin a discussion of the

second Article. Apparently the motion was not seconded. See Newspaper Report of Proceedings and Debates, 30 November, below from the *Pennsylvania Herald.*

Convention Debates

ROBERT WHITEHILL: I confess, Mr. President, that after the full exercise of his eloquence and ingenuity, the honorable delegate to the late Convention [James Wilson] has not removed those objections which I formerly submitted to your consideration in hopes of striking, indeed, from his superior talents and information a ray of wisdom to illuminate the darkness of our doubts and to guide us in the pursuit of political truth and happiness. If the learned gentleman, however, with all his opportunities of investigating this particular system, and with all his general knowledge in the science of government, has not been able to convert or convince us; far be it from me to impute this failure to the defects of his elocution or the languor of his disposition. It is no impeachment of those abilities which have been eminently distinguished in the abstruse disquisitions of law that they should fail in the insidious task of supporting, on popular principles, a government which originates in mystery and must terminate in despotism. Neither can the want of success, sir, be ascribed to the want of zeal; for, we have heard with our ears, and our eyes have seen, the indefatigable industry of the worthy member in advocating the cause which he has undertaken. But, Mr. President, the defect is in the system itself, there lies the evil which no argument can palliate, no sophistry can disguise. Permit me, therefore, sir, again to call your attention to the principles which it contains, and for a moment to examine the ground upon which those principles are defended. I have said, and with increasing confidence I repeat, that the proposed Constitution must eventually annihilate the independent sovereignty of the several states. In answer to this, the forms of election for supplying the offices of the federal head have been recapitulated; it has been thence inferred that the connection between the individual and the general governments is of so indissoluble a nature, that they must necessarily stand or fall together, and, therefore, it has been finally declared to be impossible, that the framers of this Constitution could have a premeditated design to sow in the body of their work, the seeds of its own destruction. But, sir, I think it may be clearly proved that this system contains the seeds of self-preservation, independent of all the forms referred to; seeds which will vegetate and strengthen in proportion to the decay of state authority, and which will ultimately spring up and overshadow the thirteen commonwealths of America with a deadly shade. The honorable member from the city [James Wilson] has indeed observed that every government should possess the means of its own preservation; and this Constitution is possibly the result of that proposition. For, sir, the first Article comprises the grants of powers so superlative in their nature, and so unlimited in their extent, that without the aid of any other branch of the system, a foundation rests upon this Article alone for the extension of the federal jurisdiction to the most extravagant degree of arbitrary sway. It will avail little to detect and deplore the encroachments of a government clothed in the plenitude of these powers; it will afford no consolation to reflect that we are not enslaved by the positive dereliction of our rights; but it will be well to remember, at this day, sir, that, in effect, we rob the people of their liberties when we establish a power whose usurpations they will not be able to counteract or resist. It is not alone, however, the operative force of the powers expressly given to Congress that will accomplish their independence of the states, but we find an efficient auxiliary in the clause that authorizes that body "to make all laws which shall be necessary and proper for carrying into execution the foregoing powers, and all other powers vested by this constitution in this government of the United States, or in any department or office thereof" [Article I, section 8]. Hence, sir, if it should happen, as the honorable members from the city [Thomas McKean and James Wilson] have presumed, that by the neglect or delinquency of the states, no place and manner, or an improper place and manner for conducting the elections should be appointed, will it not be said that the general government ought not for this reason to be destroyed; and will it not therefore be necessary for carrying the powers of this Constitution into execution, that the Congress should provide for its elections in such manner as will prevent the federal business from being frustrated by the listless or refractory disposition of the states individually? This event is in a great measure provided for, indeed, by the plan itself; for, "the Congress may (constitutionally) at any time by law make or alter such regulations (that is the times, places, and manner of holding elections prescribed in each state by the legislatures thereof) except as to the places of choosing senators" [Article I, section 4]. If the power here given was necessary to the preservation of the proposed government, as the honorable members have contended, does it not, at the same time, furnish the means to act independent of the connection, which has been so often represented, as the great security for the continuance of the state sovereignties? Under the sanction of this clause, the Senators may hold their seats as long as they live, and there is no authority to dispossess them. The duration of the House of Representatives may likewise be protracted to any period, since the time and place of election will always be adapted to the objects of the

Congress or its leading demagogues; and as that body will ultimately declare what shall constitute the qualification of its members, all the boasted advantages of representation must terminate in idle form and expensive parade. If the voice of complaint should not then be silenced by the dread of punishment, easy it is nevertheless to anticipate the fate of petitions or remonstrances presented by the trembling hand of the oppressed to the irritated and ambitious oppressor. Solicitation will be answered by those statutes which are to be the supreme law of the land, and reproach will be overcome by the frown of insolent authority. This, Mr. President, is but a slight view of the calamities that will be produced by the exercise of those powers which the honorable members from the city have endeavored to persuade us it is necessary to grant to the new government, in order to secure its own preservation and to accomplish the objects of the Union. But in considering, sir, what was necessary to the safety and energy of the government, some attention ought surely to have been paid to the safety and freedom of the people. No satisfactory reason has yet been offered for the omission of a bill of rights; but, on the contrary, the honorable members are defeated in the only pretext which they have been able to assign, that every thing which is not given is excepted, for we have shown that there are two articles expressly reserved, the writ of *habeas corpus* and the trial by jury in criminal cases; and we have called upon them, in vain, to reconcile this reservation with the tenor of their favorite proposition. For, if there was danger in the attempt to enumerate the liberties of the people, lest it should prove imperfect and defective, how happens it, that in the instances I have mentioned, that danger has been incurred? Have the people no other rights worth their attention, or is it to be inferred, agreeably to the maxim of our opponents, that every other right is abandoned? Surely, sir, our language was competent to declare the sentiments of the people and to establish a bar against the intrusions of the general government in other respects as well as these; and when we find some privileges stipulated, the argument of danger is effectually destroyed; and the argument of difficulty, which has been drawn from the attempt to enumerate every right, cannot now be urged against the enumeration of more rights than this instrument contains. In short, Mr. President, it is our duty to take care that the foundation of this system is so laid that the superstructure, which is to be reared by other hands, may not cast a gloom upon the temple of freedom, the recent purchase of our toil and treasure. When, therefore, I consider it as the means of annihilating the constitutions of the several states, and consequently, the liberties of the people, I should be wanting to my constituents, to myself, and to posterity did

I not exert every talent with which Heaven has endowed me to counteract the measures that have been taken for its adoption. That it was the design of the late Federal Convention to absorb and abolish the individual sovereignty of the states, I seek no other evidence but this system; for as the honorable delegate [James Wilson] to that body has recommended, I am also satisfied to judge of the tree by its fruit. When, therefore, I behold it thus systematically constructed for the accomplishment of that object, when I recollect the talents of those who framed it, I cannot hesitate to impute to them an intention corresponding with the principles and operation of their own work. Finally, sir, that the dissolution of our state constitutions will produce the ruin of civil liberty is a proposition easy to be maintained, and which, I am persuaded, in the course of these debates, will be incontrovertibly established in the mind of every member, whose judgment is open to conviction and whose vote has not been conclusively pledged for the ratification of this Constitution before its merits were discussed. [Dallas' Debates, *Pennsylvania Herald,* 29 December][1]

Whitehill: The general government may subsist after the *abolition* of the state governments. The powers of Congress are unlimited and undefined. The Senators may hold their places as long as they live, and there is no power to prevent them.

Article 1, section 8, last clause gives the power of self-preservation *independent* of the several states; for in case of their abolition it will be alleged in favor of the general government that self-preservation is the first law.

The "Time" of election is in their power and therefore they may make it as long as they please.

There are *some reservations* in this government—why not more?

It was systematically intended to abolish the state governments. [Wilson's Notes, PHi]

Whitehill: That after the state governments is destroyed [etc.].[(a)] When vacancies happen, etc. the executive, etc.[(b)] They have the time, manner, and place (1st Article, section 4th). They have also the power of saying what the qualification of the electors [is]—£10,000.[(c)] Why destroy the foundation of the state governments?[(d)] [Wayne's Notes, MiU-C]

[Wayne's marginal notes]
(a) The election biennial.
(b) These vacancies may happen when the Assembly stand adjourned. Ought they not to *be filled*?
(c) 1 Article, 2d section: the qualification of the electors.
(d) The foundation is preserved entire and whole.

Whitehill: The seeds of self-preservation are so well sown in the federal system, that the same will overshadow all the state governments. [Yeates's Notes, PPIn]

* * * *

THOMAS HARTLEY: It has been uniformly admitted, sir, by every man who has written or spoken upon the subject, that the existing Confederation of the states is inadequate to the duties of a general government. The lives, the liberties, and the property of the citizens are no longer protected and secured; so that necessity compels us to seek beneath another system, some safety for our most invaluable rights and possessions. It is, then, the opinion of many wise and good men, that the Constitution presented by the late Federal Convention will in a great measure afford the relief which is required by the wants and weakness of our present situation; but, on the other hand, it has been represented as an instrument to undermine the sovereignty of the states and destroy the liberties of the people. It is the peculiar duty of this Convention to investigate the truth of those opinions and to adopt or reject the proposed Constitution, according to the result of that investigation. For my part, I freely acknowledge, Mr. President, that, impressed with a strong sense of the public calamities, I regard the system before us as the only prospect which promises to relieve the distresses of the people and to advance the national honor and interests of America. I shall therefore offer such arguments in opposition to the objections raised by the honorable delegates from Cumberland [Robert Whitehill] and Fayette [John Smilie], as have served to establish my judgment, and will, I hope, communicate some information to the judgments of the worthy members who shall favor me with a candid attention. The first objection is, that the proposed system is not coupled with a bill of rights, and therefore, it is said, there is no security for the liberties of the people. This objection, sir, has been ably refuted by the honorable members from the city and will admit of little more animadversion than has already been bestowed upon it in the course of their arguments. It is agreed, however, that the situation of a British subject and that of an American citizen in the year 1776 were essentially different; but it does not appear to be accurately understood in what manner the people of England became enslaved before the reign of King John. Previously to the Norman Conquest, that nation certainly enjoyed the greatest portion of civil liberty then known in the world. But when William, accompanied by a train of courtiers and dependents, seized upon the Crown, the liberties of the vanquished were totally disregarded and forgotten, while titles, honors, and estates were distributed with a liberal hand among his needy and avaricious followers. The lives and fortunes of the ancient inhabitants became, thus, subject to the will of the usurper, and no stipulations were made to protect and secure them from the most wanton violations. Hence, sir, arose the successful struggles in the reign of John, and to this source may be traced the subsequent exertions of the people for the recovery of their liberties, when Charles endeavored totally to destroy, and the Prince of Orange at the celebrated era of the British Revolution was invited to support them upon the principles declared in the Bill of Rights. Some authors, indeed, have argued that the liberties of the people were derived from the prince, but how they came into his hands is a mystery which has not been disclosed. Even on that principle, however, it has occasionally been found necessary to make laws for the security of the subject, a necessity that has produced the writ of *habeas corpus,* which affords an easy and immediate redress for the unjust imprisonment of the person, and the trial by jury, which is the fundamental security for every enjoyment that is valuable in the contemplation of a freeman. These advantages have not been obtained by the influence of a bill of rights, which, after all, we find is an instrument that derives its validity only from the sanction and ratification of the prince. How different then is our situation from the circumstances of the British nation? As soon as the independence of America was declared in the year 1776, from that instant all our natural rights were restored to us, and we were at liberty to adopt any form of government to which our views or our interests might incline us. This truth, expressly recognized by the act, declaring our independence, naturally produced another maxim, that whatever portion of those natural rights we did not transfer to the government was still reserved and retained by the people; for, if no power was delegated to the government, no right was resigned by the people; and if a part only of our national rights was delegated, is it not absurd to assert that we have relinquished the whole? Where then is the necessity of a formal declaration that those rights are still retained, of the resignation of which no evidence can possibly be produced? Some articles indeed, from their preeminence in the scale of political security, deserve to be particularly specified, and these have not been omitted in the system before us. The definition of treason, the writ of *habeas corpus,* and the trial by jury in criminal cases are here expressly provided for; and in going thus far, solid foundation has been laid. The ingenuity of the gentlemen who are inimical to the proposed Constitution may serve to detect an error, but can it furnish a remedy? They have told us that a bill of rights ought to have been annexed; but, while some are for this point, and others for that, is it not evidently impracticable to frame an instrument which will be satisfactory to the wishes of every man, who thinks himself competent to propose and obviate objections. Sir, it is enough for me that the great cardinal points of a free government are here secured without the useless enumeration of privileges under the popular appellation of a bill of rights. The second objection which I have been able to collect from the arguments of the honorable members in opposition is this, that annual elections are not recognized and established by this Constitution. I confess, Mr. President, the business of elections is a very important object in the institution of a free government; but I am of opinion that their frequency must always depend upon the circumstances of the country. In a small territory, an annual election is proper and convenient, but in a jurisdiction extending 1500 miles, through various climates, even if practicable, it would be an idle and burthensome arrangement. If, for instance, a delegate to the Congress were obliged to travel 7 or 800 miles to Georgia or Carolina, he could scarcely have entered upon the duties of his appointment before the year would be past and his authority annulled. Let us look at the nations in Europe, and by way of illustration let us suppose particularly that it was necessary in Denmark to meet in Copenhagen, the seat of government, from districts at the distance of seven hundred miles, would it not be proper to extend the period of service, in proportion to the time required for collecting the scattered members of the body politic? In England, indeed, a compact and cultivated country, through which the communication is never interrupted, an annual election might be productive of great advantages, and could be attended with few inconveniencies; but, as I have already represented, the case must here be essentially different. If then, this objection is answered, so likewise must be the objection which has been next offered, that the appropriation of public monies for the maintenance of a military force may be for a period of two years, whereas in England it is only for one; since the same reasons which made it necessary to deviate from annual elections, must render it necessary to extend those appropriations. The power granted to levy taxes is another subject for opposition; and, at first view, indeed, it may naturally excite some astonishment. But, Mr. President, it is necessary that those who are authorized to contract debts upon the public faith should likewise be invested with the means for discharging those debts. We have fatally experienced that recommendations are incompetent to that object, for what part of our foreign obligations have they hitherto been able to discharge? Let us, however, suppose, that by the operation of federal recommendations, it is possible to accomplish the payment of our existing debts—where is the faith so credulous that will advance us another shilling upon the same security?

But on the other hand, establish a power which can discharge its engagement, and you insure the confidence and friendship of the world. The power of taxation is then, a great and important trust; but we lodge it with our own representatives, and as long as we continue virtuous we shall be safe, for they will not dare to abuse it. We now come, sir, to the objection which seems to spread the greatest alarm, and in support of which much labor and ingenuity have been displayed. That the rights now proposed by the states will in some degree be abridged by the adoption of the proposed system has never been denied; but it is only in that degree which is necessary and proper to promote the great purposes of the Union. A portion of our natural rights are given up, in order to constitute society; and so it is here, a portion of the rights belonging to the states individually is resigned, in order to constitute an efficient confederation. But, Mr. President, I do not know any instance in ancient history exactly similar to the situation of this country. The allusion which was made by the honorable member from Fayette [John Smilie] to the Roman annals is incapable of a just application to the subject in discussion; for the senate, at the period to which he has referred, was not created by election, but appointed by the mandate of the prince. The power of life and death was exclusively possessed by the emperor, and the senate had no authority but what he pleased to bestow. In modern history there is indeed one event which seems to be in point. When the union was about to be formed between Scotland and England, in the reign of Queen Anne, wise men of all descriptions opposed the transaction, and, particularly, it was the subject of clamor among the clergy of every denomination. Lord Peterborough compared it to Nebuchadnezzar's image of iron and clay; and then, as it is now, the annihilation of the inferior power was warmly predicted by the wise men of the north. But, sir, those fears and prognostications have been dissipated and disappointed by the event, and every liberal Scotchman will acknowledge he has gained by the bargain. Let it now be remarked that though Scotland sends only forty-five members to the British Parliament, yet its judiciary and religious establishments being secured to them by the union, it has never been alleged that the superintending power has in any degree intruded upon those rights or infringed the general tenor of the compact. Here then is an instance of a kingdom preserved, even where the law is made and proceeds from a different and distant country. With respect to the German confederation, if anything can thence be drawn, it is an inference contrary to the doctrine contended on the part of the opposition. There, sir, a number of deputies meet in general diet and make certain laws which are to pervade the Germanic body. But has this general head subverted the independence and liberties of its constituent members? No, for, on the reverse, we find the House of Austria, a single branch, has become superior to the whole, except the king of Prussia, who is likewise formidable, but it is in his power and influence over the general system. Upon the whole, Mr. President, I sincerely think that the opinions of the worthy gentlemen are mistaken, and that their fears are vain and extravagant; for it is necessary that something should be done, and this plan, waiving any compliment to its excellence, is, at least, an eligible one. [Dallas' Debates, *Pennsylvania Herald,* 2 January]

Hartley: England became enslaved at the time of the Conquest. The power of *collecting* taxes is necessary. *Recommendations* have been insufficient. *Our Representatives* have this power. In the time of the emperors, *they* appointed the senate. [Wilson's Notes, PHi]

Hartley: The Norman Conqueror usurped the liberties of the people and hence arose the claims of rights by the *people,* but different in *America.* The power of collecting taxes ought to be vested in *Congress.* [Wayne's Notes, MiU-C]

* * * *

BENJAMIN RUSH: I believe, Mr. President, that of all the treaties which have ever been made, William Penn's was the only one, which was contracted without parchment; and I believe, likewise, it is the only one that has ever been faithfully adhered to. As it has happened with treaties, so, sir, has it happened with bills of rights, for never yet has one been made which has not, at some period or other, been broken. The celebrated Magna Charta of England was broken over and over again, and these infractions gave birth to the Petition of Rights. If, indeed, the government of that country has not been violated for the last hundred years, as some writers have said, it is not owing to charters or declarations of rights, but to the balance which has been introduced and established in the legislative body. The constitution of Pennsylvania, Mr. President, is guarded by an oath, which every man employed in the administration of the public business is compelled to take; and yet, sir, examine the proceedings of the Council of Censors and you will find innumerable instances of the violation of that constitution, committed equally by its friends and enemies. In truth then, there is no security but in a pure and adequate representation; the checks and all the other desiderata of government are nothing but political error without it, and with it, liberty can never be endangered. While the Honorable Convention, who framed this system, were employed in their work, there are many gentlemen who can bear testimony that my only anxiety was upon the subject of representation; and when I beheld a legislature constituted of three branches, and in so excellent a manner, either directly or indirectly elected by the people and amenable to them, I confess, sir, that here I cheerfully reposed all my hopes and confidence of safety. Civilians having taught us, Mr. President, that occupancy was the origin of property, I think, it may likewise be considered as the origin of liberty; and as we enjoy all our natural rights from a preoccupany, antecedent to the social state, in entering into that state, whence shall they be said to be derived? Would it not be absurd to frame a formal declaration that our natural rights are acquired from ourselves, and would it not be a more ridiculous solecism to say, that they are the gift of those rulers whom we have created, and who are invested by us with every power they possess? Sir, I consider it as an honor to the late Convention that this system has not been disgraced with a bill of rights; though I mean not to blame or reflect upon those states which have encumbered their constitutions with that idle and superfluous instrument.[2] One would imagine however, from the arguments of the opposition that this government was immediately to be administered by foreigners, strangers to our habits and opinions, and unconnected with our interests and prosperity. These apprehensions, sir, might have been excused while we were contending with Great Britain; but, at this time, they are applicable to all governments, as well as that under consideration; and the arguments of the honorable members are, indeed, better calculated for an Indian council fire than the meridian of this refined and enlightened Convention. [Dallas' Debates, *Pennsylvania Herald,* 5 January]

Rush: All bills of rights have been broken. There is no security for liberty but in *two* things—just *representation* and checks. The citizens of United States have the *preoccupancy* of liberty; shall they make a deed of confirmation to themselves? [Wilson's Notes, PHi]

Rush: Voltaire says that there is but one instance of a treaty not being broke, i.e., the one made by William Penn with the *Indians. Magna Charta* has often been broke, hence arose the claims of rights, etc. [Wayne's Notes, MiU-C]

* * * *

JASPER YEATES: 1st Objection: The want of a bill of rights.

Response: Our governments differ in their formation from England and therefore, tho necessary there, not so here. New Hampshire, Rhode Island, Connecticut, New York, New Jersey, South Carolina, Georgia, and perhaps Virginia have no bill of rights. Are they not free? Do they hold their liberties as tenants at will? But an enumeration would be dangerous; part might be omitted and therefore excluded. Whatever is not expressly ceded to the federal government is still reserved.

But it is said we have adopted part of the bill of rights, as in reserving the trials by jury in criminal cases, and directing that the privilege of the *habeas corpus* act shall not be suspended except in times of immediate danger.

Response: This is restrictive of the general legislative powers of Congress. They might claim this right if not restrained. Their powers being enumerated, it became necessary to make exceptions. This clause then does not form a bill of rights, but are the express exceptions from the general delegated powers of Congress.

2d Objection: The Federal Constitution annihilates all state legislatures and is intended for that purpose and vest Congress with too large and dangerous state powers.

Response: Candor and the character of the Federal Convention forbid the idea. The work does not justify the remark. But it has been shown if the state governments fail, so must the federal government. The Representatives must be chosen by persons voting for the most numerous branch of the state legislature. The state legislatures must choose the Senate and appoint Electors to choose a President. The judicial power depends on the Senate. The 4th section of the 4th Article guarantees a republican form of government to each state (read it).

As to the large legislative powers given to Congress, they are absolutely necessary to our existence and can be lodged in no hands so safely. *They are our choice.* Their existence depends on the choice of a House of Representatives, and should have power to make regulations to prevent factions. It is only intended that this power should be used when the state would either not use or abuse their power. Will we presume that Congress *will abuse this power*? It is not possible to define and lay down power so exactly, but that it may be abused. The elements of fire and water may be abused. But shall we renounce them because they may be abused?

The supreme power must be vested somewhere, but where so naturally as in the supreme head chosen by the free suffrages of the people mediately or immediately. The objects of state legislation are different from those of the Federal Constitution. They are confined to matters within ourselves. The latter embrace the general interests of the United States and conduct them into one common channel to enrich and render happy the citizens of the whole community. Could the states individually exercise the powers given to Congress? Could they carry them into execution? Could they propose an uniform system of commerce and trade? Witness the 5 percent *impost refused by* the State of *Rhode Island*.[3] Consider the circumstances if Congress had the power they are now proposed to have? This matter is taken up by the opposition as if Congress were a separate independent body deliberately determined on destroying the liberties of the people. Surely this is not fair. They have no separate interests from ourselves. They must feel every tax, every imposition. We can remove them if we please.

It is confessed the 10th section [Article I] abridges some of the powers of the state legislature, as in preventing them from coining money, emitting bills of credit, making legal tender, impairing the obligations of contracts, etc. But is [it] not proper that they should be so restricted? What have been the effects of tender laws, emissions of paper money, or the destruction of contracts? All faith has been destroyed amongst us; speculations of the most dangerous kind have been introduced. The principles of morality have been impaired; and if virtue is the foundation of a republic, we have been sapping it as fast as we could.

If state governments are prevented from exercising these powers, it will produce respectability, and credit will immediately take place. Laws respecting the general interests of trade will take place, commerce will flourish, shipbuilding will revive again, taxes will be lessened on the landed interest, the superfluities of life will be taxed, and the luxuries of the rich will defray a considerable part of the national burthen. We shall be respectable in the eyes of all Europe. Our credit will again extend itself. Foreigners will trust us. Congress alone with the powers given them by this system, or similar powers, can effect these purposes. [Yeates's Notes, PPIn][4]

Yeates: The objections hitherto offered to this system, Mr. President, may, I think, be reduced to these general heads: first, that there is no bill of rights, and secondly, that the effect of the proposed government will be a consolidation, and not a confederation of the states. Upon the first head, it appears to me, that great misapprehension has arisen, from considering the situation of Great Britain to be parallel to the situation of this country, whereas the difference is so essential that a bill of rights, which was there both useful and necessary, becomes here at once useless and unnecessary. In England a power (by what means it signifies little) was established paramount to that of the people, and the only way which they had to secure the remnant of their liberties was, on every opportunity, to stipulate with that power for the uninterrupted enjoyment of certain enumerated privileges. But our case is widely different, and we find that, upon the opinion of this difference, seven of the thirteen United States have not added a bill of rights to their respective constitutions. Nothing, indeed, seems more clear to my judgment than this, that in our circumstances, every power which is not expressly given is, in fact, reserved. But it is asked, as some rights are here expressly provided for, why should not more? In truth, however, the writ of *habeas corpus* and the trial by jury in criminal cases cannot be considered as a bill of rights, but merely as a reservation on the part of the people and a restriction on the part of their rulers; and I agree with those gentlemen who conceive that a bill of rights, according to the ideas of the opposition, would be accompanied with considerable difficulty and danger; for, it might be argued at a future day by the persons then in power—you undertook to enumerate the rights which you meant to reserve, the pretension which you now make is not comprised in that enumeration, and, consequently, our jurisdiction is not circumscribed.

The second general head respects the consolidation of the states; but I think, sir, candor will forbid us to impute that design to the late Convention when we review the principles and texture of their work. Does it not appear that the organization of the new government must originate with the states? Is not the whole system of federal representation dependent upon the individual governments? For, we find that those persons who are qualified to vote for the most numerous branch of the state legislatures are alone qualified to vote for delegates to the House of Representatives. The Senators are to be chosen immediately by the legislatures of the states; and those legislatures likewise are to prescribe the manner for the appointment of Electors who are to elect the President. Thus, sir, is the connection between the states in their separate and aggregate capacity preserved, and the existence of the federal government made necessarily dependent upon the existence and actual operation of its constituent members. Lest anything, indeed, should be wanting to assure us of the intention of the framers of this Constitution, to preserve the individual sovereignty and independence of the states inviolate, we find it expressly declared by the 4th section of the 4th Article, that "the United States shall guarantee to every state in this union, a republican form of government." A constitutional security far superior to the fancied advantages of a bill of rights. It is urged, however, that all the security derived from this clause, and from the forms of representation, may be defeated by the exercise of the power which is vested in Congress to change the times, places, and manner of election. Sir, let it be remembered that this power can only operate in a case of necessity, after the factious or listless disposition of a particular state has rendered an interference essential to the salvation of the general government. But is it fair, is it liberal, that every presumption should impute to

Congress an abuse of the powers with which they are entrusted? We might surely on the ground of such extravagant apprehensions proscribe the use of fire and water—for fire may burn, and water may drown us. Is it, indeed, possible to define any power so accurately, that it shall reach the particular object for which it was given, and yet not be liable to perversion and abuse? If it is too much restrained it will certainly be incompetent; and, I am free to declare the opinion, that it is much better under a limited government to trust something to the discretion of the ruler, than to attempt so precise a definition of power as must defeat every salutary object which it is intended to produce. In what instance does it appear, after all, that the jurisdiction of the states will be abridged, except, indeed, in those respects from which the universal sense of mankind must forever exclude them. The general government will, and incontrovertibly should, be possessed of the power to superintend the general objects and interests of the country—the particular objects and interests of the states will still be subject to the power of the particular governments—and is this not a natural and necessary distribution of authority? What single state, for instance, is equal to the regulation of commerce? Have we not seen a sister republic [Rhode Island] by an obstinate refusal of the 5 percent impost [of 1781], involve the whole Union in difficulties and disgrace? To that refusal, indeed, may be ascribed our present embarrassments, and the continuance of a heavy debt, which must otherwise have been long since discharged. But what are the particular restrictions which this system imposes upon the authority of the states? They are contained, sir, in the tenth section of the first Article; and I appeal, cheerfully, to the candor of every man who hears me, whether they are not such as ought, for the sake of public honor and private honesty to be imposed. "No state shall enter into any treaty, alliance, or confederation, grant letters of marque and reprisal; coin money; emit bills of credit; make any thing but gold and silver coin a tender in payment of debts; pass any bill of attainder, expost facto law, or law impairing the obligation of contracts, or grant any title of nobility." These, sir, and some restraints in commercial affairs are the restrictions on the several states; we have little information from the fatal experience of past years, if we cannot perceive their propriety and rejoice in the anticipation of the beneficial consequences they must produce. What, Mr. President, has hitherto been the effect of tender laws, paper money, and iniquitous speculations these excrescences of a weak government naturally engendered? I wish not, sir, to afflict you with a painful recollection upon this subject; but it will be well to remember how much we have suffered, that we may properly estimate the hand which rescues us from poverty and disgrace. If virtue is the foundation of a republican government, has it not been fatally sapped by these means? The morals of the people have been almost sunk into depravity; and the government of laws has been almost superseded by a licentious anarchy. The day of reformation and happiness, however, rapidly approaches, and this system will be, at length, the glorious instrument of our political salvation. For, under the authority here given, our commerce will be rendered respectable among the nations of the world; the product of the impost will ease the weight of internal taxation; the land tax will be diminished; and the luxuries and conveniences of life bear a proportionate share in the public expenses. In short, sir, I perceive nothing in this system to terrify, but everything to flatter the hopes of a friend to his country, and I sincerely hope it will be adopted. [Dallas' Debates, *Pennsylvania Herald,* 5 January][5]

Yeates: Objections reducible to 2 heads—want of bill of rights—abolition of state governments.

4 Article, 4 section: Guarantee of republican government.

Power *must* be given. All power *may* be abused.

The restrictions in Article 1, section 10 will revive our commerce, restore public credit, lessen taxes. [Wilson's Notes, PHi]

Yeates: The objections are reduced to two heads—a bill of rights and the annihilation of the state constitutions. 4th Article, 4 section guarantees to each state a republican form of government. 1 Article, 10th section the same as is granted in the Confederation, Article 6th. [Wayne's Notes, MiU-C]

* * * *

WILLIAM FINDLEY: The observations made relate to what is, and what is not in the system. I confine myself to answering the remarks that have been made this forenoon.

The natural course of power is to make the many slaves to the few. This is verified by universal experience. England had always the common law. Its Charter will not apply to us. Bills of rights were great improvements there. Government will construe its own powers so as to suit its own *wishes,* which it will call *necessities.* Because *all* securities are broken, shall we have *none*? Is it not a new doctrine that, because a good government, ill-administered, produces mischief, therefore we ought to be indifferent about it? Powers *given*—powers reserved—ought to be *all* enumerated. Let us add a bill of rights to our other securities.

In Britain the appropriations are *annual.* Annual elections are absolutely necessary in this government that is not merely federal. The Senate, the principal branch, is elected for 6 years, and removes responsibility far. Number of Representatives too small. There should be more in this new and thinly settled country than in one old and populous. Pennsylvania will not have any Representatives far from Philadelphia.

This is not a *confederate* but a *consolidating* government. We ought to suppose that Congress will *abuse* its powers. The powers of the general government extend to *state* and *internal* purposes. [Wilson's Notes, PHi]

Findley: That what is not expressly given away is retained may in part be true, but not conclusive. Have we any security for an equal representation?[(a)] [Wayne's Notes, MiU-C]

> [Wayne's marginal note]
> (a) From the gentleman's argument, the Representatives may be proper for Philadelphia, but not large enough, etc. [for Pennsylvania?]. Charters had better not be mentioned. That governments all tend to enslave the people—goes *against* all *government*. The principle of despotic governments is fear.

Findley: The number of Representatives is much too few for so large a country as America.

Does any state who has a bill of rights complain of it? [Yeates's Notes, PPIn]

* * * *

BENJAMIN RUSH: Our rights are not yet all known. Why should we attempt to enumerate them? [Wilson's Notes, PHi]

* * * *

HENRY WYNKOOP moved, after some debate, that the second Article should be taken into consideration. [*Pennsylvania Herald,* 1 December]

* * * *

JOHN SMILIE: On this, Mr. Smilie observed, that he hoped so precipitate a measure would not be adopted, for, in his opinion they had not yet got over the first six words of the Preamble. [*Pennsylvania Herald,* 1 December][6]

Smilie: The state of Virginia has a bill of rights. Reads a volume of *The Remembrancer* for this purpose.[7] Says he has a French translation of it. [Yeates's Notes, PPIn]

Smilie: In *The Remembrancer* there is a bill of rights of Virginia. [Wilson's Notes, PHi]

Smilie: *Remembrancer* 2nd. Page 21 Virga. B of R—p215-p221. We have not proceeded further than the first *six words*. I wish the gentleman W[ilson] would answer the objections. [Wayne's Notes, MiU-C]

* * * *

JAMES WILSON: It's my duty, and I intend to give answers when I hear any objection worthy of an answer. Until I hear much stronger reasons, I shall not trouble the Convention with any further observations. [Wayne's Notes, MiU-C]

Wilson: I wish to hear and subsequently answer every objection against the new Constitution. [Yeates's Notes, PPIn][8]

* * * *

THOMAS MCKEAN: The gentleman [William Findley] who complains of the smallness of representation in the Union should tell us in what ratio the people should be represented instead of 30,000 for 1. Formerly representation was in this state as 750 to 1, now it is 1,000 to 1 and, perhaps in a few years, it will be 2,000 to 1. This is all matter of opinion. [Yeates's Notes, PPIn]

McKean: I wish to see what kind of bill of rights those gentlemen would propose. [Wilson's Notes, PHi]

* * * *

JOHN SMILIE: We will exhibit a bill of rights, if the Convention will receive it. (1) Great point—Is a bill of rights necessary? (2) Does this system abolish the state governments? Direct taxation, poll tax, standing army are objections.

Freedom almost unknown in the Old World. Are we to go there for precedents of liberty? Bill of rights necessary as the instrument of *original compact* and to mention the rights reservèd. The sovereignty and independence of the states should be reserved. There must be a people before there is a king; and the people, in the first instance, have inherent and inalienable rights. We ought to know what rights we *surrender*, and what we *retain*.

Suppose Congress to pass an act for the punishment of libels and restrain the liberty of the press, for they are warranted to do this. What security would a printer have, tried in one of their courts? An aristocratical government cannot bear the liberty of the press.

The Senate will swallow up any thing. What harm from a bill of rights? [Wilson's Notes, PHi]

Smilie: Pledges himself to offer a bill of rights—that bill of rights will [not] destroy the Constitution.

Two objections: 1st no safety without a bill of rights, (2) whether this is a consolidation or a confederation, (3) to a direct tax, (4) to a standing army. [Wayne's Notes, Cox Collection]

Smilie: 1st Objection. Want of a bill of rights.

2. The government is a consolidated one and will swallow up the state legislatures.

We shall object to direct taxation [and] to the power of keeping up standing armies. [Yeates's Notes, PPIn][9]

* * * *

JAMES WILSON: It is objected that the number of members in the House of Representatives is too small. This is a subject something embarrassing, and the Convention who framed the Article felt the embarrassment. Take either side of the question, and you are necessarily led into difficulties. A large representation, sir, draws along with it a great expense. We all know that expense is offered as an objection to this system of government, and certainly had the representation been greater, the clamor would have been on that side, and perhaps, with some degree of justice. But the expense is not the sole objection; it is the opinion of some writers, that a deliberative body ought not to consist of more than one hundred members. I think, however, that there might be safety and propriety in going beyond that number; but certainly there is some number so large, that it would be improper to increase them beyond it. The British House of Commons consists of upwards of five hundred. The Senate of Rome consisted, it is said, at some times, of one thousand members. This last number is certainly too great.

The Convention endeavored to steer a middle course, and when we consider the scale on which they formed their calculation, there are strong reasons why the representation should not have been larger. On the ratio that they have fixed, of one for every thirty thousand, and according to the generally received opinion of the increase of population throughout the United States, the present number of their inhabitants will be doubled in twenty-five years, and according to that progressive proportion, and the ratio of one member for thirty thousand inhabitants, the House of Representatives will, within a single century, consist of more than six hundred members; permit me to add a further observation on the numbers—that a large number is not so necessary in this case, as in the cases of state legislatures. In them there ought to be a representation sufficient to declare the situation of every county, town, and district; and if of every individual, so much the better, because their legislative powers extend to the particular interest and convenience of each, but in the general government, its objects are enumerated and are not confined in their causes or operations to a county, or even to a single state. No one power is of such a nature, as to require the minute knowledge of situations and circumstances necessary in state governments, possessed of general legislative authority; these were the reasons, sir, that I believe had influence on the Convention to agree to the number of thirty thousand, and when the inconveniencies and conveniencies on both sides are compared, it would be difficult to say what would be a number more unexceptionable. [Lloyd, *Debates,* 48–49]

Wilson: A large representation draws after it heavy expense. A deliberative body may be too large. I won't say it may not exceed 100. Great difficulties arose on this question in Convention. If we suppose, according to the common calculation, that the numbers of people in the United States double every 25 years, in the course of one century, according to the best accounts we have of our state of population, the number of Representatives in the Federal Constitution will amount to about 600 persons. Carrying our views therefore to a distant period, it appears that the ratio of 30,000 for 1 will not be improper. [Yeates's Notes, PPIn]

1. Dallas' report of debates on 30 November was published in the *Pennsylvania Herald,* 29 December, and 2 and 5 January 1788. It was reprinted in the *Independent Gazetteer* and the *Pennsylvania Packet,* 31 December, and 3 and 7 January. The *Pennsylvania Chronicle* reprinted a portion of Dallas' report on 31 January and 6 February.

2. William Petrikin, a Cumberland County Antifederalist, asked if Rush should not be rewarded for "such candid declarations with a suit of tar and feathers, or with a hempen neck-lace" (Mfm:Pa. 661). For another attack on Rush's speech, see Mfm:Pa. 308. Rush's argument was repeated by "One of the People" in the *Pennsylvania Gazette,* 9 January (Mfm:Pa. 314).

3. See CDR:IV, A for the Impost of 1781.

4. This manuscript in Yeates's handwriting is endorsed "Notes of Speech delivered in Convention 30 Novr. 1787."

5. Dallas' full reports of the debates (except for those on 12 December) end with his report of the first part of the debates on 30 November which was published in the *Pennsylvania Herald* on 5 January 1788. Shortly thereafter he was fired as editor of the *Herald.* For Federalist opposition to Dallas and his dismissal, see the Note on Sources.

6. The *Pennsylvania Herald's* summary of the day's proceedings is printed at the end of the debates for the day.

7. *The Remembrancer; or, Impartial Repository of Public Events. Part II. For the year 1776,* III (London, 1776), 221–22, printed the Virginia Bill of Rights. In the debates on 28 November Wilson had denied that Virginia had a bill of rights. Smilie brought in the *Remembrancer* to prove that Wilson and others were wrong.

8. Yeates's notes are dated "December 4," but clearly they concern the debates on 30 November.

9. As in the note above, Yeates's notes of Smilie's speech relate to the debates on 30 November.

Newspaper Report of Proceedings and Debates

Yesterday the Convention proceeded in their deliberations upon the first Article of the proposed Constitution, and Mr. Wynkoop moved, after some debate, that the second Article should be taken into consideration. On this, Mr. Smilie observed, that he hoped so precipitate a measure would not be adopted, for, in his opinion, they had not yet got over the first six words of the Preamble. He then reduced the present subject of discussion to two general heads, viz: 1st the necessity of a declaration of rights, and 2dly whether the plan was a consolidation or a confederation of the United States? After these points are ascertained, he observed, it would be proper to consider each section of the first Article particularly, in order to state the objections to the powers delegated to the Congress for imposing internal taxation, raising a poll tax, and maintaining a standing army in time of peace. The Convention adjourned at 2 o'clock.

Mr. M'Kean said yesterday in the Convention, that he wished the opponents of the proposed Constitution would not merely find out its defects, but state the remedies. Since they consider a bill of rights so essential, why do they not show us one that we may judge of its necessity? To this Mr. Smilie answered, he was happy to hear the idea suggested, for he had understood that the Convention did not mean to admit either additions or amendments, but let them agree to do this, and he pledged himself to produce such a declaration of rights and such other amendments as would conciliate the opponents of the plan in its present state, who wished not to reject it altogether, but to make it as secure as possible, in favor of the civil liberties of the people. [*Pennsylvania Herald,* 1 December][1]

1. The *Herald's* account was reprinted in the *Pennsylvania Packet,* 3 December and in nine newspapers from Massachusetts to Georgia. Two separate speeches by John Smilie seem to have been combined in the first paragraph.

The Pennsylvania Convention
Saturday
1 December 1787

Convention Proceedings

The Convention met pursuant to adjournment,

And resumed the consideration of the first Article of the proposed Constitution. After some debate on the liberty of the press, and on the legislative, executive, and judicial powers of the new government, it was agreed,

On motion of Enoch Edwards, seconded by James Wilson,

That the Convention, from and after Monday next, will meet twice a day, viz., at half after nine o'clock in the morning, and half after four o'clock in the afternoon.[1]

Adjourned until three o'clock on Monday next, P.M.

1. For complaints about the Convention's slow progress, see "A Farmer," 5 December; "One of the Gallery," 5 December; and "Ego," 8 December, all in II:F above. See also Mfm:Pa. 256, 257.

Convention Debates

TIMOTHY PICKERING: Our principal debate during the many days we have met has been whether the house should have a porch. Let us first take a survey of the mansion and see whether a porch be necessary. [Wilson's Notes, PHi]

Pickering: Moved that the members opposing the Constitution should keep to some kind of order with respect to their objections. Mr. Chambers seconded him. [Yeates's Notes, PPIn]

* * * *

STEPHEN CHAMBERS: The manner of debate is been very irregular and desultory.

"All Legislative Powers *herein* granted" (Article 1, section 1). [Wilson's Notes, PHi]

Chambers: The 1 section of the first Article limits the Congress to the powers therein granted. [Wayne's Notes, Cox Collection]

* * * *

WILLIAM FINDLEY: It has been the endeavor of many to paint our necessities highly—like persuading a man in health that [he] is sick. Our situation is such, that we are not hastened in point of time and necessity. We are enjoying liberty and happiness to a very great degree. Our difficulties arose from the requisition and heavy taxes laid in 1782.

This system not suitable to our necessities or expectations. Necessities: We could not enforce treaties, regulate commerce, and draw a revenue from it. This system goes to raise internal taxes—capitation, excises—to an extension of the judiciary power even to capital cases, a dependence of the state officers on the general government. This system is not such as was expected by me, by the people, by the legislatures, nor within their power.

It is a *consolidating government* and will abolish the state governments or reduce them to a shadow of power.

(1) From its organization: "We the People" not "We the States."[(a)] From this we could not find out that we were *United States.* The

sovereignty of the states not held forth, nor represented.[b] "Each Senator shall have one Vote." Under the present Confederation the state sovereignty is represented. In Congress they vote by *states*. A state can speak but one voice.

(2) From its powers: [Those] who can tax possess all other sovereign power. There cannot be two sovereign powers.[c] A *subordinate* sovereignty is no sovereignty. Will the people submit to two taxing powers? The power over elections gives absolute sovereignty—so of judging elections. The judicial powers are coextensive with the legislative powers. Oath of allegiance shows it to be a consolidating government. The wages paid out of the public treasury a proof of consolidated government. [Wilson's Notes, PHi]

[Wilson's marginal notes]
(a) "for the United States."
(b) "Sovereignty in the People."
(c) ~~County Taxes~~.

Findley: Draws a simile of a man in health, being by a combination of gentlemen persuaded that he was sick, which produced his *death*.[a]

The taxes fully adequate to pay the *interest* and *debts*.

My opinion is that the system is *unnecessary* and *improper*—it is not such as the people had a *right* to expect.

"We the people," not "the people of the United States," supposes us in a state of nature, and to a stranger it would appear that no states were in existence.[b]

The people [and] the assemblies are only electors, and when they have once elected, they have no power over the persons elected.[c]

The power to tax is only in the sovereign authority—there cannot exist two *sovereign powers* to tax.[d]

Judicial power: Was it ever known that *judges* took an oath to be bound by the laws of two sovereign *states*?

The wages paid out of the common stock is unequal and unjust as one state is 10 times greater than another.[e]
[Wayne's Notes, Cox Collection]

[Wayne's marginal notes]
(a) Is the present Confederation perfect? Is it in full health, etc.?
(b) *Vide* the first words of the Preamble: "We the People of the United States."
(c) Every two *years*—they have a power over one-third of the *Senators*.
(d) County taxes and counties similar to the 13 United

States. (The objection as to taxation is as absurd, when the present Constitution is in operation, as it would be for any one county in the state to object to being taxed by the other counties *because* the people of that county had not the app[ointmen]t, etc.)[1]
(e) In proportion to numbers is certainly just.
1st Objection. No *bill of rights*: We stand on higher and stronger ground than when the Declaration of Independence.
2[nd Objection.] Against taxation both *internal* and *external*: The State of Pennsylvania has the power of taxing, etc. yet the *counties* also exercise the right of *laying* and collecting *taxes*.
3[rd Objection.] No check to the Congress: The checks are effectual—the originating of money bills, the biennial elections, etc. [Congress] can do nothing injurious to their constituents, but what equally affect *themselves*.

Findley: The Constitution offered to us is a consolidated government and not a confederate republic. It will swallow up eventually all state governments. There is no sovereignty left in the state legislatures. [Yeates's Notes, PPIn]

Findley: On Saturday Mr. Findley delivered an eloquent and powerful speech to prove that the proposed plan of government amounted to a consolidation, and not a confederation of the states. Mr. Wilson had before admitted that if this was a just objection it would be strongly against the system; and, it seems, from the subsequent silence of all its advocates upon that subject (except Doctor Rush, who on Monday [3 December] insinuated that he saw and rejoiced at the eventual annihilation of the state sovereignties) Mr. Findley has established his position.[2] Previous to an investigation of the plan, that gentleman animadverted upon the argument of necessity, which had been so much insisted upon, and showed that we were in an eligible situation to attempt the improvement of the federal government, but not so desperately circumstanced as to be obliged to adopt any system, however destructive to the liberties of the people and the sovereign rights of the states. He then argued that the proposed Constitution established a general government and destroyed the individual governments, from the following evidence taken from the system itself. 1st. In the Preamble, it is said, *"We the People,"* and not *"We the States,"* which therefore is a compact between individuals entering into society, and not between separate states enjoying independent power and delegating a portion of that power for their common benefit. 2dly. That in the legislature each member has a vote, whereas in a confederation, as we have hitherto practiced it, and from the very nature of the thing, a state can only have one voice, and therefore all the delegates of any state can only give one vote. 3d. The powers given to the federal body for imposing internal taxation will necessarily destroy the state sovereignties for there cannot exist two independent sovereign taxing powers in the same community, and the strongest will, of course, annihilate the weaker. 4th. The power given to regulate and judge of elections is a proof of a consolidation, for there cannot be two powers employed at the same time in regulating the same elections, and if they were a confederated body, the individual states would judge of the elections, and the general Congress would judge of the credentials which proved the election of its members. 5th. The judiciary power, which is coextensive with the legislative, is another evidence of a consolidation. 6th. The manner in which the wages of the members is paid makes another proof, and *lastly* the oath of allegiance directed to be taken establishes it incontrovertibly, for would it not be absurd that the members of the legislative and executive branches of a sovereign state should take a test of allegiance to another sovereign or independent body? [*Pennsylvania Herald,* 5 December][3]

* * * *

JAMES WILSON: The secret is now disclosed, and it is discovered to be a dread, that the boasted state sovereignties will under this system be disrobed of part of their power. Before I go into the examination of this point, let me ask one important question. Upon what principle is it contended that the sovereign power resides in the state governments? The honorable gentleman [William Findley] has said truly, that there can be no subordinate sovereignty. Now if there cannot, my position is that the sovereignty resides in the people; they have not parted with it; they have only dispensed such portions of power as were conceived necessary for the public welfare. This Constitution stands upon this broad principle. I know very well, sir, that the people have hitherto been shut out of the federal government, but it is not meant that they should any longer be dispossessed of their rights. In order to recognize this leading principle, the proposed system sets out with a declaration, that its existence depends upon the supreme authority of the people alone. We have heard much about a consolidated government. I wish the honorable gentleman would condescend to give us a definition of what he meant by it. I think this the more necessary, because I apprehend that the term, in the numerous times it has been used, has not always been used in the same sense. It may be said, and I believe it has been said, that a consolidated government is such, as will absorb and destroy the governments of the several states. If it is taken in this view, the plan before us is not a consolidated government, as I showed on a former day, and may, if necessary, show further on some future occasion. On the other hand, if it is meant, that the general government will take from the state governments their power in some particulars, it is confessed and evident, that this will be its operation and effect.

When the principle is once settled, that the people are the source of authority, the consequence is, that they may take from the subordinate governments powers with which they have hitherto trusted them, and place those powers in the general government, if it is thought that there they will be productive of more good. They can distribute one portion of power to the more contracted circle called state governments; they can also furnish another proportion to the government of the United States. Who will undertake to say, as a state officer, that the people may not give to the general government what powers, and for what purposes they please? How comes it, sir, that these state governments dictate to their superiors, to the majesty of the people? When I say the majesty of the people, I mean the thing and not a mere compliment to them. The honorable gentleman [William Findley] went a step further and said, that the state governments were kept out of this government altogether. The truth is, and it is a leading principle in this system, that not the states only, but the people also shall be here represented. And if this is a crime, I confess the general government is chargeable with it; but I have no idea, that a safe system of power, in the government, sufficient to manage the general interest of the United States, could be drawn from any other source or rested in any other authority than that of the people at large, and I consider this authority as the rock on which this structure will stand. If this principle is unfounded, the system must fall. If honorable gentlemen, before they undertake to oppose this principle, will show that the people have parted with their power to the state governments, then I confess I cannot support this Constitution. It is asked, can there be two taxing powers? Will the people submit to two taxing powers? I think they will, when the taxes are required for the public welfare, by persons appointed immediately by their fellow citizens.

But I believe this doctrine is a very disagreeable one to some of the state governments. All the objects that will furnish an increase of revenue are eagerly seized by them; perhaps this will lead to the reason why a state government, when she was obliged to pay only about an eighth part of the loan-office certificates, should voluntarily undertake the payment of about one-third part of them.[4] This power of taxation will be regulated in the general government upon equitable principles. No state can have more than her just proportion to discharge—no longer will government be obliged to assign her funds for the payment of debts she does not owe. Another objection has been taken, that the judicial powers are coextensive with the objects of the national government. So far as I can understand the idea of magistracy in every government, this seems to be a proper arrangement; the judicial department is considered as a part of the executive authority of government. Now, I have no idea that the authority should be restrained, so as not to be able to perform its functions with full effect. I would not have the legislature sit to make laws, which cannot be executed. It is not meant here that the laws shall be a dead letter; it is meant, that they shall be carefully and duly considered, before they are enacted; and that then they shall be honestly and faithfully executed. This observation naturally leads to a more particular consideration of the government before us. In order, sir, to give permanency, stability, and security to any government, I conceive it of essential importance, that its legislature should be restrained; that there should not only be what we call a *passive,* but an *active* power over it; for of all kinds of despotism, this is the most dreadful and the most difficult to be corrected. With how much contempt have we seen the authority of the people treated by the legislature of this state—and how often have we seen it making laws in one session, that have been repealed the next, either on account of the fluctuation of party or their own impropriety.

This could not have been the case in a compound legislature; it is therefore proper to have efficient restraints upon the legislative body. These restraints arise from different sources. I will mention some of them. In this Constitution they will be produced, in a very considerable degree, by a division of the power in the legislative body itself. Under this system, they may arise likewise from the interference of those officers, who will be introduced into the executive and judicial departments. They may spring also from another source, the election by the people; and finally, under this Constitution, they may proceed from the great and last resort—from the PEOPLE themselves. I say, under this Constitution, the legislature may be restrained, and kept within its prescribed bounds, by the interposition of the judicial department. This I hope, sir, to explain clearly and satisfactorily. I had occasion, on a former day [24 November], to state that the power of the Constitution was paramount to the power of the legislature, acting under that Constitution. For it is possible that the legislature, when acting in that capacity, may transgress the bounds assigned to it, and an act may pass, in the usual *mode,* notwithstanding that transgression; but when it comes to be discussed before the judges—when they consider its principles and find it to be incompatible with the superior power of the Constitution, it is their duty to pronounce it void. And judges, independent and not obliged to look to every session for a continuance of their salaries, will behave with intrepidity and refuse to the act the sanction of judicial authority. In the same manner, the President of the United States could shield himself and refuse to carry into effect an act that violates the Constitution.

In order to secure the President from any dependence upon the legislature as to his salary, it is provided, that he shall, at stated times, receive for his services, a compensation that shall neither be increased nor diminished, during the period for which he shall have been elected, and that he shall not receive, within that period, any other emolument from the United States, or any of them.

To secure to the judges this independence, it is ordered that they shall receive for their services, a compensation which shall not be diminished during their continuance in office. The Congress may be restrained, by the election of its constituent parts. If a legislature shall make a law contrary to the Constitution, or oppressive to the people, they have it in their power, every second year, in one branch, and every sixth year in the other, to displace the men, who act thus inconsistent with their duty; and if this is not sufficient, they have still a further power; they may assume into their own hands, the alteration of the Constitution itself—they may revoke the lease when the conditions are broken by the tenant. But the most useful restraint upon the legislature, because it operates constantly, arises from the division of its power, among two branches and from the qualified negative of the President upon both. As this government is formed, there are two sources from which the representation is drawn, though they both ultimately flow from the people. *States* now exist and others will come into existence; it was thought proper that they should be represented in the general government. But, gentlemen will please to remember, this Constitution was not framed merely for the states; it was framed for the PEOPLE also; and the popular branch of the Congress will be the objects of their immediate choice.

The two branches will serve as checks upon each other; they have the same legislative authorities, except in one instance. Money bills must originate in the House of Representatives. The Senate can pass no law without the concurrence of the House of Representatives; nor can the House of Representatives without the concurrence of the Senate. I believe, sir, that the observation which I am now going to make will apply to mankind in every situation; they will act with more caution, and perhaps more integrity, if their proceedings are to be under the inspection and control of another, than when they are not. From this principle, the proceedings of Congress will be conducted with a degree of circumspection not common in single bodies, where nothing more is necessary to be done, than to carry the business through amongst themselves, whether it be right or wrong. In compound legislatures, every object must be submitted to a distinct body, not influenced by the arguments or warped by the prejudices of the other. And, I believe, that the persons who will form the Congress will be cautious in running the risk, *with a bare majority*, of having the negative of the President put on their proceedings. As there will be more circumspection in forming the laws, so there will be more stability in the laws when made. Indeed one is the consequence of the other; for what has been well considered, and founded in good sense, will, in practice, be useful and salutary, and of consequence will not be liable to be soon repealed. Though two bodies may not possess more wisdom or patriotism than what may be found in a single body, yet they will necessarily introduce a greater degree of precision. An indigested and inaccurate code of laws is one of the most dangerous things that can be introduced into any government. The force of this observation is well-known by every gentleman that has attended to the laws of this state. This, sir, is a very important advantage, that will arise from this division of the legislative authority.

I will proceed now to take some notice of a still further restraint upon the legislature—I mean the qualified negative of the President. I think this will be attended with very important advantages, for the security and happiness of the people of the United States. The President, sir, will not be a stranger to our country, to our laws, or to our wishes. He will, under this Constitution, be placed in office as the President of the whole Union, and will be chosen in such a manner that he may be justly styled THE MAN OF THE PEOPLE; being elected by the different parts of the United States, he will consider himself as not particularly interested for any one of them, but will watch over the whole with paternal care and affection. This will be the natural conduct to recommend himself to those who placed him in that high chair, and I consider it as a very important advantage, that such a man must have every law presented to him, before it can become binding upon the United States. He will have before him the fullest information of our situation; he will avail himself not only of records and official communications, foreign and domestic, but he will have also the advice of the executive officers in the different departments of the general government.

If in consequence of this information and advice, he exercise[s] the authority given to him, the effect will not be lost—he returns his objections, together with the bill, and unless two-thirds of both branches of the legislature are *now* found to approve it, it does not become a law. But even if his objections do not prevent its passing into a law, they will not be useless; they will be kept together with the law, and, in the archives of Congress, will be valuable and practical materials, to form the minds of posterity for legislation—if it is found that the law operates inconveniently, or oppressively, the people may discover in the President's objections, the source of that inconvenience or oppression. Further, sir, when objections shall have been made, it is provided, in order to secure the greatest degree of caution and responsibility, that the votes of both houses shall be determined by yeas and nays, and the names of the persons, voting for and against the bill, shall be entered in the journal of each house respectively. Thus much I have thought proper to say, with regard to the distribution of the legislative authority, and the restraints under which it will be exercised. [Lloyd, *Debates,* 49–55]

Wilson: Upon what principle can the gentleman [William Findley] defend the assertion of the supreme power being in the United States? The contrary is the fact; the supreme power is in and retained by the *people.*

The legislature may be restrained by the judicial department and by biennial elections. The President may be called the *man* of the *people.* [Wayne's Notes, Cox Collection]

Wilson: All sovereignty rests in the people. There is no sovereign authority in any state or in Congress. If the people have parted with their sovereign authority to the state legislatures, then this Constitution cannot be defended. [Yeates's Notes, PPIn]

* * * *

JOHN SMILIE: Has not Congress a power, or right, *to declare* what is a *libel*? That this government is a complete aristocracy. [Wayne's Notes, Cox Collection]

Smilie: Congress have authority to declare what is a libel (Article 1, section 8). A jury may be packed. [Wilson's Notes, PHi]

* * * *

WILLIAM FINDLEY: That the supreme power is, of right, in the people is true in all countries. *Cajole* the people. [Wilson's Notes, PHi]

Findley: It is no argument for the Federal Constitution to show that the legislature of Pennsylvania have passed laws which have been improper. [Yeates's Notes, PPIn]

* * * *

ROBERT WHITEHILL: Tho it is not declared that Congress have a power to destroy the liberty of the press; yet, in effect, they will have it. For they will have the powers of self-preservation. They have a power to secure to authors the right of their writings. Under this, they may license the press, *no doubt*; and under licensing the press, they may suppress it. Article 2 [I], section 6: The press is by this clause restrained; because the members shall not be questioned for speeches in *any other place*.

Amendments may be laid before Congress. [Wilson's Notes, PHi]

Whitehill: The Congress have the power of suppressing the liberty of the press entirely.[(a)] [Wayne's Notes, Cox Collection]

> [Wayne's marginal note]
> (a) The Congress shall have power to secure to authors the benefit of their writings [Article I] 8 section. Will the suppression of the press secure this benefit?

* * * *

DR. ENOCH EDWARDS:[5] I object to a bill of rights being brought in. [Yeates's Notes, PPIn]

* * * *

JOHN SMILIE: In the construction of a complete government all the necessary powers are given that are not restrained.

The Supreme Court shall have jurisdiction in cases when a state is a party. Crimes shall be tried by jury, ergo they have powers to declare. [Wilson's Notes, PHi]

Smilie: Congress have a power to restrain libels. [Yeates's Notes, PPIn]

* * * *

JAMES WILSON: The gentleman in opposition [John Smilie] strongly insists, that the general clause at the end of the eighth section, gives to Congress a power of legislating generally; but I cannot conceive by what means he will render the words susceptible of that expansion. Can the words, the Congress shall have power to make all laws, which shall be necessary and proper to carry into execution the foregoing powers, be capable of giving them general legislative power? I hope that it is not meant to give to Congress merely an illusive show of authority, to deceive themselves or constituents any longer. On the contrary, I trust it is meant that they shall have the power of carrying into effect the laws, which they shall make under the powers vested in them by this Constitution. In answer to the gentleman from Fayette (John Smilie) on the subject of the press, I beg leave to make an observation; it is very true, sir, that this Constitution says

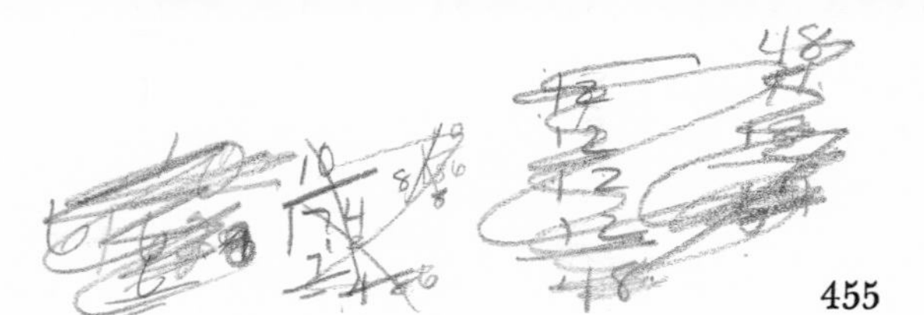

nothing with regard to that subject, nor was it necessary, because it will be found that there is given to the general government no power whatsoever concerning it; and no law in pursuance of the Constitution can possibly be enacted to destroy that liberty.

I heard the honorable gentleman make this general assertion, that the Congress was certainly vested with power to make such a law, but I would be glad to know by what part of this Constitution such a power is given? Until that is done, I shall not enter into a minute investigation of the matter, but shall at present satisfy myself with giving an answer to a question that has been put. It has been asked, if a law should be made to punish libels, and the judges should proceed under that law, what chance would the printer have of an acquittal? And it has been said he would drop into a den of devouring monsters.

I presume it was not in the view of the honorable gentleman to say there is no such thing as a libel or that the writers of such ought not to be punished. The idea of the liberty of the press is not carried so far as this in any country—what is meant by the liberty of the press is, that there should be no antecedent restraint upon it; but that every author is responsible when he attacks the security or welfare of the government or the safety, character, and property of the individual.

With regard to attacks upon the public, the mode of proceeding is by a prosecution. Now if a libel is written, it must be within some one of the United States or the district of Congress. With regard to that district, I hope it will take care to preserve this as well as the other rights of freemen; for whatever district Congress may choose, the cession of it cannot be completed without the consent of its inhabitants. Now, sir, if this libel is to be tried, it must be tried where the offense was committed; for under this Constitution, as declared in the second section of the third Article, the trial must be held in the state; therefore on this occasion it must be tried where it was published, if the indictment is for publishing; and it must be tried likewise by a jury of that state. Now I would ask, is the person prosecuted in a worse situation under the general government, even if it had the power to make laws on this subject, than he is at present under the state government? It is true, there is no particular regulation made, to have the jury come from the body of the county in which the offense was committed; but there are some states in which this mode of collecting juries is contrary to their established custom, and gentlemen ought to consider that this Constitution was not meant merely for Pennsylvania. In some states the juries are not taken from a single county. In Virginia, the sheriff, I believe, is not confined even to the inhabitants of the state, but is at liberty to take any man he pleases and put him on the jury. In Maryland I think a set of jurors serve for the whole Western Shore, and another for the Eastern Shore.

I beg to make one remark on what one gentleman [Robert Whitehill] has said, with respect to amendments being proposed to this Constitution. To whom are the Convention to make report of such amendments? He tells you, to the present Congress. I do not wish to report to that body, the representatives only of the state governments; they may not be disposed to admit the people into a participation of their power. It has also been supposed, that a wonderful unanimity subsists among those who are enemies to the proposed system. On this point I also differ from the gentleman who made the observation. I have taken every pains in my power, and read every publication I could meet with, in order to gain information; and as far as I have been able to judge, the opposition is inconsiderable and inconsistent. Instead of agreeing in their objections, those who make them bring forward such as are diametrically opposite. On one hand, it is said, that the representation in Congress is too small; on the other, it is said to be too numerous. Some think the authority of the Senate too great; some that of the House of Representatives; and some that of both. Others draw their fears from the powers of the President; and like the iron race of Cadmus, these opponents rise, only to destroy each other. [Lloyd, *Debates,* 55–57]

* * * *

WILLIAM FINDLEY: No opposition on *local* principles. This plan is *inimical* to our liberties. [Wilson's Notes, PHi]

1. The portion of Wayne's marginal note in parentheses is in the collection of his notes at the Clements Library, University of Michigan.

2. The statement in the *Pennsylvania Herald* on 5 December that William Findley had "established his position" that the Constitution provided for a consolidation rather than a confederation of the states was answered by "An Impartial Bye-Stander" in the *Herald* on 8 December: "it is insinuated that Mr. Wilson denied that the states were consolidated. He certainly acknowledged it to a certain degree, but he said upon many occasions that the new Constitution did not annihilate the state governments, but that it deprived them of their sovereignty, which he said both in the old and new government resides only in the *people.* In this opinion Doctor Rush [on 3 December] agreed with Mr. Wilson, and only added to it, that the exercise of this sovereignty happily was to be lodged by the new Constitution in Congress" (Mfm:Pa. 266).

3. This report of Findley's speech was reprinted in the *Independent Gazetteer* and *Pennsylvania Packet,* 6 December; *Pennsylvania Journal,* 8 December; and in thirteen newspapers from Maine to South Carolina.

4. Wilson is referring to the Pennsylvania funding act of 16 March 1785, which provided that the state pay both the interest and the principal on state and national securities owned by Pennsylvanians.

5. Edwards, a physician who served as an army surgeon during the Revolution, was a justice of the peace for Philadelphia County from 1777 to 1789 and a member of the state constitutional convention in 1789–1790.

The Pennsylvania Convention
Monday
3 December 1787

Convention Proceedings

The Convention met pursuant to adjournment,

And resumed the consideration of the first Article of the proposed Constitution. After some debate on the power vested in the President, by and with the consent and advice of two-thirds of the Senate, to make obligatory treaties, and a comparison of this power with the first clause of the first Article, and after some inquiry into the ninth section of the first Article,

Adjourned until half after nine o'clock tomorrow, A.M.

Convention Debates

BENJAMIN RUSH: (on the subject of the new government tending to abridge the states of their respective sovereignty) observed in the Convention, that this passion for separate sovereignty had destroyed the Grecian union. This plurality of sovereignty is in politics what plurality of gods is in religion—it is the idolatry, the heathenism of government. In marking the advantages which are secured to us by the new government, the Doctor principally enforced the following: that citizens under it will have an immediate voice in delegations to Congress; that an unoffending posterity will not (as is now the case on commission of treason) be punished for the sins of offending ancestors; that an eternal veto will be stamped on paper emissions; that religious tests would be abolished; that commerce will hold up her declining head under the influence of general, vigorous, uniform regulations; that a system of infinite mischief to this state would be counteracted; that the adopted certificates would devolve back to the continent. The Doctor concluded an animated speech by holding out the new Constitution as pregnant with an increase of freedom, knowledge, and religion. [*Pennsylvania Packet,* 5 December][1]

Rush: We sit here as representatives of *the people*—we were not appointed by the legislature.

A passion for state sovereignty dissolved the union of Greece. Britain—France—enjoyed more advantages *united* than *separate*. A plurality of sovereigns is political idolatry. The sovereignty of Pennsylvania is ceded to United States.

(1) I have now a vote for members of Congress;

(2) I am a citizen of every state;

(3) I have more security for my property; the weakness of Pennsylvania in the Wyoming business; the insurgents are Antifederal;

(4) no corruption of blood or forfeiture except. . . ;

(5) no paper money or tender laws;

(6) no religious test;

(7) commerce—its influence on agriculture;

(8) shipbuilding; iron mines;

(9) hemp;

(10) produce to load our vessels built—*one only* exists in the Southern—the *other only* in the Eastern States;

(11) the communication of the Mississippi with the Atlantic will be opened under the new Constitution. The members in Virginia from Kentucky are enthusiasts for this system.

By adopting the funding system we have assumed a great disproportion of the public debt. It must be thrown back on Congress. Distress general thro the country. [Wilson's Notes, PHi]

* * * *

William Findley and Benjamin Rush: Dr. Rush having frequently alluded with disapprobation to the funding system, in a late debate [3 December] Mr. Findley observed that the Doctor was one of the committee of public creditors who had conferred with a committee of the General Assembly upon this measure, and was at that time active in promoting it. The Doctor, for fear any unfavorable impression should be made by that assertion, observed that he did not think the system would have extended so far. [*Pennsylvania Herald,* 5 December][2]

* * * *

Benjamin Rush: The Doctor acknowledged that he had been active in procuring relief for public creditors; but that upon the appearance of the funding bill in its present form, he foresaw the extent of its mischief by including an overproportion of certificates from all the states to the injury of the original holders and by requiring paper money for its support. And that in consequence of this, he had opposed the bill in the committee, for which he was dismissed by the public creditors from their service, and Mr. Francis Wade elected in his room. The whole design of the Doctor's remarks on the funding bill was to show that the society of the public creditors, and the certainty of the interest being paid on their certificates, depended on the ratification of the proposed Constitution. ["An Impartial Bye-Stander," *Pennsylvania Herald,* 8 December][3]

* * * *

JOHN SMILIE: (1) It is admitted that the state sovereignty is given up.
(2) I never heard anything so ridiculous except a former [sentiment?] of the same gentleman [Benjamin Rush].
(3) Our preposterous commerce has been the source of our distress, together with our extravagance.
(4) We wish alterations made in the Confederation, but we wish not to sacrifice the rights of men to obtain them.
(5) Rights of conscience should be secured. They are so in the bill of rights of Pennsylvania. [Wilson's Notes,[4] PHi]

* * * *

WILLIAM FINDLEY: (6) A confederation and good government would be more to me and my family than wealth, honors, and offices.
(7) This a government of individuals, and not a confederation of states.
(8) Sovereignty is in the states and not in the people in its exercise.
(9) Vattel's description of sovereignty–it belonged originally to the body of the society (Vat. page 9. of the Sovereign).
(10) Vattel's description of a federal republic. If I am wrong, Vattel and Montesquieu are wrong (Vat. p. 11. [18] s. 10.).
(11) 1. Investigate the nature and principles of this government.
(12) 2. How will it apply to our security and interests?
(13) Gentlemen should first explain its principles.
(14) General interests are well secured.
(15) A single branch I will concede.
(16) I wish not to destroy this system. Its outlines are well laid. By amendments it may answer all our wishes.
(17) Notwithstanding the legislative power in Article I, section 1, the power of treaties is given to the President and Senate. This is branch of legislative power.
(18) Dark conclave. [Wilson's Notes, PHi]

* * * *

TIMOTHY PICKERING: According to common acceptation of words, treaties are not part of the legislative power. The king of Great Britain. [Wilson's Notes, PHi]

* * * *

WILLIAM FINDLEY: (19) The king of Great Britain makes laws *ministerially,* and the legislature confirms them.
(20) Ministers impeached for the Partition Treaty. [Wilson's Notes, PHi]

Findley: The king makes treaties ministerially and the legislature find difficulty in making *laws* to confirm them. [Wayne's Notes, Cox Collection]

* * * *

James Wilson: The President and Council in this Constitution makes the treaty ministerially. [Wayne's Notes, Cox Collection]

* * * *

John Smilie: (21) If the ministers of Great Britain make an inglorious conduct; they may be impeached and punished, but can you impeach the Senate before itself?
(22) If it is *ministerial*, the Senate are not here a legislature.
(23) Supreme laws cannot be made ministerially, but legislatively. [Wilson's Notes, PHi]

* * * *

Timothy Pickering: In Great Britain treaties are obligatory. [Wilson's Notes, PHi]

* * * *

John Smilie: (24) In Great Britain a law is frequently necessary for the execution of a treaty. [Wilson's Notes, PHi]

* * * *

Robert Whitehill: (25) When a treaty is made in Great Britain it binds not the people, if unreasonable. Treaties are binding by acts of Parliament and the consent of the people. [Wilson's Notes, PHi]

Whitehill: By this Constitution two-thirds of the Senate, "with the President," may make treaties to abolish the legislature of the United States as the section [Article VI] make those treaties the supreme law of the land in the *nature of things*. An inconsistency between the 1st and 2nd articles.[a] [Wayne's Notes, Cox Collection]

> [Wayne's marginal note]
> (a) Answer—Mon 2nd B 2 vol. [Montesquieu, I, 11–18].
> In this state the right of suffrage is secured paramount to the laws of this Constitution.

* * * *

James Wilson: Treaties in all countries have the force of laws. 1st. Blackstone [I, 252–57]. [Wayne's Notes, Cox Collection]

Wilson: Mr. Wilson said, that the manner in which the opposition treated the proposed Constitution, taking it by piecemeal without considering the relative connection and dependence of its parts, reminded him of an anecdote which occurred when it was the practice in churches to detail a single line of Sternhold and Hopkins's *Psalms*, and then set the verse to music. A sailor entered a church when the clerk gave out the following line: "The Lord will come, and he will not." The sailor stared, but when he heard the next line: "Hold your peace, but speak aloud," he instantly left the congregation, convinced that it was an assembly of lunatics. [*Pennsylvania Herald,* 5 December]

Wilson: Take detached parts of any system whatsoever, in the manner these gentlemen have hitherto taken this Constitution, and you will make it absurd and inconsistent with itself. I do not confine this observation to human performances alone; it will apply to divine writings. An anecdote, which I have heard, exemplifies this observation. When Sternhold and Hopkin's version of the *Psalms* was usually sung in churches, a line was first read by the clerk, and then sung by the congregation. A sailor had stepped in, and heard the clerk read this line: "The Lord will come, and he will not." The sailor stared; and when the clerk read the next line, "Keep silence; but speak out," the sailor left the church, thinking the people were not in their senses.

This story may convey an idea of the treatment of the plan before you; for although it contains sound sense, when connected, yet by the detached manner of considering it, it appears highly absurd. [*Pennsylvania Mercury,* 19 January][5]

* * * *

WILLIAM FINDLEY: (26) The President has a qualified negative.[6] This is *another* inconsistency. [Wilson's Notes, PHi]

Findley: My object is to point out inconsistencies in the Constitution. [Wayne's Notes, Cox Collection]

* * * *

BENJAMIN RUSH: In Great Britain the king alone makes the treaty. In the present Constitution the President and Senate make the treaty, *therefore* it is the act of the *states,* therefore the act of the whole people. [Wayne's Notes, Cox Collection]

* * * *

JAMES WILSON: Article 2, section 2nd: The power of the President and 2/3 of the Senate to *concur.* [Wayne's Notes, Cox Collection]

* * * *

JOHN SMILIE: (27) If the king of Great Britain makes a treaty contrary to act of Parliament, it cannot be executed till the law is repealed. We have not the same security here.

(28) If the Senate could be impeached as the British ministers may be; we would have more security. [Wilson's Notes, PHi]

* * * *

JASPER YEATES: I was absent for an hour. A desultory conversation took place. It was contended that an act of Parliament is necessary in England to confirm a treaty. [Yeates's Notes, PPIn]

* * * *

WILLIAM FINDLEY: (29) The manner of numbering the inhabitants is dark—"other Persons" (Article 1, section 2).
(30) Article 1, section 9, 1st clause: Migration, etc. is unintelligible. It is unfortunate if this guarantees the importation of slaves or if it lays a duty on the importation of other persons.
(31) This is a reservation; and yet the power of preventing importation is nowhere given. [Wilson's Notes, PHi]

Findley: Takes exceptions to the 9th section, 1 Article, that part admitting the importation of slaves.[a] [Wayne's Notes, Cox Collection]

> [Wayne's marginal note]
> (a) What were the Southern States to gain by the Constitution? No restraint in the *Articles* of *Confederation*. In this [Constitution] the restraint [is] 21 *years*. A duty amounting to a prohibition.

Findley: On Monday it was urged by Mr. Findley that Congress under the new system would have it in their power to lay an impost upon immigrants [*Pennsylvania Herald,* 5 December]

* * * *

JAMES WILSON: Much fault has been found with the mode of expression, used in the first clause of the ninth section of the first Article. I believe I can assign a reason, why that mode of expression was used, and why the term "slave" was not directly admitted in this Constitution; and as to the manner of laying taxes, this is not the first time that the subject has come into the view of the United States, and of the legislatures of the several states. The gentleman (William Findley) will recollect, that in the present Congress, the quota of the federal debt, and general expenses, was to be in proportion to the value of LAND, and other enumerated property, within the states. After trying this for a number of years, it was found on all hands, to be a mode that could not be carried into execution. Congress were satisfied of this, and in the year 1783, recommended, in conformity with the powers they possessed under the Articles of Confederation, that the quota should be according to the number of free people, including those bound to servitude, and excluding Indians not taxed.[7] These were the very expressions used in 1783,[a] and the fate of this recommendation was similar to all their other resolutions. It was not carried into effect, but it was adopted by no fewer than eleven out of thirteen states; and it cannot but be matter of surprise to hear gentlemen, who agreed to this very mode of expression at that time, come forward and state it as an objection on the present occasion. It was natural, sir, for the late Convention to adopt the mode after it had been agreed to by eleven states and to use the expression which they found had been received as unexceptionable before. With respect to the clause restricting Congress from prohibiting the migration or importation of such persons as any of the states now existing shall think proper to admit prior to the year 1808, the honorable gentleman [William Findley] says that this clause is not only dark, but intended to grant to Congress, for that time, the power to admit the importation of slaves. No such thing was intended; but I will tell you what was done, and it gives me high pleasure that so much was done. Under the present Confederation, the states may admit the importation of slaves as long as they please; but by this Article, after the year 1808, the Congress will have power to prohibit such importation, notwithstanding the disposition of any state to the contrary. I consider this as laying the foundation for banishing slavery out of this country; and though the period is more distant than I could wish, yet it will produce the same kind, gradual change, which was pursued in Pennsylvania. It is with much satisfaction I view this power in the general government, whereby they may lay an interdiction on this reproachful trade; but an immediate advantage is also obtained, for a tax or duty may be imposed on such importation, not exceeding ten dollars for each person; and this, sir, operates as a partial prohibition. It was all that could be obtained, I am sorry it was no more; but from this I think there is reason to hope that yet a few years and it will be prohibited altogether; and in the meantime, the new states which are to be formed will be under the control of Congress in this particular; and slaves will never be introduced amongst them.[8] The gentleman [William Findley] says, that it is unfortunate in another point of view; it means to prohibit the introduction of white people from Europe, as this tax may deter them from coming amongst us. A little impartiality and attention will discover the care that the Convention took in selecting their language. The words are, the *migration or* IMPORTATION of such persons, etc. shall not be prohibited by Congress prior to the year 1808, but a tax or duty may be imposed on such IMPORTATION; it is observable here, that the term migration is dropped when a tax or duty is mentioned; so that Congress have power to impose the tax only on those imported. [Lloyd, *Debates,* 57–59]

[Lloyd's errata]
(a) "*dele* 'these were the very expressions used in 1783'."

* * * *

ROBERT WHITEHILL: Mr. President: It has been said that Congress will have power, by the new Constitution, to lay an impost on the *importation* of slaves into these states; but that they will have no power to impose any tax upon the *migration* of Europeans. Do the gentlemen, sir, mean to insult our understandings when they assert this? Or are they ignorant of the English language? If, because of their ignorance, they are at a loss, I can easily explain this clause for them. The words "*migration*" and "*importation*" sir, being *connected* by the *disjunctive* conjunction "*or*," certainly mean either migration or importation; either the one or the other; or both. Therefore, when we say "a tax may be laid upon such *importation*," we mean, either upon the *importation* or *migration*; or upon both; for, because they are *joined together*, in the first instance, by the *disjunctive conjunction* "*or*," they are both synonymous terms for the same thing—therefore, "*such importation*," because the *comparative* word "*such*" is used, means both importation and migration. ["Puff," *Independent Gazetteer*, 6 December][9]

Whitehill: That migration and importation of persons are the same thing in section [9] of Article [I]. [Yeates's Notes, PPIn]

1. The *Packet's* account of Rush's speech was reprinted twice in Massachusetts and once in New York and in Maryland.

2. The *Herald's* report of debates on 3 December (Mfm:Pa. 266), from which the above is an excerpt, was reprinted, in whole or in part, three times in Pennsylvania and eleven times from New Hampshire to South Carolina.

3. "An Impartial Bye-Stander" (Mfm:Pa. 266) asserted that the Convention debates for 1 and 3 December (as reported by the *Pennsylvania Herald* on 5 December) contained "two mistakes." For the "first mistake," see Convention Debates, 1 December, n. 2. "The second mistake relates to Doctor Rush's reply to Mr. Findley upon the subject of the funding bill." Rush's speech, as reported by "An Impartial Bye-Stander," then follows.

4. Wilson began numbering all Antifederal objections consecutively on this day, ending with objection number 241 on 8 December. He then grouped the objections in general categories and answered them in a speech on 11 December.

5. The versions of the speech in the *Herald* on 5 December and in the *Mercury* on 19 January are the only accounts. "T.L." who was probably Thomas Lloyd, sent the version to the *Mercury* and stated that he had seen a publication about the 5th or 6th "purporting to be the language of Mr. Wilson, in justice to that gentleman, please to insert in your useful paper the following extract from the first volume of the *Debates of the Convention*, published by Thomas Lloyd." Lloyd's *Debates* were published three weeks later on 7 February and follow the *Mercury's* version word for word. There is no indication as to when Wilson made the speech, but it seems likely that it was an answer to Robert Whitehill's charge of inconsistency.

"Squib" in the *New York Journal* on 18 December declared that the "lines" quoted by Wilson from Sternhold and Hopkins were "not in that version of the Psalms, nor, I believe, in any other." "Squib" was correct. The lines are not in the original edition of Thomas Sternhold, et al., *The Whole Booke of Davids Psalmes. . .* (London, 1582), or in any of the reprints available in 1787. "Squib" was reprinted in the *Independent Gazetteer* on 27 December. For another attack on the speech see "Democritus," *New York Journal,* 28 December, Convention Debates, A.M., 11 December, n.1.

6. In a speech on the afternoon of 4 December, Wilson responded to Findley's charge that the President's qualified negative was inconsistent with Article I, section 1.

7. See Amendment to Share Expenses According to Population, CDR:IV, E.

8. The Northwest Ordinance, passed by Congress on 13 July 1787, prohibited slavery in the new states to be established in the territory northwest of the Ohio River (CDR:IV, K).

9. This version of Whitehill's speech was printed in the *Independent Gazetteer* at the beginning of an article signed "Puff" (probably Benjamin Rush). The speech was entitled "Substance of a speech, delivered by J________W_______ h_ll, Esquire, in Convention, on last Monday evening." However, Yeates credits Robert Whitehill, rather than John Whitehill with being the speaker, as does James Wilson in a speech on the morning of 4 December. "Puff's" version of the speech was followed by an attack on Whitehill's use of language (Mfm:Pa. 266). For a rejoinder to "Puff," see "One of the People," *Independent Gazetteer,* 11 December, Mfm:Pa. 266. For another attack on Whitehill's speech, see Mfm:Pa. 255.

The Pennsylvania Convention
Tuesday
4 December 1787

Convention Proceedings, A.M.

The Convention met pursuant to adjournment,

And resumed the consideration of the first Article of the proposed Constitution.

The President submitted to the Convention, whether the system under their consideration will not meet with a more full and expeditious investigation, by a general statement of the objections to it, and a subsequent reply to those objections. After some debate,

Adjourned until half after four o'clock, P.M.

Convention Debates, A.M.

JOHN SMILIE: (32) As the greatest part of the states have compound legislatures, I shall give up that point.

(33) I shall not object to the President's negative, for he will never be able to execute it. The king of Great Britain does not execute.

(34) Tho there be no separate *orders,* there is a *natural* aristocracy.

The Senate will represent *it*. House of Representatives will represent the common mass of the people.
(35) Are the rights of the people secured? Is the balance preserved? A comparison between the powers of the two houses.
(36) The number of the House of Representatives too small.
(37) They will not have the confidence of the people, because the people will not be *known* by them as to their characters, etc. Only 8 for Pennsylvania. The districts will be very large.
(38) The greatest part of the members even in this house will be attached to the natural aristocracy.
(39) This body will be subject to corruption; and the means of corruption will be in the Senate; for they have a share in the appointment of all officers.
(40) There will be people willing to receive bribes. The lower house may be corrupted, with offices, by the Senate; as the House of Commons are. There will be judges, tax gatherers, land waiters, tide waiters, excise officers.
(41) To the legislative power of the Senate are added some judicial power and an alarming share of the executive. They are to concur with the President in making treaties, which are to be the supreme *law of the land*.
(42) In Great Britain if treaties interfere with subsisting laws; they must be confirmed. Treaty of commerce between France and England, Article 14. (Bl 252–57 [Blackstone, I]).
(43) The Senate may be bribed. Ought they not to be brought to punishment? Will their colleagues convict him on impeachment?
(44) If it was not for such things as these, we would not contend against this Constitution.
(45) The Senate may forever prevent the addition of a single member to the lower house; while their own representation may be increased.
(46) This Constitution contradicts the leading principles of government (Mont. b. 11. c. 6. p. 199 [Montesquieu, I, 221–37]).
(47) We have not every security from the judicial department. The judges, for disobeying a law, may be impeached by one house, and tried by the other. [Wilson's Notes, PHi]

Smilie: The *Senate* were meant to represent an artificial *aristocracy*, and the House of *Representatives* to represent the mass of the people. I shall endeavor to prove that one branch of the legislature can and will destroy the balance intended by the other. The House of Representatives are so few in number as to have but very little influence.(a) The districts being large, the members returned will not be by the *voice* of the *people*. This body will be subject to corruption, and the means of corruption will be in the power of the *Senate*. Will you bring an impeachment? Who are to try it? The *Senate*.(b)

The treaty of commerce between Great Britain and France 1786, Article 14 (Mon 1, V *Spirit* 6 Ch 11th book).[c] [Wayne's Notes, Cox Collection]

> [Wayne's marginal notes]
> (a) The influence will be increasing every year, and the ratio being 30,000, and a *census* taken every 10 years, in the course of *25* years [the number of Representatives will] double.
> (b) The *state assemblies* have an effectual check upon the *Senate* by changing 1/3 every two years and placing men in that body who may try and punish them on impeachment.
> (c) Answer: Sir William Blackstone upon *treaties*—the power is absolutely in the king. Here, they can't be made but by the concurrence of 2 of the branches, i.e., the *President* and *Senate*.

Smilie: The Senate has a dangerous power of corrupting, by their offices, the Representatives of the people. [Yeates's Notes, PPIn][1]

* * * *

JAMES WILSON: Summary of Objections to the Constitution[2]

(1) There is no bill of rights. Many of the states have bills of rights. There are some reservations; why not more? Powers given, and powers and rights *reserved* ought all to be enumerated. What harm in a bill of rights?

(2) There is no check but the people. Our liberties are not secured but as to *habeas corpus*.

(3) There is no security for the rights of conscience.

(4) This system violates the Confederation; and the Assembly of this state could not join in it; for their powers are limited by the Constitution.

(5) There is a *mode* of *amendment* in the Confederation.

(6) "We the People," etc. This clause changes the principles of the Confederation; and introduces a *consolidating* and *absorbing* government. Will this be a proper one for the United States?

(7) The sovereignty and independence of the states is not preserved. There cannot be *two* sovereign powers. A subordinate sovereignty is no sovereignty. The *sovereignty* of the states is not represented in this Constitution. A state can speak but *one* voice; here each Senator has a vote.[a]

(8) This system unhinges and eradicates the state governments; and was systematically intended to do so.[b]

(9) Congress may prescribe the *times* and places and manner of elections, when the state governments shall be abolished. They may make the times as *distant* as they please.

(10) Article 1, section 8, last clause gives the power of self-preservation to the general government, *independent* of the states; for, in case of their *abolition,* it will be alleged on behalf of the general government, that self-preservation is the first law, and necessary to the exercise of *all other* powers.

(12) [sic] This is not a *federal* government, but a complete one, with legislative, executive, and judicial powers. It is a *consolidating* government.

(13) The *forms* of the state governments may remain; but their *power* will be destroyed. They will lose the attachment of the people by losing the power of conferring advantages.

(14) The people will not be at the expense of keeping them up.

(15) The state elections will be ill-attended and the state governments mere *electors.*

(16) There will be a rivalship between the state governments and the general governments. On each side endeavors will be made to increase power. The state governments cannot make head against the general government.

(17) The power over elections, and of judging of elections gives *absolute* sovereignty.

(18) There is a dependence of the state officers on the general government; they must swear to support it.

(19) The number of Representatives is too small. There should be more in a country lately and thinly settled, than in one old and populous. Pennsylvania will not have any Representative far from Philadelphia.

(20) Annual assemblies and annual appropriations are necessary. The *British* Parliament took seven years; but even there the appropriations are *annual.*

(21) The members of the Senate may enrich themselves; they may hold their offices as long as they live, and there is no power to prevent them. The Senate will swallow up any thing.

(22) The powers of Congress extend to taxation—to direct taxation, to internal taxation, to poll taxes, to excises—to other state and internal purposes. Those who possess the power to tax, possess all *other* sovereign powers.

(23) Congress may borrow money, keep up standing armies, and command the militia.

(24) The powers of Congress are unlimited and undefined. They will be the judges of what is *necessary* and *proper.*

(25) The liberty of the press is not secured. Congress may license the press, and declare what shall be a libel.

(26) Crimes shall be tried by a jury; therefore Congress may declare crimes.

(27) An *aristocratical* government cannot bear the liberty of the press.

(28) For speeches in Congress, members cannot be tried in any other place; therefore not by the press.

(29) Congress will have the power of self-preservation; and therefore may destroy the liberty of the press.

(30) The judicial powers are coextensive with the legislative powers; and extend even to capital cases.

(31) This is not such a system as was within the powers of the Convention. They assumed the power of *proposing*.

(32) This system was not expected by the people, the legislatures, or by us.

(33) A general government was not in contemplation. The business was only to amend the present Confederation, and give more powers to Congress.

(34) The objections are not on *local* but on *general* principles. They are *uniform* throughout the states.

(35) The plan is *inimical* to our liberties. [Wilson's Notes, PHi]

> [Wilson's marginal notes]
> (a) Sovereignty Vat. p. 5. s. 2 Lock, p. 2, s. 149, 227. Bl. 245. 161. 162. Confederacy, Vattel p. 11. s. 10 Mont. b. 9. c. 1.[3]
> (b) A general inconsistency between *this* reasoning and that against the powers of the Senate.

Wilson: I shall take this opportunity, of giving an answer to the objections already urged against the Constitution; I shall then point out some of those qualities, that entitle it to the attention and approbation of this Convention; and after having done this, I shall take a fit opportunity of stating the consequences, which I apprehend will result from rejecting it and those which will probably result from its adoption. I have given the utmost attention to the debates and the objections, that from time to time have been made by the three gentlemen who speak in opposition. I have reduced them to some order, perhaps not better than that in which they were introduced. I will state them; they will be in the recollection of the house, and I will endeavor to give an answer to them—in that answer, I will interweave some remarks, that may tend to elucidate the subject.

A good deal has already been said concerning a bill of rights; I have stated, according to the best of my recollection, all that passed in Convention relating to that business. Since that time, I have spoken with a gentleman who has not only his memory but full notes that he had taken in that body; and he assures me, that upon this subject, no direct motion was ever made at all;[4] and certainly, before we heard this so violently supported out of doors, some pains ought to have been taken to have tried its fate within; but the truth is, a bill of rights would, as I have mentioned already, have been not only unnecessary but improper. In some governments it may come within the gentleman's [John Smilie, 30 November] idea, when he says it can do no harm; but even in these governments, you find bills of rights do not uniformly obtain; and do those states complain who have them not? Is it a maxim in forming governments, that not only all the powers which are given, but also that all those which are reserved, should be enumerated? I apprehend, that the powers given and reserved form the whole rights of the people as men and as citizens. I consider that there are very few who understand the *whole* of these rights. All the political writers, from Grotius and Puffendorf down to Vattel, have treated on this subject; but in no one of those books, nor in the aggregate of them all, can you find a complete enumeration of rights, appertaining to the people as men and as citizens.

There are two kinds of government; that where general power is intended to be given to the legislature and that where the powers are particularly enumerated. In the last case, the implied result is, that nothing more is intended to be given, than what is so enumerated, unless it results from the nature of the government itself. On the other hand, when general legislative powers are given, then the people part with their authority, and on the gentleman's principle of government, retain nothing. But in a government like the proposed one, there can be no necessity for a bill of rights. For, on my principle, the people never part with their power. Enumerate all the rights of men! I am sure, sir, that no gentleman in the late Convention would have attempted such a thing. I believe the honorable speakers in opposition on this floor were members of the Assembly which appointed delegates to that Convention;[5] if it had been thought proper to have sent them into that body, how luminous would the *dark conclave* have been! So the gentleman [William Findley] has been pleased to denominate that body. Aristocrats as they were, they pretended not to define the rights of those who sent them there. We are asked repeatedly, what *harm* could the addition of a bill of rights do? If it can do no *good,* I think that a sufficient reason to refuse having any thing to do with it. But to whom are we to report this bill of rights, if we should adopt it? Have we authority from those who sent us here to make one?

It is true we may propose, as well as any other private persons; but how shall we know the sentiments of the citizens of this state and of the other states? Are we certain that any one of them will agree with our definitions and enumerations?

In the second place, we are told, that there is no check upon the government but the people; it is fortunate, sir, if their superintending authority is allowed as a check. But I apprehend that in the very construction of this government, there are numerous checks. Besides those expressly enumerated, the two branches of the legislature are mutual checks upon each other. But this subject will be more properly discussed, when we come to consider the form of government itself; and then I mean to show the reason, why the right of *habeas corpus* was secured by a particular declaration in its favor.

In the third place we are told, that there is no security for the rights of conscience. I ask the honorable gentleman [John Smilie], what part of this system puts it in the power of Congress to attack those rights? When there is no power to attack, it is idle to prepare the means of defense.

After having mentioned, in a cursory manner, the foregoing objections, we now arrive at the leading ones against the proposed system.

The very manner of introducing this Constitution, by the recognition of the authority of the people, is said to change the principle of the present Confederation, and to introduce a *consolidating* and absorbing government!

In this confederated republic, the sovereignty of the states, it is said, is not preserved. We are told, that there cannot be two sovereign powers, and that a subordinate sovereignty is no sovereignty.

It will be worthwhile, Mr. President, to consider this objection at large. When I had the honor of speaking formerly on this subject, I stated, in as concise a manner as possible, the leading ideas that occurred to me, to ascertain where the supreme and sovereign power resides. It has not been, nor, I presume, will it be denied, that somewhere there is, and of necessity must be, a supreme, absolute and uncontrollable authority. This, I believe, may justly be termed the sovereign power; for from that gentleman's (William Findley's) account of the matter, it cannot be sovereign unless it is supreme; for, says he, a subordinate sovereignty is no sovereignty at all. I had the honor of observing, that if the question was asked, where the supreme power resided, different answers would be given by different writers. I mentioned, that Blackstone will tell you, that in Britain, it is lodged in the British Parliament; and I believe there is no writer on this subject on the other side of the Atlantic but supposes it to be vested in that body. I stated further, that if the question was asked, some politician, who had not considered the subject with sufficient accuracy, where the supreme power resided in our governments, he would answer, that it was vested in the state constitutions. This opinion approaches near the truth, but does not reach it; for the truth is, that the supreme, absolute, and uncontrollable authority *remains* with the people. I mentioned also, that the practical recognition of this truth was reserved for the honor of this country. I recollect no constitution founded on this principle. But we have witnessed the improvement, and enjoy the happiness, of seeing it carried into practice. The great and penetrating mind of Locke seems to be the only one that pointed towards even the theory of this great truth.

When I made the observation, that some politicians would say the supreme power was lodged in our state constitutions, I did not suspect that the honorable gentleman from Westmoreland (William Findley) was included in that description; but I find myself disappointed; for I imagined his opposition would arise from another consideration. His position is, that the supreme power resides in the states, as governments; and mine is, that it *resides* in the PEOPLE, as the fountain of government; that the people have not—that the people mean not—and that the people ought not to part with it to any government whatsoever. In their hands it remains secure. They can delegate it in such proportions, to such bodies, on such terms, and under such limitations as they think proper. I agree with the members in opposition, that there cannot be two sovereign powers on the same subject.

I consider the people of the United States, as forming one great community; and I consider the people of the different states, as forming communities again on a lesser scale. From this great division of the people into distinct communities, it will be found necessary, that different proportions of legislative powers should be given to the governments, according to the nature, number, and magnitude of their objects.

Unless the people are considered in these two views, we shall never be able to understand the principle on which this system was constructed. I view the states as made *for* the People, as well as *by* them, and not the People as made for the states; the People, therefore, have a right, whilst enjoying the undeniable powers of society, to form either a general government, or state governments, in what manner they please; or to accommodate them to one another; and by this means preserve them all; this, I say, is the inherent and unalienable right of the people; and as an illustration of it, I beg to read a few words from the Declaration of Independence, made by the representatives of the United States and recognized by the whole Union.

"We hold these truths to be self-evident, that all men are created equal; that they are endowed by their Creator with certain unalienable rights; that among these are life, liberty, and the pursuit of happiness. That to secure these rights, *governments* are instituted among men, *deriving their just powers from the consent of the governed*; that whenever any form of government becomes destructive of these ends, it is the RIGHT of the People, to alter or to abolish it, and institute new governments, laying its foundation on such principles, and organizing its powers in such forms, as to them shall seem most likely to effect their safety and happiness."

This is the broad basis on which our independence was placed; on the same certain and solid foundation this system is erected.

State sovereignty, as it is called, is far from being able to support its weight. Nothing less than the authority of the people could either support it or give it efficacy. I cannot pass over this subject, without noticing the different conduct pursued by the late Federal Convention and that observed by the convention which framed the constitution of Pennsylvania; on that occasion you find an attempt made to deprive the people of this right, so lately and so expressly asserted in the Declaration of Independence.[6] We are told in the preamble to the declaration of rights, and frame of government, that *we* "do, by virtue of the authority vested in *us* [by our constituents], ordain, declare and establish, the following declaration of rights, and frame of government, to be the constitution of this commonwealth, and to remain in force therein UNALTERED, except in such articles as shall hereafter, on experience, be found to require improvement, and which shall, by the same authority of the people, [be] fairly delegated *as this frame of government directs*." An honorable gentleman (Stephen Chambers) was well warranted in saying, that all that could be done, was done, to cut off the people from the right of amending; for if it be amended[(a)] by any other mode than that which it directs; then any number more than one-third may control any number less than two-thirds.

But I return to my general reasoning. My position is, sir, that in this country the supreme, absolute, and uncontrollable power resides in the people at large; that they have vested certain proportions of this power in the state governments; but that the fee simple continues, resides, and remains with the body of the people. Under the practical influence of this great truth, we are now sitting and deliberating, and under its operation, we can sit as calmly, and deliberate as coolly, in order to change a constitution, as a legislature can sit and deliberate under the power of a constitution, in order to alter or amend a law. It is true the exercise of this power will not probably be so frequent, nor resorted to on so many occasions in one case as in the other; but the recognition of the principle cannot fail to establish it more firmly; because[(b)] this recognition is made in the proposed Constitution, an exception is taken to the whole of it; for, we are told, it is a violation of the present Confederation—a CONFEDERATION of SOVEREIGN STATES. I shall not enter into an investigation of the present Confederation, but shall just remark, that its principle is not the principle of free governments. The PEOPLE of the United States are not as such represented in the present Congress; and considered even as the component parts of the several states, they are not represented in proportion to their numbers and importance.

In this place I cannot help remarking on the general inconsistency which appears between one part of the gentleman's [John Smilie] objections and another. Upon the principle we have now mentioned, the honorable gentleman contended, that the powers ought to flow from the states; and that all the late Convention had to do was to give additional powers to Congress. What is the present form of Congress? A single body, with some legislative, but little executive and no effective judicial power. What are these additional powers that are to be given? In some cases legislative are wanting, in others judicial, and in others executive; these, it is said, ought to be allotted to the general government; but the impropriety of delegating such extensive trust to one body of men is evident; yet in the same day, and perhaps in the same hour, we are told, by honorable gentlemen, that these three branches of government are not kept sufficiently distinct in this Constitution; we are told also that the Senate, possessing some executive power, as well as legislative, is such a monster that it will swallow up and absorb every other body in the general government after having destroyed those of the particular states.

Is this reasoning with consistency? Is the Senate under the proposed Constitution so tremendous a body, when checked in their legislative capacity by the House of Representatives, and in their executive authority by the President of the United States? Can this body be so tremendous as the present Congress, a single body of men possessed of legislative, executive, and judicial powers? To what purpose was Montesquieu read to show that this was a complete tyranny? The application would have been more properly made by the advocates of the proposed Constitution, against the patrons of the present Confederation.

It is mentioned that this federal government will annihilate and absorb all the state governments. I wish to save as much as possible the time of the house, I shall not, therefore, recapitulate what I had the honor of saying last week [28 November] on this subject; I hope it was then shown, that instead of being abolished (as insinuated) from the very nature of things, and from the organization of the system itself, the state governments must exist, or the general government must fall amidst their ruins; indeed so far as to the forms, it is admitted they may remain; but the gentlemen seem to think their power will be gone.

I shall have occasion to take notice of this power hereafter, and, I believe, if it was necessary, it could be shown that the state governments, as states, will enjoy as much power, and more dignity, happiness, and security than they have hitherto done. I admit, sir, that some of the powers will be taken from them, by the system before you; but it is, I believe, allowed on all hands, at least it is not among us a disputed point, that the late Convention was appointed with a particular view to give more power to the government of the Union. It is also acknowledged, that the intention was to obtain the advantage of an efficient government over the United States; now, if power is to be given to that government, I apprehend it must be taken from some place. If the state governments are to retain all the powers they held before, then, of consequence, every new power that is given to Congress must be taken from the people at large. Is this the gentleman's intention? I believe a strict examination of this subject will justify me in asserting, that the states, as governments, have assumed too much power to themselves, while they left little to the people. Let not this be called cajoling the people—the elegant expression used by the honorable gentleman from Westmoreland (William Findley); it is hard to avoid censure on one side or the other. At some time it has been said, that I have not been at the pains to conceal my contempt of the people; but when it suits a purpose better, it is asserted that I cajole them. I do neither one nor the other. The voice of approbation, sir, when I think that approbation well earned, I confess is grateful to my ears; but I would disdain it, if it is to be purchased by a sacrifice of my duty or the dictates of my conscience. No, sir, I go practically into this system, I have gone into it practically when the doors were shut; when it could not be alleged that I cajoled the people, and I now endeavor to show that the true and only safe principle for a free people is a practical recognition of their original and supreme authority.

I say, sir, that it was the design of this system to take some power from the state government and to place it in the general government. It was also the design, that the people should be admitted to the exercise of some powers, which they did not exercise under the present Confederation. It was thought proper, that the citizens, as well as the states should be represented; how far the representation in the Senate is a representation of states, we shall see by and by, when we come to consider that branch of the federal government.

This system, it is said, "unhinges and eradicates the state governments, and was systematically intended so to do"; to establish the *intention,* an argument is drawn from Article Ist, section 4th on the subject of elections. I have already had occasion to remark upon this, and shall therefore pass on to the next objection.

That the last clause of the 8th section of the Ist Article gives the power of self-preservation to the general government, *independent* of the states. For in case of their *abolition,* it will be alleged in behalf of the general government, that self-preservation is the first law, and necessary to the exercise of *all other* powers.

Now let us see what this objection amounts to. Who are to have this self-preserving power? The Congress. Who are Congress? It is a body that will consist of a Senate and a House of Representatives. Who compose this Senate? Those who are *elected* by the *legislatures* of the different states. Who are the electors of the House of Representatives? Those who are *qualified* to *vote* for the most numerous branch of the *legislature* in the separate states. Suppose the state legislatures annihilated, where is the criterion to ascertain the qualification of electors? And unless this be ascertained, they cannot be admitted to vote; if a state legislature is not elected, there can be no Senate, because the Senators are to be chosen by the *legislatures only.*

This is a plain and simple deduction from the Constitution, and yet the objection is stated as conclusive upon an argument expressly drawn from the last clause of this section.

It is repeated, with confidence, "that this is not a *federal* government, but a complete one, with legislative, executive and judicial powers. It is a *consolidating* government." I have already mentioned the misuse of the term; I wish the gentleman [William Findley] would indulge us with his definition of the word. If, when he says it is a consolidation, he means so far as relates to the general objects of the Union—so far it was intended to be a consolidation, and on such a consolidation, perhaps our very existence, as a nation, depends. If, on the other hand (as something which has been said seems to indicate) he (William Findley) means that it will absorb the governments of the individual states, so far is this position from being admitted, that it is unanswerably controverted. The existence of the state government is one of the most prominent features of this system. With regard to those purposes which are allowed to be for the general welfare of the Union, I think it no objection to this plan, that we are told it is a complete government. I think it no objection, that it is alleged the government will possess legislative, executive, and judicial powers. Should it have only legislative authority! We have had examples enough of such a government to deter us from continuing it. Shall Congress any longer continue to make requisitions from the several states, to be treated sometimes with silent and sometimes with declared contempt? For what purpose give the power to make laws, unless they are to be executed? And if they are to be executed, the executive and judicial powers will necessarily be engaged in the business.

Do we wish a return of those insurrections and tumults to which a sister state was lately exposed[7] or a government of such insufficiency as the present is found to be? Let me, sir, mention one circumstance in the recollection of every honorable gentleman who hears me. To the determination of Congress are submitted all disputes between states concerning boundary, jurisdiction, or right of soil. In consequence of this power, after much altercation, expense of time, and considerable expense of money, this state was successful enough to obtain a decree in her favor, in a difference then subsisting between her and Connecticut;[8] but what was the consequence? The Congress had no power to carry the decree into execution. Hence the distraction and animosity, which have ever since prevailed, and still continue in that part of the country. Ought the government then to remain any longer incomplete? I hope not; no person can be so insensible to the lessons of experience as to desire it.

It is brought as an objection "that there will be a rivalship between the state governments and the general government; on each side endeavors will be made to increase power."

Let us examine a little into this subject. The gentlemen tell you, sir, that they expect the states will not possess any power. But I think there is reason to draw a different conclusion. Under this system their respectability and power will increase with that of the general government. I believe their happiness and security will increase in a still greater proportion; let us attend a moment to the situation of this country; it is a maxim of every government, and it ought to be a maxim with us, that the increase of numbers increases the dignity, the security, and the respectability of all governments; it is the first command given by the Deity to man, increase and multiply; this applies with peculiar force to this country, the smaller part of whose territory is yet inhabited. We are representatives, sir, not merely of the present age, but of future times; not merely of the territory along the seacoast, but of regions immensely extended westward. We should fill, as fast as possible, this extensive country, with men who shall live happy, free, and secure. To accomplish this great end ought to be the leading view of all our patriots and statesmen. But how is it to be accomplished, but by establishing peace and harmony among ourselves, and dignity and respectability among foreign nations. By these means, we may draw numbers from the other side of the Atlantic, in addition to the natural sources of population. Can either of these objects be attained without a protecting head? When we examine history, we shall find an important fact, and almost the only fact, which will apply to all confederacies. They have all fallen to pieces, and have not absorbed the subordinate government.[(c)]

In order to keep republics together they must have a strong binding force, which must be either external or internal. The situation of this country shows, that no foreign force can press us together, the bonds of our Union ought therefore to be indissolubly strong.

The powers of the states, I apprehend, will increase with the population and the happiness of their inhabitants. Unless we can establish a character abroad, we shall be unhappy from foreign restraints or internal violence. These reasons, I think, prove sufficiently the necessity of having a federal head. Under it the advantages enjoyed by the whole Union would be participated [in] by every state. I wish honorable gentlemen would think not only of themselves, not only of the present age, but of others and of future times.

It has been said, "that the state governments will not be able to make head against the general government," but it might be said with more propriety, that the general government will not be able to maintain the powers given it against the encroachments and combined attacks of the state governments. They possess some particular advantages, from which the general government is restrained. By this system, there is a provision made in the Constitution that no Senator or Representative shall be appointed to any civil office under the authority of the United States, which shall have been created, or the emoluments whereof shall have been increased during the time for which he was elected; and no person holding any office under the United States can be a member of either house; but there is no similar security against state influence, as a Representative may enjoy places and even sinecures under the state governments. On which side is the door most open to corruption? If a person in the legislature is to be influenced by an office, the general government can give him none unless he vacate his seat. When the influence of office comes from the state government, he can retain his seat and salary too. But, it is added, under this head "that state governments will lose the attachment of the people, by losing the power of conferring advantages, and that the people will not be at the expense of keeping them up." Perhaps the state governments have already become so expensive as to alarm the gentlemen on that head. I am told that the civil list of this state amounted to £40,000 in one year. Under the proposed government, I think it would be possible to obtain in Pennsylvania every advantage we now possess, with a civil list that shall not exceed one-third of that sum.[9]

How differently the same thing is talked of, if it be a favorite or otherwise! When advantages to an officer are to be derived from the general government, we hear them mentioned by the name of *bribery*, but when we are told of the states' governments losing the power of conferring advantages, by the disposal of offices, it is said they will lose the *attachment* of the people. What is in one instance corruption and bribery, is in another the power of conferring advantages.

We are informed "that the state elections will be ill-attended, and that the state governments will become mere boards of electors." Those who have a due regard for their country will discharge their duty and attend; but those who are brought only from interest or persuasion had better stay away; the public will not suffer any disadvantage from their absence. But the honest citizens, who know the value of the privilege, will undoubtedly attend to secure the man of his choice. The power and business of the state legislatures relates to the great objects of life, liberty, and property; the same are also objects of the general government.

Certainly the citizens of America will be as tenacious in the one instance as in the other. They will be interested, and I hope will exert themselves to secure their rights not only from being injured by the state governments, but also from being injured by the general government.

"The power over election, and of judging of elections, gives absolute sovereignty"; this power is given to every state legislature, yet I see no necessity, that the power of absolute sovereignty should accompany it. My general position is, that the absolute sovereignty never goes from the people.

We are told, "that it will be in the power of the Senate to prevent any addition of Representatives to the lower house."

I believe their power will be pretty well balanced, and though the Senate should have a desire to do this, yet the attempt will answer no purpose; for the House of Representatives will not let them have a farthing of public money, till they agree to it. And the latter influence will be as strong as the other.

"Annual assemblies are necessary" it is said—and I answer in many instances they are very proper. In Rhode Island and Connecticut they are elected for six months. In larger states, that period would be found very inconvenient, but in a government as large as that of the United States, I presume that annual elections would be more disproportionate, than elections for six months would be in some of our largest states.

"The British Parliament took to themselves the prolongation of their sitting to seven years. But even in the British Parliament the appropriations are annual."

But, sir, how is the argument to apply here? How are the Congress to assume such a power? They cannot assume it under the Constitution, for that expressly provides "the members of the house of representatives shall be chosen every two years, by the people of the several states, and the senators for six years." So if they take it at all, they must take it by usurpation and force.

"Appropriations may be made for two years, though in the British Parliament they are made but for one"; for some purposes, such appropriations may be made annually, but for every purpose they are not; even for a standing army, they may be made for seven, ten, or fourteen years—the civil list is established, during the life of a prince. Another objection is "that the members of the Senate may enrich themselves—they may hold their office as long as they live, and there is not power to prevent them; the Senate will swallow up everything." I am not a blind admirer of this system. Some of the powers of the Senators are not with me the favorite parts of it, but as they stand connected with other parts, there is still security against the efforts of that body. It was with great difficulty that security was obtained, and I may risk the conjecture, that if it is not now accepted, it never will be obtained again from the same states. Though the Senate was not a favorite of mine, as to some of its powers, yet it was a favorite with a majority in the Union, and we must submit to that majority, or we must break up the Union. It is but fair to repeat those reasons, that weighed with the Convention. Perhaps, I shall not be able to do them justice, but yet I will attempt to show, why additional powers were given to the Senate, rather than to the House of Representatives. These additional powers, I believe, are, that of trying impeachments, that of concurring with the President in making treaties, and that of concurring in the appointment of officers. These are the powers that are stated as improper. It is fortunate, that in the exercise of every one of them, the Senate stands controlled. If it is that monster which it [is] said to be, it can only show its teeth; it is unable to bite or devour. With regard to impeachments, the Senate can try none but such as will be brought before them by the House of Representatives.

The Senate can make no treaties; they can approve of none unless the President of the United States lay it before them. With regard to the appointment of officers, the President must nominate before they can vote. So that if the powers of either branch are perverted, it must be with the approbation of some one of the other branches of government. Thus checked on each side, they can do no one act of themselves.

"The powers of Congress extend to taxation—to direct taxation—to internal taxation—to poll taxes—to excises—to other state and internal purposes." Those who possess the power to tax, possess all other sovereign power. That their powers are thus extensive is admitted; and would any thing short of this have been sufficient? Is it the wish of these gentlemen? If it is, let us hear their sentiments—that the general government should subsist on the bounty of the states. Shall it have the power to contract, and no power to fulfill the contract? Shall it have the power to borrow money, and no power to pay the principal or interest? Must we go on, in the track that we have hitherto pursued and must we again compel those in Europe, who lent us money in our distress, to advance the money to pay themselves interest on the certificates of the debts due to them?

This was actually the case in Holland, the last year.[10] Like those who have shot one arrow, and cannot regain it, they have been obliged to shoot another in the same direction, in order to recover the first. It was absolutely necessary, sir, that this government should possess these rights, and why should it not, as well as the state governments? Will this government be fonder of the exercise of this authority, than those of the states are? Will the states, who are equally represented in one branch of the legislature, be more opposed to the payment of what shall be required by the future, than what has been required by the present Congress? Will the people, who must indisputably pay the whole, have more objections to the payment of this tax, because it is laid by persons of their own immediate appointment, even if those taxes were to continue as oppressive as they now are? But under the general power of this system, that cannot be the case in Pennsylvania. Throughout the Union, direct taxation will be lessened, at least in proportion to the increase of the other objects of revenue. In this Constitution, a power is given to Congress to collect imposts, which is not given by the present Articles of Confederation. A very considerable part of the revenue of the United States will arise from that source; it is the easiest, most just, and most productive mode of raising revenue; and it is a safe one, because it is voluntary. No man is obliged to consume more than he pleases, and each buys in proportion only to his consumption. The price of the commodity is blended with the tax, and the person is often not sensible of the payment. But would it have been proper to have rested the matter there? Suppose this fund should not prove sufficient, ought the public debts to remain unpaid or the exigencies of government be left unprovided for? Should our tranquility be exposed to the assaults of foreign enemies, or violence among ourselves, because the objects of commerce may not furnish a sufficient revenue to secure them all? Certainly Congress should possess the power of raising revenue from their constituents, for the purpose mentioned in the eighth section of the first Article, that is "to pay the debts and provide for the common defence and general welfare of the United States." It has been common, with the gentlemen on this subject, to present us with frightful pictures. We are told of the hosts of tax gatherers that will swarm through the land; and whenever taxes are mentioned, military force seems to be an attending idea. I think I may venture to predict, that the taxes of the general government (if any shall be laid) will be more equitable, and much less expensive, than those imposed by the state government.

I shall not go into an investigation of this subject; but it must be confessed, that scarcely any mode of laying and collecting taxes can be more burdensome than the present.

Another objection is, "that Congress may borrow money, keep up standing armies, and command the militia." The present Congress possesses the power of borrowing money and of keeping up standing armies. Whether it will be proper at all times to keep up a body of troops will be a question to be determined by Congress; but I hope the necessity will not subsist at all times; but if it should subsist, where is the gentleman that will say that they ought not to possess the necessary power of keeping them up?

It is urged, as a general objection to this system, that "the powers of Congress are unlimited and undefined, and that they will be the judges, in all cases, of what is necessary and proper for them to do." To bring this subject to your view, I need do no more than point to the words in the Constitution, beginning at the 8th section, Article 1st. "The Congress," it says, "shall have power, etc." I need not read over the words, but I leave it to every gentleman to say whether the powers are not as accurately and minutely defined, as can be well done on the same subject, in the same language. The old constitution is as strongly marked on this subject; and even the concluding clause, with which so much fault has been found, gives no more, or other powers; nor does it in any degree go beyond the particular enumeration; for when it is said, that Congress shall have power to make all laws which shall be necessary and proper, those words are limited, and defined by the following, "for carrying into execution the foregoing powers." It is saying no more than that the powers we have already particularly given shall be effectually carried into execution.

I shall not detain the house, at this time, with any further observations on the liberty of the press, until it is shown that Congress have any power whatsoever to interfere with it, by licensing it, or declaring what shall be a libel.

I proceed to another objection, which was not so fully stated as I believe it will be hereafter; I mean the objection against the judicial department. The gentleman from Westmoreland [William Findley] only mentioned it to illustrate his objection to the legislative department. He said "that the judicial powers were coextensive with the legislative powers, and extend even to capital cases." I believe they ought to be coextensive, otherwise laws would be framed, that could not be executed. Certainly, therefore, the executive and judicial departments ought to have power commensurate to the extent of the laws; for, as I have already asked, are we to give power to *make* laws, and no power to *carry them into effect*?

I am happy to mention the punishment annexed to one crime. You will find the current running strong in favor of humanity. For this is the first instance in which it has not been left to the legislature, to extend the crime and punishment of treason so far as they thought proper. This punishment and the description of this crime are the great sources of danger and persecution, on the part of government against the citizen. Crimes against the state! and against the officers of the state!; history informs us, that more wrong may be done on this subject than on any other whatsoever. But under this Constitution, there can be no treason against the United States, except such as is defined in this Constitution. The manner of trial is clearly pointed out; the positive testimony of two witnesses to the same overt act or a confession in open court is required to convict any person of treason. And after all, the consequences of the crime shall extend no further than the life of the criminal; for no attainder of treason shall work corruption of blood, or forfeiture, except during the life of the person attainted.

I come now to consider the last set of objections that are offered against this Constitution. It is urged, that this is not such a system as was within the powers of the Convention; they assumed the *power of proposing*. I believe they might have made proposals without going beyond their powers. I never heard before, that to make a proposal was an exercise of power. But if it is an exercise of power, they certainly did assume it; yet they did not act as that body who framed the present constitution of Pennsylvania acted; they did not by an ordinance attempt to rivet the constitution on the people, before they could vote for members of Assembly under it.[11] Yet such was the effect of the ordinance that attended the constitution of this commonwealth. I think the late Convention have done nothing beyond their powers. The fact is, they have exercised no power at all. And in point of validity, this Constitution, proposed by them for the government of the United States, claims no more than a production of the same nature would claim, flowing from a private pen. It is laid before the citizens of the United States, unfettered by restraint; it is laid before them to be judged by the natural, civil, and political rights of men.

By their FIAT, it will become of value and authority; without it, it will never receive the character of authenticity and power. The business, we are told, which was entrusted to the late Convention was merely to amend the present Articles of Confederation. This observation has been frequently made, and has often brought to my mind a story that is related of Mr. [Alexander] Pope, who, it is well known, was not a little deformed. It was customary with him to use this phrase, "God mend me," when any little accident happened. One evening a linkboy was lighting him along, and coming to a gutter, the boy jumped nimbly over it. Mr. Pope called to him to turn, adding, "God mend me." The arch rogue turned to light him—looked at him, and repeated "God mend you! He would sooner make half a dozen new ones." This would apply to the present Confederation; for it would be easier to make another than to mend this. The gentlemen urge, that this is such a government as was not expected by the people, the legislatures, nor by the honorable gentlemen who mentioned it. Perhaps it was not such as was expected, *but it may be* BETTER; and is that a reason why it should not be adopted? It is not worse, I trust, than the former. So that the argument of its being a system not expected is an argument more strong in its favor than against it. The letter which accompanies this Constitution, must strike every person with the utmost force. "The friends of our country have long seen and desired the power of war, peace, and treaties, that of levying money and regulating commerce, and the corresponding executive and judicial authorities, should be fully and effectually vested in the general government of the union; but the impropriety of delegating such extensive trust to one body of men, is evident. *Hence results the necessity of a different organization*."[12] I therefore do not think that it can be urged as an objection against this system, that it was not expected by the people. We are told, to add greater force to these objections, that they are not on local, but on general principles, and that they are uniform throughout the United States. I confess I am not altogether of that opinion; I think some of the objections are inconsistent with others, arising from a different quarter, and I think some are inconsistent, even with those derived from the same source. But, on this occasion, let us take the fact for granted, that they are all on general principles, and uniform throughout the United States. Then we can judge of their full amount; and what are they, BUT TRIFLES LIGHT AS AIR? We see the whole force of them; for according to the sentiments of opposition, they can nowhere be stronger, or more fully stated than here. The conclusion, from all these objections, is reduced to a point, and the plan is declared to be inimical to our liberties. I have said nothing, and mean to say nothing, concerning the dispositions or characters of those that framed the work now before you. I agree that it ought to be judged by its own intrinsic qualities. If it has not merit, weight of character ought not to carry it into effect. On the other hand, if it has merit, and is calculated to secure the blessings of liberty, and to promote the general welfare, then such objections as have hitherto been made ought not to influence us to reject it.

I am now led to consider those qualities that this system of government possesses, which will entitle it to the attention of the United States. But as I have somewhat fatigued myself, as well as the patience of the honorable members of this house, I shall defer what I have to add on this subject until the afternoon. [Lloyd, *Debates,* 59–77]

[Lloyd's errata]
(a) "read 'for it *cannot* be amended.' "
(b) "*but* because."
(c) "government*s*."

Wilson: In a general government there is no necessity of a bill of rights, for in my opinion all rights are in the people, nor would I attempt to define the *rights of those people* who sent me *here.*

In every community there is supreme controlling power, which I call *sovereign* power. Sir William Blackstone informs us that this power is in the British Parliament (Vatel p: 9. on Sovg Govt). Mr. Finley's position is that the sovereign power resides in the state governments; mine is that it resides in the *people.* That it is [a] consolidating government, if it is meant that it is annihilating the state government, it cannot be admitted. The Constitution itself pointedly contradicts *it* for it can *exist* only as long as the state governments *exist.* Altho this Constitution will necessarily take some powers from the state governments, yet when it is once in *operation,* it will add to the power and happiness of the state governments. Confederacies have not been *absorbed,* but fell to *pieces.* Powers of *taxing,* etc. *Answers* to the objections to the judicial department.

The limited power of punishment in cases of *treason* show that the current runs *strong* in favor of *humanity* and gives security to every individual, for from this principle, oppression may operate with dreadful effect. [Wayne's Notes, Cox Collection]

1. This account of Smilie's speech appears on a sheet of paper endorsed "December 4." Immediately preceding this entry Yeates noted two additional comments by Smilie and a comment by James Wilson which appear to have been made on 30 November. See Convention Debates, 30 November and Mfm:Pa. 265.

2. This undated six-page manuscript in the Wilson Papers is the outline of

Wilson's speech on 4 December. The first four pages, headed "Objections," contain thirty-four objections to the Constitution. The last two pages list seventeen "Reasons for adopting the Constitution." The "Objections" are placed before Lloyd's version of Wilson's speech in the morning session. The "Reasons for adopting the Constitution" are placed in the afternoon session.

Wilson's list of "Objections" was compiled from his notes of debates on 28 and 30 November, and 1 December.

3. Vattel, 16; Locke, II, sections 149, 227; Blackstone, I, 161–62, 245; Vattel, 18; Montesquieu, I, 185–87.

4. See Convention Debates, 28 November, n. 5. As for the "gentleman" who had "full notes," one possibility was James Madison. Another might have been William Jackson, secretary of the Convention, who told John Quincy Adams in 1819 that he had taken "extensive minutes" of the debates (Farrand, III, 426, 476). Such "minutes" have never been located.

5. Findley and Whitehill were members of the Assembly which elected the delegates to the Constitutional Convention.

6. The procedure of the Pennsylvania convention in 1776 was the reverse of what Wilson declared it to be. On 5 September 1776 the convention ordered its draft constitution printed for public consideration. Two-thirds of the draft was altered significantly as a result of public criticism and of further convention discussion. See John N. Shaeffer, "Public Consideration of the 1776 Pennsylvania Constitution," *Pennsylvania Magazine of History and Biography,* XCVIII (1974), 415–37.

7. The reference is to Shays's Rebellion in Massachusetts.

8. On 28 August 1782 Congress established a special court to examine the conflicting land claims in the Wyoming Valley. In the "Trenton Decree" on 30 December 1782 the court ruled that the land in question was under the jurisdiction of Pennsylvania. Connecticut renounced its claim to the land, but settlers from Connecticut resisted. (See JCC, XXIV, 6–32; Taylor, VII, 144–246, "The Trenton Trial Proceedings and Related Documents.")

9. Federalist writers all insisted that the new government would save the state governments money. "Federal Constitution," in the *Pennsylvania Gazette,* 10 October (CC:150-B) estimated that the Constitution "will necessarily reduce the expenses of our government from nearly £50,000 to £10,000 or, at most, £15,000 a year." This item was reprinted six times in Pennsylvania. Another article in the *Gazette* on 17 October (II:C above) stated that the adoption of the new Constitution would reduce the expenses of the state government by £35,000 annually.

10. For the Dutch loans to America, see E. James Ferguson, *The Power of the Purse . . .* (Chapel Hill, N.C., 1961), 260–61.

11. See note 6 above.

12. The President of the Convention to the President of Congress, 17 September, CDR:VIII, A.

Convention Proceedings, P.M.

The Convention met pursuant to adjournment,

Resumed the consideration of the first Article of the proposed Constitution, and after some debate,

Adjourned until half past nine o'clock tomorrow, A.M.

Convention Debates, P.M.

James Wilson interrupted the prepared speech he began in the morning session to answer John Smilie's speech in the morning session.

JAMES WILSON: Before I proceed to consider those qualities in the Constitution before us, which I think will insure it our approbation, permit me to make some remarks, and they shall be very concise, upon the objections that were offered this forenoon, by the member from Fayette (John Smilie). I do it, at this time, because I think it will be better to give a satisfactory answer to the whole of the objections, before I proceed to the other part of my subject. I find that the doctrine of a single legislature is not to be contended for in this Constitution. I shall therefore say nothing on that point. I shall consider that part of the system, when we come to view its excellencies. Neither shall I take particular notice of his observation on the qualified negative of the President, for he finds no fault with it; he mentions, however, that he thinks it a vain and useless power, because it can never be executed. The reason he assigns for this is, that the king of Great Britain, who has an absolute negative over the laws proposed by Parliament, has never exercised it, at least, not for many years. It is true, and the reason why he did not exercise it was, that during all that time, the king possessed a negative before the bill had passed through the two houses, a much stronger power than a negative after debate. I believe, since the Revolution, at the time of William III, it was never known that a bill disagreeable to the Crown passed both houses. At one time in the reign of Queen Anne, when there appeared some danger of this being effected, it is well-known that she created twelve peers, and by that means effectually defeated it. Again, there was some risk of late years in the present reign, with regard to Mr. [Charles James] Fox's East India bill, as it is usually called, that passed through the House of Commons, but the king had interest enough in the House of Peers, to have it thrown out; thus it never came up for the royal assent. But that is no reason why this negative should not be exercised here, and exercised with great advantage. Similar powers are known in more than one of the states. The governors of Massachusetts and New York have a power similar to this; and it has been exercised frequently to good effect.[1]

I believe the governor of New York, under this power, has been known to send back five or six bills in a week; and I well recollect that at the time the funding system was adopted by our legislature, the people in that state considered the negative of the governor as a great security, that their legislature would not be able to encumber them by a similar measure. Since that time an alteration has been supposed in the governor's conduct, but there has been no alteration in his power.

The honorable gentleman from Westmoreland (William Findley) [on 3 December], by his highly refined critical abilities, discovers an inconsistency in this part of the Constitution, and that which declares in [Article I,] section first: "All legislative powers, herein granted, shall be vested in a congress of the United States, which shall consist of a senate and a house of representatives," and yet here, says he, is a power of legislation given to the President of the United States, because every bill, before it becomes a law, shall be presented to him. Thus he is said to possess legislative powers. Sir, the Convention observed on this occasion strict propriety of language; "if he approve the bill when it is sent, he shall sign it, but if not he shall return it"; but no bill passes in consequence of having his assent—therefore he possesses no legislative authority.

The effect of his power upon this subject is merely this, if he disapproves a bill, two-thirds of the legislature become necessary to pass it into a law, instead of a bare majority. And when two-thirds are in favor of the bill, it becomes a law, not by his, but by authority of the two houses of the legislature. We are told, in the next place, by the honorable gentleman from Fayette (John Smilie) that in the different orders of mankind, there is that of a natural aristocracy. On some occasions, there is a kind of magical expression, used to conjure up ideas, that may create uneasiness and apprehension. I hope the meaning of the words is understood by the gentleman who used them. I have asked repeatedly of gentlemen to explain, but have not been able to obtain the explanation of what they meant by a consolidated government. They keep round and round about the thing, but never define. I ask now what is meant by a natural aristocracy? I am not at a loss for the etymological definition of the term, for, when we trace it to the language from which it is derived, an aristocracy means nothing more or less than a government of the best men in the community, or those who are recommended by the words of the constitution of Pennsylvania, where it is directed, that the representatives should consist of those most noted for wisdom and virtue. Is there any danger in such representation? I shall never find fault, that such characters are employed. Happy for us, when such characters can be obtained. If this is meant by a natural aristocracy, and I know no other, can it be objectionable, that men should be employed that are most noted for their virtue and talents? And are attempts made to mark out these as the most improper persons for the public confidence?

I had the honor of giving a definition, and I believe it was a just one, of what is called an aristocratic government. It is a government where the supreme power is not retained by the people, but resides in a select body of men, who either fill up the vacancies that happen, by their own choice and election, or succeed on the principle of descent, or by virtue of territorial possessions, or some other qualifications that are not the result of personal properties. When I speak of personal properties, I mean the qualities of the head and the disposition of the heart.

We are told that the Representatives will not be known to the people, nor the people to the Representatives, because they will be taken from large districts where they cannot be particularly acquainted. There has been some experience in several of the states, upon this subject, and I believe the experience of all who have had experience demonstrates that the larger the district of election, the better the representation. It is only in remote corners of a government, that little demagogues arise. Nothing but real weight of character can give a man real influence over a large district. This is remarkably shown in the Commonwealth of Massachusetts. The members of the House of Representatives are chosen in very small districts, and such has been the influence of party cabal and little intrigue in them, that a great majority seem inclined to show very little disapprobation of the conduct of the insurgents in that state.

The governor is chosen by the people at large, and that state is much larger than any district need be under the proposed Constitution. In their choice of their governor, they have had warm disputes; but however warm the disputes, their choice only vibrated between the most eminent characters. Four of their candidates are well-known: Mr. [John] Hancock, Mr. [James] Bowdoin, General [Benjamin] Lincoln, and Mr. [Nathaniel] Gorham, the late President of Congress.

I apprehend it is of more consequence to be able to know the true interest of the people, than their faces, and of more consequence still, to have virtue enough to pursue the means of carrying that knowledge usefully into effect. And surely when it has been thought hitherto, that a representation in Congress of from five to two members was sufficient to represent the interest of this state, is it not more than sufficient to have ten members in that body and those in a greater comparative proportion than heretofore? The citizens of Pennsylvania will be represented by eight, and the state by two. This, certainly, though not gaining enough, is gaining a good deal; the members will be more distributed through the state, being the immediate choice of the people, who hitherto have not been represented in that body. It is said that the House of Representatives will be subject to corruption, and the Senate possess the means of corrupting, by the share they have in the appointment to office. This was not spoken in the soft language of attachment to government. It is perhaps impossible, with all the caution of legislators and statesmen, to exclude corruption and undue influence entirely from government. All that can be done, upon this subject, is done in the Constitution before you. Yet it behooves us to call out, and add, every guard and preventative in our power. I think, sir, something very important on this subject is done in the present system. For it has been provided, effectually, that the man that has been bribed by an office shall have it no longer in his power to earn his wages. The moment he is engaged to serve the Senate, in consequence of their gift, he no longer has it in his power to sit in the House of Representatives. For "no representative shall, during the term for which he was elected, be appointed to any civil office, under the authority of the United States, which shall have been created, or the emoluments whereof shall have been encreased during such time." And the following annihilates corruption of that kind: "And no person holding any office under the United States, shall be a member of either house, during his continuance in office." So that the mere acceptance of an office as a bribe effectually destroys the end for which it was offered. Was this attended to when it was mentioned that the members of the one house could be bribed by the other? "But the members of the Senate may enrich themselves" was an observation made as an objection to this system. As the mode of doing this has not been pointed out, I apprehend the objection is not much relied upon. The Senate are incapable of receiving any money, except what is paid them out of the public treasury. They cannot vote to themselves a single penny, unless the proposition originates from the other house. This objection therefore is visionary, like the following one, "that pictured group, that numerous host, and prodigious swarm of officers, which are to be appointed under the general government." The gentlemen tell you that there must be judges of the supreme, and judges of the inferior courts, with all their appendages; there will be tax gatherers swarming throughout the land. Oh! say they, if we could enumerate the offices, and the numerous officers that must be employed every day, in collecting and receiving, and comptrolling the monies of the United States, the number would be almost beyond imagination. I have been told, but I do not vouch for the fact, that there are in one shape or another, more than a thousand persons in this very state, who get their living in assessing and collecting our revenues from the other citizens. Sir, when this business of revenue is conducted on a general plan, we may be able to do the business of the thirteen states, with an equal, nay, with a less number—instead of thirteen comptrollers general, one comptroller will be sufficient. I apprehend that the number of officers under this system will be greatly reduced from the number now employed. For as Congress can now do nothing effectually, the states are obliged to do everything. And in this very point, I apprehend, that we shall be great gainers.

Sir, I confess I wish the powers of the Senate were not as they are. I think it would have been better if those powers had been distributed in other parts of the system. I mentioned some circumstances in the forenoon, that I had observed on this subject. I may mention now, we may think ourselves very well off, sir, that things are as well as they are, and that that body is even so much restricted. But surely objections of this kind come with a bad grace from the advocates, or those who prefer the present Confederation, and who wish only to increase the powers of the present Congress. A single body not constituted with checks, like the proposed one, who possess not only the power of making treaties, but executive powers, would be a perfect despotism; but, further, these powers are, in the present Confederation, possessed without control.

As I mentioned before, so I will beg leave to repeat, that this Senate can do nothing without the concurrence of some other branch of the government. With regard to their concern in the appointment to offices, the President must nominate before they can be chosen; the President must acquiesce in that appointment. With regard to their power in forming treaties, they can make none, they are only auxiliaries to the President. They must try all impeachments; but they have no power to try any until presented by the House of Representatives; and when I consider this subject, though I wish the regulations better, I think no danger to the liberties of this country can arise even from that part of the system. But these objections, I say, come with a bad grace from those who prefer the present Confederation, who think it only necessary to add more powers to a body organized in that form. I confess, likewise, that by combining those powers, of trying impeachments, and making treaties, in the same body, it will not be so easy as I think it ought to be, to call the Senators to an account for any improper conduct in that business.

Those who proposed this system were not inattentive to do all they could. I admit the force of the observation made by the gentleman from Fayette (John Smilie) that when two-thirds of the Senate concur in forming a bad treaty, it will be hard to procure a vote of two-thirds against them, if they should be impeached. I think such a thing is not to be expected; and so far they are without that *immediate* degree of responsibility, which I think requisite, to make this part of the work perfect. But this will not be *always* the case. When a member of Senate shall behave criminally, the criminality will not expire with his office. The Senators may be called to account after they shall have been changed, and the body to which they belonged shall have been altered. There is a rotation; and every second year one-third of the whole number go out. Every fourth year two-thirds of them are changed. In six years the whole body is supplied by a new one. Considering it in this view, responsibility is not entirely lost. There is another view in which it ought to be considered, which will show that we have a greater degree of security. Though they may not be convicted on impeachment before the Senate, they may be tried by their country; and if their criminality is established, the law will punish. A grand jury may present, a petit jury may convict, and the judges will pronounce the punishment. This is all that can be done under the present Confederation, for under it there is no power of impeachment; even here then we gain something. Those parts that are exceptionable in this Constitution are improvements on that concerning which so much pains are taken to persuade us, that it is preferable to the other.

The last observation respects the judges. It is said that if they dare to decide against the law, one house will impeach them, and the other will convict them. I hope gentlemen will show how this can happen, for bare supposition ought not to be admitted as proof. The judges are to be impeached because they decide an act null and void that was made in defiance of the Constitution! What House of Representatives would dare to impeach, or Senate to commit judges for the performance of their duty? These observations are of a similar kind to those with regard to the liberty of the press. [Lloyd, *Debates*, 77–84]

JAMES WILSON: Reasons for Adopting the Constitution

The practical recognition of the supreme power of the people.

The legislative, executive, and judicial powers kept distinct and independent.

The legislative authority *divided*—beneficence—wisdom.

The executive authority, *one*—stability—vigor—responsibility.

The judicial authority independent—restraining the excesses of legislative and executive power. Property and personal security.

The result of this distribution of power—mutually to *prevent* and check excesses—to procure the advantages and avoid the inconveniencies of the different kinds of government.[a]

All authority is derived by representation from the people; the democratic principle is carried into every part of the government.

Right of suffrage, fundamental to republics, secured (Article 1, section 2).[b]

Representation and *direct* taxation according to numbers (Article 1, section 2).[c]

Members of the legislature cannot hold offices in government (Article 1, section 6).

Everything almost is transacted by a *majority*. The minority do not govern.[d]

The powers of the general government are necessary and well-defined.

The restraints on it and the state governments are salutary (Article 1, section 9).[e]

The power of punishing on impeachment for crimes and misdemeanors in office (Article 2, section 4).[f]

The accurate description of treason—its consequences confined to the criminal (Article 3, section 3).[g]

A republican government is guaranteed to each state (Article 4, section 4).[h]

The seeds of improvement by amendment (Article 5).[i] [Wilson's Notes, PHi]

> [Wilson's marginal notes]
> (a) The accurate line drawn between the powers of the general and those of the state governments.
> (b) Mont. b. 2. c. 2 [Montesquieu, I, 11–18].
> (c) Mont b. 9. c. 3 [Montesquieu, I, 188–89]. Neckar. 308 [I, 320].
> (d) Burl, 72 [J. J. Burlamaqui, *The Principles of Natural and Politic Law* (2nd ed., 2 vols., London, 1763), II, 72].
> (e) Paley's *Philos.* 270–272 [380–82]. Neckar 329, 332 [I, 332–34].
> (f) Mont. b. 11. c. 6. [Montesquieu, I, 221–37]. Bl 155 [Blackstone, I].
> (g) Mont. b. 12. c. 7. 11. 18 [Montesquieu, I, 278–79, 282, 289–91].
> (h) Mont. b. 9. c. 2. [Montesquieu, I, 187–88].
> (i) Mont. b. 11. c. 8. [Montesquieu, I, 238–40].

Wilson: I will now proceed to take some notice of those qualities in this Constitution, that I think entitle it to our respect and favor. I have not yet done, sir, with the great principle on which it stands; I mean the practical recognition of this doctrine, that in the United States the people retain the supreme power.

In giving a definition of the simple kinds of government known throughout the world, I had occasion to describe what I meant by a democracy; and I think I termed it, that government in which the people retain the supreme power, and exercise it either collectively or by representation—this Constitution declares this principle in its terms and in its consequences, which is evident from the manner in which it is announced: "WE, THE PEOPLE OF THE UNITED STATES." After all the examination, which I am able to give the subject, I view this as the only sufficient and the most honorable basis, both for the people and government, on which our Constitution can possibly rest. What are all the contrivances of states, of kingdoms, and empires? What are they all intended for? They are all intended for man, and our natural character and natural rights are certainly to take place, in preference to all artificial refinements that human wisdom can devise.

I am astonished to hear the ill-founded doctrine, that states alone ought to be represented in the federal government; these must possess sovereign authority forsooth, and the people be forgot. No, let us *reascend* to first principles. That expression is not strong enough to do my ideas justice. Let us RETAIN first principles. The people of the United States are now in the possession and exercise of their original rights, and while this doctrine is known, and operates, we shall have a cure for every disease.

I shall mention another good quality, belonging to this system. In it the legislative, executive, and judicial powers are kept nearly independent and distinct. I express myself in this guarded manner, because I am aware of some powers that are blended in the Senate. They are but few; and they are not dangerous. It is an exception, yet that exception consists of but few instances, and none of them dangerous. I believe [that] in no constitution for any country on earth is this great principle so strictly adhered to, or marked with so much precision and accuracy, as in this. It is much more accurate, than that which the honorable gentleman [John Smilie] so highly extols, I mean the constitution of England. There, sir, one branch of the legislature can appoint the members of another. The king has the power of introducing members into the House of Lords. I have already mentioned that in order to obtain a vote, twelve peers were poured into that house at one time; the operation is the same, as might be under this Constitution, if the President had a right to appoint the members of the Senate. This power of the king's extends into the other branch, where, though he cannot immediately introduce a member, yet he can do it remotely by virtue of his prerogative, as he may create boroughs with power to send members to the House of Commons. The House of Lords form a much stronger exception to this principle than the Senate in this system; for the House of Lords possess judicial powers, not only that of trying impeachments, but that of trying their own members, and civil causes when brought before them, from the courts of chancery, and the other courts in England.

If we therefore consider this Constitution, with regard to this special object, though it is not so perfect as I would wish, yet it is more perfect than any other government that I know.

I proceed to another property which I think will recommend it to those who consider the effects of beneficence and wisdom. I mean the *division of this legislative authority* into two branches. I had an opportunity of dilating somewhat on this subject before. And as it is not likely to afford a subject of debate, I shall take no further notice of it, than barely to mention it. The next good quality, that I remark is, that the *executive authority is one*; by this means we obtain very important advantages. We may discover from history, from reasoning, and from experience, the security which this furnishes. The executive power is better to be trusted when it has no *screen.* Sir, we have a responsibility in the person of our President; he cannot act improperly, and hide either his negligence, or inattention; he cannot roll upon any other person the weight of his criminality. No appointment can take place without his nomination; and he is responsible for every nomination he makes. We secure *vigor*; we well know what numerous executives are. We know there is neither vigor, decision, nor responsibility in them. Add to all this, that officer is placed high, and is possessed of power, far from being contemptible, yet not a *single privilege* is annexed to his character; far from being *above the laws,* he is *amenable* to them in his *private character* as a *citizen,* and in his public character by impeachment.

Sir, it has often been a matter of surprise, and frequently complained of even in Pennsylvania, that the independence of the judges is not properly secured. The servile dependence of the judges, in some of the states that have neglected to make proper provision on this subject, endangers the liberty and property of the citizen; and I apprehend that whenever it has happened that the appointment has been for a less period than during good behavior, this object has not been sufficiently secured—for if every five or seven years, the judges are obliged to make court for a reappointment to office, they cannot be styled independent. This is not the case with regard to those appointed under the general government. For the judges here shall hold their offices during good behavior. I hope no further objections will be taken, against this part of the Constitution, the consequence of which will be, that private property (so far as it comes before their courts) and personal liberty, so far as it is not forfeited by crimes, will be guarded with firmness and watchfulness.

It may appear too professional to descend into observations of this kind, but I believe, that public happiness, personal liberty, and private property depend essentially upon the able and upright determinations of independent judges.

Permit me to make one more remark on the subject of the judicial department. Its objects are intended *beyond* the bounds or power of every particular state, and therefore must be proper objects of the general government. I do not recollect any instance where a case can come before the judiciary of the United States, that could possibly be determined by a particular state, except one, which is, where citizens of the same state claim lands under the grant of different states, and in that instance, the power of the two states necessarily comes in competition; wherefore there would be great impropriety in having it determined by either.

Sir, I think there is another subject with regard to which this Constitution deserves approbation. I mean the *accuracy* with which the *line is drawn* between the powers of the *general government,* and that of the *particular state governments.* We have heard some general observations on this subject, from the gentlemen who conduct the opposition. They have asserted that these powers are unlimited and undefined. These words are as easily pronounced as limited and defined. They have already been answered by my honorable colleague (Thomas M'Kean) therefore, I shall not enter into an explanation; but it is not pretended, that the line is drawn with mathematical precision; the inaccuracy of language must, to a certain degree, prevent the accomplishment of such a desire. Whoever views the matter in a true light will see that the powers are as minutely enumerated and defined as was possible, and will also discover that the general clause [Article I, section 8], against which so much exception is taken, is nothing more than what was necessary to render effectual the particular powers that are granted.

But let us suppose (and the supposition is very easy in the minds of the gentlemen on the other side) that there is some difficulty in ascertaining where the true line lies. Are we therefore thrown into despair? Are disputes between the general government and the state governments to be necessarily the consequence of inaccuracy? I hope, sir, they will not be the enemies of each other, or resemble comets in conflicting orbits mutually operating destruction. But that their motion will be better represented by that of the planetary system, where each part moves harmoniously within its proper sphere, and no injury arises by interference or opposition. Every part, I trust, will be considered as a part of the United States. Can any cause of distrust arise here? Is there any increase of risk, or rather are not the enumerated powers as well defined here, as in the present Articles of Confederation?

Permit me to proceed to what I deem another excellency of this system—all authority of every kind *is derived by* REPRESENTATION *from the* PEOPLE, *and the* DEMOCRATIC *principle is carried into every part of the government.* I had an opportunity when I spoke first of going fully into an elucidation of this subject. I mean not now to repeat what I then said.

I proceed to another quality that I think estimable in this system—*it secures in the strongest manner the right of suffrage.* Montesquieu, book 2d, ch. 2d [I, 11–18], speaking of laws relative to democracy, says, "when the body of the people is possessed of the SUPREME POWER, this is called a *democracy.* When the SUPREME POWER is lodged in the hands of a part of the people, it is then an *aristocracy.*

"In a democracy the people are in some respects the sovereign, and in others the subject.

"There can be no exercise of sovereignty but by their suffrages, which are their own will; now, the sovereign's will is the sovereign himself. The laws, therefore, which establish the right of suffrage are fundamental to this government. And indeed it is as important to regulate, in a republic, in what manner, by whom, to whom, and concerning what, suffrages are to be given, as it is in a monarchy, to know who is the prince, and after what manner he ought to govern."

In this system it is declared, that the electors in each state shall have the qualification requisite for electors of the most numerous branch of the state legislature. This being made the criterion of the right of suffrage, it is consequently secured, because the same Constitution *guarantees* to every state in the Union a *republican* form of government. The right of suffrage is fundamental to republics.

Sir, there is another principle that I beg leave to mention. *Representation and direct taxation,* under this Constitution, are to be according to numbers. As this is a subject which I believe has not been gone into in this house, it will be worthwhile to show the sentiments of some respectable writers thereon. Montesquieu, in considering the requisites in a confederate republic, book 9th, ch. 3d [I, 188–89], speaking of Holland observes, "it is difficult for the united states to be all of equal power and extent. The Lycian republic[a] was an association of twenty-three towns; the large ones had three votes in the common council, the middling ones two, and the small towns one. The Dutch republic consists of seven provinces, of different extent of territory, which have each one voice."

The cities of Lycia[b] *contributed to the expenses of the state, according to the proportion of suffrages.* The provinces of the United Netherlands cannot follow this proportion; they must be directed by that of their power.

In Lycia[c] the judges and town magistrates were elected by the common council, *and according to the proportion already mentioned.* In the republic of Holland, they are not chosen by the common council, but each town names its magistrates. Were I to give a model of an excellent confederate republic, I should pitch upon that of Lycia.

I have endeavored, in all the books that I could have access to, to acquire some information relative to the Lycian republic, but its history is not to be found; the few facts that relate to it are mentioned only by Strabo; and however excellent the model it might present, we were reduced to the necessity of working without it. Give me leave to quote the sentiments of another author, whose peculiar situation and extensive worth throws a luster on all he says, I mean Mr. Neckar, whose ideas are very exalted both in theory and practical knowledge on this subject. He approaches the nearest to the truth in his calculations from experience, and it is very remarkable that he makes use of that expression. His words are,[d] "population can therefore be only looked on as an exact measure of comparison, when the provinces have resources nearly equal; but even this imperfect rule of proportion ought not to be neglected; and of all the objects which may be subjected to a determined and positive calculation, that of the taxes, to the population, approaches nearest to the truth."

Another good quality in this Constitution is, that the members of the *legislature cannot hold offices under the authority of this government.* The operation of this I apprehend would be found to be very extensive, and very salutary in this country, to prevent those intrigues, those factions, that corruption, that would otherwise rise here, and have risen so plentiful in every other country. The reason why it is necessary in England to continue such influence is that the Crown, in order to secure its own influence against two other branches of the legislature, must continue to bestow places, but those *places* produce the opposition which frequently runs so strong in the British Parliament.

Members who do not enjoy offices combine against those who do enjoy them. It is not from principle, that they thwart the ministry in all its operations. No, their language is, let us turn them out and succeed to their places. The great source of corruption in that country is that persons may hold offices under the Crown, and seats in the legislature at the same time.

I shall conclude at present, and I have endeavored to be as concise as possible, with mentioning, that in my humble opinion, the powers of the general government are necessary, and well defined—that the restraints imposed on it, and those imposed on the state governments, are rational and salutary, and that it is entitled to the approbation of those for whom it was intended.

I recollect, on a former day, the honorable gentleman from Westmoreland (William Findley) and the honorable gentleman from Cumberland (Robert Whitehill) took exceptions against the first clause of the 9th section, Article I, arguing very unfairly, that because Congress might impose a tax or duty of ten dollars on the importation of slaves, within any of the United States, Congress might therefore permit slaves to be imported within this state, contrary to its laws. I confess I little thought that this part of the system would be excepted to.

I am sorry that it could be extended no further; but so far as it operates, it presents us with the pleasing prospect, that the rights of mankind will be acknowledged and established throughout the Union.

If there was no other lovely feature in the Constitution, but this one, it would diffuse a beauty over its whole countenance. Yet the lapse of a few years and Congress will have power to exterminate slavery from within our borders.

How would such a delightful prospect expand the breast of a benevolent and philanthropic European? Would he cavil at an expression? Catch at a phrase? No, sir, that is only reserved for the gentleman [William Findley] on the other side of your chair to do. What would be the exultation of that great man, whose name I have just now mentioned, we may learn from the following sentiments on this subject. They cannot be expressed so well as in his own words.[e]

"The colonies of France contain as we have seen, near five hundred thousand slaves, and it is from the number of these wretches, that the inhabitants set a value on their plantations. What a fatal prospect and how profound a subject for reflection! Alas! How inconsequent we are, both in our morality, and our principles. We preach up humanity, and yet go every year to bind in chains twenty thousand natives of Africa! We call the Moors barbarians and ruffians, because they attack the liberty of Europeans, at the risk of their own; yet these Europeans go, without danger, and as mere speculators, to purchase slaves, by gratifying the cupidity of their masters; and excite all those bloody scenes which are the usual preliminaries of this traffic! In short, we pride ourselves on the superiority of man, and it is with reason that we discover this superiority, in the wonderful and mysterious unfolding of the intellectual faculties; and yet a trifling difference in the hair of the head, or in the color of the epidermis, is sufficient to change our respect into contempt, and to engage us to place beings like ourselves, in the rank of those animals devoid of reason, whom we subject to the yoke; that we may make use of their strength, and of their instinct, at command.

"I am sensible, and I grieve at it, that these reflections which others have made much better than me, are unfortunately of very little use!

The necessity of supporting sovereign power has its peculiar laws, and the wealth of nations is one of the foundations of this power. Thus the sovereign who should be the most thoroughly convinced of what is due to humanity, would not singly renounce the service of slaves in his colonies; time alone could furnish a population of free people to replace them, and the great difference that would exist in the price of labor, would give so great an advantage to the nation that should adhere to the old custom, that the others would soon be discouraged in wishing to be more virtuous. And yet, would it be a chimerical project to propose a general compact, by which all the European nations should unanimously agree to abandon the traffic of African slaves! They would in that case, find themselves exactly in the same proportion relative to each other as at present; for it is only on comparative riches that the calculations of power are founded.

"We cannot as yet indulge such hopes; statesmen in general, think that every common idea must be a low one; and since the morals of private people stand in need of being curbed, and maintained by the laws, we ought not to wonder, if those of sovereigns conform to their independence.

"The time may nevertheless arrive, when, fatigued of that ambition which agitates them, and of the continual rotation of the same anxieties, and the same plans, they may turn their views to the great principles of humanity; and if the present generation is to be witness of this happy revolution, they may at least be allowed to be unanimous in offering up their vows for the perfection of the social virtues, and for the progress of public beneficial institutions." These are the enlarged sentiments of that great man.

Permit me to make a single observation in this place on the restraints placed on the state governments. If only the following lines were inserted in this Constitution, I think it would be worth our adoption: "No state shall hereafter *emit bills of credit*; make any thing, but gold and silver coin, a *tender* in payment of debts; pass any bills of attainder; ex post facto law; *or law impairing the obligation of contracts.*" Fatal experience has taught us, dearly taught us, the value of these restraints. What is the consequence even at this moment? It is true we have no tender law in Pennsylvania; but the moment you are conveyed across the Delaware you find it haunts your journey and follows close upon your heels. The paper passes commonly at twenty-five or thirty percent discount.[2] How insecure is property!

These are a few of those properties in this system, that I think recommend it to our serious attention, and will entitle it to receive the adoption of the United States. Others might be enumerated, and others still will probably be disclosed by experience. [Lloyd, *Debates,* 84–92]

[Lloyd's notes]
(a) Strabo, lib. 14 [Horace L. Jones, trans., *The Geography of Strabo* (8 vols., London, 1917–1932), VI, 313–15].
(b) Ibid.
(c) Ibid.
(d) Neckar on Finance, Vol. 1. p. 308 [I, 320].
(e) Ibid., Vol. 1, page 329 [I, 330–34].

Wilson: The meaning of a natural aristocracy—trace it to the original, and it is the men most noted for *virtue* and *abilities.* It is only in little remote corners where demagogues arise. In large districts the man of abilities and virtue can only be appointed.

Taxes levying and collecting: there are 1,000 in this state, including comptrollers, etc.[a]

Paper money has been lately suspected by all *parties, vide* the Journals of the House of Assembly of Pennsylvania, *March 1786.*[3]

In the Massachusetts government the election of governor was confined to 4 men of virtue and knowledge. That men must return to the common mass, etc.

[Wayne's marginal note]
(a) Neckers Book: on the Finances of France [I, 332–34]: taxation in the *ratio* of numbers the best *criterion.*

[Wayne's miscellaneous notes]
A power to compel the *requisitions* of Congress—we *concede.* Could any powers less than those granted answer this purpose?
400,000 souls in Pennsylvania.
When 21 years comes round the Congress may continue it.
They have redeemed their paper money better than *Congress*—therefore this Constitution is *necessary,* for it prohibits paper currency from being ever made a *tender.*
[Wayne's Notes, Cox Collection]

1. Vetoes by the governor of Massachusetts could be overridden by a two-thirds vote of each house. The veto power in New York was exercised by the governor, the chancellor, and the judges of the supreme court sitting as the Council of Revision. Its vetoes could be overridden by a two-thirds vote of each house. In the Constitutional Convention Wilson had been one of the minority which had argued for an absolute veto power for the President.

2. The reference is to the £100,000 of legal tender paper money authorized by the New Jersey legislature in May 1786.

3. Probably a reference to the petition campaign in March 1786 to support the recharter of the Bank of North America. Between 3 and 29 March petitions signed by 2,947 people were submitted to the Assembly. The Bank's charter had been repealed by the Constitutionalist-controlled Assembly on 13 September 1785, and the recharter campaign was viewed as an attack on the state paper currency. The Bank was given a limited charter in March 1787 (Mathew Carey, ed., *Debates and Proceedings of the General Assembly of Pennsylvania . . .* [Philadelphia, 1786]).

The Pennsylvania Convention
Wednesday
5 December 1787

Convention Proceedings, A.M.

The Convention met pursuant to adjournment,

And resumed the consideration of the first Article of the proposed Constitution. After some inquiry into the qualified negative of the President, and the general construction of the new government,

Adjourned until half after four o'clock, P.M.

Convention Debates, A.M.

William Findley: (48) The states made bills of rights, not because they were known in Britain; but because they were proper.
(49) A majority of the states have them.
(50) M. b. 2. c. 2. [Montesquieu, I, 11–18.] "The People, in whom the Supreme Power resides."
(51) Vat. b. 1. s. 1. 2. [Vattel, 15–16.] "Sovereignty."
(52) The sovereignty is essentially in the people; but is vested in a senate or a monarch.
(53) Vat. b. 1. s. 11. 10 [Vattel, 18].
(54) If all the powers of sovereignty are vested in one *man* or *body*; it is a tyranny.
(55) The states have already parted with a portion of their sovereignty. It is now proposed to give more. But the people did not mean that the whole should be given up to the general government.
(56) The state governments are not subordinate to the general government as to *internal taxes* and other *internal* purposes.
(57) Congress may, with safety, raise a revenue from commerce.
(58) The general government is farther removed from the people than the state governments.
(59) There cannot be two taxing powers on the same subject—taxation draws legislation with it. There will [be] no sovereignty in the states with regard to taxation.
(60) There is no sovereignty left in the state governments—the only one is in the general government.
(61) The general interests of Pennsylvania were not represented in the [Constitutional] Convention.
(62) Sovereignty essentially resides in the people, but they have *vested*

certain parts of it in the state governments, and other parts in the present Congress.
(63) We never said that the people were made for the states.
(64) Who denied that sovereignty was inalienably in the people?
(65) There is a declaration in the bill of rights of Pennsylvania that the people may change the constitution—and they only add a constitutional right—which is also done in the system before us. The same thing has also been done in some of the other states.
(66) The checks on the Senate are not *sufficient*.
(67) We ought to draw instruction from the state constitutions. Many of them—Virginia in particular—declare that the legislative, executive and judicial departments should be kept distinct and independent.
(68) What can be a greater source of corruption than for the legislature to appoint officers and fix salaries?
(69) I would be at any expense rather than submit to the beginnings of corruption such as this.
(70) There can be no legislation without taxation. The states will not be able to raise a civil list.
(71) I mean by a consolidating government that which puts all the thirteen states into one.
(72) This is a consolidating government as to all useful purposes of sovereignty.
(73) In the Senate, a citizen of Delaware enjoys ten votes for one that a citizen of Pennsylvania enjoys.
(74) It is not all one for a citizen of Pennsylvania to be taxed by a Representative from Georgia, as for by his own Representative.
(75) The smaller states have a majority in the Senate; and they may lay taxes on the larger states.
(76) Congress may make the number of Representatives as few as they please.
(77) In Pennsylvania before the Revolution, the new counties were unequally represented.
(78) Pennsylvania is unequally represented in the House of Representatives.
(79) 100 members are enough for a deliberative body. And, on the present plan, the *number* will be either too large, or the representation too small. To avoid this, let us have a federal government. Internal power in a federal government is *inadmissible*. See next page but one.[1]
(80) To state the danger of refusing this plan is improper. It is the tyrant's plea: Take this or nothing.[2] [Wilson's Notes, PHi]

Findley: Montesquieu *Lib*. 2. cap. 2 [I, 11–18]. The people in whom the supreme power resides ought to have the management of everything within their reach. What exceeds their abilities must be conducted by their ministers (Vattel *Lib.* 1 fol. 1) [15–16]. The supreme power is placed in the people (Vattel. c. 2. pa. 10. 11 [18]).

States forming a federal republic: The federal head should regulate commerce, but its powers should go no further. The powers of legislation will follow taxation. The sovereignty of the state legislatures will be entirely destroyed by the Federal Constitution. The general interests of Pennsylvania were not represented in the late Convention. Had I been in the Convention, I would have opposed the shutting of the doors, and would have collected intelligence from the sentiments of my friends.

Sovereignty essentially resides in the people, but they may vest what portion of it they please in state legislatures. I agree that states were made for the people and not the people for the states.

If the constitution of Pennsylvania is wrong, we ought not to adopt for that reason a wrong federal system. Our constitution points out a constitutional mode of altering our systems if found improper.

The state constitution of Virginia expressly directs that the legislative, executive, and judicial departments should be kept separate. So says Montesquieu and reason.

There is no rotation of offices under the present federal system as proposed to us.

Means are not left in each state to support a civil list.

The smaller states have an equal vote in the Senate with the larger states, but this is rather to be lamented than avoided.

There will be no saving of public expense in the different states by adopting the new Constitution.

The people are not sufficiently represented in the House of Representatives. The number is too small for an extended empire. [Yeates's Notes, PPIn]

Findley: Contends for a bill of rights, the liberty of the *press,* trial by *jury.*

I mean by sovereignty,[(a)] speaking on Roman government—the people in whom the supreme power resides.[(b)]

When I was proposed as a member of the late Convention, I declined it as I thought it too great an undertaking *for me* to *represent* and *guard* all the rights and liberties of the people of Pennsylvania.

The Congress may lessen the R[epresentatives?] to one from each state.[(c)]

The D[eclaration of Rights] in the state constitution say that the people have a *right* to alter, etc.

Biennial elections 1/3 [of the Senate] *may* be changed. The appointment to office removes those who may be appointed [from the requirement of rotation in office]; and if the appointments have been wrong, etc., [those appointed cannot be removed?].[(d)]

Taxes:[(e)]

The Senate and *Council* of *Censors.*

To be taxed by government. The *counties* may object; [that?] the citizens of Philadelphia. [Wayne's Notes, Cox Collection]

[Wayne's marginal notes]
(a) Mont: *S.L.* B 2nd. C 2nd [Montesquieu, I, 11–18].
(b) V. 1 . . 1 Book 12 Ch: Page 19 C:4-p:10. p 11 [Vattel, 15–16, 18].
(c) *Vide* 3C 2 sect [Article I, section 2, clause 3].
(d) bienl Electns. & Impeachments.
Page 218 last clause in 6th sect [Article I, section 6].
(e) 3 Cl 2 sect: 4C 9th sect [Article I, section 2, clause 3; section 9, clause 4].

1. Wilson refers to objection number 95, which appears on the following page of his manuscript notes.

2. Wilson answered this charge by stating that "the argument of necessity is the patriot's defense, as well as the tyrant's plea" (Convention Debates, P.M., 11 December).

Convention Proceedings, P.M.

The Convention met pursuant to adjournment,

Resumed the consideration of the first Article of the proposed Constitution, and after some debate,

Adjourned until half after nine o'clock tomorrow, A.M.

Convention Debates, P.M.

WILLIAM FINDLEY: (81) The partial negative of the President is a part of legislative authority, as no bill can become a law without his revision.

(82) Mr. [John] Adams defines a natural aristocracy. "Such as have a separate interest from the community." "Those that, in most countries, are called the nobles."

(83) The larger the districts, the purer the elections is a novel doctrine to us, and opposed to the very end of elections.

(84) Adam's, *Def.* Pref. p. 3 [*Defence,* preface].[1]

(85) The voice of the people is the law of the land.[(a)]

(86) Are 8 members a better representation of Pennsylvania than what they now enjoy?

(87) While the *forms* of state governments continue, all their apparatus of offices continue.

(88) We all mean the same thing about the sovereignty of the people. Sovereignty remains *essentially* in them.
(89) Annual elections are an annual recognition of the sovereignty of the people.
(90) Are the state governments a snare? They are not wrapped in mystery and darkness.(b)
(91) I believe that there are governments that keep the several powers more distinct than the system before us.
(92) We are agreed as to the independence of the judges.
(93) The present system has increased the difficulty of drawing the line between general and state governments by encroaching into *internal* objects.
(94) The President may aid the aristocratical Senate—and must aid it.
(95) Internal powers in a federal government are inadmissible.
(96) There is no guard against Congress making paper money.
(97) The states have redeemed their paper money better than Congress have done.
(98) Amendments will always take more power from the people and give more to the government.
(99) There is no security for such amendments as we want. If we don't obtain them now; we shall probably never procure them.
(100) The system ought to speak for itself; and not need explanations. [Wilson's Notes, PHi]

[Wilson's marginal notes]
(a) But not the voice of *districts.*
(b) An attempt was made to trap the people of Pennsylvania at the time of forming its constitution.

* * * *

STEPHEN CHAMBERS: From the silence on the other side, I conclude they have no more to say against the first Article. I move to proceed to the consideration of the second Article. [Wilson's Notes, PHi]

* * * *

ANTHONY WAYNE: I second the motion. I hope the reasons in favor of the proposed Constitution will induce many of the opposition to come over. [Wilson's Notes, PHi]

* * * *

ROBERT WHITEHILL: (101) If we go to the 2d Article, shall we be permitted to draw our objections from the first, to show that this is a consolidating government and will annihilate the states?
(102) Article 1, section 3: How shall the seats of the first, etc. class of the Senators be vacated? This must be made by law of the Senators and Representatives. But they may make or not make this law at their pleasure.

(103) The present Congress or some other body should have decided this matter.
(104) The Senate may be enlarged under the 5th Article. "Its equal Suffrage" may mean a suffrage in proportion to numbers; and consequently would increase the numbers and influence of the Senate.
(105) Such members may be chosen as the city of Philadelphia shall please—men of wealth, etc.
(106) Article 5: To whom are Congress to propose amendments? To a few men of the different states if they please.
(107) Congress, when they propose amendments, will have it in their power to regulate the elections of convention; or may order one election and one convention for the whole Union.
(108) As long as the world stands, there never will be another amendment if the present system be confirmed.
(109) Even post roads are in the power of Congress.
(110) A citizen of one state may sue a citizen of another state for an inheritance of land claimed by will under the law of the state where the land is.
(111) They may establish the right of primogeniture. [Wilson's Notes, PHi]

Whitehill: How are two of the Senators to take *rotation* (the 4th section, 1 Article)? How are the proposals, and to whom are they to be made—to the legislatures or to conventions—or [the organization of] Congress may be proposed by *that body* [itself] (*vide* [Article I], 5th section)?

The [Congress] may have power to regulate the wills of the *people*. [Wayne's Notes, Cox Collection]

* * * *

JOHN SMILIE: (112) Has not this day been pretty closely occupied by us in the opposition? [Wilson's Notes, PHi]

1. Adams declared that smaller election districts and shorter distances to polling places were "great advances towards the annihilation of corruption" (CC:16).

The Pennsylvania Convention
Thursday
6 December 1787

Convention Proceedings

The Convention met pursuant to adjournment,

And resumed the consideration of the first Article of the proposed

Constitution. After some debate on the powers vested in Congress to raise and support armies, to organize and superintend the militia, to regulate elections, and on the responsibility of Congress in the exercise of these powers,

Adjourned until half after nine o'clock tomorrow, A.M.

Convention Debates

John Smilie: (113) I object to the power of Congress over the militia and to keep a standing army.

(114) What I mean by a consolidating government is one that will transfer the sovereignty from the state governments to the general government.

(115) It is properly an aristocracy,

(116) because the Representatives are too few, and will be elected only by a few tools in very large districts.

(117) In Pennsylvania before the Revolution, the little county towns governed the elections.

(118) The people will not attend the election; only the tools of government will attend.

(119) If Congress exercise their powers over the times, places, and manner of elections, where are we? 8 men may be elected in one ticket and at one place. Should anybody have this power?

(120) The balance of power is in the Senate. Their share in the executive department will corrupt the legislature, and detracts from the proper power of the President, and will make the President merely a tool to the Senate.

(121) The President should have had the appointment of all officers, with the advice of a council.

(122) The Senate will overset the balance of government by having the purse and the sword. The President will act in concert with them.

(123) In a free government there never will be need of standing armies; for it depends on the confidence of the people. If it does not so depend, it is not free.

(124) The Convention, in framing this government, knew it was not a free one; otherwise they would not have asked the power of the purse and the sword.

(125) The last resource of a free people is taken away; for Congress are to have the command of the militia.

(126) The laws of Pennsylvania have hitherto been executed without the aid of the militia.

(127) The governor of each state will be only the drill sergeant of Congress.

(128) The militia officers will be obliged by oath to support the general government against that of their own state.
(129) Congress may give us a select militia which will, in fact, be a standing army—or Congress, afraid of a general militia, may say there shall be no militia at all.
(130) When a select militia is formed; the people in general may be disarmed.
(131) Will the states give up to Congress their last resource—the command of the militia?
(132) Will the militia laws be as mild under the general government as under the state governments? Militia men may be punished with whipping or death. They may [be] dragged from one state to any other.
(133) "Congress guarantees to each State a *Republican* Form of Government." Is this a security for a *free* government? (Mr. Adams's *Defence,* 86, Poland is a republic.)
(134) Can even the shadow of state governments be continued if Congress please to take it away?
(134) [*sic*] The Senate and President may dismiss the Representatives, when once a standing army is established with funds; and there this government will terminate. [Wilson's Notes, PHi]

Smilie: The President has no powers—he is only a tool to the *Senate.* The officers of the army will obey those who appoint them.

Vide the last clause but 2 in 8 section 1 [Article]. Will the mild laws of the states for governing the *militia* be continued by Congress? No, we shall find laws to inflict corporal punishment.

Section 4th Article 6: Congress shall guarantee to each state a republican form of government. [Wayne's Notes, Cox Collection]

Smilie: I mean to consider the consequences of the power of Congress over the militia and their keeping up a standing army. [Yeates's Notes, PPIn]

* * * *

WILLIAM FINDLEY: (135) The objections of the member from Fayette [John Smilie] are founded, important, and of extensive practical influence. Tax and militia laws are of universal operation.
(136) The militia will be taken from home; and when the militia of one state has quelled insurrections and destroyed the liberties, the militia of the last state may, at another time, be employed in retaliating on the first.
(137) No provision in behalf of those who are conscientiously scrupulous of bearing arms. [Wilson's Notes, PHi]

Findley: By the silence of the gentlemen on the *other side* I take that they concede and admit the force of the arguments offered by the member from Fayette [John Smilie].

The militia may be ordered from New Hampshire to Georgia to suppress an *insurrection.* [Wayne's Notes, Cox Collection]

* * * *

JOHN SMILIE: (138) As citizens, we are all equally interested. Let us have a friendly, free, and fair discussion. [Wilson's Notes, PHi]

Smilie: I have [hope] the gentlemen will not take advantage of the sickness of one of our members. [Wayne's Notes, Cox Collection]

* * * *

WILLIAM FINDLEY: (139) The power of regulating elections remains to be considered.
(140) Article 1, section 4 as to the "Place" of elections struck the public more suddenly and with more force than any other. The "*Time*" may be justified.
(141) Congress may say that none shall vote by ballot.
(142) The *modes* of election will be appointed in such way as to give the greatest influence to government.
(143) The "Places" of elections are of more importance than the time or manner.
(144) The states were competent as to the places by their knowledge and responsibility. This is entrusted by our constitution to the state legislature.
(145) This can have no *virtuous* or *pure* use.
(146) The *place* of elections may be removed so as to take it out of the reach of the lower and middling classes of men.
(147) By this clause the government may mold and influence elections as it shall please.
(148) This government may go into the channel of monarchy; but more likely of aristocracy.
(149) Under the present Confederation, Congress have not both the power of raising standing armies and the means of paying them.
(150) I could not contrive a better plan [than] this for introducing aristocracy. [Wilson's Notes, PHi]

Findley: Has another objection to the power of regulating elections. Mr. Finley objects to the manner of holding elections (4th section, 1st Article). This state may have its representation reduced to 4, 3, and even to 1.

Query: What will be the proportion of the Delaware representation? 1 member for every *30,000*? [Wayne's Notes, Cox Collection]

* * * *

JOHN SMILIE: (151) Mr. Adams says there is in all societies a natural aristocracy. [Adams, *Defence,*] Letter. 53. p. 362. Three branches of government in every society. The executive ought to have a negative on the legislature.
(152) The people of United States thought a single branch sufficient for Congress, which is not a legislative but a *diplomatique* body, etc. (ibid.).
(153) [Adams, *Defence,*] Letter. 55. 372[-82]. [Wilson's Notes, PHi]

Smilie: Adams's book takes this direction (53L 362—55L 372P [Adams, *Defence,* Letters 53, 55, pp. 362-64, 372-82]). [Wayne's Notes, Cox Collection]

* * * *

ANTHONY WAYNE: [Objections to the Constitution and Answers][1]
Take notice of:

(1) The declamatory rep[robation?] and abuse of the members of the General Convention.

The late Convention have been frequently charged with intending to deprive the citizens of America of their nearest and dearest rights.

(2) The expenses of the present organization of the militia.

3,000 militia including pay, arms, rations, etc. for three months—the first [month] £40,000, the second and 3rd, £30,000. *Vide* Page XXVI Article 6; XXVII, Article 9 of the *Confederation*: troops to *garrison posts.* Mr. Smilie, the expenses of a standing army, *nothing* to the present expense of the *militia.*

(3) The mild militia laws, etc.

I recollect that in 1785 an attempt was made to lay a fine on the tender conscience to pay in proportion to per his estate.

(4) The Senate appoint officers and try the impeachment.

The President and [Supreme Executive] Council [of Pennsylvania] appoint and try impeachments.[2] [Wayne's Notes, Cox Collection]

1. Wayne's notes of debates on 6, 7, 8, and 11 December are on a single sheet of paper folded in half to make four pages. The notes for 6 December appear on pages one and three, those for the 7th appear on pages three and four, and the notes for the 8th on page four. Scraps of notes for the 11th appear on page one, while page two is blank. Each page is divided vertically into two columns—the right column for notes of debates, and the left for Wayne's marginal notes. On the bottom of the last page he wrote: "Take notice," and then listed four objections to the Constitution. Elaborations and answers to these objections appear on the first page in the left-hand column. Wayne's answers were not arranged in the exact order in which he listed the objections, but are so arranged here. For Wayne's manuscript notes, see Mfm:Pa. 263.

2. Section 20, Pennsylvania constitution of 1776 (Thorpe, V, 3087).

The Pennsylvania Convention
Friday
7 December 1787

Convention Proceedings

The Convention met pursuant to adjournment.

On motion of Stephen Chambers, seconded by James Wilson,

The Convention proceeded to the consideration of the remaining articles of the proposed Constitution; and after some inquiry into the construction and powers of the judiciary department,

Adjourned until half after nine o'clock tomorrow, A.M.

Convention Debates

ROBERT WHITEHILL: (154) The Vice President will be an useless and perhaps a dangerous officer; as he will be more blended with the legislature, and will have a voice when the votes are equal. Salaries may depend on his vote.
(155) The power of Congress to fix the time of choosing the Electors of the President is improper. We have no power to oblige Congress to act.
(156) The power of the Senate to make treaties is dangerous.
(157) The extent of this government is too great. It cannot be executed. We have proved it to be a consolidating government. [Wilson's Notes, PHi]

Whitehill: Vice President will be a dangerous officer. He has the casting vote in the Senate. It blends the legislative and executive departments. [Yeates's Notes, PPIn]

* * * *

JOHN SMILIE: It was said by Mr. Wilson that this government could not be executed. [Yeates's Notes, PPIn]

* * * *

WILLIAM FINDLEY: (158) Only a part of the executive power is vested in the President. The most influential part is in the Senate, and he only acts as *primus inter pares* of the Senate; only he has the sole right of nomination.
(159) The officers of government are the creatures of the Senate. The Senate should not, therefore, be the judges on impeachments.
(160) The great objection is the blending of executive and legislative power. Where they are blended, there can be no liberty. Mr. Adams

says so. This great subject is better understood by the people and attended to by the legislatures than any other. It is my duty to insist, and I will insist, that the distribution of power in the present system be amended. [Wilson's Notes, PHi]

Findley: President in appointing officers will generally nominate such persons as will be agreeable to the Senate. The legislative and executive departments are mixed in this Constitution [Yeates's Notes, PPIn]

* * * *

ROBERT WHITEHILL: (161) Why is the sovereignty of the people always brought to view? There are 13 sovereignties in the United States; and 13 different governments. Why knock down all distinction of different governments?
(162) The judicial department is blended with and will absorb the judicial powers of the several states; and nothing will be able to stop its way.
(163) The Supreme Court will have very extensive powers indeed. They must be as extensive as the United States.
(164) There must be a great number of inferior courts in the several states. One for a large state would not be enough. Shall an action for 5 or 10£ be brought in it? There ought to be one in every county. The number of judicial officers will be multiplied.
(165) Appeals will be to the Supreme Court; which will put it in the power of the wealthy to oppress the poor.
(166) The powers will be too extensive for the safety and happiness of the people. Justice cannot be administered.
(167) Any kind of action may, by contrivance, be brought into the federal courts.
(168) There may be courts of equity as well as law.
(169) Can the federal courts give relief to the complaints of the people in proper time? The state courts have much business. How much more will the general courts have?
(170) The general courts may alter the rights of descent and the division of real property. They may establish the rights of primogeniture.
(171) The trial of *crimes* is to be by jury; therefore the trial of civil causes is supposed not to be by jury.
(172) We preserved the trial by jury against the attempts of the British Crown.
(173) I wish, for the honor of the Convention, this had not been omitted.
(174) Article 3, section 2: "the Laws of the United States." Laws may be made in *pursuance* of the Constitution tho not *agreeably* to it. The laws may be unconstitutional.

(175) Treaties may be so made as to absorb the liberty of conscience, trial by jury, and all our liberties.
(176) "Citizens of another State" must mean *all* the citizens.
(177) There is no line drawn, in the judicial department, between the general and state governments.
(178) Houses may be broke open by the officers of the general government. They will not be bound by this Constitution. [Wilson's Notes, PHi]

Whitehill: The judicial powers will swallow up all the state courts' jurisdictions. The people will be dragged a great distance to attend the inferior federal courts. There must be a federal court in every county which, with the expense of officers attending it, will be a great burthen. The appeals will be very dangerous to the people. The wealthy must also succeed. Bonds will be sued for. Titles to lands will be tried in the federal courts. The direction of trials of crimes by a jury excludes trials in civil cases by a jury. The enumeration of the former excludes the latter.

The liberties of the people may be absorbed by a treaty. [Yeates's Notes, PPIn]

Whitehill: Contends that the judiciary powers granted to Congress will totally *absorb* the state *courts*. This power may extend to defeat and regulate the *wills* of the *citizens*. *Congress* can by this Constitution give all the real estate to the *eldest son*.

The Congress may deprive the citizens of America of the *liberty* of *conscience* by *treaty*.

The power to decide in controversies "between Citizens of different *States*."[(a)] [Wayne's Notes, Cox Collection]

> [Wayne's marginal note]
> (a) Answer: Shall the citizens of this state having a debt due to him in *Georgia* be paid in a paper currency @ 5 for one discount?

* * * *

James Wilson: This is the first time that the Article respecting the judicial department has come directly before us. I shall therefore take the liberty of making such observations as will enable honorable gentlemen to see the extent of the views of the Convention in forming this Article, and the extent of its probable operation.

This will enable gentlemen to bring before this house their objections more pointedly than, without any explanation, could be done. Upon a distinct examination of the different powers, I presume it will be found, that not one of them is unnecessary. I will go further—there is not one of them but will be discovered to be of such nature, as to be attended with very important advantages. I shall beg leave to premise one remark, that the Convention, when they formed this system, did not expect they were to deliver themselves, their relations, and their posterity into the hands of such men as are described by the honorable gentlemen in opposition. They did not suppose that the legislature under this Constitution would be an *association of demons*. They thought that a proper attention would be given by the citizens of the United States, at the general election, for members to the House of Representatives; they also believed, that the particular states would nominate as good men as they have heretofore done, to represent them in the Senate. If they should now do otherwise, the fault will not be in Congress, but in the people or states themselves. I have mentioned oftener than once, that for a people wanting to themselves, there is no remedy.

The Convention thought further (for on this very subject, there will appear caution, instead of imprudence in their transactions) they considered, that if suspicions are to be entertained, they are to be entertained with regard to the objects in which government have separate interests and separate views, from the interests and views of the people. To say that officers of government will oppress, when nothing can be got by oppression, is making an inference, bad as human nature is, that cannot be allowed. When persons can derive no advantage from it, it can never be expected they will sacrifice either their duty or their popularity.

Whenever the general government can be a party against a citizen, the trial is guarded and secured in the Constitution itself, and therefore it is not in its power to oppress the citizen. In the case of treason, for example, though the prosecution is on the part of the United States, yet the Congress can neither define nor try the crime. If we have recourse to the history of the different governments that have hitherto subsisted, we shall find that a very great part of their tyranny over the people has arisen from the extension of the definition of treason. Some very remarkable instances have occurred, even in so free a country as England. If I recollect right, there is one instance that puts this matter in a very strong point of view. A person possessed a favorite buck, and on finding it killed wished the horns in the belly of the person who killed it; this happened to be the king; the injured complainant was tried and convicted of treason, for wishing the king's death.

I speak only of free governments, for in despotic ones, treason depends entirely upon the will of the prince. Let this subject be attended to, and it will be discovered where the dangerous power of the government operates to the oppression of the people. Sensible of this, the Convention has guarded the people against it, by a particular and accurate definition of treason.

It is very true, that trial by jury is not mentioned in civil cases; but I take it, that it is very improper to infer from hence, that it was not meant to exist under this government. Where the people are represented—where the interest of government cannot be separate from that of the people (and this is the case in trial between citizen and citizen)—the power of making regulations with respect to the mode of trial may certainly be placed in the legislature; for I apprehend that the legislature will not do wrong in an instance, from which they can derive no advantage. These were not all the reasons that influenced the Convention to leave it to the future Congress to make regulations on this head.

By the constitutions of the different states, it will be found that no particular mode of trial by jury could be discovered that would suit them all. The manner of summoning jurors, their qualifications, of whom they should consist, and the course of their proceedings are all different, in the different states; and I presume it will be allowed a good general principle, that in carrying into effect the laws of the general government by the judicial department, it will be proper to make the regulations as agreeable to the habits and wishes of the particular states as possible; and it is easily discovered that it would have been impracticable, by any general regulation, to have given satisfaction to all. We must have thwarted the custom of eleven or twelve to have accommodated any one. Why do this, when there was no danger to be apprehended from the omission? We could not go into a particular detail of the manner that would have suited each state.

Time, reflection, and experience will be necessary to suggest and mature the proper regulations on this subject; time and experience were not possessed by the Convention; they left it therefore to be particularly organized by the legislature—the representatives of the United States, from time to time, as should be most eligible and proper. Could they have done better?

I know in every part, where opposition has risen, what a handle has been made of this objection; but I trust upon examination it will be seen that more could not have been done with propriety. Gentlemen talk of bills of rights! What is the meaning of this continual clamor, after what has been urged, though it may be proper in a single state, whose legislature calls itself the sovereign and supreme power? Yet it would be absurd in the body of the people, when they are delegating from among themselves persons to transact certain business, to add an enumeration of those things, which they are not to do. "But trial by jury is secured in the bill of rights of Pennsylvania; the parties have a right to trials by jury, which OUGHT to be held sacred," and what is the consequence? There has been more violations of this right in Pennsylvania, since the Revolution, than are to be found in England, in the course of a century.

I hear no objection made to the tenure by which the judges hold their offices. It is declared that the judges shall hold them during good behavior; nor to the security which they will have for their salaries. They shall at stated times receive for their services, a compensation which shall not be diminished during their continuance in office.

The Article respecting the judicial department is objected to as going too far and is supposed to carry a very indefinite meaning. Let us examine this—the judicial power shall extend to all cases in law and equity, *arising under this Constitution and the laws of the United States.* Controversies may certainly arise under this Constitution and the laws of the United States, and is it not proper that there should be judges to decide them? The honorable gentleman from Cumberland (Robert Whitehill) says, that laws may be made inconsistent with the Constitution; and that therefore the powers given to the judges are dangerous; for my part, Mr. President, I think the contrary inference true. If a law should be made inconsistent with those powers vested by this instrument in Congress, the judges, as a consequence of their independence, and the particular powers of government being defined, will declare such law to be null and void. For the power of the Constitution predominates. Anything, therefore, that shall be enacted by Congress contrary thereto will not have the force of law.

The judicial power extends to all cases arising under treaties made, or which shall be made, by the United States. I shall not repeat, at this time, what has been said with regard to the power of the states to make treaties; it cannot be controverted, that when made, they ought to be observed. But it is highly proper that this regulation should be made; for the truth is, and I am sorry to say it, that in order to prevent the payment of British debts, and from other causes, our treaties have been violated, and violated too by the express laws of several states in the Union. Pennsylvania, to her honor be it spoken, has hitherto done no act of this kind; but it is acknowledged, on all sides, that many states in the Union have infringed the treaty; and it is well-known, that when the minister of the United States [John Adams] made a demand of Lord Carmarthen, of a surrender of the western posts, he told the minister, with truth and justice, "The treaty, under which you claim those possessions, has not been performed on your part. Until that is done, those possessions will not be delivered up." This clause, sir, will show the world, that we make the faith of treaties a constitutional part of the character of the United States; that we secure its performance no longer nominally, for the judges of the United States will be enabled to carry them into effect, let the legislatures of the different states do what they may.[1]

The power of the judges extends to all cases affecting ambassadors, other public ministers, and consuls. I presume very little objection will be offered to this clause; on the contrary, it will be allowed proper and unexceptionable.

This will also be allowed with regard to the following clause, "all cases of admiralty and maritime jurisdiction."

The next is "to controversies to which the United States shall be a party." Now I apprehend it is something very incongruous, that, because the United States are a party, it should be urged, as an objection, that their judges ought not to decide, when the universal practice of all nations have and unavoidably must admit of this power. But say the gentlemen, the sovereignty of the states is destroyed, if they should be engaged in a controversy with the United States, because a suitor in a court must acknowledge the jurisdiction of that court, and it is not the custom of sovereigns to suffer their names to be made use of in this manner. The answer is plain and easy. The government of each state ought to be subordinate to the government of the United States.

"To controversies between two or more states." This power is vested in the present Congress, but they are unable, as I have already shown [4 December, A.M.], to enforce their decisions. The additional power of carrying their decrees into execution, we find is therefore necessary, and I presume no exception will be taken to it.

"Between a state, and citizens of another state." When this power is attended to, it will be found to be a necessary one. Impartiality is the leading feature in this Constitution; it pervades the whole. When a citizen has a controversy with another state, there ought to be a tribunal where both parties may stand on a just and equal footing.

"Between citizens of different states, and between a state, or the citizens thereof, and foreign states, citizens or subjects." This part of the jurisdiction, I presume, will occasion more doubt than any other part, and at *first view* it may seem exposed to objections well-founded and of great weight; but I apprehend this can be the case only *at first view*. Permit me to observe here, with regard to this power, or any other of the foregoing powers given to the Federal Court, that they are not exclusively given. In all instances the parties may commence suits in the courts of the several states. Even the United States may submit to such decision if they think proper.

Though the citizens of a state, and the citizens or subjects of foreign states, *may* sue in the Federal Court, it does not follow that they *must* sue.[2] These are the instances in which the jurisdiction of the United States may be exercised; and we have all the reason in the world to believe, that it will be exercised impartially; for it would be improper to infer, that the judges would abandon their duty, the rather for being independent. Such a sentiment is contrary to experience and ought not to be hazarded. If the people of the United States are fairly represented, and the President and Senate are wise enough to choose men of abilities and integrity for judges, there can be no apprehension; because, as I mentioned before, the government can have no interest in injuring the citizens.

But when we consider the matter a little further, is it not necessary, if we mean to restore either public or private credit, that foreigners, as well as ourselves, have a just and impartial tribunal to which they may resort? I would ask, how a merchant must feel to have his property lay at the mercy of the laws of Rhode Island?[3] I ask further, how will a creditor feel, who has his debts at the mercy of tender laws in other states? It is true, that under this Constitution, these particular iniquities may be restrained in future; but, sir, there are other ways of avoiding payment of debts. There have been installment acts, and other acts of a similar effect. Such things, sir, destroy the very sources of credit.

Is it not an important object to extend our manufactures and our commerce? This cannot be done unless a proper security is provided for the regular discharge of contracts. This security cannot be obtained unless we give the power of deciding upon those contracts to the general government.

I will mention further, an object that I take to be of particular magnitude, and I conceive these regulations will produce its accomplishment. The object, Mr. President, that I allude to is the improvement of our domestic navigation, the instrument of trade between the several states. That decay of private credit which arose from the destruction of public credit, by a too inefficient general government, will be restored, and this valuable intercourse among ourselves must give an increase to those useful improvements, that will astonish the world. At present, how are we circumstanced! Merchants of eminence will tell you that they can trust their correspondents without law; but they cannot trust the laws of the state in which their correspondents live. Their friend may die, and may be succeeded by a representative of a very different character. If there is any particular objection that did not occur to me on this part of the Constitution, gentlemen will mention it; and I hope when this

Article is examined, it will be found to contain nothing but what is proper to be annexed to the general government. The next clause, so far as it gives original jurisdiction in cases affecting ambassadors, I apprehend is perfectly unexceptionable.

It was thought proper to give the citizens of foreign states full opportunity of obtaining justice in the general courts, and this they have by its appellate jurisdiction; therefore, in order to restore credit with those foreign states, that part of the Article is necessary. I believe the alteration that will take place in their minds, when they learn the operation of this clause, will be a great and important advantage to our country, nor is it any thing but justice; they ought to have the same security against the state laws that may be made, that the citizens have, because regulations ought to be equally just in the one case as in the other. Further, it is necessary, in order to preserve peace with foreign nations. Let us suppose the case, that a wicked law is made in some one of the states, enabling a debtor to pay his creditor with the fourth, fifth, or sixth part of the real value of the debt, and this creditor, a foreigner, complains to his prince or sovereign, of the injustice that has been done him. What can that prince or sovereign do? Bound by inclination as well as duty to redress the wrong his subject sustains from the hand of perfidy, he cannot apply to the particular guilty state, because he knows that by the Articles of Confederation, it is declared that no state shall enter into treaties. He must therefore apply to the United States. The United States must be accountable. "My subject has received a flagrant injury; do me justice, or I will do myself justice." If the United States are answerable for the injury, ought they not to possess the means of compelling the faulty state to repair it? They ought, and this is what is done here. For now, if complaint is made in consequence of such injustice, Congress can answer, "why did not your subject apply to the General Court, where the unequal and partial laws of a particular state would have had no force?"

In two cases the Supreme Court has original jurisdiction; that affecting ambassadors, and when a state shall be a party. It is true, it has appellate jurisdiction in more, but it will have it under such restrictions as the Congress shall ordain. I believe that any gentleman, possessed of experience or knowledge on this subject, will agree that it was impossible to go further with any safety or propriety, and that it was best left in the manner in which it now stands.

"In all the other cases before mentioned, the supreme court shall have appellate jurisdiction, both as to law and fact." The jurisdiction as to fact may be thought improper, but those possessed of information on this head see that it is necessary. We find it essentially necessary from the ample experience we have had in the courts of admiralty with regard to captures. Those gentlemen, who during the late war had their vessels retaken, know well what a poor chance they would have had, when those vessels were taken into other states and tried by juries, and in what a situation they would have been, if the court of appeals had not been possessed of authority to reconsider and set aside the verdict of those juries. Attempts were made by some of the states to destroy this power, but it has been confirmed in every instance.

There are other cases in which it will be necessary; and will not Congress better regulate them as they rise from time to time, than could have been done by the Convention? Besides, if the regulations shall be attended with inconvenience, the Congress can alter them as soon as discovered. But any thing done in Convention must remain unalterable, but by the power of the citizens of the United States at large.

I think these reasons will show, that the powers given to the Supreme Court are not only safe, but constitute a wise and valuable part of this system. [Lloyd, *Debates,* 92–100]

Wilson: Care has been taken to prevent the government from doing acts of oppression in government matters. Trials by jury are secured in criminal cases. It is not to be supposed that individuals or a government will do oppressive things, unless from principles of interest, ambition, or emolument. There have been more violations of the rights of trial by jury in Pennsylvania since the Revolution than in England in the course of a century, notwithstanding a boasted bill of rights.

There are no instances of exclusive jurisdiction in the federal courts. There are but few cases of their having original jurisdiction. [Yeates's Notes, PPIn]

* * * *

John Smilie: (179) In common law cases there ought not to be an appeal as to facts. Facts found by a jury should never be reexamined.

(180) I doubt whether there has not been an intention to substitute the civil law instead of the common law.

(181) There may be danger in the execution of the judicial department, as in the case of a rigorous collection of direct taxes. A quarrel between a collector and a citizen would drag the citizen into the court of Congress.

(182) The courts must be very *numerous* or very *few*. Either will be inconvenient. They must be numerous.

(183) If the state governments are to continue, the people will not

be able to bear the expense of them and the general government. Will this save expense? [Wilson's Notes, PHi]

Smilie: In the case of the sloop *Active,*[4] the law passed in Pennsylvania[5] was founded on the immediate recommendation of Congress,[6] to try prize cases by jury. Jury trials may be superseded in civil cases. Appellate jurisdiction is a civil law term. There can be no appeal after jury trials. I fear there is an intention to substitute the civil law in the room of the common law. Think of the expense of the different courts and of the federal system at large. [Yeates's Notes, PPIn]

Smilie: In collecting direct taxes, whether the collector might have a quarrel with one of the citizens, may not that citizen be dragged away to the appellate court of *Congress*? The expenses will [be] *accumulated* by the additional *inferior courts*. [Wayne's Notes, Cox Collection]

* * * *

William Findley: (184) The Convention, no doubt, thought they were forming a contract or compact of the greatest importance.
(185) The judges are better for [because of] the guard of juries in all possible cases. The mistakes of juries are never systematical. The laws can never be so enacted, as to prevent the judges from doing wrong.
(186) I admit that it would have been impossible to have accommodated the trial by jury to all the states; but power ought not to have been given applying to such *internal* objects.
(187) There might have been a declaration that the trial by jury in civil cases as it hath hitherto been in the several states; or in the state, where the cause arose.
(188) The jurisdiction will, I believe, be chiefly appellate; and therefore, chiefly without jury.
(189) The states can make "no [ex] post facto Laws &c." Therefore there was no occasion for introducing the clause "between Citizens of different States."
(190) This clause may produce doubts in the dealings between citizens of this state and New Jersey.
(191) "Compensation" is a new term. Does it denote salary or perquisites? [Judges] should be incapable of holding offices under the states, or other offices under the general government. They may hold sinecures. I have only lately discovered this objection.
(192) A treaty is not constitutionally guarded. It may be superior to the legislature itself. The House of Representatives have nothing to do with treaties. [Wilson's Notes, PHi]

Findley: The powers vested by the new Constitution are not accurately and precisely defined. The liberties of the people are always safest where juries (who never go wrong by system) are called in and control the conduct of the judges.

Tho the individual states are restricted from making *ex post facto* laws, yet the general legislative authority is not prevented by the Constitution from making such laws.[7] [Yeates's Notes, PPIn]

Findley: I have my doubts respecting the independence of the judges, such as to stated times of paying the *salaries*. The judges are eligible to any other office—they may hold seats in the *legislature* or *Senate*.[(a)]

The power of making treaties ought to be confined. They are declared the supreme laws of the land, therefore they may be of such a nature as to repeal or infringe the very Constitution. [Wayne's Notes, Cox Collection]

> [Wayne's marginal note]
> (a) *Vide* last [clause] of the 6th section [Article I]: No Person holding any Office under the U[nited] S[tates] shall be a member of either house, etc.

* * * *

John Smilie: (193) I cannot see the great difficulty of securing at least the substance of jury [trial] in civil cases. It might have been said that the legislature should make regulations for the trial by jury in them.

(194) Whatever is not given is reserved. The trial by jury is given in criminal cases therefore reserved in civil cases.

(195) The judges may be bribed by holding other offices. [Wilson's Notes, PHi]

1. According to Wayne's notes Wilson said: "The faith of treaties are made a part of the Constitution of the United *States* and the *judges* are to be *bound* by them" (Cox Collection).

2. According to Wayne's notes Wilson said: "It does not follow that citizens of different states *must* sue, because they *may* sue." Wayne then noted: "but there are Pine Barren Law and installment *laws* (*vide* South Carolina)" (Cox Collection). For the Pine Barren Act, which served debtors as a stay law, see Thomas Cooper and David J. McCord, eds., *Statutes at Large of South Carolina* (10 vols., Columbia, S.C., 1836–1841), IV, 710–12.

3. Wilson is referring to Rhode Island legislation which forced creditors to accept the state's paper money at face value.

4. For the jurisdictional dispute between Congress and Pennsylvania over the sloop *Active* which remained unsettled in 1787, see J. Franklin Jameson, "The Predecessor of the Supreme Court," *Essays in the Constitutional History of the United States in the Formative Period, 1775–1789* (Boston, 1889), 17–23.

5. This law, enacted on 9 September 1778, established a state court of admiralty with trial by jury (*Pa. Statutes,* IX, 277–83).

6. See the resolution of Congress, 25 November 1775 (JCC, III, 371–75).
7. Findley was in error. Article I, section 9, of the Constitution forbade Congress to pass *ex post facto* laws.

Newspaper Report of Proceedings and Debates

It was said in the Convention, that the opposition conceived every man would be possessed by a daemon who had any share in the administration of the proposed government; to which Mr. Smilie answered, that in framing a political system it was proper to presume that every person in power would do wrong if he could; and therefore every restraint should be provided, for if the rulers were honest, no harm was done, but if they were otherwise, a security was obtained against their machinations.

The Convention has again returned to one meeting in each day. The first Article of the proposed Constitution having been fully discussed, the second, respecting the executive power was yesterday taken into consideration. As the whole of the plan has in a great degree been investigated in the argument on the first Article, it is supposed that the Convention will break up in the course of the ensuing week.

Yesterday Mr. Wilson entered into an investigation of the judiciary power contained in the proposed Constitution, and asserted, that so far from unnecessary or improper, it was a valuable and indispensable acquisition to the federal government. He observed that, bad as human nature was, it could hardly be presumed that the governors would act improperly without an object. In every case therefore where they could have an interest in the oppression of a citizen, the trial by jury is to be inviolably preserved. With respect to treason, likewise, he remarked that the definition of that crime, which had been always a prolific instrument of tyranny, was not left to the Congress, but was ascertained in the Constitution itself. He then proceeded to examine the different points of jurisdiction given to the Supreme Court, and concluded with declaring that they were all essential to public and private credit and the impartial administration of justice.

It was argued by the opponents of the proposed plan, that the independency of the judges was not secured, for if any law were passed contrary to the Constitution, and they should refuse to execute it, the House of Representatives and the Senate, who made the law, would impeach them, and then it would be the duty of the Senate to determine whether or not the law was unconstitutional and whether the judges were not bound by it. Mr. Wilson on this occasion asserted that the judges would be governed by the Constitution and not by the contradicting law, which would be, *ipso facto,* nugatory and void. *Query,* whether the same doctrine has been held in the Supreme Court of Pennsylvania. [*Pennsylvania Herald,* 8 December][1]

1. This account, sometimes in excerpted form, was reprinted eleven times from Vermont to South Carolina.

The Pennsylvania Convention
Saturday
8 December 1787

Convention Proceedings

The Convention met pursuant to adjournment,

Resumed the consideration of the remaining articles, and after some debate,

Adjourned until three o'clock on Monday next, P.M.

Convention Debates

JOHN SMILIE: (196) This system puts the government in a situation, in which the officers are not responsible.

(197) Every door is shut against democracy.

(198) It was the design and intention of the Convention to divest us of the liberty of trial by jury in civil cases; and to deprive us of the benefits of the common law.

(199) The word "appeal" is a civil law term; and therefore the Convention meant to introduce the *civil* law.

(200) On an appeal the judges may set aside the verdict of a jury.

(201) Appeals are not admitted in the common law.

(202) If a jury give a false verdict, a writ of attaint lies or the verdict may be set aside. A writ of error lies as to matters of law; but on that writ the facts are not reexamined.

(203) 3. Bl. [Blackstone, III,] 378. Concerning trials by jury.[(a)]

(204) 3. Bl. [Blackstone, III,] 392. The *expense* of civil law proceedings.

(205) 3. Bl. [Blackstone, III,] 390, 391. The propriety of new trials.

(206) 3. Bl. [Blackstone, III,] 452. Chancery frequent[ly] directs the trial of facts by a jury.

(207) 3. Bl. [Blackstone, III,] 336. Trial by witness is the only mode known to the civil law.

(208) The case of *Forsey v. Cunningham,* New York.[1] Appeal to the governor and council. Reasons of the chief justice for the conduct of the judges.[(b)]
(209) "All the appeals we have yet had have been in error."
(210) If such an attempt was made in England; what would the people of that country do? It would set the whole nation in a flame.
(211) Securing the trial by jury in criminal cases is worse than saying nothing.
(212) The Convention might have said, that Congress should establish trials by jury in civil cases. [Wilson's Notes, PHi]

[Wilson's marginal notes]
(a) At the will of Parliament.
(b) The question here was whether instructions from the Crown could or were meant to alter the law.

Smilie: The appellate jurisdiction is borrowed from the civil law and will exclude trials by jury. Writ of attaint lies against a jury for giving a false verdict [e.g.,] case of *Forsey v. Cunningham* at New York in 1764. Appeal from the general verdict of a jury assessing damages in the case of a trespass and assault to the governor and council refused in the supreme court by the judges. England, corrupt as she is, would not bear an innovation like our appellate jurisdiction.

The trials in criminal cases by jury is secured, but, not being mentioned in civil cases, it is clearly excepted in such latter cases. [Yeates's Notes, PPIn]

* * * *

ROBERT WHITEHILL: (213) Are we to trust all to judges, who will have their favorites?
(214) There is no security, by this Constitution, for people's houses or papers.
(215) Farmer's Letters, Letter 9.[2] The king cannot punish till a person be found guilty by his peers. Excellence and description of trial by jury in criminal cases.
(216) These privileges (described in the Letter) are not secured by this Constitution.
(217) The case of Mr. [John] Wilkes, and the doctrine of general warrants show that judges may be corrupted.[3]
(218) A wicked use may be made of search warrants.
(219) If such men execute as formed this Constitution, all alterations will be for the worse.
(220) The people will not submit to this government.
(221) Article 6, clauses 2 and 3 are concluding clauses that the state governments will be abolished.

(222) The oath here required is contrary to the oath required by the constitution of Pennsylvania. No member of Assembly will hereafter take the latter oath.
(223) The next thing will be to call conventions to alter the state governments.
(224) All our constitutions may be altered by treaties made by a few Senators.
(225) This lordly domination will not do.
(226) Our greatest liberties will, by this Constitution, be sacrificed to the will of men.
(227) The trial by jury is given up to the will of Congress.[(a)]
[Wilson's Notes, PHi]

[Wilson's marginal note]
(a) New Hampshire Bill of Rights, section 20, 21. Massachusetts Bill of Rights, section 15.

Whitehill: The Federal Convention found the task too great for them to ascertain the mode of trial in civil cases. We are solemnly bound to our God not to give away the rights and liberties of the people. The rich will swallow up the poor—we shall have no security for our property. Why need we obtain property if it is insecure?
There is no security for people's houses or papers by the Constitution. All depends on the goodwill of Congress and the judges. It is a solemn mockery of Heaven to say that our rights are [preserved?] by the Constitution. Cites 9th Letter of the Farmer's Letters published in Pennsylvania. [Yeates's Notes, PPIn]

Whitehill: We have no right to give away many of the rights which are cont[aine]d in the Con [Pennsylvania Constitution?] [Wayne's Notes, Cox Collection]

* * * *

THOMAS MCKEAN: Too much time has been spent in this business. The whole matter might have been dispatched in a few days. [Yeates's Notes, PPIn]

McKean: I have read as well as heard the objections mentioned here, in the Centinel, Brutus, Cincinnatus. [Wilson's Notes, PHi][4]

* * * *

WILLIAM FINDLEY: (228) The state has had but two months to consider this system.
(229) Trial by jury is not secured in civil cases as in criminal ones. It is at the mercy of the legislature.
(230) By the appellate clause, an appeal lies from the verdict of a jury, a thing hitherto unknown.

(231) Personal liberty cannot be enjoyed without trial by jury.
(232) All the northern countries have been zealous of freedom. Sweden till lately had trials by jury—and certainly a free government well-balanced, consisting of four branches.[5] [Wilson's Notes, PHi]

Findley: On Saturday last, in the course of an argument to prove the dissolution of the trial by jury, if the proposed system was adopted, and the consequent sacrifice of the liberties of the people, Mr. Findley observed, that when the trial by jury, which was known in Sweden so late as the middle of the last century, fell into disuse, the commons of that nation lost their freedom and a tyrannical aristocracy prevailed. [*Pennsylvania Herald,* 12 December]

* * * *

JAMES WILSON and THOMAS MCKEAN interrupted Mr. Findley and called warmly for his authority to prove that the trial by jury existed in Sweden, Mr. Wilson declaring that he had never met with such an idea in the course of his reading; and Mr. M'Kean asserting that the trial by jury was never known in any other country than England and the governments descended from that kingdom. Mr. Findley answered that he did not, at that moment, recollect his authority, but having formerly read histories of Sweden, he had received and retained the opinion which he now advanced, and would on a future occasion, perhaps, refer immediately to the book.[6] [*Pennsylvania Herald,* 12 December]

* * * *

WILLIAM FINDLEY: (233) Trial by jury is inconsistent with a complete aristocracy.
(234) The lower class of people will be oppressed without trial by jury.
(235) This part is explanatory of other parts of the plan.
(236) The people never expressed a wish to give up the trial by jury.
(237) In Pennsylvania the trial by jury must be by a jury of the proper county. [Wilson's Notes, PHi]

Findley: Future ages will be surprised at America's adopting this Constitution. Englishmen would not do it and would wonder at freemen's adopting it.

If there is no bill of rights, there should be ample security given that our rulers should be honest and virtuous; and that if they themselves were virtuous, they should not be imposed on by the vicious. If otherwise, our liberties are held on the most precarious tenures. [Yeates's Notes, PPIn]

* * * *

JOHN SMILIE: (238) In all times a minority, contending for the rights of mankind, have been treated with contempt.

(239) The people should be represented, by juries, in the administration of justice.
(240) 3. Bl. [Blackstone, III,] 380. Every new tribunal, without jury, is a step towards an aristocracy. [Wilson's Notes, PHi]

Smilie: 3 Blackst. 380. Eulogy on Juries. Aristocracy is the most oppressive of all tyrannical governments. The Convention deliberately planned the system of taking away the trials by jury. [Yeates's Notes, PPIn]

* * * *

An altercation between the Chief Justice and Mr. Smiley. Mr. Chambers defended the Chief Justice and berated the opposition.[7] [Yeates's Notes, PPIn]

Newspaper Report of a "Warm Altercation"

On Saturday last a very warm altercation passed in the Convention, of which we submit to our readers the following impartial statement.

Mr. M'Kean, rising in consequence of the repeated call of the opposition for an answer to their arguments, observed, that the observations and objections were so often reiterated, that most of them had already been replied to, and in his opinion, all the objections which had been made to the proposed plan might have been delivered in the space of two hours; so he concluded, that the excess of time had been consumed in trifling and unnecessary debate. In reply to these observations, Mr. Smilie remarked, that the honorable gentleman had treated the opposition with contempt; and with *a magisterial air* had condemned their arguments. He was about to proceed in his animadversion upon the conduct of the majority, who presumed thus, he added, upon their numbers, when several members started up, but at length, Mr. Chambers claimed the attention of the President. He began a speech of some length with terming Mr. Smilie's language *indecent,* because, he said, it alluded to Mr. M'Kean as a judge. He then proceeded with great heat to reprobate the behavior of the *three* gentlemen who managed the arguments against the proposed system, and declared that they had *abused* the *indulgence* which the other side of the house had *granted* to them in consenting to hear all their reasons. He next animadverted upon the characters of those who composed the opposition, and loudly asked, where had they been found in the day of danger? Thence drawing a contrast between them and the representatives of Pennsylvania in the late Federal Convention, who were, he remarked, men of as great talents and patriotism, as good generals and statesmen, as any that had appeared in the business of the Revolution. From this ground he took an opportunity of saying something about those Englishmen who had arrived in this country since the peace, and who had presumed to judge for themselves respecting the politics of Pennsylvania. He referred to Mr. Findley's having no more than two votes as a delegate to the Federal Convention, in order to show the insignificance of his character, and the wisdom of Pennsylvania, which would not admit of his being elected on that occasion. He then adverted to the character of Mr. M'Kean, which he asserted was superior to all attacks, and concluded with declaring that everything which had been offered by the opposition was, in his judgment, trifling and unnecessary. When Mr. Chambers had finished, Mr. Smilie appealed to the candor of the Convention, whether he had used a single word which could be deemed *indecent* and which was not fairly justified by the conduct to which he had alluded. He feelingly exclaimed that he was pleading for the interests of his country, and that no character should influence, and no violence overawe his proceedings. For, he not only claimed the free exercise of speech as a right, but he would exercise it as a duty. Mr. Findley followed, promising that he should take very little notice of the speech delivered by Mr. Chambers, as, indeed, he had never found occasion to take much notice of anything that dropt from that quarter. He would observe, however, that the characteristic of the conduct of the honorable member in public bodies was to discourse without reason and to talk without argument. Here a considerable cry of order arose, and Mr. Findley said he would only add, that he always wished to avoid an investigation of characters, but at least, he would take care never to engage on that subject but with a competent judge. During some disturbance in the house, Mr. Chambers retorted that he had a perfect contempt both for Mr. Findley's arguments and person, and Mr. Findley closed the altercation with declaring that he saw no reason for dispute, since he and Mr. Chambers were in that respect so perfectly agreed. Mr. M'Pherson stated to the chair the impropriety of such proceedings, and observed that the member from Fayette [John Smilie] had not satisfactorily shown in what manner the member from the city (Thomas McKean) had spoken indecent language to justify the retort that had been made. Mr. Findley then remarked that when a member undertook personally to dictate to the Convention, he was an object of personal animadversion, for, it was only by motion and resolve of the whole body that their proceedings were to be governed.

Mr. Smilie said, he had in his opinion satisfactorily shown the ground upon which he had spoken, for he had referred to the recollection of the Convention, that Mr. M'Kean treated the arguments of the opposition as trifling and contemptible, and this with *a magis-*

terial air which was all the retort he had made. To this Mr. Findley subjoined that he did not rise to argue upon the question, but to claim what was just and right; he therefore referred it to the President to determine, whether he or his coadjutors had transgressed any of the established rules of the Convention? Upon this the President said, it was true that no positive rule had been transgressed, but he could not avoid considering Mr. Smilie's language highly improper. On this there was a unanimous cry of adjourn, which at last, put a stop to the altercation. [*Pennsylvania Herald,* 12 December][8]

1. The case of *Forsey v. Cunningham* (1764) and the issue of the appeal of jury trials "produced . . . a flame of patriotic and successful opposition that will not be easily forgotten" ("Centinel" II, CC:190). The proceedings of the case were printed in 1764 by John Holt. See Milton M. Klein, "Prelude to Revolution in New York: Jury Trials and Judicial Tenure," *William and Mary Quarterly,* 3rd series, XVII (1960), 439–62.

2. A reference to John Dickinson's "Letters From A Farmer in Pennsylvania" published in the *Pennsylvania Chronicle* between 2 December 1767 and 15 February 1768. See Paul L. Ford, ed., *The Writings of John Dickinson* (Philadelphia, Pa., 1895), 277–417.

3. For Wilkes and the issue of general warrants, see Horace Bleackley, *Life of John Wilkes* (London, 1917), 87–109.

4. McKean was correct in stating that Antifederalists in the Convention used the arguments of such writers as "Centinel," "Brutus," and "Cincinnatus." For instance, in his speech on this day John Smilie relied heavily upon the discussion of trial by jury in "Centinel" II, 24 October (CC:190). Smilie also used the same sources as "Centinel," such as the case of *Forsey v. Cunningham* (1764), Blackstone's *Commentaries,* and the ninth letter of John Dickinson's "Letters From A Farmer in Pennsylvania."

5. The issue of trial by jury in Sweden was first raised in "Centinel" II, 24 October (CC:190), which stated that "The northern nations of the European continent, have all lost this invaluable privilege [trial by jury in civil cases]: *Sweden,* the last of them, by the artifices of the *aristocratic* senate, which depressed the king and reduced the house of commons to insignificance. But the nation a few years ago, preferring the absolute authority of a monarch to the *vexatious* domination of the *wellborn* few, an end was suddenly put to their power."

6. "One of the People," *Independent Gazetteer,* 11 December, reported that McKean and Wilson "interrupted a member while speaking, and declared that jury trial never existed in Sweden or in any other country, out of Great Britain and America" (Mfm:Pa. 266). For the continuation of the dispute over trial by jury in Sweden, see speeches by Findley on 10 December and Wilson on 11 December, and William Shippen, Jr. to Thomas Lee Shippen, 18 December, Mfm:Pa. 271.

7. In the Yeates manuscript, the note about the "altercation" immediately precedes the note of Smilie's speech. The order is reversed here because, according to the newspaper account, the "altercation" led to adjournment for the day.

8. The *Herald's* account of the altercation was reprinted in the *Independent Gazetteer* and *Pennsylvania Packet,* 13 December, and in five newspapers from Rhode Island to South Carolina.

The Pennsylvania Convention
Monday
10 December 1787

Convention Proceedings

The Convention met pursuant to adjournment,

Resumed the consideration of the remaining articles of the proposed Constitution, and after some debate,

Adjourned until past nine o'clock tomorrow, A.M.

Convention Debates

WILLIAM FINDLEY: . . . on Monday afternoon, he produced the *Modern Universal History*,[1] and the 3d volume of Blackstone's *Commentaries*, which incontrovertibly established his position [that Sweden had jury trials]. Having read his authorities, he concluded in the following manner: "I am not accustomed, Mr. President, to have my word disputed in public bodies upon the statement of a fact; but in this Convention it has already occurred more than once. It is now evident, however, that I was contradicted on this subject improperly and unjustly by the learned Chief Justice [Thomas McKean] and Counselor [James Wilson] from the city. That the account given in the *Universal History* should escape the recollection or observation of the best informed man is not extraordinary, but this I will observe, that if my son had been at the study of the law for six months and was not acquainted with the passage in Blackstone, I should be justified in whipping him. But the contradiction coming from the quarter known to this Convention, I am at a loss whether to ascribe it to the want of veracity or the ignorance of the learned members."[2] [*Pennsylvania Herald,* 12 December]

Findley: 33d Vol. *Universal History,* fol. 21. Trials by jury are in disuse in Sweden except in the lower courts. 3 Blackst. 349, 380. 381. Every new tribunal without a jury is an introduction of aristocracy, the worst of all tyrannies. Trials by jury in Sweden have been in disuse for near a century past. [Yeates's Notes, PPIn]

Findley: As to the trial by jury in Sweden (*Mod Un His* Vol. 33, p. 21 22). Juries remain *in office for life* (3. Bl. 349, 380. 381). [Wilson's Notes, PHi]

* * * *

THOMAS MCKEAN: Sir, you have under your consideration a matter of very great weight and importance, not only to the present generation but to posterity; for where the rights and liberties of the people are concerned, there certainly it is fit to proceed with the utmost caution and regard. You have done so hitherto. The power of this Convention, being derived from the people of Pennsylvania, by a *positive* and *voluntary* grant, cannot be extended further than what this *positive grant* hath conveyed. You have been chosen by the people, for the sole purpose of "assenting to and ratifying the Constitution, proposed for the future government of the United States, with respect to their general and common concerns," or of rejecting it. It is a sacred trust; and, as on the one hand, you ought to weigh well the innovations it will create in the governments of the individual states and the dangers which may arise by its adoption; so upon the other hand, you ought fully to consider the benefits it may promise and the consequences of a rejection of it. You have hitherto acted strictly conformably to your delegated power; you have agreed, that a single question can come before you; and it has been accordingly moved, that you resolve, "to assent to and ratify this Constitution."[3] Three weeks have been spent in hearing the objections that have been made against it, and it is now time to determine whether they are of such a nature as to overbalance any benefits or advantages that may be derived to the State of Pennsylvania by your accepting it.

Sir, I have as yet taken up but little of your time; notwithstanding this, I will endeavor to contract what occurs to me on the subject. And in what I have to offer, I shall observe this method: I will first consider the arguments that have been used against this Constitution, and then give my reasons why I am for the motion.

The arguments against the Constitution are, I think, chiefly these.

First. That the elections of Representatives and Senators are not frequent enough to insure responsibility to their constituents.

Second. That one Representative for thirty thousand persons is too few.

Third. The Senators have a share in the appointment of certain officers and are to be the judges on the impeachment of such officers. This is blending the executive with the legislative and judicial departments, and is likely to screen the offenders impeached, because of the concurrence of a majority of the Senate in their appointment.

Fourth. That the Congress may by law deprive the electors of a fair choice of their Representatives, by fixing improper times, places, and modes of election.

Fifth. That the powers of Congress are too large, particularly in laying internal taxes and excises, because they may lay excessive taxes and leave nothing for the support of the state governments.

In raising and supporting armies, and that the appropriation of money for that use, should not be for so long a term as two years.

In calling forth the militia on necessary occasions; because they may call them from one end of the continent to the other, and wantonly harrass them; besides they may coerce men to act in the militia, whose consciences are against bearing arms in any case.

In making all laws which shall be necessary and proper for carrying into execution the foregoing powers, and all other powers vested by this Constitution in the government of the United States, or in any department or officer thereof.

And in declaring, that this Constitution, and the laws of the United States which shall be made in pursuance thereof, and all treaties made, or which shall be made, under the authority of the United States, shall be the supreme law of the land.

That migration or importation of such persons, as any of the states shall admit, shall not be prohibited prior to 1808, nor a tax or duty imposed on such importation exceeding ten dollars for each person.

Sixth. That the whole of the executive power is not lodged in the President alone, so that there might be one responsible person.

That he has the sole power of pardoning offenses against the United States, and may therefore pardon traitors for treasons committed in consequence of his own ambitious and wicked projects or those of the Senate.

That the Vice President is a useless officer, and being an executive officer, is to be President of the Senate, and in case of a division is to have the casting voice.

Seventh. The judicial power shall be vested in one Supreme Court. An objection is made, that the *compensation* for the services of the judges shall not be *diminished* during their continuance in office, and this is contrasted with the compensation to the President, which is to be neither *increased* nor *diminished* during the period for which he shall have been elected. But that of the judges may be increased, and the judge may hold other offices of a lucrative nature, and his judgment be thereby warped.

That in all the cases enumerated, except where the Supreme Court has original jurisdiction, "they shall have *appellate* jurisdiction, both as to law and facts, with such exceptions, and under such regulations as the congress shall make." From hence is inferred that the trial by jury is not secured.

That they have jurisdiction between citizens of different states.

Eighth. That there is no bill or declaration of rights in this Constitution.

Ninth. That this is a *consolidation* of the several states, and not a *confederation.*

Tenth. It is an *aristocracy* and was intended to be so by the framers of it.

The first objection that I heard advanced against this Constitution, I say, sir, was that the elections of Representatives and Senators are not frequent enough to insure responsibility to their constituents.

This is a subject that most men differ about, but there are more considerations than that of mere responsibility. By this system the House of Representatives is composed of persons chosen every second year by the people of the several states; and the Senators every six years by the legislatures. Whether the one or the other of these periods are of too long duration is a question to which various answers will be given; some persons are of opinion that three years in the one case, and seven in the other, would be a more eligible term than that adopted in this Constitution. In Great Britain, we find the House of Commons elected for seven years; the House of Lords is perpetual; and the king never dies. The Parliament of Ireland is octennial; in various other parts of the British dominions, the house of representatives are during the royal pleasure, and have been continued twenty years; this, sir, is a term undoubtedly too long. In a single state, I think annual elections most proper, but then there ought to be more branches in the legislature than one. An annual legislature possessed of supreme power may be properly termed an annual despotism—and, like an individual, they are subject to caprice, and act as party spirit or spleen dictates; hence that instability to our laws, which is the bane of republican governments. The framers of this Constitution wisely divided the legislative department between two houses subject to the qualified negative of the President of the United States, tho this government embraces only enumerated powers. In a single state, annual elections may be proper, the more so, when the legislative powers extend to all cases; but in such an extent of country as the United States, and when the powers are circumscribed, there is not that necessity, nor are the objects of the general government of that nature as to be acquired immediately by every capacity. To combine the various interests of thirteen different states requires more extensive knowledge than is necessary for the legislature of any one of them; two years are therefore little enough, for the members of the House of Representatives to make themselves fully acquainted with the views, the habits, and interests of the United States. With respect to the Senate, when we consider the trust reposed in them, we cannot hesitate to pronounce, the period assigned to them is short enough; they possess, in common with the House of Representatives, legislative power; with its concurrence they also have power to declare war; they are joined with the President in concluding treaties; it therefore behooves them to be conversant with the politics of the nations of the world and the dispositions of the sovereigns, and their ministers; this requires much reading and attention. And believe me, the longer a man bends his study to any particular subject, the more likely he is to be master of it. Experience and practice will assist genius and education. I therefore think the time allowed, under this system, to both houses to be extremely proper. This objection has been made repeatedly, but it can only have weight with those who are not at the pains of thinking on the subject. When anything, sir, new or great is done, it is very apt to create a ferment among those out of doors who, as they cannot always enter into the depth and wisdom of councils, are too apt to censure what they do not understand; upon a little reflection and experience, the people often find that to be a singular *blessing* which at first they deemed a *curse*.

Second. "That one Representative for thirty thousand persons is too few."

There will be, sir, sixty-five in the House of Representatives and twenty-six in the Senate, in all ninety-one, who, together with the President, are to make laws in the several particular matters entrusted to them, and which are all enumerated and expressed. I think the number sufficient at the present, and in three years time, when a census or actual enumeration must take place, they will be increased, and in less than twenty-five years they will be more than double. With respect to this, different gentlemen in the several states will differ, and at last the opinion of the majority must govern.

Third. "The Senators have a share in the appointment of certain officers, and are to be the judges on the impeachment of such officers. This is blending the executive with the legislative and judicial departments, and is likely to screen the offenders impeached because of the concurrence of a majority of the Senate in their appointment."

The President is to nominate to office, and with the advice and consent of the Senate appoint officers, so that he is the responsible person, and when any such impeachment shall be tried, it is more than probable, that not one of the Senate, who concurred in the appointment, will be a Senator, for the seats of a third part are to be vacated every two years, and of all in six.

As to the Senators having a share in the executive power, so far as to the appointment of certain officers, I do not know where this restraint on the President could be more safely lodged. Some may think a privy councillor might have been chosen by every state, but this could little mend the matter if any, and it would be a considerable additional expense to the people. Nor need the Senate be under any necessity of sitting constantly, as has been alleged, for there is an express provision made to enable the President to fill up all vacancies that may happen during their recess; the commissions to expire at the end of the next sessions.

As to impeachments, the objection is much stronger against the Supreme Executive Council of Pennsylvania.

The House of Lords in Great Britain are judges in the last resort in all civil causes and besides have the power of trying impeachments.

On the trial of impeachments the Senators are to be under the sanction of an oath or affirmation besides the other ties upon them to do justice; and the bias is more likely to be against the officer accused, than in his favor, for there are always more persons disobliged than the contrary when an office is given away, and the expectants of office are more numerous than the possessors.

Fourth. "That the Congress may by law deprive the electors of a fair choice of their Representatives by fixing improper times, places and modes of election."

Every House of Representatives are of necessity to be the judges of the elections, returns, and qualifications of its own members. It is therefore their province, as well as duty, to see, that they are fairly chosen, and are the legal members; for this purpose, it is proper they should have it in their power to provide that the times, places, and manner of election should be such as to insure free and fair elections.

Annual *congresses* are expressly secured; they have only a power given to them to take care that the *elections* shall be at convenient and suitable times and places, and conducted in a proper manner; and I cannot discover why we may not entrust these particulars to the representatives of the United States with as much safety as to those of the individual states.

In some states the electors vote *viva voce,* in others by ballot; they ought to be uniform, and the elections held on the same day throughout the United States to prevent corruption or undue influence. Why are we to suppose that Congress will make a bad use of this power, more than the representatives in the several states?

It is said "that the powers of Congress, under this Constitution are too large, particularly in laying internal taxes and excises, because they *may* lay excessive taxes and leave nothing for the support of the state governments." Sir, no doubt but you will discover, on consideration, the necessity of extending these powers to the government of the Union. If they have to borrow money, they are certainly bound in honor and conscience to pay the interest, until they pay the principal, as well to the foreign as to the domestic creditor; it therefore becomes our duty to put it in their power to be honest. At present, sir, this is not the case, as experience has fully shown. Congress have solicited and required the several states to make provision for these purposes; has one state paid its quota? I believe not one of them; and what has been the result? Foreigners have been compelled to advance money, to enable us to pay the interest due them on what they furnished to Congress during the late war. I trust, we have had experience enough to convince us that Congress ought no longer to depend upon the force of requisition. I heard it urged, that Congress ought not to be authorized to collect taxes until a state had refused to comply with this requisition. Let us examine this position. The engagements entered into by the general government render it necessary that a certain sum shall be paid in one year; notwithstanding this, they must not have power to collect it until the year expires, and then it is too late. Or is it expected that Congress would borrow the deficiency? Those who lent us in our distress have little encouragement to make advances again to our government; but give the power to Congress to lay such taxes as may be just and necessary, and public credit will revive. Yet, because they have the power to lay taxes and excise, does it follow that they *must*? For my part, I hope it may not be necessary; but if it is, it is much easier for the citizens of the United States to contribute their proportion, than for a few to bear the weight of the whole principal and interest of the domestic debt; and there is perfect security on this head, because the regulation must equally affect every state, and the law must originate with the immediate Representatives of the people, subject to the investigation of the state representatives. But is the abuse an argument against the use of power? I think it is not; and, upon the whole, I think this power wisely and securely lodged in the hands of the general government; though on the first view of this work, I was of opinion they might have done without it; but, sir, on reflection, I am satisfied that it is not only proper, but that our political salvation may depend upon the exercise of it.

The next objection is against "the power of raising and supporting armies, and the appropriation of money for that use should not be for so long a term as two years." Is it not necessary that the authority superintending the general concerns of the United States should have the power of raising and supporting armies? Are we, sir, to stand defenseless amidst conflicting nations? Wars are inevitable, but war cannot be declared without the consent of the immediate Representatives of the people; there must also *originate* the law which appropriates the money for the support of the army, yet they can make no appropriation for a longer term than two years; but does it follow that because they *may* make appropriations for that period, that they *must* or even *will* do it? The power of raising and supporting armies is not only necessary, but is enjoyed by the present Congress, who also judge of the expediency or necessity of keeping them up. In England there is a standing army, though in words it is engaged but for one year. Yet is it not kept constantly up? Is there a year that Parliament refuses to grant them supplies? Though this is done annually, it might be done for any longer term. Are not their officers commissioned for life, and when *they* exercise this power with so much prudence, shall the representatives of this country be suspected the more, because they are restricted to two years?

It is objected that the powers of Congress are too large, because "they have the power of calling forth the militia on necessary occasions, and may call them from one end of the continent to the other and wantonly harrass them; besides they may coerce men to act in the militia, whose consciences are against bearing arms in any case." It is true, by this system, power is given to Congress to organize, arm, and discipline the militia, but everything else is left to the state governments; they are to officer and train them. Congress have also the power of calling them forth, for the purpose of executing the laws of the Union, suppressing insurrections, and repelling invasions; but can it be supposed they would call them in such case from Georgia to New Hampshire? Common sense must oppose the idea.

Another objection was taken from these words of the Constitution: "to make all laws which shall be necessary and proper for carrying into execution the foregoing powers, and all other powers vested by this Constitution in the government of the United States, or in any department, or officer thereof." And in declaring "that this Constitution, and the laws of the United States which shall be made in pursuance thereof, and all treaties made, or which shall be made, under the authority of the United States, shall be the supreme law of the land." This has at last been conceded, that though it is explicit enough, yet it gives to Congress no further powers than those already enumerated. Those that first said it gave to Congress the power of superseding the state governments cannot persist in it; for no person can, with a tolerable face, read the clauses over and infer that such may be the consequence.

Provision is made that Congress shall have power to prohibit the importation of slaves after the year 1808, but the gentlemen in opposition accuse this system of a crime, because it has not prohibited them at once. I suspect those gentlemen are not well acquainted with the business of the diplomatic body, or they would know that an agreement might be made, that did not perfectly accord with the will and pleasure of any one person. Instead of finding fault with what has been gained, I am happy to see a disposition in the United States to do so much.

The next objections have been against the executive power; it is complained of, "because the whole of the executive power is not lodged in the President *alone,* so that there might be one responsible person; he has the *sole* powers of pardoning offenses against the United States, and may therefore pardon traitors for treasons committed in consequence of his own ambitious or wicked projects or those of the Senate."

Observe the contradiction, sir, in these two objections; one moment the system is blamed for not leaving all executive authority to the President *alone,* the next it is censured for giving him the *sole* power to pardon traitors. I am glad to hear these objections made, because it forebodes an amendment in that body in which amendment is necessary. The President of the United States must nominate to all offices, before the persons can be chosen; he here consents and becomes liable. The Executive Council of Pennsylvania appoint officers by ballot, which effectually destroys responsibility. He may pardon offense, and hence it is inferred that he may pardon traitors for treason committed in consequence of his own ambitious and wicked projects. The Executive Council of Pennsylvania can do the same. But the President of the United States may be impeached before the Senate and punished for his crimes.

"The Vice President is an useless officer." Perhaps the government might be executed without him, but there is a necessity of having a person to preside in the Senate to continue a full representation of each state in that body. The chancellor of England is a judicial officer, yet he sits in the House of Lords.

The next objection is against the judicial department. The judicial power shall be vested in one Supreme Court. An objection is made that the compensation for the services of the judges shall not be *diminished* during their continuance in office, and this is contrasted with the compensation of the President, which is to be neither *increased* nor *diminished* during the period for which he shall be elected. But that of the judges may be increased, and the judges may hold other offices of a lucrative nature, and his judgment be thereby warped.

Do gentlemen not see the reason why this difference is made? Do they not see that the President is appointed but for four years, whilst the judges may continue for life, if they shall so long behave themselves well? In the first case, little alteration can happen in the value of money; but in the course of a man's life, a very great one may take place from the discovery of silver and gold mines and the great influx of those metals; in which case an increase of salary may be requisite. A security that their compensation shall not be lessened, nor they have to look up to every session for salary, will certainly tend to make those officers more easy and independent.

"The judges may hold other offices of a lucrative nature." This part of the objection reminds me of the scheme that was fallen upon in Pennsylvania to prevent any person from taking up large tracts of land. A law was passed restricting the purchaser to a tract not exceeding three hundred acres; but all the difference it made was that the land was taken up by several patents, instead of one, and the wealthy could procure, if they chose it, three thousand acres. What, though the judges could hold no other office, might they not have brothers, children and other relations, whom they might wish to see placed in the offices forbidden to themselves? I see no apprehensions that may be entertained on this account.

That in all cases enumerated, except where the Supreme Court has original jurisdiction, "they shall have appellate jurisdiction both as to law and fact, with such exceptions and under such regulations as the Congress shall make." From this is inferred, that the trial by jury is not secured; and an objection is set up to the system, because they have jurisdiction between citizens of different states. Regulations, under this head, are necessary, but the Convention would form no one that would have suited each of the United States. It has been a subject of amazement to me to hear gentlemen contend that the verdict of a jury shall be without revision in all cases. Juries are not infallible because they are twelve in number. When the law is so blended with the fact, as to be almost inseparable, may not the decision of a jury be erroneous? Yet notwithstanding this, trial by jury is the best mode that is known. Appellate jurisdiction, sir, is known in the common law, and causes are removed from inferior courts by writ of error into some court of appeal. It is said that the lord chancellor, in all cases, sends down to the lower courts when he wants to determine a fact, but that opinion is not well-founded, because he determines nineteen out of twenty without the intervention of any jury. The power to try causes between citizens of different states was thought by some gentlemen invidious; but I apprehend they must see the necessity of it, from what has been already said by my honorable colleague [James Wilson].

"That there is no bill or declaration of rights in this Constitution."

To this I answer, such a thing has not been deemed essential to liberty excepting in Great Britain, where there is a king and an House of Lords quite distinct with respect to power and interest from the rest of the people; or in Poland, the *Pacta Conventa,* which the king signs before he is crowned, and in six states of the American United States.

Again, because it is unnecessary, for the powers of Congress, being derived from the people in the mode pointed out by this Constitution, and being therein enumerated and *positively* granted, can be no other than what this positive grant conveys.[(a)]

With respect to executive officers, they have no manner of authority, any of them, beyond what is, by *positive* grant and commission, delegated to them.

"That this is a *consolidation* of the several states and not a *confederation.*"

To this I answer, the name is immaterial—the thing unites the several states and makes them like one in particular instances and for particular purposes, which is what is ardently desired by most of the sensible men in this country. I care not, whether it is called a consolidation, confederation, or national government, or by what other name, if it is a good government and calculated to promote the blessings of liberty, tranquility and happiness.

"It is an *aristocracy* and was intended to be so by the framers of it."

Here again, sir, the name is immaterial, if it is a good system of government for the general and common concerns of the United States. But after the definition which has already been given of an aristocratic government, it becomes unnecessary to repeat arguments to prove that this system does not establish an aristocracy.

There have been some other small objections to, or rather criticisms on this work, which I rest assured the gentlemen who made them will, on reflection, excuse me in omitting to notice them.

Many parts of this Constitution have been wrested and tortured, in order to make way for shadowy objections, which must have been observed by every auditor. Some other things were said with acrimony; they seemed to be personal; I heard the sound, but it was inarticulate. I can compare it to nothing better than the feeble noise occasioned by the working of small beer.

[Mr. M'Kean said, in the course of his speech on Monday, that the apprehensions of the opposition respecting the new plan, amounted to this, that *if the sky falls, we shall catch larks; if the rivers run dry, we shall catch eels;* and he compared their arguments to a sound—but then it was a mere sound like *the working of small beer.* (*Pennsylvania Herald,* 12 December, Mfm:Pa. 266)]

It holds in argument as well as nature, that *destructio unius est generatio alterius*—the refutation of an argument begets a proof.

The objections to this Constitution having been answered, and all done away, it remains pure and unhurt, and this alone is a forcible argument of its goodness.

Mr. President, I am sure nothing can prevail with me to give my vote for ratifying this Constitution, but a conviction from comparing the arguments on both sides, that the not doing it is liable to more inconvenience and danger than the doing it.

I. If you do it, you strengthen the government and people of these United States, and will thereby have the wisdom and assistance of all the states.

II. You will settle, establish, and firmly perpetuate our independence, by destroying the vain hopes of all its enemies, both at home and abroad.

III. You will encourage your allies to join with you; nay to depend, that what hath been stipulated or shall hereafter be stipulated and agreed upon will be punctually performed, and other nations will be induced to enter into treaties with you.

IV. It will have a tendency to break our parties and divisions, and by that means, lay a firm and solid foundation for the future tranquility and happiness of the United States in general, and of this state in particular.

V. It will invigorate your commerce and encourage shipbuilding.

VI. It will have a tendency not only to prevent any other nation from making war upon you, but from offering you any wrong or even insult.

In short, the advantages that must result from it are obviously so numerous and important, and have been so fully and ably pointed out by others, that it appears to be unnecessary to enlarge on this head.

Upon the whole, sir, the law has been my study from my infancy, and my only profession. I have gone through the circle of office, in the legislative, executive, and judicial departments of government; and from all my study, observation, and experience, I must declare, that from a full examination and due consideration of this system, it appears to me the *best the world has yet seen.*

I congratulate you on the fair prospect of its being adopted, and am happy in the expectation of seeing accomplished, what has been long my ardent wish—that you will hereafter have a SALUTARY PERMANENCY, in *magistracy* and STABILITY IN THE LAWS. [Lloyd, *Debates,* 135–47)[4]

[Lloyd's note]
(a) "Locke on civil government, vol. 2, b. 2, chap. ii. sect. 141, and in the xiiith chap. sect. 152" [Locke, II, sections 141, 152].

McKean: The following are objections to the system.

Objection 1. The election of Representatives and Senators is not frequent enough to secure their responsibility.

Response 1. People greatly differ on these points. Annual elections may be proper in a single branch but not so of the present system where their objects are to matters which particular states are not competent to.

2. 30,000 people represented by one delegate is too small a representation.

Response 2. In England Parliament exercise general legislative powers in all cases. Here the powers of the legislative body are restricted to more general matters reaching over the whole Union.

3. Senators have a share in the appointment of certain officers, and yet must try them on impeachment which blends the executive and judicial offices.

Response 3. This resembles the constitution of Great Britain which is deemed the best balanced in the world. It holds in the strongest light in the constitution of Pennsylvania where the Executive Council *alone* appoint and try impeachments.

4. Congress may affix improper modes of election in their control of the legislatures of the states.

Response 4. The United States at large have a greater interest in the due election of Representatives than any one state has, and this power is absolutely necessary to their preservation.

5. Powers of Congress too large in laying internal direct taxations, their power over militia too great, the appropriations of money for too long a time. The people have no control over them.

Response 5. Congress owe large debts and ought to have the powers of compelling the payment of money. The power of raising armies and paying them must be lodged somewhere and where so properly as in Congress? It is absolutely necessary for the salvation of the United States.

6. The whole executive power not lodged in the President—his power of pardoning treasons enormous. Vice President is an useless office.

Response 6. Is it an objection that the President is bound to consult the Senate? This is contending for his monarchy. But he clearly is responsible to the people. The objection of his solely having the power of granting pardons is inconsistent with the first objection. This power should be lodged in one person. The Vice President's office is grounded on the practice in England.

7. Objection against the judiciary department. The salary of the

judges may be increased and they may hold lucrative offices. The President's salary may not be increased or diminished.

Response 7. The judges hold their offices during life and great changes may happen in the value of money. Not so of the President who can only continue for 4 years. You cannot avoid their getting offices, for they may elude these provisions by getting the office conferred on a son, etc.

8. No bill of rights to secure the liberties of the people.

Response 8. It is not necessary where there is no king or prerogative. All that is not granted is reserved (cites Locke, on Govt. pt. 2. sect. 141, 152).

9. A consolidation of the several states.

Response 9. This is a mere criticism on terms. It will, by uniting the states, secure us against exterior force.

10. An aristocracy and so intended by the Federal Convention.

Response 10. The frequent changes in the Senate, every 2 years some going out, will prevent all danger of caballing which is the greatest danger of an aristocracy.

Objection 11. The trial by jury not secured under the appellate jurisdiction.

Response 11. The verdicts of juries should in some instances be revised. The House of Lords have an appellate jurisdiction both as to law and in fact. So have the Supreme Court in matters in the orphans court, so of the court of errors and appeals in disputes about wills, so of chancery who determines it *jus testes*. In Massachusetts and New Hampshire, cases are removed into the supreme courts by appeal instead of writs of error.

By acceding to the Constitution you have the wisdom and experience of the United States brought to your aid.

(2) You will thereby perpetuate our independence by destroying the hopes of foreign and domestic enemies.

(3) You will encourage your allies and other powers will make treaties with us.

(4) It will break our parties and divisions in every state and particularly in this.

(5) It will invigorate your commerce; your shipbuilding will flourish under it. If you [do] not accede to it, there is no prospect of getting another constitution. It has the seeds of amendment in it. Upon the most mature deliberation, I pronounce the Constitution to be the best on the face of the earth. [Yeates's Notes, PPIn]

McKean: 1. Consider Objections. 2. Give Reasons in Favor of the Plan.

Objections: 1. Elections not frequent enough. 2. Number of Representatives too few. 3. Senate have too many blended powers. 4. Congress times, etc. elections. 5. Powers of Congress too large. Appropriations too long. 6. Whole of the executive power not lodged in President alone. Vice President should not have a voice in Senate. 7. Compensation of judges may be incidentally increased. 8. No bill of rights. 9. A consolidating government—not a federal one. 10. An aristocracy.

[Responses to Objections]

I. Elections not [i.e., are] frequent enough. The different durations of Parliament. Service of Senators should be longer than that of Representatives.

II. The representation is large enough. Before 25 years the number will be doubled.

III. None of the simple forms of government are the best. There is no writer of reputation but has allowed that the British government was the best in the world before the emancipation of United States.

When a judge, etc. is impeached, it is probable that none of those who appointed him will be present. The danger lies from the desire of removal. In Pennsylvania, Executive Council *appoint* and *impeach* officers.

IV. Article 1, section 4 [5]: Every house is judge of qualification and elections. Are not *all* the states interested in the elections?

V. Power of *internal* taxes not too great. Foreigners may *compel* payment of their debts. Have we not had experience enough of requisitions? Is it not necessary that Congress should have a power of raising and supporting armies and the command and discipline of the militia?

"All Laws necessary & proper," etc. This liable to no just exceptions.

"This Constitution," etc. "shall be the Supreme Law."

"Importation, &c." Subject of applause.

VI. In Pennsylvania, there is no responsibility in Council; because the president has given up his right of nomination. And they appoint by ballot, and therefore are not responsible. There is scarce a king in Europe that has not some check upon him in the appointment of officers.

VII. Offices to judges' relations the same as to themselves.

There might be improvements in the institution of juries; particularly as to the mode of appointing them. The House of Lords have an appellate jurisdiction in law and *fact*. Appellate jurisdiction from orphans courts. In the Eastern States, causes tried by juries are removed on appeal.

VIII. What occasion for a bill of rights when only delegated powers are given? One possessed of 1000 acres, conveys 250. Is it necessary to reserve the 750? (Locke on Gov. p. 2. s. 141. 152.)

IX. I shall not quarrel about names.

X. An aristocracy is the best security against external force.

Consequences of accepting: strengthen the government, assistance from the people of all the states, settle and perpetuate our independence, encourage our allies and make *new* treaties, break our parties and divisions, invigorate commerce, shipbuilding.

The clause of amendment, Article 5. This is the best system this world can now produce. [Wilson's Notes, PHi]

* * * *

WILLIAM FINDLEY: The principle of our argument not stated—consolidating government. In connection with this principle were all our arguments. [Wilson's Notes, PHi]

Findley: The principle on which the Chief Justice [speaks] is that the government should be consolidated. [Yeates's Notes, PPIn]

The spectators in the gallery applauded at the end of McKean's speech. According to Wilson and Yeates, Findley replied to McKean and then Smilie attacked the gallery for applauding.

* * * *

JOHN SMILIE: Those who clap and laugh are not the people of Pennsylvania. If the gallery was filled with bayonets, it would not intimidate me.

It is a great misfortune that another state [Delaware] has been before us in the surrender of their liberties.[5] [Wilson's Notes, PHi]

Smilie: I never found we had the worst of the argument until tonight. We have no people to laugh for us. We are not to be intimidated tho the gallery were armed with bayonets. [Yeates's Notes, PPIn]

Smilie: As soon as Mr. M'Kean had closed his speech, a loud and general tribute of applause was expressed by the citizens in the gallery; which gave occasion to the following philippic from Mr. Smilie. "Mr. President, I confess that hitherto I have persuaded myself that the opposition had the best of the argument on the present important question; but I have found myself mistaken, for the gentlemen on the other side have, indeed, an argument which surpasses and supersedes all others—a party in the gallery prepared to clap and huzza in affirmance of their speeches.[6] But, sir, let it be remembered that this is not the voice of the people of Pennsylvania; for, were I convinced of that, I should consider it as a conclusive approbation of the proposed system and give a ready acquiescence. No, sir, this is not the voice of the people of Pennsylvania; and were this Convention assembled at another place, the sound would be of a different nature, for the sentiments of the citizens are different indeed. Even there, however, it would pain me were I to see the majority of this body treated with such gross insult and disrespect by my friends as the minority now experience from theirs. In short, Mr. President, this is not the mode which will prevail on the citizens of Pennsylvania to adopt the proposed plan, let the decision here be what it may; and I will add that such conduct, nay were the gallery filled with bayonets, such appearance of violence would not intimidate me, or those who act with me, in the conscientious discharge of a public duty." [*Pennsylvania Herald,* 12 December][7]

* * * *

THOMAS McKEAN: When Mr. Smilie had finished, Mr. M'Kean remarked that the worthy gentleman seemed mighty angry, merely because somebody was pleased. [*Pennsylvania Herald,* 12 December]

1. *The Modern Part of an Universal History, From the Earliest Account of Time,* XXXIII (London, 1761), 21–22.
2. For Wilson's response to Findley, see Convention Debates, A.M., 11 December.
3. For McKean's motion, see Convention Proceedings, 24 November.
4. Lloyd misdated McKean's speech, placing it after James Wilson's speech on Tuesday, P.M., 11 December. Both Wilson's and Yeates's notes, as well as the newspaper accounts, indicate that McKean's speech was given on Monday, 10 December.
5. Delaware ratified the Constitution on 7 December.
6. For other Pennsylvania responses to the Federalists' use of the gallery, see Mfm:Pa. 269, 300. James Winthrop, a leading Massachusetts Antifederalist, commented that the Pennsylvania Federalists "had not themselves full confidence in their own reasons at Philadelphia is evident from the method they took to bias the state Convention. Messrs. Wilson and M'Kean, two Scottish names, were repeatedly worsted in the argument. To make amends for their own incapacity, the gallery was filled with a rabble, who shouted their applause, and these heroes of aristocracy were not ashamed, though modesty is their national virtue, to vindicate such a violation of decency" ("Agrippa," *Massachusetts Gazette,* 8 January 1788, RCS:Mass.).
7. Smilie's speech and McKean's response are excerpted from the *Herald's* account of 12 December, which was reprinted, in whole or in part, three times in Pennsylvania and twelve times from Massachusetts to South Carolina. For the *Herald's* complete account, see Mfm:Pa. 266.

Newspaper Report of Proceedings and Debates

On Monday last Mr. M'Kean delivered a learned and sensible speech in the Convention, of near three hours in length, in which he fully and ably answered every objection that had been made to the proposed Constitution, and afterwards pointed out the influence which the adoption of it would have upon the character and prosperity of the United States, both at home and abroad. He concluded by declaring, that, after full examination, he thought the proposed Constitution was the BEST THE WORLD EVER SAW.

Mr. Smilie and Mr. Findley having, in some of their speeches, treated Mr. M'Kean with indecent language, he took no other notice of them than comparing their speeches to the feeble noise occasioned by the working of small beer.

So very acceptable was Mr. M'Kean's speech to the gallery, which was unusually crowded, that contrary to custom in a popular assembly, they expressed their approbation by clapping him. This threw Mr. Smilie into a rage, and led him to use many fiery *sharp-pointed expressions,* which were coolly answered by Mr. M'Kean with the following short observation: "The gentleman, sir, is *angry*—because other folks are *pleased.*" [*Pennsylvania Gazette,* 12 December][1]

1. The *Gazette's* account was reprinted, in whole or in part, ten times from New Hampshire to Virginia.

William Shippen, Jr. to Thomas Lee Shippen, Philadelphia, 18 December (excerpt)[1]

I long to send you the debates. [William] Findley has gained great honor and proved himself vastly superior to [James] Wilson and the whole Convention. In one particular instance he triumphed over [Thomas] McKean and Wilson to their infinite mortification. He asserted in a speech that when Sweden lost the trial by jury, it lost its freedom. Wilson warmly and in his dictatorial manner called for his authority to show that Sweden ever had a trial by jury, and the Chief [Justice, McKean] called aloud on the orator to show it and declared, no country but England and her dependencies ever enjoyed trial by jury. Mr. F[indley] modestly replied, he could not immediately name his authors but was sure he had read it when reading some history of Sweden. Next day he produced the *Modern Universal History* and [the] 3d [volume of] Blackstone, and severely remarked that it might be excusable in the Chief Justice of Pennsylvania and counselor of the city to forget such a circumstance in a history, but I will observe that had my son been at the study of the law 6 months and not know such a passage in Blackstone, I would be justifiable in whipping him. What a stroke to the pride of two men who think themselves the greatest in the United States! Wilson attempted a flimsy excuse for his colleague alleging that in such a magazine of knowledge, twas impossible not to forget some, etc. [Eleazer] Oswald will never forget to mention the incident to his friend Jefferies, his honor [McKean]. Today a writer in his [Oswald's] paper concluded a severe piece by saying that he [McKean] is no longer worthy of the rank he possesses, and that there are sufficient grounds for an impeachment.[2] Your grandfather is sitting by me reading the Dissent of the Minority[3] and says he would not have had such a thing happen to Tom [McKean] for 100 pounds.

1. RC, Shippen Family Papers, DLC. For the complete letter, see Mfm:Pa. 271.
2. See "A By-Stander," *Independent Gazetteer,* 18 December, Mfm:Pa. 266.
3. Dissent of the Minority of the Convention, 18 December, III below.

The Pennsylvania Convention
Tuesday
11 December 1787

Convention Proceedings, A.M.

The Convention met pursuant to adjournment.

Petitions from sundry inhabitants and landholders of the county of Philadelphia (offering the said county, or any part thereof, for the seat of the general government, and for the exclusive legislation of Congress) were read; also petitions from sundry inhabitants of the counties of Philadelphia, Bucks, and Montgomery, offering a tract of country, situate between Pennipack and Neshaminy creeks, on the west side of the river Delaware, for the above purposes.[1]

Ordered to lie on the table.

The Convention then resumed the consideration of the remaining articles of the proposed Constitution, and after some debate,

Adjourned until half past three o'clock, P.M.

1. On 4 December a meeting at Germantown agreed that Philadelphia County should be offered to Congress as the seat of government, and petitions were distributed (Mfm:Pa. 248, 254). The *Pennsylvania Herald* report of 12 December, stating that petitions signed by inhabitants of the county had been presented to the Convention, was reprinted six times in Pennsylvania and eleven times from Massachusetts to South Carolina.

Convention Debates, A.M.

JAMES WILSON: Mr. Wilson again adverted to the subject [of jury trials in Sweden] in the following manner. "I will, Mr. President, take some notice of a circumstance, which, for want of something more important, has made considerable noise. I mean what respects the assertion of the member from Westmoreland [William Findley] that trials by jury were known in Sweden. I confess, sir, when I heard that assertion it struck me as new and contrary to my idea of the fact, and, therefore, in as decent terms as I could, I asked for the honorable member's authority. The book in which it is found convinces me I must before have read it, but I do not pretend to remember everything I read. This remark is made more for the sake of my colleague [Thomas McKean], who supported my opinion, than for my own. But I will add, sir, that those whose stock of knowledge is limited to a few items may easily remember and refer to them; but many things may be overlooked and forgotten in a magazine of literature. It may therefore with propriety be said, by my honorable colleague, as it was formerly said by Sir John Maynard to a petulant student who reproached him with an ignorance of a trifling point: "Young man, I have forgotten more law than ever you learned." [*Pennsylvania Herald,* 12 December][1]

JAMES WILSON: 2d List of Objections[2]

The Convention, no doubt, thought they were forming a compact or contract of the greatest importance (No. 184).[(a)]

The present Confederation should have been continued; but additional powers should have been given (Page 5, 6, 16, No. 4, 7, *79,* 149, *152*). The extent of the government is too great. It cannot be executed (No. 157). The general government ought not to possess power for internal purposes (No. 56, 57, *79, 95,* 186). There is no sovereignty left in the state governments (No. 60). This is a consolidating government; and will abolish the state governments (No. *71,* 72, *114,* 157, 162, *221, 222, 223,* 224).

The powers of the several parts of this government are not kept distinct and independent (No. 46, *54, 67, 160*). The number of Representatives is too small (No. 36, 37, 38, 116), and may be made smaller (No. 76). The districts will be too great (No. 37, 83, 116). They may be bribed by the Senate (39, 40, 68, 69, 120). The powers of the Senate are too great (No. 17, 41, 66, 122, 156, 158, 159, 175, 192), and representation unequal (No. 75). The Senate may be bribed (No. 43).

The power of internal taxation ought not to be given (No. 59, 135). The power over elections is dangerous (No. 119, 140, 141, 142, 143, 144, 145, 146, 147).

The President is only a tool of the Senate (No. 120, 122, 158). He should have had the appointment of all officers with the advice of a council (No. 121).

The judges are not sufficiently independent (No. 47, 92). Their powers are too extensive (No. 162, 163, 164, 165, *166,* 167, 168, 169, *170,* 177, 178, 181, 182). They may hold sinecures (No. 191, 195). [Wilson's Notes, PHi]

[Wilson's marginal note]
(a) *Vide* No. 8, 9, 10, 52, 62, 64, 161.

Wilson: Three weeks have now elapsed since this Convention met. Some of the delegates attended on Tuesday the 20th November; a great majority within a day or two afterwards, and all but one on the 4th day. We have been since employed in discussing the business for which we are sent here. I think it will now become evident to every person who takes a candid view of our discussions, that it is high time our proceedings should draw towards a conclusion. Perhaps our debates have already continued as long, nay, longer than is sufficient for every good purpose. The business which we were intended to perform is necessarily reduced to a very narrow compass. The single question to be determined is, shall we assent to and ratify the Constitution proposed?

As this is the first state whose Convention has met on the subject, and as the subject itself is of very great importance not only to Pennsylvania, but to the United States, it was thought proper, fairly, openly, and candidly, to canvass it. This has been done. You have heard, Mr. President, from day to day, and from week to week, the objections that could be offered from any quarter. We have heard those objections once—we have heard a great number of them repeated much oftener than once. Will it answer any valuable end, sir, to protract these debates longer? I suppose it will not. I apprehend it may serve to promote very pernicious and destructive purposes. It may perhaps be insinuated to other states, and even to distant parts of this state, by people in opposition to this system, that the expediency of adopting is at most very doubtful, and that the business labors among the members of the Convention.

This would not be a true representation of the fact; for there is the greatest reason to believe that there is a very considerable majority who do not hesitate to ratify the Constitution. We were sent here to express the voice of our constituents on the subject, and I believe that many of them expected to hear the echo of that voice before this time.

When I consider the attempts that have been made on this floor, and the many misrepresentations of what has been said among us that have appeared in the public papers, printed in this city, I confess that I am induced to suspect that opportunity may be taken to pervert and abuse the principles on which the friends of this Constitution act. If attempts are made here, will they not be repeated when the distance is greater, and the means of information fewer? Will they not at length produce an uneasiness, for which there is, in fact, no cause? Ought we not to prohibit any such uses being made of the continuance of our deliberations? We do not wish to preclude debate—of this our conduct has furnished the most ample testimony. The members in opposition have not been prevented a repetition of all their objections, that they could urge against this plan.

The honorable gentleman from Fayette (Mr. Smilie) the other evening [10 December] claimed for the minority, the merit of contending for the rights of mankind; and he told us, that it has been the practice of all ages, to treat such minorities with contempt. He further took the liberty of observing, that if the majority had the power, they do not want the inclination to consign the minority to punishment. I know that claims, self-made, form no small part of the merit, to which we have heard undisguised pretenses; but it is one thing to claim, and it is another thing, very different indeed, to support that claim. The minority, sir, are contending for the rights of mankind; what then are the majority contending for? If the minority are contending for the rights of mankind, the majority must be contending for the doctrines of tyranny and slavery. Is it probable that that is the case? Who are the majority in this assembly? Are they not the people? Are they not the representatives of the people, as well as the minority? Were they not elected by the people as well as the minority? Were they not elected by the greater part of the people?[3] Have we a single right separate from the rights of the people? Can we forge fetters for others, that will not be clasped round our own limbs? Can we make heavy chains, that shall not cramp the growth of our own posterity? On what fancied distinction shall the minority assume to themselves the merit of contending for the rights of mankind?

Sir, if the system proposed by the late Convention, and the conduct of its advocates, who have appeared in this house, deserve the declarations and insinutions that have been made concerning them—well may we exclaim—ill-fated America! thy crisis was approaching! perhaps it was come! Thy various interests were neglected—thy most sacred rights were insecure. Without a government! without energy! without confidence internally! without respect externally! the advantages of society were lost to thee! In such a situation, distressed but not despairing, thou desiredst to reassume thy native vigor, and to lay the foundation of future empire! Thou selectedst a number of thy sons, to meet together for the purpose. The selected and honored characters met; but horrid to tell, they not only consented, but they combined in an aristocratic system, calculated and intended to enslave their country! Unhappy Pennsylvania! thou, as a part of the Union, must share in its unfortunate fate! For when this system, after being laid before thy citizens, comes before the delegates selected by you for its consideration, there are found but three of the numerous members that have virtue enough to raise their voices in support of the rights of mankind! America, particularly Pennsylvania, must be ill-starred indeed, if this is a true state of the case! I trust we may address our country in far other language.

Happy America! Thy crisis was indeed alarming, but thy situation was not desperate. We had confidence in our country; though on whichever side we turned, we were presented with scenes of distress. Though the jarring interests of the various states, and the different habits and inclinations of their inhabitants, all lay in the way, and rendered our prospect gloomy and discouraging indeed, yet such were the generous and mutual sacrifices offered up, that amidst forty-two members, who represented twelve of the United States, there were only three who did not attest the instrument as a confirmation of its goodness—happy Pennsylvania! this plan has been laid before thy citizens for consideration, they have sent delegates to express their voice; and listen, with rapture listen! From only three [of the] opposition has been heard against it.

The singular unanimity that has attended the whole progress of their business will in the minds of those considerate men, who have not had opportunity to examine the general and particular interest of their country, prove to their satisfaction, that it is an excellent Constitution, and worthy to be adopted, ordained, and established by the people of the United States.

After having viewed the arguments drawn from *probability,* whether this is a good or a bad system, whether those who contend for it, or those who contend against it, contend for the rights of mankind, let us step forward and examine the *fact.*

We were told some days ago [7 December], by the honorable gentleman from Westmoreland (William Findley) when speaking of this system and its objects, that the Convention, no doubt, thought they were forming a compact or contract of the greatest importance. Sir, I confess I was much surprised at so late a stage of the debate, to hear such principles maintained. It was matter of surprise to see the great leading principle of this system still so very much misunderstood. "The Convention, no doubt, thought they were forming a compact!"[(a)] I cannot answer for what every member thought; but I believe it cannot be said, that they thought they were making a compact,[(b)] because

I cannot discover the least trace of a compact in that system. There can be no compact unless there are more parties than one. It is a new doctrine, that one can make a compact with himself. "The Convention were forming compacts!" With whom? I know no bargains that were made there. I am unable to conceive who the parties could be. The state governments make a bargain with one another; that is the doctrine that is endeavored to be established, by gentlemen in opposition, their state sovereignties wish to be represented! But far other were the ideas of the Convention, and far other are those conveyed in the system itself.

As this subject has been often mentioned and as often misunderstood, it may not be improper to take some further notice of it. This, Mr. President, is not a government founded upon compact; it is founded upon the power of the people. They express in their name and their authority, "*We the People do ordain and establish,*" etc. from their ratification, and their ratification alone, it is to take its constitutional authenticity; without that, it is no more than *tabula rasa*.

I know very well all the commonplace rant of state sovereignties, and that government is founded in original compact. If that position was examined, it will be found not to accede very well with the true principle of free government. It does not suit the language or genius of the system before us. I think it does not accord with experience, so far as I have been able to obtain information from history.

The greatest part of government have been founded on conquest; perhaps a few early ones may have had their origin in paternal authority. Sometimes a family united, and that family afterwards extended itself into a community. But the greatest governments which have appeared on the face of the globe have been founded in conquest. The great empires of Assyria, Persia, Macedonia, and Rome were all of this kind. I know well that in Great Britain, since the Revolution [of 1688], it has become a principle, that the constitution is founded in contract; but the form and time of that contract, no writer has yet attempted to discover. It was, however, recognized at the time of the Revolution, therefore is politically true. But we should act very imprudently to consider our liberties as placed on such foundation.

If we go a little further on this subject, I think we see that the doctrine of original compact cannot be supported consistently with the best principles of government. If we admit it, we exclude the idea of amendment; because a contract once entered into between the governor and governed becomes obligatory, and cannot be altered but by the mutual consent of both parties. The citizens of United

America, I presume do not wish to stand on that footing, with those to whom, from convenience, they please to delegate the exercise of the general powers necessary for sustaining and preserving the Union. They wish a principle established by the operation of which the legislatures may feel the direct authority of the people. The people possessing that authority will continue to exercise it by amending and improving their own work. This Constitution may be found to have defects in it; amendments hence may become necessary; but the idea of a government founded on contract destroys the means of improvement. We hear it every time the gentlemen are up, "shall we violate the Confederation, which directs every alteration that is thought necessary to be established by the state legislatures only." Sir, those gentlemen must ascend to a higher source; the people fetter themselves by no contract. If your state legislatures have cramped themselves by compact, it was done without the authority of the people, who alone possess the supreme power.

I have already shown, that this system is not a compact or contract; the system itself tells you what it is; it is an ordinance and establishment of the people. I think that the force of the introduction to the work must by this time have been felt. It is not an unmeaning flourish. The expressions declare, in a practical manner, the principle of this Constitution. It is ordained and established by the people themselves; and we, who give our votes for it, are merely the proxies of our constituents. We sign it as their attorneys, and as to ourselves, we agree to it as individuals.

We are told by honorable gentlemen in opposition, "that the present Confederation should have been continued, but that additional powers should have been given to it. That such was the business of the late Convention, and that they had assumed to themselves, the power of proposing another in its stead; and that which is proposed is such an one as was not expected by the legislatures nor by the people." I apprehend this would have been a very insecure, very inadequate, and a very pernicious mode of proceeding. Under the present Confederation, Congress certainly do not possess sufficient power; but one body of men we know they are; and were they invested with additional powers, they must become dangerous. Did not the honorable gentleman [William Findley] himself tell us, that the powers of government, vested either in one man, or one body of men, formed the very description of tyranny? To have placed in the present, the legislative, the executive, and judicial authority, all of which are essential to the general government, would indubitably have produced the severest despotism. From this short deduction, one of these two things must have appeared to the Convention, and must appear to every man, who is at the pains of thinking on the subject. It was indispensably necessary, either to make a new distribution of the powers of government or to give such powers to one body of men, as would constitute a tyranny. If it was proper to avoid tyranny, it becomes requisite to avoid placing additional powers in the hands of a Congress, constituted like the present; hence the conclusion is warranted, that a different organization ought to take place.

Our next inquiry ought to be, whether this is the most proper disposition and organization of the necessary powers. But before I consider this subject, I think it proper to notice one sentiment, expressed by an honorable gentleman from the county of Cumberland (Robert Whitehill); he asserts [7 December] the extent of the government is too great, and this system cannot be executed. What is the consequence if this assertion is true? It strikes directly at the root of the Union.

I admit, Mr. President, there are great difficulties in adopting a system of good and free governments to the extent of our country. But I am sure that our interests as citizens, as states, and as a nation depend essentially upon an Union. This Constitution is proposed to accomplish that great and desirable end. Let the experiment be made; let the system be fairly and candidly tried before it is determined that it cannot be executed.

I proceed to another objection; for I mean to answer those that have been suggested since I had the honor of addressing you last week [4 December]. It has been alleged by honorable gentlemen, that this general government possesses powers, for *internal* purposes, and that the general government cannot exercise internal powers. The honorable member from Westmoreland (William Findley) dilates on this subject and instances the opposition that was made by the colonies against Great Britain, to prevent her imposing internal taxes or excises. And before the federal government will be able to impose the one, or obtain the other, he considers it necessary that it should possess power for every internal purpose.

Let us examine these objections; if this government does not possess internal as well as external power, and that power for internal as well as external purposes, I apprehend, that all that has hitherto been done must go for nothing. I apprehend a government that cannot answer the purposes for which it is intended is not a government for this country. I know that Congress, under the present Articles of Confederation, possess no internal power, and we see the consequences; they can recommend; they can go further, they can make requisitions, but there they must stop. For as far as I recollect, after making a law, they cannot take a single step towards carrying it into execution. I believe it will be found in experience, that with regard to the exercise of internal powers, the general government will not be unnecessarily rigorous. The future collection of the duties and imposts will, in the opinion of some, supersede the necessity of having recourse to internal taxation. The United States will not, perhaps, be often under the necessity of using this power at all; but if they should, it will be exercised only in a moderate degree. The good sense of the citizens of the United States is not to be alarmed by the picture of taxes collected at the point of the bayonet. There is no more reason to suppose, that the delegates and representatives in Congress, any more than the legislature of Pennsylvania, or any other state, will act in this manner. Insinuations of this kind, made against one body of men, and not against another, though both the representatives of the people, are not made with propriety, nor will they have the weight of argument. I apprehend the greatest part of the revenue will arise from external taxation. But certainly it would have been very unwise in the late Convention to have omitted the addition of the other powers; and I think it would be very unwise in this Convention, to refuse to adopt this Constitution, because it grants Congress power to lay and collect taxes for the purpose of providing for the common defense and general welfare of the United States.

What is to be done to effect these great purposes if an impost should be found insufficient? Suppose a war was suddenly declared against us by a foreign power possessed of a formidable navy; our navigation would be laid prostrate, our imposts must cease; and shall our existence as a nation depend upon the peaceful navigation of our seas? A strong exertion of maritime power, on the part of an enemy, might deprive us of these sources of revenue in a few months. It may suit honorable gentlemen, who live at the western extremity of this state, that they should contribute nothing, by internal taxes, to the support of the general government. They care not what restraints are laid upon our commerce, for what is the commerce of Philadelphia to the inhabitants on the other side the Allegheny Mountain? But though it may suit them, it does not suit those in the lower part of the state, who are by far the most numerous. Nor can we agree that our safety should depend altogether upon a revenue arising from commerce.

Excise may be a necessary mode of taxation; it takes place in most states already.

The capitation tax is mentioned as one of those that are exceptionable. In some states, that mode of taxation is used; but I believe in many, it would be received with great reluctance; there are one or two states where it is constantly in use, and without any difficulties and inconveniences arising from it. An excise, in its very principles, is an improper tax, if it could be avoided; but yet it has been a source of revenue in Pennsylvania, both before the Revolution and since; during all which time, we have enjoyed the benefit of free government.

I presume, sir, that the executive powers of government ought to be commensurate with the government itself, and that a government which cannot act in every part is so far defective. Consequently it is necessary, that Congress possess powers to tax internally, as well as externally.

It is objected to this system, that under it there is no sovereignty left in the state governments. I have had occasion to reply to this already; but I should be very glad to know at what period the state governments became possessed of the supreme power. On the principle on which I found my arguments, and that is the principle of this Constitution, the supreme power resides in the people. If they choose to indulge a part of their sovereign power to be exercised by the state governments, they may. If they have done it, the states were right in exercising it; but if they think it no longer safe or convenient, they will resume it, or make a new distribution, more likely to be productive of that good, which ought to be our constant aim.

The power both of the general government, and the state governments, under this system, are acknowledged to be so many emanations of power from the people. The great object now to be attended to, instead of disagreeing about who shall possess the supreme power, is to consider whether the present arrangement is well calculated to promote and secure the tranquility and happiness of our common country. These are the dictates of sound and unsophisticated sense, and what ought to employ the attention and judgment of this honorable body.

We are next told, by the honorable gentlemen in opposition (as indeed we have been from the beginning of the debates in this Convention to the conclusion of their speeches yesterday) that this is a consolidated government and will abolish the state governments. Definitions of a consolidated government have been called for; the gentlemen gave us what they termed definition, but it does not seem, to me at least, that they have as yet expressed clear ideas upon that subject. I will endeavor to state their different ideas upon this point. The gentleman from Westmoreland (William Findley) when speaking on this subject [4 December], says, that he means by a consolidation, that government which puts the thirteen states into one.

The honorable gentleman from Fayette (John Smilie) gives you this definition [6 December]: "What I mean by a consolidated government is one that will transfer the sovereignty from the state governments to the general government."

The honorable member from Cumberland (Robert Whitehill) instead of giving you a definition, sir, tells you again [7 December], that "it is a consolidated government, and we have proved it so."

These, I think, sir, are the different descriptions given us of a consolidated government. As to the first, that it is a consolidated government, that puts the thirteen United States into one; if it is meant, that the general government will destroy the governments of the states, I will admit that such a government would not suit the people of America. It would be improper for *this* country, because it could not be proportioned to *its extent* on the principles of freedom. But that description does not apply to the system before you. This, instead of placing the state governments in jeopardy, is founded on their existence. On this principle, its organization depends; it must stand or fall, as the state governments are secured or ruined. Therefore, though this may be a very proper description of a consolidating government, yet it must be disregarded as inapplicable to the proposed Constitution. It is not treated with decency when such insinuations are offered against it.

The honorable gentleman (John Smilie) tells you, that a consolidating government, "is one that will transfer the sovereignty from the state governments to the general government." Under this system, the sovereignty is not in the possession of the state governments, therefore it cannot be transferred from them to the general government. So that in no point of view of this definition can we discover that it applies to the present system.

In the exercise of its powers will be insured the exercise of their powers to the state government; it will insure peace and stability to them; their strength will increase with its strength; their growth will extend with its growth.

Indeed narrow minds, and some such there are in every government—narrow minds, and intriguing spirits, will be active in sowing dissensions and promoting discord between them. But those whose understandings, and whose hearts are good enough to pursue the general welfare, will find, that what is the interest of the whole must, on the great scale, be the interest of every part. It will be the duty of a state, as of an individual, to sacrifice her own convenience to the general good of the Union.

The next objection that I mean to take notice of is that the powers of the several parts of this government are not kept as distinct and independent as they ought to be. I admit the truth of this general sentiment. I do not think, that in the powers of the Senate, the distinction is marked with so much accuracy as I wished, and still wish; but yet I am of opinion, that real and effectual security is obtained, which is saying a great deal. I do not consider this part as *wholly* unexceptionable; but even where there are defects in this system, they are improvements upon the old. I will go a little further; though in this system, the distinction and independence of power is not adhered to with entire theoretical precision, yet it is more strictly adhered to than in any other system of government in the world. In the constitution of Pennsylvania, the executive department exercises judicial powers, in the trial of public officers; yet a similar power in this system is complained of; at the same time the constitution of Pennsylvania is referred to as an example for the late Convention to have taken a lesson by.

In New Jersey, in Georgia, in South Carolina, and in North Carolina the executive power is blended with the legislative. Turn to their constitutions and see in how many instances.

In North Carolina, the Senate and House of Commons elect the governor himself; they likewise elect seven persons, to be a council of state, to advise the governor in the execution of his office. Here we find the whole executive department under the nomination of the legislature, at least the most important part of it.

In South Carolina, the legislature appoint the governor and commander in chief, lieutenant governor, and privy council. "Justices of the peace shall be nominated by the legislature and commissioned by the governor," and what is more, they are appointed during pleasure. All other judicial officers are to be appointed by the senate and house of representatives. I might go further and detail a great multitude of instances in which the legislative, executive, and judicial powers are blended, but it is unnecessary; I only mention these to show that though this Constitution does not arrive at what is called perfection, yet, it contains great improvements, and its powers are distributed with a degree of accuracy, superior to what is termed accuracy, in particular states.

There are four instances in which improper powers are said to be blended in the Senate. We are told, that this government is imperfect, because the Senate possess the power of trying impeachments. But here, sir, the Senate are under a check, as no impeachment can be tried until it is made; and the House of Representatives possess the sole power of making impeachments. We are told that the share which the Senate have in making treaties is exceptionable; but here they are also under a check, by a constituent part of the government, and nearly the immediate representative of the people, I mean the President of the United States. They can make no treaty without his concurrence. The same observation applies in the appointment of officers. Every officer must be nominated solely and exclusively, by the President.

Much has been said on the subject of treaties, and this power is denominated a blending of the legislative and executive powers in the Senate. It is but justice to represent the favorable, as well as unfavorable side of a question, and from thence determine, whether the objectionable parts are of a sufficient weight to induce a rejection of this Constitution.

There is no doubt, sir, but under this Constitution, treaties will become the supreme law of the land; nor is there any doubt but the Senate and President possess the power of making them. But though treaties are to have the force of laws, they are in some important respects very different from other acts of legislation. In making laws, our own consent alone is necessary. In forming treaties, the concurrence of another power becomes necessary; treaties, sir, are truly contracts, or compacts, between the different states, nations, or princes, who find it convenient or necessary to enter into them. Some gentlemen are of opinion, that the power of making treaties should have been placed in the legislature at large; there are, however, reasons that operate with a great force on the other side. Treaties are frequently (especially in time of war) of such a nature, that it would be extremely improper to publish them, or even commit the secret of their negotiation to any great number of persons. For my part I am not an advocate for secrecy in transactions relating to the public; not generally even in forming treaties, because I think that the history of the diplomatic corps will evince, even in that great department of politics, the truth of an old adage, that "honesty is the best policy," and this is the conduct of the most able negotiators; yet sometimes secrecy may be necessary, and therefore it becomes an argument against committing the knowledge of these transactions to too many persons. But in their nature treaties originate differently from laws. They are made by equal parties, and each side has half of the bargain to make; they will be made between us and the powers at the distance of three thousand miles. A long series of negotiation will frequently precede them; and can it be the opinion of these gentlemen, that the legislature should be in session during this whole time? It well deserves to be remarked, that though the House of Representatives possess no active part in making treaties, yet their legislative authority will be found to have strong restraining influence upon both President and Senate. In England, if the king and his ministers find themselves, during their negotiation, to be embarrassed, because an existing law is not repealed, or a new law is not enacted, they give notice to the legislature of their situation and inform them that it will be necessary, before the treaty can operate, that some law be repealed or some be made. And will not the same thing take place here? Shall less prudence, less caution, less moderation take place among those who negotiate treaties for the United States, than among those who negotiate them for the other nations of the earth? And let it be attended to, that even in the making treaties the states are immediately represented, and the people mediately represented; two of the constituent parts of government must concur in making them. Neither the President nor the Senate solely can complete a treaty; they are checks upon each other and are so balanced, as to produce security to the people.

I might suggest other reasons, to add weight to what has already been offered, but I believe it is not necessary; yet let me however add one thing: the Senate is a favorite with many of the states, and it was with difficulty that these checks could be procured; it was one of the last exertions of conciliation in the late Convention, that obtained them.

It has been alleged, as a consequence of the small number of Representatives, that they will not know as intimately as they ought, the interests, inclinations, or habits of their constituents.

We find on an examination of all its parts, that the objects of this government are such as extend beyond the bounds of the particular states. This is the line of distinction between this government and the particular state governments.

This principle I had an opportunity of illustrating on a former occasion. Now when we come to consider the objects of this government, we shall find, that in making our choice of a proper character to be a member of the House of Representatives, we ought to fix on one, whose mind and heart are enlarged; who possesses a general knowledge of the interests of America and a disposition to make use of that knowledge for the advantage and welfare of his country. It belongs not to this government to make an act for a particular township, county, or state.

A defect in *minute* information has not certainly been an objection in the management of the business of the United States; but the want of enlarged ideas has hitherto been chargeable on our councils; yet even with regard to minute knowledge, I do not conceive it impossible to find eight characters, that may be very well informed as to the situation, interests and views of every part of this state; and who may have a concomitant interest with their fellow citizens. They could not materially injure others without affecting their own fortunes.

I did say, that in order to obtain that enlarged information in our Representatives, a large district for election would be more proper than a small one. When I speak of large districts, it is not agreeable to the idea entertained by the honorable member from Fayette (John Smilie) who tells you, that elections for large districts must be ill-attended, because the people will not choose to go very far on this business [4, 6 December]. It is not meant, sir, by me, that the votes should be taken at one place; no, sir, the elections may be held thro this state, in the same manner as elections for members of the General Assembly, and this may be done too without any additional inconvenience or expense.

If it could be effected, all the people of the same society ought to meet in one place and communicate freely with each other on the great business of representation. Though this cannot be done in fact, yet we find that it is the most favorite and constitutional idea. It is supported by this principle too, that every member is the representative of the whole community, and not of a particular part. The larger therefore the district is, the greater is the probability of selecting wise and virtuous characters, and the more agreeable it is to the constitutional principle of representation.

As to the objection that the House of Representatives may be bribed by the Senate, I confess I do not see that bribery is an objection against *this system*; it is rather an objection against human nature. I am afraid that bribes in every government may be offered and received; but let me ask of the gentlemen who urge this objection, to point out where any power is given to bribe *under this Constitution*? Every species of influence is guarded against as much as possible. Can the Senate procure money to effect such design? All public monies must be disposed of by law, and it is necessary that the House of Representatives originate such law. Before the money can be got out of the treasury, it must be appropriated by law. If the legislature had the effrontery to set aside three or four hundred thousand pounds for this purpose, and the people would tamely suffer it, I grant it might be done; and in Pennsylvania the legislature might do the same; for by a law, and that conformably to the constitution, they might divide among themselves what portion of the public money they pleased. I shall just remark, sir, that the objections, which have repeatedly been made, with regard to "the number of Representatives being too small, and that they may possibly be made smaller; that the districts are too large, and not within the reach of the people; and that the House of Representatives may be bribed by the Senate"; these objections come with an uncommon degree of impropriety, from those who would refer us back to the Articles of Confederation. For under those, the representation of this state cannot exceed seven members, and may consist of only two; and these are wholly without the reach or control of the people. Is there not also greater danger that the majority of such a body might be more easily bribed, than the majority of one, not only more numerous, but checked by a division of two or three distinct and independent parts? The danger is certainly better guarded against in the proposed system, than in any other yet devised.

The next objections which I shall notice are, "that the powers of the Senate are too great, that the representation therein is unequal, and that the Senate, from the smallness of its number, may be bribed." Is there any propriety in referring us to the Confederation on this subject? Because, in one or two instances, the Senate possess more power than the House of Representatives, are these gentlemen supported in their remarks when they tell you they wished and expected more powers to be given to the present Congress, a body certainly much more exceptionable than any instituted under this system?

"That the representation in the Senate is unequal," I regret, because I am of opinion, the states ought to be represented according to their importance; but in this system there is considerable improvement; for the true principle of representation is carried into the House of Representatives, and into the choice of the President; and without the assistance of one or the other of these, the Senate is inactive and can do neither good or evil.

It is repeated again and again, by the honorable gentlemen, "that the power over elections, which is given to the general government in this system, is a dangerous power." I must own I feel myself surprised that an objection of this kind should be persisted in, after what has been said by my honorable colleague [Thomas McKean] in reply. I think it has appeared by a minute investigation of the subject, that it would have been not only unwise, but highly improper in the late Convention, to have omitted this clause, or given less power, than it does over elections. Such powers, sir, are enjoyed by every state government in the United States. In some, they are of a much greater magnitude; and why should this be the only one deprived of them? Ought not these, as well as every other legislative body, to have the power of judging of the qualifications of its own members? "The times, places and manner of holding elections for Representatives may be altered by Congress." This power, sir, has been shown to be necessary, not only on some particular occasions, but even to the very existence of the federal government. I have heard some very improbable suspicions indeed suggested with regard to the manner in which it will be exercised. Let us suppose it may be improperly exercised. Is it not more likely so to be by the particular states, than by the government of the United States? Because the general government will be more studious of the good of the whole, than a particular state will be; and therefore, when the power of regulating the time, place, or manner of holding elections is exercised by the Congress, it will be to correct the improper regulations of a particular state.

I now proceed to the second Article of this Constitution, which relates to the executive department.

I find, sir, from an attention to the arguments used by the gentlemen on the other side of the house, that there are but few exceptions taken to this part of the system. I shall take notice of them and afterwards point out some valuable qualifications, which I think this part possesses in an eminent degree.

The objection against the powers of the President is not that they are too many or too great, but to state it in the gentleman's own language [John Smilie, 6 December], they are so trifling that the President is no more than the *tool* of the Senate.

Now, sir, I do not apprehend this to be the case, because I see that he may do a great many things independent of the Senate; and with respect to the executive powers of government in which the Senate participate, they can do nothing without him. Now I would ask, which is most likely to be the tool of the other? Clearly, sir, he holds the helm, and the vessel can proceed neither in one direction nor another, without his concurrence. It was expected by many, that the cry would have been against the powers of the President as a monarchical power; indeed the echo of such sound was heard, some time before the rise of the late Convention. There were men at that time, determined to make an attack upon whatever system should be proposed, but they mistook the point of direction. Had the President possessed those powers, which the opposition on this floor are willing to consign him, of making treaties, and appointing officers, with the advice of a council of state, the clamor would have been, that the House of Representatives and the Senate were the *tools* of the monarch. This, sir, is but conjecture, but I leave it to those who are acquainted with the current of the politics pursued by the enemies to this system to determine whether it is a reasonable conjecture or not.

The manner of appointing the President of the United States I find is not objected to, therefore I shall say little on that point. But I think it well worthwhile to state to this house how little the difficulties, even in the most difficult part of this system, appear to have been noticed by the honorable gentlemen in opposition. The Convention, sir, were perplexed with no part of this plan so much as with the mode of choosing the President of the United States. For my own part, I think the most unexceptionable mode, next after the one prescribed in this Constitution, would be that practiced by the Eastern States and the State of New York; yet if gentlemen object, that an 8th part of our country forms a district too large for elections, how much more would they object, if it was extended to the whole Union? On this subject, it was the opinion of a great majority in Convention, that the thing was impracticable; other embarrassments presented themselves.

Was the President to be appointed by the legislature? Was he to continue a certain time in office, and afterward was he to become ineligible?

To have the executive officers dependent upon the legislative would certainly be a violation of that principle so necessary to preserve the freedom of republics, that the legislative and executive powers should be separate and independent. Would it have been proper, that he should be appointed by the Senate? I apprehend, that still stronger objections could be urged against that—cabal, intrigue, corruption—everything bad would have been the necessary concomitant of every election.

To avoid the inconveniences already enumerated, and many others that might be suggested, the mode before us was adopted. By it we avoid corruption, and we are little exposed to the lesser evils of party and intrigue; and when the government shall be organized, proper care will undoubtedly be taken to counteract influence even of that nature—the Constitution, with the same view has directed, that the day on which the Electors shall give their votes shall be the same throughout the United States. I flatter myself the experiment will be a happy one for our country.

The choice of this officer is brought as nearly home to the people as is practicable; with the approbation of the state legislatures, the people may elect with only one remove; for "each state shall appoint, in such manner as the legislature thereof may direct, a number of electors equal to the whole number of senators and representatives, to which the state may be entitled in congress." Under this regulation, it will not be easy to corrupt the Electors, and there will be little time or opportunity for tumult or intrigue. This, sir, will not be like the elections of a Polish diet, begun in noise and ending in bloodshed.

If gentlemen will look into this Article and read for themselves, they will find, that there is no well-grounded reason to suspect the President will be the *tool* of the Senate. "The president shall be commander in chief of the army and navy of the United States, and of the militia of the several states, when called into the actual service of the United States. He may require the opinion in writing of the principal officers in each of the executive departments, upon any subject relative to the duties of their respective offices; and he shall have power to grant reprieves and pardons, for offenses against the United States." Must the President, after all, be called the *tool* of the Senate? I do not mean to insinuate, that he has more powers than he ought to have, but merely to declare that they are of such a nature as to place him above expressions of contempt.

There is another power of no small magnitude entrusted to this officer. "He shall take care, that the laws be faithfully executed."

I apprehend, that in the administration of this government, it will not be found necessary for the Senate always to sit. I know some gentlemen have insinuated and conjectured, that this will be the case, but I am inclined to a contrary opinion. If they had employment every day, no doubt but it might be the wish of the Senate to continue their session; but from the nature of their business, I do not think it will be necessary for them to attend longer than the House of Representatives. Besides their legislative powers, they possess three others, viz., trying impeachments, concurring in making treaties, and in appointing officers. With regard to their power in making treaties, it is of importance, that it should be very seldom exercised—we are happily removed from the vortex of European politics, and the fewer, and the more simple our negotiations with European powers, the better they will be. If such be the case, it will be but once in a number of years, that a single treaty will come before the Senate. I think, therefore, that on this account it will be unnecessary to sit constantly. With regard to the trial of impeachments, I hope it is what will seldom happen. In this observation, the experience of the ten last years support me. Now there is only left the power of concurring in the appointment of officers; but care is taken, in this Constitution, that this branch of business may be done without their presence. The President is authorized to fill up all vacancies, that may happen during the recess of the Senate, by granting commissions, which shall expire at the end of their next session. So that on the whole the Senate need not sit longer than the House of Representatives, at the public expense; and no doubt if apprehensions are entertained of the Senate, the House of Representatives will not provide pay for them one day longer than is necessary. But what (it will be asked) is this great power of the President? He can fill the offices only by temporary appointments. True; but every person knows the advantage of being once introduced into an office; it is often of more importance than the highest recommendation.

Having now done with the legislative and executive branches of this government, I shall just remark, that upon the whole of the executive, it appears that the gentlemen in opposition state nothing as exceptionable, but the deficiency of powers in the President; but rather seem to allow some degree of political merit in this department of government.

I now proceed to the judicial department; and here, Mr. President, I meet an objection, I confess I had not expected; and it seems it did not occur to the honorable gentleman (William Findley) who made it until a few days ago [7 December].

He alleges, that the judges, under this Constitution, are not rendered sufficiently independent, because they may hold other offices; and though they may be independent as judges, yet their other office may depend upon the legislature. I confess, sir, this objection appears to me to be a little wiredrawn in the first place; the legislature can appoint to no office, therefore the dependence could not be on them for the office, but rather on the President and Senate; but then these cannot add the salary, because no money can be appropriated, but in consequence of a law of the United States. No sinecure can be bestowed on any judge, but by the concurrence of the whole legislature and of the President; and I do not think this an event that will probably happen.

It is true, that there is a provision made in the constitution of Pennsylvania, that the judges shall not be allowed to hold any other office whatsoever; and I believe they are expressly forbidden to sit in Congress; but this, sir, is not introduced as a principle into this Constitution. There are many states in the Union, whose constitutions do not limit the usefulness of their best men, or exclude them from rendering such services to their country, for which they are found eminently qualified. New York, far from restricting their chancellor or judges of the Supreme Court from a seat in Congress, expressly provide for sending them there on extraordinary occasions. In Connecticut, the judges are not precluded from enjoying other offices. Judges from many states have sat in Congress. Now it is not to be expected, that eleven or twelve states are to change their sentiments and practice on this subject to accommodate themselves to Pennsylvania.

It is again alleged against this system, that the powers of the judges are too extensive; but I will not trouble you, sir, with a repetition of what I had the honor of delivering the other day [7 December]; I hope the result of those arguments gave satisfaction, and proved that the judicial were commensurate with the legislative powers; that they went no further, and that they ought to go so far.

The laws of Congress being made for the Union, no particular state can be alone affected, and as they are to provide for the general purposes of the Union, so ought they to have the means of making the provisions effectual over all that country included within the Union. [Lloyd, *Debates,* 100–20]

> [Lloyd's errata]
> (a), (b). [The word in the text of the debates is "contract," but the correct word is "compact," which Lloyd notes in his errata.]

Wilson: I congratulate you on this business drawing to a conclusion. It is of great consequence to us and our posterity whether we shall continue under a Confederation without efficient powers to carry its purposes into execution, despised abroad and without credit at home; or whether we shall adopt a system of Union; with energetic powers, which can effectually carry into execution such measures as may be calculated and devised for the common safety.

The gentlemen in opposition cannot complain of precipitancy or hurry. I beg to ask whether we have not, on the other hand, delayed and procrastinated the main question *perhaps* unnecessarily and improvidently. The objections to the new Federal Constitution have been urged repeatedly in different lights and the same arguments have been brought before the Convention in a variety of shapes.

Objection 1. They have urged the want of a bill of rights; that the right of conscience and liberty of the press are not thereby secured to us.

Response 1. We answer such an enumeration is unnecessary and at best dangerous. In the instances where power is not delegated to our rulers, the rights still remain in the people. Whatever is not given is reserved. Many of the states have no bills of rights in the formation of their constitutions.

Objection 2. It is said to be a consolidated government, annihilating and absorbing all the state legislatures which must necessarily fall of themselves.

Response 2. The government is consolidated to certain purposes and vigor given to the general Union. The sovereignty rests with the people. In them consists the supreme power. We are a confederate republic with proper balancing powers vested in certain bodies for the benefit of the whole. The existence of the Federal Constitution must depend on the continuance of the state legislatures in the case of the election of the House of Representatives, the Senate, the President and the judges. A republican form of government is guaranteed to each state and are to be guarded from foreign as well as domestic violence. The powers given to the new Congress reach to objects beyond the compass of the state legislatures. They [Congress] only are competent to it. [Yeates's Notes, PPIn][4]

1. For James Wilson's and Thomas McKean's denials that Sweden once had jury trials, see the debate on 8 December; and for William Findley's presentation of proof that Sweden had had jury trials, see the debate on 10 December. The *Herald's* report was reprinted in the *Independent Gazetteer* and *Pennsylvania Packet* on 13 December and in seven newspapers from Massachusetts to South Carolina. In a satirical article, "Democritus" marvelled that James Wilson had forsaken his "profane studies" and betook himself to the perusal of pious and holy books." "Democritus" added that "though by profession a lawyer; yet he forgets a remarkable passage in Blackstone, about the trial by jury in Sweden—while he recollects two whole lines in Sternhold and Hopkins's *Psalms*" (*New York Journal,* 28 December, RCS:N.Y.).

2. This undated manuscript in the Wilson Papers, entitled "2d List of Objections," is the outline for James Wilson's speech in the Convention on 11 December. Wilson began the speech in the morning session and completed it in the afternoon. The section of the "List" that outlines the morning portion of the speech is placed in the A.M. session, and the remainder of the "List" is in the P.M. session. The "No." in the "List" refers to the objections which Wilson had numbered consecutively in his notes of debates between 3 and 8 December. The "Page" in the "List" refers to the numbered pages of Wilson's notes of debates before 3 December.

3. On 5 December articles in the *Independent Gazetteer* and the *Freeman's Journal* (II:D above) declared that the minority in the Convention had received over 1,000 more votes than the majority and that many freemen had not voted for delegates to the Convention because they considered that it had been called in a riotous and illegal manner "as well as with dangerous and unconstitutional precipitancy." For additional comments on the numbers voting, see the speeches of William Findley and Thomas Hartley, Convention Debates, 12 December, A.M.

4. Yeates wrote at the top of his notes of Wilson's speech: "22 minutes past 10 o'clock, A.M. began, and ended at 1 o'clock, P.M."

Convention Proceedings, P.M.

The Convention met pursuant to adjournment,

Resumed the consideration of the proposed Constitution, and after some inquiry into the principles, construction, and probable operation of the new government,

Adjourned until half past nine o'clock tomorrow, A.M.

Convention Debates, P.M.

JAMES WILSON: 2d List of Objections.[1]

The trial by jury was intended to be given up;[(a)] and the civil law introduced in civil cases[(b)] (No. 171, 172, 173, 180, 185, 186, 187, *194, 193,* 198, 199, *201,* 209, 203–207, *210, 212,* 215, 227, 229, 231, 232, 233, 234, 236, 237, 239, 240). The appellate jurisdiction as to facts improper; appeals are unknown to the common law (No. 179, 188, 200, 202, 208, 209, 230).

The expense of the general government and of the state governments will be too great (No. 183).

Standing armies should not be among the powers given to Congress (No. 113, 123, *149*). Nor should the command of the militia (No. 113, 125–132, 136, 137).

This government is too far removed from the people. There is not sufficient responsibility in it (No. 58, 196). The Convention *knew* this was not a free government; otherwise they would not have asked the power of the purse and the sword (No. 124). This government is, and was intended to be an aristocracy (No. 34, 35, 38, *82,* 115, *134, 148, 150,* 151, *219*). [Wilson's Notes, PHi]

> [Wilson's marginal notes]
> (a) "The trial by jury was intended to be given up." [Under this heading, Wilson emphasized the objection numbered 185 and 198.]
> (b) "The civil law introduced in civil cases." [Under this heading, Wilson emphasized the objections numbered 180, 198, 199, and 209.]

Wilson: I shall now proceed, Mr. President, to notice the remainder of the objections that have been suggested by the honorable gentlemen who oppose the system now before you.

We have been told, sir, by the honorable member from Fayette (John Smilie) "that the trial by jury was *intended* to be given up, and the civil law was *intended* to be introduced into its place in civil cases."

Before a sentiment of this kind was hazarded, I think, sir, the gentleman ought to be prepared with better proof in its support, than any he has yet attempted to produce. It is a charge, sir, not only unwarrantable, but cruel; the idea of such a thing, I believe, never entered into the mind of a single member of that Convention; and I believe further, that they never suspected there would be found within the United States, a single person that was capable of making such a charge. If it should be well-founded, sir, they *must* abide by the consequences, but if (as I trust it will fully appear) it is ill-founded, then he or they who make it *ought* to abide by the consequences.

Trial by jury forms a large field for investigation, and numerous volumes are written on the subject; those who are well acquainted with it may employ much time in its discussion; but in a country where its excellence is so well understood, it may not be necessary to be very prolix, in pointing them out. For my part, I shall confine myself to a few observations in reply to the objections that have been suggested.

The member from Fayette (John Smilie) has labored to infer, that under the Articles of Confederation, the Congress possessed no appellate jurisdiction; but this being decided against him, by the words of that instrument, by which is granted to Congress the power of "establishing courts for receiving and determining, finally, appeals in all cases of capture." He next attempts a distinction and allows the power of appealing from the decisions of the judges, but not from the verdict of a jury; but this is determined against him also, by the practice of the states. For in every instance which has occurred, this power has been claimed by Congress and exercised by the court of appeals; but what would be the consequence of allowing the doctrine for which he contends? Would it not be in the power of a jury, by their verdict, to involve the whole Union in a war? They may condemn the property of a natural[(a)] or otherwise infringe the law of nations; in this case ought their verdict to be without revisal? Nothing can be inferred from this, to prove that trials by jury were intended to be given up. In Massachusetts, and all the Eastern States, their causes are tried by juries, though they acknowledge the appellate jurisdiction of Congress.

I think I am not now to learn the advantages of a trial by jury; it has excellencies that entitle it to a superiority over any other mode, in cases to which it is applicable.

Where jurors can be acquainted with the characters of the parties and the witnesses, where the whole cause can be brought within their knowledge and their view, I know no mode of investigation equal to that by a jury; they hear everything that is alleged; they not only hear the words, but they see and mark the features of the countenance; they can judge of [the][(b)] weight due to such testimony; and moreover, it is a cheap and expeditious manner of distributing justice. There is another advantage annexed to the trial by jury; the jurors may indeed return a mistaken, or ill-founded verdict, but their errors cannot be systematical.

Let us apply these observations to the objects of the judicial department under this Constitution. I think it has been shown already, that they all extend beyond the bounds of any particular state; but further, a great number of the civil causes there enumerated depend either upon the law of nations or the marine law, that is, the general law of mercantile countries. Now, sir, in such causes, I presume it will not be pretended that this mode of decision ought to be adopted; for the law with regard to them is the same here as in every other country, and ought to be administered in the same manner. There are instances, in which I think it highly probable, that the trial by jury will be found proper; and if it is highly probable that it will be found proper, is it not equally probable, that it will be adopted? There may be causes depending between citizens of different states, and as trial by jury is known and regarded in all the states, they will certainly prefer that mode of trial before any other. The Congress will have the power of making proper regulations on this subject, but it was impossible for the Convention to have gone minutely into it; but if they could, it must have been very improper, because alterations, as I observed before, might have been necessary; and whatever the Convention might have done would have continued unaltered, unless by an alteration of the Constitution. Besides, there was another difficulty with regard to this subject. In some of the states they have courts of chancery and other appellate jurisdictions, and those states are as attached to that mode of distributing justice, as those that have none are to theirs.[2]

I have desired, repeatedly, that honorable gentlemen, who find fault, would be good enough to point out what they deem to be an improvement. The member from Westmoreland (William Findley) tells us, that the trial between citizens of different states ought to be by a jury of that state in which the cause of action arose. Now it is easy to see, that in many instances, this would be very improper and very partial, for besides the different manner of collecting and forming juries in the several states, the plaintiff comes from another state; he comes a stranger, unknown as to his character or mode of life, while the other party is in the midst of his friends, or perhaps his dependents. Would a trial by jury in such a case insure justice to the stranger? But again, I would ask that gentleman, whether, if a great part of his fortune was in the hands of some person in Rhode Island, he would wish, that his action to recover it should be determined by a jury of that country under its present circumstances?[3]

The gentleman from Fayette (John Smilie) says, that if the Convention found themselves embarrassed, at least they might have done thus much: they should have declared, that the substance should be secured by Congress; this would be saying nothing unless the cases were particularized.

* * * *

JOHN SMILIE: I said the Convention ought to have declared, that the legislature should establish the trial by jury by proper regulations.[4]

* * * *

JAMES WILSON: The legislature shall establish it by proper regulations! So after all, the gentleman has landed us at the very point from which we set out. He wishes them to do the very thing they have done, to leave it to the discretion of Congress. The fact, sir, is, nothing more could be done.

It is well-known, that there are some cases that should not come before juries; there are others, that in some of the states never come before juries, and in these states where they do come before them, appeals are found necessary, the facts reexamined, and the verdict of the jury sometimes is set aside. But I think in all cases, where the cause has come originally before a jury, that the last examination ought to be before a jury likewise.

The power of having appellate jurisdiction, as to facts, has been insisted upon as a proof, "that the Convention *intended* to give up the trial by jury in civil cases and to introduce the civil law." I have already declared my own opinion on this point and have shown, not merely, that it is founded on reason and authority. The express declaration of Congress[(c)] is to the same purpose. They insist upon this power as requisite to preserve the peace of the Union; certainly, therefore, it ought always to be possessed by the head of the Confederacy.

We are told, as an additional proof, that the trial by jury was intended to be given up, "that appeals are unknown to the common law; that the term is a civil law term, and with it the civil law is intended to be introduced." I confess I was a good deal surprised at this observation being made; for Blackstone, in the very volume which the honorable member (John Smilie) had in his hand and read us several extracts from, has a chapter entitled "Of Proceeding in the Nature of Appeals" [chapter 25]; and in that chapter says, that the "principal method of redress for erroneous judgments, in the king's courts of record, is by writ of error to some superior court of appeal."[(d)] Now it is well-known, that his book is a commentary upon the common law. Here then is a strong refutation of the assertion, "that appeals are unknown to the common law."

I think these were all the circumstances adduced to show the truth of the assertion, that in this Constitution, the trial by jury was *intended* to be given up by the late Convention in framing it. Has the assertion been proved? I say not, and the allegations offered, if they apply at all, apply in a contrary direction. I am glad that this objection has been stated, because it is a subject upon which the enemies of this Constitution have much insisted. We have now had an opportunity of investigating it fully, and the result is, that there is no foundation for the charge, but it must proceed from ignorance or something worse.

I go on to another objection which has been taken to this system, "that the expense of the general government and of the state governments will be too great, and that the citizens will not be able to support them." If the state governments are to continue as cumbersome and expensive as they have hitherto been, I confess it would be distressing to add to their expenses, and yet it might be necessary; but I think I can draw a different conclusion on this subject from more conjectures than one. The additional revenue to be raised by a general government will be more than sufficient for the additional expense; and a great part of that revenue may be so contrived as not to be taken from the citizens of this country; for I am not of opinion, that the consumer always pays the impost that is laid on imported articles; it is paid sometimes by the importer and sometimes by the foreign merchant who sends them to us. Had a duty of this nature been laid at the time of the peace, the greatest part of it would have been the contribution of foreigners. Besides, whatever is paid by the citizens is a voluntary *payment*.

I think, sir, it would be very easy and laudable to lessen the expenses of the state governments. I have been told (and perhaps it is not very far from the truth), that there are *two thousand* members of assembly in the several states; the business of revenue is done in consequence of requisitions from Congress, and whether it is furnished or not, it commonly becomes a subject of discussion. Now when this business is executed by the legislature of the United States, I leave it to those who are acquainted with the expense of long and frequent sessions of assembly to determine the great saving that will take place. Let me appeal to the citizens of Pennsylvania, how much time is taken up in this state every year, if not every session, in providing for the payment of an amazing interest due on her funded debt. There will be many sources of revenue, and many opportunities for economy, when the business of finance shall be administered under one government; the funds will be more productive, and the taxes, in all probability, less burthensome than they are now.

I proceed to another objection, that is taken against the power given to Congress of raising and keeping up standing armies. I confess I have been surprised that this objection was ever made, but I am more so that it is still repeated and insisted upon. I have taken some pains to inform myself how the other governments of the world stand with regard to this power; and the result of my inquiry is, that there is not one which has not the power of raising and keeping up standing armies. A government without the power of defense! It is a solecism!

I well recollect the principle insisted upon by the patriotic body in Great Britain; it is, that in time of peace, a standing army ought not to be kept up without the consent of Parliament. Their only apprehension appears to be, that it might be dangerous was the army kept up without the concurrence of the representatives of the people. Sir, we are not in the millennium. Wars may happen—and when they do happen, who is to have the power of collecting and appointing the force then become immediately and indispensably necessary?

It is not declared in this Constitution, that the Congress *shall* raise and support armies. No, sir, if they are not driven to it by necessity, why should we suppose they would do it by choice, any more than the representatives of the same citizens in the state legislatures? For we must not lose sight of the great principle upon which this work is founded. The authority here given to the general government flows from the same source as that placed in the legislatures of the several states.

It may be frequently necessary to keep up standing armies in time of peace. The present Congress have experienced the necessity; and seven hundred troops are just as much a standing army as seventy thousand. The principle which sustains them is precisely the same. They may go further, and raise an army, without communicating to the public the purpose for which it is raised. On a particular occasion, they did this. When the commotions existed in Massachusetts, they gave orders for enlisting an additional body of two thousand men.[5] I believe it is not generally known on what a perilous tenure we held our freedom and independence at that period. The flames of internal insurrection were ready to burst out in every quarter; they were formed by the correspondents of some state officers (to whom an allusion was made on a former day) and from one end to the other of the continent, we walked on ashes, concealing fire beneath our feet; and ought Congress to be deprived of power to prepare for the defense and safety of our country? Ought they to be restrained from arming until they divulge the motive which induced them to arm? I believe the *power* of raising and keeping up an army, in time of peace, is essential to every government. No government can secure its citizens against dangers, internal and external, without possessing it and sometimes carrying it into execution. I confess it is a power in the exercise of which all wise and moderate governments will be as prudent and forbearing as possible. When we consider the situation of the United States, we must be satisfied, that it will be necessary to keep up some troops for the protection of the western frontiers and to secure our interest in the internal navigation of that country. It will be not only necessary, but it will be economical on the great scale. Our enemies finding us invulnerable will not attack us, and we shall thus prevent the occasion for larger standing armies. I am now led to consider another charge that is brought against this system.

It is said, that Congress should not possess the power of calling out the militia to execute the laws of the Union, suppress insurrections, and repel invasions, nor the President have the command of them when called out for such purposes.

I believe any gentleman who possesses military experience will inform you, that men without an uniformity of arms, accoutrements, and discipline are no more than a mob in a camp; that in the field, instead of assisting, they interfere with one another. If a soldier drops his musket, and his companion, unfurnished with one, takes it up, it is of no service because his cartridges do not fit it. By means of this system, a uniformity of arms and discipline will prevail throughout the United States.

I really expected that for this part of the system at least, the framers of it would have received plaudits, instead of censures, as they here discover a strong anxiety to have this body put upon an effective footing, and thereby, in a great measure, to supersede the necessity of raising, or keeping up, standing armies.

The militia formed under this system, and trained by the several states, will be such a bulwark of internal strength as to prevent the attacks of foreign enemies. I have been told, that about the year 1744, an attack was intended by France upon Massachusetts Bay, but was given up on reading the militia law of that province.

If a single state could deter an enemy from such attempts, what influence will the proposed arrangement have upon the different powers of Europe!

In every point of view, this regulation is calculated to produce the best effects. How powerful and respectable must the body of militia appear, under general and uniform regulations! How disjointed, weak, and inefficient are they at present! I appeal to military experience for the truth of my observations.

The next objection, sir, is a serious one indeed; it was made by the honorable gentleman from Fayette (John Smilie). "The Convention knew this was not a free government, otherwise they would not have asked the powers of the purse and sword." I would beg to ask the gentleman, what free government he knows that has not the powers of both? There was indeed a government under which we unfortunately were for a few years past, that had them not, but it does not now exist. A government without those powers is one of the improvements with which opposition wish to astonish mankind.

Have not the freest government those powers, and are they not in the fullest exercise of them? This is a thing so clear, that really it is impossible to find facts or reason more clear in order to illustrate it. Can we create a government without the power to act; how can it act without the assistance of men, and how are men to be procured without being paid for their services? Is not the one power the consequence of the other?

We are told, and it is the last and heaviest charge, "that this government is an aristocracy, and was *intended* so to be by the late Convention"; and we are told (the truth of which is not disputed) that an aristocratical government is incompatible with freedom. I hope, before this charge is believed, some stronger reasons will be given in support of it than any that have yet been produced.

The late Convention were assembled to devise some plan for the security, safety, and happiness of the people of the United States; if they have devised a plan, that robs them of their power, and constitutes an aristocracy, they are the parricides of their country, and ought to be punished as such. What part of this system is it that warrants the charge?

What is an aristocratic government? I had the honor of giving a definition of it at the beginning of our debates; it is, sir, the government of a few over the many, elected by themselves, or possessing a share in the government by inheritance, or in consequence of territorial rights, or some quality independent of the choice of the people. This is an aristocracy, and this Constitution is said to be an aristocratical form of government, and it is also said that it was intended so to be by the members of the late Convention who framed it. What peculiar rights have been reserved to any class of men on any occasion? Does even the first magistrate of the United States draw to himself a single privilege or security that does not extend to every person throughout the United States? Is there a single distinction attached to him in this system more than there is to the lowest officer in the republic? Is there an office from which any one set of men whatsoever are excluded? Is there one of any kind in this system but is as open to the poor as to the rich, to the inhabitant of the country, as well as to the inhabitant of the city? And are the places of honor and emoluments confined to a few, and are these few the members of the late Convention? Have they made any particular provisions in favor of themselves, their relations, or their posterity? If they have committed their country to the demon of aristocracy, have they not committed themselves also, with everything they held near and dear to them?

Far, far other is the genius of this system. I have had already the honor of mentioning its general nature; but I will repeat it, sir. In its principle, it is purely democratical; but its parts are calculated in such manner as to obtain those advantages also which are peculiar to the other forms of government in other countries. By appointing a single magistrate, we secure strength, vigor, energy, and responsibility in the executive department. By appointing a Senate, the members of which are elected for six years, yet by a rotation already taken notice of, they are changing every second year, we secure the benefit of experience, while, on the other hand, we avoid the inconveniences that arise from a long and detached establishment. This body is periodically renovated from the people, like a tree, which, at the proper season, receives its nourishment from its parent earth.

In the other branch of the legislature, the House of Representatives, shall we not have the advantages of benevolence and attachment to the people, whose immediate representatives they are?

A free government has often been compared to a pyramid. This allusion is made with peculiar propriety in the system before you; it is laid on the broad basis of the people; its powers gradually rise, while they are confined, in proportion as they ascend, until they end in that most permanent of all forms. When you examine all its parts, they will invariably be found to preserve that essential mark of free governments—a chain of connection with the people.

Such, sir, is the nature of this system of government; and the important question at length presents itself to our view. Shall it be ratified, or shall it be rejected by this Convention? In order to enable us still further to form a judgment on this truly momentous and interesting point, on which all we have or can have dear to us on earth is materially depending, let us for a moment consider the consequences that will result from one or the other measure. Suppose we reject this system of government, what will be the consequence? Let the farmer say, he whose produce remains unasked for; nor can he find a single market for its consumption, though his fields are blessed with luxuriant abundance. Let the manufacturer and let the mechanic say, they can feel and tell their feelings. Go along the wharves of Philadelphia, and observe the melancholy silence that reigns. I appeal not to those who enjoy places and abundance under the present government; they may well dilate upon the easy and happy situation of our country. Let the merchants tell you, what is our commerce; let them say what has been their situation since the return of peace. An era which they might have expected would furnish additional sources to our trade and a continuance, and even an increase, to their fortunes. Have these ideas been realized, or do they not lose some of their capital in every adventure and continue the unprofitable trade from year to year, subsisting under the hopes of happier times under an efficient general government? The ungainful trade carried on by our merchants has a baneful influence on the interests of the manufacturer, the mechanic, and the farmer, and these I believe are the chief interests of the people of the United States.

I will go further. Is there now a government among us that can do a single act, that a national government ought to do? Is there any power of the United States that can *command* a single shilling? This is a plain and a home question.

Congress may recommend, they can do more, they may require, but they must not proceed one step further. If things are bad now, and that they are not worse is only owing to hopes of improvement or change in the system, will they become better when those hopes are disappointed? We have been told by honorable gentlemen on this floor (John Smilie, William Findley, and Robert Whitehill) that it is improper to urge this kind of argument in favor of a new system of government, or against the old one. Unfortunately, sir, these things are too severely felt to be omitted; the people feel them; they pervade all classes of citizens and every situation from New Hampshire to Georgia; the argument of necessity is the patriot's defense, as well as the tyrant's plea.[6]

Is it likely, sir, that, if this system of government is rejected, a better will be framed and adopted? I will not expatiate on this subject, but I believe many reasons will suggest themselves to prove that such expectation would be illusory. If a better could be obtained at a future time, is there anything essentially wrong in this? I go further, is there anything wrong that cannot be amended more easily by the mode pointed out in the system itself, than could be done by calling convention after convention before the organization of the government. Let us now turn to the consequences that will result if we assent to and ratify the instrument before you; I shall trace them as concisely as I can, because I have trespassed already too long on the patience and indulgence of the house.

I stated on a former occasion one important advantage; by adopting this system, we become a NATION; at present we are not one. Can we perform a single national act? Can we do anything to procure us dignity or to preserve peace and tranquility? Can we relieve the distress of our citizens? Can we provide for their welfare or happiness? The powers of our government are mere sound. If we offer to treat with a nation, we receive this humiliating answer: "You cannot in propriety of language make a treaty because you have no power to execute it." Can we borrow money? There are too many examples of unfortunate creditors existing, both on this and the other side of the Atlantic, to expect success from this expedient. But could we borrow money, we cannot command a fund to enable us to pay either the principal or interest; for, in instances where our friends have advanced the principal, they have been obliged to advance the interest also, in order to prevent the principal from being annihilated in their hands by depreciation. Can we raise an army? The prospect of a war is highly probable. The accounts we receive by every vessel from Europe mention that the highest exertions are making in the ports and arsenals of the greatest maritime powers; but, whatever the consequence may be, are we to lay supine? We know we are unable under the Articles of Confederation to exert ourselves, and shall we continue so until a stroke be made on our commerce or we see the debarkation of an hostile army on our unprotected shores? Who will guarantee that our property will not be laid waste, that our towns will not be put under contribution by a small naval force and subjected to all the horror and devastation of war? May not this be done without opposition, at least effectual opposition, in the present situation of our country? There may be safety over the Appalachian Mountains, but there can be none on our seacoast. With what propriety can we hope our flag will be respected, while we have not a single gun to fire in its defense?

Can we expect to make internal improvement, or accomplish any of those great national objects, which I formerly alluded to, when we cannot find money to remove a single rock out of a river?

This system, sir, will at least make us a nation, and put it in the power of the Union to act as such. We will be considered as such by every nation in the world. We will regain the confidence of our own citizens and command the respect of others.

As we shall become a nation, I trust that we shall also form a national character; and that this character will be adapted to the principles and genius of our system of government; as yet we possess none—our language, manners, customs, habits, and dress depend too much upon those of other countries. Every nation in these respects should possess originality. There are not on any part of the globe finer qualities, for forming a national character, than those possessed by the children of America: activity, perseverance, industry, laudable emulation, docility in acquiring information, firmness in adversity, and patience and magnanimity under the greatest hardships. From these materials, what a respectable national character may be raised! In addition to this character, I think there is strong reason to believe, that America may take the lead in literary improvements and national importance. This is a subject, which I confess, I have spent much pleasing time in considering. That language, sir, which shall become most generally known in the civilized world will impart great importance over the nation that shall use it. The language of the United States will, in future times, be diffused over a greater extent of country, than any other that we now know. The French, indeed, have made laudable attempts toward establishing an universal language, but, beyond the boundaries of France, even the French language is not spoken by one in a thousand. Besides the freedom of our country, the great improvements she has made and will make in the science of government will induce the patriots and literati of every nation to read and understand our writings on that subject, and hence it is not improbable that she will take the lead in political knowledge.

If we adopt this system of government, I think we may promise security, stability, and tranquility to the governments of the different states. They will not be exposed to the danger of competition on questions of territory or any other that have heretofore disturbed them. A tribunal is here founded to decide, justly and quietly, any interfering claim; and now is accomplished, what the great mind of Henry IV of France had in contemplation, a system of government, for large and respectable dominions, united and bound together in peace, under a superintending head, by which all their differences may be accommodated, without the destruction of the human race! We are told by Sully, that this was the favorite pursuit of that good king during the last years of his life, and he would probably have carried it into execution had not the dagger of an assassin deprived the world of his valuable life. I have, with pleasing emotion, seen the wisdom and beneficence of a less efficient power under the Articles of Confederation in the determination of the controversy between the states of Pennsylvania and Connecticut;[7] but, I have lamented, that the authority of Congress did not extend to extinguish, entirely, the spark which has kindled a dangerous flame in the district of Wyoming.

Let gentlemen turn their attention to the amazing consequences which this principle will have in this extended country. The several states cannot war with each other; the general government is the great arbiter in contentions between them; the whole force of the Union can be called forth to reduce an aggressor to reason. What an happy exchange for the disjointed contentious state sovereignties!

The adoption of this system will also secure us from danger and procure us advantages from foreign nations. This, in our situation, is of great consequence. We are still an inviting object to one European power at least, and, if we cannot defend ourselves, the temptation may become too alluring to be resisted. I do not mean, that, with an efficient government, we should mix with the commotions of Europe. No, sir, we are happily removed from them and are not obliged to throw ourselves into the scale with any. This system will not hurry us into war; it is calculated to guard against it. It will not be in the power of a single man, or a single body of men, to involve us in such distress, for the important power of declaring war is vested in the legislature at large; this declaration must be made with the concurrence of the House of Representatives. From this circumstance we may draw a certain conclusion, that nothing but our national interest can draw us into a war. I cannot forbear, on this occasion, the pleasure of mentioning to you the sentiments of the great and benevolent man whose works I have already quoted on another subject. Mr. Neckar has addressed this country in language important and applicable in the strictest degree to its situation and to the present subject. Speaking of war, and the great caution that all nations ought to use in order to avoid its calamities: "And you, rising nation," says he, "whom generous efforts have freed from the yoke of Europe! let the universe be struck with still greater reverence at the sight of the privileges you have acquired, by seeing you continually employed for the public felicity. Do not offer it as a sacrifice at the unsettled shrine of political ideas, and of the deceitful combinations of warlike ambition; avoid, or at least delay participating in the passions of our hemisphere; make your own advantage of the knowledge which experience alone has given to our old age, and preserve for a long time, the simplicity of childhood. In short, honor human nature, by showing that when left to its own feelings, it is still capable of those virtues that maintain public order, and of that prudence which insures public tranquility."[8]

Permit me to offer one consideration more that ought to induce our acceptance of this system. I feel myself lost in the contemplation of its magnitude. By adopting this system, we shall probably lay a foundation for erecting temples of liberty in every part of the earth. It has been thought by many, that on the success of the struggle America has made for freedom will depend the exertions of the brave and enlightened of other nations. The advantages resulting from this system will not be confined to the United States; it will draw from Europe many worthy characters who pant for the enjoyment of freedom. It will induce princes, in order to preserve their subjects, to restore to them a portion of that liberty of which they have for many ages been deprived. It will be subservient to the great designs of Providence with regard to this globe; the multiplication of mankind, their improvement in knowledge, and their advancement in happiness. [Lloyd, *Debates,* 120–35]

[Lloyd's notes and errata]
(a) The word "neutral" to be substituted for the word "natural."
(b) "judge of *the* weight."
(c) "Journals of congress, March 6, 1779" [JCC, XIII, 283].
(d) "III. Blackstone, 406" [405].

Wilson: That government is founded on contract does not appear to be founded on experience or supported upon the principles of freedom and reason. The doctrine is politically true in Great Britain because it was recognized at the Revolution [of 1688]. It destroys the rights of amendment, because the contract, if made, ought to be pursued and kept up.

In America the supreme power resides [in] the people who have it in their power to ordain such systems as may be most suitable to their interests. In this instance they differ from Great Britain. Why then talk of a violation of the Confederation? Cannot the people change their constitution if they find thereby their common safety endangered? [Yeates's Notes, PPIn][9]

1. This is the last portion of Wilson's "2d List of Objections" which outlines the continuation of the speech he began in the morning session.

2. According to Wayne's notes, Wilson said: "Appellate jurisdiction both as to *law* and *fact*. The *chancery courts* in many of the states judge of the *fact* as well as of law. Appellate jurisdiction must necessarily place the same powers in the *Federal* Court" (Wayne's Notes, Cox Collection).

3. This is a reference to various acts passed by the Rhode Island legislature issuing paper money and requiring creditors to accept it at face value.

4. This remark by John Smilie is the only statement by an opponent of ratification that Thomas Lloyd published in his *Debates*.

5. 20 October 1786, JCC, XXXI, 891–93.

6. William Findley had declared that "To state the danger of refusing this plan is improper. It is the tyrant's plea: Take this or nothing" (Convention Debates, 5 December).

7. For the "Trenton Decree" see Convention Debates, A.M., 4 December, n. 8.

8. Necker, III, 306–7.

9. According to Yeates: "Mr. Wilson began to speak 10 minutes after 4 P.M. and spoke again 2 hours."

Newspaper Reports of Debates

Yesterday Mr. Wilson replied, in the forenoon and afternoon, in a summary way to every objection that had been made in the Convention to the new Constitution. His arguments were strong and irresistible in favor of the government. He proved it, to the satisfaction of everyone (the leaders of the minority only excepted), to be a wise, safe, and free one. He showed the excellencies and perfections of each of its parts and thereby increased the confidence and attachment of all who heard him to it. [*Pennsylvania Gazette,* 12 December][1]

* * * *

Yesterday morning Mr. Wilson entered into a general answer of all the objections urged by the opposition, but, being fatigued, the conclusion of his speech was postponed till the afternoon. The substance of this, and of the several speeches of the members on both sides, will be given in the regular course of the debates. [*Pennsylvania Herald,* 12 December][2]

1. Reprinted once in Pennsylvania and twelve times from New Hampshire to Virginia.

2. Reprinted: *Pennsylvania Packet,* 13 December; and Charleston *Columbian Herald,* 27 December.

Timothy Pickering to John Gardner, Philadelphia, 11 December (excerpt)[1]

I am here the member from Luzerne [County] in the state Convention assembled to ratify the new Constitution for the United States. The question will probably be taken tomorrow, and by a very great majority the Constitution will be adopted. Delaware State made short work. Their Convention assembled on a Monday, and on the following Thursday (last week) *unanimously* adopted it. We have a number of opposers; but they evidently oppose from interested and from party views. They are all Constitutionalists; and some of their party are continually publishing the most abominable lies and perverse misrepresentations to deceive the people, and raise a clamor among them against it. But all their wicked efforts will be fruitless.

1. RC, Gardner Family Papers, MHi. Gardner, Pickering's nephew, was a Charlestown, Mass., merchant.

The Pennsylvania Convention
Wednesday
12 December 1787

Convention Proceedings, A.M.

The Convention met pursuant to adjournment,

Resumed the consideration of the remaining articles of the proposed Constitution, and after some debate,

Adjourned until half past three o'clock, P.M.

Convention Debates, A.M.

WILLIAM FINDLEY: On Wednesday morning Mr. Findley closed his arguments in opposition to the proposed federal system. [Dallas' Debates, *Pennsylvania Herald,* 15 December][1]

Findley: Sovereignty. Vat. [Vattel] p. 9. 19.

Locke, on Gov. [II] c. 13 [chapter XIII]. There is but one supreme power, viz., the legislative; but it is accompanied with a trust, and there is still an inherent right and power in the people for self-preservation. But this inherent power can never be exercised, till the government be dissolved.

Confederation. p. 11. 2. 10 [reference not located].

Mont. [Montesquieu] b. 9. c. 1 [I, 185–87]. Confederate Republic.

There should have been a council of advice to the President responsible to their conduct. The Senate and President *may* make a monarchy.

The power of *regulating* elections includes the power of *elections*.

It is not unreasonable to suppose that this system may be made better. [Wilson's Notes, PHi]

Findley: On Wednesday, Mr. Findley in the course of an eloquent and argumentative speech, suddenly introduced the following observation: "Mr. President, I have observed a person [William Jackson?] who has introduced himself among the members of this Convention, laughing for some time at everything I have said. This conduct does not, sir, proceed from a superiority of understanding, but from the want of a sense of decency and order. If he were a member, I should certainly call him to order; but as it is, I shall be satisfied with despising him."[2]

"What," said Mr. Findley, "would we have thought of Congress, if, at the time that body made the requisition for an impost of five percent, the powers and jurisdiction contained in the proposed plan had been required? It would have been thought at once impudent and ridiculous. How great then is the revolution of our sentiments in so short a space of time!" [Dallas' Debates, *Pennsylvania Herald,* 15 December]

Findley, at the conclusion of the speech which he delivered on Friday [i.e., Wednesday] last, animadverted upon the previous steps that had been taken to call the Convention which, he said, were marked with disgraceful precipitancy and violence. He then added that from the returns, and upon the best information he could otherwise obtain, it did not appear that above one-sixth of the people had voted at the elections for delegates. Hence he drew an inference that there might be a majority of the state averse to the measure, and, therefore, he insinuated the propriety of postponing the decision of this great question till the general sentiments of the people could be obtained. He concluded with declaring that he did not conceive, under all the circumstances of the case, the minority of the state could be bound by the proceedings at this day, but would still have a right, which he thought would be exercised, to object to the ratification of the proposed Constitution, and, if they pleased, to associate under another form of government. [*Pennsylvania Herald,* 19 December][3]

* * * *

THOMAS HARTLEY [?]: In answer to Mr. Findley's declaration on the day of the ratification, of only one-sixth part of the State of Pennsylvania having voted for the late Convention, Colonel Hartley, or one of the Federalists, observed that this was a very unfair mode of determining the strength or number of the friends of the new government—that the whole of the state seldom voted upon any occasion, except in contested elections, and that the reason why so few voted was because, in the city of Philadelphia, and in all the large and populous counties, there was nearly a perfect unanimity upon the subject of the new Constitution. The speaker added, that the Convention that framed the constitution of Pennsylvania was chosen only by about 6,000 votes and that the members of the first legislature that sat under it were elected by a little more than 1,500 votes. ["A By-Stander," *Pennsylvania Packet,* 25 December][4]

1. The *Herald's* account of the debates on the 12th was reprinted, in part or in whole, four times in Pennsylvania, seven times in Massachusetts, and twice in New York. For the entire account, see Mfm:Pa. 266.

2. William Shippen, Jr. wrote to his son: "As your friend Jackson was sitting in the Convention opposite to and laughing and grinning at honest Findley while he was speaking—Findley stopped short and said. . . ." Shippen then quoted the account from the *Herald verbatim,* and concluded: "Even Jackson's impudence was not able to bear this merited stroke. He grew pale, laughed no more and did not appear in the afternoon. A crowded house were delighted and thought Findley should have moved his expulsion from the house. You know his contemptuous grin" (to Thomas Lee Shippen, 18 December, Mfm:Pa. 271).

3. Findley's remarks summarized in the *Herald* on 19 December were evidently a part of his closing speech in opposition to ratification given on Wednesday the 12th. (See "A By-Stander" printed immediately after the *Herald's* report.) The *Herald's* account was reprinted in the *Pennsylvania Packet,* 20 December; *Independent Gazetteer,* 21 December; and once each in Maine, Massachusetts, and Maryland.

4. If Thomas Hartley was the Federalist who replied to Findley, it is possible he replied in the afternoon session since James Wilson lists Hartley as speaking in the afternoon. However, Hartley moved ratification in the afternoon session, and it is possible that Wilson's listing of his name indicates that fact.

Convention Proceedings, P.M.

The Journal's account of the events of the afternoon session is incomplete. The Journal misplaces the motion to ratify the Constitution and omits the fifteen amendments to the Constitution submitted by Robert Whitehill. The principal events of the afternoon session are as follows:

1. John Smilie's speech
2. Motion by Thomas Hartley and Stephen Chambers to ratify the Constitution
3. Benjamin Rush's speech
4. Stephen Chambers' speech
5. Robert Whitehill presents Cumberland County petitions requesting amendments

6. Thomas McKean's speech
7. Robert Whitehill presents fifteen amendments to the Constitution and submits written motion to adjourn the Convention to consider amendments
8. James Wilson's speech
9. John Smilie's speech
10. Whitehill's motion to adjourn defeated 46 to 23
11. Hartley's motion to ratify adopted 46 to 23
12. Wilson, McKean, and Yeates appointed a committee to draft a Form of Ratification
13. Convention orders the secretary to engross two copies of the Form of Ratification on parchment
14. Convention resolves that the ratification of the Constitution is to be read in public at noon on 13 December and requests the Supreme Executive Council to make the arrangements.

The Convention met pursuant to adjournment,

And resumed the consideration of the remaining articles of the proposed Constitution.

Petitions from sundry inhabitants of the county of Cumberland, praying that the proposed Constitution may not be adopted without amendments, etc. were read, and

Ordered to lie on the table.[1]

It was moved by Robert Whitehill, and seconded by William Findley,

"That this Convention do adjourn until the __________ day of _________ next, to meet in the city of *Philadelphia,* in order that the propositions for amending the proposed Constitution[2] may be considered by the people of this state, that we may have an opportunity of knowing what amendments or alterations may be proposed by the other states, and that these propositions, together with such other amendments as may be proposed by other states, may be offered to Congress, and taken into consideration by the United States, before the proposed Constitution shall be finally ratified."[3]

The question being put, the yeas and nays were called by John Smilie and Stephen Chambers, and were as follow.

YEAS [23]
1 John Whitehill
2 John Harris
3 John Reynolds
4 Robert Whitehill
5 Jonathan Hoge
6 Nicholas Lutz
7 John Ludwig
8 Abraham Lincoln
9 John Bishop
10 Joseph Heister
11 James Martin
12 Joseph Powell
13 William Findley
14 John Baird
15 William Todd
16 James Marshall
17 James Edgar
18 Nathaniel Breading
19 John Smilie
20 Richard Bard
21 William Brown
22 Adam Orth
23 John A. Hanna

NAYS [46]
1 George Latimer
2 Benjamin Rush
3 Hilary Baker
4 James Wilson
5 Thomas M'Kean
6 William M'Pherson
7 John Hunn
8 George Gray
9 Samuel Ashmead
10 Enoch Edwards
11 Henry Wynkoop
12 John Barclay
13 Thomas Yardley
14 Abraham Stout
15 Thomas Bull
16 Anthony Wayne
17 William Gibbons
18 Richard Downing
19 Thomas Cheney
20 John Hannum
21 Stephen Chambers
22 Robert Coleman
23 Sebastian Graff
24 John Hubley
25 Jasper Yeates
26 Henry Slagle
27 Thomas Campbell
28 Thomas Hartley
29 David Grier
30 John Black
31 Benjamin Pedan
32 John Arndt
33 Stephen Balliott
34 Joseph Horsefield
35 David Deshler
36 William Wilson
37 John Boyd
38 Thomas Scott
39 John Nevill
40 John Allison
41 Jonathan Roberts
42 John Richards
43 Frederick A. Muhlenberg
44 James Morris
45 Timothy Pickering
46 Benjamin Elliott

So it was negatived.

On motion of Thomas Hartley, seconded by Stephen Chambers,

The original question, as moved by Mr. M'Kean [on 24 November], viz.: "Will this Convention assent to and ratify the Constitution agreed to on the 17th of September last, by the Convention of the United States of America, held in Philadelphia?" was put.[4]

The yeas and nays were called by John Smilie and Jasper Yeates, and are as follow.

YEAS [46]
1 George Latimer
2 Benjamin Rush
3 Hilary Baker
4 James Wilson
5 Thomas M'Kean
6 William M'Pherson
7 John Hunn
8 George Gray
9 Samuel Ashmead
10 Enoch Edwards
11 Henry Wynkoop
12 John Barclay
13 Thomas Yardley
14 Abraham Stout
15 Thomas Bull
16 Anthony Wayne
17 William Gibbons
18 Richard Downing
19 Thomas Cheyney
20 John Hannum
21 Stephen Chambers
22 Robert Coleman
23 Sebastian Graff
24 John Hubley
25 Jasper Yeates
26 Henry Slagle
27 Thomas Campbell
28 Thomas Hartley
29 David Grier
30 John Black
31 Benjamin Pedan
32 John Arndt
33 Stephen Balliott
34 Joseph Horsefield
35 David Deshler

36 William Wilson
37 John Boyd
38 Thomas Scott
39 John Nevill
40 John Allison
41 Jonathan Roberts
42 John Richards
43 Frederick A. Muhlenberg
44 James Morris
45 Timothy Pickering
46 Benjamin Elliott

NAYS [23]
1 John Whitehill
2 John Harris
3 John Reynolds
4 Robert Whitehill
5 Jonathan Hoge
6 Nicholas Lutz
7 John Ludwig
8 Abraham Lincoln
9 John Bishop
10 Joseph Heister
11 James Martin
12 Joseph Powell
13 William Findley
14 John Baird
15 William Todd
16 James Marshall
17 James Edgar
18 Nathaniel Breading
19 John Smilie
20 Richard Bard
21 William Brown
22 Adam Orth
23 John Andre Hanna

So it was carried in the affirmative.

Ordered, That Mr. Wilson, Mr. M'Kean, and Mr. Yeates be a committee to prepare and report a Form of Ratification.[5]

Ordered, That the secretary have the Constitution, and the ratification of it, engrossed on parchment, an original and a duplicate.

On motion of Thomas M'Kean, seconded by Stephen Chambers,

Resolved, That this Convention will proceed in a body tomorrow, at twelve o'clock, to the courthouse, where the ratification of the Constitution shall be publicly read and that the honorable the Supreme Executive Council be requested to attend the procession, and to make the necessary arrangements for announcing this ratification to the People.[6]

Adjourned until half past nine o'clock tomorrow, A.M.

1. For the Cumberland County petition to the Convention, 12 December, see II:F above.

2. The propositions referred to were presented to the Convention by Robert Whitehill. See Convention Debates, P.M., 12 December.

3. Whitehill's motion was printed in the *Pennsylvania Packet* on 14 December and the *Independent Gazetteer* on 15 December. It was reprinted once in New York, New Jersey, and Maryland.

4. This motion and the roll-call vote was printed in the *Pennsylvania Packet* on 13 December. Within six days, the *Packet's* account was reprinted in seven Pennsylvania newspapers. By 21 January the *Packet's* complete account was also reprinted three times in both New York and South Carolina, and twice in both Connecticut and Maryland. By 14 January twenty-four other newspapers from New Hampshire to Virginia reprinted only the motion to ratify and the final vote total.

5. For a draft version of the Form of Ratification in Jasper Yeates's handwriting, see Mfm:Pa. 265.

6. For the Council's response, see the Public Reading of the Form of Ratification, Thursday, 13 December, III below.

Convention Debates, P.M.

JOHN SMILIE: . . . in the afternoon Mr. Smilie, taking a general view of the subject, stated briefly the leading principles which influenced his vote. [Dallas' Debates, *Pennsylvania Herald,* 15 December]

Smilie: The case of the *Active*. Are not the persons to be entrusted with power, parties to this government? British Liberties, p. 98. 99. 21 [121] [*British Liberties, Or The Free-born Subject's Inheritance* . . . (London, 1766)].[1]

Powers undefined are extremely favorable for the increase of power. If there was an explicit declaration that the people had a right to alter this system; all matters would be easy. The rights of conscience are not secured. [Priestcraft?] useful to all tyrannical governments. Congress may establish any religion.

Aristocracy is the government of the few over the many.

This government cannot be executed, because the same means must be employed for this purpose as are necessary to execute a despotism. But discontent and opposition will arise in every quarter. If executed at all, it must be by force. The framers of this Constitution must have seen that force would be necessary. This will be the case; and if this be so, we have struggled and fought in vain.

Since the peace there has been a set of men from New Hampshire to Georgia who could not bear to be on the same footing with the other citizens. I cannot tell how many of them were in the Convention.

Congress, by the powers they have already, have contributed to throw things into confusion to produce the present great event. A change of habits is necessary to relieve the present distresses of the people. The adoption of the present system will not accomplish this. If this Constitution is adopted, I look upon the liberties of America as gone, until they shall be recovered by arms. [Wilson's Notes, PHi][2]

* * * *

[A motion was made to consider the original question as put by Thomas McKean on 24 November, viz., "Will this Convention assent to and ratify the Constitution agreed to on the 17th of September last, by the Convention of the United States of America, held in Philadelphia?"]

* * * *

BENJAMIN RUSH: The important question was now called for, when Doctor Rush requested the patience of the Convention for a few minutes. He then entered into a metaphysical argument, to prove that the morals of the people had been corrupted by the imperfections of the government, and while he ascribed all our vices and distresses to the existing system, he predicted a millennium of virtue and happiness as the necessary consequence of the proposed Constitution. To illustrate the depraved state of society, he remarked, among other things, the disregard which was notorious in matters of religion, so that between the congregation and the minister scarcely any communication or respect remained; nay, the Doctor evinced that they were not bound by the ties of common honesty, on the evidence of two facts, from which it appears that several clergymen had been lately cheated by their respective flocks of the wages due for their pastoral care and instruction. Dr. Rush then proceeded to consider the origin of the proposed system, and fairly deduced it from heaven, asserting that he as much believed the hand of God was employed in this work, as that God had divided the Red Sea to give a passage to the children of Israel or had fulminated the Ten Commandments from Mount Sinai![3] Dilating some time upon this new species of *divine right,* thus transmitted to the future governors of the Union, he made a pathetic appeal to the opposition, in which he deprecated the consequences of any further contention and pictured the honorable and endearing effects of an unanimous vote, after the full and fair investigation which the great question had undergone. "It is not, sir, a majority (continued the Doctor), however numerous and respectable, that can gratify my wishes—nothing short of an unanimous vote can indeed complete my satisfaction. And, permit me to add, were that event to take place, I could not preserve the strict bounds of decorum; but, flying to the other side of this room, I should cordially embrace every member, who has hitherto been in the opposition, as a brother and a patriot. Let us then, sir, this night bury the hatchet and smoke the calumet of peace!" [Dallas' Debates, *Pennsylvania Herald,* 15 December]

Thomas Lloyd charged that Dallas' report of Rush's speech was "a gross misrepresentation both as to opinions and language" and printed his own version in the *Pennsylvania Gazette,* the *Independent Gazetteer,* and the *Pennsylvania Packet* on 19 December. His version was reprinted four times in Pennsylvania and seven times from Massachusetts to South Carolina (see CC:357). Lloyd promised that he would publish "every word" of Rush's speech in his forthcoming volume of debates, but he did not do so.

The *Pennsylvania Herald* reprinted Lloyd's version on 22 December with a prefatory statement (probably by William Spotswood, the owner) asserting that the *Herald's* reporter "did not intend to misrepresent it," and that Lloyd's version would hopefully "correct the error." On the same day, Dallas, the editor of the *Herald,* wrote a statement, published in the *Independent Gazetteer* on 24 December, that Lloyd's charge was *"a gross falsehood"* (Mfm:Pa. 286).

"P.Q." printed both versions of the speech in parallel columns in the *Independent Gazetteer* on 29 December, and declared: "I cannot, for my life and soul, find any difference in the features of either of these bantlings which have been laid at the Doctor's door" (Mfm:Pa. 295). Lloyd's version follows.

Rush: The Doctor began by recapitulating the many harsh epithets that had been given to the new government by the opposition. Mr. Findley having in a debate a few days before [3 December] said, there was a bright and dark side to every question, and having illustrated it by mentioning the doctrine of predestination, the Doctor applied the remark to the present government, and said Mr. Findley had unfortunately chosen the reprobation side of it. But as the darkness of that doctrine was in the human mind only, and not in the doctrine itself, so he hoped the misery and evil Mr. Findley had discovered in the new Constitution was in the minds of the members who opposed it, and not in the Constitution itself. The Doctor then proceeded to mention several reasons for adopting the new government. These were derived:

1st. From the influence which the example of a good government might have upon the nations of Europe, who had already shown a a disposition to imitate us in asserting their liberties.

2d. From the effects of good government in securing liberty, for where there was no law, there could be no liberty. Here the Doctor remarked, that man was naturally an ungovernable animal. That in Europe it had been found necessary to add ecclesiastical and military to civil power, in order to govern him. In America it would be improper to introduce the first two species of government; for which reason much higher degrees of civil government were necessary in this country, than had hitherto been established in the United States.

3. From the distresses of the country, which the Doctor said had been before enumerated, and which he said originated only in the want of an efficient government.

4. From the present state of morals in the country. Here the Doctor showed the connection between the want of justice and fidelity in government to individuals, and of individuals to government, and every branch of moral obligation. From this failure of political obligation arose the want of justice between man and man, the difficulty of borrowing and the danger of lending money, the oppressions of landlords, the frauds of tenants, and the numerous instances of conjugal infelicity and divorces, etc. among the lower classes of people; and lastly, the deficiency in parishes to pay their ministers agreeably to their subscriptions. This last instance of a failure in moral obliga-

tion, the Doctor lamented, as having a melancholy influence upon the happiness of our country; for, said he, where public worship is not maintained, it will be difficult to preserve religion; and where there is no religion, there will be no morals. Where there are no morals, there can be no government, and where there is no government, there can be no liberty. It is true, said the Doctor, we hear much of the liberality and humanity discovered by our citizens in the establishment of charitable and benevolent institutions; but these are the sorrowful marks of the declension of our country. They prove, that we have some virtue, but much more vice among us; and if Pennsylvania has been distinguished from her sister states by the number and perfection of these humane institutions, it is only because there is more weakness in the *form,* and more *corruption* in the *administration* of her government, than in any of the states in the Union.

After this the Doctor proceeded to show the source of obligation to government, and asserted from a late writer, Mr. Paley, that it was founded "in obedience to the will of God, collected from expediency."[4] He then mentioned the unanimity of the Convention, the general approbation of the Constituion by all classes of people, and the zeal which appeared everywhere, in votes and instructions, in favor of the government, from New Hampshire to Georgia, as reasons to believe that the adoption of the government was agreeable to the will of Heaven, for the *Vox Populi—Vox Dei*—was a truth, when it applied to the feelings of the people. Here the Doctor added, that *he believed* the same voice that thundered on Mount Sinai, "thou shalt not steal," now proclaimed in our ears, by a number of plain and intelligible providences, "thou shalt not reject the new federal government."

The Doctor then proceeded as follows: "If the forms and degrees of government are so essential to the preservation of liberty, religion, and morals in our country, then," said he, "I call upon every member of this Convention to lay his hand on his heart, and to ask himself whether he can, consistent with his duty to his Maker, refuse to assent to the ratification of the proposed Constitution. If there is any man in this assembly, who feels a struggle between the inclinations of his constituents and the dictates of his conscience, let him obey the dictates of his conscience. It is the voice of God speaking in his heart. And let him reflect further, that in giving a vote upon this question, he is bound to consult the interests and wishes, not of a particular county, but of the whole state.

"I have no doubt," concluded the Doctor, "but a respectable majority will rise to the question of the ratification, but, Mr. President, this will not come up to my wishes. Nothing will satisfy me perfectly, but an unanimous vote. Lord Belhaven, in a speech delivered in the Scotch Parliament upon the subject of the union, observes very justly, that 'unanimity in a *wrong* measure is often better than division in a *right* one.' Suppose the measure before us should be wrong. Unanimity would better enable us to recover from the evils that would arise from it. Think, sir, of the effects of an unanimous vote upon our sister states. It would probably check Rhode Island in her career of iniquity, and produce even paleness and distress at the Court of St. James's.[5] Think, sir, of its effects upon the State of Pennsylvania. Let this Constitution be the umpire of all our past disputes. Here let us this night bury the hatchet of civil discord and smoke the calumet of peace together! When the great question is called, should we be so happy as to see every chair in this assembly deserted, what a triumph would it be of reason and humanity over prejudice and party spirit! Should this be the case, Mr. President, I should find it difficult to restrain myself by the rules of the house. I should feel myself strongly disposed to run across the room, and take every member of the opposition in my arms. I should think it, sir, the beginning of a year of jubilee in Pennsylvania." [*Pennsylvania Gazette,* 19 December]

* * * *

STEPHEN CHAMBERS: When Dr. Rush had concluded, Mr. Chambers remarked upon the Doctor's wish of conciliation and unanimity, that *it was an event which he neither expected nor wished for.* [Dallas' Debates, *Pennsylvania Herald,* 15 December]

* * * *

ROBERT WHITEHILL now rose, and having animadverted upon Doctor Rush's metaphysical arguments, and regretted that so imperfect a work should have been ascribed to God, he presented several petitions from 750 inhabitants of Cumberland County, praying, for the reasons therein specified, that the proposed Constitution should not be adopted without amendments, and, particularly, without a bill of rights.[6] [Dallas' Debates, *Pennsylvania Herald,* 15 December]

* * * *

THOMAS MCKEAN: The petitions being read from the chair, Mr. M'Kean said, he was sorry that at this stage of the business so improper an attempt should be made. He repeated that the duty of the Convention was circumscribed to the adoption or rejection of the proposed plan, and such had certainly been the sense of the members when it was agreed that only one question could be taken on the important subject before us. He hoped, therefore, that the petitions would not be attended to.[7]

. . . .

Mr. M'Kean pronounced an animated eulogium on the character, information and abilities of Mr. George Mason, but concluded that the exclusion of juries in civil causes was not among the objections which had governed his [Mason's] conduct. [Dallas' Debates, *Pennsylvania Herald,* 15 December]

* * * *

ROBERT WHITEHILL: On this assertion Mr. Whitehill quoted the following passage from Mr. Mason's objections: "There is no declaration of any kind for preserving the liberty of the press, *the trial by jury in civil causes,* nor against the danger of standing armies in time of peace."[8]

. . . .

Mr. Whitehill then read, and offered as the ground of a motion for adjourning to some remote day, the consideration of the following articles,[9] which he said might either be taken collectively as a bill of rights, or separately as amendments to the general form of government proposed.

1. The rights of conscience shall be held inviolable, and neither the legislative, executive, nor judicial powers of the United States shall have authority to alter, abrogate, or infringe any part of the constitutions of the several states, which provide for the preservation of liberty in matters of religion.

2. That in controversies respecting property, and in suits between man and man, trial by jury shall remain as heretofore, as well in the federal courts, as in those of the several states.

3. That in all capital and criminal prosecutions, a man has a right to demand the cause and nature of his accusation, as well in the federal courts, as in those of the several states; to be heard by himself or his counsel; to be confronted with the accusers and witnesses, to call for evidence in his favor, and a speedy trial, by an impartial jury of the vicinage, without whose unanimous consent, he cannot be found guilty, nor can he be compelled to give evidence against himself; that no man be deprived of his liberty, except by the law of the land or the judgment of his peers.

4. That excessive bail ought not to be required nor excessive fines imposed, nor cruel or unusual punishments inflicted.

5. That warrants unsupported by evidence, whereby any officer or messenger may be commanded or required to search suspected places, or to seize any person or persons, his or their property, not particularly described, are grievous and oppressive, and shall not be granted either by the magistrates of the federal government or others.

6. That the people have a right to the freedom of speech, of writing, and of publishing their sentiments, therefore, the freedom of the press shall not be restrained by any law of the United States.

7. That the people have a right to bear arms for the defense of

themselves and their own state, or the United States, or for the purpose of killing game; and no law shall be passed for disarming the people or any of them, unless for crimes committed, or real danger of public injury from individuals; and as standing armies in the time of peace are dangerous to liberty, they ought not to be kept up; and that the military shall be kept under strict subordination to and be governed by the civil power.

8. The inhabitants of the several states shall have liberty to fowl and hunt in seasonable times, on the lands they hold, and on all other lands in the United States not enclosed, and in like manner to fish in all navigable waters, and others not private property, without being restrained therein by any laws to be passed by the legislature of the United States.

9. That no law shall be passed to restrain the legislatures of the several states, from enacting laws for imposing taxes, except imposts and duties on goods exported and imported, and that no taxes, except imposts and duties upon goods imported and exported, and postage on letters shall be levied by the authority of Congress.

10. That elections shall remain free, that the House of Representatives be properly increased in number and that the several states shall have power to regulate the elections for Senators and Representatives, without being controlled either directly or indirectly by any interference on the part of Congress, and that elections of Representatives be annual.

11. That the power of organizing, arming, and disciplining the militia (the manner of disciplining the militia to be prescribed by Congress) remain with the individual states, and that Congress shall not have authority to call or march any of the militia out of their own state, without the consent of such state and for such length of time only as such state shall agree.

12. That the legislative, executive, and judicial powers be kept separate, and to this end, that a constitutional council be appointed to advise and assist the President, who shall be responsible for the advice they give (hereby, the Senators would be relieved from almost constant attendance); and also that the judges be made completely independent.

13. That no treaties which shall be directly opposed to the existing laws of the United States in Congress assembled shall be valid until such laws shall be repealed or made conformable to such treaty, neither shall any treaties be valid which are contradictory to the Constitution of the United States, or the constitutions of the individual states.

14. That the judiciary power of the United States shall be confined

to cases affecting ambassadors, other public ministers and consuls, to cases of admiralty and maritime jurisdiction, to controversies to which the United States shall be a party, to controversies between two or more states—between citizens claiming lands under grants of different states, and between a state or the citizens thereof and foreign states, and in criminal cases, to such only as are expressly enumerated in the Constitution, and that the United States in Congress assembled shall not have power to enact laws, which shall alter the laws of descents and distributions of the effects of deceased persons, the title of lands or goods, or the regulation of contracts in the individual states.

15. That the sovereignty, freedom, and independency of the several states shall be retained, and every power, jurisdiction and right which is not by this Constitution expressly delegated to the United States in Congress assembled.

Some confusion arose on these articles being presented to the chair, objections were made by the majority to their being officially read, and, at last, Mr. Wilson desired that the intended motion might be reduced to writing, in order to ascertain its nature and extent. Accordingly, Mr. Whitehill drew it up, and it was read from the chair in the following manner.

"That this Convention do adjourn to the ________ day of ________ next, then to meet in the city of Philadelphia, in order that the propositions for amending the proposed Constitution may be considered by the people of this state; that we may have an opportunity of knowing what amendments or alterations may be proposed by other states, and that these propositions, together with such other amendments as may be proposed by other states, may be offered to Congress, and taken into consideration by the United States, before the proposed Constitution shall be finally ratified." [Dallas' Debates, *Pennsylvania Herald,* 15 December]

* * * *

JAMES WILSON: As soon as the motion was read, Mr. Wilson said, he rejoiced that it was by this means ascertained upon what principles the opposition proceeded, for, he added, the evident operation of such a motion would be to exclude the people from the government and to prevent the adoption of this or any other plan of confederation. For this reason he was happy to find the motion reduced to certainty, that it would appear upon the Journals, as an evidence of the motives which had prevailed with those who framed and supported it, and that its merited rejection would permanently announce the sentiments of the majority respecting so odious an attempt. [Dallas' Debates, *Pennsylvania Herald,* 15 December]

* * * *

JOHN SMILIE followed Mr. Wilson, declaring that he too rejoiced that the motion was reduced to a certainty, from which it might appear to their constituents, that the sole object of the opposition was to consult with, and obtain the opinions of the people upon a subject, which they had not yet been allowed to consider. "If," exclaimed Mr. Smilie, "those gentlemen who have affected to refer all authority to the people, and to act only for the common interest, if they are sincere, let them embrace this last opportunity to evince that sincerity. They all know the precipitancy with which the measure has hitherto been pressed upon the state, and they must be convinced that a short delay cannot be injurious to the proposed government if it is the wish of the people to adopt it; if it is not their wish, a short delay which enables us to collect their real sentiments may be the means of preventing future contention and animosity in a community, which is, or ought to be, equally dear to us all." [Dallas' Debates, *Pennsylvania Herald,* 15 December]

* * * *

The question being taken on the motion [Whitehill's motion for adjournment], there appeared for it 23, against it 46. The great and conclusive question was then taken, that "this Convention do assent to and ratify the plan of federal government, agreed to and recommended by the late Federal Convention?" when the same division took place, and the yeas and nays being called by Mr. Smilie and Mr. Chambers, were as follow.[10]

[For the yeas and nays, see the Convention Proceedings, P.M., 12 December.]

This important decision being recorded, Thomas M'Kean moved that the Convention do tomorrow proceed in a body to the courthouse, there to proclaim the ratification, and that the Supreme Executive Council be requested to make the necessary arrangements for the procession on that occasion, which motion was agreed to, and the Convention adjourned till the next morning at half past nine o'clock. [Dallas' Debates, *Pennsylvania Herald,* 15 December]

1. According to Wilson's notes this portion of Smilie's speech was given in the morning session.

2. Immediately after the notes of Smilie's speech, Wilson listed the following men's names: "Mr. Hartley, Dr. Rush, Mr. Chambers. Mr. Whitehill, Mr. McKean." No notes of speeches given by these five men were taken by Wilson.

3. "P.Q." asserted that "This allusion, and nearly in these words, the Doctor certainly made. Citizens who were in the gallery can attest it" (Mfm:Pa. 295). William Findley, writing as "Hampden" in the *Pittsburgh Gazette,* 16 February 1788, attacked the assertion that the Constitution "was accompanied with such miraculous divine energy as divided the Red Sea and spake with thunder on Mount Sinai," IV:A below.

4. Paley, VI, Chapter IV, "Of the Duty of Civil Obedience as Stated in the Christian Scriptures," 356–64.
5. This assertion was attacked by "Philadelphiensis" VI, 26 December (CC:382).
6. For the Cumberland County petition, 12 December, see II:F above.
7. See "Philadelphiensis" V, 19 December, for an attack on the Federalists' position on these petitions (CC: 356).
8. See Mason's Objections, CC:138–B, 276–A.
9. These articles, or propositions, with minor variations, are identical to the propositions in the "Dissent of the Minority," 18 December, III below.
10. According to the Convention *Minutes,* Smilie and Yeates called for the yeas and nays on the final question. Smilie and Chambers had called for the yeas and nays on the vote on Whitehill's motion for adjournment.

Private Commentaries on the Vote for Ratification

Samuel Powel to George Washington, Philadelphia, 12 December (excerpt)[1]

I had, this day, the pleasure of your very obliging letter,[2] for which I return you my best thanks.

The important question is at length decided and Pennsylvania has had virtue enough to adopt the proposed Federal Constitution by a majority of forty-six against twenty-three. On this event I sincerely felicitate my country, and trust that her example will be followed by the other states. So Federal are we that an invitation has been handed to the Convention, signed by the landholders of Philadelphia County, offering the said county as the seat of the future government. This measure was taken at a very respectable meeting.[3]

All ranks of people here rejoice in the event of this evening's deliberations, which was proclaimed thro the city by repeated shouts and huzzas. The Convention will sign the Ratification tomorrow morning.

New Jersey will probably adopt the Constitution this week and Massachusetts next month. I think and hope it will be generally accepted.

William Shippen, Jr. to Thomas Lee Shippen, Philadelphia, 12 December (excerpt)[4]

My dear cruel son: It is almost 4 months since your last letter was dated; it appears an age. Where are you?

The new Constitution has been ably opposed by honest [William] Findley and ably defended by the sensible [James] Wilson for 3 weeks. This evening the question was put to adopt or reject it *in toto* and a great majority rose to adopt it; and the mob in the streets are huzzaing triumphantly on the great event, perfectly ignorant whether it will make them free or slaves.

The minority will protest and [Thomas] Lloyd will publish the whole debates as soon as possible. They will be a treat to you and Mr. [Thomas] Jefferson.

The State of Delaware are before us. They met on Monday the 3d instant and adopted it unanimously on the following Thursday. New Jersey tis said will do it next week. The other states give themselves time to consider and understand before they receive or reject a matter of such infinite magnitude.

I hope it will be amply commented upon by the learned and unprejudiced on your side of the water. Your observations I think should be confined to me or your Uncle R[ichard] H[enry] L[ee] unless you think tis a good and safe system. I confess I am not enough versed in matters of government to give a well-founded judgment, but fear it will not preserve or secure the liberty and safety of America. I think too it cannot be executed in so widely extended an empire but by such an army as the people will not submit to. Tis still doubtful whether nine states will adopt it without alteration.

The county of Philadelphia have offered the new government 10 miles square for their residence on their own terms and a committee of 9 are to say tomorrow which is the most eligible part of the county.[5]

Mrs. Robert Morris to Robert Morris, Philadelphia, 13 December (excerpt)[6]

I intended my dear Mr. Morris by today's post writing you a long letter in answer to your tender and affectionate one of yesterday but am prevented saying much by a provoking headache. As you know that I am something of a politician, I therefore could not forbear informing you that the federal government is agreed to by our Convention. They finished last evening; great demonstrations of joy were expressed by the populace. They did not forget *you*. We had three cheers.

1. RC, Washington Papers, DLC. Powel, one of the wealthiest men in Philadelphia, was the city's last prewar mayor in 1775 and the first mayor after the city received a new charter in 1789.

2. Washington wrote Powel from Mount Vernon on 30 November that "By this evening's post . . . we expect to know the decision of your state Convention on the federal government" (RC, ViMtvL).

3. For the Philadelphia County petitions, see Convention Proceedings, A.M., 11 December.

4. RC, Shippen Family Papers, DLC.

5. See note 3 above.

6. RC, Robert Morris Papers, CSmH. The letter, evidently written on 13 December although it was dated "Novr. 12," was endorsed, "Mr. Morris, Richmond Virginia." For Morris's trip to Virginia, see Gouverneur Morris to George Washington, 30 October, II.C above.

The Pennsylvania Convention
Thursday
13 December 1787

Convention Proceedings, A.M.

Convention met pursuant to adjournment.

The committee appointed to draft a Form of Ratification made report of the following, viz.:

"In the Name of the PEOPLE of Pennsylvania.

"BE IT KNOWN UNTO ALL MEN,—That We, the Delegates of the PEOPLE of the Commonwealth of Pennsylvania, in General Convention assembled, have assented to and ratified, and by these Presents DO, in the Name and by the Authority of the same PEOPLE, and for ourselves, assent to and ratify the foregoing Constitution for the UNITED STATES of AMERICA."

By special order, this Form was taken up for a second reading, and adopted.

The Convention then proceeded (agreeably to the resolution of yesterday) to the courthouse, where the above Ratification was publicly read.

Convention Debates, A.M.

On Thursday the Convention being assembled, Mr. Whitehill remarked that the bill of rights, or articles of amendment, which he had the day before presented to the chair, were not inserted upon the Journals together with the resolution which referred to them. This he declared an improper omission, and desired they might be inserted. This was opposed by the majority, but as there was no motion before the Convention, the President did not see how a determination could take place, though he wished to know the sense of the members upon this occasion. Mr. Smilie in consequence of this intimation, moved for the insertion of Mr. Whitehill's articles. Mr. Wilson continued his opposition, and called on Mr. Smilie to reduce his motion to writing. "Indeed, sir," observed Mr. Smilie, "I know so well that if the honorable member from the city says the articles shall not, they will not be admitted, that I am not disposed to take the useless trouble of reducing my motion to writing, and therefore I withdraw it." Mr. Chambers exclaimed that the member from Fayette [John Smilie] and his friends might be accustomed to the arrangement which he alluded to, but neither Mr. Wilson nor those who agreed in sentiments with him were to be led by a mere *fiat*. The Form being presented by Mr. M'Kean, who with Mr. Wilson and Mr. Yates were appointed as a committee to prepare it, it was agreed that the Convention should proceed to proclaim the Ratification before it was signed, which was accordingly done. [*Pennsylvania Herald,* 15 December] [1]

1. The *Herald's* account was reprinted in the *Independent Gazetteer* and *Pennsylvania Packet* on 17 December, and twice each in Massachusetts and New York.

Public Reading of the Form of Ratification, Thursday Noon, 13 December[1]

Supreme Executive Council Proceedings, 13 December

At the request of the Convention, Council agreed to attend the procession to the courthouse this day at twelve o'clock to announce to the people the Ratification of the proposed Constitution.

The procession was as follows, vizt.:

Order of Procession

To be observed on Thursday, December the thirteenth, 1787 at twelve o'clock, upon announcing to the public the Ratification of the Federal Constitution by this State.

Constables with their staves,
Sub-Sheriffs with their wands,
High Sheriff and Coroner with their wands,
Judges of the Supreme Court and Judges of the High Court of Errors and Appeals,
Attorney General and Prothonotary of the Supreme Court,
Marshal of the Admiralty,
Judge and Register of the Admiralty,
Wardens of the Port of Philadelphia,
Naval Officer, Collector of the Customs, and Tonnage Officer,
Treasurer and Comptroller General,
Secretary of the Land Office,
Receiver General and Surveyor General,
Justices of the Peace,
Prothonotary of the Court of Common Pleas, and Clerk of the Court of Quarter Sessions,
Clerk of the City Court,
Master of the Rolls and Register of Wills,
Assistant Secretary of the Council,
Secretary of the Council,

His Excellency the President, and Honorable the Vice President,
Members of the Council, two and two,
Doorkeeper of the Council,
Messenger of the Convention,
Secretary of the Convention,
Honorable the President of the Convention,
Members of the Convention, two and two,
Doorkeeper of the Convention,
Delegates of Congress,
Provost and Faculty of the University,
Officers of the Militia,
Citizens.

1. See Newspaper Reports of the Public Celebration of Ratification on 13 December, below.

Convention Proceedings, P.M.

The Convention returned, and subscribed the Ratification of the Constitution on an original and duplicate.

It was moved by Thomas M'Kean, and seconded by Hilary Baker,

That the secretary deliver to the master of the rolls (for the purpose of having it recorded) one of the scrolls, containing the Constitution, Ratification, and names subscribed, as they here follow.

[At this point the Journals contain the Constitution and the names of the thirty-nine delegates who signed it in the Constitutional Convention.]

RATIFICATION.

In the Name of the PEOPLE of Pennsylvania.

BE IT KNOWN UNTO ALL MEN,—That We, the Delegates of the PEOPLE of the Commonwealth of Pennsylvania, in General Convention assembled, have assented to and ratified, and by these Presents DO, in the Name and by the Authority of the same PEOPLE, and for ourselves, assent to and ratify the foregoing Constitution for the UNITED STATES of AMERICA.

DONE in Convention, the Twelfth Day of December, in the Year one thousand seven hundred and eighty-seven, and of the Independence of the United States of America the Twelfth. In witness whereof, we have hereunto subscribed our Names.[1]

[At this point the Journals contain the names of the forty-six delegates who voted for ratification and the attestation of Secretary James Campbell. For the official Form of Ratification sent to the Confederation Congress, see Frederick A. Muhlenberg to the President of Congress, 15 December, III below.]

Adjourned until half past nine o'clock tomorrow, A.M.

1. The Form of Ratification has been transcribed literally. On 15 December this Form of Ratification was printed in the *Pennsylvania Packet* and was reprinted six times in the state. Outside Pennsylvania it was reprinted twenty times from Vermont to Maryland by 7 January. For a preliminary draft of the Form of Ratification, see Yeates's Notes, Mfm:Pa. 265.

Convention Debates, P.M.

On the return of the members to the Convention, Mr. Hartley hoped that the opposition might yet be induced to sign the Ratification as a fair and honorable acquiescence in the principle, that a majority should govern. To which Mr. Smilie replied, that speaking for himself, he never would allow his hand, in so gross a manner, to give the lie to his heart and tongue. Two copies of the proposed Constitution were then formally ratified by the members who had voted in favor of it, Mr. Harris observing, that though he had voted against it, and would still abide by that vote, so far as to decline putting his signature to the Ratification, yet he did now, and always should consider himself to be bound by the sense of the majority of any public body of which he had the honor to be appointed a member. The Convention then adjourned till yesterday morning at half past nine o'clock. [*Pennsylvania Herald,* 15 December]

Newspaper Reports of the Public Celebration of Ratification on 13 December

And yesterday, between the hours of 12 and 1 o'clock, the above resolution was publicly read at the courthouse, by the secretary of the Convention, to a large concourse of citizens, who testified their applause by *three cheers.* The members of Council and Convention, some militia officers and citizens composed a procession. A detachment of the militia train of artillery fired a federal salute on Market Street wharf, and the bells of Christ Church were rung on the solemn occasion. [*Independent Gazetteer,* 14 December]

* * * *

Yesterday the Convention of this state (accompanied by His Excellency the President, the Vice President and the members of the Supreme Executive Council; also by several members of Congress, the faculty of the university, the magistrates, and militia officers of the city) went in procession to the courthouse, where the Ratification of the Constitution of the United States was read, amidst the acclamations of a great concourse of citizens—13 cannon[1] were fired and the bells were rung on this joyful occasion;[2] after this the Convention returned to the State House and subscribed the two copies of the Ratification.

At three o'clock they met and dined with the members of the Supreme Executive Council, several members of Congress and a number of citizens, at Mr. Epple's tavern;[3] where the remainder of the day was spent in mutual congratulations upon the happy prospect of enjoying, once more, order, justice, and good government in the United States. The following is the list of the toasts given on the occasion.

1. The *People* of the United States.
2. The President and members of the late Convention of the United States.
3. The President of the State of Pennsylvania.
4. May the citizens of America display as much wisdom in adopting the proposed Constitution to *preserve* their liberties, as they have shown fortitude in *defending* them.
5. May order and justice be the pillars of the American Temple of Liberty.
6. May the agriculture, manufactures, and commerce of the United States speedily flourish under the new Constitution.
7. The Congress.
8. The virtuous minority of Rhode Island.
9. The powers of Europe in alliance with the United States.
10. May the flame kindled on the Altar of Liberty in America lead the patrons[4] of the world to a knowledge of their rights and to the means of recovering them.
11. The memory of the heroes who have sacrificed their lives in defense of the liberties of America.
12. May America diffuse over Europe a greater portion of political light than she has borrowed from her.
13. Peace and free governments to all the nations in the world. [*Pennsylvania Packet,* 14 December][5]

* * * *

A correspondent says, "It is worthy of remark, that amongst the various classes of citizens who consider their interests and happiness essentially combined with, and dependent upon the adoption of the proposed Constitution for the United States of America, the ship carpenters of Philadelphia have given the most irrefragable proof of their approbation of the same by conducting, on the evening of its ratification by this state, a vessel on wheels through the streets of this city, decorated with flags and insignia emblematical of their fixed expectation of the revival of commerce and navigation under this happy government." [*Pennsylvania Packet,* 15 December][6]

* * * *

On the evening of the public rejoicing for the ratification of the Federal Constitution, a number of ship carpenters and sailors conducted a boat, on a wagon drawn by five horses, through the city, to the great amusement of many thousand spectators. On their way through the different streets, they frequently threw a sounding line, and cried out, "three and twenty fathoms, *foul* bottom"; and in other places, "six and forty fathoms, *sound* bottom—safe anchorage"; alluding to the numbers that composed the minority and majority of the late Convention of Pennsylvania, which ratified the Federal Constitution. [*Pennsylvania Gazette,* 19 December][7]

* * * *

A correspondent observes, he was much surprised to see so very short a procession on Thursday last, at the proclaiming and publishing the Ratification and adoption of the new plan of government; which is of so solemn and important concern to all of us. The delinquency of the officers, of (our present) government on this occasion, is easily accounted for; but that so few militia officers as 17, and such a small number of other citizens should think it worth their attention, is very strange. The gentlemen of the university were as scarce on this occasion as any others. Our friends in Convention and Council deserve credit for their exertions; they distributed invitations and copies of the order of the procession all round; and did their utmost to procure as respectable a company on that day as the occasion merited. And the common people appeared to be as inattentive as the rest. A batteau was carried on a cart in the evening, thro the back streets, dressed with several flags (an emblem of our future commerce) and notwithstanding the hearty sailors who conducted it, used all their honest endeavors, by huzzaing and playing on a fiddle, to attract the admiration, yet it was remarkable, that the people did not seem much pleased with it; none but a few children followed. With such astonishing indifference is this great subject treated. [*Freeman's Journal,* 19 December][8]

* * * *

The conduct of our fellow citizens on the late *glorious* occasion of *solemnly* proclaiming to the people the Ratification and adoption of the *proposed new* Constitution, by the Convention of *this* state does them no honor; for, notwithstanding due notice having been given by our friends in the Convention and Council, to the members of Council, judges, justices, and other state officers, the faculty of the university, militia officers, and citizens, of the order and time of the procession; yet few of any of these attended. The citizens and militia officers in particular were uncommonly scarce. They should at least have given their countenance to this very important business; it is not very unaccountable that more officers of government did not come forth, but that more of the professors, etc. in the university, the militia officers, and citizens did not appear to celebrate this grand affair which concerns them all, so materially, is wonderful.

And the common people, I observed, were as inattentive as the others. They did not seem to show any attention to a fine little batteau (dressed off with colors) that was industriously carried on a cart through some of the back streets, as an emblem of our *future* commerce; although the sailors, etc. who conducted it, used all their generous endeavors to excite admiration. They huzzaed at the corners, had the sweet music of a fiddle, etc. I followed them many squares, and could not find any but children with them. O strange behavior! the people do not seem to know what grandeur is preparing for them and their posterity.

But to come to the point; our friends, the majority, after dining together, enjoyed much happiness, in the pleasures of the social bottle till late at night, when our worthy *Chief J[u]st[i]ce,* that great patron and protector of the press, was a little affected by the *working of small beer,* and so retired.[9]

Some of the toasts that were drank were middling, but most of them were not to the purpose; for we should now forget our past national transactions; and it will be ridiculous to give 13 toasts hereafter, as we are all *to be* united and bound together into 1. For the same reason it was wrong to fire 13 guns, *one great gun* ought only to have been fired; and we must immediately alter our flags and remove the 13 stripes and stars, and in their places insert the spread eagle, or some other great monster, emblematical of our future Unison.

I think the conduct of our people in the majority in Convention was from the beginning a true emblem of our future unanimity and grandeur. They were from the first united in and under J[ames] W[ilso]n, Esquire, without whose direction nothing was done or said; in short, none of our party attempted to argue except him, and he deserves much credit for his industry and ingenuity on the occasion; to be sure, he had the best right to defend it, for it was framed by him and our worthy friend Mr. G[ouverneu]r M[orri]s in the Federal Convention. I think, Mr. Oswald, that if we had not put him in our Convention, the business would have been lost. The yellow whigs were *so arch,* and upon the whole, they both deserve great *promotion* and the *highest* offices. I am sure they shall have the vote of A UNITARIAN. [*Independent Gazetteer,* 21 December]

1. On 15 December the *Pennsylvania Herald* reported that "A gentleman being asked why only *twelve* guns were discharged on announcing the ratification of the proposed Constitution gave the following reason: because *twelve* states were represented in the late Federal Convention, and their system was adopted by this state on the *twelfth* day of the *twelfth* month, in the *twelfth* year of the

independency of America." This item was reprinted three times in Pennsylvania and sixteen times from Vermont to South Carolina.

2. The Supreme Executive Council requested Joseph Dolby to "ring the bells immediately upon the ratification of the Federal Constitution by this state being announced to the public from the courthouse steps, which will be at 12 o'clock this day." Dolby was paid £6 for his services. See Mfm:Pa. 268.

3. Henry Epple's tavern, "The Sign of the Rainbow," No. 117 Sassafras Street.

4. On 15 December the *Independent Gazetteer* and *Pennsylvania Herald* changed "patrons" to "nations," while the *Pennsylvania Journal* changed it to "patriots."

5. Reprinted five times in Philadelphia, once in Lancaster, and, in part or in whole, thirty-one times from Maine to South Carolina.

6. This report was reprinted once each in Philadelphia, Pittsburgh, and Charleston, and twice in New York City.

7. Reprinted twenty-six times from Maine to South Carolina by 22 January.

8. Reprinted eight times from Massachusetts to Georgia by 9 February.

9. See McKean's comment that Antifederalists' arguments sounded like "the feeble noise occasioned by the working of small beer," Convention Debates, 10 December.

The Pennsylvania Convention
Friday
14 December 1787

Convention Proceedings

The Convention met pursuant to adjournment.

It was moved by James Wilson, and seconded by Hilary Baker,

That when the Constitution, proposed by the late General Convention shall have been organized, this commonwealth will cede to the Congress the jurisdiction over any place in *Pennsylvania,* not exceeding ten miles square, which, with the consent of the inhabitants, the Congress may choose for the seat of the government of the United States.

On motion of Anthony Wayne, seconded by Thomas Bull,

Ordered, That a committee be appointed, to take the foregoing motion into consideration, and make report thereon.

The committee agreed on consists of Mr. Wilson, Mr. M'Pherson, Mr. Gray, Mr. Wynkoop, Mr. Coleman, Mr. Wayne, Mr. Grier, Mr. Morris, and Mr. Pickering.[1]

On motion of George Gray, seconded by William M'Pherson,

The petitions relative to the cession of a district to the Congress, for the seat of the general government, were read a second time, and referred to the above committee.[2]

Ordered, That Mr. Baker, Mr. Balliott and Mr. Hoge be a committee of accounts, that they ascertain the mileage of each member, and such other expenses as are to be provided for by this Convention.

Adjourned until half after nine o'clock tomorrow, A.M.

1. Wilson's motion and the appointment of the committee were reported in the *Pennsylvania Packet,* 15 December and reprinted in the *Pittsburgh Gazette,* 5 January. By 15 January the *Packet's* account, in part or in whole, was reprinted fourteen times from Maine to Maryland.

2. For the Philadelphia County petitions, see Convention Proceedings, A.M., 11 December.

Newspaper Report of Proceedings

Yesterday the Convention appointed a committee to consider and report upon the overtures which have been made by the county of Philadelphia, and likewise by part of the county of Philadelphia, Montgomery, and Bucks united, respecting the cession of 10 miles square to the future Congress of the United States. This the opposition to the federal system deemed a matter upon which the Convention could not, and ought not to act; for, they represented it as a violation of the constitution of the state, which still existed, and which, while in existence, it was the duty of every citizen to support. Upon this principle they refused either to vote for or against the appointment of a committee, which produced a temporary embarrassment as the majority were not at first agreed in the number, but ultimately concurred in making it nine. The Convention likewise appointed a committee to receive and state the account of their expenses, etc. and then adjourned till tomorrow at half past nine o'clock, which will certainly be the last time of their meeting. [*Pennsylvania Herald,* 15 December]

The Pennsylvania Convention
Saturday
15 December 1787

Convention Proceedings[1]

The Convention met pursuant to adjournment.

The committee appointed to consider the motion of James Wilson, relative to a cession to the United States of a district for the seat of the federal government, report the following resolution,

That when the Constitution, proposed by the late General Convention, shall have been organized, this commonwealth will cede to the Congress of the United States the jurisdiction over any place in Pennsylvania, not exceeding ten miles square, which, with the consent of the inhabitants, the Congress may choose, for the seat of the government of the United States, excepting only the city of Philadelphia, the district of Southwark, and that part of the Northern Liberties included within a line running parallel with Vine street, at the distance of one mile northward thereof, from the river Schuylkill to the southern side of the main branch of Cohockshink Creek, thence down the said creek to its junction with the river Delaware; but the marshland, and so much of the adjoining bank on the same side of the said creek as shall be necessary for the erecting any dams, or works to command the water thereof, are excluded from this exception.

On the question being put, the yeas and nays were called by Thomas M'Kean and Robert Whitehill, and were as follow.

YEAS [46]
1 George Latimer
2 Benjamin Rush
3 Hilary Baker
4 James Wilson
5 Thomas M'Kean
6 William M'Pherson
7 John Hunn
8 George Gray
9 Samuel Ashmead
10 Enoch Edwards
11 Henry Wynkoop
12 John Barclay
13 Thomas Yardley
14 Abraham Stout
15 Thomas Bull
16 Anthony Wayne
17 William Gibbons
18 Richard Downing
19 Thomas Cheney
20 John Hannum
21 Stephen Chambers
22 Robert Coleman
23 Sebastian Graff
24 John Hubley
25 Jasper Yeates
26 Henry Slagle
27 Thomas Campbell
28 Thomas Hartley
29 David Grier
30 John Black
31 Benjamin Pedan
32 Nicholas Lutz
33 John Arndt
34 Stephen Balliott
35 Joseph Horsefield
36 David Deshler
37 William Wilson
38 John Boyd
39 John Nevill
40 John Allison
41 Jonathan Roberts
42 John Richards
43 Frederick A. Muhlenberg
44 James Morris
45 Timothy Pickering
46 Benjamin Elliott

NAYS [16]
1 John Harris
2 John Reynolds
3 Robert Whitehill
4 Jonathan Hoge
5 John Ludwig
6 John Bishop
7 James Martin
8 Joseph Powell
9 William Findley
10 John Baird
11 William Todd
12 James Edgar
13 Nathaniel Breading
14 John Smilie
15 Richard Bard
16 Adam Orth

So it was carried in the affirmative.

On motion of Timothy Pickering, seconded by Stephen Chambers,

Resolved, That it is the opinion of this Convention, that until the Congress shall have made their election of a district for the place of their permanent residence, and provided buildings for their accommodation, they may have the use of such of the public buildings within the city of Philadelphia, or any other part of this state, as they may find convenient.

On the question being put, the yeas and nays were called by Anthony Wayne and Stephen Chambers, and were as follow.

YEAS [48]
1 George Latimer
2 Benjamin Rush
3 Hilary Baker
4 James Wilson
5 Thomas M'Kean
6 William M'Pherson
7 John Hunn
8 George Gray
9 Samuel Ashmead
10 Enoch Edwards
11 Henry Wynkoop
12 John Barclay
13 Thomas Yardley
14 Abraham Stout
15 Thomas Bull
16 Anthony Wayne
17 William Gibbons
18 Richard Downing
19 Thomas Cheney
20 John Hannum
21 Stephen Chambers
22 Robert Coleman
23 Sebastian Graff
24 John Hubley
25 Jasper Yeates
26 Henry Slagle
27 Thomas Campbell
28 Thomas Hartley
29 David Grier
30 John Black
31 Benjamin Pedan
32 John Harris
33 Nicholas Lutz
34 John Arndt
35 Stephen Balliott
36 Joseph Horsefield
37 David Deshler
38 Joseph Powell
39 William Wilson
40 John Boyd
41 John Nevill
42 John Allison
43 Jonathan Roberts
44 John Richards
45 Frederick A. Muhlenberg
46 James Morris
47 Timothy Pickering
48 Benjamin Elliott

NAYS [11]
1 John Reynolds
2 Robert Whitehill
3 John Ludwig
4 John Bishop
5 James Martin
6 John Baird
7 James Edgar
8 Nathaniel Breading
9 John Smilie
10 Richard Bard
11 Adam Orth

So it was carried in the affirmative.

On motion of Stephen Chambers, seconded by Anthony Wayne,

Resolved, That the President be directed to transmit to His Excellency the President of Congress, by the secretary [James Campbell], the Constitution as ratified by this Convention, together with the resolution respecting the cession of territory and the temporary residence of the honorable the Congress of the United States.

On motion of Thomas Hartley, seconded by Stephen Chambers,

Resolved, That three thousand copies of the Federal Constitution, and the Ratification thereof by this Convention, be printed in the English language, and two thousand copies in the German language, and delivered to the President, for the several members of this body, in proportion to the number of deputies from the several counties, to be distributed amongst their constituents.[2]

The committee of accounts made report;[3] whereupon

Resolved, That the President draw an order on the treasurer, in favor of James Campbell, Esquire for forty-one pounds, for his services as secretary to the Convention, including fifteen days' allowance for completing the business.

In favor of Andrew Burkhard, messenger, for his services, including four days' allowance, for fifteen pounds.

In favor of Joseph Fry, doorkeeper, for his services, including four days' allowance, for fifteen pounds.

In favor of James Martin, for his services, for six pounds fifteen shillings.

In favor of the secretary, for carrying the new Constitution of the United States, and Ratification thereof by this state, to Congress, for twenty pounds.

In favor of the secretary for four hundred pounds, to defray the printing of the Minutes and other contingent expenses, and that he account with the comptroller general for the same.

On motion, Resolved, That Mr. M'Kean, Mr. Latimer and Mr. Baker be a committee, for the purpose of revising the Minutes and superintending the printing thereof.

On motion of Thomas M'Kean, seconded by Stephen Chambers,

Resolved, unanimously, That the thanks of this Convention be presented to the President, for the able and faithful manner in which he has discharged the duties of the chair.[4]

Adjourned *sine die.* James Campbell, Secretary

1. The first two resolutions and the final resolution on this day were printed in the *Pennsylvania Packet,* 17 December. They were reprinted five times in Pennsylvania and eight times from Massachusetts to Maryland.

2. The English version was printed by Hall and Sellers. No copy of the German version has been located.

3. See Convention Expenses, 15 December 1787, Mfm:Pa. 268.

4. According to the *Pennsylvania Packet,* 17 December, Muhlenberg responded: "Gentlemen, I feel with the utmost gratitude the honor you have just now done me, and I shall always esteem your approbation as my highest reward for performing my duty to you, or rendering any services to my fellow citizens."

Newspaper Report of Proceedings

The state Convention being assembled on Saturday, the committee to whom was referred the proposals for ceding a tract of ten miles square in the county of Philadelphia, etc. made a report, which was as follows:

[For the resolution reported by the committee, see the Convention Proceedings.]

This report was objected to, as well with respect to the authority of the Convention to make the cession, as to the propriety of offering the public buildings for the accommodation of the future Congress, but it was finally adopted. The accounts of the Convention being then arranged, and the warrants for allowance delivered to the members, Mr. M'Kean moved that thanks be given to the President for the able and faithful discharge of his duty, which was accordingly agreed to, and Mr. Muhlenberg, returned his acknowledgments for this testimony of approbation, which he added was the highest reward he could receive for this or any other service he might render his fellow citizens. The Convention then adjourned *sine die.* [*Pennsylvania Herald,* 19 December]

Frederick Augustus Muhlenberg, President of the Convention, to the President of Congress, in Convention, 15 December[1]

Sir: In compliance with the directions of the Convention of the State of Pennsylvania, I have now the honor of transmitting, by the secretary [James Campbell], the Ratification of the Constitution of the late General Convention, together with sundry resolutions respecting a cession of territory and temporary residence of the honorable the Congress of the United States.

1. RC, RG 11, Certificates of Ratification of the Constitution and the Bill of Rights . . . , 1787–92, DNA. This letter was endorsed, "Letter Decr. 15th 1787—President of Convention of state of Pensa. transmitting ratification of the New Constitution, Offer of ten Mile Square &c.—Read Jany. 24th. 1788. See file—Offers of the States—with Acts &c."

The Pennsylvania Form of Ratification, 13 December[1]

In the Name of the People of Pennsylvania. Be it Known unto all Men that We the Delegates of the People of the Commonwealth of Pennsylvania in general Convention assembled Have assented to, and ratifyed, and by these presents Do in the Name and by the authority of the same people, and for ourselves, assent to, and ratify the foregoing Constitution for the United States of America. Done in Convention at Philadelphia the twelfth day of December in the year of our Lord one Thousand seven hundred and eighty seven and of the Independence of the United States of America the twelfth. In Witness whereof we have hereunto subscribed our Names.

Frederick Augustus Muhlenberg President

George Latimer
Benjn Rush
Hilary Baker
James Wilson
Thomas M'Kean
W Macpherson
John Hunn
George Gray
Samuel Ashmead
Enoch Edwards
Henry Wynkoop
John Barclay
Thos. Yardley
Abraham Stout
Thomas Bull
Anthony Wayne
William Gibbons
Richard Downing
Thomas Cheyney
John Hannum
Stephen Chambers
Robert Coleman
Sebastian Graff
John Hubley
Jasper Yeates
Heny Slagle
Thomas Campbell
Thomas Hartley
David Grier
John Black
Benjamin Pedan
John Arndt
Stephen Balliet
Joseph Horsfield
David Deshler
William Wilson
John Boyd
Tho Scott
John Nevill
Jno Allison
Jonathan Roberts
John Richards
James Morris
Timothy Pickering
Benjn Elliot

Attest James Campbell Secretary

1. Engrossed MS (LT), RG 11, Certificates of Ratification of the Constitution and the Bill of Rights . . . , 1787–92, DNA. The Form of Ratification retained by Pennsylvania is in RG 26, Records of the Department of State, Division of Public Records, PHarH. For photographic copies of both forms, see Mfm:Pa. 267.

The first part of the Form of Ratification consists of a hand-written copy of the Constitution with the names of its signers. Congress received the Form on 22 January (PCC, Item 185, Despatch Books, 1779–89, Vol. 4, p. 21, DNA).

B. THE DISSENT OF THE MINORITY OF THE CONVENTION

The "Dissent of the Minority of the Convention" was signed by twenty-one of the twenty-three members who had voted against ratification of the Constitution. The "Dissent" summarized the arguments against the Constitution set forth in the newspaper essays and pamphlets printed in Pennsylvania and elsewhere since mid-September, and the arguments Robert Whitehill, John Smilie, and William Findley had used in the state Convention. It attacked the secrecy of the Constitutional Convention and its lack of authority to write a new constitution. It denounced both the force used to secure a quorum of the Pennsylvania Assembly to make the calling of a state convention possible and the procedures of the state Convention and the behavior of the majority of its members.

However, the "Dissent" was more than a political attack upon political opponents. The document provided a detailed analysis of the Constitution from the point of view of men who believed in the sovereignty of the states, and who believed that the new government would destroy state sovereignty and deprive individual citizens of their rights and liberties.

Most importantly of all, the "Dissent," as the "official" statement of the minority of the Convention, presented the amendments to the Constitution that Robert Whitehill had submitted to the Convention on 12 December. The majority of the Convention had refused to consider the amendments or to allow them to be placed on the Convention Journals. Although not an official document in a strict sense, the "Dissent" gave formal sanction to the growing demand for amendments in Pennsylvania, and it provided an example for men in other states as their conventions met to consider the Constitution.

In 1807, in applying for office under the administration of Thomas Jefferson, Samuel Bryan, the author of "Centinel," declared that he had written the "Dissent of the Minority." If so, he must have had the help of minority members of the Convention.

The "Dissent" was published on 18 December in the *Pennsylvania Packet* and as a broadside by Eleazer Oswald. By 9 February 1788 it had been reprinted in the *Freeman's Journal, Pennsylvania Mercury, Carlisle Gazette, American Museum, Lancaster Zeitung, Philadelphische Correspondenz,* and the *Pittsburgh Gazette.* For Pennsylvania responses to the "Dissent," see the *Pennsylvania Gazette,* 26 December and 9 January 1788, and "A Citizen of Philadelphia," 23 January, all in IV:A below; "A Freeman" I, II, III, *Pennsylvania Gazette,* 23, 30 January, 6 February and "Centinel" XVIII, *Independent Gazetteer,* 9 April, all in *Commentaries on the Constitution;* and Mfm:Pa. 278, 288, 430, 503. The "Dissent" circulated throughout the country in newspaper, broadside, and pamphlet form (see CC:353).

The version of the "Dissent" printed below is from the *Pennsylvania Packet* and follows the *Packet* and the broadside version in omitting the use of capital letters. It may or may not be significant that the two first printings do not capitalize such words as "Convention," "Constitution," "President," "Senator" and the like, but capitalize "Congress" consistently.

In the *Packet* and the broadside versions, the "Dissent" is followed by the roll-call vote on ratification, which is dated *"Philadelphia,* Dec. 12, 1787." That vote is omitted below.

The Address and Reasons of Dissent of the Minority of the Convention of the State of Pennsylvania to their Constituents.

It was not until after the termination of the late glorious contest, which made the people of the United States an independent nation, that any defect was discovered in the present confederation. It was formed by some of the ablest patriots in America. It carried us successfully through the war; and the virtue and patriotism of the people, with their disposition to promote the common cause, supplied the want of power in Congress.

The requisition of Congress for the five percent impost was made before the peace, so early as the first of February 1781,[1] but was prevented taking effect by the refusal of one state; yet it is probable every state in the union would have agreed to this measure at that period had it not been for the extravagant terms in which it was demanded. The requisition was new molded in the year 1783, and accompanied with an additional demand of certain supplementary funds for 25 years.[2] Peace had now taken place, and the United States found themselves laboring under a considerable foreign and domestic debt, incurred during the war. The requisition of 1783 was commensurate with the interest of the debt, as it was then calculated; but it has been more accurately ascertained since that time. The domestic debt has been found to fall several millions of dollars short of the calculation, and it has lately been considerably diminished by large sales of the western lands. The states have been called on by Congress annually for supplies until the general system of finance proposed in 1783 should take place.

It was at this time that the want of an efficient federal government was first complained of, and that the powers vested in Congress were found to be inadequate to the procuring of the benefits that should result from the union. The impost was granted by most of the states, but many refused the supplementary funds; the annual requisitions were set at naught by some of the states, while others complied with them by legislative acts, but were tardy in their payments, and Congress found themselves incapable of complying with their engagements, and supporting the federal government. It was found that our national character was sinking in the opinion of foreign nations. The Congress could make treaties of commerce, but could not enforce the observance of them. We were suffering from the restrictions of foreign nations, who had shackled our commerce, while we were unable to retaliate; and all now agreed that it would be advantageous to the union to enlarge the powers of Congress; that they should be enabled in the amplest manner to regulate commerce, and to lay and collect duties on the imports throughout the United States. With this view a convention was first proposed by Virginia,[3] and finally recommended by Congress for the different states to appoint deputies to meet in convention, "for the purposes of revising and amending the present articles of confederation, so as to make them adequate to the exigencies of the union."[4] This recommendation the legislatures of twelve states complied with so hastily as not to consult their constituents on the subject; and though the different legislatures had no authority from their constituents for the purpose, they probably apprehended the necessity would justify the measure; and none of them extended their ideas at that time further than "revising and amending the present articles of confederation." Pennsylvania by the act appointing deputies expressly confined their powers to this object;[5] and though it is probable that some of the members of the assembly of this state had at that time in contemplation to annihilate the present confederation, as well as the constitution of Pennsylvania, yet the plan was not sufficiently matured to communicate it to the public.

The majority of the legislature of this commonwealth were at that time under the influence of the members from the city of Philadelphia. They agreed that the deputies sent by them to convention should have no compensation for their services, which determination was calculated to prevent the election of any member who resided at a distance from the city. It was in vain for the minority to attempt electing delegates to the convention, who understood the circumstances, and the feelings of the people, and had a common interest with them. They found a disposition in the leaders of the majority of the house to choose themselves and some of their dependents. The minority attempted to prevent this by agreeing to vote for some of the leading members, who they knew had influence enough to be appointed at any rate, in hopes of carrying with them some respectable citizens of Philadelphia, in whose principles and integrity they could have more confidence; but even in this they were disappointed, except in one member [Jared Ingersoll]: the eighth member [Benjamin Franklin] was added at a subsequent session of the assembly.[6]

The Continental convention met in the city of Philadelphia at the time appointed. It was composed of some men of excellent characters; of others who were more remarkable for their ambition and cunning, than their patriotism; and of some who had been opponents to the independence of the United States. The delegates from Pennsylvania were, six of them, uniform and decided opponents to the constitution of this commonwealth. The convention sat upwards of four months. The doors were kept shut, and the members brought under the most solemn engagements of secrecy.[(a)] Some of those who opposed their going so far beyond their powers retired, hopeless, from the convention, others had the firmness to refuse signing the plan altogether; and many who did sign it, did it not as a system they wholly approved, but as the best that could be then obtained, and notwithstanding the time spent on this subject, it is agreed on all hands to be a work of haste and accommodation.

Whilst the gilded chains were forging in the secret conclave, the meaner instruments of despotism without were busily employed in alarming the fears of the people with dangers which did not exist, and exciting their hopes of greater advantages from the expected plan than even the best government on earth could produce.

The proposed plan had not many hours issued forth from the womb of suspicious secrecy, until such as were prepared for the purpose were carrying about petitions for people to sign, signifying their approbation of the system, and requesting the legislature to call a convention. While every measure was taken to intimidate the people against opposing it, the public papers teemed with the most violent threats against those who should dare to think for themselves, and *tar and feathers*[7] were liberally promised to all those who would not immediately join in supporting the proposed government be it what it would. Under such circumstances petitions in favor of calling a convention were signed by great numbers in and about the city, before they had leisure to read and examine the system, many of whom, now they are better acquainted with it, and have had time to investigate its principles, are heartily opposed to it. The petitions were speedily handed into the legislature.[8]

Affairs were in this situation when on the 28th of September last, a resolution was proposed to the assembly by a member [George Clymer] of the house who had been also a member of the federal convention, for calling a state convention, to be elected within *ten* days for the purpose of examining and adopting the proposed constitution of the United States, though at this time the house had not received it from Congress. This attempt was opposed by a minority, who after offering every argument in their power to prevent the precipitate measure, without effect, absented themselves from the house as the only alternative left them, to prevent the measure taking place previous to their constituents being acquainted with the business. That violence and outrage which had been so often threatened was now practiced; some of the members were seized the next day by a mob collected for the purpose, and forcibly dragged to the house, and there detained by force whilst the quorum of the legislature, *so formed,* completed their resolution. We shall dwell no longer on this subject, the people of Pennsylvania have been already acquainted therewith. We would only further observe that every member of the legislature, previously to taking his seat, by solemn oath or affirmation, declares, "that he will not do or consent to any act or thing whatever that shall have a tendency to lessen or abridge their rights and privileges, as declared in the constitution of this state." And that constitution which they are so solemnly sworn to support cannot legally be altered but by a recommendation of the council of censors, who alone are authorized to propose alterations and amendments, and even these must be published at least *six months,* for the consideration of the people. The proposed system of government for the United States, if adopted, will alter and may annihilate the constitution of Pennsylvania; and therefore the legislature had no authority whatever to recommend the calling a convention for that purpose. This proceeding could not be considered as binding on the people of this commonwealth. The house was formed by violence, some of the members composing it were detained there by force, which alone would have vitiated any proceedings, to which they were otherwise competent; but had the legislature been legally formed, this business was absolutely without their power.

In this situation of affairs were the subscribers elected members of the convention of Pennsylvania. A convention called by a legislature in direct violation of their duty, and composed in part of members, who were compelled to attend for that purpose, to consider of a constitution proposed by a convention of the United States, who were not appointed for the purpose of framing a new form of government, but whose powers were expressly confined to altering and amending the present articles of confederation. Therefore the members of the continental convention in proposing the plan acted as individuals, and not as deputies from Pennsylvania.[(b)] The assembly who called the state convention acted as individuals, and not as the legislature of Pennsylvania; nor could they or the convention chosen on their recommendation have authority to do any act or thing, that can alter or annihilate the constitution of Pennsylvania (both of which will be done by the new constitution) nor are their proceedings in our opinion, at all binding on the people.

The election for members of the convention was held at so early a period and the want of information was so great, that some of us did not know of it until after it was over, and we have reason to believe that great numbers of the people of Pennsylvania have not yet had an opportunity of sufficiently examining the proposed constitution. We apprehend that no change can take place that will affect the internal government or constitution of this commonwealth, unless a majority of the people should evidence a wish for such a change; but on examining the number of votes given for members of the present state convention, we find that of upwards of *seventy thousand* freemen who are entitled to vote in Pennsylvania, the whole convention has been elected by about *thirteen thousand* voters, and though *two-thirds* of the members of the convention have thought proper to ratify the proposed constitution, yet those *two-thirds* were elected by the votes of only *six thousand and eight hundred* freemen.

In the city of Philadelphia and some of the eastern counties, the junto that took the lead in the business agreed to vote for none but such as would solemnly promise to adopt the system *in toto,* without exercising their judgment. In many of the counties the people did not attend the elections as they had not an opportunity of judging of the plan. Others did not consider themselves bound by the call of a set of men who assembled at the state house in Philadelphia, and assumed the name of the legislature of Pennsylvania; and some were prevented from voting by the violence of the party who were determined at all events to force down the measure.[9] To such lengths did the tools of despotism carry their outrage, that in the night of the election for members of convention, in the city of Philadelphia, several of the subscribers (being then in the city to transact your business) were grossly abused, ill-treated and insulted while they were quiet in their lodgings, though they did not interfere, nor had anything to do with the said election, but, as they apprehend, because they were supposed to be adverse to the proposed constitution, and would not tamely surrender those sacred rights, which you had committed to their charge.[10]

The convention met, and the same disposition was soon manifested in considering the proposed constitution, that had been exhibited in every other stage of the business. We were prohibited by an express vote of the convention, from taking any question on the separate articles of the plan, and reduced to the necessity of adopting or rejecting *in toto*. Tis true the majority permitted us to debate on each article, but restrained us from proposing amendments. They also determined not to permit us to enter on the minutes our reasons of dissent against any of the articles, nor even on the final question our reasons of dissent against the whole. Thus situated we entered on the examination of the proposed system of government, and found it to be such as we could not adopt, without, as we conceived, surrendering up your dearest rights. We offered our objections to the convention, and opposed those parts of the plan, which, in our opinion, would be injurious to you, in the best manner we were able; and closed our arguments by offering the following propositions to the convention.

1. The right of conscience shall be held inviolable; and neither the legislative, executive, nor judicial powers of the United States shall have authority to alter, abrogate, or infringe any part of the constitution of the several states, which provide for the preservation of liberty in matters of religion.

2. That in controversies respecting property, and in suits between man and man, trial by jury shall remain as heretofore, as well in the federal courts, as in those of the several states.

3. That in all capital and criminal prosecutions, a man has a right to demand the cause and nature of his accusation, as well in the federal courts, as in those of the several states; to be heard by himself and his counsel; to be confronted with the accusers and witnesses; to call for evidence in his favor, and a speedy trial by an impartial jury of his vicinage, without whose unanimous consent, he cannot be found guilty, nor can he be compelled to give evidence against himself; and that no man be deprived of his liberty, except by the law of the land or the judgment of his peers.

4. That excessive bail ought not to be required, nor excessive fines imposed, nor cruel nor unusual punishments inflicted.

5. That warrants unsupported by evidence, whereby any officer or messenger may be commanded or required to search suspected places, or to seize any person or persons, his or their property, not particularly described, are grievous and oppressive, and shall not be granted either by the magistrates of the federal government or others.

6. That the people have a right to the freedom of speech, of writing and publishing their sentiments, therefore, the freedom of the press shall not be restrained by any law of the United States.

7. That the people have a right to bear arms for the defense of themselves and their own state, or the United States, or for the purpose

of killing game; and no law shall be passed for disarming the people or any of them, unless for crimes committed, or real danger of public injury from individuals; and as standing armies in the time of peace are dangerous to liberty, they ought not to be kept up; and that the military shall be kept under strict subordination to and be governed by the civil powers.

8. The inhabitants of the several states shall have liberty to fowl and hunt in seasonable times, on the lands they hold, and on all other lands in the United States not enclosed, and in like manner to fish in all navigable waters, and others not private property, without being restrained therein by any laws to be passed by the legislature of the United States.

9. That no law shall be passed to restrain the legislatures of the several states from enacting laws for imposing taxes, except imposts and duties on goods imported or exported, and that no taxes, except imposts and duties upon goods imported and exported, and postage on letters shall be levied by the authority of Congress.

10. That the house of representatives be properly increased in number; that elections shall remain free; that the several states shall have power to regulate the elections for senators and representatives, without being controlled either directly or indirectly by an interference on the part of the Congress; and that elections of representatives be annual.

11. That the power of organizing, arming, and disciplining the militia (the manner of disciplining the militia to be prescribed by Congress) remain with the individual states, and that Congress shall not have authority to call or march any of the militia out of their own state, without the consent of such state, and for such length of time only as such state shall agree.

That the sovereignty, freedom, and independency of the several states shall be retained, and every power, jurisdiction, and right which is not by this constitution expressly delegated to the United States in Congress assembled.

12. That the legislative, executive, and judicial powers be kept separate; and to this end that a constitutional council be appointed, to advise and assist the president, who shall be responsible for the advice they give, hereby the senators would be relieved from almost constant attendance; and also that the judges be made completely independent.

13. That no treaty which shall be directly opposed to the existing laws of the United States in Congress assembled shall be valid until such laws shall be repealed, or made conformable to such treaty; neither shall any treaties be valid which are in contradiction to the

constitution of the United States, or the constitutions of the several states.

14. That the judiciary power of the United States shall be confined to cases affecting ambassadors, other public ministers and consuls; to cases of admiralty and maritime jurisdiction; to controversies to which the United States shall be a party; to controversies between two or more states—between a state and citizens of different states—between citizens claiming lands under grants of different states; and between a state or the citizens thereof and foreign states, and in criminal cases, to such only as are expressly enumerated in the constitution, and that the United States in Congress assembled shall not have power to enact laws, which shall alter the laws of descents and distribution of the effects of deceased persons, the titles of lands or goods, or the regulation of contracts in the individual states.

After reading these propositions, we declared our willingness to agree to the plan, provided it was so amended as to meet those propositions, or something similar to them; and finally moved the convention to adjourn, to give the people of Pennsylvania time to consider the subject, and determine for themselves; but these were all rejected, and the final vote was taken, when our duty to you induced us to vote against the proposed plan, and to decline signing the ratification of the same.

During the discussion we met with many insults, and some personal abuse; we were not even treated with decency, during the sitting of the convention, by the persons in the gallery of the house; however, we flatter ourselves that in contending for the preservation of those invaluable rights you have thought proper to commit to our charge, we acted with a spirit becoming freemen, and being desirous that you might know the principles which actuated our conduct, and being prohibited from inserting our reasons of dissent on the minutes of the convention, we have subjoined them for your consideration, as to you alone we are accountable. It remains with you whether you will think those inestimable privileges, which you have so ably contended for, should be sacrificed at the shrine of despotism, or whether you mean to contend for them with the same spirit that has so often baffled the attempts of an aristocratic faction, to rivet the shackles of slavery on you and your unborn posterity.

Our objections are comprised under three general heads of dissent, viz.:

We dissent, first, because it is the opinion of the most celebrated writers on government, and confirmed by uniform experience, that a very extensive territory cannot be governed on the principles of freedom, otherwise than by a confederation of republics, possessing all the powers of internal government; but united in the management of their general, and foreign concerns.

If any doubt could have been entertained of the truth of the foregoing principle, it has been fully removed by the concession of Mr. [James] Wilson, one of majority on this question; and who was one of the deputies in the late general convention. In justice to him, we will give his own words; they are as follows, viz.:[11] "The extent of country for which the new constitution was required produced another difficulty in the business of the federal convention. It is the opinion of some celebrated writers that to a small territory, the democratical; to a middling territory (as Montesquieu has termed it) the monarchical; and to an extensive territory, the despotic form of government is best adapted. Regarding then the wide and almost unbounded jurisdiction of the United States, at first view, the hand of despotism seemed necessary to control, connect, and protect it; and hence the chief embarrassment rose. For, we know that, altho our constituents would cheerfully submit to the legislative restraints of a free government, they would spurn at every attempt to shackle them with despotic power." And again in another part of his speech he continues. "Is it probable that the dissolution of the state governments and the establishment of one *consolidated empire* would be eligible in its nature and satisfactory to the people in its administration? I think not, as I have given reasons to show that so extensive a territory could not be governed, connected, and preserved, but by the *supremacy of despotic power*. All the exertions of the most potent emperors of Rome were not capable to keeping that empire together, which in extent was far inferior to the dominion of America."

We dissent, secondly, because the powers vested in Congress by this constitution must necessarily annihilate and absorb the legislative, executive, and judicial powers of the several states, and produce from their ruins one consolidated government, which from the nature of things will be *an iron-handed despotism*, as nothing short of the supremacy of despotic sway could connect and govern these United States under one government.

As the truth of this position is of such decisive importance, it ought to be fully investigated, and if it is founded to be clearly ascertained; for, should it be demonstrated, that the powers vested by this constitution in Congress will have such an effect as necessarily to produce one consolidated government, the question then will be reduced to this short issue, viz.: whether satiated with the blessings of liberty; whether repenting of the folly of so recently asserting their unalienable rights, against foreign despots at the expense of so much blood and treasure, and such painful and arduous struggles, the people of America are now willing to resign every privilege of freemen, and submit to the dominion of an absolute government, that will embrace all America in one chain of despotism; or whether they will with virtuous indignation spurn at the shackles prepared for them, and confirm their liberties by a conduct becoming freemen.

That the new government will not be a confederacy of states, as it ought, but one consolidated government founded upon the destruction of the several governments of the states, we shall now show.

The powers of Congress under the new constitution are complete and unlimited over the *purse* and the *sword,* and are perfectly independent of, and supreme over, the state governments; whose intervention in these great points is entirely destroyed. By virtue of their power of taxation, Congress may command the whole, or any part of the property of the people. They may impose what imposts upon commerce; they may impose what land taxes, poll taxes, excises, duties on all written instruments, and duties on every other article that they may judge proper; in short, every species of taxation, whether of an external or internal nature is comprised in section the 8th, of Article the 1st, viz.: "The Congress shall have power to lay and collect taxes, duties, imposts, and excises, to pay the debts, and provide for the common defence and general welfare of the United States."

As there is no one article of taxation reserved to the state governments, the Congress may monopolize every source of revenue, and thus indirectly demolish the state governments, for without funds they could not exist. The taxes, duties, and excises imposed by Congress may be so high as to render it impracticable to levy further sums on the same articles; but whether this should be the case or not, if the state governments should presume to impose taxes, duties, or excises, on the same articles with Congress, the latter may abrogate and repeal the laws whereby they are imposed, upon the allegation that they interfere with the due collection of their taxes, duties, or excises, by virtue of the following clause, part of section 8th, Article 1st, viz.: "To make all laws which shall be necessary and proper for carrying into execution the foregoing powers, and all other powers vested by this constitution in the government of the United States, or in any department or officer thereof."

The Congress might gloss over this conduct by construing every purpose for which the state legislatures now lay taxes, to be for the *"general welfare,"* and therefore as of their jurisdiction.

And the supremacy of the laws of the United States is established by Article 6th, viz.: "That this constitution and the laws of the United States, which shall be made in pursuance thereof, and *all treaties* made, or which shall be made, under the authority of the United States, shall be the *supreme law* of the *land*; and *the judges in every state shall be bound thereby; any thing in the constitution or laws of any state to the contrary notwithstanding.*" It has been alleged that the words "pursuant to the constitution" are a restriction upon the authority of Congress; but when it is considered that by other sections they are invested with every efficient power of government, and which may be exercised to the absolute destruction of the state governments, without any violation of even the forms of the constitution, this seeming restriction, as well as every other restriction in it, appears to us to be nugatory and delusive; and only introduced as a blind upon the real nature of the government. In our opinion, "pursuant to the constitution" will be coextensive with the *will* and *pleasure* of Congress, which, indeed, will be the only limitation of their powers.

We apprehend that two coordinate sovereignties would be a solecism in politics. That therefore as there is no line of distinction drawn between the general and state governments; as the sphere of their jurisdiction is undefined, it would be contrary to the nature of things, that both should exist together, one or the other would necessarily triumph in the fullness of dominion. However the contest could not be of long continuance, as the state governments are divested of every means of defense, and will be obliged by "the supreme law of the land" *to yield at discretion.*

It has been objected to this total destruction of the state governments, that the existence of their legislatures is made essential to the organization of Congress; that they must assemble for the appointment of the senators and president general of the United States. True, the state legislatures may be continued for some years, as boards of appointment, merely, after they are divested of every other function, but the framers of the constitution foreseeing that the people will soon be disgusted with this solemn mockery of a government without power and usefulness have made a provision for relieving them from the imposition, in section 4th, of Article 1st, viz.: "The times, places, and manner of holding elections for senators and representatives shall be prescribed in each state by the legislature thereof; *but the Congress may at any time, by law make or alter such regulations; except as to the place of chusing senators.*"

As Congress have the control over the time of the appointment of the president general, of the senators and of the representatives of the United States, they may prolong their existence in office, for life, by postponing the time of their election and appointment, from period to period, under various pretenses, such as an apprehension of invasion, the factious disposition of the people, or any other plausible pretense that the occasion may suggest; and having thus obtained life estates in the government, they may fill up the vacancies themselves, by their control over the mode of appointment; with this exception in regard to the senators, that as the place of appointment for them must, by the constitution, be in the particular state, they may depute somebody in the respective states, to fill up the vacancies in the senate occasioned by death, until they can venture to assume it themselves. In this manner may the only restriction in this clause be evaded. By virtue of the foregoing section, when the spirit of the people shall be gradually broken; when the general government shall be firmly established, and when a numerous standing army shall render opposition vain, the Congress may complete the system of despotism, in renouncing all dependence on the people, by continuing themselves, and [their] children in the government.

The celebrated Montesquieu, in his *Spirit of Laws,* vol. 1, page 12th, says, "That in a democracy there can be no exercise of sovereignty, but by the suffrages of the people, which are their will; now the sovereign's will is the sovereign himself; the laws therefore, which establish the right of suffrage, are fundamental to this government. In fact, it is as important to regulate in a republic in what manner, by whom, and concerning what suffrages are to be given, as it is in a monarchy to know who is the prince, and after what manner he ought to govern." The *time, mode,* and *place* of the election of representatives, senators and president general of the United States ought not to be under the control of Congress, but fundamentally ascertained and established.

The new constitution, consistently with the plan of consolidation, contains no reservation of the rights and privileges of the state governments, which was made in the confederation of the year 1778, by Article the 2d, viz.: "That each state retains its sovereignty, freedom and independence, and every power, jurisdiction and right, which is not by this confederation expressly delegated to the United States in Congress assembled."

The legislative power vested in Congress by the foregoing recited sections is so unlimited in its nature; may be so comprehensive, and boundless its exercise, that this alone would be amply sufficient to annihilate the state governments, and swallow them up in the grand vortex of general empire.

The judicial powers vested in Congress are also so various and extensive, that by legal ingenuity they may be extended to every case, and thus absorb the state judiciaries, and when we consider the decisive influence that a general judiciary would have over the civil polity of the several states, we do not hesitate to pronounce that this power, unaided by the legislative, would effect a consolidation of the states under one government.

The powers of a court of equity, vested by this constitution in the tribunals of Congress; powers which do not exist in Pennsylvania unless so far as they can be incorporated with jury trial, would, in this state, greatly contribute to this event. The rich and wealthy suitors would eagerly lay hold of the infinite mazes, perplexities, and delays, which a court of chancery, with the appellate powers of the supreme court in fact as well as law would furnish him with, and thus the poor man being plunged in the bottomless pit of legal discussion would drop his demand in despair.

In short, consolidation pervades the whole constitution. It begins with an annunciation that such was the intention. The main pillars of the fabric correspond with it, and the concluding paragraph is a confirmation of it. The preamble begins with the words, "We the people of the United States," which is the style of a compact between individuals entering into a state of society, and not that of a confederation of states. The other features of consolidation, we have before noticed.

Thus we have fully established the position, that the powers vested by this constitution in Congress will effect a consolidation of the states under one government, which even the advocates of this constitution admit could not be done without the sacrifice of all liberty.

3. We dissent, thirdly, because if it were practicable to govern so extensive a territory as these United States includes, on the plan of a consolidated government, consistent with the principles of liberty and the happiness of the people, yet the construction of this constitution is not calculated to attain the object, for independent of the nature of the case, it would of itself, necessarily produce a despotism, and that not by the usual gradations, but with the celerity that has hitherto only attended revolutions effected by the sword.

To establish the truth of this position, a cursory investigation of the principles and form of this constitution will suffice.

The first consideration that this review suggests is the emission of a BILL OF RIGHTS ascertaining and fundamentally establishing those unalienable and personal rights of men, without the full, free, and secure enjoyment of which there can be no liberty, and over which it is not necessary for a good government to have the control. The principal of which are the rights of conscience, personal liberty by the clear and unequivocal establishment of the writ of *habeas corpus,* jury trial in criminal and civil cases, by an impartial jury of the vicinage or county; with the common law proceedings, for the safety of the accused in criminal prosecutions; and the liberty of the press, that scourge of tyrants, and the grand bulwark of every other liberty and privilege; the stipulation heretofore made in favor of them in the state constitutions are entirely superseded by this constitution.

The legislature of a free country should be so formed as to have a competent knowledge of its constituents, and enjoy their confidence. To produce these essential requisites, the representation ought to be fair, equal, and sufficiently numerous, to possess the same interests, feelings, opinions, and views, which the people themselves would possess were they all assembled; and so numerous as to prevent bribery and undue influence, and so responsible to the people, by frequent and fair elections, as to prevent their neglecting or sacrificing the views and interests of their constituents, to their own pursuits.

We will now bring the legislature under this constitution to the test of the foregoing principles, which will demonstrate, that it is deficient in every essential quality of a just and safe representation.

The house of representatives is to consist of 65 members; that is one for about every 50,000 inhabitants, to be chosen every two years. Thirty-three members will form a quorum for doing business, and 17 of these, being the majority, determine the sense of the house.

The senate, the other constituent branch of the legislature, consists of 26 members, being *two* from each state, appointed by their legislatures every six years—fourteen senators make a quorum; the majority of whom, eight, determines the sense of that body; except in judging on impeachments, or in making treaties, or in expelling a member, when two-thirds of the senators present must concur.

The president is to have the control over the enacting of laws, so far as to make the concurrence of *two*-thirds of the representatives and senators present necessary, if he should object to the laws.

Thus it appears that the liberties, happiness, interests, and great concerns of the whole United States may be dependent upon the integrity, virtue, wisdom, and knowledge of 25 or 26 men. How inadequate and unsafe a representation! Inadequate, because the sense and views of 3 or 4 millions of people diffused over so extensive a territory comprising such various climates, products, habits, interests, and opinions cannot be collected in so small a body; and besides, it is not a fair and equal representation of the people even in proportion to its number, for the smallest state has as much weight in the senate as the largest, and from the smallness of the number to be chosen for both branches of the legislature; and from the mode of election and appointment, which is under the control of Congress; and from the nature of the thing, men of the most elevated rank in life will alone be chosen. The other orders in the society, such as farmers, traders, and mechanics, who all ought to have a competent number of their best-informed men in the legislature, will be totally unrepresented.

The representation is unsafe because in the exercise of such great powers and trusts, it is so exposed to corruption and undue influence, by the gift of the numerous places of honor and emolument, at the disposal of the executive; by the arts and address of the great and designing; and by direct bribery.

The representation is moreover inadequate and unsafe, because of the long terms for which it is appointed, and the mode of its appointment, by which Congress may not only control the choice of the people, but may so manage as to divest the people of this fundamental right, and become self-elected.

The number of members in the house of representatives *may* be increased to one for every 30,000 inhabitants. But when we consider, that this cannot be done without the consent of the senate, who from their share in the legislative, in the executive, and judicial departments, and permanency of appointment, will be the great efficient body in this government, and whose weight and predominancy would be abridged by an increase of the representatives, we are persuaded that this is a circumstance that cannot be expected. On the contrary, the number of representatives will probably be continued at 65, although the population of the country may swell to treble what it now is; unless a revolution should effect a change.

We have before noticed the judicial power as it would effect a consolidation of the states into one government; we will now examine it, as it would affect the liberties and welfare of the people, supposing such a government were practicable and proper.

The judicial power, under the proposed constitution, is founded on the well-known principles of the *civil law,* by which the judge determines both on law and fact, and appeals are allowed from the inferior tribunals to the superior, upon the whole question; so that *facts* as well as *law,* would be reexamined, and even new facts brought forward in the court of appeals; and to use the words of a very eminent civilian, "The cause is many times another thing before the court of appeals, than what it was at the time of the first sentence."

That this mode of proceeding is the one which must be adopted under this constitution is evident from the following circumstances: 1st. That the trial by jury, which is the grand characteristic of the common law, is secured by the constitution, only in criminal cases. 2d. That the appeal from both *law* and *fact* is expressly established, which is utterly inconsistent with the principles of the common law, and trials by jury. The only mode in which an appeal from law and fact can be established is by adopting the principles and practice of the civil law; unless the United States should be drawn into the absurdity of calling and swearing juries, merely for the purpose of contradicting their verdicts, which would render juries contemptible and worse than useless. 3d. That the courts to be established would decide on all cases *of law and equity,* which is a well-known characteristic of the civil law, and these courts would have conusance [cognizance] not only of the laws of the United States and of treaties, and of cases affecting ambassadors, but of all cases of *admiralty and maritime jurisdiction,* which last are matters belonging exclusively to the civil law, in every nation in Christendom.

Not to enlarge upon the loss of the invaluable right of trial by an unbiased jury, so dear to every friend of liberty, the monstrous expense and inconveniences of the mode of proceeding to be adopted are such as will prove intolerable to the people of this country. The lengthy proceedings of the civil law courts in the chancery of England, and in the courts of Scotland and France, are such that few men of moderate fortune can endure the expense of; the poor man must therefore submit to the wealthy. Length of purse will too often prevail against right and justice. For instance, we are told by the learned Judge Blackstone, that a question only on the property of an ox, of the value of three guineas, originating under the civil law proceedings in Scotland, after many interlocutory orders and sentences below, was carried at length from the court of sessions, the highest court in that part of Great Britain, by way of *appeal* to the House of Lords, where the question of law and fact was finally determined. He adds, that no pique of spirit could in the court of king's bench or common pleas at Westminster have given continuance to such a cause for a tenth-part of the time, nor have cost a twentieth-part of the expense. Yet the costs in the courts of king's bench and common pleas in England are infinitely greater than those which the people of this country have ever experienced. We abhor the idea of losing the transcendent privilege of trial by jury, with the loss of which, it is remarked by the same learned author, that in Sweden, the liberties of the commons were extinguished by an aristocratic senate; and *trial by jury* and the liberty of the people went out together. At the same time we regret the intolerable delay, the enormous expenses and infinite vexation to which the people of this country will be exposed from the voluminous proceedings of the courts of civil law, and especially from the appellate jurisdiction, by means of which a man may be drawn from the utmost boundaries of this extensive country to the seat of the supreme court of the nation to contend, perhaps with a wealthy and powerful adversary. The consequence of this establishment will be an absolute confirmation of the power of aristocratical influence in the courts of justice; for the common people will not be able to contend or struggle against it.

Trial by jury in criminal cases may also be excluded by declaring that the libeler, for instance, shall be liable to an action of debt for a specified sum, thus evading the common law prosecution by indictment and trial by jury. And the common course of proceeding against a ship for breach of revenue laws by information (which will be classed among civil causes) will at the civil law be within the resort of a court, where no jury intervenes. Besides, the benefit of jury trial, in cases of a criminal nature, which cannot be evaded, will be rendered of little value, by calling the accused to answer far from home; there being no provision that the trial be by a jury of the neighborhood or country. Thus an inhabitant of Pittsburgh, on a charge of crime committed on the banks of the Ohio, may be obliged to defend himself at the side of the Delaware, and so *vice versa*. To conclude this head, we observe that the judges of the courts of Congress would not be independent, as they are not debarred from holding other offices during the pleasure of the president and senate, and as they may derive their support in part from fees alterable by the legislature.

The next consideration that the constitution presents is the undue and dangerous mixture of the powers of government: the same body possessing legislative, executive, and judicial powers. The senate is a constituent branch of the legislature, it has judicial power in judging on impeachments, and in this case unites in some measure the characters of judge and party, as all of the principal officers are appointed by the president general, with the concurrence of the senate and therefore they derive their offices in part from the senate. This may bias the judgments of the senators, and tend to screen great delinquents from punishment. And the senate has, moreover, various and great executive powers, viz.: in concurrence with the president general, they form treaties with foreign nations, that may control and abrogate the constitutions and laws of the several states. Indeed, there is no power, privilege, or liberty of the state governments, or of the people, but what may be affected by virtue of this power. For all treaties, made by them, are to be the "supreme law of the land; any thing in the constitution or laws of any state, to the contrary notwithstanding."

And this great power may be exercised by the president and 10 senators (being two-thirds of 14 which is a quorum of that body). What an inducement would this offer to the ministers of foreign powers to compass by bribery *such concessions* as could not otherwise be obtained. It is the unvaried usage of all free states, whenever treaties interfere with the positive laws of the land, to make the intervention of the legislature necessary to give them operation. This became necessary, and was afforded by the parliament of Great Britain in consequence of the late commercial treaty between that kingdom and France. As the senate judges on impeachments, who is to try the members of the senate for the abuse of this power! And none of the great appointments of office can be made without the consent of the senate.

Such various, extensive, and important powers combined in one body of men are inconsistent with all freedom; the celebrated Montesquieu tells us, that "when the legislative and executive powers are united in the same person, or in the same body of magistrates, there can be no liberty, because apprehensions may arise, lest the same monarch or *senate* should enact tyrannical laws, to execute them in a tyrannical manner."

"Again, there is no liberty, if the power of judging be not separated from the legislative and executive powers. Were it joined with the legislative, the life and liberty of the subject would be exposed to arbitrary control: for the judge would then be legislator. Were it joined to the executive power, the judge might behave with all the violence of an oppressor. There would be an end of everything, were the same man, or the same body of the nobles, or of the people, to exercise those three powers; that of enacting laws; that of executing the public resolutions; and that of judging the crimes or differences of individuals."

The president general is dangerously connected with the senate; his coincidence with the views of the ruling junto in that body is made essential to his weight and importance in the government, which will destroy all independency and purity in the executive department, and having the power of pardoning without the concurrence of a council, he may screen from punishment the most treasonable attempts that may be made on the liberties of the people, when instigated by his coadjutors in the senate. Instead of this dangerous and improper mixture of the executive with the legislative and judicial, the supreme executive powers ought to have been placed in the president, with a small independent council made personally responsible for every appointment to office or other act, by having their opinions recorded; and that without the concurrence of the majority of the quorum of this council, the president should not be capable of taking any step.

We have before considered internal taxation, as it would effect the destruction of the state governments, and produce one consolidated government. We will now consider that subject as it affects the personal concerns of the people.

The power of direct taxation applies to every individual, as Congress, under this government, is expressly vested with the authority of laying a capitation or poll tax upon every person to any amount. This is a tax that, however oppressive in its nature, and unequal in its operation, is certain as to its produce and simple in its collection; it cannot be evaded like the objects of imposts or excise, and will be paid, because all that a man hath will he give for his head. This tax is so congenial to the nature of despotism, that it has ever been a favorite under such governments. Some of those who were in the late general convention from this state have long labored to introduce a poll tax among us.

The power of direct taxation will further apply to every individual, as Congress may tax land, cattle, trades, occupations, etc. to any amount, and every object of internal taxation is of that nature, that however oppressive, the people will have but this alternative, either to pay the tax, or let their property be taken, for all resistance will be vain. The standing army and select militia would enforce the collection.

For the moderate exercise of this power, there is no control left in the state governments, whose intervention is destroyed. No relief, or redress of grievances can be extended, as heretofore, by them. There is not even a declaration of RIGHTS to which the people may appeal for the vindication of their wrongs in the court of justice. They must therefore, implicitly, obey the most arbitrary laws, as the worst of them will be pursuant to the principles and form of the constitution, and that strongest of all checks upon the conduct of administration, *responsibility to the people,* will not exist in this government. The permanency of the appointments of senators and representatives, and the control the Congress have over their election, will place them independent of the sentiments and resentment of the people, and the administration having a greater interest in the government than in the community, there will be no consideration to restrain them from oppression and tyranny. In the government of this state, under the old confederation, the members of the legislature are taken from among the people, and their interests and welfare are so inseparably connected with those of their constituents, that they can derive no advantage from oppressive laws and taxes, for they would suffer in common with their fellow citizens; would participate in the burthens they impose on the community, as they must return to the common level, after a short period; and notwithstanding every exertion of influence, every means of corruption, a necessary rotation excludes them from permanency in the legislature.

This large state is to have but ten members in that Congress which is to have the liberty, property, and dearest concerns of every individual in this vast country at absolute command, and even these ten persons, who are to be our only guardians, who are to supersede the legislature of Pennsylvania, will not be of the choice of the people, nor amenable to them. From the mode of their election and appointment they will consist of the lordly and high-minded; of men who will have no congenial feelings with the people, but a perfect indifference for, and contempt of them; they will consist of those harpies of power, that prey upon the very vitals; that riot on the miseries of the community. But we will suppose, although in all probability it may never be realized in fact, that our deputies in Congress have the welfare of their constituents at heart, and will exert themselves in their behalf. What security could even this afford; what relief could they extend to their oppressed constituents? To attain this, the majority of the deputies of the twelve other states in Congress must be alike well disposed; must alike forego the sweets of power, and relinquish the pursuits of ambition, which from the nature of things is not to be expected. If the people part with a responsible representation in the legislature, founded upon fair, certain, and frequent elections, they have nothing left they can call their own. Miserable is the lot of that people whose every concern depends on the WILL and PLEASURE of their rulers. Our soldiers will become Janissaries, and our officers of government bashaws; in short, the system of despotism will soon be completed.

From the foregoing investigation, it appears that the Congress under this constitution will not possess the confidence of the people, which is an essential requisite in a good government; for unless the laws command the confidence and respect of the great body of the people, so as to induce them to support them, when called on by the civil magistrate, they must be executed by the aid of a numerous standing army, which would be inconsistent with every idea of liberty; for the same force that may be employed to compel obedience to good laws, might and probably would be used to wrest from the people their constitutional liberties. The framers of this constitution appear to have been aware of this great deficiency; to have been sensible that no dependence could be placed on the people for their support; but on the contrary, that the government must be executed by force. They have therefore made a provision for this purpose in a permanent STANDING ARMY, and a MILITIA that may be subjected to as strict discipline and government.

A standing army in the hands of a government placed so independent of the people may be made a fatal instrument to overturn the public liberties; it may be employed to enforce the collection of the most oppressive taxes, and to carry into execution the most arbitrary measures.

An ambitious man who may have the army at his devotion may step up into the throne, and seize upon absolute power.

The absolute unqualified command that Congress have over the militia may be made instrumental to the destruction of all liberty, both public and private; whether of a personal, civil, or religious nature.

First, the personal liberty of every man probably from sixteen to sixty years of age may be destroyed by the power Congress have in organizing and governing of the militia. As militia they may be subjected to fines to any amount, levied in a military manner; they may be subjected to corporal punishments of the most disgraceful and humiliating kind, and to death itself, by the sentence of a court martial. To this our young men will be more immediately subjected, as a select militia, composed of them, will best answer the purposes of government.

Secondly, the rights of conscience may be violated, as there is no exemption of those persons who are conscientiously scrupulous of bearing arms. These compose a respectable proportion of the community in the state. This is the more remarkable, because even when the distresses of the late war, and the evident disaffection of many citizens of that description, inflamed our passions, and when every person, who was obliged to risk his own life, must have been exasperated against such as on any account kept back from the common danger, yet even then, when outrage and violence might have been expected, the rights of conscience were held sacred.

At this momentous crisis, the framers of our state constitution made the most express and decided declaration and stipulations in favor of the rights of conscience;[12] but now when no necessity exists, those dearest rights of men are left insecure.

Thirdly, the absolute command of Congress over the militia may be destructive of public liberty; for under the guidance of an arbitrary government, they may be made the unwilling instruments of tyranny. The militia of Pennsylvania may be marched to New England or Virginia to quell an insurrection occasioned by the most galling oppression, and aided by the standing army, they will no doubt be successful in subduing their liberty and independency; but in so doing, although the magnanimity of their minds will be extinguished, yet the meaner passions of resentment and revenge will be increased, and these in turn will be the ready and obedient instruments of despotism to enslave the others; and that with an irritated vengeance. Thus may the militia be made the instruments of crushing the last efforts of expiring liberty, of riveting the chains of despotism on their fellow citizens, and on one another. This power can be exercised not only without violating the constitution, but in strict conformity with it;

it is calculated for this express purpose, and will doubtless be executed accordingly.

As this government will not enjoy the confidence of the people, but be executed by force, it will be a very expensive and burthensome government. The standing army must be numerous, and as a further support, it will be the policy of this government to multiply officers in every department: judges, collectors, tax gatherers, excisemen, and the whole host of revenue officers will swarm over the land, devouring the hard earnings of the industrious, like the locusts of old, impoverishing and desolating all before them.

We have not noticed the smaller, nor many of the considerable blemishes, but have confined our objections to the great and essential defects; the main pillars of the constitution, which we have shown to be inconsistent with the liberty and happiness of the people, as its establishment will annihilate the state governments, and produce one consolidated government, that will eventually and speedily issue in the supremacy of despotism.

In this investigation, we have not confined our views to the interests or welfare of this state, in preference to the others. We have overlooked all local circumstances; we have considered this subject on the broad scale of the general good; we have asserted the cause of the present and future ages, the cause of liberty and mankind.

Nathaniel Breading
John Smilie
Richard Baird
Adam Orth
John A. Hanna
John Whitehill
John Harris
Robert Whitehill
John Reynolds
Jonathan Hoge
Nicholas Lutz
John Ludwig
Abraham Lincoln
John Bishop
Joseph Heister
Joseph Powel
James Martin
William Findley
John Baird
James Edgar
William Todd

a. *The Journals of the conclave are still concealed.*

b. The continental convention in direct violation of the 13th Article of the confederation have declared, "that the ratification of nine states shall be sufficient for the establishment of this constitution, between the states so ratifying the same." Thus has the plighted faith of the states been sported with! They had solemnly engaged that the confederation now subsisting should be inviolably preserved by each of them, and the union thereby formed, should be perpetual, unless the same should be altered by mutual consent.

1. For the Impost of 1781, see CDR:IV, A.

2. For the Impost of 1783 and the request for supplementary funds, see CDR:IV, D.

3. For Virginia's call of the Annapolis Convention, see CDR:V, A.

4. For the congressional resolution of 21 February 1787, see CDR:V, C.

5. For the act of 30 December 1786 appointing delegates to the Constitutional Convention, see CDR:VI, C.

6. Franklin was appointed to the Constitutional Convention on 28 March 1787.

7. See "Tar and Feathers," 28 September and 2 October, II:A above.

8. For the petitions sent to the Assembly, see the Assembly Proceedings, 24, 26, 27, and 28 September and Mfm:Pa. 61.

9. See the *Independent Gazetteer* and the *Freeman's Journal,* 5 December, II:D above.

10. For the election night riot on 6 November, see II:D above.

11. This and the subsequent quotation are taken from the Version of Wilson's Speech by Alexander J. Dallas, 24 November.

12. Article II of the Pennsylvania Declaration of Rights (Thorpe, V, 3082).

IV

The Aftermath of Ratification in Pennsylvania

Introduction

Instead of subsiding, the public debate in Pennsylvania mounted in quantity and intensity (and occasionally in scurrility) after the state Convention voted to ratify the Constitution. The debate centered around such issues as (1) the need for amendments to the Constitution; (2) charges that the post office prevented the distribution of Antifederalist material through the mails; (3) charges that men such as Robert Morris were corrupt and supported the Constitution in order to escape paying the debts they owed the United States; and (4) the publication of fake letters by Federalists and Antifederalists alike to discredit their opponents.

The intensity of feeling generated by the public debate manifested itself in several concrete ways. Almost immediately, Antifederalists defended the minority of the Convention and praised its "Dissent" which emphasized the need to protect the rights and liberties of the people. Federalists countered by attacking the minority for not accepting the majority's will and for trying to foment a civil war.

One event which received national attention was a riot at Carlisle in Cumberland County on the 26th of December when Antifederalists used force to prevent a Federalist celebration of ratification. A second and more important development was an Antifederalist petition campaign. By the spring of 1788 several thousand signers of petitions requested the Assembly to refuse to confirm the ratification of the Constitution by the state Convention.

The debate over amendments to the Constitution had begun in the fall of 1787, but it was given new impetus by the refusal of the Convention to consider amendments and by the publication of the "Dissent of the Minority" of the Convention. Some Federalists asserted that a bill of rights was unnecessary in a democratic republic, and they urged the people to trust their elected leaders to establish a moderate government and to protect individual rights and liberties. Other Federalists argued that if amendments were needed, the people should wait until the new Congress recommended them. Above all, a second constitutional convention, which many Antifederalists demanded, would not have the spirit of compromise that characterized the Constitutional Convention, and might well destroy the new government.

The Antifederalists argued that the new Congress could not be trusted and demanded that a second constitutional convention be called immediately to adopt a bill of rights to protect the people. They argued that the vast powers of Congress under the Constitution would corrupt its members, who would never relinquish such power. In particular, Antifederalists demanded guarantees of trial by jury in civil cases, religious freedom and liberty, and the freedom of the press.

Such Antifederalists as "Centinel" (Samuel Bryan) and "Philadelphiensis" (Benjamin Workman) were particularly insistent upon a bill of rights. They argued that the Constitution was a "conspiracy" against the rights, liberties, and property of the American people because it established an aristocratic government which would almost certainly become a "despotic monarchy." "Philadelphiensis" described the "monarchy men" in the Constitutional Convention as "a set of the basest conspirators that ever disgraced a free country." (The "Centinel" and "Philadelphiensis" essays are published in *Commentaries on the Constitution.*)

The Antifederalists, led by "Centinel" (XVI and XVII, *Independent Gazetteer,* 26 February and 24 March), declared there were conspiracies of other kinds. They charged that Robert Morris, William Bingham, and Thomas Mifflin had pocketed millions of dollars of public funds during the War for Independence, and that the *ex post facto* clause of the Constitution would enable them to avoid paying their just debts (for examples, see Mfm:Pa. 455, 457, 487, 511, 522, 538). Robert Morris replied that it was through no fault of his own that his remaining accounts had never been settled (Mfm:Pa. 613), while Mifflin's supporters declared that he had done everything possible to settle his accounts as quartermaster general of the Continental Army (Mfm:Pa. 493).

Charges that Federalists used their influence with postal officials to prevent the circulation of Antifederalist material through the mails were made throughout the United States, but most heatedly in Pennsylvania. On 1 January, Ebenezer Hazard, postmaster general of the United States, with the consent of Congress, transferred the carrying of mail from stagecoaches to postriders. The stagecoaches had carried newspapers from one publisher to another without charge, but the postriders refused to carry newspapers without being paid to do so.

Antifederalists led by "Centinel" (IX, *Independent Gazetteer,* 8 January) charged that Hazard's decision was a plot to prevent the circulation of Antifederalist material, while others declared that Federalists paid postmasters and postriders to destroy Antifederalist material. Federalists denied such charges and insisted that the Antifederalists were merely trying to stir up trouble. (For documents on the controversy over the mails, see CC:Vol. III, Appendix, and Mfm:Pa. 372, 394.)

While the Antifederalists published more than the Federalists after 15 December 1787, the Federalists counterattacked vigorously. Much of their fire was focused on Benjamin Workman, the author of "Philadelphiensis," and a tutor in mathematics at the University of Pennsylvania, which, under its provost, the Reverend Dr. John Ewing, was an Antifederalist stronghold (for examples, see Mfm:Pa. 519, 552, 579, 590, 603, 632, 646, 654). Nor did the Federalists forget their old antagonist "Centinel," whom they believed to be Justice George Bryan of the state Supreme Court.

Late in March they published two letters in the *Pennsylvania Gazette,* purportedly written by Bryan. The "letters" were prefaced with a statement referring to "Centinel" as an "indefatigable Monster," ever zealous in the production of mischief. Moreover, the letters were supposedly written to John Ralston of Northampton County, "one of the sourest, narrowest, and most illiterate creatures in the state." The Federalists also branded Bryan as a sower of sedition, who, with the help of out-of-state incendiaries, was bent upon starting a civil war (Mfm:Pa. 575, 599, 600).

Some Antifederalists declared that the letters were fraudulent and unfair attacks upon two worthy and patriotic individuals, while others declared that the letters showed how Federalists controlled the post offices and intercepted private correspondence. Such Federalist activity, they said, along with the stoppage of newspapers and the campaign against amendments, was yet another conspiracy against the rights and liberties of the people (Mfm:Pa. 582, 595, 609, 617).

The fake letter or essay was common in the months following ratification of the Constitution. For instance, on 16 February the Federalist *Pennsylvania Mercury,* which allegedly employed Benjamin Rush as one of its writers, published a bogus "Centinel" XV, which circulated throughout the United States (see *Commentaries on the Constitution*). Five days later the *Mercury* published the first of eight "Letters of Margery" (i.e., George Bryan), described by William Findley as "trifling and scurrilous" (Mfm:Pa. 444, 507). In turn, according to Findley, the Antifederalist *Independent Gazetteer* "produced the more masterly though perhaps not less scurrilous" purported exchange of four letters between "James de Caledonia" (i.e., James Wilson) and James Bowdoin, former governor of Massachusetts (Mfm:Pa. 457, 481, 512, 522). Shortly afterwards, the Antifederalist *Freeman's Journal* published two purported letters from Benjamin Rush to Alexander Hamilton (Mfm:Pa. 487).

Such exchanges prompted elder-statesman Benjamin Franklin to submit an essay entitled "On the Abuse of the Press" to the *Pennsylvania Gazette.* Franklin deplored "the spirit of rancor, malice, and *hatred*" which breathed in the state's newspapers. Reading these newspapers, he said, gave one the impression that Pennsylvania "is peopled by a set of the most unprincipled, wicked, rascally, and quarrelsome scoundrels upon the face of the globe." Franklin called upon printers to be more discreet about what they published. He did not want men to die before newspapers eulogized them as "good husbands, good fathers, good friends, good citizens, and good Christians." It is perhaps significant that the newspaper which Franklin had founded did not print his essay (Mfm:Pa. 588).

Such documents are among the 435 items from newspapers and pamphlets illustrating the varieties of public debate after ratification by Pennsylvania which have been placed in the microform supplement. Others are printed in *Commentaries on the Constitution.* It should be remembered, however, that these documents, though voluminous, represent only a sample of the material to be found in Pennsylvania newspapers between the end of the state Convention in December 1787 and the early summer of 1788.

Documents concerning (1) the response to ratification and the "Dissent of the Minority," (2) the Carlisle riot and its aftermath, and (3) the petition campaign requesting the Assembly that the ratification of the Constitution "not be confirmed," are printed below to illustrate the continuing debate over the Constitution in Pennsylvania.

A. RESPONSES TO RATIFICATION AND TO THE DISSENT OF THE MINORITY

York Celebration, 18 December[1]

Yesterday, one of the delegates of the honorable the Convention returned home to this borough and announced the ratification of the Federal Constitution, when the inhabitants, fired with honest zeal, exhibited their approbation by ringing of bells and other demonstrations of joy.

1. This item was printed in the Winchester *Virginia Gazette,* 28 December under the dateline of "York, Dec. 19," and reprinted in the *Pennsylvania Journal,* 2 January 1788. It was probably first printed in the York *Pennsylvania Chronicle,* 19 December, an issue not located.

Lancaster Celebration, 19 December[1]

It is with pleasure I inform you, that the people here continue to be warmly federal. The new Constitution has the advantage of all great truths. The more it is examined, the more it is admired.

The inhabitants of our town, on the morning of the day their deputies in Convention were to return, fired a morning gun, and at twelve o'clock thirteen rounds were fired out of a piece of artillery belonging to the state. From that time, until night, all the bells in town were ringing. I never have been a witness of so much respect being paid by the people to their delegates, or of more general joy upon any occasion.

1. *Pennsylvania Gazette,* 2 January 1788. This account, headed "Extract of a letter from Lancaster, dated December 20," was reprinted three times in Philadelphia, once in Pittsburgh, and fourteen times from Maine to Georgia by 21 February 1788. For another account of the Lancaster celebration, see the *Lancaster Zeitung,* 26 December, which stated that the celebration took place on 19 December.

Northampton County Meeting, 20 December[1]

At a meeting of sundry respectable inhabitants of the county of Northampton, held at Easton, the twentieth day of December, 1787, Alexander Patterson, Esquire, in the chair.

The meeting took into consideration the report made to the people of this county by their deputies to the state Convention. Whereupon,

Resolved unanimously: First, That we highly approve of the conduct of our deputies in assenting to and ratifying the Constitution of the United States, as proposed by the late Federal Convention.

Second, That the chairman be requested to return our hearty thanks to the said deputies for the patriotism, public spirit, and faithful discharge of their duty, as representatives of this county.

Third, That their report, together with these resolutions, be transmitted by the chairman to Philadelphia for publication.

Signed, by order of the meeting, Alexander Patterson,[2] Chairman.

Attest. James Pettigrew, Secretary.

Friends and Fellow Citizens of Northampton County.

The representatives of this county in the late Convention of this state think it their duty, as servants of the public, to lay before you, their constituents, the result of their deliberations upon the new Constitution for the United States submitted to their consideration by a resolve of the legislature for calling a state convention.

The debates at large, we have reason to expect, will be published, wherein those whose inclination may lead them to it will find a detail of all the arguments made use of either for or against the adoption of the Constitution. Our intention, therefore, is not to enter fully into an investigation of the component parts of it, but only to inform our constituents that it has been carefully examined in all its parts; that every objection that could be offered to it has been heard and attended to; and that upon mature deliberation, two-thirds of the whole number of deputies from the city and counties in this state have, in the name and by the authority of the people of this state, fully ratified it upon the most clear conviction.

1st. That the state of America required a concentration and union of the powers of government for all general purposes of the United States.

2dly. That the Constitution proposed by the late Convention of the United States, held at Philadelphia, was the best form that could be devised and agreed upon.

3dly. That such a Constitution will enable the representatives of the different states in the Union to restore the commerce of all the states in general, and this in particular, to its former prosperity.

4thly. That by a diminution of taxes upon real estates, agriculture may be encouraged and the prices of lands, which have of late greatly declined, will be increased to their former value.

5thly. That by imposing duties on foreign luxuries, not only arts and manufactures will be encouraged in our own country, but the public creditors of this state and the United States will be rendered secure in their demands without any perceptible burthen on the people.

6thly. That all disputes which might otherwise arise, concerning territory or jurisdiction, between neighboring states, will be settled in the ordinary mode of distributing justice without war or bloodshed.

7thly. That the support of government will be less expensive than under the present constitutions of the different states.

8thly. That all partial laws of any particular state for the defeating contracts between parties, or rendering the compliance therewith on one part easier than was originally intended and fraudulent to the other party, are effectually provided against by a prohibition of paper money and tender laws. And,

9thly. That peace, liberty, and safety, the great objects for which the late united colonies, now free independent states, expended so much blood and treasure can only be secured by such an union of interests as this Constitution has provided for.

In full confidence that our unanimous conviction and concurrence in favor of this Constitution will meet the entire approbation of our constituents, the freemen and citizens of this county, we have the honor to subscribe ourselves, their devoted servants. John Arndt, Stephen Balliot, Jos. Horsefield, David Deshler. Easton, December 20, 1787.

1. *Pennsylvania Gazette,* 2 January 1788. This account was reprinted five times in Philadelphia, once in Carlisle, and three times in New England by the end of the first week in February 1788. "Centinel" IX, 8 January (CC:427) charged that the resolutions were the work of "a despicable few" who were trying deceitfully to make it appear that Northampton County strongly supported the Constitution. "Centinel's" allegations touched off a heated exchange between Patterson, the meeting's chairman, and the publishers of the *Freeman's Journal* and of the *Independent Gazetteer* for printing such charges (Mfm:Pa. 382, 405, 406, 470, 482).

For correspondence between John Nicholson and James Pettigrew, the meeting's secretary, concerning a derogatory remark that Pettigrew supposedly made about Nicholson at this, or some other Northampton County meeting, see Mfm:Pa. 508, 566, 589.

2. Captain Patterson was the leader of the Pennsylvania claimants in the Wyoming Valley in 1783 and 1784. He favored using force against the Connecticut claimants.

John Armstrong, Sr. to Benjamin Franklin, Carlisle, 25 December (excerpt)[1]

I beg you may accept my thanks for your favor enclosing a copy of the Federal Constitution, some time ago delivered to me by young Mr. Wharton. . . .

You must be so tired of various and perverse speculation on the new Constitution that I must not add to the common trespass but as little as possible. I confess I am far from pretending to know what is the best system of government, and ready to question whether any man knows it, otherwise than by a general knowledge of human nature and the particular circumstances of the people for whom it is framed. The people of best discernment this way instead of caviling are rather amazed that so many states with their different prejudices have been brought to meet on so good ground. Dr. [Charles] Nesbit, with great strength of reason is clear for adopting it, keeping in view such amendments as experience and a fitter time shall point out.[2] And indeed when we consider our situation at home (on the confines of anarchy) and our need of reputation abroad, it appears to me in the light of moral certainty, that immediate adoption is not only our wisest course, but also the shortest and safest mode to obtain such amendments as may either be found to be really salutary in themselves, or only calculated merely to please. In this view my small support shall not be wanting; more apprehensive as I am of a failure in the duty of the people, than of any early encroachment of a new Congress—nor would the body of the people but by undue influence give any opposition. Stale and careless jealousy, or prejudice and private motives, have thrown too many men into a political phrenzy, which in Pennsylvania we now have to regret. Your last speech in the Federal Convention, being just up, will be in our paper tomorrow.[3] It is come in good time, and I think can scarcely fail of some good effects.

The tenor of the minority's Dissent and particularly a few explicit [sentences?] appears to have a wild and pernicious tendency![4] We must not pray God to reward them according to their works, but beseech Him to restrain the residue of their wrath, to still the tumults of the people which they seem to provoke; and forgive their abettors for the Mediator's sake, for they either care not, or know not what they do.

1. RC, Franklin Papers, PPAmP.

2. Nisbet, a Presbyterian clergyman, was president of Dickinson College at Carlisle. For his support of the Constitution, see Mfm:Pa. 259, 642.

3. Franklin's speech on 17 September was reprinted in the *Carlisle Gazette,* 26 December (see CC:77).

4. The *Carlisle Gazette* published the first installment of the "Dissent" on 26 December, the day after Armstrong made this observation.

Pennsylvania Gazette, 26 December

A correspondent has read, with astonishment, that part of the address of the minority of our state Convention, wherein they say, that the new Federal Constitution enables the President, Senate, and Representatives to perpetuate their political existence, when it expressly declares they shall continue for four, six, and two years, and no longer. He is restrained from giving its proper name to such an assertion by respect, not for those uncandid men, but for the public.

The members of the opposition to the new federal government in this state are well-known to be attached to *a single legislative body,* and to be very much opposed to a second and third branch; yet they have not had firmness and sincerity enough to say so in their address to their constituents, because they know the objection would be considered as a great and palpable political error by the conventions of all the other states, to whom, and not to their constituents, have the dissenters wished to address themselves. The federal legislature not being a single house is, however, *their great objection.* The good people of the Union, and particularly those skilled in political science, will form their own opinions of such men, and such politicians.

It is asserted that the Federal Constitution will annihilate the state constitutions. Several arguments have been adduced to evince the error of such an assertion, but the following detail will show it is impossible that government could be carried on, without the continuance of the state constitutions. The federal government neither makes, nor can without alteration make, any provision for the choice of probates of wills, land officers and surveyors, justices of the peace, county lieutenants, county commissioners, receivers of quitrents, sheriffs, coroners, overseers of the poor, and constables; nor does it provide in any way for the important and innumerable trials that must take place among the citizens of the same state, nor for criminal offenses, breaches of the peace, nuisances, or other objects of the state courts; nor for licensing marriages, and public houses; nor for county roads, nor any other roads than the great post roads; nor the erection of ferries and bridges, unless on post roads; nor for poorhouses; nor incorporating religious and political societies, towns and boroughs; nor for charity schools, administrations on estates, and many other matters essential to the advancement of human happiness, and to the existence of civil society.

John Clark to Jasper Yeates, York, 28 December (excerpt)[1]

I congratulate you on your safe return and your success in Convention in support of the new Constitution; I flatter myself much good will flow from it. The people of Chambersburg, at the court, demonstrated their joy on the arrival of the news with thirteen discharges of cannon, and the madeira flowed plentifully. What must the minority think, when at this place they expected support, to find themselves so disappointed? I hope it will be [the] case everywhere.

1. RC, Yeates-Burd Collection, PHi. Clark was a York lawyer.

Northampton County Meeting, 1 January 1788[1]

At a meeting of a number of respectable inhabitants of the second election district, in the county of Northampton, held at the town of Northampton the first day of January, 1788, Peter Rhoads, Esquire was chosen chairman.

The Constitution proposed for the government of the United States by the late Federal Convention held at Philadelphia, and the report of the honorable the deputies from this county in the state Convention to the people thereof, were read.

On consideration, it was *unanimously Resolved*:

1st. That it is of the greatest importance to the good people of these states, that the United States in Congress assembled be vested with all the necessary powers of a free and sovereign people in order to command respect with foreign nations, and keep domestic peace and good order among these states, and the citizens thereof.

2dly. That we are fully convinced the proposed Constitution (wisely built on the grand foundation of free government, the sovereignty of the people) will effect these inestimable national blessings.

3dly. That this meeting highly approves of the conduct of the honorable the deputies from this county in the late state Convention, in assenting to the ratification of the said Federal Constitution.

4thly. That the proceedings of this meeting be published in one or more of the newspapers in this state.

Signed, by order of the meeting, Peter Rhoads, Chairman.

1. *Pennsylvania Gazette,* 30 January. The *Gazette's* account, translated from the *Philadelphische Correspondenz,* 22 January, was reprinted four times in Philadelphia and three times outside Pennsylvania.

An Address to the Minority of the Convention, Carlisle Gazette, 2 January[1]

The history of mankind is pregnant with frequent, bloody, and almost imperceptible transitions from freedom to slavery. Rome, after she had been long distracted by the fury of the patrician and plebeian parties, at length found herself reduced to the most abject slavery under a Nero, a Caligula, etc. The successive convulsions, which happened at Rome, were the immediate consequence of the aspiring ambition of a few great men, and the very organization and construction of the government itself. The republic of Venice, by the progressive and almost imperceptible encroachments of the nobles, has at length degenerated into an odious and permanent aristocracy. This we are convinced, by indubitable demonstration, will be the final consequence of the proposed Federal Constitution; and because we prize the felicity and freedom of our posterity equally with our own, we esteem it our indispensable duty to oppose it with that determined resolution and spirit that becomes freemen. That fire for liberty which was kindled in every patriotic breast during the late glorious contention, though in a latent state, will be easily rekindled; and upon the contact of a very spark will devour by its direful explosion, not only the enemies of liberty, but both parties promiscuously. Discontent, indignation, and revenge already begins to be visible in every patriotic countenance; and civil discord already raises her sneaky head. And we are well convinced that nothing less than a total recantation and annihilation of the proposed aristocratic delusion will appease the insulted and enraged defenders of liberty. If the lazy and great wish to ride, they may lay it down as an indubitable position or axiom, that the people of America will make very refractory and restiff hackneys. Although the designing and artful Federalists have effected their scheme so far as to have the Constitution adopted in this state by surprise, notwithstanding the people are pretty generally convinced of their delusion, and little less than the lives of their betrayers will satiate their revenge. Not even the authority of the clergy, who seem generally to have been a set of men decidedly opposed to popular freedom, can give sanction to such a government. The people of America understand their rights better than, by adopting such a constitution, to rivet the fetters of slavery; or to sacrifice their liberty at the shrine of aristocracy or arbitrary government. We, the subscribers, are a society united for the express purpose of reciprocal or mutual improvement; we meet once a week, and political matters are frequently the subjects of litigation and debate. We have read and endeavored fully to comprehend the proposed Federal Constitution; and also the arguments for and against it; and after mature deliberation, we unanimously acquiesce with, and cordially thank you the minority in the late state Convention: First, for your patriotic and spirited endeavors to support the drooping cause of liberty and rights of your constituents. Secondly, for your integrity and firmness in stemming the torrent of popular clamor, insult, and flattery. Thirdly, for your unanswerable, solid, and well-founded arguments and reason of dissent. Lastly, we rejoice to think that your names will shine illustriously in the page of history, and will be read with honor and grateful remembrance in the annals of fame; while the names of the majority, and their ignorant tools will be spurned and execrated by the succeeding generations as the pillars of slavery, tyranny, and despotism.

James M'Cormick
David Boyd
William Gelson
James Irvin
Andrew Irvin
Wm. Carothers, Sr.
William Addams
Wm. Carothers, Jr.
John Douglass
Arch. Hamilton
Joseph Junkin
John Clandinen
Thomas Henderson
Robert Bell
John Junkin
James Bell
Thomas Atchley
William Irvin
William Douglass
John Walker
William Greason
David Walker
Jonathan Walker
John Buchanan
Francis M'Guire
John Armstrong
Benj. Junkin
John Carothers, Jr.
James Fleming
Thomas Carothers

1. Reprinted: *Independent Gazetteer,* 9 January. Outside Pennsylvania the address was reprinted five times from Massachusetts to Maryland by 1 March. For an answer, see "Hermenius," *Carlisle Gazette,* 16 January, IV:B below. The *Gazette,* however, refused to publish on 9 January "Junius's Address to one of the minority of the state Convention [because it] is fraught with too much invective and personal reflections. . . ."

Pennsylvania Gazette, 9 January[1]

The rest of the Union, says a correspondent, may judge how sincere the minority of our Convention are in their jealousies about the federal government, when they are informed of the following facts:

1st. That these gentlemen are *to a man* what are called Constitutionalists here, that is, friends to our state constitution, which they call *admirable* in their protest. And

2dly. That this constitution gives *all* legislative power to a *single house* of representatives.

3dly. That instead of a governor and council of three or five, we have an Executive Council of nineteen equal members on every vote.

4thly. That the county of Chester sends only one of these councillors, though it has 6,000 electors; and the county of Luzerne sends one also, though it has not 1,000 electors.

5thly. That this *Executive* Council is our *court of impeachment,* with power to inflict all the punishments usually attendant on conviction of impeachable offenses—by which the highest criminal court of the state is centered in the same hands with the supreme executive power.

6thly. That our constitution cannot be changed without a recommendation of two-thirds of *a Council of Censors,* a body chosen septennially in such a manner that seven counties (Luzerne, Huntingdon, Fayette, Franklin, Dauphin, Bedford, Northumberland) having 13 members and 13,000 electors can prevent any alteration from being *even considered by a convention,* though desired by all the rest of the counties, who have 57 members and 57,000 electors.

That these are serious truths, nobody can deny. Now let the minority of the Pennsylvania Convention point out to impartial America such departures from the evident principles of justice and liberty in the federal government, of which they so roundly complain.

1. This item was reprinted in the *Pennsylvania Journal,* 12 January, and once in New York and in Maryland.

Hermenius, Carlisle Gazette, 16 January

The Address to the Minority of the State Convention of Pennsylvania, Explained.[1]

The next day after the address to the minority of the state Convention of Pennsylvania appeared in the *Carlisle Gazette,* I happened to be in company with a number of respectable and intelligent gentlemen, at least they are generally esteemed so. The subject of their discourse was the address. One asserted that "it was the most bombastical and nonsensical composition he had ever read." Another affirmed "it was the sublime of nonsense." Another, "that the person who had composed it was undoubtedly a poor, smattering pedant." Another declared, "that though he was opposed to the new Federal Constitution, yet he detested that address as a foolish, inconsistent jargon."

However, I was so far from agreeing with these gentlemen in exclaiming against the address, that I esteemed it an excellent composure of the kind; to vindicate this opinion of its merit, the following short remarks are presented to the public, designed principally to explain the most difficult terms and sentences in that performance, that it may not be rashly condemned or misunderstood. By an address in this place, must not be understood an application made by the party addressing to the party addressed, desiring to have something done for them; nor an indication of anything to the party addressed, which ought in a particular manner to be taken into their consideration; though this is the common acceptation of the word. But by this address is meant, a medley composition made up of remarks and assertions upon different and unconnected subjects. The term being explained, the address itself is next to be considered. In the first place, observe that history is assumed as the foundation and standard of the arguments used in the first part of this address; you may take notice also that by history being pregnant is not meant that it is great with young breeding or fruitful, which are the common senses of the word; but only that history informs or makes known what has been. We are informed in the address, "that the successive convulsions that happened at Rome were the immediate consequence" (that is, a consequence that proceeds from its cause, without the intervention of secondary causes or means) "of the aspiring ambition of a few great men," that is, of the minority of great men, or men in public offices. I say the minority, because history is the standard in this matter; and it informs us that there were many great men in the Roman commonwealth; therefore, these few great men were the minority, who occasioned the successive convulsions of Rome.

Again, these "convulsions were the immediate consequence of the very organization and construction of the government itself"; therefore, since there was means, there must have been a continued and uninterrupted convulsion in the Roman state, from the first day that the Roman government was organized and constructed till it was totally erased. Away then with all the fabulous descriptions of the glory, peace, happiness, liberty, and grandeur of the Roman state, that are handed down to us by the historians of all ages since the Roman state first existed; these historians have been ignorant fools and ill-designing blockheads to impose such gross falsehoods upon the world! Falsehoods so glaring, that thirty men in Cumberland County, many centuries after, have detected? The address informs us also that "Venice by the encroachments of her nobles has degenerated into an odious and permanent aristocracy." But America has no nobles to dread in this respect. Now in the first place, the minority of great men at Rome occasioned their convulsions. Secondly, the organization and construction of the Roman government was not the cause of these convulsions; for then there would have been an uninterrupted convulsion in the Roman state; but history informs us otherwise. Thirdly, the nobles of Venice brought about an odious and permanent aristocracy; therefore, if the new Federal Constitution be similar to the Roman constitution, there will be no danger of convulsions being the immediate consequence of adopting it. And if the convulsions that happened at Rome were the immediate consequence of the aspiring ambition of the few great men, or minority, certainly, from a similarity of causes, similar consequences will happen [to] the Americans, if they should follow their minority; especially, as we shall show afterwards, that they are very probably actuated by the same principles as the minority at Rome were. Again nothing can be proved by the comparison of Venice to America, because there are no nobles in America, and so the causes being dissimilar, the consequences cannot be proved to be similar. We may, indeed, suppose that all the Americans are nobles; but then it would be unreasonable to suppose that they would bring an odious and permanent aristocracy over themselves; therefore, the indubitable demonstration must fall to the ground. The phrases, "fire of liberty" and "the contact of a very spark" are so metaphorically plain and easy to be understood, that I need not explain them, but only to show that the spark is to come into contact with the fire of liberty, and then, "by its direful explosion, it will devour not only the enemies of liberty, but both parties" (that is, both its enemies and friends) "promiscuously." This is the glorious liberty, tending to the destruction of both its friends and enemies promiscuously, which is so much endangered by the new Federal Constitution! Oppose therefore, O Americans, like freemen! Next, let us observe, that discontent, indignation, and revenge are the principles mentioned in the address, that are visible in every patriotic countenance. Patriotic principles indeed! exactly suited to the defenders of that liberty, or fire of liberty, that will devour both its enemies and friends! Hail happy patriots! Nero, Caligula, Clodius, and Cataline! It was by these patriotic principles you were actuated, when you committed all your outrages, and it was in defense of that liberty, that devours both friends and enemies promiscuously! Eternal disgrace be on Demosthenes, Cicero, Cato, and others who suppressed these patriotic principles, and managed matters of state with justice, benevolence, and clemency! No wonder the addressers have said, "that little less than the lives of their betrayers will satiate their revenge; that nothing but an annihilation of the Federal Constitution will appease the enraged defenders of liberty." No wonder, indeed, when actuated by the patriotic principles of discontent, indignation, rage, and revenge, in defense of a liberty, that will devour both friends and enemies. "Civil discord already raises her sneaky head." The public, I hope, will pardon this romantic phrase. The next sentence that needs a little explanation is where the addressers reject the authority of the clergy, with respect to the Federal Constitution, because, "they seem generally to have been a set of men decidedly opposed to popular freedom." This is to be understood that they are opposers of that freedom and liberty that will devour both its friends and enemies. For with regard to that liberty that is inconsistent with, and tends to promote the mutual interest, advantage, and support of the citizens, all America can testify, that the greater part of the clergy in America have exerted themselves in the support and defense of it. But as this is a species of liberty diametrically opposed to the [one line unreadable] friends and enemies promiscuously, it is not strange that the authority of the clergy is rejected in this case.

The addressers very modestly proclaim to the public, that "they are a society united for the express purpose of mutual improvement." The public are much obliged to them for this information, as it is of great importance to know it. Lastly, by taking notice of the remarks already made in explaining this address, we may easily discern the reasons why the addressers so highly applauded the minority of the late state Convention, and so severely execrate the majority. The minority are esteemed patriots by the addressers; that is, according to their idea of patriotism, men actuated by discontent, indignation, and revenge; and stand in the defense of a liberty, that will devour both its friends and enemies promiscuously; but the majority are for another kind of liberty, and act from different principles. Hoping the public will understand the address better by these remarks, I beg leave to subscribe myself, HERMENIUS.

1. See "An Address to the Minority of the Convention," 2 January, IV:B above.

Independent Gazetteer, 22 January[1]

A correspondent says, that the present situation of public affairs is truly alarming. The minority of the state Convention of Pennsylvania have declared in their protest, that the Continental Convention have no power to annihilate the old Articles of Confederation without the consent of every one of the thirteen states in the Union; that two members of the late Assembly of the State of Pennsylvania were forcibly dragged to the House for the purpose of making a quorum to call a convention, whereby the proceedings of such an Assembly are by no means binding upon the people; and that the constitution of the State of Pennsylvania cannot be set aside although nine states should agree to the ratification of the new Constitution. In these opinions they are supported not only by their constituents but by a very considerable part of the whole body of the people of Pennsylvania, who, it is expected, will soon confederate under these sentiments. It would be the part therefore of wisdom in some of the states who have not yet adopted the new Constitution, to pause a while before they proceed to the ratification of it. A civil war with all its dreadful train of evils will probably be the consequence of such a proceeding. Whereas, if we have patience, we may at more convenient opportunity determine upon some alteration in government which will be peaceably adopted by the people.

1. This item was not reprinted in any other Pennsylvania newspaper and was reprinted only once outside the state: in the *Maryland Journal* on 29 January.

A Citizen of Philadelphia, Pennsylvania Gazette, 23 January[1]

In the list of the signers of the protest of the minority of the Convention against the Federal Constitution, we find six (and three of them the only speakers against it in the Convention)[2] whose names are upon record as the friends of *paper money,* and the advocates for the late unjust *test law* of Pennsylvania, which for near *ten* years excluded the *Quakers, Mennonists, Moravians,* and several other sects scrupulous against war, from a representation in our government.

In the *Minutes* of the second session of the Ninth General Assembly of the Commonwealth of Pennsylvania, we find in the 212th page the following persons among the yeas, who voted for the emission of paper money, which has, by its depreciation, so much injured the trade and manufactures of the state, and which, by impairing its funds, has weakened the strength of our government, and thereby destroyed the hopes and support of the public creditors. The persons are *William Findley, John Smilie, Robert Whitehill, Adam Orth, Nicholas Lutz, Abraham Lincoln.*

In the 302d page of the same book, we find a report declaring the Quakers, Moravians, etc. who, from conscientious scruples, decline taking part in the war, to be "enemies to liberty and the rights of mankind—British subjects, aliens and cowards—who had no share in the declaration of independence, in the formation of our constitution, or in establishing them by arms"; which report is agreed to, as appears in the list of the yeas, by the same *William Findley, John Smilie, Robert Whitehill, Adam Orth, Nicholas Lutz, Abraham Lincoln.*

These men certainly are not in earnest when they talk and write of *liberty* and of the sacred rights of *conscience.* Their conduct contradicts all their speeches and publications; and, if they were truly sensible of their folly and wickedness in opposing the new government instead of trying to excite a civil war (in which they will bear no more part than they did in the late war with Great Britain), they ought rather to acknowledge, with gratitude, the lenity of their fellow citizens in permitting them to live among us with impunity after thus transgressing and violating the great principles of liberty, government, and conscience.

In the Centinel No. XI[3] we are told that General Washington (under God the deliverer of our country) is a poor creature with many *constitutional* infirmities; and that he has, from ambitious motives, united with the *conspirators* of Delaware, Pennsylvania, New Jersey, and Connecticut to enslave his country. Can human nature sink so low as to be guilty of such base ingratitude to a man to whom America owes her independence and liberties? or will the more grateful sons of America suffer the author of such a declaration to continue to insult their opinions and feelings? There was a time when the liberties of our country were at the mercy of this great and good man. There was a time when a defrauded and clamorous army, devoted to his will, and a Congress without power of credit would have rendered it an easy matter for him to have established a monarchy in the United States. But how nobly did he behave in this alarming crisis of our affairs. He composed the turbulent and punished the mutinous spirit of the army. He strengthened by his influence the hands of Congress and finally bequeathed, as his last legacy to his country, his parting advice to form such a union as would forever perpetuate her liberties.

In the same Centinel we are told, that *anarchy* and a *civil war* are less evils than the despotism (as he calls it) of the new government. It would be an affront to the understandings of my readers to controvert these two opinions. I shall only ask the author of them, whether he will risk himself, at the head of a company of his Carlisle *white* boys, in case he should succeed in his beloved scheme of exciting a civil war, or whether he would not rather shelter himself under a safe office, as he did during the late war, until the bloody storm was over?

The people of Pennsylvania have been so often told of *an appeal to arms,* when power and office (not liberty) were in danger, by the leaders of the old Constitutional junto, that they now regard the threat no more than the scolding of the apple women in Market Street, when they are disturbed by the country people on a market day. They remember how much these men boasted, and how little they did, during the late war. They know full well that not only wealth, but that numbers, virtue, courage, and military skill are all on the federal side of the question in Pennsylvania. They know, that the brave and tried militia of Delaware and New Jersey will not be neutral spectators of a contest in Pennsylvania, which involves in it the safety of a government, which they have unanimously and joyfully adopted. They, therefore, pity the poor madmen who sport these threats and anticipate no other consequence from their being carried further than the certain ruin of two or three seditious individuals in the city of Philadelphia.

In a republic, the majority should certainly govern. Now a majority have decided in favor of the new Constitution. The opposition to it after this, by a minority, is not only an attempt to establish an aristocracy, or a government of a *few* over the *many,* but it is downright rebellion.

But we are told, this majority have adopted a system of despotism. This is false, for the new government is the best bulwark of freedom that ever was framed in the world. But I will suppose this was not the case, and that the new Constitution was as bad as it is said to be. What then? The minority are still bound to submit to it; for it is the choice of the *majority,* and they cannot be *free* unless it be adopted. If it is rejected, then the majority, who are deprived of what they love and *prefer,* yield to the minority, which is contrary to every principle of democracy.

I wish the public creditors to look to themselves. The funding system of Pennsylvania is on its last legs. It cannot exist another year without convulsing our state. All the distress, oppression, speculation, idleness, peculation in government, and bankruptcies, not of merchants only, but of *tradesmen* and *farmers* (a thing unheard of before and unknown in other countries) are owing to the funding law. Pennsylvania has assumed a million and an half of dollars in certificates, above her quota of the public debt. It is only by adopting the federal government that this enormous, unequal, and oppressive burthen can be taken off our shoulders, and the state rescued out of the hands of speculators, sharpers, and public defaulters. It is, moreover, only from a federal treasury that the public creditors, of all descriptions, can expect substantial and permanent justice.

1. "A Citizen of Philadelphia" was a pseudonym which had been used by Pelatiah Webster ever since the late 1770s. This item was reprinted in the *New York Morning Post,* 30 January.

2. The three signers of the protest who spoke against the Constitution in the Convention were William Findley, John Smilie, and Robert Whitehill.

3. "Centinel" XI was printed in the *Independent Gazetteer* and in the *Freeman's Journal,* 16 January.

John Black to Benjamin Rush, Marsh Creek, 13 February[1]

That morning I left Philadelphia the Dissent of the Minority appeared in the public prints. I certainly expected, agreeably to our plan, that the reply and vindication of the majority would have followed in a few days; and signified it to my acquaintances at my return home. I have not yet, however, seen, nor heard of a single sentence published to that purpose.[2] This, you may naturally suppose, would produce some speculation—I can neither satisfy myself nor others upon the subject. In the meantime the Antifederalists are triumphing, as if the publications on their side were unanswerable. [Have you?], in the city, determined not to publish any reply? If so, I should be [glad?] to know the reasons. It may, perhaps, be best. Yet I cannot help thinking there is some attention, or, if you please, compassion due to those who, tho well-meaning, are in danger of being prejudiced against a good cause by the silence of its friends and the constant exertions of its enemies.

Some of the people of Franklin County (instigated, I suppose, by Messrs. [James] McClean and [Abraham] Smith) are preparing a petition to the Assembly to interpose their authority that the new Constitution may not be adopted.[3] Amazing infatuation! Whilst they are setting the state in an uproar for liberty, they themselves are, in fact, declaring that the Assembly are legally possessed of sovereign power and authority, and have a right to control the solemn decisions of the *body* of the people—consequently, that the people have, of right, no power at all.

1. RC, Rush Papers, PPL. Black, a Presbyterian clergyman, had represented York County in the Pennsylvania Convention and voted for ratification.
2. For an Antifederalist's explanation of why the majority did not publish any "reply and vindication," see Mfm:Pa. 288.
3. See IV:C below for the petition campaign requesting that the ratification of the Constitution "not be confirmed" by the Assembly.

An Address of Thanks, Freeman's Journal, 13 February[1]

An address of Thanks from a number of the Inhabitants of the borough of Carlisle, to the minority of the late State Convention, in general, and the representatives of Cumberland County, in particular.

Gentlemen: WE return you our hearty thanks for the magnanimous and spirited opposition which you made in the late state Convention, to that instrument of oppression, injustice, and tyranny, which was then the subject of your deliberations, viz., the proposed Constitution for the United States.

We assure you, that your conduct meets with our most cordial approbation, and fully answers the expectation we formed of you when we voted you to represent us. Altho we did not tie up your hands, by dictating to you how to behave or what side to take, nor did we preclude you from investigating its properties or discussing its principles in the most ample manner, according to the dictates of your own enlightened understanding, by extorting from you, previous to your election, or afterwards, any promises or engagements to vote for or against the proposed plan; this would have been treating you like machines or tools, and for such a purpose as this parrots and magpies trained to prattle would have answered the purpose much better than freemen. Nevertheless, gentlemen, the measures you have taken have fully justified the confidence we reposed in you, and comes up to our most sanguine wishes.

We, gentlemen, with you, deprecate the impending ruin, and deplore the unhappy fate of our dear country and innocent posterity, should this engine of slavery ever be established. We sincerely grieve to see the people of this state plunge themselves into the jaws of destruction, and sacrifice their dearest interests to gratify the ambition of a few selfish despots. Yet we sorrow not as those who have no hope. We are happy to find that a formidable opposition is made to it in some of our sister states. We rejoice in the expectation of your cogent arguments and spirited protest being disseminated through America, and rousing multitudes from their supine lethargy, and opening the eyes of others who are blinded with prejudice, and misled by artful men; we comfort ourselves with the hope that your example will animate such citizens of our own state, whose generous souls recoil at the idea of slavery, and who have not yet degenerated so far from their original principles as to be content to live in fetters, to oppose it. We hope it is not yet too late, although the chains are making they are not yet riveted on, and their Constitution is not yet "the supreme law of the land," and we flatter ourselves it never will. When liberty was the grand question, America combated an infinitely more formidable power than the partisans of the proposed Constitution; when her rights and privileges were invaded by one of the most puissant monarchs on earth, she bravely resisted the attack, and laughed at the shaking of their spear—she despised their menaces, and returned their threats with redoubled vengeance on their own heads. Will her brave freeborn yeomen, then, tamely submit to be circumvented or cajoled out of their freedom and invaluable rights by a few petty domestic tyrants? No, we are persuaded they never will.

It is, gentlemen, with the most agreeable surprise that we behold a very few country farmers and mechanics nonplus the great rabbis and doctors of the schools, who no doubt summoned in all the rhetoric, logic, and sophistry they were capable of on this occasion. We rejoice to see scholastic learning and erudition fly before simple reason, plain truth, and common sense. But though you defeated them in argument, they exceeded you in numbers; however, should the worst happen (which Heaven avert) this will be your consolation, that in the time of danger you exerted every effort to prevent the calamity;

you exonerated your consciences by a faithful discharge of your duty. Your names will descend to posterity with admiration and esteem, when those of your opponents will be loaded with infamy and execration. It will be said, These were the Demosthenes's, the Bruti, the Cato's of America, when your antagonists will be classed with the vilest tyrants that ever disgraced human nature. This will be a sufficient compensation for all the outrage and insult you have received from the senseless, ignorant rabble in Philadelphia, and the harsh rude treatment given you by such of the aristocratical junto as were members of the Convention; so that your reward is sure, suppose this Constitution should even be adopted universally, which we are persuaded will never be. The late glorious Revolution is too recent in the memory of American freemen, to suffer this. It may occasion a small conflict, but the cause of liberty is worth contending for, and we firmly believe there are yet numbers who will account it their highest honor to unite with you in the glorious struggle. That the same spirit which actuated you from the first appearance of this baneful instrument may predominate in the breast of every brave American is, gentlemen, the most ardent desire of your inflexible adherents.

Signed by order of the meeting, William Brown, in the chair. George Logue, Clerk.[2]

1. According to John Jordan, the "Address of Thanks" was written before the riot in Carlisle on 26 December but that the "commotions" prevented its publication in the *Carlisle Gazette*. Jordan therefore sent it to John Nicholson for publication in Philadelphia newspapers (Jordan to Nicholson, 26 January, IV:B below). By 17 March the "Address" had been reprinted in the *Carlisle Gazette* and in three Antifederalist newspapers: the *Independent Gazetteer*, the *New York Journal*, and the Boston *American Herald*.

2. Logue had taken part in the Carlisle Riot of 26–27 December 1787 (see Pennsylvania Supreme Court to Sheriff Charles Leeper, 23 January, IV:B below).

Hampden, Pittsburgh Gazette, 16 February[1]

The Constitution proposed for the government of the United States is of such importance to the present age, as fully to justify an honest and free discussion thereof. Yet the magnitude of the subject certainly requires that such as offer their sentiments respecting it to the public should themselves have a competent knowledge of its principles. It may be freely granted, that from a mistaken zeal in favor of that political liberty which was so recently purchased at so costly a rate, even good men may give it unreasonable opposition, but such men cannot reasonably be charged with sordid personal interest as their motive; because it is great and sudden changes which produces opportunities of preferment; but that class of men, who either prompted by their own ambition or desperate fortunes, are expecting employments under the proposed plan, or those weak and ardent men who always expect to be gainers by revolutions, and who are never contented, but always hastening from one difficulty to another; may be expected to ascribe every excellence to the proposed system and to urge a thousand reasons for our real or supposed distresses, to induce our adopting thereof. Such characters may also be expected to promise us such extravagantly flattering advantages to arise from it, as if it was accompanied with such miraculous divine energy as divided the Red Sea and spake with thunder on Mount Sinai.[2]

Sober-minded citizens, however, will not be intimidated with bugbears, nor will they expect magical wonders. They know well that it is only our industry and frugality that can pay our debts and make us respectable; that the utmost which the best regulated governments can do is only to protect and encourage our industry, and in some moderate degree, to correct luxury. All the friends to our country have wished that the powers of regulating commerce and levying imposts should be vested in the general government. Pennsylvania and most of the other states agreed by law to surrender these powers several years since, when Congress required it; the opposition of one state rendered a federal convention necessary. All in this state who oppose the proposed system are willing to invest the general government with all the power that ever Congress asked for or declared to be necessary. Many sensible patriots, from their earnest desire of giving sufficient federal powers, and their honest unsuspecting confidence in the Federal Convention, were well pleased with the proposed system at the first examination thereof, who have since entirely changed their opinion of it, having by a more strict scrutiny penetrated the mystery with which much of it is enwrapped, and understood the extent of the powers to be given up, as well as the highly dangerous combination of the legislative and executive departments. I make no doubt but this is the case with such of the inhabitants of the town of Pittsburgh, who, on the 9th of November last, published sentiments highly favorable to the proposed system.[3] As that is the only publication which hath, to my knowledge, originated in this western country upon the subject, I hope my taking some notice of a few expressions therein contained will not give offense to so respectable a town meeting. The expressions to which I confine my remarks, run thus—"We are of opinion that it is the result of much political wisdom, good sense, and candor in those who framed it." I shall address my attention chiefly to the character of candor, as it relates either to the Convention itself or to the system which they have proposed. Things are come to that crisis which justify a free examination and it is happy that to examine freely is not yet declared to be treason, or that the liberty of the press is not already restrained. Was it the result of candor? Let us first examine facts. The State of Virginia set the example and eleven other states followed the example in appointing delegates to hold a federal convention, and Congress recommended the measure. The delegates were strictly limited by the law of their appointment solely to the revising the existing Confederation and reporting the result to Congress.[4] In the meantime the people at large had great hopes and few jealousies, because the Convention had powers to brace, but not to destroy the Confederation; they had authority to recommend more extensive federal powers to the general government, but not dissolve the constitutions of the several states, and give ultimately the whole internal sovereign power to Congress, was as far from being included in their appointment, as it was from the expectation and wishes of the people. If they had strengthened the Confederation, and increased the federal powers; if they had clothed Congress with every general power belonging to the United States, would they not have done their duty? Would they not have fulfilled their trust according to the law of their appointment? Would they then not have merited the character of candor? But if it doth not appear that they have discharged any part of the sacred trust reposed in them, but that they, on the contrary, as far as in them lay, destroyed the very object of their appointment; whatever may be said of them otherwise, I hope the character of candor will be given up. But to be more particular; that honorable body, after entering into a bond of secrecy which, however plausible and artful the reasons might be which brought that measure about, was certainly not necessary at least after their business was brought into form; because the secret transactions of government, such as making treaties, conducting war, and the like, was not the object of their deliberations.

When four months was spent in mysterious secrecy, a system of a very novel and unexpected nature was transmitted to Congress, who though vehemently urged (by a number of such as were members both of the Convention and of Congress) to signify their approbation of the system, entirely refused to do it, and [----] [----] transmit it to the states without any [recomm]endation. With respect to such members of the Federal Convention, who were also members of the Pennsylvania Assembly, they, upon the designed last day of the sitting of that House, moved and urged the calling a convention for adopting the Constitution before the people could be acquainted with it, and they finally compelled a vote of the House by the aid of a mob, and imposed upon the people a declaration that it had been transmitted to them by Congress, whereas the truth is, it was not so transmitted until a number of days after the House had gone through the business and rose.

It ought to be noticed that, as members of the Assembly, those very men were solemnly sworn to preserve the [state] constitution inviolate, though, under the bond of that sacred oath, they were using the utmost violence to destroy it. I ask the advocates of this conduct (if there are any) if this merits the character of candor? If it doth, the term must certainly have changed its meaning. But call it what you will, the impartial page of future history will doubtless record the whole transaction taken together as an uncommon instance of insidious usurpation, fraught with a solemn lesson to future ages and rising nations.

But I shall proceed to examine how far candor is the genuine characteristic of the system, which was the result of such conduct.

The first clause of the Constitution assures us that the legislative powers shall be vested in a Congress, which shall consist of a Senate and House of Representatives; and in the second clause of the second Article, it is declared that the President, by and with the consent of the Senate, is to make treaties. Here the supreme executive magistrate is officially connected with the highest branch of the legislature; and in Article sixth, clause second, we find that all treaties made, or which shall be made, under the authority of the United States, shall be the supreme law of the land, and the judges in every state shall be bound thereby; any thing in the constitution or laws of any state to the contrary notwithstanding. When we consider the extent of treaties; that in fixing the tariff of trade, the imposts and port duties generally are or may be fixed; and by a large construction, which interested rulers are never at a loss to give to any constitutional power. Treaties may be extended to almost every legislative object of the general government. Who is it that doth not know that by treaties in Europe the succession and constitution of many sovereign states hath been regulated. The Partition Treaty, and the War of the Grand Alliance, respecting the government of Spain, are well remembered; nor is it long since three neighboring powers established a nobleman of that nation upon the throne and regulated and altered the fundamental laws of that country, as well as divided the territory thereof, and all this was done by treaty. And from this power of making treaties, the House of Representatives, which hath the best chance of possessing virtue and public confidence is entirely excluded. Indeed, I see nothing to hinder the President and Senate, at a convenient crisis, to declare themselves hereditary and supreme, and the lower house altogether useless, and to abolish what shadow of the state constitutions remain by this power alone; and as the President and Senate have all that influence which arises from the creating and appointing of all offices and officers, who can doubt but at a proper occasion they will succeed in such an attempt? and who can doubt but that men will arise who will attempt it? Will the doing so be a more flagrant breach of trust, or a greater degree of violence and perfidy, than hath already been practiced, in order to introduce the proposed plan? Do these inconsistent arrangements and contradictory declarations of power merit the character of candor? Of the same kind, and full as inconsistent and dangerous, is the first clause of the second Article compared with the second clause of the second section, we first find the President fully and absolutely vested with the executive power, and presently we find the most important and most influential portion of the executive power, viz., the appointment of all officers vested in the Senate; with whom the President only acts as a nominating member. It is on this account that I have said above that the greatest degree of virtue may be expected in the House of Representatives, for if any considerable part of the executive power be joined with the legislature, it will as surely corrupt that branch with which it is combined, as poison will the human body; therefore, though the small House of Representatives will consist of the natural aristocracy of the country, as well as the Senate, yet not being dangerously combined with the executive branch, it hath not such certain influential inducements to corruption. Doth this contradiction justify the character of candor? To the character of being inconsistent, I shall add that of being mysterious and hard to be understood, or at least very liable of being misunderstood. What reader will say that the other persons, three-fifths of which are to be taken with a view to taxation and representation, or the clause respecting the raising of a revenue from, or prohibiting the importation of persons in the first and ninth sections, is expressed with candid clearness? If slaves, or emigrant servants only are designed, why are they not so expressed? Candor certainly required a manner of expression suitable to the people's uptakings.

I find that most readers believe that the House of Representatives are certainly to consist of one to 30,000 whereas the truth is they are to consist of one to 50,000 and may be reduced to one to [?]00,000 if our future rulers see fit. The number of 30,000 was inserted out of compliment to General Washington, near the close of their sitting, who, being confined to his chair, had no vote nor share in the arguments, but was so much displeased with the smallness of the representation that he requested an alteration. They complimented him with a nominal change in the ratio, but not with an increased representation.[5] But passing other instances which repeated and attentive reading will discover, I would ask what is meant by the guarantee of a republican form of government to each of the states? Why not guarantee to them their own forms of government or free forms of government? It is but too well-known that under aristocratical republics, there is often less personal freedom and political importance enjoyed by the people at large than under despotic forms, witness, Poland, Venice, and other aristocracies. In the official letter from the Convention to Congress, they say that the proposed plan is the result of that mutual deference and concession, which the peculiarity of our political situation rendered indispensable.[6] It is well-known that all the states have by their own constitution reserved unalienably unto their citizens, the right of trial by jury, in civil as well as in criminal cases; and the liberty of the press, as well as restrictions against standing armies in times of peace, etc. Surely then, these rights to the arbitrary will of our future rulers could not arise from the political situation of the different states. Candor would have dictated a more honest reason. No doubt remains with me, but an aristocracy was the design, at least of those who prevailed so far as to vitiate a plan, the outlines of which I believe were at first well arranged and is yet capable of being made a good government, and I trust in the virtue of the United States that the dark and dangerous paths thereof will be properly altered and then adopted. But it will be asked, no doubt, who is this that dares so boldly to arraign the conduct and censure the production of a Convention composed of so chosen a band of patriots? To this I answer, that I am a freeman, and it is the character of freemen to examine and judge for themselves; they know that implicit faith respecting politics is the handmaid to slavery, and that the greatness of those names who frame a government cannot sanctify its faults, nor prevent the evils that result from its imperfections. Delicacy forbids that scrutiny into particular characters, which the boasting advocates of the new system seem to invite; and indeed the adding so much weight on the gilding of great names betrays a want of more substantial aid. However, I cheerfully grant that the names of Franklin and Washington would do honor to any deliberative body; their patriotism is unquestionable; but had those great men been the framers of the system, we ought not for this to give up our right of judging, but the case is quite otherwise. We know that General Washington, being President, was obliged to sign officially, whatsoever the majority resolved upon, let it be ever so contrary to his own sentiments; and though the general proceedings of that body are still a secret, we yet certainly know that he expressed a considerable degree of disapprobation of the system, by breaking through the established rules, in order to have it amended, in the important instance before mentioned. With respect to Dr. Frankin, it is now also well-known that he was all along in the minority; that after long labor the patriots of the minority procured some alterations to the better; that Doctor Franklin never approved of it in the Federal Convention, but even to the last expressed his apprehension that it would end in despotism, though he and several others joined it out of submission to the majority, and as the best they could obtain to lay before the people. Messrs. [George] Mason, [Elbridge] Gerry, and [Edmund] Randolph, who refused absolutely to sign the system, were also patriots who souls had been tried, and many such characters retired hopeless before the question was taken.

With respect to the majority, I do not doubt the testimony of a dignified supporter of the system that they were all, or nearly all, eminent lawyers; but I do doubt the patriotism and political virtue of several of the most eminently active of them, but it is not with the men, but with the plan to which they gave birth, we have to contend, and to contend with such a degree of moderation and firmness as will best promote political security shall be the endeavor of HAMPDEN.

1. "Hampden" was apparently William Findley. Thomas Scott stated: "Mr. Finley I am told behaves with considerable moderation, but he republished the Dissent of the Minority in the *Pittsburgh Gazette*. and published his Hampden, which I enclose you" (to Benjamin Rush, Washington, 3 March, Mfm:Pa. 476).

2. On 12 December 1787 Benjamin Rush declared that the hand of God was employed in the creation of the new Constitution in the same manner as "God had divided the Red Sea to give a passage to the children of Israel or had fulminated the Ten Commandments from Mount Sinai" (Convention Debates, P.M., 12 December, III above).

3. See "Pittsburgh Meeting," 9 November, II:F above.

4. The Pennsylvania act of 30 December 1786 elected delegates for "the purpose of revising the Foederal Constitution" (CDR:VI, C).

5. For the action of the Constitutional Convention on the ratio of representation on 17 September 1787, and for Washington's statement, see CC:75 and *Pennsylvania Herald,* 7 November, CC:233–B.

6. See President of the Convention to the President of Congress, 17 September 1787, CDR:VIII, A.

B. THE CARLISLE RIOT AND ITS AFTERMATH 26 December 1787–20 March 1788

On 26 December at Carlisle in Cumberland County a Federalist celebration of Pennsylvania's ratification of the Constitution was broken up by a riot, and the next day opponents of the Constitution burned effigies of Chief Justice Thomas McKean and James Wilson, the two principal speakers in behalf of the Constitution in the state Convention.

Depositions were collected and sent to the Supreme Court which issued a warrant on 23 January for the apprehension of twenty-one named rioters, including John Jordan, presiding judge of the Cumberland County Court of Common Pleas. The men named in the warrant appeared before two justices of the Court of Common Pleas on 25 February. Most of the men accepted the offer of a parole until their cases could be heard, but seven men refused and were jailed.

Shortly thereafter hundreds of Cumberland County militiamen, and a few militiamen from Dauphin and York counties, started for Carlisle to release the prisoners. On Friday, 29 February, some "Anticonstitutionalists" and others offered to provide bail, but the prisoners refused to accept it. Meanwhile, before the militiamen entered the town early on Saturday morning, 1 March, each militia company had appointed a man to serve on a militia committee. Furthermore, a delegation of five men from Dauphin County arrived in Carlisle. They met with the "new Federalists," and proposed "terms of accommodation." The "new Federalists" then met with the militia committee and reached an agreement to request the Supreme Executive Council to end the proceedings against the men named in the warrant issued by the Supreme Court on 23 January. The prisoners then consented to leave the jail, the militiamen left town, and on 20 March the Council instructed the Attorney General to drop the prosecution.

An Old Man, Carlisle Gazette, 2 January 1788[1]

As the riot on Wednesday last [26 December], and the burning of the effigies of two of the most distinguished characters in the state, in the public streets of Carlisle, by a mob on Thursday, has already made a considerable noise in the county, an impartial spectator desirous of furnishing the public with a just and true state of facts, to enable them to form a proper judgment of the conduct of the parties concerned—begs leave to lay before them the following representation, for the truth of which he pledges himself, and which will appear by the depositions of a cloud of reputable and respectable witnesses, in the possession of John Agnew, Esquire.[2]

About five o'clock on Wednesday afternoon, public notice being given by ringing the bell and beating the drum, a number of persons met at the public square, to testify their approbation of the proceedings of the late Convention, in the most decent and orderly manner. A piece of artillery having been brought to the ground, and materials collected for a bonfire; a number of men armed with bludgeons came in regular order from one quarter of the town, while others sallied forth from different streets armed in the same manner. Major James A. Wilson (having been appointed with two other gentlemen, to make the necessary arrangements for the occasion), was preparing to have the gun loaded, when he was ordered by many of the armed party to desist, and many threats thrown out against any person who would attempt to kindle the bonfire; to which the Major replied, that those who were not disposed to rejoice might withdraw; and that he hoped people so pregnant with liberty as they appeared to be would not wish to hinder their neighbors to show marks of joy, when they were pleased. Immediately after a number of barrels and staves were thrown at him, one of which struck him on the breast. He then sprung forward to the persons who threw at him, and struck one of them with a small pine stick, to which a piece of match rope was fixed; he was then beat down by a number of blows from six or seven persons with bludgeons, who continued beating him after he fell. They would have taken his life had not a trusty old soldier thrown himself on the Major and received the blows aimed at him; a general confusion took place.[3] Mr. Robert Miller, Jr. was attacked by a person, who with both hands wielded a massy bludgeon, and while he was engaged with the first, received several blows from one who stood behind him. The persons met for the purpose of the celebration, altogether unprepared for such an assault (being even without walking canes), were forced to return. The armed party having accomplished their premeditated designs of preventing the public rejoicing, proceeded to spike the cannon, and having made a large fire, committed to the flames the cannon and its carriage, together with a sledge on which it had been drawn to the ground. They then sent for an almanac, containing the Federal Constitution, which was formally burned. Loud huzzas were repeated, with damnation to the 46 members, and long live the virtuous 23.

On Thursday at 12 o'clock, I understood that the friends to government intended to carry into execution their resolution of the celebration of the event from which the evening before they had been so violently prevented. I went to the place, found them at the courthouse armed chiefly with muskets and bayonets; they discovered every pacific disposition, but at the same time the most determined resolution to repel, at the risk of their lives any attack which might be made on them. A bonfire was made, and the ratification of the Constitution by this state was read, accompanied by the acclamation of all the people present, repeated volleys of musketry and firing of cannon.

I cannot help giving my praise to the good order and coolness and determined spirit with which the business was conducted, although the mob made their appearance in several places, armed with guns and bludgeons, and even came close to where the Federalists were firing the cannon, and used threatening language, which was treated with every possible contempt, and no violence offered to them. The Federalists remained 2 hours on the ground, testified their joy, with every appearance of harmony and good humor, and returned without any disturbance to their homes. Immediately after, a drum beat—the mob gathered—collected barrels, and proceeded to the courthouse with noise and tumult, when there was brought from an adjacent lot two effigies with labels on their breasts, THOMAS M'KEAN,[4] Chief Justice and JAMES WILSON the Caledonian. They formed in order, had the effigies carried in front, preceded only by a noted captain of militia [Joseph Frazier], who declared he was inspired from Heaven, paraded the streets, and with shouts and most dreadful execrations committed them to the flames. It is remarkable that some of the most active people in the riot of Wednesday evening, and the mob of Thursday, have come to this country within these two years—men perfectly unknown, and whose characters were too obscure to attract the notice of the inhabitants of this place, and others who but lately have stripped off the garb of British soldiers. I think it improper to prejudice the public by naming the persons concerned in these atrocious riots, as prosecutions are about to be commenced in the name of the state against them. Every lover of good order must lament the wound the dignity of the state has received in burning in the public street, in one of the largest towns in open day, the effigy of the first magistrate of the commonwealth. Proceedings of this kind are really alarming, directly tend to the dissolution of all governments, and must receive the reprobation of every honest citizen.

I was invited, being an old man, to spend the evening with the Federalists, at Mr. Joseph Postlethwait's tavern, where an elegant supper had been prepared. A number of the respectable inhabitants of Carlisle convened there and spent the evening with the most perfect harmony, good humor, and conviviality. After supper, the following toasts were drank.

1. The Federal Constitution.
2. General Washington, and the Federal Convention.
3. The states who acceded to the Federal Constitution.

4. A speedy accession and ratification of the Constitution by all the states.

5. The patriotic forty-six.

6. The president of the state.

7. The chief justice of Pennsylvania, and member of the late Convention.

8. The Hon. James Wilson, Esquire of Philadelphia.

9. Major James Armstrong Wilson.

10. An increase of the agriculture, manufactures, and commerce of America.

11. May the flag of United States fly triumphant in all the ports of the world.

12. Our friends in Europe.

1. The article is not signed, but the writer refers to himself as "an old man" as do those who reply to him. According to John Montgomery (to William Irvine, 9 January, printed below) "An Old Man" was written by "Mr. Duncan." There were two Duncan brothers in Carlisle: Thomas, a lawyer, and Stephen, a merchant. For a reply to "An Old Man," see "One of the People," *Carlisle Gazette,* 9 January, IV:B below. "An Old Man" was reprinted five times in Philadelphia, once in Lancaster, and thirty-one times from Maine to Georgia by 10 March (see CC:407).

2. Agnew was one of the judges of the Court of Common Pleas for Cumberland County. For attacks upon him, see "The Scourge," 23 January and William Petrikin to John Nicholson, 24 February, n. 3 (both IV:B below).

3. On 18 March the *Carlisle Gazette* reported that Wilson died at the age of thirty-six after "a short illness."

4. A former Constitutionalist, McKean aroused the bitter enmity of other Constitutionalists because he supported the Constitution. For instance, on 10 May Thomas Rodney was told that if McKean ever appeared in Washington County, he would be put to death (Mfm:Pa. 676).

John Shippen to Joseph Shippen, Carlisle, 3 January (excerpt)[1]

The paper I enclose will afford you news highly displeasing to every true well-wisher to his country—the riot of Wednesday, the 26th, and the address of the 30 wise men to the minority of the state Convention.[2] I cannot but commend and admire the reasonable and judicious reply of Major James A. Wilson to the bludgeon-bearing company, when some through anger and revenge against the victorious Federalists, and others, who knew nothing about the Constitution, thro vain and puffed-up ideas of their own strength and courage, all marched forward under honorable arms, headed by a noble captain, who being a clerk of the meeting, was inspired from Heaven, who all, pretending to be filled with liberty, strove to prevent the praiseworthy rejoicers from showing marks of joy and gladness at the adoption of the Federal Constitution in this their state. I wish them not a corporal, but a mental punishment; that they may be brought to a sense of their foolishness; that they may hide their faces with shame at the thoughts of their madness; that they may repent of their wickedness, and sin no more; and that this their example may be [a] lesson to them and to posterity in deterring them from folly and madness, and be the mean of preserving them to wisdom and prudence in hereafter actions.

I am convinced *(by indubitable demonstration)* that the upright, honorable, virtuous, and judicious 46 will in history attract the eyes of praise and approbation, while on the other hand, the self-interested 23 and the self-conceited 30, will allure those of censure and contempt.

This conduct of the Antifederalists here will not, I think or at least I hope, be imitated by any county throughout the 12 states.

1. RC, Shippen Papers, PHi. John Shippen was a student at Dickinson College in Carlisle. His father, Joseph, was a judge in Lancaster County.

2. Shippen enclosed the *Carlisle Gazette,* 2 January, which contained "An Old Man" (printed immediately above) and "An Address to the Minority of the Convention," 2 January, IV:A above.

One of the People, Carlisle Gazette, 9 January

According to John Jordan, presiding judge of the Court of Common Pleas, who was named as one of the rioters, a single person was the author of "One of the People," "The Scourge" (printed below), and of an Antifederalist pamphlet (to John Nicholson, 26 January, IV:B below). The author of the pamphlet, published in Carlisle in April with the title *The Government of Nature Delineated . . .* (Mfm:Pa. 661), was William Petrikin (John Montgomery to William Irvine, Carlisle, 27 April, Mfm:Pa. 662). Petrikin's personal letters are eloquent but written without regard for spelling, punctuation, or capitalization (see his letter to John Nicholson, 24 February, printed below). It is evident that his newspaper articles and pamphlet were "edited," although whoever edited his writing did not tamper with his vigorous style.

Petrikin, an immigrant from Scotland, was a tailor in Carlisle. Evidently he was also a landowner, since the warrant issued for the apprehension of the rioters listed him as a "yeoman." Petrikin was one of the seven men who refused bail and insisted on staying in jail from 25 February to 1 March when an agreement was reached to request the Supreme Executive Council to drop the prosecution of all the rioters.

AN OLD MAN, who pretends to be an impartial spectator, has taken upon him to furnish the public with a state of the facts, respecting what he calls "the riot on Wednesday the 26th of December last; as also of the burning the effigies of two of the most distinguished characters in the state."[a] The vein of misrepresentation and falsehood that runs through this production renders its legitimacy very dubious. From its complexion and features it appears to be the brat of some attorney, who durst not father it himself; therefore procured the old sage to act as sponsor. However, as his respectableness has pledged himself for the truth of what is there represented, I shall consider him as the parent, and treat him accordingly. After having pledged himself for the truth of what he represents, he says, "About 5 o'clock on Wednesday afternoon, public notice being given by ringing the bell, etc." But I would ask his gravity, if a town meeting was called to consult the people, whether they approved of the measure or not? Without this precaution, their public notice was to no purpose. It is unknown to the borough charter, and therefore the intended rejoicers were an unhallowed riotous mob. This impartial spectator has neglected to take notice of a subscription paper that was handed about the same day, binding the subscribers to illuminate their windows, with a menace, that such windows as would not be illuminated should be broken. This was one great cause which induced the people to oppose the rejoicing; and an order of time ought to have been narrated before the ringing of the bell, etc. if the spectator had acted an impartial part; but perhaps the old man was not trusted with the secret; for tho a very good spy, he may be a bad secretary. A man cannot be expected to possess talents suitable to every sphere of life. It is necessary to observe as we go along, that when it was remonstrated to the intended rejoicers, by a number of respectable inhabitants in the most peaceable manner, that their conduct was contrary to the minds of three-fourths of the inhabitants, and must therefore produce bad consequences if they persisted; their reply was, "They would fire the cannon in spite of any who would oppose them; and if they would not clear the way, they would blow them up in the air." Such imperious language was too grating for the ears of freemen, and produced a short conflict which ended in the total rout of the new Federalists. The old sage further says, "that three gentlemen were appointed to make the necessary arrangements"; in this business they employed a certain John Rinn, and promised him five shillings for his service, but ran away without paying him; to revenge which he collected such of the rabble as the intended rejoicers had gathered together to assist them in hauling the cannon from Mr. Forster's tavern to the courthouse (but deserted them when they were defeated), and with their assistance burnt the sledge and cannon carriage, contrary to the express prohibition of such of the inhabitants who opposed the rejoicing as were then present. This old man says, "The persons met for the purpose of the celebration were altogether unprepared for such an assault, being even without walking canes." True, but they had much more formidable weapons, viz., muskets and fixed bayonets and bludgeons, so that all the preparation they wanted was spirit and courage (Major James A. Wilson excepted) for they had weapons, and numbers more than sufficient. He says again, "that loud huzzas were repeated, with damnation to the 46 members, etc." Here his gravity has pledged himself for a palpable falsehood; for no such words were used as "damnation to the 46 members."

He again adds, "that the friends of government intended on Thursday at 12 o'clock to carry into execution their resolution of rejoicing." Why the old man cannot be serious! What spirit possessed him, when he called them friends to government? Pray what government do they befriend? They are determined enemies to the government of Pennsylvania, to the Confederation of the United States, and to every government that ever existed in the world (a despotism excepted). The government which they are so enthusiastically fond of is as yet an ideal phantom, a chimera, a mere theory detested and execrated by every true friend to government. He again tells us, "he went to the courthouse, found them armed, chiefly with guns and bayonets, that they discovered every pacific disposition, but at the same time, the most determined resolution to repel at the risk of their lives, any attack which might be made on them." What a palpable contradiction is this, "they were armed with guns and bayonets" (he ought to have added, they were loaded with powder and musket ball, as has been proven on oath) "determined to repel all who should oppose them at the risk of their lives, and at the same time to discover every pacific disposition." I appeal to common sense, if they could possibly have discovered a more hostile disposition; however their disposition appeared more pacific upon hearing the militia drum beat. They immediately left the ground, after firing three discharges of cannon; whereas their original declaration was, that if the devil should come from hell to oppose them, they would fire thirteen. Our old man again says, "although the mob made their appearance in several places and used threatening language which was treated with every possible contempt, and no violence offered to them." Was it not violence to draw a sword, and present a loaded gun and fixed bayonet at an unarmed man, for no other reason, than treating them with a little irony, which it was difficult for any person of a moderate share of vivacity to forbear on this occasion; for the whole transaction had every appearance of a funeral ceremony awkwardly performed, but not the least resemblance of rejoicing. He further tells us, "there are prosecutions about to be commenced in the name of the state, against the persons whom he is pleased to call rioters." Tis very well to be prepared, but would advise, that the prosecutions be deferred, until the new Federal Constitution is adopted, where they may have a trial at a federal court, without the detestable interference of a jury. He says again, "that every lover of good order must lament the wound, the dignity of the state has received, in burning etc. the effigy of the first magistrate of the commonwealth." This is the first time I heard of this transaction, I presume it owes its origin to the inventive genius of the old man; for my part I took His Excellency Doctor Franklin to be the first magistrate of the commonwealth; and I never so much as heard a reproachful word spoke of him. But perhaps he meant the Chief Justice, to whom no indignity was offered in his judicial character, but his conduct in the late Convention has given the State a much greater wound, and justly merits the resentment of the People. The old man observes, "it is remarkable that some of the most active people in the riot of Wednesday and the mob of Thursday have come to this country, within these two years, men perfectly unknown and whose characters were too obscure to attract the notice of the inhabitants of this place." Some of these characters, however, are so obvious as to be noticed with an envious eye, even by the old man himself, and several others of his party, but does the old man think newcomers are to be deprived of their rights as men? But in this his spirit is exactly similar to that of their darling Constitution, which has laid newcomers under many legal disabilities and given all the discourgement that it durst safely do, by empowering Congress to lay a tax of ten dollars on each immigrant.

The old man talks of some who opposed the rejoicing, that had but lately stripped off the garb of British soldiers; here he is mistaken again, but I suppose he means the wheelbarrow garb which Rinn, their artillery man, had so lately been stripped of.[1] He again exclaims, "proceedings of this kind are really alarming, and directly tend to the dissolution of all government." Now of all others, the new Federalists ought to be silent about the dissolution of governments, for they professedly avow the dissolution of all governments, and is endeavoring to establish an unheard of monster on their ruins. He tells us further "that being an old man, he was invited to spend the evening with the Federalists (or rather incendiaries) at Mr. Joseph Postlethwait's tavern."

What! has our impartial spectator degenerated into a palpable partisan, by his own confession at the banquet of wine? However he might have saved himself the trouble of the declaration, as any person who reads his narrative would have easily discerned his cloven foot without the help of spectacles; but it seems he was invited, indeed, it would have been the basest ingratitude of the new Federalists, if they had not invited their faithful spy, who had watched the motions of their opposers with such unwearied assiduity, that day and the preceding evening. I would recommend thus much to the old gentleman (if it is not profanity to call him so) should his vanity prompt him to father another bastard of this kind, to beware of inserting such palpable falsehoods, for mankind has not as yet refined so much upon good breeding as to pass them by unnoticed, out of deference to his antiquated genius. I shall therefore dismiss his gravity, with an old proverb, "old people are twice children."

> (a) One of them [James Wilson] is peculiarly distinguished for his cowardice and timidity in the day of trial, for his opposition to the independence of America; and for inventing every possible scheme to destroy the liberty of her citizens.

1. "Wheelbarrow garb" was worn by prisoners released from jail to work on public improvements and who used wheelbarrows. Prisoners accused of more serious crimes wore a ball and chain in addition, and were chained to the barrows.

John Montgomery to William Irvine, Carlisle, 9 January[1]

I hope that you had an agreeable Chrismas times & a happey new Year which more than your friends has injoyed in this place our myreth was interuped with tumult and wite a Statement of which youll see in the inclosed news pepars from Both Sides the one in this pepar is totley falss in many particlurs the federalist not Exspecting oposition did not Come prepared nor was thire a gun or boynet in one of thire hands Rhin was not imployed he was brought up by Barker and they two were the active person in Distroying the Canon Carrage one Fraiser a Captn spiked hir the old man aluded too in the peace signed one of the people is Mr. Duncan[2] the Effigie of the Chief Justics [Thomas McKean] was pretty well Dressed a good Coat but not black a pretty good hat & wig & Rufld Shirt the fellow who give the Coat will repent of his Liberality before the End of Winter as I am Certain that he will have occasion for it himself thire is no hops of accomadating this unhapy affair both parties are preparing for the Law the Deposn. taken by the federalists are sent to Philada what will be the Essue I know not but our Situation is Exsceeding—Disagreeable neaghbours [snubbing neighbors?] as they pass and not a word Spoken great pains are taking to inflame the mind of the Countray People and thire is now a great Majoritty in oposition to the new Constitution the pice in the 2d of this month signed by 30[3] are Chiefly Boys Calculated to intimdate the protest of the minority laid the foundation for all this Disturbance it is a wicked Divilish pice and will do more harm than the authours will or Can Cure we have formed ourselves in to a Committee with a Design to seport the Law. Peace and Good order and to protect Each other from outrage and insult

I have sean sevral numbers of the federalists I Esteem [it] highly I think it the Best wrote of any thing that has been yet Published we are told that writer is Mr [John] Jay but I Rather think that it is wrote by Mr [Alexander] Hamilton if I Had all the numbers I woud Endeavour to have them Republished in our news pepar we have no news from the westward genrl Butler is at pittsburge shall be glad to hear from You

1. RC (LT), Irvine Papers, PHi.
2. See "An Old Man," 2 January, and "One of the People," 9 January, both IV:B above.
3. See "An Address to the Minority of the Convention," 2 January, IV:A above.

Another of the People, Carlisle Gazette, 16 January[1]

The base untruths, the infamous falsehoods contained in the publication under the signature of One of the People, require a refutation, which would be unnecessary were the characters of the authors known to the public. A decent, a candid, and true representation of the conduct of the rabble, who interrupted the rejoicing Wednesday the 26th December, and burned the effigies on Thursday, was given to the public, and the authority of it depended not on the respectability of the writer, but on a proof of the facts; and those who doubted those facts were referred to depositions in the hands of John Agnew, Esquire. It depended then, not on an anonymous publication, but on testimony. The names of the authors were left with the printers. It was not the work of an attorney, nor the production of needy, obscure, and starving adventurers, whose precarious freedom depends on the nod of their numerous creditors, nor of a man who lives in the violation of every divine precept, and every moral duty, nor of one who has basely deserted a constitution which he approved by an uplifted hand in a town meeting, and who under the smile of complacency and benevolence conceals a black and most treacherous heart; and under the specious mantle of religion covers a depraved mind and the most detestable hypocrisy. It never was fathered by him, whom they basely attempt to calumniate under the appellation of an old spy. A man who despises their impotent efforts to injure him, equally as he does their persons or characters, and whose unblemished character I would no more place in competition with that of his calumniators than I would put virtue in competition with vice, honesty with dishonesty, integrity with knavery, or truth with falsehood. A contest with them I know is as if a well-dressed man were to engage with a chimney sweep in a wrestling bout, where if he threw the sweep, soot and dirt are the only consequences of the victory. It seems a matter of surprise to One of the People, that a town meeting was not called agreeable to the charter.[2] I never knew that the charter prescribed a mode of rejoicing, or that it was necessary to have a meeting of the borough, and ask their permission to be pleased, and for liberty to express their pleasure. I now proceed to state the falsehoods contained in the publication of One of the People. The first assertion is the most abominable falsehood that ever polluted paper; it is asserted that a subscription paper was handed about, binding the subscribers to illuminate, containing a menace that such windows as were not illuminated should be broken. To whom was this subscription paper handed? Who saw it? This is a tale fabricated to excuse their wicked, abandoned, and unprovoked attack—to catch the country whom they have through the whole of this transaction endeavored to delude and inflame, by the grossest misrepresentation and matchless untruths. A subscription paper did not exist. They say the intended rejoicers were remonstrated to by a number of respectable inhabitants; here are two falsehoods in as many lines. I dare declare to the public, that they are not amongst the respectable inhabitants of Carlisle, and that they are men equally void of credit, character, and understanding; that they came up in a most tumultuous, daring, and insolent manner, armed with budgeons, and their only remonstrances were desperate threats, their only arguments oaken cudgels. [John] Rinn, lately released from his chains at the wheelbarrow, it is asserted was hired to assist the party who attempted to rejoice, and from revenge, as they had run off without paying him, had gathered the rabble, burned the carriage of the cannon, and placed the cannon in the flames. Do not act so ungratefully by your best friend as to give him up; his valiant and faithful services in your cause deserve a better return, for his worthy keeper instilled your glorious principles into his patriotic breast. He caught a spark of that sacred fire of liberty, which, when it explodes, destroys promiscuously its friends and enemies; and when the Constitution was burned, he declared that he never would part with his dear-bought liberty. But then to disown your guide and general, for shame! for shame! Do not add the crime of ingratitude to that of lying, for if you thus desert him, ________ and ________ and must be left out of the catalogue of your adherents.

When you say that Rinn collected the rabble and burnt the carriage of the cannon, if you mean yourselves, I readily subscribe to it; for when you were collected, you contained the body of the rabble of this place. That Rinn was one of the blessed freemen and respectable inhabitants who remonstrated with clubs, burnt the carriage, and put in the flames the cannon is an indubitable truth. It is a fact in testimony, that one of their party spiked the cannon, and this was justified by their declaration that the cannon was the property of the United States, that what belonged to the United States belonged to the People;[3] that they were the People, and had consequently a right to burn the carriage and spike the cannon; that is, the vile rabble of Carlisle had a right to destroy the public property, or convert it to their own use, as was done in this instance with some of the iron of the cannon. It is said that the people who came to rejoice were armed with muskets, bayonets, and bludgeons; this like the rest of their assertions is totally false, for at the time of their rout they had neither musket, bayonet, nor bludgeon. After their rout, indeed, one person returned with a musket and bayonet and kept the whole mob at bay. Here comes the strangest of all assertions, that the Federalists had numbers more than sufficient, if they had but resolution to have repelled their attack. The writer who has made use of one proverb should have recollected another, "That liars should have good memories." He should have recollected, that a little above he had said, "that the opponents to the rejoicing, were three-fourths of the inhabitants." Truth is consistent; it appears strange that this inconsistency should have remained uncorrected; one might have expected it from the pens of its vile and contemptible composers.

But when it came forth from the wise, the learned, and the venerable committee met in secret conclave at the Lamb, better things were to have been looked for. The charge of want of courage in the Federalists, one would be led to imagine that their adversaries possessed that virtue in a high degree. Yes, their conduct on that glorious field gives them a claim to some pretensions. It certainly was a bold heroic and glorious achievement for twenty men armed with bludgeons to beat down one unarmed man. Ye, worthy captains who headed the victorious band, after the toils of that ever-memorable day, you may repose yourselves in peace, in quiet, lay aside the bloody acts of war, and suffer your well-tried swords to rest in their peaceful scabbards. Believe me noble sirs, it was an exploit worthy your martial genius, and that posterity will mention with applause and veneration your names, when those of Alexander and Caesar shall be forgotten. But this man of the people advances to Thursday, he denies that the Federalists are friends to government; if a submission to the laws and support of civil authority constitute a friend to government, then they are the friends to government; but if a declaration that if the laws are executed, the jail will be pulled down and the town reduced to ashes constitute a real friend to government, then most certainly their adversaries are entitled to that honorable appellation.

It is admitted by the Federalists that they did assemble at the public square; that they were armed with muskets and bayonets; that they had balls in their pockets and cartouches; that there were several discharges of the cannon and firings of musketry; and I can assure the world that they were not prevented by fear, from firing the cannon thirteen times. They gave but a discharge for each of those states who had acceded to Constitution; they remained on the ground two hours; it was some time before they could unspike the gun. The ratification was read—every countenance beamed with joy, gladness, and happiness, except those of a few worthless ragamuffins, who were made drunk for the purpose of burning the effigies. The contempt displayed by the men under arms must have grated their leaders. One cub insulted a young gentleman and provoked him so far as to lay his hand on his sword, but he immediately staggered off. This is the man of vivacity, who treated them with a little irony—he is certainly a young man of great vivacity, but his natural vivacity, on this occasion, must have been increased by the artificial vivacity of New England rum. The drum of the mob had not beat until the Federalists left the ground. One of the captains had not slept off his night's drunkenness; the other was unfit to appear, as he had provoked a Federalist to bung his eyes on Wednesday evening. The vapor about the beating of the drum resembles the declaration of one of the partisans when the cannon was in the fire, "Damn the cannon, if I was not afraid of breaking my stick, O how I could beat it." One of the People says, that a pacific disposition and determined resolution are palpable contradictions. I think not. A man might possess a very pacific disposition, and at the same time take his life, if he attempted to burn his house, to rob, or to assassinate him. The whole transaction, they say, had the appearance of a funeral ceremony. If they allude to the rejoicing, it is false, if to a meeting of a knot of their demagogues at a spunging house upon the first intelligence of ratification, it may be true, for they held down their disappointed and disconsolate heads and mourned with bitterness, the ruin, the destruction of that anarchy and confusion, which raised them to any kind of consequence; they lamented the loss of their beloved popularity, and shed tears at sinking again into that state of insignificance and contempt, which nature intended they should occupy. This sagacious writer denies that the Chief Justice is the first magistrate of the state; the person from whom he received this information must have derived his law knowledge from being some bum bailiff, or perhaps have disgraced the more dignified office of a justice of the peace. But let me inform him, that the Chief Justice is the first judicial magistrate in the state, and the vile subterfuge of burning him, not as Chief Justice, but as a member of the Convention, will not serve their turn. The label affixed to his breast was in these words, "THOMAS M'KEAN, Chief Justice," and their conduct is approved by the authors of their contemptible and scurrilous justification; for they have the audacity to declare, that his conduct in the Convention has given the state a greater wound—a greater wound than he has given the state in his judicial character is the obvious meaning; and that he surely merits the resentment of the people, that is, the mob have done right in burning his effigy. But it seemed the old man looked with an envious eye, upon the rising consequence and dignity of the newcomers (some of the newcomers are respectable characters, and reprobate the conduct of their apostate countrymen); poor old man, he must be envious indeed! What qualities and possessions he envies them for, I wish the public had been informed. He would scarcely wish to barter respect for contempt; good report for infamy; an unembarrassed situation for poverty. Old as he is, he is not reduced to that state of dotage. There is some reason in their opposition to the proviso in the Constitution, which requires a residence of fourteen years, as a qualification for the President of the United States. Had the Federal Convention known, that in Carlisle there lived persons who possessed the understanding and abilities of a Solon or a Lycurgus, a Montesquieu or an Adams, they would, unless they had beheld them with the envious eye of the old man, have made a reservation for those enlightened men, who have since the Revolution honored America with their habitations, and chosen Carlisle as the spot on which to commence their political career. If the representation of the 9th of January was true, then those people may be under no apprehension from a prosecution, but if it contained not one syllable of truth, then they may justly tremble! So conscious of the latter being the case were their four counselors (perhaps secret instigators) that they, with the most anxious solicitude, pressed the justice [John Agnew] before whom the depositions were taken to destroy them and bury the whole transaction in oblivion; and accompanied their request with a menace, that if this was not done, Carlisle might be laid in ashes. Had this the appearance of that innocence which they now proclaim to the world [---] [---] [---] [---] the terror of guilt, and dread of punishment; this insidious proposition was spurned at with contempt by the upright magistrate.

They have now fled to stubborn impudence, and infamous, unhallowed falsehoods as the last presage of guilt. The threat in the concluding paragraph is most despicable. They know or might have known the authors by applying to the printers. The reputation of the authors is safe, for their account contained nothing but the truth, and as for any other safety they are not very solicitous. The public are requested to lend an ear to a publication, every line of which contains an untruth; but if a doubt of the truth of the first account remains in their mind, to remove the doubt by a candid inquiry, by reading the depositions in the hands of John Angew, Esquire, who will readily grant them that permission.

1. John Montgomery commented upon the 16 January issue of the *Gazette*: "thire is nothing but Stuff in it when our Bickering will be over I Know not for they are Violent on Both Sides" (to William Irvine, 19 January, RC[LT], Mfm:Pa. 346).
2. Carlisle was an incorporated borough.
3. A United States military depot and arsenal, Carlisle Barracks, had been located in Carlisle since the War for Independence.

Pennsylvania Supreme Court to Sheriff Charles Leeper, 23 January[1]

The Commonwealth of Pennsylvania To [Charles] Leeper, Esquire, Sheriff of the County of Cumberland.

Whereas, information is given to the Honorable William Augustus Atlee, Jacob Rush, and George Bryan, esquires, justices of our Supreme Court of the said commonwealth, That John Jordan of the borough of Carlisle in the county of Cumberland aforesaid esquire, William Petriken of the same county yeoman, Samuel Gray of the same county yeoman, Joseph Young of the same county yeoman, Mathew Allison of the same county yeoman, William Barker of the same county yeoman, Thomas Briceland of the same county yeoman, George Logue of the same county yeoman, James Wallace of the same county yeoman, John Steel of the same county yeoman, Joseph Steel of the same county yeoman, John Rine of the same county yeoman, Joseph Frazier of the same county yeoman, Andrew Steel of the same county yeoman, James Lamberton of the same county yeoman, Samuel Grier of the same county yeoman, Bartholomew White of the same county yeoman, Thomas Dixon of the same county yeoman, Samuel Stewart of the same county yeoman, John Rhea of the same county yeoman, and John Wren of the same county yeoman at the borough of Carlisle in the county of Cumberland aforesaid on Wednesday the twenty-sixth day of December now last past in a riotous, routous, and unlawful manner, armed with sticks, staves, and clubs, did assemble themselves and meet together to the great terror and disturbance of the inhabitants of the said borough of Carlisle and then and there in a riotous, routous, and unlawful manner did assault, beat, and wound James Armstrong Wilson of the same county esquire and Robert Miller the younger of the said county yeoman and divers others of the citizens and inhabitants of the said commonwealth then and there being to the great injury of the persons so by them assaulted and beaten, to the great terror, annoyance, and disturbance of the citizens and inhabitants of the said borough of Carlisle and against the peace and dignity of the said commonwealth. These are therefore in the name of the said commonwealth to require and command you forthwith to apprehend the said John Jordan, William Petricken, Samuel Gray, Joseph Young, Mathew Allison, William Barker, Thomas Briceland, George Logue, James Wallace, John Steel, Joseph Steel, John Rine, Joseph Frazier, Andrew Steel, James Lamberton, Samuel Grier, Batholomew White, Thomas Dixon, Samuel Stewart, John Rhea, and John Wren and each and every of them and bring them before some or one of our said justices of our said Supreme Court or any one of the justices of the peace of the county of Cumberland to answer in the premises, and that they may be dealt with according to law. Hereof fail not. Given under the hands and seals of the said William Augustus Atlee, Jacob Rush, and George Bryan, esquires at Philadelphia the twenty-third day of January in the year of our Lord one thousand seven hundred and eighty-eight.

1. MS (Copy), Peter Force Collection, Pennsylvania Miscellany, DLC.

The Scourge, Carlisle Gazette, 23 January[1]

JUDGES.—3, Chap.—21, v.—And Ehud put forth his left hand and took the dagger from his right thigh and thrust it into his belly, verse 22, and the dirt came out—My father chastised you with whips but I will chastise you with scorpions. First Kings. 19th Chap. 11th V.

The various and repeated defeats which that party who arrogates to themselves the appellation of federalists has received from the friends of liberty in Carlisle has almost tortured their souls to distraction; many schemes of revenge has been devised which have proved unsuccessful—Immediately after their last attempt to rejoice was baffled, they betook themselves to law for revenge; as this was their native region (some of the principal partizans being attornies) they assured themselves of an easy victory, and solaced their ravenous souls with an ample and speedy glut of revenge; threats, menaces and awful denounciations was now issued out; nothing less than gaols, dungeons, chains and fetters, were to be the portion of their adversaries, but their bravadoes were all visionary, their dastardly souls shrunk back into their own native cowardice, and their sanguinary hopes of vengeance was again disappointed. They then betook themselves to scribbling; here again they promised themselves the advantage, having the learned professions on their side, and by the help of their invention they fabricated a system of falshood and misrepresentations, and procured an old man whom they before employed as a spy to father them, which they published in the Carlisle Gazette; this provoked one of the people to draw forth the dagger of truth and thrust it into their bellies, which had the very effect he expected, and which naturally results from such causes, viz. the dirt came out. I don't undertake the disagreeable task of wading through such heaps of putrid matter from any design to point forth their nauseous qualities to the public; to suppose they needed this, would be an insult upon their understanding, but I am a pationate friend to liberty which makes me delight in tormenting tyrants; I must therefore give the dagger another thrust, for there is more dirt yet. The authors of the piece signed, another of the people, conscious that reason and truth detested their cause like the rest of their new federal brethren, betake themselves to personal slander, defamation and detraction, in order to vent their spleen and emit their disappointed malice: after a most virulent declamation by way of introduction they exclaim that "their piece is not the work of an attorney," in this I grant they have justly corrected one of the people, perhaps it is not the work of one attorney, I will believe it employed the heads of all the attorneys then in town, and all the auxillaries they could procure to compose it; and it certainly does honour to their literary acquisitions. They may without presumption vie with a Solon, a Lycurgus, a Montesquieu or an Adams; they add "nor of needy obscure and starving adventurers whose precarious freedom depends on the nod of their numerous creditors;" it is evident this alludes to the new-incomers; large quantities of dirt of the same kind is disgorged in other places—they say, that "they are men equally void of credit, character or understanding;" and again, that "the old man would scarcely wish to barter an unembarrassed situation for poverty." By all these dirty and malicious hints, it is evident that the old man and his party, envies the rising consequence of the new-incomers, notwithstanding they affect to deny it; for it is manifest that such of the new-incomers as is here pointed at, is in much better credit than many of their malicious adversaries, whose credit would not permit them to appear in Philadelphia this fall (Some of them has not gone down these nine, twelve and eighteen months, and some of their greatest nabobs these two years; we would despise mentioning such circumstances, were it not to contrast these unembarrassed characters with those whom they are pleased to represent as needy, starving adventurers, &c.) least they should have a disagreeable interview with some of their "numerous creditors." Who rose from a state of insignificancy and contempt to an appearance of affluence, at the expence of the public, and retains that appearance at the nod of "their numerous creditors." I wish the public to examine into the truth of these facts, and then say who has reason to boast of an unembarrassed situation. They further add, "nor of a man who lives in violation of every divine precept and moral duty;" perhaps the authors of the old man's adopted brat may be very pious men for ought I know, but if they are, they have certainly sworn to conceal it from the rest of mankind, but men differ in opinion about religious as well as civil matters, perhaps they account it divine precepts and moral duties, to print falshoods, threaten the lives of their neighbours, go to church once or twice of a Sunday to hear a solemn lecture on politics, blended with geography and astronomy, and interspersed with a few religious hints, and spend the remainder of the day in sacrificing to Bacchus; but it is evident this pious parade is not so much intended to embellish their own character as it is to defame that of another man's, but as his character is established in Pennsylvania infinitely above the reach of their malicious insinuations, and as Cumberland county hath already given demonstration to the world that they esteem him a better man than any of their fraternity; I shall therefore leave the public indignation to be their scourge; and only observe, that it is evident the dagger has made a large orrifice when such large quantities of dirt comes out. Yet notwithstanding this great fluxion there is more dirt yet. The next passage that represents itself is of the same diabolical nature, they say, "nor of one who basely deserted a constitution which he approved by an uplifted hand in a town meeting, and who under the smile of complacency and benevolence conceals a black and most treacherous heart, and under the specious mantle of religion covers a most depraved mind, &c." It is really astonishing the distracted frenzy that disappointed rage will drive men to. One man they stigmatize as a violator of every divine precept, &c. because he does not make a specious profession of religion—another they brand with detestable hypocrisy because he makes a profession of religion, and practices the duties thereof too, with much more uprightness, at least to human appearance (and we can judge no further) than any of his calumniators can pretend to; but the more good qualities he possesses the more obnoxious he is to their envenomed malevolence; they hate him because he is a man of honesty and integrity, and dare think for himself, and avow his principles; would he prostitute his understanding to act the deceitful Parisite; the cringing tool, or fawning minion to our pretended quality. He would with the greatest alacrity be admitted "into the councils of the great," but his magnanimous soul disdains such servile disimulation. They talk of a well dressed man wrestling with a chimney sweep; this is the comparison they draw between themselves and the people. Candid public: these are the men who endeavour by fraud and force, to cram down your throats a constitution which would immediately create them your rulers; they here present you with a small specimen of what treatment you may expect when their favourite constitution becomes "the supreme law of the land." The most contemptuous and degrading epithets, is given to all such as are not of their faction; no better names than "rabble, mob, chimney sweeps, ragamuffins, vile, contemptible, senseless, ignorant, suited only by nature to a state of insignificance and contempt, is conferred on such citizens as oppose the ambitious views of this imperious junto—Rouse then my fellow citizens before it be too late; act with a spirit becoming freemen; convince the world and your adversaries to, who wish to become your tyrants—That you are not insensible of the invaluable blessings of liberty—That you esteem life and property, but secondary objects; when your liberty comes to be attacked.

Teach these domineering despots who wish to rejoice, because they have a prospect of rioting on your spoils; that you perceive their designs, that you can both read and understand their constitution, & spurn it with contempt. They make a flourish about deserting [John] Rinn, and pray who deserted him. It is a certain fact that he was released from his chains at the request and intercession of our new federalists; that one of their champanions brought his pardon from Philadelphia,—That they hired him for five shillings to assist them, his good friends and benefactors, in carrying on their rejoicing; that they deserted him without paying him his wages, and that he, unmindful of recent favours, gratified his revenge by burning their hackney sled, and the cannon carriage. May it not then be retorted on them with the strictest propriety, "for shame! for shame! Do not act so ungratefully by your worthy friend, for whom you had so lately discovered such a kindness by procuring for him his dear bought liberty, his valiant and faithfull services in your cause, (for which you never paid him), deserve a better return; pray then do not disown your guide and Captain of Artillery. [I understand the passage in their first piece "that some who opposed the rejoicing, had but lately stripped of the garb of British soldiers," is pointed to a certain gentleman who belonged to a Volunteer Company in Ireland. (Men who bravely espoused the cause of liberty in their own country; nor will they desert it here). The gentleman alluded to, challenges the Poother Anatomy who circulated the insidious falshood of a British soldier, to step forth and prove the assertion, otherwise he will be looked on with contempt, and treated accordingly. If his Pootership declines this reasonable demand, he may expect the public will consider him what he really is, a blazing meteor, or mere sky-rocket; but as the public are already in full possession of his [---] faculty, and as he has formerly given a specimen of his vindictive, slanderous disposition, I shall dismiss him at present with wishing nothing worse to befal him, than he procured lately to a man of principles much superior to himself]; this would be adding the crime of ingratitude to that of lying, defaming and cheating the hireling of his wages."

It is denied by them that the rejoicers had muskets, bayonets and bludgeons at the time of their rout, I know not what they had at the time of their rout, perhaps they threw them away that they might not incumber them in their flight; but that they had them immediately before their rout is a fact given in testimony, where no party riden lawyers were admitted as inquisitors, nor was the truth partly heard, and partly stifled, but the truth, the whole truth, and nothing but the truth was required and stated with the utmost precision; neither was self-accusation extorted from the simple and ignorant, by terror and menace, so that any person who may be solicitous to ascertain a true state of facts, may have information from other depositions besides those in the "upright magistrates" inquisition; upright indeed! rather the dupe and creature of a domineering faction. They affirm "the drum of the mob had not beat until the federalists left the ground," the drum of the mob was their own drum, but if they mean the people's drum it is a palpable falsehood; it can be proven by more than fifty witnesses, that the people's drum beat around two squares before they (the federalists) left the ground.—They seem to be mightily chagrined at calling the intended rejoicers a mob, but why so much offended, they were only acting in unison with their new federal brethren in the city, whose conduct they [have?] [most?] cordially approved [and?] chearfully recognized the authority of the mob in Philadelphia, who broke open private houses, and dragged two of the members through the streets to the State-House, and then guarded the Assembly while they were passing the resolutions for calling the state convention.[2] The midnight mob headed by Jemey the Caledonian [James Wilson], who attacked the lodgings of the western members of Assembly and Council, on the night of the elections for convention men, was an upright, orderly association, and highly servicable to the federal junto. The mob who insulted the western members, when advocating the rights of the people in convention, was of great utility, as they served to keep the members who were advocates for the proposed constitution, &c. in countenance when reason and argument had deserted them[3]—In a word were it not for the mob the new constitution would not yet have been adopted in Pennsylvania; and our Carlisle rejoicers would have wanted this cause "to be pleased," and to assemble in a mobocratical manner, to express that pleasure. They further say "one of the captains had not slept off his night's drunkenness;" what more dirt yet, will the fluxion never cease. It is notoriously known that the person here alluded to, maintains a character the very reverse of what they represent; and that his opposition to the rejoicing, proceeded from that love of freedom which stimulated him, to expose himself to perils and dangers, during the late struggle for American independence; when their old man, and other ringleaders of these pretended federalists, basely sculked behind the curtain. They say, "the other was unfit to appear as he had provoked a federalist, to bung his eyes on Wednesday evening;" I expected shame would have deterred them from mentioning falsehood, as the federalist carryed the bung [for?] one of his eyes to the sham rejoicing [that?] day; and although the order appeared publickly, no such thing was to be [———] but every thing combines to prove "the dirt came out."

The passage in one of the people, which says, "that the rejoicers had weapons and numbers more than sufficient," seems to give the dagger a violent thrust, and consequently draws forth a great eruption of dirt; they endeavour to represent it as an inconsistency with the passage, which says, "the rejoicing was contrary to the minds of three fourths of the inhabitants;" but I would wish to know where the inconsistency lies; might not three fourths of the inhabitants be against the rejoicing, and yet not one eighth of them be on the spot to oppose it; very few of the inhabitants knew any thing of the rejoicing, (the spunging club at the glimmering attorney's excepted), until it was ripe for execution; so that only a few who catched the report by chance, were on the ground to oppose it. They say, "that some of the new comers are respectable characters, and reprobate the conduct of their apostate countrymen." Yes! such of them as are under petticoat government which is certainly a very respectable situation; I think those who submit to it, may be pretty easy what constitution is the "supreme law of the land." They say "the threat in the concluding paragraph is the most despicable; they knew or might have known the authors by applying to the printers." What! is it granted that the old man was not the author, then it seems, one of the people was right in his conjecture, that the piece was a bastard, and the old man only the adopting father, or rather grand-father.—Gentlemen, apply your own proverb, "lyers should have good memories," applying to the printers for the authors names we detest. We know it is the practice of our despotic opponents; but we contend for a free press, and abhor every thing that has the least tendency to shackle it. Neither do we employ pimps and spies to catch what intelligence they can, by obtruding themselves upon companies, where their presence is as disagreeable and surfeiting as the fluxion of dirt which is emitted by the authors of another of the people.

Thus I have so far dissected this putrid carcase, were I to take notice of all the dirt which it contains, I must transcribe the whole; but this is a task by far too laborious, disagreeable and nauseous.—Other persons pointed at will therefore excuse me, if I omit saying any thing in their behalf; it greatly accelerates our business in this affair, that we have the good-will, faith, and credit of the country on our side. We are struggling for their rights and liberties, as well as our own; which entitles us at least to their approbation, and (to the mortification of our adversaries), we have it in the most [line unreadable] course with the following new song, entitled,

The FEDERAL JOY, to the tune of
Alexander, hated thinking.

I. AWAKE my muse in copious numbers,
Sing the federal joy compleat,
The loud huzzas the cannon thunders
Announce their triumphs to be great.

II. Behold they march with curls flying,
Weary steps, and powdered heads,
Soften'd hands, with eyes espying
Crowds of whigs assembled.

III. But see they halt, & now are forming
Regular as veteran bands,
Breathing defiance, scoffing, scorning,
The low opposers of their plans.

IV. But now a crew for constitution,
Harshly then began to treat them,
Despising federal institution,
Nor aw'd by powder or pomatum.

V. From words to blows, those vile aggressors,
Rudely drove our harmless band,
Despoil'd the work of their hair-dressers,
Daring assumed the chief command.

VI. Now helter skelter in disorder,
Flew our heroes to their homes,
Happy their legs were in good order,
To save from geting broken bones.

VII. Lawyers, doctors and store-keepers,
Forsook their general in his need.
And from their windows began peeping
Viewing their valliant hero bleed.
VIII. But like veterans in the morning,
Appear'd in arms bright array,
Revenge, Revenge, they cry'd when forming
We ne'er again will run away.
IX. Full thirteen rounds for federal honor
Shall thunder loud, tho' hell oppose;
Display our new terrific banner,
To intimidate our scurvy foes.
X. Undauntedly three rounds they fir'd,
When lo a drum, most dreadful sound
Awak'd new fears, courage retir'd,
Paleness in every face was found.
XI. Again their shanks were put in motion,
With rapid strides they homewards stretches,
Or to avoid another portion,
Or s--t a second pair of breeches.
XII. And now the pannic being over,
When not afraid of club or rope,
Descends to law for to recover
Money for to purchase soap.
XIII. But not a souse for all their swearing,
Tho' shirt and breeches both were foul'd;
Liberties sons are presevering,
Nor will by fed'rals be controul'd.
XIV. And if those harpies seek preferment
Thro' their countries streaming blood,
They'll dig graves for their interment,
Or smother in the purple flood.

1. LT. In this same issue of the *Gazette,* another writer declared that the accounts which the *Gazette* had published about the riots, were "fraught with the grossest falsehoods," and asked the printers to stop publishing such material (Mfm:Pa. 354). The printers promised to discontinue the publication of items filled with personal invective (Mfm:Pa. 357).

2. See Assembly Proceedings and Debates, 29 September, I:A above.

3. For the election night riot in Philadelphia on 6 November, see II:D above.

John Jordan to John Nicholson, Carlisle, 26 January[1]

I received the petitions you sent me. I delivered the packets to the persons they were directed to. The petitions is signing very fast.

The new Constitution has a great many cordial enemies in this place. We sent down a state of facts respecting the affray that happened here on the 26th–27th of December last to be published in the Philadelphia papers but have received no certain intelligence whether it was done or not.[2] Our opponents who intended to rejoice, but was prevented, stated the facts in their way which we heard was published in Philadelphia.[3] In one of the enclosed newspapers, viz., that of the 9th January, you will see an answer to them signed One of the People.[4] In the paper of 16th, you'll see their reply signed Another of the People.[5] In the 23, our answer concluded with a song, signed The Scourge.[6] We wish to have them published in the city [Philadelphia] as it will show the public the spirit of opposition that takes place here against the Constitution. I could wish you would be so good as [to] send up a few papers with them when printed. The subscription paper for printing, which I have sent you thinking perhaps you would get a few subscribers in the city.[7] I think it would be a pity that it should not be published. The author is the same who wrote our pieces in the papers. It will cost a good deal to have it printed and our friends here is not of the richest sort. I really think the piece might be of use, however, exercise your own judgment, but please to write me immediately whether you think proper to apply for subscribers or not. I would have sent the manuscript but it could not be spared. The Address to the Minority was voted a considerable time ago and was originally intended to be published in the *Carlisle Gazette* but the late commotions breaking out about that time prevented it, and we have since agreed to have it rather published in the city.[8] I am requested to solicit you to have it published in as many papers as you conveniently can. We have it in contemplation to appoint a committee here to correspond with the committee in Philadelphia and other places. We wish to have intelligence from time to time what measures you think most advisable to break this formidable conspiracy. We are determined here to do everything in our power to retain that liberty without which life is not worth the enjoying. Our adversaries leave no method untried to break our spirit. They, in a particular manner, have endeavored to wreak their vengeance on me, but I regard them not. I understand they have sent an anonymous letter to Council setting forth that I headed a mob at the courthouse.[9] This is such a malicious falsehood as I thought none that retained the least regard to veracity or shame would have dared to assert. During the whole affray I was sitting in my own house drinking a dish of tea when being solicited to go and try if I could not do something to stop the quarrel. I went, but found the people quiet, peaceable, and without interfering, less or more, I returned home again. Notwithstanding I never considered the citizens who opposed the rejoicing a mob, but rather the rejoicers, as you will see by the enclosed newspapers and as depositions now in my hands prove. I could wish you would particularly send up some papers with the address by some careful person direct for the [---] to W[illia]m Blair, Sr., W[illia]m Brown, or myself. I have reason to believe that papers have been sent to persons here who have suppress[ed] them.

1. RC, Nicholson Papers, PHarH. Endorsed: "Recd Feby 2d 1788."
2. Jordan probably refers to the articles signed "One of the People," dated "Carlisle, Jan. 1, 1788," which was published in the *Independent Gazetteer* on 7 February (Mfm:Pa. 409).
3. "An Old Man," *Carlisle Gazette,* 2 January, IV:B above, was reprinted in the *Independent Gazetteer* on 9 January.
4. "One of the People," 9 January, IV:B above.
5. "Another of the People," 16 January, IV:B above.
6. "The Scourge" is printed immediately above.
7. The reference is presumably to the pamphlet by William Petrikin (see headnote to "One of the People," 9 January, IV:B above).
8. "An Address of Thanks," published in the *Freeman's Journal,* 13 February, is printed in IV:A above.
9. Jordan was charged with being a rioter in the warrant issued by the Supreme Court (see Pennsylvania Supreme Court to Sheriff Charles Leeper, 23 January, IV:B above).

William Petrikin to John Nicholson, Carlisle, 24 February[1]

Altho I am astranger to your person I am nevertheless intimately acquainted with your political principles I therefor Beg leave to inform you of some transactions that hath taken place here since you recd the accounts by Squire Brown from Mr. Jordan about three weeks ago a warrant came up here signed by Attly & Rush ordering the Shiriff to take 20 persons therin mentioned of which I have the honor to be one and bring them before a Justice of the peace to have them bound over to the Supreme Court to answer for a Riot comited at the Court-house in this Borough on the 26 Decr. last[2] this sir is for the opposing of the Federal Rejoicing the warrants has still lyen over till yesterday when we were notifyed by the Shiriff to appear befor the upright Majistrat (whose Character you will see Delineated in the Scourge)[3] and enter Bail or go to Jail the last is our full Determination the Country is almost unanimously on our Side and seems to wish for an opportunity to signalize themselvs I am almost certain that the Federalist by their mad fury is preparing afattle Blow both for themselves and Constitution. We are at agreat loss here for Intelegence you our friends in Philadelphia entirly neglects us we never hear aword from you we want advice and information in many cases but no one takes the least notice of us while our advarsary carrys on aconstant intercourse with their confedrates every where. The Pamphlet[4] for which we sent you the Subscription paper is in the Press and will be out emediatly we have engaged to pay the Printers 15 Pound for Printing 1400 Copies I am persuaded 3 times that number of them would sell befor the 1t of may when you see it I think you will say that it is both good Satir and good reasoning we would wish to know if any has subscribed for it in the City and how many the money for Printing must all be paid in hand before the Books is taken away. The Bearer is atrusty friend. The correspondent Commitee here would have wrote with him had they known of his going I hope you will not fail to send what Intelegence you know worth the communicating with him we have not heard yet whether our address of thanks &c[5] or any of our other peices have been printed but We depend if you recd. them you would not fail to have it done we are very anxious to see afew of the Papers up here be so kind Sir to take the trouble to send them by the Bearer afew of the Centinals would be very acceptable they are much admired here & we have seen one since the 9th[6] if business permit your writing a few lines would very much oblidge your humble servt.

P.S. I expect in short time to have the Pleasure of informing you what the issue of our going to Jail will be In the inclosed newspaper you will observe aspurious letter pretend to be wrote by the author of the Centinal[7] &c. but wrote in Carlisle as we imagine I could wish you would show it to the real author of the Centinal and request him to send an answer to it by the Bearer to be published here I hope he-ll treat the author according to his deserts we would have answered it here but were of opinion it would come best from the Centinal himself it is necessary to answer it as some people in the Country beleive that it realy came from the Centinal. Perhaps you could furnish us with a peice to publish by way of retaliation for the letter under the Carlisle head said [to] be from a Getleman in the Mercantile line in Philadelphia but I am certain was done in Carlisle—Both the Clergymen in this town are against us, but particularly Davidson[8] is our inviterate enemy, he declares he-ll leave the Congregation if the mob (as he calls them) that opposed the rejoicing is not prosecuted with rigor; the truth is he is an insignificant tool to the mock gentry here. John Chriegh is our most Malicious enemy:[9] the reason why I mention these, is, that it is supposed, you and some other of our friends in the City, have derected intelegence to them (they being formerly proffesed friends to the constitution of Pensylvania) intended for us, and they have suppressed it, and we been deprived of usefull information. The people here in this County and Franklin

County are forming Societys for the purpose of opposing this detastable Fedrall conspiracy: we almost every day here of some new society of this nature being formed, it is proposed to have agenral meeting in the spring, consisting of delegates from the sevral township and societys in the Countys of York Dauphin Cumberland and Franklin.[10] perhaps if some persons from Phia. and the lower Countys could be procured to meet along with them, their meeting might be of more extensive utility. the Society in the City might consider of this and send their opinion to the Commitee in this town, it is proposed to chuse the delegates at the township meetings in March for the purpose of chusing Township officers. the People in this County is so much enraged against the sticklers for new Constitution that agreat number of them have resolved to have no dealings with them either Social or Comercial this is bringing some of the Federal Merchants and Taveran-keepers to astate of repentance for the active part they have taken in its favour but whether their repentance will be unto life or unto death I shall not take upon me to determine

1. RC (LT), Nicholson Papers, PHarH. Endorsed: "Letter from William Petriken Recd March 5h 1788 per Geo. Hackett."

2. See the Pennsylvania Supreme Court to Sheriff Charles Leeper, 23 January, IV:B above.

3. The "upright Majistrat" was John Agnew. See "The Scourge," 23 January, IV:B above.

4. Petrikin's pamphlet, signed "Aristocrotis" and entitled *The Government of Nature Delineated. . . ,* was published in April by Kline and Reynolds of the *Carlisle Gazette* (Mfm:Pa. 661).

5. See "An Address of Thanks," 13 February, IV:A above.

6. "Centinel" IX was published in the *Independent Gazetteer,* 8 January (CC: 427) and reprinted in the *Carlisle Gazette,* 5 March.

7. One of two spurious letters attributed to the author of "Centinel" was printed in the *Carlisle Gazette,* 6 February. It was first published in the *Pennsylvania Gazette,* 23 January (Mfm:Pa. 366).

8. Robert Davidson, a Presbyterian, taught at Dickinson College. The other clergyman was probably Dr. Charles Nisbet, president of Dickinson College.

9. Creigh, a member of the Assembly in 1785 and 1786, was a trustee of Dickinson College.

10. For examples of such "societies," see "An Address to the Minority of the Convention," 2 January and "An Address of Thanks," 13 February, both in IV:A above; and Mfm:Pa. 403. For Francis Hopkinson's satire about the societies, see Mfm:Pa. 440.

Frederick Watts to John Agnew, Philadelphia, 25 February (excerpt)[1]

I am sorry to hear that the troubles in your county has not yet subsided; I was afraid it might be carried to too great a degrees of extremes; and for that purpose applied to Council for the direction in the case. They directed two of their members to call upon the Chief Justice [Thomas McKean], and to let him know that it was the wish of Council that the operation of the warrant signed by two of the judges of the Supreme Court might be suspended.[2] The gentleman seemed to be good humored, and said he would write to Judge [William A.] Atley and John Montgomery, esquires, of Carlisle for that purpose. I am sorry to hear that the Chief Justice of the state has been treated with so much indignity in Carlisle; but it is over now and cannot be helped, and I hope all your animosity will cease and forever be buried in oblivion. The gentleman, I believe, forgives their folly and thinks it beneath him to take notice thereof.

1. "Copy of an Extract," Watts Papers, PHarH. Watts, a former brigadier general of militia, represented Cumberland County in the Supreme Executive Council. He had defeated Robert Whitehill in the election for councillor on 9 October 1787.

2. Others also thought the warrant should be suspended. Walter Stewart declared: "The papers handed Mr. McKean will be laid by, as he could not be so very ridiculous as to blow up a coal which now seems expiring by investigating them, or calling to account any of the people concerned in the affair at Carlisle. It is now over, and the less that is said publicly on the subject the better" (to William Irvine, 30 January, Mfm:Pa. 380). See also Walter Stewart to William Irvine, 20 February, IV:C below.

Justices John Agnew and Samuel Irwin Explain Why Seven Men Were Jailed on 25 February[1]

Whereas, we understand that a report has been propagated in the country by some persons respecting the manner in which the following persons have been committed to jail by John Agnew and Samuel Irwin, esquires, viz., Joseph Young, Samuel Greer, Thomas Dickson, Joseph Steel, Bartholemew White, William Petrekin, and James Wallace, upon the charges of being guilty of a riot. We think it expedient to testify that the said persons, together with several others being brought before us upon the said charge, and being doubtful as to the direction of a warrant from the judge of the Supreme Court, whether it was in our power to investigate the said charge, and go into evidence thereon, to commit absolutely in case bail was not offered. We thought proper to signify that they might all go at large on parole until the 25th of March, to give us time to consult the Chief Justice [Thomas McKean] upon said warrant, but all the above persons insisted to have a trial, refused to give bail, altho they could have easily obtained bail; but they would rather go to jail than accept of a parole as others did in the like situation. We therefore conceived it our duty to commit them. The above is a true state of the affair. Witness our hand this 26th day of February, 1788.

1. *Carlisle Gazette,* 27 February. Reprinted: *Independent Gazetteer,* 22 March.

Six Prisoners Explain Why They Refused Bail and Were Imprisoned on 25 February[1]

Whereas a publication has appeared in the last Gazette, signed John Agnew and Samuel Irvin, in which our conduct is misrepresented in the most glaring manner; our own vindication, therefore, calls upon us to set before you a true state of facts; for the truth of which we appeal to every spectator who was present during the transaction. By the appointment of the sheriff [Charles Leeper] we appeared before John Agnew, Esquire, at his office on Monday last [25 February 1788] in the afternoon, who laid before us a warrant and a number of depositions containing the charge alleged against us. Upon perusal of the warrant and depositions aforesaid, we prayed a hearing or investigation of the premises, which, if granted, we proposed to exculpate ourselves from every part of the accusation; but this was positively refused. We then, with some degree of spirit, contended that the warrant required a hearing, there being no oath set forth in it, which we pleaded was absolutely necessary according to the constitution and laws of this state, before any person should be held to bail or deprived of their liberty. For this we had every reason to believe the Chief Justice [Thomas McKean] (who issued the warrant), had neither oath or affirmation before them at the time of granting the warrant, Thomas Duncan, Esquire having declared on his honor, at the late orphans' court, in a reputable meeting at Mr. William Rainey's, that no deposition had been sent down to the Chief Justice. We again pleaded that as freemen we had a right to an impartial investigation of the affair, but still the old cant was reiterated by John Agnew, Esquire that he could grant us no hearing. The only alternative was to enter bail or be committed, for he would not be browbeat. At length Samuel Irvin, Esquire arrived and retired with John Agnew, Esquire to a separate apartment, in order to consult what would be best to be done. On their return they proposed to write to the chief justices to know whether they would grant us a hearing or not; and in the meantime remain in the custody of the sheriff, until the 25th day of March next, and then appear to know their determination. Although we considered that the chief justices had no power to supersede our rights as freemen, yet we agreed to postpone it to the time proposed provided we were assured of a full discussion at that period. But this also was refused us. We then again demanded to be confronted by the witnesses. This being again refused, we said we would not engage to appear a second time, on the same warrant; but, willing to submit to the decision of his worship, our *mittimus* was then written, and we were about to be sent to limbo, when we made a demand of the prosecutors and witnesses being recognized to prosecute previous to our commitment. This legal request was obstinately and peremptorily refused. On this ground we refused bail and consequently were committed.

William Petrikin, Samuel Greer, Joseph Young, Joseph Steel, James Wallace, Barthol. White. Carlisle, March 1, 1788.

1. *Carlisle Gazette,* 5 March. Reprinted: *Independent Gazetteer,* 22 March.

The Release of the Prisoners, 1 March[1]

A narrative of facts, respecting the manner by which the prisoners were liberated from their confinement, in the gaol of Cumberland County, on Saturday the first of March instant.

It is presumed the public are already in full possession of the cause which gave rise to the following transactions, viz., the opposition made by some of the inhabitants of the borough of Carlisle to the rejoicing intended to be celebrated by the new Federalists, on the 26th and 27th of December last. It is already known that a number of depositions were taken in the office of John Agnew, Esquire with an intention to criminate the several persons who were active in opposing said rejoicing, on which depositions or other information laid before the honorable the supreme justices of the State of Pennsylvania, a warrant was issued charging the said opposers with divers unlawful acts, etc. and commanding the sheriff of this county to apprehend 20 persons therein named, and take them before some of the justices of the Supreme Court, or any of the justices of Cumberland County, to answer to the premises and be dealt with according to law. Some time after the sheriff received the warrant, and called upon the defendants, and informed them such warrant was in his hands; each person willingly agreed to appear at any time he might think proper before any magistrate of this county. He thought proper to appoint Monday the 25th of February last for them to appear before John Agnew, Esquire which they readily complied with. The warrant being read, which exhibited the charge of a riot against the defendants, who demanded that they should be confronted with the witnesses, and offered, if permitted, to produce sufficient evidence to exculpate themselves from the charge alleged against them, which was refused, as the magistrate was of opinion that it was not in his power to supersede a warrant issued by the supreme justices. In the interim a country magistrate [Samuel Irwin] arrived, who had been previously sent for by John Agnew, Esquire. After a short consultation, they came forth, and the country justice told the defendants that in his opinion the warrant admitted of a hearing, but added that he was determined not to act in the matter and advised the defendants to accept of a proposal made by Mr. Agnew, which was to remain in the custody of the sheriff unto the 25th of March next, at which time Mr. Agnew hoped to have instructions from the supreme justices. Seven of the defendants absolutely refused the proposal, unless they were assured of an investigation of the premises at the time mentioned, which was likewise refused. Bail was then demanded by the justice. The defendants answered they were conscious that they were guilty of no crime against the laws of their country; and as they were prosecuted to gratify party spite, they were determined not to enter bail on the occasion, but would otherwise willingly comply with the orders of his worship, upon which Mr. Agnew wrote and signed their commitment, and gave it to the sheriff, who conducted the prisoners to the county gaol. Immediately the country took the alarm on hearing that a number of persons was confined in prison for opposing a measure that was intended to give sanction to the proposed Federal Constitution. The people who composed the different companies of militia in this county thought proper to collect, and appointed to meet in Carlisle on Saturday last to inquire why those persons were confined, and at the same time determined to act agreeable to the opposition offered them by the rejoicing party. Accordingly about sunrise the bell began to ring, and the men under arms made their appearance from different quarters, who previously had appointed one person from each company to represent them in a committee, for the purpose of consulting on such measures as might be most expedient on the occasion. Previous to their meeting, five persons with delegated power from the people of Dauphin County had met a number of new Federalists and had proposed terms of accommodation. In one hour the new Federalists promised to give them an answer, at which time they accordingly met, together with the committee appointed by the different companies, who immediately agreed on terms of accommodation, and mutually consented to transmit a petition to Council, signed by a number of respectable persons on both sides of the question. They then agreed that the sheriff would sign the following discharge:

Be it known that I Charles Leeper, Esquire, Sheriff of Cumberland County, do hereby discharge from their imprisonment in the jail of this county of Cumberland, the following persons, viz., James Wallace,

William Petrikin, Thomas Dickson, Samuel Greer, Bartholomew White, Joseph Young, and Joseph Steel. Charles Leeper, Sheriff.

After the above agreement was ratified, the militia were marched under their respective officers from the public square to the jail, where the sheriff conducted the prisoners to the street. Having read the above discharge, they were restored to their former liberty with loud huzzas and a *feu-de-joie* from right to left of the companies, who then marched out of town in good order, without injuring any person or property, except two balls which was fired through a tavernkeeper's sign who is said to be a warm Federalist.[2]

It is with pleasure we announce to the public that the militia who appeared on this occasion amounted to about 1,500 men who are generally men of property and good characters, who all evinced both by words and actions, that they intended to persevere in every measure that would oppose the establishment of the new Constitution at the risk of their lives and fortunes.

1. *Carlisle Gazette,* 5 March. By 26 April this item had been reprinted five times in Pennsylvania and reprinted or summarized thirteen times in other states from Maine to South Carolina.

2. Probably Joseph R. Postlethwaite's tavern, a meeting place of Carlisle Federalists (see "An Old Man," 2 January, IV:B above).

John Montgomery to James Wilson, Carlisle, 2 March[1]

I beg leave to inform you that a scene was exhibited at this place yesterday, which it was apprehended would have been the first act of a tragedy; but which turned out to be a harmless comic opera. You have no doubt heard that about Christmas last the people of this place received the account of the adoption of the Federal Constitution by two-thirds of the Convention of this state. That thereupon, a number of the people, who believed that Constitution was well calculated to render us respected abroad, as a nation, and to secure tranquility, freedom, and happiness among ourselves on the most firm and lasting basis, resolved to testify their approbation of the vote of adoption, by the firing of a cannon, etc., at the courthouse. That they met there for that purpose and were interrupted by a number, who immediately made their appearance armed with bludgeons and made an attack upon the unsuspecting and unarmed Federalists and drove them off the ground; after having nearly killed one of them and much hurt another. That the next day the Federalists met again at the same place for the same purpose and prepared to repel any attacks which might be attempted to be made on them again. That the party who had made the attack on them the preceding day perceiving that it would be dangerous to renew it, appeared soon after the federal friends had separated and paraded the streets with the effigies of the Chief Justice of this state [Thomas McKean] and of Mr. [James] Wilson, which they afterwards committed to the flames. That complaints were afterwards made to a justice of the riot, assault and battery committed the first day. That the parties injured demanded a warrant from the justice against the rioters. That the justice being a cautious, prudent, and rather a timid man, transmitted the affidavits, which were made in the premises, to the judges of the Supreme Court. That two of the said judges granted a warrant to apprehend the rioters (it is presumed that the Chief Justice declined acting in the affair, because his own political character had been attacked next day by the same party). The warrant came up two or three weeks ago, directed to the sheriff [Charles Leeper]. The rioters had notice of it immediately, although no attempt was made, I believe, to take them for about ten days, during which time they had an opportunity of forming combinations, and it will appear that they instantly embraced and made the best of it, by riding, and sending their emissaries through the country inflaming the minds of the people by representing themselves as in danger of becoming victims in the cause of liberty, and for daring to lift up their voices against the most detestable system of tyranny and arbitrary power that was ever devised for the total and final destruction of freedom. Although the sheriff is by no means a decided character, I can hardly impute his improper conduct to corrupt motives—he asked the advice of every person and was too timid to act with firmness, and the advice of those to whom he applied was so various, that it distracted his irresolute mind. About a week ago he gave notice to *all* the rioters to appear *the same afternoon* before Justice [John] Agnew. Mr. Agnew, believing the affair to be of some importance and delicacy, requested the assistance of the three nearest justices. Justice [Samuel] Irwin attended—the others did not. Those named in the warrant appeared—they started some objections to the *form* and *effect* of it. The justices, being cautious, thought it proper to give the parties day until the 25 March in order that they might in the meantime apply for the directions of the judges, on the points in question; but six [seven] of the rioters refused to have the matter postponed and insisted on being discharged altogether or of going to prison. The justices told them they could not discharge them, therefore they went to gaol the same evening. Immediately the drum beat to arms and the bell was rung. A few creatures of no character and a number of the blackguard boys collected;[2] but not being joined by the party whom they expected, they dispersed in a short time—damning the fools, who would not accept the terms which the others had done, but had gone to gaol, where they might stay and hatch lies till they were tired. A party consisting chiefly of such boys and fellows of dissolute character went through town every night afterwards beating the drum, and information was given that in consequence of a preconcerted plan, riders had gone out to all quarters warning the friends of freedom to collect and rescue their persecuted brethren. Very exact intelligence was communicated from time to time of their proceedings. Meetings of the friends of good order were had where it was proposed by some ardent men to oppose the rescuers by force, and a plan was suggested by the adoption of which a dreadful carnage might have been made, among our misguided fellow citizens at the onset. Many lives might have been lost on both sides afterwards, and at least *parts* of Pennsylvania might have been involved in the horrors of a civil war;[3] but happily the most temperate councils prevailed almost universally—not to attempt to prevent a rescue—to avoid giving the most distant pretext of offense either by word or action; but to be in readiness to repair with our arms in order at a moment's warning, and to act under proper command, according to the contingency.

It was known that the people from all parts of the country were to be in yesterday morning to take the prisoners out of gaol; but on the preceding day, some Anticonstitutionalists of character and property, apprehending fatal consequences, came to town and, joining with people equally disposed to preserve peace and good order, entered bail for the prisoners; but the obstinate tools refused to go out of gaol until they were taken out by force of arms.

Yesterday at break of day, according to appointment and expectation, the bell began to ring, the militia armed and under their officers, from all parts of the county and a few from Dauphin County and from the Redlands of York County, came into town to the number of, I suppose, about five hundred; but I cannot, be very certain as to their numbers, as they made several ingenious military maneuvers to make their numbers appear as large as possible, to people unacquainted with such devices.[4] You will now naturally expect to hear that when so many people met, with minds highly inflamed and irritated by the numerous aggravating falsehoods which had been industriously propagated among them by designing men, they would not separate without committing desperate outrage or doing or suffering some mischief. You will therefore sincerely rejoice when I inform you that a few of their most intelligent officers met some of the inhabitants, some in favor of and some opposed to the Federal Constitution, and it being agreed that the prosecutors should request the Executive Council to recommend to the Attorney General to enter a *nolle prosequi,* and that the militia should return to their homes. They marched to the gaol where the voluntary prisoners presented themselves, and were received and conducted to the courthouse in triumph. There the militia discharged their guns and after they had again paraded the streets as they had done during four hours before from the time of their coming to town. They left town by different routes, without being guilty of the least mischief or insult, excepting what I shall mention respecting the printers.

Thus the hopes and expectations of the unprincipled and desperate wretches who have for some time past, from the worst of motives, inflamed the minds of the unsuspecting people, have been happily defeated. I have good reason to believe that the most respectable and the honest part of those who came to town yesterday, with minds highly inflamed, went home with very different sentiments; and I believe they now begin to look with their own eyes and to think for themselves. You may be assured that if these people are left to the dispassionate exercise of their own good sense, they will think rightly. The incendiaries well know this, and therefore it is a fundamental point with them to keep the minds of the honest unsuspecting men in a continual state of inflammation, by the most impudent declamatory falsehoods—and we all know that in this state of mind, the wisest and most upright men are very credulous and easily imposed upon.

Those who went so willingly and unnecessarily to gaol are only the tools of tools. I verily believe that they, and those here who immediately urged them on, wished and expected to foment a civil war. Happily their attempts, as well as the machinations of those at the bottom of this wickedness, have proved abortive on this occasion and will, I hope, be brought to nought ultimately. I must, however, do many respectable characters, whose minds were for some time greatly adverse to that Constitution, which most of the wisest and best men on the continent so highly approve of, the justice to observe that they seemed upon this occasion as anxious to preserve peace and good order, as any others. Upon the whole, seeming evil has often since the Revolution been productive of real good in our public affairs, and I trust that when the people reflect upon what a trifling and unnecessary occasion they were led to collect in such numbers (and many from a distance) at this inclement season of the year—when they become sensible (indeed some expressed themselves to be so before they left the town) how much their minds have been inflamed by groundless insinuations, they will in earnest think for themselves and act according to the dictates of reason—not the impulse of passions.

The incendiaries here have iniquitously attempted to set the country at variance with the town by asserting that the inhabitants of the town are enemies to equal liberty, and that they are in favor of the Constitution, because they expect to be enabled under it to make dependents of the farmers, who will be reduced to a sort of vassalage. Absurd as this falsehood is, the inflamed mind believes it as proofs of Holy Writ.

Thus, sir, have I taken the liberty of giving you a short and simple narrative of a transaction which may be variously represented. The party in Philadelphia, who by their incendiary publications, and by their deputies in this county, fomented the spirit of jealousy among the people,[5] may enlarge upon it in such varied and aggravated forms as they may think most likely to excite opposition or strengthen the opposition which exists in the two neighboring southern states.

The Antifederal Party will publish their account of it here in such manner as they think best calculated to answer their own purposes, and the printers must, upon this occasion, publish whatever that party sends them, for reasons of which the bearer can give you full information. He will tell you that the printers [Kline and Reynolds] were sent for yesterday by some of the leaders of that party, accused of partiality, and their printing office threatened. Any account of the transaction which we could publish here would be disregarded. It is for this reason that I have furnished you with these materials of which you can make such use as you think proper in the Philadelphia papers; only I wish that it may not appear as if the account came from any *resident* in this place, while the people are in their present temper of mind. The bearer can give you such further information, as will enable you to publish a true and accurate account of the transaction, which I wish to see published in your papers immediately, for obvious reasons. I need not mention that the foregoing hints are not fit for publication in their present form.

Had the warrant been executed when it came up, I am satisfied by reasons, which professional duty forbids me to mention, that the rioters would all have given bail.

1. RC(?), James Wilson Correspondence, James A. Montgomery Collection, PHi. This undated and unsigned letter is in the handwriting of John Montgomery, who marked it "Confidential." The content of the letter reveals that it was written on 2 March, the day after the prisoners left the jail.

2. "Veritas" described these individuals as "desperate and abandoned fellows" and "men of infamous characters and bankrupt fortunes" (*Federal Gazette*, 22 March, Mfm:Pa. 556). Richard Butler, however, claimed that some rioters were men of property (to William Irvine, Philadelphia, 11 March, Mfm:Pa. 505).

3. For other expressions of fear of anarchy and civil war, see Mfm:Pa. 506, 556.

4. Contemporary estimates of the number of armed men varied from 250 to 1,500 (Mfm:Pa. 491, 544, 554, 556, 629, 652). Before the marchers reached Carlisle,

a rumor circulated in Philadelphia that 5,000 men were moving toward the town from every direction (Mfm:Pa. 479).

5. Others also blamed Philadelphia Antifederalist leaders for the march on Carlisle. For instance, John Vaughan declared that "The pupils of our inveterate town [Philadelphia] leaders and teachers have shown themselves at Carlisle" (to John Dickinson, Philadelphia, 9 March, RC, Dickinson Papers, PPL).

John Shippen to Joseph Shippen, Carlisle, 3 March[1]

I know not how to introduce the present subject, nor, indeed, do I think it is in the power of words to express fully the transactions of the people of Cumberland. However difficult it may be, I shall attempt it, hoping to give you the outlines, after a fashion, that you may complete the picture and have some small idea of their conduct. It will not seem a credible story to people who are unacquainted with the inhabitants of the county, but when attested by the hand and name of your son, you can have no doubt of the truth of it.

I presume papa remembers the contents of a *Carlisle Gazette,* which I sent him, with respect to the riot of December.[2] The sheriff of this county [Charles Leeper], receiving warrants (state) from the Chief Justice, [Thomas] McKean, against twenty-one rioters, took said persons before Mr. [John] Agnew and Mr. [Samuel] Erwin (justices), who being in some doubt with respect to the warrants, offered them a privilege to remain on parole a month, viz., to the 25th of March, till they should have opportunity to consult the Chief Justice. The twenty-one taking into consideration the above offer, seventeen [seven] of them insisted upon a trial, refused to give bail, though they might have obtained it, and declared they would rather go to jail than accept of a parole, as others did in the same situation. They were accordingly committed. The report of their imprisonment having spread through the country, Mr. Agnew and Mr. Erwin thought it expedient to publish in the paper the above account, which by the country people was thought to be a lie, as well as the procession in the town of Boston. I may here remark that whatever account favorable to the Federalists appears in the paper, it is esteemed as a lie and a falsehood by the adverse party—I mean the Antifederalists. Of the conduct of the latter I mean now to treat.

On Saturday [1 March], by daylight, a company from the lower settlement entered the town singing "Federal Joy" (a song composed by one of their party and published in the newspapers),[3] took possession of the courthouse, and rung the bell all the morning. (I should have mentioned, they were armed.) Several other companies came in from different parts of the country, the last of which about ten o'clock.

They then marched to the jail and demanded the prisoners; upon which they received them, placed them in their front, and marched through town huzzaing, singing, hallooing, firing, and the like. It is thought there was upwards of eight hundred. Such a number of dirty, rag-a-muffin-looking blackguards I never beheld.

It was feared they would all remain (at night) in town in order to do mischief; but their leaving it in the afternoon produced an agreeable disappointment. It may seem strange that they should thus be permitted to do as they pleased; but for want of a sufficient number to repel them, the gentlemen of town, who are men of sense and forethought, as well as men of true courage, thought it most proper to let them alone. Not that they were afraid, for if they could but have raised two or three hundred men, well armed, they would have marched in front; but the matter would not rest here; they could have raised nearly as many more, which would have been the cause of a civil war, to prevent them, viz., the Antifederalists.

Thus, our Federalists acted their before-mentioned character, which, considering their situation, was, in my humble opinion, very proper and becoming.

I drank tea at General [Richard] Butler's yesterday. He told me he was going to Lancaster and is so good as to take care of this letter. I wish to be remembered with the greatest respect and love to my dear mamma, sisters and brothers, as also to Mr. [Jasper] Yeates, and General [Edward] Hand's family, Mr. [Thomas] Hutchins and Miss Patty.

1. Printed: Thomas Balch, ed., *Letters and Papers Relating Chiefly to the Provincial History of Pennsylvania . . .* (Philadelphia, Pa., 1855), 288–90.

2. See John Shippen to Joseph Shippen, 3 January, and "An Old Man," 2 January, both IV:B above.

3. See "The Scourge," 23 January, IV:B above.

The Supreme Executive Council and the Carlisle Petition, March 1788

Letter to Councillor Frederick Watts[1]

We enclose you the representation and petition of a number of the inhabitants of this borough to the Honorable Council. It contains the joint wishes of both parties. It is much to be regretted that this unhappy dispute ever took place in our county, but we hope and trust it will be buried in eternal silence and oblivion. We know the pleasure this communication will give to you and doubt not of your good offices in bringing about a happy conclusion of the transaction. This event seems ardently to be sought after by both the friends and enemies of the proposed Constitution. We will consider ourselves under particular obligations to you if you will favor us with the determination of Council by the earliest opportunity.

***Petition to the Council*[2]**

To the Honorable the Supreme Executive Council of the State of Pennsylvania.

We the undernamed, being desirous of preserving the peace of the county of Cumberland, do hereby signify and declare our wishes and desire that the prosecutions commenced respecting certain riots said to have been committed upon Wednesday and Thursday the twenty-sixth and twenty-seventh of December last should be discontinued; and that your honors will be pleased to direct the Attorney General to enter *nolle prosequi* to the said prosecutions.

John Montgomery, John Agnew, Stephen Duncan, James Hamilton, Samuel A. M'Coskery, Robert Magaw, Joseph Thornburgh, John Holmes, John Creigh, Richard Butler.

William Blair, John Wray, William Brown, Mathew Alison, John Jordon, James Lemberton, Samuel Gray, George Logan [Logue].

N.B. John Montgomery, etc. are in favor of the new Constitution, and William Blair, etc. against it.

***Council Proceedings, Thursday, 20 March*[3]**

Agreeably to the Minute of yesterday, Council resumed the consideration of General [Frederick] Watts's motion "That the attorney general be directed to discontinue the prosecutions commenced respecting certain riots said to have been committed in Cumberland County on the twenty-sixth and twenty-seventh of December last" agreeably to the petition of divers inhabitants of the said county; thereupon,

Ordered, That the Attorney General be directed to enter a *nolle prosequi* in this case.

1. FC, Manuscript Box 21–9, PCarlH. This undated and unsigned letter was addressed to "Dr. Sir" and endorsed "Copy of Letter to Council March 1788." "Dr. Sir" was probably Frederick Watts, the councillor from Cumberland County.

2. *Independent Gazetteer,* 14 March. Immediately preceding the petition, the *Gazetteer* reprinted the *Carlisle Gazette's* account of "The Release of the Prisoners," 1 March, IV:B above. The petition was reprinted once in Massachusetts and twice in both New York and South Carolina by 3 April.

3. According to the Council Minutes for 19 March, Watts's motion "That Council direct the attorney general to discontinue the prosecutions commenced respecting certain riots said to have been committed in Cumberland County on the twenty-sixth and twenty-seventh December last" was postponed until the next day.

C. THE PETITION CAMPAIGN FOR LEGISLATIVE REJECTION OF RATIFICATION
2 January–29 March 1788

John Nicholson, comptroller general of Pennsylvania, inaugurated the campaign, possibly in cooperation with other Philadelphia opponents of the Constitution. The petition requested (1) that the Assembly censure the Pennsylvania delegates to the Constitutional Convention for exceeding their authority; (2) that ratification of the Constitution by the state Convention "not be confirmed"; and (3) that the Pennsylvania delegates in the Confederation Congress be instructed that the Constitution not be "adopted in the said United States. . . ." Nicholson drafted the petition in late December 1787 or early January 1788, since a copy reached Lancaster County by 14 January.

Nicholson sent copies to opponents of the Constitution in at least nine counties. It is possible that the petition was circulated as a printed broadside, but no copy has been found. The first printed version located is in the *Carlisle Gazette* on 30 January (Mfm:Pa. 381). It was reprinted in three Antifederalist newspapers: Philadelphia *Independent Gazetteer,* 19 February; *New York Journal,* 3 March; Boston *American Herald,* 6 March. Only one manuscript copy, signed by 156 people in Franklin County, has been located (Mfm:Pa. 558).

Between 17 and 29 March petitions signed by 6,005 people in Northampton, Dauphin, Bedford, Franklin, Cumberland, and Westmoreland counties were presented to the Assembly. In addition, at least seven other petitions were signed in Northumberland County but evidently did not reach the Assembly in time for them to be "tabled" with the other petitions before the Assembly adjourned on 29 March. According to a newspaper account, petitions were signed in Huntingdon County but were destroyed by supporters of the Constitution. Lancaster County was so strongly Federalist that opponents of the Constitution decided not to circulate the petition. Only one petition opposing the petition campaign is recorded. It was signed by thirty-one men in Wayne Township, Cumberland County, and was presented to the Assembly on 1 March.

Opponents of the Constitution did not give up after the legislature adjourned. On 3 July, after news of ratification by the ninth and tenth states reached Carlisle, Cumberland County Antifederalists sent out a circular letter calling a convention to meet at Harrisburg in September to nominate candidates for the United States House of Representatives in the first federal elections and to draft amendments to the Constitution (see Merrill Jensen and Robert A. Becker, eds., *The Documentary History of the First Federal Elections, 1788–1790,* I [Madison, Wis., 1975], 240–41).

Freeman's Journal, 2 January 1788[1]

A correspondent informs us, that from the general temper of the farmers and the complexion of the Assembly, it is almost certain that we will have another convention in a legal constitutional manner called in this state, for amending the proposed Constitution, and annexing a bill of rights thereto. We may expect a power of petitions will be laid before the Assembly (at their sitting next month) for this purpose.[2] What a pleasure, adds he, must it give to every friend to order and good government that we have so easy a method of accommodating such an important business to the satisfaction of all classes of citizens, and thereby prevent much disorder, confusion, and anarchy.

1. By 31 January this item was reprinted in eight newspapers in Massachusetts, Rhode Island, and New York, four of which were Antifederalist.

2. On 4 January, William Shippen, Jr. reported that "There will be much opposition in the western part of the state, and numerous petitions to the next Assembly to call a new convention to reconsider the Constitution" (to Thomas Lee Shippen, Philadelphia, Mfm:Pa. 271). See also Mfm:Pa. 304.

Petition Against Confirmation of the Ratification of the Constitution, January 1788[1]

To the Honorable the Representatives of the Freemen of the Commonwealth of Pennsylvania in General Assembly Met.

The petition of the subscribers, freemen and inhabitants of the county of ________, most respectfully showeth, That your petitioners are desirous that order and good government should prevail, and that the constitution of this state should not be violated or subverted.

That as the members of your honorable body are all sworn or affirmed to do no act or thing prejudicial or injurious to the constitution or government of this state as established by the convention [of 1776], they look up to you as the guardians of the rights and liberties therein secured to your petitioners, and pray that they may be protected therein.

That your petitioners are much alarmed at an instrument called a Constitution for the United States of America; framed by a Convention which had been appointed by several of the states, "solely to revise the Articles of the Confederation, and report such alterations and provisions therein as should when agreed to in Congress, And confirmed by the several states, render the Federal Constitution Adequate to the exigencies of government, and the preservation of the Union"[2] inasmuch as the liberties, lives and property of your petitioners are not secured thereby.

That the powers therein proposed to be granted to the government of the United States are too great, and that the proposed distribution of those powers are dangerous and inimical to liberty and equality amongst the people.

That they esteem frequent elections and rotation in offices as the greatest bulwark of freedom.

That they conceive standing armies in times of peace are not only expensive but dangerous to liberty, and that a well-organized militia will be the proper security for our defense.

That the liberty of the press, that palladium of freedom, should not be insecure or in danger.

That the rights of conscience should be secured to all men, that no man should be molested for his religion, and that none should be compelled contrary to their principles and inclination to hear or support the clergy of any one religion.

That the right of trial by jury should be secured both in civil and criminal cases.

That the government as proposed would be burthensome, expensive, and oppressive, and that your petitioners are averse from paying taxes to support a numerous train of offices erected thereby, which would be not only unnecessary but dangerous to our liberties.

That your petitioners conceive the majority of the deputies of the General Convention, who have been appointed by this state, have exceeded the powers with which they were delegated, that their conduct is reprehensible, and that they should be brought to account for the same as the precedent is highly dangerous and subversive of all government.

That your petitioners observe this proposed Constitution hath not been approved by the Congress of the United States as directed by the Articles of the Confederation; and your petitioners desire that it may not be confirmed by the legislature of this state, nor adopted in the said United States, and that the delegates of Congress from this state be instructed for that purpose.

1. MS, Nicholson Papers, PHarH. This undated document in John Nicholson's handwriting was endorsed "Copy of A Petition Agt The Proceedings of the Convention."

2. See the resolution of the Confederation Congress, 21 February 1787, CDR:V, C.

Samuel Turbett to John Nicholson, Lancaster, 14, 28 January (excerpts)[1]

Your very agreeable favors 27th ult. and 11 inst. at hand, half an hour since. The pamphlet[2] and petition enclosed. Tomorrow I shall feel the sentiment of our friends here and, if consistent, the petition shall be warmly promoted; but this by the bye. There are a large majority in the borough that are strong Federalist.

* * * *

I took the necessary and confidential steps with the petition by showing it to some warm friends, but it was adjudged best not to attempt anything at this place, as there are a large majority in the other side of the question.

1. RC, Nicholson Papers, PHarH. The letter of 14 January (first paragraph) is endorsed by Nicholson as received on 16 or 17 January and answered on 18 January. The letter of 28 January (second paragraph) is endorsed by Nicholson as received on 31 January. Both letters were addressed: "Handed by Mr. Beckham." Turbett was collector of excise for Lancaster County and became postmaster for the borough of Lancaster in 1790.

2. Turbett probably refers to Nicholson's pamphlet published in mid-October 1787 (Mfm:Pa. 141).

Richard Bard to John Nicholson, Franklin County, 1 February[1]

I lately received a Letter from Coll: [Abraham] Smith[2] which I would suppos was directed to me by you, I found it contained a Petition to the Assembly respecting the late proposed constitution. I have coppyed it and has sent coppyes thereof to the several Townships in the County. The Coppy that I drew off for the Township [Mercersburg] in which I live will be sighnd by the people in general very willingly. If I was to judge of Franklin County by the Township in which I live I think there will be at [least] ten persons that will sighn the petition for one that will refuse to do it. By a Letter that I lately received from my Brothr at Bedford I am informed that Peopele in general in that County are sighning the petitions that were sent to them—I think it would be well done if some Gentlemen would send petitions to the different Countyes with particular Instructions to particular Persons to take the care of them.

I have frequent opertunity to hear what the people beyond the Allegany Mountain thinks of the new Constitution. They are enraged at it, and even in york county where all the members in the late Convention voted for [sd?] constitution there are great numbers of the people much dissatisfyd I am very confident that on the West side of the Susquehanna in this state there is at least nine out of every ten that would at the risk of their lives & property be as willing to oppose the new constitution as they were the British in their late desighns—There is some of your neighbors in Philadelphia which if they should have any occastion to travel toward the Westenen end of this state I think that it would be prudent in them to make their Wills before they leve Home

P.S: Sir please to excuse this hurried piece—

1. RC (LT), Nicholson Papers, PHarH. This letter is endorsed: "Letter from Richard Beard Esqr. Recd Feby 6th 1788—." Bard had represented Franklin County in the state Convention, where he voted against ratification.

2. Colonel Smith, one of the seceding assemblymen in September 1787, was elected to represent Franklin County in the Supreme Executive Council on 9 October 1787.

James Marshel to John Nicholson, Washington, 2 February[1]

The new Federal Constitution is seldom mentioned in this county [Washington]. The people's minds are so well prepared for a change that even those who opposed it with considerable warmth appear to be in suspense whether it is not our true interest to receive it; therefore a spirited opposition is not to be expected, unless the government in its operation (should it ever operate) prepare the minds of the people as well for another change.[2] Nor do I believe that a petition would be very generally signed for calling another convention. At any rate, it would require considerable address and the same degree of address would no doubt prevail with a great number to contradict themselves and sign a petition of a contrary nature. The truth is the people at large do not understand the subject and an appeal to them is certainly dangerous. While men of influence in every part of the state are so much divided, of consequence so will the people. I freely confess that I'm not able to determine with precision what is our true interest as a people in the present crisis for I neither think the proposed government so diabolical as some in the opposition seem to hold forth nor so good as its advocates represent. I feel strongly inclined to wait with patience the decision of other states before I take up strong and rooted prejudices against it, for it may be I shall be obliged to live under it and a rash and unadvised opposition might be attended with the worst consequence.

1. RC, Nicholson Papers, PHarH. This letter, addressed "(Private) pr favr. Jas Allison Esqr.," was endorsed by Nicholson "Recd Feby 21st 1788—Answered March 26th 1788." Marshel had represented Washington County in the state Convention and voted against ratification.

2. A report published in the *Pennsylvania Gazette,* 16 April, stated that there was "but a small opposition" to the Constitution in Washington County (Mfm:Pa. 631). On 10 May, however, Thomas Rodney reported that eight men lost their lives in a battle between the advocates and the opponents of the Constitution in Washington County (Mfm:Pa. 676).

George Bryan to George Clinton, 9 February (excerpt)[1]

As soon as the season permit, we plan to hold at some convenient point a meeting of delegates who shall decide how far the majority of the people of this state are to abide by the decision of the violent and tyrannous minority. Our action will much depend on the complexion of the acts of those states which we look to to hold up the standard of liberty—and I must beg that you will write me, by Mr. Aldis, who returns to this city shortly, of the probable action of your state, and that you will keep me informed of any change in sentiment.

1. Printed: Paul L. Ford, *The Origin, Purpose and Result of the Harrisburg Convention of 1788. A Study in Popular Government* (Brooklyn, N.Y., 1890), 13. Clinton was governor of New York and leader of the New York Antifederalists.

Benjamin Blyth, Sr. to John Nicholson, Near Shippensburg, 11 February[1]

It has not been in My power as yet to discharge aney part of that Publick debt due by me to you, Som privet Contractes which I was under, & the defeet of payment to me of those indebted to me, has not put it in my power as I would wish to discharg it. I have a favourable prospect to pay one hundreed pounds by next fall, & you may be ashurd I anchously wish to pay it off. Aas I Never was on a Law Docket I wish to keep my Self So as Much as I Can: I thank you Sir for your lenaty: My Misfortan in the Chaing of Many So much in favour of the State, May plead in my favour in Som degree. Aand I hope I Shall make tolerable Speedy payment by the help of John Reynolds who Says he will help me—

Our Publick offers that Respect this Constatution Seems to make havock of our Peace. A zealious & Powerfull party of Citizens who wish to Goveren the Rest, ever restless for Power uncontrowled, has formed A Cistom, which if Affected will Suffisantly Ansure ther turn. Nothing has Surprised me more then to see so mainey of our People who it would Seam an affront to their understandings to think they realy Chose it from Judgment, are intoxacated with the prospect of its being Established. But those are fare from the Majaraty of the People. Last week I went thrue the Town of Sheppensburg with a Pition to the Genral Assembley, not to Conferm the Sd. Cistom, in which I had More then ordonary Sucksess, having got Ninty nine Substanshall Subscribers, Maney of whome Declairs they will defind their Established Constitunal Liberty with the risk of their Lives—The affear at Carlisle may give you a Speciman of the temper that prevales hear, that matter may yet be attended with Serious Conseiquences: if those who are Sued Should be Proseicuted, I thinke Much Mischeaf will ensue.—I do not know how Judg McKain will hold Court in this County. Shuld Nine States Agree to the proposed plan of Goverment, I am of the opinion it will not lay the warmness of the Mealcontents, but they may agree with Such Stat or Stats as may have warmness anough to apose the Mishure. We have one Consolation that A Soverain Power directes all Human affears—

P.S. Mr Henderson of our town is a great Frend to the New Cistom

1. RC (LT), Nicholson Papers, PHarH. Endorsed: "Recd Feby 1788." Addressed: "John Nichalson Esqr C. G. Hand by Magor James M'Calmont." Blyth, a farmer, served as sublieutenant of Cumberland County during the Revolution. On 3 July 1788 he served as chairman of an Antifederalist meeting which issued the call for the Harrisburg Convention (Mfm:Pa. 697, 698).

Walter Stewart to William Irvine, Philadelphia, 20 February (excerpt)[1]

Yesterday our Assembly were to meet, and I suppose they will be able to make a house this week. It is expected by the Antifederal Party that very extensive petitions will be laid before them against the new Constitution. I however think they have abated much in their warmth since they see Massachusetts have come into it. And they at last say they think amendments may possibly be made.[2] I sincerely hope they will, as it would be a means of reconciling all parties and enable us to carry it through; without them, the opposition will be so powerful as to clog its execution in too great a degree.

Mr. [Thomas] Fitzsimmons is clearly of opinion an official letter from the delegates of Pennsylvania to either the Assembly or some one of the members, stating the situation in which Congress are, might have a desirable effect. To himself I think it might be as properly addressed as any other person.

I much fear matters will be carried to great lengths against the people concerned in the riot at Carlisle. I have spoken to many on the subject, some of whom think it would be best to bury the whole in oblivion, whilst others fear the people there might conceive it a want of ability in government to punish the offenders [———][3] letting the prosecution drop.

The river still unnavigable. Money scarce, and everything dull here.

1. Copy, Irvine Papers, PHi. Stewart, a Philadelphia merchant, retired from the Continental Army in 1783 at the age of twenty-six as a brevet brigadier general. Irvine was a Pennsylvania delegate to the Confederation Congress.

2. The Massachusetts Convention ratified the Constitution on 6 February and recommended nine amendments to the Constitution. Three Philadelphia newspapers printed the amendments between 14 and 22 February.
3. Marked "indistinct" by copyist.

Thomas FitzSimons to William Irvine, Philadelphia, 22 February (excerpt)[1]

Our Assembly met yesterday, and from anything that appears, at present I am induced to believe the session will be a short one. Except the provision to be made for Congress and the Wyoming business, I see little to be done; for tho great reforms in many branches of our domestic administration are wanting, yet as there is so good a prospect of obtaining a federal government, it seems to be agreed to postpone all these objects till that event takes place.

I am told there are a great many petitions, nine dozen, against the act of the late Convention and desiring that a new one should be called; but I suspect the result of the Massachusetts business will either prevent their being presented or at least of their being attended to. It would seem, however, that the nearer we approach to the completion of this business the more vindictive and virulent is the conduct of the opposition.

1. Copy, Irvine Papers, PHi.

Assembly Proceedings, Saturday, 1 March

A petition from a number of the inhabitants of Wayne Township, in the county of Cumberland, was read praying that this House may not oppose the adoption of the Constitution for the government of the United States proposed by the late Federal Convention.

Ordered to lie on the table.

Wayne Township Petition, 1 March[1]

To the Honorable the Representatives of the Freemen of the Commonwealth of Pennsylvania in General Assembly Met.

The petition of the subscribers, freemen inhabitants of the county of Cumberland, most respectfully showeth,

That your petitioners are desirous that order and good government should prevail and that the laws and civil government should not be violated or subverted.

That as the members of your honorable body are all sworn or affirmed to do no act or thing that may be prejudicial or injurious to the constitution of this state as established by the convention [of 1776], they look up to you as the guardians of their rights and liberties therein secured to your petitioners.

That as the [state] constitution expressly declares that the people have a right to change alter or abolish their form of government when they think it will be conducive to their interest or happiness, your petitioners believe there is ample provision made for any change that may be occasioned by adopting the proposed Federal Constitution.

That as the constitution of Pennsylvania was not formed with a direct view of a federal government, the right of the people thereto could not be declared in more express terms.

That the necessity of an efficient federal government is so great as to require no proof or illustration.

That the proposed Federal Constitution cannot be very dangerous while the legislature[s] of the different states possess the power of calling a convention, appointing the delegates and instructing them in the articles they wish altered or abolished.

That your petitioners believe it is more the duty of their representatives to cooperate with the legislatures of the different states in amending the parts that may yet appear to be defective, than to endeavor to deprive them of the benefit of what is indisputably useful and necessary.

That the objections to the Federal Constitution are founded on the absurd supposition that the Representatives in Congress must have an interest different from and contrary to that of their constituents.

That as the proposed plan of government hath been approved by Congress and adopted by a Convention appointed by the citizens of this state for the express purpose of approving or condemning the same, the opposition of the legislature would in our humble opinion be a deviation from the line of their conduct, a wanton usurpation of undelegated power and a flagrant violation of the liberty of their constituents.

That petitions requesting the intervention of the legislature can only proceed from a desire of authorizing the disorder and confusion now spreading through the state by the example of your august body. And,

That their promoters ought to be inquired after and published, that they might be treated with that indignation and contempt justly due to the traitors of their country.

1. DS, John A. McAllister Papers, PPL. Endorsed: "Petition of A Number of Inhabitants of Wayne Township in Cumberland County Praying that the Assembly may not Directly or Indirectly Oppose the Adoption of the Feoderal Constitution

& for other Purposes therein Mentioned—Read 1 time Mar. 1, 1788." Lloyd, *Assembly Debates* (Mfm:Pa. 468) states that John Oliver, an assemblyman from Cumberland County, presented the petition. For a photographic copy of the petition with the names of the thirty-one signers, see Mfm:Pa. 469.

Freeman's Journal, 19 March[1]

In consequence of the outrageous behavior of the mock-federal faction of the county of Huntingdon, in publicly tearing the petitions of the inhabitants of the county, which they had signed to the Assembly, against the proposed Constitution; a number of people of the town of Standing Stone collected and conducted upon the backs of old *scabby* ponies the EFFIGIES of the principals of the junto, viz., John Cannon,[2] Esquire, member of Council and president of the court, and Benjamin Elliot[3], Esquire, a member of Convention of that county. The effigies passing near the door of the court, His Honor Mr. Cannon, who was then sitting on the bench, thinking his dignity wounded, ordered the officers of the court to assist his partisans in apprehending the effigy-men, which they effected in part (as they were not numerous), and a number of persons were thrown into jail. Immediately the county took the alarm, assembled, and liberated the sons of liberty, so unjustly confined; who passed down the jail steps, under loud huzzas and repeated acclamations of joy from a large concourse of people; who soon after retired from the town declaring their intention to *duck* the junto if they repeated their insults.

1. This item, headed "Federal Intelligence," was reprinted in three Antifederalist newspapers: the *New York Morning Post,* 22 March, the *New York Journal,* 27 March, and the Boston *American Herald,* 10 April; and in the *Vermont Gazette,* 7 April.
2. Cannon had represented Bedford County in the Assembly in September 1787 and voted to call the state Convention. He was elected to the Supreme Executive Council from Huntingdon County on 9 October 1787, about a month after the county was created.
3. Elliott, Huntingdon County's only representative in the state Convention, voted to ratify the Constitution.

John Simpson to John Nicholson, Northumberland, 26 March (excerpt)[1]

I received your packet, also one for Colonel [William] Mongomery[2] and others, with petitions to be signed against the Federal Constitution, which are rapidly signing and seven come in already signed that will be forwarded soon.

1. RC, Nicholson Papers, PHarH. Endorsed: "Answered Apl 30h 1788." Simpson was register of wills and recorder of deeds for Northumberland County. There is

no evidence that the petitions from Northumberland were presented to the Assembly.

2. Montgomery was elected to the Confederation Congress in 1784 and the next year was appointed a justice of the Court of Common Pleas of Northumberland County.

Assembly Proceedings on the Petitions Against the Adoption of the New Constitution, 17–29 March[1]

Assembly Proceedings, Monday, 17 March

The House met pursuant to adjournment.

Petitions from 231 inhabitants of the county of Northampton were read praying that the Constitution proposed by the late Federal Convention may not be adopted, and that the delegates representing this state in the Congress of the United States may be instructed to that purpose.

Ordered to lie on the table.

Assembly Proceedings, Saturday, 22 March

Petitions from 600 inhabitants of the county of Dauphin, 450 inhabitants of the county of Bedford, 1884 inhabitants of the county of Franklin, and 930 inhabitants of the county of Cumberland were read, remonstrating against the Constitution proposed by the late Federal Convention for the government of the United States, and adopted by the Convention of this state.

Ordered to lie on the table.

Assembly Proceedings, Monday, 24 March

A petition from 387 inhabitants of the county of Cumberland, remonstrating against the Constitution proposed by the late Federal Convention for the government of the United States, and adopted by the Convention of this state, was read and

Ordered to lie on the table.

Assembly Proceedings, Wednesday, 26 March

The House met pursuant to adjournment.

Petitions from 1004 inhabitants of the county of Cumberland were read remonstrating against the Constitution proposed by the late Federal Convention for the government of the United States and adopted by the Convention of this state.

Ordered to lie on the table.

Assembly Proceedings, Saturday, 29 March

The House met pursuant to adjournment.

Petitions from 519 inhabitants of the county of Westmoreland were read praying that the Constitution proposed for the government of the United States of America by the late Federal Convention may not be adopted, and setting forth the conduct of the majority of the deputies of the General Convention, appointed by this state, is reprehensible, and that they should be brought to account for the same.

Ordered to lie on the table.

. . . .

The letter from the honorable the Vice President of this state [Peter Muhlenberg], read February 28th last, transmitting a letter from His Excellency the Governor of the State of Massachusetts [John Hancock], together with the amendments proposed by the late Convention of that state to the Federal Constitution recommended for the government of the United States, was read the second time. Whereupon,

Ordered, That the letter from His Excellency the Governor of Massachusetts, together with the proposed amendments, be inserted on the Minutes, viz.:

[Text of Hancock's letter of 16 February 1788 and the proposed amendments of the Massachusetts Convention. Shortly after the documents were read into the Minutes, the Assembly adjourned until the first Tuesday in September.]

Summary of Petitions Against the Adoption of the New Constitution Presented to the Assembly, March 1788[2]

Petitions presented in session of March 1788 against the adoption of the new Constitution:

Northampton	presented	by	Mr. [Peter] Trexler [Jr.],	Signed	by	230[3]
Dauphin	″	″	Mr. [Robert] Clarke	″	″	600
Bedford	″	″	Mr. [John] Piper	″	″	450
Franklin	″	″	Mr. [James] McCalmont	″	″	1884
Cumberland	″	″	Mr. [Thomas] Beal	″	″	930
						4094
Cumberland	″	″	Mr. [John] Oliver	″	″	387
						4481
Cumberland	″	″	Mr. [Thomas] Kennedy	″	″	1004
						5485
Westmoreland	″	″	Mr. [James] Bar	″	″	519
						[6004]

Petitions in favor of it presented in the former year, signed by 4310 of which 3681 were from the city [Philadelphia].[4]

1. Between 22 March and 5 April, all of the proceedings, except those on 29 March, were printed in either the *Federal Gazette* or the *Pennsylvania Packet*. Except for the Journal entry for 26 March, all of the Assembly proceedings were also published in Thomas Lloyd's *Assembly Debates* (Mfm:Pa. 534).

2. MS, RG 7, Records of General Assembly, Minute Book, Feb. 19–March 29, 1788, Division of Public Records, PHarH. This undated document is at the end of the manuscript Minute Book, separated from the last entry by twenty-five blank pages.

Five of the men presenting the petitions—Clark, Piper, M'Calmont, Kennedy, and Barr—had been among the seceding assemblymen in the September 1787 session of the Assembly. Trexler voted for a state convention in that session, while Beale did not attend, and Oliver was not a member.

3. According to the Assembly Proceedings, 17 March, there were 231 signers.

4. For the petitions presented to the Assembly in September 1787, see I:A above.

Newspaper Commentaries on the Petition Campaign, 19 March–9 April

The following examples of newspaper commentaries indicate how the newspapers continued to disagree about the extent of opposition to and support for the Constitution. The commentaries are also noteworthy because writers on both sides either did not know or deliberately misstated the facts concerning the origin of the petition campaign, the number of counties petitioning, and the number of people signing the petitions.

Having procured the enclosed copy of an extract of a letter in the hands of a gentleman in this city, I hand it to you for publication, together with the following estimate of the strength of the advocates of the new Constitution in the counties on the eastern side of the Susquehanna; which I trust will be allowed as just and accurate an account as the best information now had will admit of, viz.:

In Dauphin County they count 38 friends to the new system.

Berks	do.	53	do.
Northampton	do.	about 1/6	of the county.
Lancaster	do.	about 1/3	do.
Montgomery	do.	about 1/4	do.
Bucks	do.	about 1/3	do.
Chester	do.	do.	do.
Luzerne	do.	(The state of this little county is not known.)	

It is to be observed, that *most* of those counted as friends to the new Constitution are to be reckoned as doubtful or wavering friends, who allow great defects, and say that they will not interfere on either side. These are chiefly composed of that respectable denomination of people called Quakers; but at the same time it is proper to remark that the most of the first characters of that society are warm in the opposition; and the Quakers, as a society, have directed their people not to interfere on either side. This alone shows a pointed disapprobation of theirs to the new Constitution.[1]

This being established, what danger is there of a civil war? None! For who would be the parties in the war? Would a city faction venture to face the majesty of a free people? No! like the Carlisle junto, the best man among them would be, he who had the best pair of heels. And even in the city and county, we may count a large third in the opposition, and a very small part of the two-thirds would choose to fight under the banners of despotism, to protect the mock-federal faction, whose leaders are the principal public defaulters!

The idea of a civil war, then, must only be held out by the junto to intimidate the people from procuring the necessary amendments. But it cannot have any effect, only upon those who are really no men at all. ["Investigator," *Freeman's Journal,* 19 March][2]

* * * *

An extract of a letter from a gentleman of veracity in Franklin County to his correspondent in this city, dated 2d March, 1788.

Every hour the new Constitution loses ground in this part of the state. I find too, from the information of travelers from the counties adjacent to the Delaware, that the most of the inhabitants of those counties are with us in sentiment; and that the advocates of this system are confined chiefly within the city, the majority of whom are under the influence and direction of the Bank [of North America]. I wish you may write me soon on the subject.

In the counties this side the Susquehanna, we are pretty well in unison, determined to oppose the chains forged for us by the Wellborn. I shall endeavor to give you some idea of the situation of the proposed Constitution in the counties this side of the river.

In Washington County they count 27 advocates of the new Constitution.

Westmoreland	do.	33 do.
Fayette	do.	2 do.
Bedford	do.	7 do.
Huntingdon	do.	26 do.
Franklin	do.	33 do.
Cumberland	do.	31 1/4 do.
Northumberland	do.	very few, number not yet ascertained,
York	do.	do. do.[3]

A report having been circulated in your city, that the delegates from Fayette County [John Smilie and Nathaniel Breading] had voted against the sense of their constituents, a county meeting was called, and a numerous concourse of the inhabitants having assembled at the courthouse, the matter was discussed, and the thanks of the county unanimously tendered to their delegates; and after much search and inquiry, it was found that there were two men in the county who advocated the system, one of whom had been promised a colonel's commission in the *Standing Army*. These two men were ashamed to appear at the meeting.

I am told that the 33 friends of the Wellborn in the county of Westmoreland consist of shopkeepers, packhorsemen, half-pay officers, Cincinnati, attorneys-at-law, public defaulters, and Jews. And the 31 and 1/4 in Carlisle (Cumberland County) are of the same species. Scarce a farmer is to be found in this country in favor of this system of military power.

The season has been so severe, and the snow so deep, that we have not been able to do anything; but when it moderates we shall have regular county meetings and appoint proper persons to meet gentlemen that I understand are to be nominated by the lower counties. *Reading* is talked of for the place of meeting. I wish our friends in the lower counties would exert themselves in forwarding the business as early in April as possible. [*Freeman's Journal,* 19 March][4]

* * * *

The people of Carlisle and its vicinity are the only persons in Pennsylvania who have shown any public symptoms of disapprobation of the new Federal Constitution. It is a small minority to carry things with so high a hand. We understand no county in the state is so much in arrear for taxes; that is, none have so much avoided to pay *the soldiers* who have *fought* for us, *the ally* who has *assisted* us, and *the public creditor* who has *lent* us money *in the time of need.* Oh gratitude and justice, whither are ye fled! [*Pennsylvania Gazette,* 19 March][5]

* * * *

The Antifederal junto in this city and in the counties, observes a correspondent, are using all their endeavors to stir up the people of this state, and to throw us all into confusion. Already we recognize some of the first fruits of their labors, in the rising of the people of Cumberland County to let out of jail the rioters confined there. This junto seem disposed to sacrifice the peace and order of the state, and indeed every other consideration, at the shrine of popularity, to obtain which they prostitute everything that is valuable to men of any character. Their base attacks upon that great statesman, Dr. Franklin, whom they style *a public defaulter,* ought to be held in abhorrence by every good man. It is well-known that this truly venerable Philosopher would have adjusted his public accounts long since, but for his extreme age. As to his signing the new Constitution on account of the *ex post facto* and other clauses in it, which they say cancels all debts due by delinquent states and *public defaulters,* it is most absurd. Would anybody suppose that the venerable Franklin would be swayed by such motives? No! He signed it as a cure for all our evils, as a government which would restore this devoted land to its proper station among the nations of the earth. [*Pennsylvania Gazette,* 19 March][6]

* * * *

All the petitions against the new Constitution have now been presented to the legislature. Taken together, the petitioners are much fewer than those in the city and county of Philadelphia only, who petitioned in favor of it within a few days after it was published. They can do the Constitution no injury, for they are not signed by one-twentieth part of the people of the state. [*Pennsylvania Gazette,* 26 March][7]

* * * *

I observed in some late newspapers remarks upon the smallness of the number of the petitions against the new Constitution. It is well-known this measure was started by an individual in *Franklin County,* who took this step notwithstanding he was desired to desist by the party who oppose the new Constitution; and with his sole exertions in the counties of Franklin and Cumberland procured the signatures of above four thousand of the freemen of those two counties; and, if we may be allowed to judge from the tenor of the petitions of the temper of the people, they exhibit a strong picture; for they not only petition and remonstrate against the Constitution, but desire that the deputies from this state to the Federal Convention be called to account. Some few of the same petitions had, indeed, come in from other counties; but those were obtained by straggling copies of those from Franklin, and had begun so late that the Assembly adjourned before they could make any head. All the counties beyond the mountains, it is well-known, are unanimously against the Constitution, and not a single petition came from there; no, it was against the advice of the party in opposition. For it is well-known if they had adopted this measure universally in the state, they could have procured the names of above forty thousand of the inhabitants to petitions against the Constitution, but other measures much more *solid* are on the carpet, and which, I make no doubt, will procure the desired amendments, and so restore peace and concord to this distracted land. ["Valerius," *Independent Gazetteer,* 4 April (excerpt)][8]

1. For differing accounts of Quaker attitudes toward the Constitution in general in the first part of 1788, see Mfm:Pa. 324, 333, 334, 461; and for Quaker attitudes

concerning the slave trade clause of the Constitution, see Mfm:Pa. 489, 644, 667, 668 and CC:Vol. II, Appendix.

2. This item, dated "Philad. March 17, 1788," was reprinted in two Antifederalist newspapers: *New York Journal,* 29 March and the Boston *American Herald,* 18 April. For a Federalist reply, see Mfm:Pa. 547.

3. On 3 March the *Independent Gazetteer* printed an extract of a letter from York County dated 25 February, which stated: "You may depend upon it, whatever you in the city may think of the business, we country people do not consider the new Constitution adopted by this state. We look upon all yet done to be the work of the junto in the city, etc. We shall be very apt to make some *experiments* in the spring."

4. This item was reprinted in two Antifederalist newspapers: the *New York Journal,* 29 March and the Boston *American Herald,* 18 April.

5. This item was reprinted six times from New Hampshire to South Carolina by 17 April. On 2 April the *Pennsylvania Gazette* also attacked the inhabitants of Carlisle for circulating petitions for "a further emission of paper money, to be made a legal tender" (Mfm:Pa. 602).

6. This item was reprinted in two Philadelphia newspapers and one New Jersey newspaper by 25 March.

7. This item was reprinted three times in Philadelphia and fourteen times from Maine to South Carolina by 5 May.

8. For the first part of this item, see Mfm:Pa. 610.

Biographical Gazetteer

The following sketches outline the political careers of the principal Pennsylvania leaders. When known, their political positions are indicated (1) in state politics prior to 1787; (2) on the Constitution in 1787; (3) in national politics after 1787.

BRACKENRIDGE, HUGH H. (1748–1816)
Republican/Federalist/Federalist
Born Scotland; came to Pennsylvania, 1753; graduate College of New Jersey, 1771. Army chaplain in War for Independence. Admitted to practice before state Supreme Court, 1780; moved to Pittsburgh, 1781; helped establish *Pittsburgh Gazette*, 1786; Westmoreland County assemblyman, 1786–87. Published essays and poems supporting Constitution in *Pittsburgh Gazette*, 1787–88. Justice of state Supreme Court, 1799–1806.

BRYAN, GEORGE (1731–1791)
Constitutionalist/Antifederalist
Born Dublin, Ireland; came to Philadelphia, 1752; entered mercantile partnership. Member Anti-Proprietary party; opposed Stamp Act; delegate Stamp Act Congress, 1765. Appointed judge of Court of Common Pleas and Orphans' Court, 1765; appointed naval officer port of Philadelphia, 1776. Member Supreme Executive Council from Philadelphia, 1776–79; Philadelphia assemblyman, 1779–80; leading supporter of act abolishing slavery, 1780. Justice state Supreme Court, 1780–91. Delegate Council of Censors, opposed revision of state constitution, 1784. Supported revocation of Bank of North America charter, 1785. Opposed ratification of Constitution, 1787–88; was believed to be author of "Centinel" essays; delegate Harrisburg Convention, 1788.

CHAMBERS, STEPHEN (1750?–1789)
Republican/Federalist
Born northern Ireland; came to Pennsylvania before 1776; lawyer in Sunbury. Officer Pennsylvania regiment, 1776–78. Northumberland County assemblyman, 1778–79. Member Republican Society, 1779; admitted to Philadelphia bar, 1779. Moved to Lancaster, 1780; delegate Council of Censors, supported revision of state constitution, 1783–84. Delegate state Convention, voted to ratify, 1787. Defeated for election to U.S. House of Representatives, 1788.

CLYMER, DANIEL (1748–1810)
Republican/Federalist/?
Born Philadelphia; cousin George Clymer; graduate College of New Jersey, 1766; admitted to Chester County bar, 1769; admitted to practice before state Supreme Court, 1770. Lieutenant colonel Pennsylvania regiment, 1776; U.S. deputy commissary general of prisoners, 1777. Moved to Reading, Berks County, 1778; assemblyman, 1782–84, 1786–87.

CLYMER, GEORGE (1739–1813)
Republican/Federalist/Federalist
Born Philadelphia; merchant. Member Common Council, 1767–70. Member council of safety, 1775–76; member Continental Congress, 1776–77, 1780–82; signed

Declaration of Independence. Member Republican Society, 1779; helped establish Bank of North America, 1781. Philadelphia assemblyman, 1785–89. Delegate Constitutional Convention, 1787. Elected U.S. House of Representatives, 1788; declined reelection, 1790. Federal collector of excise, Pennsylvania, 1791–94.

DALLAS, ALEXANDER J. (1759–1817)
Antifederalist/Democratic-Republican
Born Jamaica, West Indies; attended Edinburgh University, Scotland; returned to Jamaica, 1780; admitted to bar. Came to Philadelphia, 1783; admitted to Philadelphia bar and to practice before state Supreme Court, 1785. Editor *Columbian Magazine*, 1787–89; *Pennsylvania Herald*, 1787–88. Reported debates in Pennsylvania Convention, 1787. Secretary of Pennsylvania, 1790–1801; U.S. district attorney Eastern District of Pennsylvania, 1801–14; U.S. Secretary of Treasury, 1814–16. Editor, *Reports of Cases Ruled and Adjudged in the Several Courts of the United States and of Pennsylvania, etc.* (4 vols., 1790–1807).

EWING, JOHN (1732–1802)
Constitutionalist/Antifederalist/Democratic-Republican
Born Maryland; graduated College of New Jersey, 1754; pastor First Presbyterian Church, Philadelphia, 1759–1802; degree of doctor of divinity Edinburgh University, Scotland, 1773; provost University of Pennsylvania, 1779–1802. Opposed ratification of Constitution, 1787–88; accused of writing "Centinel" essays.

FINDLEY, WILLIAM (1741–1821)
Constitutionalist/Antifederalist/Democratic-Republican
Born northern Ireland; came to Cumberland County, Pennsylvania, 1763; weaver, school teacher, lawyer. Captain of militia, 1776–77; moved to Westmoreland County, 1782. Delegate Council of Censors, opposed revision of state constitution, 1783–84. Assemblyman, 1784–88; delegate state Convention, voted against ratification, 1787. Delegate Harrisburg Convention, 1788. Member Supreme Executive Council, 1789–90; delegate state constitutional convention, chairman of committee which wrote new state constitution, 1789–90. Member: state House of Representatives, 1790–91; U.S. House of Representatives, 1791–99, 1803–17; state Senate, 1799–1803.

FITZSIMONS, THOMAS (1741–1811)
Republican/Federalist/Federalist
Born Ireland, Roman Catholic parents; came to Philadelphia, 1761; wealthy merchant. Raised militia company, 1776; member Republican Society, 1779. A founder of Bank of North America, 1781; director of Bank, 1781–1803. Member Confederation Congress, 1782–83; delegate Council of Censors, supported revision of state constitution, 1783–84. Philadelphia assemblyman, 1785–89; delegate Constitutional Convention, 1787. Member U.S. House of Representatives, 1789–95. A founder, director, and president Insurance Company of North America; president Philadelphia Chamber of Commerce.

FRANKLIN, BENJAMIN (1706–1790)
Constitutionalist/Federalist
(See DAB for his life and career prior to his return to America from France, Sept. 1785.) Claimed as leader by Constitutionalists; nominated for councillor from Philadelphia; elected unanimously, Oct. 1785; president, Supreme Executive Council, 1785–88. Delegate to Constitutional Convention, 1787; delivered conciliatory address at close of Convention which was widely published by Federalists late 1787 and early 1788. Nominated for state Convention by Constitutionalists, but defeated, 1787. Last public act was to sign a petition to Congress encouraging abolition of slavery, 1790.

HUTCHINSON, JAMES (1752–1793)
Constitutionalist/Antifederalist/Democratic-Republican

Born Bucks County; attended College of Philadelphia; studied medicine in England, 1775–77; returned to America, 1777. Surgeon General of Pennsylvania, 1777–84; member committee of safety. Elected to Assembly, May 1780 to complete George Bryan's term; defeated in election to Continental Congress, 1780. Opposed ratification of Constitution, 1787–88; possibly one author of "An Old Whig" essays. On medical staff, Pennsylvania Hospital almost continuously, 1777–93; taught at University of Pennsylvania, 1789–93; consulting physician port of Philadelphia, 1790–93.

LEWIS, WILLIAM (1751–1819)
Republican/Federalist/Federalist

Born Chester County, Quaker parents; admitted to Philadelphia bar, 1773. Took test oath during War for Independence; defended Quakers accused of treason. Philadelphia assemblyman, 1787–89. Delegate state constitutional convention, supported revision of state constitution, 1789–90. Appointed U.S. attorney, District of Pennsylvania, 1789; appointed judge federal district court, Eastern District of Pennsylvania, 1791. Retired to private law practice, 1792. Lifelong opponent of slavery; helped pass act abolishing slavery, 1780.

LLOYD, THOMAS (1756–1827)
Federalist/?

Born London, England, Roman Catholic parents; came to St. Mary's County, Maryland, 1771. Lieutenant Maryland regiment, 1775–79; captain quartermaster's department, 1779. Superintended printing *Journals* of Continental Congress, 1779; appointed clerk to treasurer of U.S., ca. 1782. Settled in Philadelphia; attained reputation as shorthand writer and teacher. Employed by *Pennsylvania Packet* to take notes of Assembly debates; published four volumes Assembly debates, 1787–88; published partial notes of debates of Pennsylvania Convention, Feb. 1788. Commissioned by Philadelphia Federalists to take notes of debates in Maryland Convention but debates never published. Published debates of U.S. House of Representatives, 1789–90. Lived in England, 1791–96. Returned to America; held various reporting jobs, taught shorthand; published work on stenography, 1819.

LOGAN, GEORGE (1753–1821)
Republican/Federalist/Democratic-Republican

Born Germantown, wealthy Quaker parents; apprenticed to merchant; received medical degree, University of Edinburgh, Scotland, 1779. Returned to America, 1780; never practiced medicine. Rebuilt "Stenton," family estate; agricultural reformer; helped found Philadelphia Society for the Promotion of Agriculture; encouraged American manufactures. Philadelphia County assemblyman, 1785–89, 1795–97, 1799–1800. Private mission to France to bring about peace between U.S. and France, 1798, resulted in passage of "Logan Act" forbidding such missions, 1799. U.S. Senator, 1801–7.

M'CALMONT, JAMES (1727–1809)
Constitutionalist/Antifederalist/Democratic-Republican?

Born Cumberland County, son of immigrant from northern Ireland; major Pennsylvania regiment, War for Independence. Influential in establishing Franklin County, 1784; assemblyman, 1784–88. Judge Court of Common Pleas, Franklin County, 1789–91; associate judge Fourth (later Ninth) Pennsylvania Judicial District, 1791–1809.

McKEAN, THOMAS (1734–1817)
Constitutionalist/Federalist/Democratic-Republican
Born Chester County; moved to Delaware, admitted to Delaware bar, 1754; admitted to Chester County bar, 1755; delegate Stamp Act Congress, 1765. Clerk Delaware Assembly, 1757–59; Delaware assemblyman, 1762–79; Assembly speaker, 1772–73, 1776; appointed collector port of New Castle, 1771; delegate Delaware state constitutional convention, 1776; acting president Delaware, Sept.-Nov. 1777. Moved to Philadelphia, 1774. Member Congress from Delaware, 1774–76, 1778–83; signed Declaration of Independence; member committee that drafted Articles of Confederation; president of Congress, July–Nov. 1781. Chief Justice Pennsylvania Supreme Court, 1777–99. Philadelphia delegate state Convention, voted to ratify, 1787. Delegate state constitutional convention, supported revision of state constitution, 1789–90. Presidential Elector, 1796; governor, 1799–1808; as governor was "father" of "spoils system" in Pennsylvania; and opposed efforts to call state convention to revise constitution of 1790.

McLENE, JAMES (1730–1806)
Constitutionalist/Antifederalist/Democratic-Republican?
Born Chester County; settled in Cumberland County, 1754. Delegate provincial conference, 1776; delegate state constitutional convention, 1776; assemblyman, 1776–78; member Supreme Executive Council, 1778–79. Member Continental Congress, 1779–80; delegate Council of Censors, opposed revision of state constitution, 1783–84. Represented newly-organized Franklin County, Supreme Executive Council, 1784–87; Assembly, 1787–89; state constitutional convention, 1789–90; state House of Representatives, 1790–91, 1793–94. Appointed justice of the peace, 1800.

MIFFLIN, THOMAS (1744–1800)
Republican/Federalist/Democratic-Republican?
Born Philadelphia, Quaker parents; graduate College of New Jersey, 1760; formed mercantile partnership with brother, 1765. Opposed Stamp Act, 1765. Member First and Second Continental Congress, 1774–76. Appointed Washington's aide-de-camp, 1775; quartermaster general Continental Army, 1775–78; major general Continental Army, 1777–79. Philadelphia assemblyman, 1778–79. Member Confederation Congress, 1782–84; president of Congress, Dec. 1783–June 1784. Philadelphia County assemblyman, 1785–88; Assembly Speaker, 1785–88. Delegate Constitutional Convention, 1787. President Supreme Executive Council, 1788–90; president state constitutional convention, supported revision of state constitution, 1789–90; governor, 1790–99; member state House of Representatives, Dec. 1799–Jan. 1800.

MORRIS, GOUVERNEUR (1752–1816)
Republican/Federalist/Federalist
Born New York; graduate King's College, 1768. Member New York Provincial Congress, 1775; delegate state convention, helped write new state constitution, 1776–77. Member Continental Congress, 1778–79. Became citizen of Pennsylvania, 1779; allied with Republican Party; admitted to Philadelphia bar, 1781. Assistant in U.S. office of finance, 1781–85. Delegate Constitutional Convention, delivered more speeches than any other delegate, member Committee of Style, 1787. Returned to New York and went to France as Robert Morris's business agent, 1788; minister to France, 1792–94. Returned to America, 1798; U.S. Senator 1800–3; opposed War of 1812; supported Hartford Convention, 1814.

MORRIS, ROBERT (1734–1806)
Republican/Federalist/Federalist
Born England; arrived in Maryland, 1747; apprenticed to Philadelphia merchant Charles Willing; formed mercantile partnership with Thomas Willing. Member Continental Congress, 1775–76; voted against independence, but signed Declaration

of Independence; contracted with Congress for war supplies 1775 onwards. U.S. Superintendent of Finance, 1781–84, formulated long-range plans to strengthen central government. Political plans, business methods, and charges of corruption forced resignation in 1784. Elected Philadelphia assemblyman, 1776, 1778, 1780, 1785, 1786; delegate Constitutional Convention, 1787. U.S. Senator, 1789–95. Land speculation led to bankruptcy; in debtors' prison, 1798–1801.

MUHLENBERG, FREDERICK AUGUSTUS CONRAD (1750–1801)
Republican/Federalist/Federalist
Born Philadelphia County; attended University of Halle, Germany; Lutheran minister, 1770–79. Member Continental Congress, 1779–80. Philadelphia assemblyman, 1780–83; Assembly speaker, 1780–83. Philadelphia County delegate to and president Council of Censors, supported revision of state constitution, 1783–84. Appointed justice of the peace, register of wills, recorder of deeds of newly-organized Montgomery County, 1784. Delegate state Convention, President of Convention, voted to ratify, 1787. Member U.S. House of Representatives, 1789–97; Speaker of House, 1789–91, 1793–95. Receiver general Pennsylvania land office, 1800–1.

NICHOLSON, JOHN (1757–1800)
Constitutionalist/Antifederalist/Democratic-Republican/Federalist
Born Wales; came to Cumberland County before 1775. Sergeant Pennsylvania regiment early in War for Independence; clerk chamber of accounts, Continental Board of Treasury, 1778–81. Appointed state auditor of accounts, 1781; comptroller general, 1782; receiver general of taxes, 1785; escheator general to liquidate estates of those attainted for treason, 1787; resigned all offices, 1794. Opposed Constitution, wrote pamphlet attacking it, 1787; organized petition campaign against legislative confirmation of Constitution after state Convention adjourned; had major role in calling Harrisburg Convention, 1788. Became partner of Robert Morris in land speculation, 1794; went bankrupt and died in debtors' prison.

OSWALD, ELEAZER (1755–1795)
Republican/Antifederalist/Democratic-Republican
Born England; came to America, 1770; settled in New Haven, Connecticut; apprenticed to New York newspaper publisher John Holt; married Holt's daughter, 1772. Continental Army officer, 1775–79; in regiment of Colonel John Lamb, 1777–79. Published Baltimore *Maryland Journal* with William Goddard, 1779–81. Moved to Philadelphia, established *Independent Gazetteer,* 1782; opened City Coffee House, 1783. Helped Holt operate *Independent Gazette; or the New-York Journal,* 1782–84, and Holt's widow, 1784–87. Supported Constitution, then became opponent late in 1787. Went to England, 1792 and then to France; commissioned colonel in French revolutionary army; sent by French to Ireland in 1793 to see if Irish would rebel against British. Returned to America, Nov. 1793, and became active in Democratic societies of New York and Philadelphia.

PETERS, RICHARD (1744–1828)
Republican/Federalist/Federalist
Born Philadelphia; graduate College of Philadelphia, 1761; admitted to Philadelphia bar, 1763. Secretary Continental Board of War, 1776; member Board of War, 1777–81; member Confederation Congress, 1782–83. Philadelphia County assemblyman, 1787–90; Assembly Speaker, 1788–90. Judge, federal district court, Eastern District of Pennsylvania, 1792–1828.

PETRIKIN, WILLIAM (1761?–1821)
Antifederalist/Democratic-Republican
Born Scotland; came to Carlisle, Cumberland County, some time in mid-1780s; tailor, merchant. Arrested and then released for part in Carlisle riot of 26 Dec.

1787; wrote newspaper articles and a pamphlet opposing Constitution, 1788; delegate Harrisburg Convention, 1788; justice of the peace, Cumberland County, 1795. Moved to Bellefonte, Mifflin County(?), Dec. 1795. Appointed justice of the peace of newly-organized Centre County, 1800. County register and recorder, 1809–21; county notary, 1813.

PETTIT, CHARLES (1736–1806)
Constitutionalist/Antifederalist/Democratic-Republican
Born New Jersey; son of Philadelphia merchant; appointed deputy secretary New Jersey, 1769; admitted to New Jersey bar, 1770; secretary of New Jersey, 1776–78. Assistant quartermaster general Continental Army, 1778–81. Moved to Philadelphia after war; merchant, insurance broker, speculator in national debt. Philadelphia assemblyman, 1784–85; principal author of state funding act, 1785; member Confederation Congress, 1785–87; defeated in election to state Convention, 1787; opposed Constitution. Delegate Harrisburg Convention, 1788; defeated in election to U.S. House of Representatives, 1788.

PICKERING, TIMOTHY (1745–1829)
Republican/Federalist/Federalist
Born Massachusetts; graduate Harvard College, 1763; admitted to Massachusetts bar, 1768; register of deeds Essex County, 1774. Militia colonel, 1775; adjutant general Continental Army, 1777–78; quartermaster general Continental Army, 1780–83. Moved to Pennsylvania, 1787; appointed to help organize Luzerne County. Delegate state Convention, voted to ratify, 1787. Delegate state constitutional convention, supported revision of state constitution, 1789–90. U.S. Postmaster General, 1791–94; Secretary of War, 1795; Secretary of State, 1795–1800. Returned to Massachusetts, 1800; U.S. Senator, 1803–11; member Massachusetts Executive Council, 1812–13; member U.S. House of Representatives, 1813–17. Opposed War of 1812; supported establishment of Northern confederacy.

RUSH, BENJAMIN (1745–1813)
Republican/Federalist/Democratic-Republican
Born near Philadelphia; educated College of New Jersey; received medical degree, University of Edinburgh, Scotland. Began medical practice in Philadelphia, 1769. Member Continental Congress, 1776–77; signed Declaration of Independence. Appointed surgeon general, Middle Department, 1777; member Republican Society, 1779; helped found Dickinson College at Carlisle, 1782. Delegate to state Convention, voted to ratify, 1787; wrote newspaper articles supporting Constitution and campaigned for revision of state constitution. Member Pennsylvania Democratic Society, 1794. Treasurer of the United State Mint, 1797–1813. Supported movements for prison reform, educational reform, temperance, and abolition of slavery.

SMILIE, JOHN (1742–1813)
Constitutionalist/Antifederalist/Democratic-Republican
Born northern Ireland; came to Lancaster County, Pennsylvania, 1760. Member provincial conferences, 1775, 1776; private Pennsylvania regiment, 1776–77; assemblyman, 1778–80. Moved to Westmoreland County, 1781; delegate Council of Censors, opposed revision of state constitution, 1783–84. Assemblyman newly-organized Fayette County, 1784–86. Supported revocation of Bank of North America charter, 1785. Member Supreme Executive Council, 1786–89. Delegate state Convention, voted against ratification, 1787; delegate Harrisburg Convention, 1788. Member: state constitutional convention, 1789–90; state Senate, 1790–92; state House of Representatives, 1795–98; U.S. House of Representatives, 1793–95, 1799–1813. Presidential Elector, 1796.

SMITH, JONATHAN BAYARD (1742–1812)
Constitutionalist/Antifederalist/Democratic-Republican

Born Philadelphia; graduate College of New Jersey, 1760; merchant. Member committee of safety, 1775; council of safety, 1777. Member Continental Congress, 1777, but resigned to help defend Philadelphia. Prothonotary Court of Common Pleas of city and county of Philadelphia, 1777–88; appointed justice of that court, 1778 and associate justice, 1791. Opposed ratification of Constitution. Alderman, city of Philadelphia, 1792–94; state auditor general, 1794–95. Son-in-law of George Bryan.

WAYNE, ANTHONY (1745–1796)
Republican/Federalist/Federalist

Born Chester County; surveyor, owner of tannery. Delegate provincial conference, 1775; colonel Chester County regiment, 1776; brigadier general Continental Army, 1777; served in battles of Brandywine, Germantown, Stony Point, Yorktown; defeated Creeks and Cherokees (British allies) in Georgia, 1782; negotiated treaties with them, 1782–83; retired as brevet major general, 1783. Delegate Council of Censors, favored revision of state constitution, 1783–84. Chester County assemblyman, 1784–86; delegate state Convention, voted to ratify, 1787. Moved to Georgia and elected to U.S. House of Representatives, March 1791; seat declared vacant, March 1792, because of election irregularities and residence qualification. Appointed major general commanding U.S. Army in Northwest Territory, 1791; defeated Indians at Fallen Timbers, 1794; negotiated treaty of Fort Greenville, 1795; appointed sole government commissioner for dealing with western Indians and receiver of military posts given up by British.

WHITEHILL, ROBERT (1738–1813)
Constitutionalist/Antifederalist/Democratic-Republican

Born Lancaster County, son of immigrant from northern Ireland; moved to Cumberland County, 1770. Delegate state constitutional convention and leader in writing first state constitution, 1776. Member: Assembly, 1776–78, 1783–87; Supreme Executive Council, 1779–81; Council of Censors, opposed revision of state constitution, 1783–84. Led Assembly fight to revoke Bank of North America charter, 1785. Delegate state Convention, voted against ratification, 1787; proposed amendments to Constitution in Convention. Delegate Harrisburg Convention, 1788. Delegate state constitutional convention, 1789–90, refused to sign new state constitution. Member: state House of Representatives, 1797–1801; state Senate, 1801–5; U.S. House of Representatives, 1805–13.

WILSON, JAMES (1742–1798)
Republican/Federalist/Federalist

Born Scotland; educated St. Andrews, Glasgow, and Edinburgh universities; came to Pennsylvania, 1765; studied law with John Dickinson; admitted to Philadelphia bar, 1767. Moved to Reading and then Carlisle. Elected to Continental Congress, May 1775; opposed independence, but voted for it on 2 July 1776. Moved to Philadelphia, 1778. Opponent of state constitution; a member Republican Society, 1779. Reelected to Congress, 1776, 1777, 1782, 1785; advocated measures to strengthen central government; defended Bank of North America. Delegate Constitutional Convention, member Committee of Detail, 1787. Speech at State House Yard, 6 Oct. 1787, provided standard arguments for supporters of Constitution. Delegate state Convention, voted to ratify, 1787. Presidential Elector, 1789; delegate state constitutional convention and principal author of new state constitution, 1789–90. Associate justice U.S. Supreme Court, 1789–98. Failure of land speculations led to flight to New Jersey in 1797 and then to North Carolina to escape imprisonment for debt in Pennsylvania. Died in North Carolina.

YEATES, JASPER (1745–1817)
Republican/Federalist/Federalist
Born Philadelphia; graduate College of Philadelphia, 1761; admitted to Philadelphia bar, 1765. Moved to Lancaster. Chairman committee of correspondence, 1775; captain of associators, 1776; congressional commissioner at Fort Pitt conference with Indians, 1776. Delegate state Convention, voted to ratify, 1787. Associate justice, state Supreme Court, 1791–1817; federal commissioner to confer with Whiskey insurrectionists, 1794; acquitted in impeachment trial (along with two other justices), 1805; four volumes of his reports of Supreme Court cases (1791–1808) published after his death.

The Constitution

We the People of the United States, in Order to form a more perfect Union, establish Justice, insure domestic Tranquility, provide for the common defence, promote the general Welfare, and secure the Blessings of Liberty to ourselves and our Posterity, do ordain and establish this Constitution for the United States of America.

Article. I.

Section. 1. All legislative Powers herein granted shall be vested in a Congress of the United States, which shall consist of a Senate and House of Representatives.

Section. 2. The House of Representatives shall be composed of Members chosen every second Year by the People of the several States, and the Electors in each State shall have the Qualifications requisite for Electors of the most numerous Branch of the State Legislature.

No Person shall be a Representative who shall not have attained to the Age of twenty five Years, and been seven Years a Citizen of the United States, and who shall not, when elected, be an Inhabitant of that State in which he shall be chosen.

Representatives and direct Taxes shall be apportioned among the several States which may be included within this Union, according to their respective Numbers, which shall be determined by adding to the whole Number of free Persons, including those bound to Service for a Term of Years, and excluding Indians not taxed, three fifths of all other Persons. The actual Enumeration shall be made within three Years after the first Meeting of the Congress of the United States, and within every subsequent Term of ten Years, in such Manner as they shall by Law direct. The Number of Representatives shall not exceed one for every thirty Thousand, but each State shall have at Least one Representative; and until such enumeration shall be made, the State of New Hampshire shall be entitled to chuse three, Massachusetts eight, Rhode-Island and Providence Plantations one, Connecticut five, New-York six, New Jersey four, Pennsylvania eight, Delaware one, Maryland six, Virginia ten, North Carolina five, South Carolina five, and Georgia three.

When vacancies happen in the Representation from any State, the Executive Authority thereof shall issue Writs of Election to fill such Vacancies.

The House of Representatives shall chuse their Speaker and other Officers; and shall have the sole Power of Impeachment.

Section. 3. The Senate of the United States shall be composed of two Senators from each State, chosen by the Legislature thereof, for six Years; and each Senator shall have one Vote.

Immediately after they shall be assembled in Consequence of the first Election, they shall be divided as equally as may be into three Classes. The Seats of the Senators of the first Class shall be vacated at the Expiration of the second Year, of the second Class at the Expiration of the fourth Year, and of the third Class at the Expiration of the sixth Year, so that one third may be chosen every second Year; and if Vacancies happen by Resignation, or otherwise, during the Recess of the Legislature of any State, the Executive thereof may make temporary Appointments until the next Meeting of the Legislature, which shall then fill such Vacancies.

No Person shall be a Senator who shall not have attained to the Age of thirty Years, and been nine Years a Citizen of the United States, and who shall not, when elected, be an Inhabitant of that State for which he shall be chosen.

The Vice President of the United States shall be President of the Senate, but shall have no Vote, unless they be equally divided.

The Senate shall chuse their other Officers, and also a President pro tempore, in the Absence of the Vice President, or when he shall exercise the Office of President of the United States.

The Senate shall have the sole Power to try all Impeachments.

When sitting for that Purpose, they shall be on Oath or Affirmation. When the President of the United States is tried, the Chief Justice shall preside: And no Person shall be convicted without the Concurrence of two thirds of the Members present.

Judgment in Cases of Impeachment shall not extend further than to removal from Office, and disqualification to hold and enjoy any Office of honor, Trust or Profit under the United States: but the Party convicted shall nevertheless be liable and subject to Indictment, Trial, Judgment and Punishment, according to Law.

Section. 4. The Times, Places and Manner of holding Elections for Senators and Representatives, shall be prescribed in each State by the Legislature thereof; but the Congress may at any time by Law make or alter such Regulations, except as to the Places of chusing Senators.

The Congress shall assemble at least once in every Year, and such Meeting shall be on the first Monday in December, unless they shall by Law appoint a different Day.

Section. 5. Each House shall be the Judge of the Elections, Returns and Qualifications of its own Members, and a Majority of each shall constitute a Quorum to do Business; but a smaller Number may adjourn from day to day, and may be authorized to compel the Attendance of absent Members, in such Manner, and under such Penalties as each House may provide.

Each House may determine the Rules of its Proceedings, punish its members for disorderly Behaviour, and, with the Concurrence of two thirds, expel a Member.

Each House shall keep a Journal of its Proceedings, and from time to time publish the same, excepting such Parts as may in their Judgment require Secrecy; and the Yeas and Nays of the Members of either House on any question shall, at the Desire of one fifth of those Present, be entered on the Journal.

Neither House, during the Session of Congress, shall, without the Consent of the other, adjourn for more than three days, nor to any other Place than that in which the two Houses shall be sitting.

Section. 6. The Senators and Representatives shall receive a Compensation for their Services, to be ascertained by Law, and paid out of the Treasury of the United States. They shall in all Cases, except Treason, Felony and Breach of the Peace, be privileged from Arrest during their Attendance at the Session of their respective Houses, and in going to and returning from the same; and for any Speech or Debate in either House, they shall not be questioned in any other Place.

No Senator or Representative shall, during the Time for which he was elected, be appointed to any civil Office under the Authority of the United States which shall have been created, or the Emoluments whereof shall have been encreased during such time; and no Person holding any Office under the United States, shall be a Member of either House during his Continuance in Office.

Section. 7. All Bills for raising Revenue shall originate in the House of Representatives; but the Senate may propose or concur with Amendments as on other Bills.

Every Bill which shall have passed the House of Representatives and the Senate shall, before it become a Law, be presented to the President of the United States; If he approve he shall sign it, but if not he shall return it, with his Objections to that House in which it shall have originated, who shall enter the Objections at large on their Journal, and proceed to reconsider it. If after such Reconsideration two thirds of that House shall agree to pass the Bill, it shall be sent, together with the Objections, to the other House, by which it shall likewise be reconsidered, and if approved by two thirds of that House, it shall become a Law. But in all such Cases the Votes of both Houses shall be determined by yeas and Nays, and the Names of the Persons voting for and against the Bill shall be entered on the Journal of each House respectively. If any Bill shall not be returned by the President within ten Days (Sundays excepted) after it shall have been presented to him, the Same shall be a Law, in like Manner as if he had signed it, unless the Congress by their Adjournment prevent its Return, in which Case it shall not be a Law.

Every Order, Resolution, or Vote to which the Concurrence of the Senate and House of Representatives may be necessary (except on a question of Adjournment) shall be presented to the President of the United States; and before the Same shall take Effect, shall be approved by him, or being disapproved by him, shall be repassed by two thirds of the Senate and House of Representatives, according to the Rules and Limitations prescribed in the Case of a Bill.

Section. 8. The Congress shall have Power To lay and collect Taxes, Duties, Imposts and Excises, to pay the Debts and provide for the common Defence and general Welfare of the United States; but all Duties, Imposts and Excises shall be uniform throughout the United States;

To borrow Money on the credit of the United States;

To regulate Commerce with foreign Nations, and among the several States, and with the Indian Tribes;

To establish an uniform Rule of Naturalization, and uniform Laws on the subject of Bankruptcies throughout the United States;

To coin Money, regulate the Value thereof, and of foreign Coin, and fix the Standard of Weights and Measures;

To provide for the Punishment of counterfeiting the Securities and current Coin of the United States;

To establish Post Offices and post Roads;

To promote the Progress of Science and useful Arts, by securing for limited Times to Authors and Inventors the exclusive Right to their respective Writings and Discoveries;

To constitute Tribunals inferior to the supreme Court;

To define and punish Piracies and Felonies committed on the high Seas, and Offences against the Law of Nations;

To declare War, grant Letters of Marque and Reprisal, and make Rules concerning Captures on Land and Water;

To raise and support Armies, but no Appropriation of Money to that Use shall be for a longer Term than two Years;

To provide and maintain a Navy;

To make Rules for the Government and Regulation of the land and naval Forces;

To provide for calling forth the Militia to execute the Laws of the Union, suppress Insurrections and repel Invasions;

To provide for organizing, arming, and disciplining, the Militia, and for governing such Part of them as may be employed in the Service of the United States, reserving to the States respectively, the Appointment of the Officers, and the Authority of training the Militia according to the discipline prescribed by Congress;

To exercise exclusive Legislation in all Cases whatsoever, over such District (not exceeding ten Miles square) as may, by Cession of particular States, and the Acceptance of Congress, become the Seat of the Government of the United States, and to exercise like Authority over all Places purchased by the Consent of the Legislature of the State in which the same shall be, for the Erection of Forts, Magazines, Arsenals, dock-Yards, and other needful Buildings;—And

To make all Laws which shall be necessary and proper for carrying into Execution the foregoing Powers, and all other Powers vested by this Constitution in the Government of the United States, or in any Department or Officer thereof.

Section. 9. The Migration or Importation of such Persons as any of the States now existing shall think proper to admit, shall not be prohibited by the Congress prior to the Year one thousand eight hundred and eight, but a Tax or duty may be imposed on such Importation, not exceeding ten dollars for each Person.

The Privilege of the Writ of Habeas Corpus shall not be suspended, unless when in Cases of Rebellion or Invasion the public Safety may require it.

No Bill of Attainder or ex post facto Law shall be passed.

No Capitation, or other direct, Tax shall be laid, unless in Proportion to the Census or Enumeration herein before directed to be taken.

No Tax or Duty shall be laid on Articles exported from any State.

No Preference shall be given by any Regulation of Commerce or Revenue to the Ports of one State over those of another: nor shall Vessels bound to, or from, one State, be obliged to enter, clear, or pay Duties in another.

No Money shall be drawn from the Treasury, but in Consequence of Appropriations made by Law; and a regular Statement and Account of the Receipts and Expenditures of all public Money shall be published from time to time.

No Title of Nobility shall be granted by the United States: And no Person holding any Office of Profit or Trust under them, shall, without the Consent of the Congress, accept of any present, Emolument, Office, or Title, of any kind whatever, from any King, Prince, or foreign State.

Section. 10. No State shall enter into any Treaty, Alliance, or Confederation; grant Letters of Marque and Reprisal; coin Money; emit Bills of Credit; make any Thing but gold and silver Coin a Tender in Payment of Debts; pass any Bill of Attainder, ex post facto Law, or Law impairing the Obligation of Contracts, or grant any Title of Nobility.

No State shall, without the Consent of the Congress, lay any Imposts or Duties on Imports or Exports, except what may be absolutely necessary for executing it's inspection Laws: and the net Produce of all Duties and Imposts, laid by any State on Imports or Exports, shall be for the Use of the Treasury of the United States; and all such Laws shall be subject to the Revision and Controul of the Congress.

No State shall, without the Consent of Congress, lay any Duty of Tonnage, keep Troops, or Ships of War in time of Peace, enter into any Agreement or Compact with another State, or with a foreign Power, or engage in War, unless actually invaded, or in such imminent Danger as will not admit of delay.

Article. II.

Section. 1. The executive Power shall be vested in a President of the United States of America. He shall hold his Office during the

Term of four Years, and, together with the Vice President, chosen for the same Term, be elected, as follows

Each State shall appoint, in such Manner as the Legislature thereof may direct, a Number of Electors, equal to the whole Number of Senators and Representatives to which the State may be entitled in the Congress: but no Senator or Representative, or Person holding an Office of Trust or Profit under the United States, shall be appointed an Elector.

The Electors shall meet in their respective States and vote by Ballot for two Persons, of whom one at least shall not be an Inhabitant of the same State with themselves. And they shall make a List of all the Persons voted for, and of the Number of Votes for each; which List they shall sign and certify, and transmit sealed to the Seat of the Government of the United States, directed to the President of the Senate. The President of the Senate shall, in the Presence of the Senate and House of Representatives, open all the Certificates, and the Votes shall then be counted. The Person having the greatest Number of Votes shall be the President, if such Number be a Majority of the whole Number of Electors appointed; and if there be more than one who have such Majority, and have an equal Number of Votes, then the House of Representatives shall immediately chuse by Ballot one of them for President; and if no Person have a Majority, then from the five highest on the List the said House shall in like Manner chuse the President. But in chusing the President, the Votes shall be taken by States, the Representation from each State having one Vote; A quorum for this Purpose shall consist of a Member or Members from two thirds of the States, and a Majority of all the States shall be necessary to a Choice. In every Case, after the Choice of the President, the Person having the greatest Number of Votes of the Electors shall be the Vice President. But if there should remain two or more who have equal Votes, the Senate shall chuse from them by Ballot the Vice President.

The Congress may determine the Time of chusing the Electors, and the Day on which they shall give their Votes; which Day shall be the same throughout the United States.

No Persons except a natural born Citizen, or a Citizen of the United States, at the time of the Adoption of this Constitution, shall be eligible to the Office of President; neither shall any Person be eligible to that Office who shall not have attained to the Age of thirty five Years, and been fourteen Years a Resident within the United States.

In Case of the Removal of the President from Office, or of his Death, Resignation, or Inability to discharge the Powers and Duties of the said Office, the Same shall devolve on the Vice President, and the Congress may by Law provide for the Case of Removal, Death, Resignation or Inability, both of the President and Vice President, declaring what Officer shall then act as President, and such Officer shall act accordingly, until the Disability be removed, or a President shall be elected.

The President shall, at stated Times, receive for his Services, a Compensation, which shall neither be encreased nor diminished during the Period for which he shall have been elected, and he shall not receive within that Period any other Emolument from the United States, or any of them.

Before he enter on the Execution of his Office, he shall take the following Oath or Affirmation:—"I do solemnly swear (or affirm) that I will faithfully execute the Office of President of the United States, and will to the best of my Ability, preserve, protect and defend the Constitution of the United States."

Section. 2. The President shall be Commander in Chief of the Army and Navy of the United States, and of the Militia of the several States, when called into the actual Service of the United States; he may require the Opinion, in writing, of the principal Officer in each of the executive Departments, upon any Subject relating to the Duties of their respective Offices, and he shall have Power to grant Reprieves and Pardons for Offences against the United States, except in Cases of Impeachment.

He shall have Power, by and with the Advice and Consent of the Senate, to make Treaties, provided two thirds of the Senators present concur; and he shall nominate, and by and with the Advice and Consent of the Senate, shall appoint Ambassadors, other public Ministers and Consuls, Judges of the supreme Court, and all other Officers of the United States, whose Appointments are not herein otherwise provided for, and which shall be established by Law: but the Congress may by Law vest the Appointment of such inferior Officers, as they think proper, in the President alone, in the Courts of Law, or in the Heads of Departments.

The President shall have Power to fill up all Vacancies that may happen during the Recess of the Senate, by granting Commissions which shall expire at the End of their next Session.

Section. 3. He shall from time to time give to the Congress Information of the State of the Union, and recommend to their Consideration such Measures as he shall judge necessary and expedient; he may, on extraordinary Occasions, convene both Houses, or either of them, and in Case of Disagreement between them, with Respect to the Time of Adjournment, he may adjourn them to such Time as he shall think proper; he shall receive Ambassadors and other public Ministers; he shall take Care that the Laws be faithfully executed, and shall Commission all the Officers of the United States.

Section. 4. The President, Vice President and all civil Officers of the United States, shall be removed from Office on Impeachment for, and Conviction of Treason, Bribery, or other high Crimes and Misdemeanors.

Article III.

Section. 1. The judicial Power of the United States, shall be vested in one supreme Court, and in such inferior Courts as the Congress may from time to time ordain and establish. The Judges, both of the supreme and inferior Courts, shall hold their Offices during good Behaviour, and shall, at stated Times, receive for their Services, a Compensation, which shall not be diminished during their Continuance in Office.

Section. 2. The judicial Power shall extend to all Cases, in Law and Equity, arising under this Constitution, the Laws of the United States, and Treaties made, or which shall be made, under their Authority;—to all Cases affecting Ambassadors, other public Ministers and Consuls;—to all Cases of admiralty and maritime Jurisdiction;—to Controversies to which the United States shall be a Party;—to Controversies between two or more States;—between a State and Citizens of another State;—between Citizens of different States,—between Citizens of the same State claiming Lands under Grants of different States, and between a State, or the Citizens thereof, and foreign States, Citizens or Subjects.

In all Cases affecting Ambassadors, other public Ministers and Consuls, and those in which a State shall be Party, the supreme Court shall have original Jurisdiction. In all the other Cases before mentioned, the supreme Court shall have appellate Jurisdiction, both as to Law and Fact, with such Exceptions, and under such Regulations as the Congress shall make.

The Trial of all Crimes, except in Cases of Impeachment, shall be by Jury; and such Trial shall be held in the State where the said Crimes shall have been committed; but when not committed within any State, the Trial shall be at such Place or Places as the Congress may by Law have directed.

Section. 3. Treason against the United States, shall consist only in levying War against them, or in adhering to their Enemies, giving them Aid and Comfort. No Person shall be convicted of Treason unless on the Testimony of two Witnesses to the same overt Act, or on Confession in open Court.

The Congress shall have Power to declare the Punishment of Treason, but no Attainder of Treason shall work Corruption of Blood, or Forfeiture except during the Life of the Person attainted.

Article. IV.

Section. 1. Full Faith and Credit shall be given in each State to the public Acts, Records, and judicial Proceedings of every other State. And the Congress may by general Laws prescribe the Manner in which such Acts, Records and Proceedings shall be proved, and the Effect thereof.

Section. 2. The Citizens of each State shall be entitled to all privileges and Immunities of Citizens in the several States.

A Person charged in any State with Treason, Felony, or other Crime, who shall flee from Justice, and be found in another State, shall on Demand of the executive Authority of the State from which he fled, be delivered up, to be removed to the State having Jurisdiction of the Crime.

No Person held to Service or Labour in one State, under the Laws thereof, escaping into another, shall, in Consequence of any Law or Regulation therein, be discharged from such Service or Labour, but shall be delivered up on Claim of the Party to whom such Service or Labour may be due.

Section. 3. New States may be admitted by the Congress into this Union; but no new State shall be formed or erected within the Jurisdiction of any other State; nor any State be formed by the Junction of two or more States, or Parts of States, without the Consent of the Legislatures of the States concerned as well as of the Congress.

The Congress shall have Power to dispose of and make all needful Rules and Regulations respecting the Territory or other Property belonging to the United States; and nothing in this Constitution shall be so construed as to Prejudice any Claims of the United States, or of any particular State.

Section. 4. The United States shall guarantee to every State in this Union a Republican Form of Government, and shall protect each of them against Invasion; and on Application of the Legislature, or of the Executive (when the Legislature cannot be convened) against domestic Violence.

Article. V.

The Congress, whenever two thirds of both Houses shall deem it necessary, shall propose Amendments to this Constitution, or, on the Application of the Legislatures of two thirds of the several States, shall call a Convention for proposing Amendments, which, in either Case, shall be valid to all Intents and Purposes, as Part of this Constitution, when ratified by the Legislatures of three fourths of the several States, or by Conventions in three fourths thereof, as the one or the other Mode of Ratification may be proposed by the Congress; Provided that no Amendment which may be made prior to the Year One thousand eight hundred and eight shall in any Manner affect the first and fourth Clauses in the Ninth Section of the first Article; and that no State, without its Consent, shall be deprived of it's equal Suffrage in the Senate.

Article. VI.

All Debts contracted and Engagements entered into, before the Adoption of this Constitution, shall be as valid against the United States under this Constitution, as under the Confederation.

This Constitution, and the Laws of the United States which shall be made in Pursuance thereof; and all Treaties made, or which shall be made, under the Authority of the United States, shall be the supreme Law of the Land; and the Judges in every State shall be bound thereby, any Thing in the Constitution or Laws of any State to the Contrary notwithstanding.

The Senators and Representatives before mentioned, and the Members of the several State Legislatures, and all executive and judicial Officers; both of the United States and of the several States, shall be bound by Oath or Affirmation, to support this Constitution; but no religious Test shall ever be required as a Qualification to any Office or public Trust under the United States.

Article. VII.

The Ratification of the Conventions of nine States, shall be sufficient for the Establishment of this Constitution between the States so ratifying the Same.

The Word, "the," being interlined between the seventh and eighth Lines of the first Page, The Word "Thirty" being partly written on an Erazure in the fifteenth Line of the first Page,

done in Convention by the Unanimous Consent of the States present the Seventeenth Day of September in the Year of our Lord one thousand seven hun-

The Words "is tried" being interlined between the thirty second and thirty third Lines of the first Page and the Word "the" being interlined between the forty third and forty fourth Lines of the second Page.

Attest William Jackson Secretary

dred and Eighty seven and of the Independance of the United States of America the Twelfth In Witness whereof We have hereunto subscribed our Names,

Go: Washington—Presidt.
and deputy from Virginia

Delaware: Geo: Read, Gunning Bedford junr, John Dickinson, Richard Bassett, Jaco: Broom

Maryland: James McHenry, Dan of St Thos. Jenifer, Danl Carroll

Virginia: John Blair—, James Madison Jr.

North Carolina: Wm. Blount, Richd. Dobbs Spaight., Hu Williamson

South Carolina: J. Rutledge, Charles Cotesworth Pinckney, Charles Pinckney, Pierce Butler

Georgia: William Few, Abr Baldwin

New Hampshire: John Langdon, Nicholas Gilman

Massachusetts: Nathaniel Gorham, Rufus King

Connecticut: Wm: Saml. Johnson, Roger Sherman

New York. . . Alexander Hamilton

New Jersey: Wil: Livingston, David Brearley, Wm. Paterson., Jona: Dayton

Pensylvania: B Franklin, Thomas Mifflin, Robt Morris, Geo. Clymer, Thos. FitzSimons, Jared Ingersoll, James Wilson, Gouv. Morris

Index

NOTE: Users of this index are reminded that more material relating to many of the entries is to be found in the microform supplement to this volume and in *Commentaries on the Constitution: Public and Private.*

THE DOCUMENTARY HISTORY OF THE RATIFICATION OF THE CONSTITUTION
was composed on the Linotype in
a type face called Baskerville,
and is printed on Warren's Library
Text.